New Perspectives on

W9-DDD-614

MICROSOFT® FRONTPAGE® 2000

Comprehensive

JESSICA EVANS

ROGER HAYEN
Central Michigan University

APPROVED COURSEWARE

EXPERT

COURSE
TECHNOLOGY

Thomson Learning™

ONE MAIN STREET, CAMBRIDGE, MA 02142

Australia • Canada • Mexico • Singapore • Spain • United Kingdom • United States

New Perspectives on Microsoft® FrontPage® 2000—Comprehensive is published by Course Technology.

Senior Editor	Donna Gridley
Senior Product Manager	Rachel A. Crapser
Acquisitions Editor	Christine Guivernau
Product Manager	Catherine V. Donaldson
Product Manager	Karen Shortill
Associate Product Manager	Melissa Dezotell
Editorial Assistant	Jill Kirn
Developmental Editor	Catherine Skintik
Production Editor	Jennifer Goguen
Text Designer	Meral Dabcovich
Cover Designer	Douglas Goodman

For more information contact:

Course Technology
One Main Street
Cambridge, MA 02142
Or find us on the World Wide Web at: http://www.course.com.

For permission to use material from this text or product, contact us by

- Web: www.thomsonrights.com

- Phone: 1-800-730-2214

- Fax: 1-800-730-2215

Trademarks

Disclaimer

ISBN 0-7600-6472-5
Printed in the United States of America

1 2 3 4 5 6 7 8 9 10 BM 04 03 02 01 00

PREFACE

The New Perspectives Series

About New Perspectives

Course Technology's **New Perspectives Series** is an integrated system of instruction that combines text and technology products to teach computer concepts, the Internet, and microcomputer applications. Users consistently praise this series for innovative pedagogy, use of interactive technology, creativity, accuracy, and supportive and engaging style.

How is the New Perspectives Series different from other series?

The **New Perspectives Series** distinguishes itself by **innovative technology**, from the renowned Course Labs to the state-of-the-art multimedia that is integrated with our Concepts texts. Other distinguishing features include **sound instructional design, proven pedagogy,** and **consistent quality.** Each tutorial has students learn features in the context of solving a realistic case problem rather than simply learning a laundry list of features. With the **New Perspectives Series,** instructors report that students have a complete, integrative learning experience that stays with them. They credit this high retention and competency to the fact that this series incorporates critical thinking and problem-solving with computer skills mastery. In addition, we work hard to ensure accuracy by using a multi-step quality assurance process during all stages of development. Instructors focus on teaching and students spend more time learning.

Choose the coverage that's right for you

New Perspectives applications books are available in the following categories:

Brief

2-4 tutorials

Brief: approximately 150 pages long, two to four "Level I" tutorials, teaches basic application skills.

Introductory

6 or 7 tutorials, or Brief + 2 or 3 more tutorials

Introductory: approximately 300 pages long, four to seven tutorials, goes beyond the basic skills. These books often build out of the Brief book, adding two or three additional "Level II" tutorials.

Comprehensive

Introductory + 4 or 5 more tutorials. Includes Brief Windows tutorials and Additional Cases

Comprehensive: approximately 600 pages long, eight to twelve tutorials, all tutorials included in the Introductory text plus higher-level "Level III" topics. Also includes three or four fully developed Additional Cases. The book you are holding is a Comprehensive book.

Advanced

Quick Review of basics + in-depth, high-level coverage

Advanced: approximately 600 pages long, covers topics similar to those in the Comprehensive books, but offers the highest-level coverage in the series. Advanced books assume students already know the basics, and therefore go into more depth at a more accelerated rate than the Comprehensive titles. Advanced books are ideal for a second, more technical course.

Office

Office suite components + integration + Internet

Office: approximately 800 pages long, covers all components of the Office suite as well as integrating the individual software packages with one another and the Internet.

Custom Editions

Choose from any of the above to build your own Custom Editions or CourseKits

Custom Books The New Perspectives Series offers you two ways to customize a New Perspectives text to fit your course exactly: *CourseKits*™ are two or more texts shrink-wrapped together, and offer significant price discounts. *Custom Editions*® offer you flexibility in designing your concepts, Internet, and applications courses. You can build your own book by ordering a combination of topics bound together to cover only the subjects you want. There is no minimum order, and books are spiral bound. Contact your Course Technology sales representative for more information.

What course is this book appropriate for?

New Perspectives on Microsoft FrontPage 2000—Comprehensive can be used in any course in which you want students to learn all the most important topics of FrontPage 2000, including creating a new Web site on a Web server, integrating a database with a FrontPage Web, using Office components and styles, and working with HTML code. It is particularly recommended for a full-semester course on Microsoft FrontPage 2000. This book assumes that students have learned basic Windows navigation and file management skills from Course Technology's *New Perspectives on Microsoft Windows 95—Brief*, or the equivalent book for Windows 98 or NT.

What is the Microsoft Office User Specialist Program?

APPROVED COURSEWARE

The Microsoft Office User Specialist Program provides an industry-recognized standard for measuring an individual's mastery of an Office application. Passing one or more MOUS Program certification exam helps your students demonstrate their proficiency to prospective employers and gives them a competitive edge in the job marketplace. Course Technology offers a growing number of Microsoft-approved products that cover all of the required objectives for the MOUS Program exams. For a complete listing of Course Technology titles that you can use to help your students get certified, visit our Web sit at **www.course.com**.

New Perspectives on Microsoft FrontPage 2000—Comprehensive has been approved by Microsoft as courseware for the Microsoft Office User Specialist (MOUS) Program. After completing the tutorials and exercises in this book, students may be prepared to take the MOUS Expert exam for Microsoft FrontPage 2000. For more information about certification, please visit the MOUS program site at **www.mous.net**.

Proven Pedagogy

CASE

Tutorial Case Each tutorial begins with a problem presented in a case that is meaningful to students. The case turns the task of learning how to use an application into a problem-solving process.

45-minute Sessions Each tutorial is divided into sessions that can be completed in about 45 minutes to an hour. Sessions allow instructors to more accurately allocate time in their syllabus, and students to better manage their own study time.

1.
2.
3.

Step-by-Step Methodology We make sure students can differentiate between what they are to *do* and what they are to *read*. Through numbered steps—clearly identified by a gray shaded background—students are constantly guided in solving the case problem. In addition, the numerous screen shots with callouts direct students' attention to what they should look at on the screen.

TROUBLE?

TROUBLE? Paragraphs These paragraphs anticipate the mistakes or problems that students may have and help them continue with the tutorial.

"Read This Before You Begin" Page Located opposite the first tutorial's opening page for each level of the text, the Read This Before You Begin Page helps introduce technology into the classroom. Technical considerations and assumptions about software are listed to save time and eliminate unnecessary aggravation. Notes about the Data Disks help instructors and students get the right files in the right places, so students get started on the right foot.

Quick Check Questions Each session concludes with meaningful, conceptual Quick Check questions that test students' understanding of what they learned in the session. Answers to the Quick Check questions are provided at the end of each tutorial.

Reference Windows Reference Windows are succinct summaries of the most important tasks covered in a tutorial, and they preview actions students will perform in the steps to follow.

Task Reference Located as a table at the end of the book, the Task Reference contains a summary of how to perform common tasks using the most efficient method, as well as references to pages where the task is discussed in more detail.

End-of-Tutorial Review Assignments, Case Problems, and Lab Assignments Review Assignments provide students with additional hands-on practice of the skills they learned in the tutorial using the same case presented in the tutorial. These Assignments are followed by three to four Case Problems that have approximately the same scope as the tutorial case but use a different scenario. In addition, some of the Review Assignments or Case Problems may include Exploration Exercises that challenge students and encourage them to explore the capabilities of the program they are using, and/or further extend their knowledge. Finally, if a Course Lab accompanies a tutorial, Lab Assignments are included after the Case Problems.

File Finder Chart This chart, located in the back of the book, visually explains how students should set up their Data Disk, what files should go in what folders, and what they'll be saving the files as in the course of their work.

MOUS Certification Chart In the back of the book, you'll find a chart that lists all the skills for the Microsoft Office User Specialist Expert Exam on FrontPage 2000. With page numbers referencing where these skills are covered in this text and where students get hands-on practice in completing the skills, the chart can be used as an excellent study guide in preparing for the FrontPage MOUS Expert exam.

The Instructor's Resource Kit for this title contains:

- Electronic Instructor's Manual
- Data Files
- Solution Files
- Course Labs
- Course Test Manager Testbank
- Course Test Manager Engine
- Figure files
- Sample Syllabus

These teaching tools come on CD-ROM. If you don't have access to a CD-ROM drive, contact your Course Technology customer service representative for more information.

The New Perspectives Supplements Package

Electronic Instructor's Manual Our Instructor's Manuals include tutorial overviews and outlines, technical notes, lecture notes, solutions, and Extra Case Problems. Many instructors use the Extra Case Problems for performance-based exams or extra credit projects. The Instructor's Manual is available as an electronic file, which you can get from the Instructor Resource Kit (IRK) CD-ROM or download from **www.course.com.**

Data Files Data Files contain all of the data that students will use to complete the tutorials, Review Assignments, Case Problems, and Additional Case Problems. A Readme file includes instructions for using the files. See the "Read This Before You Begin" page/pages for more information on Data Files.

Solution Files Solution Files contain every file students are asked to create or modify in the tutorials, Tutorial Assignments, Case Problems, and Additional Case Problems. A Help file on the Instructor's Resource Kit includes information for using the Solution files.

Course Labs: Concepts Come to Life These highly interactive computer-based learning activities bring concepts to life with illustrations, animations, digital images, and simulations. The Labs guide students step-by-step, present them with Quick Check questions, let them explore on their own, test their comprehension, and provide printed feedback. Lab icons at the beginning of the tutorial and in the tutorial margins indicate when a topic has a corresponding Lab. Lab Assignments are included at the end of each relevant tutorial. The Labs available with this book and the tutorials in which they appear are:

TUTORIAL 1

TUTORIAL 1

TUTORIAL 3

TUTORIAL 8

TUTORIAL 9

Figure Files Many figures in the text are provided on the IRK CD-ROM to help illustrate key topics or concepts. Instructors can create traditional overhead transparencies by printing the figure files, or they can create electronic slide shows by using the figures in a presentation program such as PowerPoint.

Course Test Manager: Testing and Practice at the Computer or on Paper Course Test Manager is cutting-edge, Windows-based testing software that helps instructors design and administer practice tests and actual examinations. Course Test Manager can automatically grade the tests students take at the computer and can generate statistical information on individual as well as group performance.

Online Companions: Dedicated to Keeping You and Your Students Up-To-Date Visit our faculty sites and student sites on the World Wide Web at **www.course.com.** Here instructors can browse this text's password-protected Faculty Online Companion to obtain an online

Instructor's Manual, Solution Files, Data Files, and more. Students can also access this text's Student Online Companion, which contains Data Files and all the links that the students will need to complete their tutorial assignments.

More Innovative Technology

Course CBT

Enhance your students' Office 2000 classroom learning experience with self-paced computer-based training on CD-ROM. Course CBT engages students with interactive multimedia and hands-on simulations that reinforce and complement the concepts and skills covered in the textbook. All the content is aligned with the MOUS (Microsoft Office User Specialist) program, making it a great preparation tool for the certification exams. Course CBT also includes extensive pre- and post-assessments that test students' mastery of skills. These pre- and post-assessments automatically generate a "custom learning path" through the course that highlights only the topics students need help with.

SAM

How well do your students *really* know Microsoft Office? SAM is a performance-based testing program that measures students' proficiency in Microsoft Office 2000. SAM is available for Office 2000 in either a live or simulated environment. You can use SAM to place students into or out of courses, monitor their performance throughout a course, and help prepare them for the MOUS certification exams.

WebCT

WebCT is a tool used to create Web-based educational environments and also uses WWW browsers as the interface for the course-building environment. The site is hosted on your school campus, allowing complete control over the information. WebCT has its own internal communication system, offering internal e-mail, a Bulletin Board, and a Chat room.

Course Technology offers pre-existing supplemental information to help in your WebCT class creation, such as a suggested Syllabus, Lecture Notes, Figures in the Book/Course Presenter, Student Downloads, and Test Banks in which you can schedule an exam, create reports, and more.

Acknowledgments

I would like to thank the following reviewers who contributed to the development of this book for their excellent comments and suggestions: Brandon Hamilton, Ivy Technical State College; Rebekah Tidwell, Carson Newman College; and Kathie Doole, Asheville Buncombe Technical College. I would like to extend my special thanks to Brandon for his help in determining the book's table of contents and to Rebekah for preparing the Instructor's Manual. This book is a better product because of your efforts.

I have always been blessed to be a part of the best publishing team in the business. I would like to thank all of the people at Course Technology who have made this book possible, and especially Catherine Donaldson, Jennifer Goguen, Rachel Crapser, Melissa Dezotell, and Donna Gridley. You are simply the best. I would also like to thank my Developmental Editor, Cat Skintik, for her patience, humor, excellent suggestions, and willingness to turn things around on a tight schedule.

And finally, to my daughter Hannah and my husband Richard: Thank you for all of the support along the way. To the best dad in the world, Buck Sherman: Yes, now we can head to Colorado. And to Richard, thanks for your confidence in me and for encouraging me to take a few chances every now and then.

Jessica Evans
November 19, 1999

BRIEF CONTENTS

TABLE OF CONTENTS

Reference **Window List**

Tutorial Tips

These tutorials will help you learn about Microsoft FrontPage 2000. The tutorials are designed to be worked through at a computer. Each tutorial is divided into sessions. Watch for the session headings, such as Session 1.1 and Session 1.2. Each session is designed to be completed in about 45 minutes, but take as much time as you need. It's also a good idea to take a break between sessions.

To use the tutorials effectively, read the following questions and answers before you begin.

Where do I start?

Each tutorial begins with a case, which sets the scene for the tutorial and gives you background information to help you understand what you will be doing. Read the case before you go to the lab. In the lab, begin with the first session of a tutorial.

How do I know what to do on the computer?

Each session contains steps that you will perform on the computer to learn how to use Microsoft FrontPage 2000. Read the text that introduces each series of steps. The steps you need to do at a computer are numbered and are set against a shaded background. Read each step carefully and completely before you try it.

How do I know if I did the step correctly?

As you work, compare your computer screen with the corresponding figure in the tutorial. Don't worry if your screen display is somewhat different from the figure. The important parts of the screen display are labeled in each figure. Check to make sure these parts are on your screen.

What if I make a mistake?

Don't worry about making mistakes—they are part of the learning process. Paragraphs labeled "TROUBLE?" identify common problems and explain how to get back on track. Follow the steps in a TROUBLE? paragraph only if you are having the problem described. If you run into other problems:

- Carefully consider the current state of your system, the position of the pointer, and any messages on the screen.

- Complete the sentence, "Now I want to…" Be specific, because identifying your goal will help you rethink the steps you need to take to reach that goal.

- If you are working on a particular piece of software, consult the Help system.

- If the suggestions above don't solve your problem, consult your technical support person for assistance.

How do I use the Reference Windows?

Reference Windows summarize the procedures you will learn in the tutorial steps. Do not complete the actions in the Reference Windows when you are working through the tutorial. Instead, refer to the Reference Windows while you are working on the assignments at the end of the tutorial.

How can I test my understanding of the material I learned in the tutorial?

At the end of each session, you can answer the Quick Check questions. The answers for the Quick Checks are at the end of that tutorial.

After you have completed the entire tutorial, you should complete the Review Assignments and Case Problems. They are carefully structured so that you will review what you have learned and then apply your knowledge to new situations.

What if I can't remember how to do something?

You should refer to the Task Reference at the end of the book; it summarizes how to accomplish tasks using the most efficient method.

Before you begin the tutorials, you should know the basics about your computer's operating system. You should also know how to use the menus, dialog boxes, Help system, and My Computer.

How can I prepare for MOUS Certification?

The Microsoft Office User Specialist (MOUS) logo on the cover of this book indicates that Microsoft has approved it as a study guide for the FrontPage 2000 MOUS Expert exam. At the back of this text, you'll see a chart that outlines the specific Microsoft certification skills for FrontPage 2000 that are covered in the tutorials. You'll need to learn these skills if you're interested in taking a MOUS exam. If you decide to take a MOUS exam, or if you just want to study a specific skill, this chart will give you an easy reference to the page number on which the skill is covered. To learn more about the MOUS certification program, refer to the preface in the front of the book or go to http://www.mous.net.

Now that you've read Tutorial Tips, you are ready to begin.

New Perspectives on

MICROSOFT®

FRONTPAGE® 2000

Read This Before You Begin

To the Student

Data Disks

To complete the Level I Tutorials, Review Assignments, and Case Problems in this book, you need six Data Disks. Your instructor will either provide you with the Data Disks or ask you to make your own.

If you are making your own Data Disks, you will need six blank, formatted high-density disks. You will need to copy a set of folders from a file server or standalone computer or the Web onto your disks. Your instructor will tell you which computer, drive letter, and folders contain the files you need. You could also download the files by going to www.course.com, clicking Data Disk Files, and following the instructions on the screen.

The following list shows you which folders go on your disks, so that you will have enough disk space to complete all the Tutorials, Review Assignments, and Case Problems:

Data Disk 1

Write this on the disk label:
Data Disk 1: Level I Tutorial 1

Put these folders on the disk:
My Webs\Carpenter
My Webs\SunnyMorningProducts

Data Disk 2

Write this on the disk label:
Data Disk 2: Level I Tutorials 2-6 & Review Assignments (Tutorials 2-6)

Put these folders on the disk:

My Webs	Tutorial.04
Tutorial.02	Tutorial.05
Tutorial.03	Tutorial.06

Data Disk 3

Write this on the disk label:
Data Disk 3: Level I Case Problem 1 (Tutorials 2-6)

Put these folders on the disk:

My Webs	Tutorial.04
Tutorial.02	Tutorial.05
Tutorial.03	Tutorial.06

Data Disk 4

Write this on the disk label:
Data Disk 4: Level I Case Problem 2 (Tutorials 2-6)

Put these folders on the disk:

My Webs	Tutorial.04
Tutorial.02	Tutorial.05
Tutorial.03	Tutorial.06

Data Disk 5

Write this on the disk label:
Data Disk 5: Level I Case Problem 3 (Tutorials 2-6)

Put these folders on the disk:

My Webs	Tutorial.04

Tutorial.02	Tutorial.05
Tutorial.03	Tutorial.06

Data Disk 6

Write this on the disk label:
Data Disk 6: Level I Case Problem 4 (Tutorials 2-6)

Put these folders on the disk:

My Webs	Tutorial.04
Tutorial.02	Tutorial.05
Tutorial.03	Tutorial.06

Hard Drive Disk Structure

In Session 6.3 and in the end-of-tutorial exercises for Tutorial 6, you must be able to publish Web sites from your Data Disk to your computer's PWS. Web sites published to the PWS go into the directory c:\Inetpub\wwwroot\ as individual folders in this path on the hard drive or the network server.

When you begin each tutorial, be sure you are using the correct Data Disk. See the inside front or inside back cover of this book for more information on Data Disk files, or ask your instructor or technical support person for assistance.

Using Your Own Computer

If you are going to work through this book using your own computer, you need:

■ **Computer System** Microsoft FrontPage 2000, Internet Explorer 5, Windows 98, and Microsoft Personal Web Server 4.0 or higher must be installed on your computer. You also must have the FrontPage 2000 Server Extensions installed and configured for the PWS 4.0. This book assumes a complete installation of FrontPage 2000.

■ **Data Disks** You will not be able to complete the tutorials or exercises in this book using your own computer until you have Data Disks.

■ **Course Lab** See your instructor or technical support person to obtain the Course Lab software for use on your own computer.

Course Lab

The Level I tutorials in this book feature three interactive Course Labs to help you understand The Internet: World Wide Web, Computer History Hypermedia, and Web Pages & HTML concepts. There are Lab Assignments at the end of Tutorials 1 and 3 that relate to these Labs.

To start a Lab, click the **Start** button on the Windows taskbar, point to **Programs**, point to **Course Labs**, point to **New Perspectives Applications**, and click the appropriate lab.

Visit Our World Wide Web Site

Additional materials designed especially for you are available on the World Wide Web. Go to **http://www.course.com**.

To the Instructor

The Data Files and labs are available on the Instructor's Resource Kit for this title. Follow the instructions in the Help file on the CD-ROM to install the programs to your network or standalone computer. For information on creating the Data Disk, see the "To the Student" section above.

You are granted a license to copy the Data Files and labs to any computer or computer network used by students who have purchased this book.

In this tutorial you will:

- Learn about the Internet, the World Wide Web, and Hypertext Markup Language

- Start Internet Explorer and explore a Web site

- Use different kinds of Web pages

- Print a Web page

- Learn what FrontPage is and how it works

- Start FrontPage and explore a Web site

- Open a Web site in different views

- View the HTML code for a Web page

- Use FrontPage Help

LABS

Computer History Hypermedia

The Internet: World Wide Web

INTRODUCING FRONTPAGE 2000

Exploring the Web Site for Sunny Morning Products

Sunny Morning Products

Sunny Morning Products is an international bottler and distributor of Olympic Gold brand fresh orange juice and thirst-quencher sports drink. Olympic Gold products are sold in grocery stores, convenience stores, and many other outlets. Located in Garden Grove, California, the company was established in 1909 by Edwin Towle. Edwin's grandson, Andrew Towle, now serves as the company's president. To better accommodate the customers and visitors who often tour the citrus groves of Sunny Morning Products, Andrew opened the Sunshine Country Store in 1951. In addition to selling Olympic Gold juice products, the Country Store sells its fresh produce, such as oranges and grapefruits. In 1987, Andrew expanded the Sunshine Country Store to include the handling of mail orders of citrus products.

Amanda Bay has been working for Sunny Morning Products for two years as a marketing manager. Her main responsibility is to assist Andrew in promoting and marketing Sunny Morning Products. One of Amanda's latest projects was to create a Web site for Sunny Morning Products to reach new and existing customers online. Because of the overwhelming success of this initial Web site, Andrew decided to expand the company's Web activities into other areas of the business. He assigned Amanda the task of training employees in Web site development so that each department will have at least one employee who can plan, develop, create, and manage Web pages for his or her department.

In response, Amanda prepared a Web site development-training program that uses Microsoft FrontPage 2000. During the first part of the training program, participants explore the current Web site for Sunny Morning Products in order to build Web development skills. Then participants use FrontPage to create a new Web site and Web pages. Upon completing the training program, employees are ready to work on new Web development projects in their own departments.

As a management intern in the marketing department, you will participate in Amanda's training program. Once you've completed the program, you will have the necessary skills to plan, develop, create, and manage Web pages for your department.

SESSION 1.1	In this session, you will learn about the Internet and the World Wide Web. You will start Internet Explorer and open and explore a Web site. You will use different kinds of Web pages. Finally, you will use Internet Explorer to print a Web page.

The Internet

The **Internet** is a large, worldwide collection of computer networks that are connected to each other. A **network** consists of two or more computers connected to one another for purposes of sharing resources and communication. Within each network, one computer is designated as the network **server**, or **host**, which functions as the network's central computer. The server is a powerful computer that stores and distributes information and resources across the network to individual computers. The Internet is not a single, massive computer, but rather a collection of millions of connected computers through which users exchange information. The Internet allows you to communicate and share data with people in the next office, across the street, or around the world. Today, the Internet is the world's largest and most widely used computer network.

The Internet's resources are organized in a **client/server architecture**. The server runs computer software that coordinates and communicates with the other computers connected to it. These other computers are called **clients**; a personal computer that is connected to the Internet is one example of a client. The server to which the client is connected stores information and processes requests by the client for that information. When a client requests information from a server, that request is transferred in the form of a file. The server finds the information and returns the requested information, also in the form of a file. This file travels over the Internet from one server to another until the file reaches the client that requested it. Sometimes the file travels through many different servers before finally reaching the client that requested it.

To access the Internet, you need an account with a commercial information service provider, commonly called an Internet service provider. An **Internet service provider (ISP)** is a business that provides a connection to the Internet for individuals, businesses, and organizations for a fee. An ISP might be a small, local business or a large, national provider, such as the Microsoft Network or America Online. Many colleges, universities, and large businesses have their own direct connections to the Internet and are, in effect, their own ISPs.

The World Wide Web

The **World Wide Web** (or simply, the **Web**) is a part of the Internet that provides information stored on servers that are connected to the Internet around the world. The Web organizes its resources in a common way so that information is easily stored, transferred, and displayed among the various types of computers connected to it. Hundreds of thousands of businesses regularly use the Web for everything from advertising to retailing.

An electronic document of information on the Web is called a **Web page**. Each page contains information ranging from simple text to complex multimedia. A **Web site** is a related set of Web pages available from the Web server on which they are stored. A **Web server** is an Internet server that stores Web pages. Each Web server can have multiple Web sites. For example, a college or university might maintain a single Web server, on which each faculty member or student might maintain a separate Web site with his or her collection of related Web pages. When a single Web site contains different, smaller Web sites, the smaller sites are called **subwebs**.

Most Web sites consist not of a single Web page, but rather of a series of Web pages that are linked together. **Hyperlinks**, or **links**, are keywords, phrases, or pictures in a Web page that when clicked using a mouse will connect you to related information located in the same Web page in the same Web site, or in another Web site. A hyperlink might open another Web page or play a video clip or a sound file. The process of connecting to another location on the Web using a hyperlink is called **linking**. When you use your mouse to click a hyperlink, you retrieve the hyperlink's file from the Web server on which it resides. Then your Web browser opens or plays the file retrieved by the hyperlink on your computer. A **Web browser** is the software program that requests, retrieves, interprets, and displays the content of a Web page on a client. A browser can locate a Web page on a server anywhere in the world. Microsoft Internet Explorer, or **Internet Explorer**, is a powerful and easy-to-use Web browser. You will learn more about Internet Explorer later in this session. Figure 1-1 shows a simplified version of how a client in Texas might receive a file from a university library's Web server in England. The entire transfer might take anywhere from a few seconds to several minutes, depending on various factors, such as the page's content and the speed of your Internet connection.

| Figure 1-1 | HOW INFORMATION IS TRANSFERRED OVER THE INTERNET |

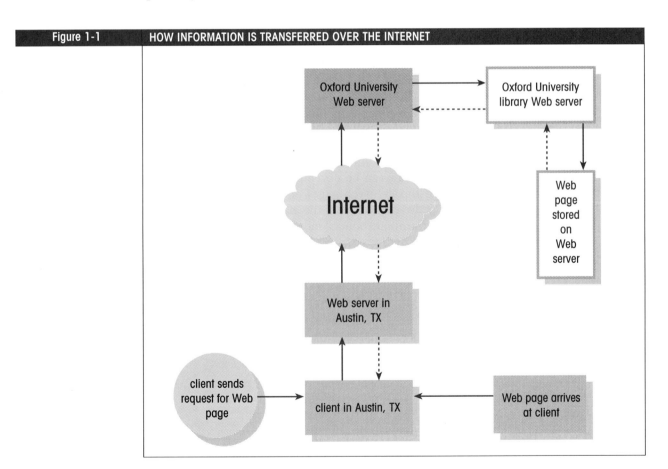

Hypertext Markup Language Documents

The Internet connects many different types of computers on servers around the world. Computers connected to the Internet can vary in terms of which file formats they can display, so the function of a client's Web browser is to determine how information will be displayed on the client. This **portability**, or the ability of software to run on many computers, means that the software does not depend on a particular type of hardware in order to run, so Web page developers are freed from having to make their Web pages compatible with many types of computers that run different operating systems.

The most common device for storing information for transfer and display on the various computers that are connected to the Internet is the **hypertext document**. Hypertext documents are prepared using a programming language called **Hypertext Markup Language (HTML)**. Because hypertext documents are created using HTML, they are also known as **HTML documents**. HTML documents use a standard set of characters, called a **character set**, which all computers recognize. In addition, each HTML document contains special codes that a Web browser interprets in order to display data in the desired format on a client. A Web page is, in fact, an HTML document that is stored on a Web server. You will learn more about HTML in Session 1.3.

Web Servers

To function as a Web server, a server connected to the Internet must run special software that enables it to receive and execute clients' requests for Web pages. Microsoft provides three versions of Web server software: the FrontPage Personal Web Server, the Microsoft Personal Web Server, and the Internet Information Server. The FrontPage Personal Web Server is used with either Windows 95/98 or Windows NT. The Microsoft Personal Web Server is used only with Windows 95/98, whereas the Internet Information Server is used only with Windows NT. A personal Web server is adequate for developing and testing most Web sites. The Internet Information Server is designed for use with commercial Web sites.

Many Web pages can be developed and tested using a **disk-based Web**, which lets you store and retrieve Web pages on a computer's disk drive. You access a disk-based Web using a drive letter and the page's pathname with backslashes, such as a:\My Webs\SunnyMorningProducts\index.htm. The testing of several more advanced features of a Web site, such as processing forms and conducting searches, requires a server-based Web. A **server-based Web** uses Web server software that is installed either on a client or on a server. A server-based Web is accessed using the prefix "http:" and the file's pathname with forward slashes, such as http://localhost/SunnyMorningProducts/index.htm.

If you are storing the Data Files for this book on your computer's floppy, hard, or network drive (the steps in this tutorial assume that you are storing your Data Files on drive A), you will examine the Web site for Sunny Morning Products as a disk-based Web. If the Data Files for this book are loaded on a Web server, then you will examine the same Web site as a server-based Web. You will work with both types of Web sites in this book. (You will use a server-based Web and learn more about Web servers in Tutorial 6.) Your instructor or technical support person will advise you of any differences that you might encounter while working through the tutorials in this book.

Getting **Started with Internet Explorer**

Recall that Internet Explorer is a Web browser that displays HTML documents on a client. Internet Explorer 5 installs automatically when you install FrontPage 2000 using the Microsoft Office 2000 CD, or you can download and install it from the Microsoft Web site (www.microsoft.com). This book uses Internet Explorer 5 as the default Web browser. If you are using a different version of Internet Explorer or a different Web browser, such as Netscape Navigator, your instructor will provide you with specific instructions for its use. In these cases, your screens might look different from the figures in these tutorials, but these differences should not affect your work in FrontPage.

Unlike some software programs, Internet Explorer does not always open with a standard start-up screen, or start page. A **start page** is the first page that opens when you start your Web browser. The address for your start page is called a **Uniform Resource Locator** (**URL**). Every resource on the Internet has its own URL. If there is no start page defined for your browser, then a blank or default Web page opens from your computer's hard drive. If the start page contains a URL for a Web site, then the Home Page for that Web site opens. A **Home Page** is the first page that opens for a Web site. This page often contains information about the host computer or sponsoring organization or individual, hyperlinks to other Web sites, and associated pictures and sounds. Figure 1-2 shows an example of a Home Page and identifies some key components of the Internet Explorer window.

Figure 1-2	SAMPLE HOME PAGE FOR THE AMERICAN CARPENTERS SOCIETY

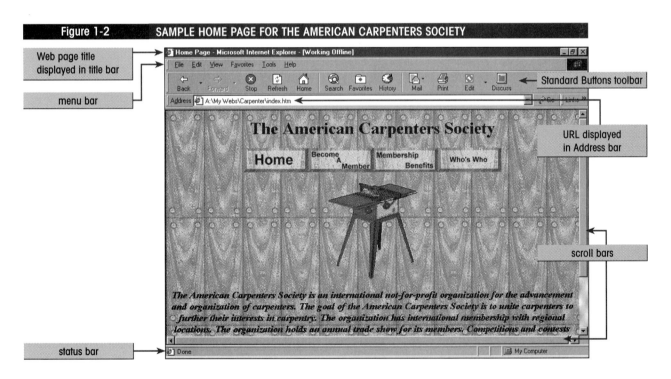

Figure 1-3 describes some of the components of the Internet Explorer window in more detail.

Figure 1-3	COMPONENTS OF THE INTERNET EXPLORER 5 WINDOW

COMPONENT	DESCRIPTION
Address bar	Located below the Standard Buttons toolbar, displays the URL of the currently displayed Web page
Menu bar	Located below the title bar, provides access to all of the commands available in Internet Explorer
Scroll bar	Located at the right and bottom of the window, moves the window's contents vertically or horizontally when the Web page exceeds the window's size
Standard Buttons toolbar	Located below the menu bar, includes icons that represent shortcuts to commonly used commands
Status bar	Located at the bottom of the window, indicates messages concerning the status of the current Web page or browser action
Title bar	Located at the top of the screen, indicates the title of the current Web page and the name of the browser program

Starting Internet Explorer

You start Internet Explorer just like any other program. When you start Internet Explorer, you might see any one of the following pages:

- The Microsoft Home Page
- Your educational institution's Home Page
- A Home Page that you or your technical support person set as the default
- A blank page
- A page indicating that no start page is available

You can customize Internet Explorer to open any Web page as its start page. For example, when Amanda starts Internet Explorer from her office, the Home Page for Sunny Morning Products opens as her start page because she often uses this Web site during the day.

You are ready to begin exploring the Web site for Sunny Morning Products as the first phase of your training. Once you have a better understanding of the different Web pages that can be created for a Web site, you will learn how to create similar Web pages using FrontPage. First, you need to start Internet Explorer.

To start Internet Explorer:

1. Make sure that your computer is on and that the Windows desktop appears. See Figure 1-4.

Figure 1-4	WINDOWS 98 DESKTOP

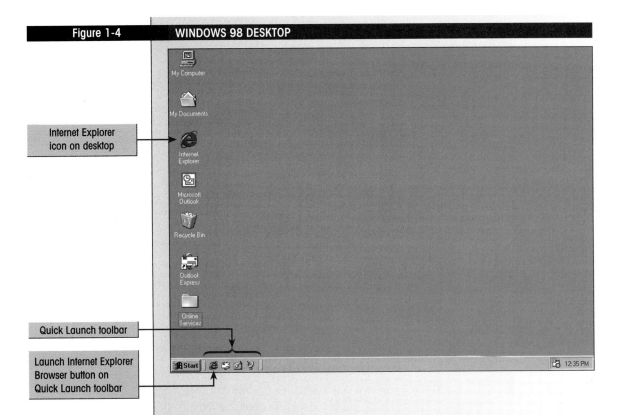

**Internet Explorer
icon on desktop**

Quick Launch toolbar

**Launch Internet Explorer
Browser button on
Quick Launch toolbar**

TROUBLE? If you do not see the Quick Launch toolbar on your taskbar, this is not a problem. Continue with Step 2.

TROUBLE? Your desktop might look different from the one shown in Figure 1-4 and contain different icons; this is not a problem.

2. Click the **Launch Internet Explorer Browser** button on the Quick Launch toolbar to start the program. If you do not see the Quick Launch toolbar on your taskbar, double-click the **Internet Explorer** icon on the desktop.

The start page for your copy of Internet Explorer opens in the browser. In Figure 1-5, the Home Page for Sunny Morning Products opens. Depending on your system configuration, your start page might be different, but this is not a problem. Figure 1-5 identifies the key components of a Home Page.

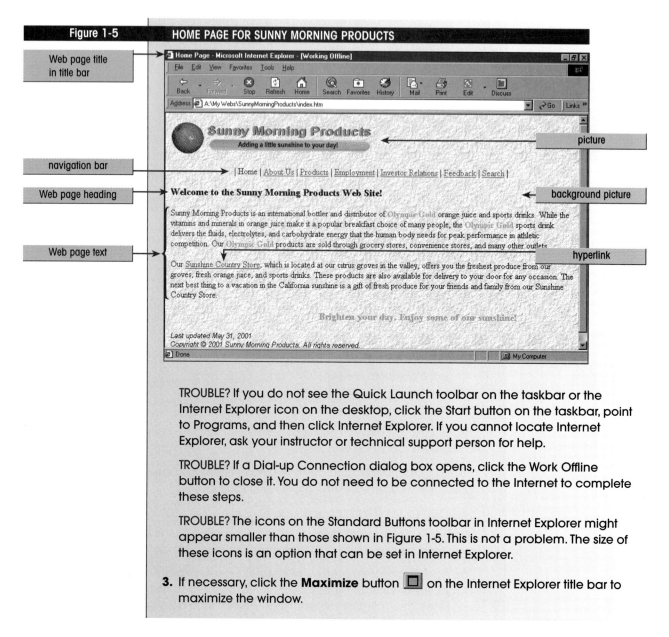

Figure 1-5   HOME PAGE FOR SUNNY MORNING PRODUCTS

TROUBLE? If you do not see the Quick Launch toolbar on the taskbar or the Internet Explorer icon on the desktop, click the Start button on the taskbar, point to Programs, and then click Internet Explorer. If you cannot locate Internet Explorer, ask your instructor or technical support person for help.

TROUBLE? If a Dial-up Connection dialog box opens, click the Work Offline button to close it. You do not need to be connected to the Internet to complete these steps.

TROUBLE? The icons on the Standard Buttons toolbar in Internet Explorer might appear smaller than those shown in Figure 1-5. This is not a problem. The size of these icons is an option that can be set in Internet Explorer.

3. If necessary, click the **Maximize** button ☐ on the Internet Explorer title bar to maximize the window.

Figure 1-6 describes some common elements in a Home Page that are identified in Figure 1-5.

Figure 1-6	COMMON ELEMENTS IN A HOME PAGE

ELEMENT	DESCRIPTION
Background	Enhances the appearance of a Web page by using a color or picture. Text and pictures appear on top of the Web page's background if one is used.
Heading	Provides a formatted heading in the Web page to differentiate Web page sections.
Hyperlink	When clicked, a hyperlink opens another Web page or scrolls to a new location in the current Web page. A hyperlink usually appears in a different color and is underlined to distinguish it from other Web page text.
Navigation bar	Contains hyperlinks to other Web pages. The navigation bar can be located anywhere on the Web page and can include text, buttons, or pictures that contain hyperlinks.
Picture	An image on a Web page that might contain a hyperlink.
Text	The content of the Web page.
Title	Located in the browser's title bar, identifies the title of the open Web page.

Opening a Web Page with a URL

Recall that each Web page is identified by a URL. A URL contains the address for the Web server or computer that stores the Web site, and an optional pathname to a specific Web page at that site. The most common method of identifying individual servers or computers on a network is to use an Internet Protocol address. An **Internet Protocol (IP) address** is a unique number that consists of four sets of numbers, separated by periods (such as 141.209.151.119), that identifies a specific server or computer. IP addresses are hard to remember, so most users rely on domain names to find Web sites. A **domain name** is an IP address that uses names instead of numbers, such as www.whitehouse.gov, instead of its IP address equivalent. Whether you use an IP address or a domain name, a Web page's URL identifies its location on the Web so that client computers can find and retrieve it. A URL can be broken down as follows:

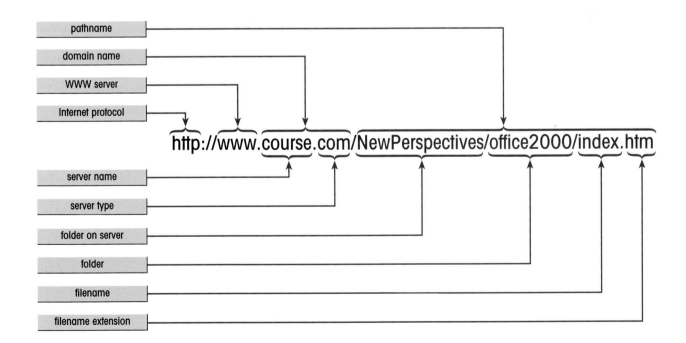

This URL identifies the exact address of the server or computer on which the page resides, and the type of organization that owns and operates it. The Internet protocol *http* is the communications protocol for accessing a page on the Web; *www* indicates that the server is a Web server; *course* indicates the name of the organization that owns the server; and *com* indicates that the server is owned by a commercial entity. Other common types of servers in the United States are education (edu), organization (org), and governmental (gov).

Finally, all files stored on a Web server must have a unique pathname, just like files stored on a disk. The pathname that follows the domain name *www.course.com* specifies the file named index.htm, which is stored in the office2000 folder, which is stored in the NewPerspectives folder. The **pathname** in a URL includes the folder name, filename, and filename extension for locating the Web page. The extension for all Web pages is either *html* or *htm*, both of which indicate an HTML document. (The html extension is used with computers that run the UNIX operating system, whereas the htm extension is used most often with personal computers running Windows or Macintosh operating systems.) Internet Explorer processes files with either of these extensions as HTML documents.

To access a particular Web site or to open a location, type its URL in the Address bar, and then press the Enter key. Internet Explorer connects to the server specified by the URL, sends a request for information, opens the Home Page or a specific file identified in the URL, and then displays the information.

The Internet: World Wide Web

REFERENCE WINDOW	RW

Opening a Web Site in Internet Explorer
- Click in the Address bar to select the current URL.
- Type the URL of the Web site you want to open in the Address bar.
- Press the Enter key.

Amanda wants you to examine the Web site for Sunny Morning Products to familiarize yourself with its features. As you work through the tutorials in this book, you will use FrontPage to create a similar Web site and Web pages. Don't be concerned if you can't remember all of the details of this Web site. You will learn about each element described in this overview throughout the tutorials as you progress through Amanda's training course. Because you are using a disk-based Web, your URL will include the pathname to the Web site that is stored on your Data Disk, instead of a URL to a Web page stored on a Web server.

To open a Web site in Internet Explorer:

1. Make sure that Internet Explorer is open and that your Data Disk is in the appropriate disk drive.

   TROUBLE? You must have a Data Disk to complete the tutorials in this book. If you do not have a Data Disk, ask your instructor or technical support person for help.

2. Click in the **Address bar** to select the entire URL that currently appears there.

   TROUBLE? If the URL is not selected, then you double-clicked the insertion point in the Address bar and changed to editing mode. Double-click the URL in the Address bar to select the entire URL, and then continue with Step 3.

3. Type **a:\My Webs\SunnyMorningProducts\index.htm** in the Address bar.

This URL identifies the location of the Home Page of the disk-based Web that is stored on your Data Disk. In this book, you will store all Web sites in the My Webs folder on your Data Disk.

As you type the Web address, Internet Explorer's **AutoComplete** feature might complete the address for you, or it might open a drop-down menu of previously opened URLs that are similar to or match the one that you are typing. The suggested match is highlighted in the Address bar. You can press the Enter key to open the selected URL, click another URL in the list, or just continue typing.

TROUBLE? If your instructor provides you with a different access method than the one described in Step 3, use that method.

4. Press the **Enter** key. The Home Page for Sunny Morning Products opens. See Figure 1-7. If your computer can play sound and your speakers are turned on, a background sound plays.

Figure 1-7	OPENING A WEB PAGE WITH A URL

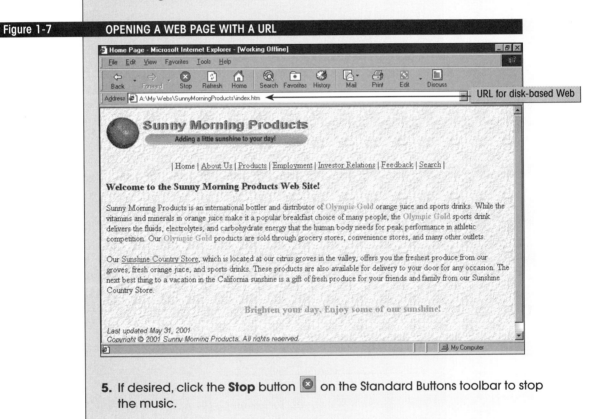

5. If desired, click the **Stop** button ⊗ on the Standard Buttons toolbar to stop the music.

Next, you will examine the various hyperlinks in the Home Page.

Linking **to and within Web Pages**

A hyperlink on the Internet, like a link in a chain, connects two end points. The Home Page for Sunny Morning Products contains several text hyperlinks, which appear as underlined text in the page. Clicking a hyperlink opens the linked Web page in your browser. A hyperlink can connect you to another location within the current Web page or to an entirely different Web page or Web site.

Because you will create and test Web page hyperlinks while learning how to develop a Web site, Amanda wants you to practice using hyperlinks to move from one Web page to another.

To link to a new Web page:

1. Point to the **Products** hyperlink in the navigation bar at the top of the page. Most Web pages include a **navigation bar** that contains hyperlinks which open other pages in the Web site. Note that the pointer changes from a ⍏ shape to a ⍡ shape to indicate that you are pointing to a hyperlink. In addition, the pathname for the linked page (products.htm) appears in the lower-left corner of the status bar.

2. Point to the **Sunshine Country Store** hyperlink in the second paragraph in the Web page. Notice that the status bar shows that this hyperlink also points to the products.htm page. You can create more than one hyperlink to the same Web page, using different hyperlink text.

3. Click the **Employment** hyperlink in the navigation bar. The Employment Web page, which contains a bulleted list of hyperlinks within the Web page, opens in the browser and replaces the Home Page. See Figure 1-8.

Figure 1-8	EMPLOYMENT WEB PAGE

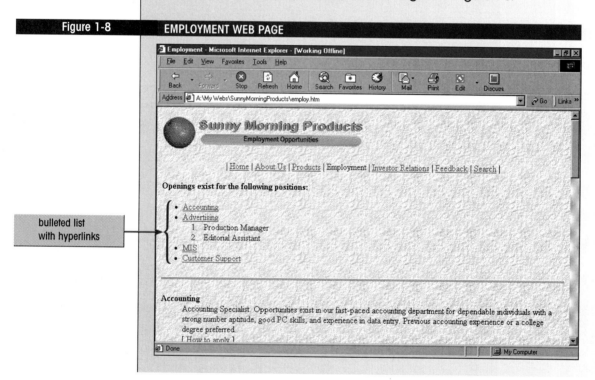

bulleted list
with hyperlinks

Next, Amanda wants you to examine an **internal hyperlink**, which is a hyperlink that connects to another location within the same Web page. A common usage of an internal hyperlink in a Web page is one that lets the user return to the top of the page as an alternative to using the vertical scroll bar to scroll up the page. A "top of page" hyperlink is particularly useful with long Web pages, such as the Employment Web page that currently appears in your browser.

To link to a location within a Web page:

1. Point to the **MIS** text in the bulleted list. Notice that the status bar displays the text #MIS, which identifies the location of the internal hyperlink.

The pound sign (#) in the hyperlink indicates that the location is within the same document. See Figure 1-9.

| Figure 1-9 | EXAMINING AN INTERNAL HYPERLINK IN A WEB PAGE |

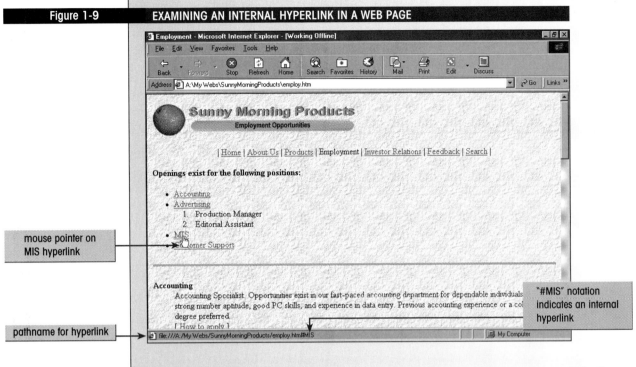

mouse pointer on MIS hyperlink

pathname for hyperlink

"#MIS" notation indicates an internal hyperlink

2. Click the **MIS** hyperlink. The Employment Web page automatically scrolls to the MIS section. See Figure 1-10.

| Figure 1-10 | MIS SECTION IN THE EMPLOYMENT WEB PAGE |

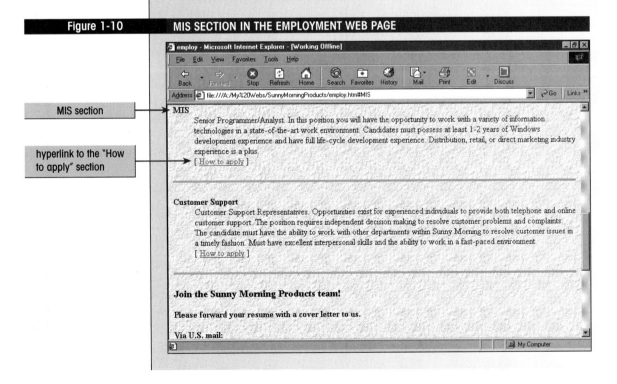

MIS section

hyperlink to the "How to apply" section

3. Click the **How to apply** hyperlink at the end of the MIS job description. The Employment Web page automatically moves to the "How to apply" section.

   Clicking any of the "How to apply" hyperlinks in this Web page moves you to this same location. In addition to creating a hyperlink to another location in the same Web page, you can create a hyperlink for sending e-mail messages. For example, the Employment Web page contains the e-mail address of the Human Resources manager.

4. Press **Ctrl + End** to move to the bottom of the Web page. See Figure 1-11.

| Figure 1-11 | BOTTOM OF THE EMPLOYMENT WEB PAGE |

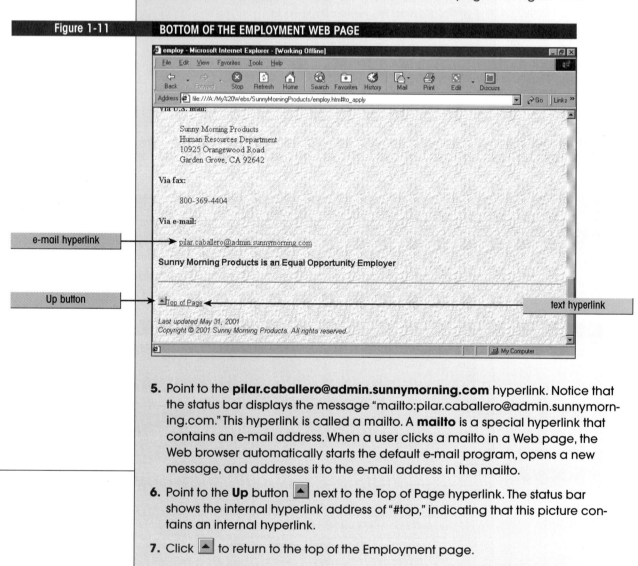

5. Point to the **pilar.caballero@admin.sunnymorning.com** hyperlink. Notice that the status bar displays the message "mailto:pilar.caballero@admin.sunnymorning.com." This hyperlink is called a mailto. A **mailto** is a special hyperlink that contains an e-mail address. When a user clicks a mailto in a Web page, the Web browser automatically starts the default e-mail program, opens a new message, and addresses it to the e-mail address in the mailto.

6. Point to the **Up** button ▲ next to the Top of Page hyperlink. The status bar shows the internal hyperlink address of "#top," indicating that this picture contains an internal hyperlink.

7. Click ▲ to return to the top of the Employment page.

The pages in the SunnyMorningProducts Web site that you have viewed so far were all single pages. Now that you've examined several individual Web pages, Amanda wants you to use a different kind of Web page that enables you to display multiple pages on your screen at once.

Examining a Frames Page

You can divide one Web page into several different windows, called **frames**, and display a different Web page in each frame. For example, one frame can continuously display a table of contents, while a second frame displays a page selected from that table of contents. You then can easily select pages from the table of contents because it remains displayed. A Web page that is divided into several frames that display other Web pages is called a **frames page** (or a **frameset**). You can scroll the contents of each frame up or down if the Web page is larger than the frame's size. Clicking a hyperlink in one frame might change the Web page displayed in another frame.

Amanda used a frames page to create the Products Web page that you will examine next.

To examine a frames page:

1. Click the **Products** hyperlink in the navigation bar at the top of the Employment Web page. The Products Web page opens. See Figure 1-12.

   TROUBLE? Depending on your monitor's resolution, your frames page might display pages with sizes different from those shown in Figure 1-12, and you might see scroll bars in all of the frames. This is not a problem.

Figure 1-12	PRODUCTS FRAMES PAGE

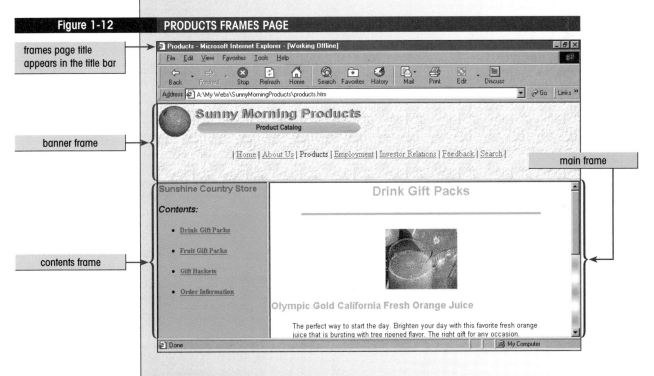

frames page title appears in the title bar

banner frame

contents frame

main frame

The Products Web page is a frames page that is divided into three frames; you can also use FrontPage to create frames pages with two, four, or more frames. In this frames page, the top frame, called the **banner frame**, contains the Sunny Morning Products logo and a navigation bar with hyperlinks that open other Web pages in the SunnyMorningProducts Web site. Clicking a hyperlink in the navigation bar opens the linked page and replaces the frames pages.

The left frame, called the **contents frame**, contains a bulleted list of hyperlinks that open pages in the main frame. The right frame, called the **main frame**, contains a scrollable Web page that opens after clicking a hyperlink in the contents frame. The Drink Gift Packs Web page currently appears in the main frame.

2. Click the **Fruit Gift Packs** hyperlink in the contents frame to open this Web page in the main frame. See Figure 1-13.

Figure 1-13	FRUIT GIFT PACKS WEB PAGE IN MAIN FRAME

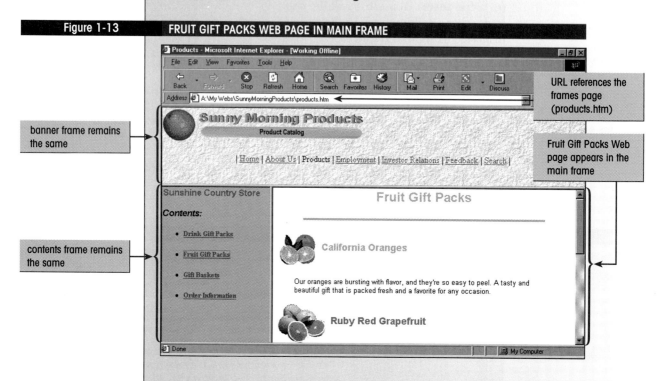

banner frame remains the same

contents frame remains the same

URL references the frames page (products.htm)

Fruit Gift Packs Web page appears in the main frame

3. Scroll down to view the contents of the Fruit Gift Packs Web page. Notice that this Web page does not use a background picture or color, but does include a centered heading, a horizontal line, and several pictures.

4. If necessary, scroll up the page until you see the California Oranges picture, and then place your mouse pointer on it. The text "Oranges" appears in a box for a moment and then disappears; this is **alternative text**. If your Web browser could not display or find the file for this picture, then the alternative text "Oranges" would appear in its place. Notice that no filename appears in the status bar when the pointer is on top of the picture, which indicates that this picture does not contain a hyperlink.

5. Click the **Gift Baskets** hyperlink in the contents frame to open this Web page in the main frame. Scroll down until you see a table listing available products and their prices. See Figure 1-14. Tables are often used in Web pages to control the arrangement of information on a page. You will learn more about tables in Tutorial 4.

| Figure 1-14 | GIFT BASKETS WEB PAGE IN MAIN FRAME |

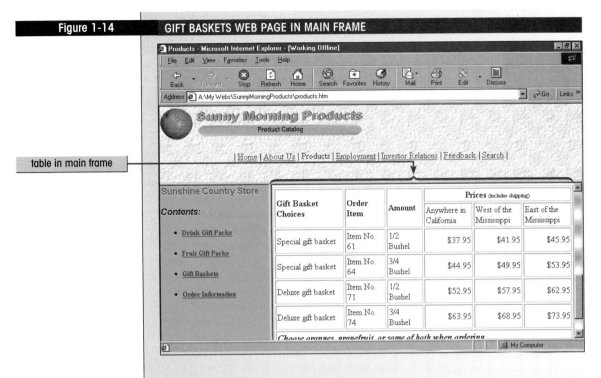

table in main frame

6. Click the **Order Information** hyperlink in the contents frame to open the Order Information page. Notice that this Web page uses a picture as its background.

Using FrontPage Components

So far in this tutorial, all of the Web pages you have viewed have been static. A **static Web page** is a Web page that you request from the server and that opens in your browser. Web pages also can be interactive. An **interactive**, or **dynamic**, **Web page** is one that doesn't already exist as a file on the server, but rather is created based on data entered by the user. For example, to complete a survey on the Web, you would use a Web page to enter your responses to the various questions, and then use your browser to send your responses to the server for processing. The server would process the data and return a response in the form of a Web page, whose content would be based in whole or in part on the data you entered.

In a FrontPage Web site, a feature called a FrontPage component handles the processing of this type of user input on the server. A **FrontPage component** is a prewritten program that carries out a particular processing function. FrontPage contains many components that you can include in Web pages for implementing various server-processing activities. An example is the **search component**, which is used to create a Search Web page that accepts a user's search request and then performs a search across all of the pages of a Web site to find matching Web pages.

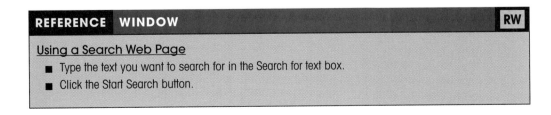

REFERENCE WINDOW **RW**

Using a Search Web Page
- Type the text you want to search for in the Search for text box.
- Click the Start Search button.

The SunnyMorningProducts Web site contains a Search Web page that enables users to locate matching keywords in any Web page in the Web site. Amanda wants you to use the Search page so that you can see the effectiveness of this type of component when designing a Web site. Keep in mind, however, that a component requires the processing capabilities of a server in order to generate a response. Because you are using a disk-based Web in this tutorial, you won't receive a response based on your search request. (Your Web page would display a search results page if it were stored on a Web server.)

To use the Search Web page:

1. Click the **Search** hyperlink in the banner frame at the top of the Products page. The Search page opens, replacing the entire frames page in the browser.

2. If necessary, scroll down the page so that you can see the **Start Search** and **Clear** buttons. See Figure 1-15.

Figure 1-15   SEARCH WEB PAGE

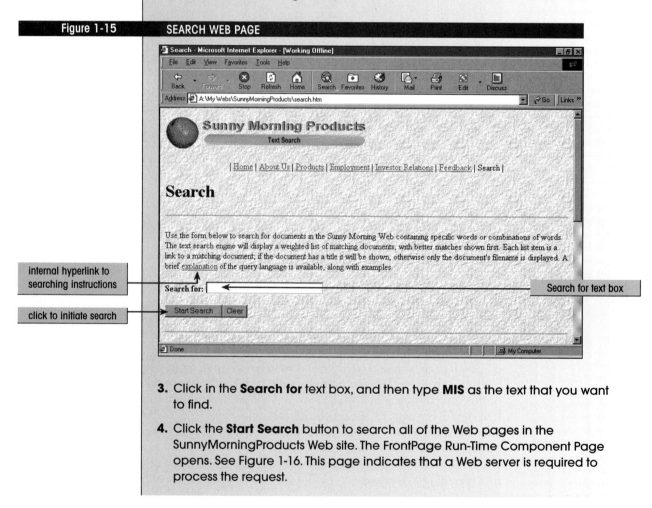

internal hyperlink to searching instructions

Search for text box

click to initiate search

3. Click in the **Search for** text box, and then type **MIS** as the text that you want to find.

4. Click the **Start Search** button to search all of the Web pages in the SunnyMorningProducts Web site. The FrontPage Run-Time Component Page opens. See Figure 1-16. This page indicates that a Web server is required to process the request.

Figure 1-16   **FRONTPAGE RUN-TIME COMPONENT PAGE**

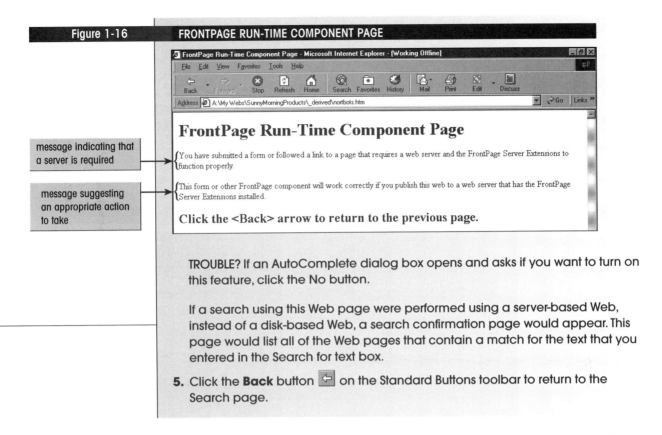

message indicating that a server is required

message suggesting an appropriate action to take

TROUBLE? If an AutoComplete dialog box opens and asks if you want to turn on this feature, click the No button.

If a search using this Web page were performed using a server-based Web, instead of a disk-based Web, a search confirmation page would appear. This page would list all of the Web pages that contain a match for the text that you entered in the Search for text box.

5. Click the **Back** button on the Standard Buttons toolbar to return to the Search page.

You will perform this type of search using a server-based Web in Tutorial 6. At that time, you will see how the Search Web page returns a page of hyperlinks to Web pages that contain your search text.

Using a Form Web Page

Often, Web pages are forms that a user completes and then submits to a Web server for processing. You use a **form Web page** to gather input from users. The information is then sent to the Web server for processing with the results saved to a text file or to a Web page on the server. A form Web page usually contains form objects, such as text boxes and check boxes, into which users input the requested information.

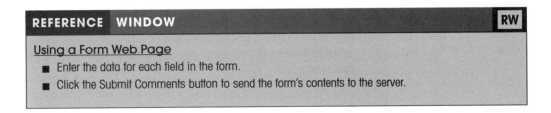

REFERENCE   WINDOW   **RW**

Using a Form Web Page
- Enter the data for each field in the form.
- Click the Submit Comments button to send the form's contents to the server.

The SunnyMorningProducts Web site contains two form Web pages: the customer order form, which processes customer orders, and the feedback form, which gathers customer feedback. A FrontPage component is used to process these forms on the server.

Amanda wants you to use a form Web page because it will be a key component in future Web sites that you will develop for your department.

To use a form Web page:

1. With the Search Web page displayed in your browser window, scroll up (if necessary) so that you can see the navigation bar, and then click the **Feedback** hyperlink to open the Feedback Web page.

2. Scroll down the Feedback Web page until you see several form objects, including option buttons, a drop-down menu, and a scrolling text box. See Figure 1-17.

Figure 1-17	FORM OBJECTS IN THE FEEDBACK WEB PAGE

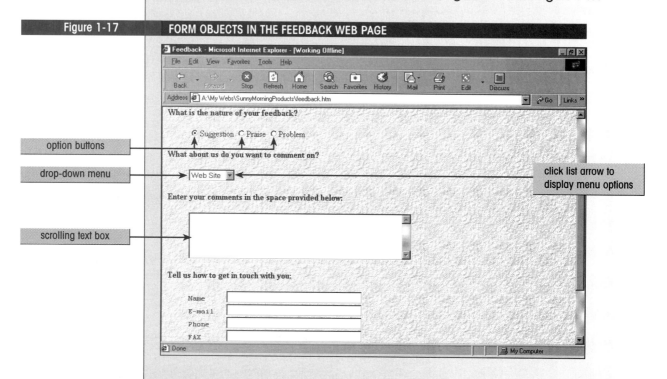

3. Click the **Praise** option button under "What is the nature of your feedback?" to select it.

4. Click the **list arrow** under "What about us do you want to comment on?" to display the menu options, and then click **Products**.

5. Click in the scrolling text box, and then type the following message: **Your Olympic Gold sports drink is great stuff. It really gives us the extra energy we need to keep going during our slow-pitch softball games. Without it, we wouldn't have won the company trophy. The new lemon-mango-strawberry flavor is super.**

6. Scroll down until you see additional form objects at the bottom of the page. See Figure 1-18. This part of the form uses several text boxes, a check box, and two buttons.

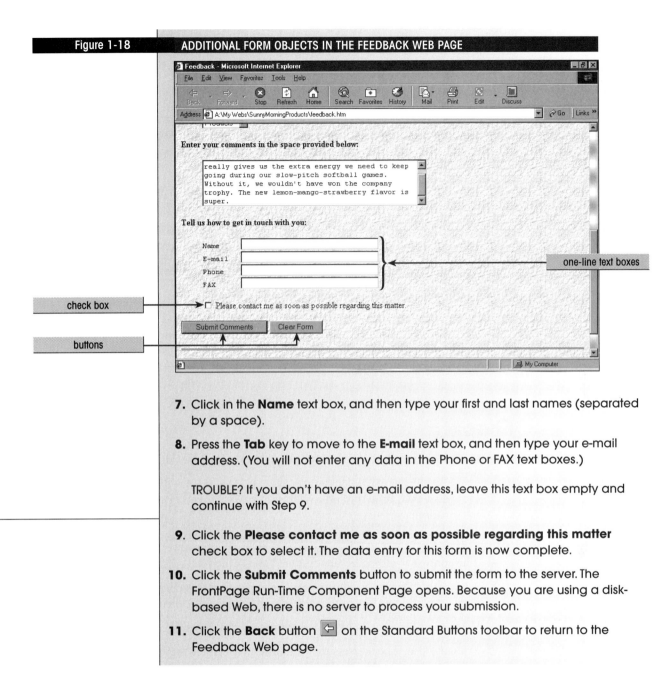

Figure 1-18   ADDITIONAL FORM OBJECTS IN THE FEEDBACK WEB PAGE

7. Click in the **Name** text box, and then type your first and last names (separated by a space).

8. Press the **Tab** key to move to the **E-mail** text box, and then type your e-mail address. (You will not enter any data in the Phone or FAX text boxes.)

   TROUBLE? If you don't have an e-mail address, leave this text box empty and continue with Step 9.

9. Click the **Please contact me as soon as possible regarding this matter** check box to select it. The data entry for this form is now complete.

10. Click the **Submit Comments** button to submit the form to the server. The FrontPage Run-Time Component Page opens. Because you are using a disk-based Web, there is no server to process your submission.

11. Click the **Back** button ⇐ on the Standard Buttons toolbar to return to the Feedback Web page.

When a form is submitted using a server-based Web, a default confirmation Web page is displayed in your window and your results are stored in a file on the server. You will learn about creating and processing forms in Tutorial 6.

Printing a Web Page

Sometimes you might want to print a Web page, such as when you need a paper copy of the information you have viewed or if you plan to give the information to someone who doesn't have Internet access. Also, when you visit other Web sites and find an interesting page, you might want to keep a printout to use as a reference as you design your own Web pages. In general, you can print any Web page that you can open. You continue your training by printing the Investor Relations Web page.

To print a Web page and close Internet Explorer:

1. Scroll up to the top of the Feedback Web page, and then click the **Investor Relations** hyperlink in the navigation bar. The Investor Relations Web page contains two tables that provide a summary of the company's financial performance and current stock information.

2. Click the **Print** button 🖨 on the Standard Buttons toolbar to print the current Web page.

   You have successfully examined several Web pages and printed the Investor Relations page. Next, close Internet Explorer.

3. Click the **Close** button ☒ on the Internet Explorer title bar to close the browser.

You have completed the first part of your training by examining the main features of the SunnyMorningProducts Web site. In the next session, you will explore this Web site using FrontPage.

Session 1.1 QUICK CHECK

1. A worldwide collection of computer networks that are connected to each other is the _____.

2. How do a Web browser and a Web server work together to provide you with information?

3. A(n) _____ page is the first page that a browser opens when it starts.

4. The address of a specific file on the Web is called its _____.

5. A keyword, phrase, or picture in a Web page that you click to open another Web page or a different location in the same Web page is called a(n) _____.

6. What are the two main differences between a disk-based Web and a server-based Web?

7. True or False: The address that identifies a specific computer on the Internet is called an Internet Protocol address.

8. True or False: A Web site is a set of related Web pages that are available from a Web server.

In this session, you will learn how to use FrontPage to create and maintain a Web site. You will open a Web site in different views to see its contents, navigation structure, available reports, and hyperlinks.

What Is FrontPage?

Microsoft FrontPage simplifies the development, maintenance, and publication of a Web site. Using this program, you can create, view, and edit your Web pages; insert and edit text and pictures; import and export files; and add, test, and repair hyperlinks to and within your pages. FrontPage lets you create, view, and manage your entire Web site. It includes features that make Web site creation easy, such as templates for creating Web pages and built-in functions for processing Web pages.

To create professional-looking Web pages, you don't need to know HTML. Instead, you use FrontPage's graphical interface to create Web pages and to develop and publish Web sites. When you **publish** a Web site, you store the Web site's files and folders on a Web server, which makes the Web site available to people using the Internet. FrontPage creates the HTML code for you that a Web browser interprets to display the data in your Web pages correctly.

A **FrontPage Web site**, or simply, a **Web site**, consists of the Web pages, files, and folders that make up the content of your Web site. It also includes the specific FrontPage server extension support files that allow your Web site to function correctly when accessed by people using the Internet. **FrontPage Server Extensions** are a set of programs and scripts that support FrontPage and allow a Web browser to send and receive Web pages that are processed by a Web server. When you create a Web site using FrontPage, these server extensions are created and included in the Web site automatically. You will learn more about the FrontPage Server Extensions in Tutorial 6.

You can create and publish a FrontPage Web site either on your computer, on a local area network, or on the Internet so that people can access it using a Web browser. A **local area network**, or **LAN**, is a group of computers that are located near each other and that are connected in order to share data, files, software, and hardware. The computers in the offices of Sunny Morning Products are an example of a LAN.

Starting FrontPage and Opening a Web Site

You are now ready to begin your training by starting FrontPage and using it to examine the Web site for Sunny Morning Products. You start FrontPage in the same manner as other Windows programs. After you examine Amanda's existing Web site, you will use FrontPage to create and manage a similar site as you complete the tutorials in this book.

REFERENCE   WINDOW   **RW**

__Opening a Web Site__
- Click the list arrow for the Open button on the Standard toolbar.
- Click Open Web in the list.
- Click the folder that contains your Web site.
- Click the Open button.

To start FrontPage and open the SunnyMorningProducts Web site:

1. Click the **Start** button on the taskbar, point to **Programs**, and then click **Microsoft FrontPage** to open FrontPage. A blank page opens in the FrontPage program window. See Figure 1-19.

Figure 1-19   **FRONTPAGE PROGRAM WINDOW**

TROUBLE? FrontPage might open the previously used Web site, instead of the blank page shown in Figure 1-19. If you see a Web site name listed in the title bar, instead of "Microsoft FrontPage," click File on the menu bar, click Close Web, and then continue with Step 2.

TROUBLE? FrontPage might open in a view different from the one shown in Figure 1-19, in which case your desktop might look different. This is not a problem; continue with Step 2.

TROUBLE? If necessary, maximize the program window so that it fills the desktop by clicking the Maximize button 🔲 on the title bar.

2. Click the list arrow for the **Open** button 🖻 on the Standard toolbar. You can use the Open button to open either a single Web page or an entire Web site. You will open a Web site next.

3. Click **Open Web** in the list. The Open Web dialog box opens.

TROUBLE? If the Open File dialog box opens, then you clicked Open in the list instead of Open Web. Click the Cancel button, and then repeat Steps 2 and 3.

You need to change to the drive or folder that contains your Data Disk to open the SunnyMorningProducts Web site.

4. Click the **Look in** list arrow, and then click the drive or folder that contains your Data Disk.

5. Double-click the **My Webs** folder, click the **SunnyMorningProducts** folder to select the folder that contains the files for the Web site for Sunny Morning Products, and then click the **Open** button in the dialog box to open the Web site in FrontPage.

6. Click the **Folders** button 📁 on the Views bar to change to Folders view. See Figure 1-20.

| Figure 1-20 | SUNNYMORNINGPRODUCTS WEB SITE IN FOLDERS VIEW |

The various components of the FrontPage window that appear in Figure 1-20 are described in detail in Figure 1-21.

| Figure 1-21 | COMPONENTS OF THE FRONTPAGE WINDOW |

COMPONENT	DESCRIPTION
Contents pane	Contains the open Web page or Web site
Folder List	Contains the folders and files that make up the open Web site
Menu bar	Located below the title bar, provides access to all options available in the current FrontPage view
Scroll bar	Located at the right and bottom of the window, scrolls the window vertically and horizontally as necessary
Status bar	Located at the bottom of the window, displays messages about the current Web page or FrontPage action; also displays the name of a toolbar button when you position the pointer over the button
Title bar	Located at the top of the window, displays the program's name and the name of the open Web site
Toolbars	Located below the menu bar, contain different icons that represent shortcuts to commonly used commands
Views bar	Provides the list of available views for your Web site

Using **Views**

FrontPage **views** provide different ways of looking at the information in your Web site so that you can effectively create and manage it. You click the buttons on the Views bar to switch among the different views, such as Folders or Page view. Six views are available, as described in Figure 1-22 and in the following sections.

Figure 1-22	FRONTPAGE VIEWS	
VIEW	**BUTTON**	**DESCRIPTION**
Page		Use to create, edit, and format the content of a Web page
Folders		Use to view, create, delete, copy, and move folders in the open Web site
Reports		Use to analyze, summarize, and produce reports about a Web site
Navigation		Use to display a Web site as a diagram that shows its navigation structure
Hyperlinks		Use to graphically display the hyperlinks between Web pages in a Web site
Tasks		Use to maintain a list of the tasks required to complete a Web site

Page View

You use **Page view** to create, edit, and format the content of your Web page. The filename of the open Web page in Page view appears in the title bar of the Contents pane. You can customize Page view in many ways.

■ To see more of the open Web page in the Contents pane, you can close the Views bar and/or the Folder List. Click View on the menu bar, and then click Views Bar and/or Folder List as needed. To open these items again, repeat the process.

■ To show or hide the formatting symbols in your document, click the Show All button ¶ on the Standard toolbar. To hide the formatting symbols again, click ¶ again.

■ To see more of the open Web page in Page view, you can display the Standard and Formatting toolbars on one row. Click View on the menu bar, point to Toolbars, and then click Customize. Next, click the Standard and Formatting toolbars share one row check box on the Options tab. The disadvantage of the toolbars sharing one row is that some buttons at the end of the toolbar do not appear on the screen. To see them, click the More Buttons button ⚡ at the end of the toolbar. The figures in these tutorials assume that your toolbars appear on two rows so that you can more easily locate and click the toolbar buttons.

Next, Amanda asks you to open the Home Page of the SunnyMorningProducts Web site in Page view.

To open and preview a page in Page view:

1. Double-click **index.htm** in the Contents pane to open the Home Page in Page view. See Figure 1-23. Notice that the toolbars change to display options that you can use to edit this page.

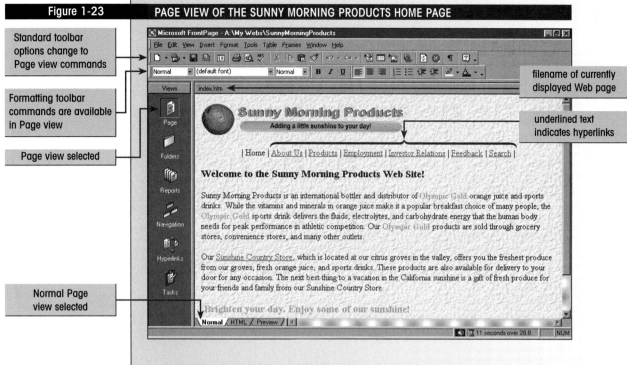

Figure 1-23   PAGE VIEW OF THE SUNNY MORNING PRODUCTS HOME PAGE

Standard toolbar options change to Page view commands

Formatting toolbar commands are available in Page view

Page view selected

Normal Page view selected

filename of currently displayed Web page

underlined text indicates hyperlinks

TROUBLE? If your Folder List does not close automatically, click the Folder List button 🔲 on the Standard toolbar so that your screen matches Figure 1-23.

Page view has three views you can use to examine your Web page: Normal, HTML, and Preview. You click the tabs in the lower-left corner of the Contents pane, as shown in Figure 1-23, to switch among these views. Most of the time, you will work in **Normal view**, where you enter and revise your Web page. When you open a Web page in Page view, it usually opens in Normal view. **HTML view** lets you view and edit the HTML code for your Web page. **Preview view** lets you quickly see your page as it will appear in a Web browser without your having to start the browser program.

By default, the Views bar is open so that it is easy to switch among the different FrontPage views. When you are working in a view, you can close the Views bar to permit more of the view to appear on the screen.

2. Click **View** on the menu bar, and then click **Views Bar**. The Views bar closes and the Home Page fills the screen. You can turn the Views bar back on by repeating Step 2. For now, however, you will leave the Views bar hidden so that you can see more of the Web page. (Showing or hiding the Views bar is a matter of personal preference.)

3. Point to the **Products** hyperlink at the top of the page. Notice that when you move the mouse pointer over the hyperlink, the name of the linked file appears in the lower-left corner of the status bar. Also, notice that the ScreenTip indicates that you can press the Ctrl key and click the hyperlink (Ctrl + Click) to follow the hyperlink.

4. Click the **Preview** tab at the bottom of the window. The view changes to show how your Web page will look when viewed by a Web browser on the Internet. See Figure 1-24.

| Figure 1-24 | PREVIEW OF THE HOME PAGE |

Preview in
Browser button

scrolling marquee
animates on the
Preview tab

download time for
this page using a
28.8 bps modem

Notice that the lower-right corner of the status bar shows how much time is required for a Web browser with a 28.8 bits per second (bps) modem connection to download this page. Also notice that this page contains an active element, called a **marquee**, which causes the text "Brighten your day. Enjoy some of our sunshine!" to scroll across the bottom of the screen.

5. Click the **Preview in Browser** button 🔍 on the Standard toolbar to open the Web page in Internet Explorer. If necessary, maximize the Internet Explorer program window by clicking the **Maximize** button 🔲 on the title bar. See Figure 1-25.

| Figure 1-25 | HOME PAGE IN INTERNET EXPLORER |

TROUBLE? This book assumes that you are using Internet Explorer 5 as your Web browser. If you are using Netscape Navigator version 4.5 or lower, or an earlier version of Internet Explorer, then your Web page might not animate the text in the marquee. In addition, your instructor might provide you with different steps so that you can use your Web browser correctly.

Notice that the page looks approximately the same in Internet Explorer as when you viewed it using the Preview tab in FrontPage. The Preview tab does not always provide an accurate rendering of the page as it ultimately appears in the browser, so it is important to open a Web page in the browser periodically as you are developing it to ensure that your design is displayed correctly.

Folders View

You use **Folders view** to view and navigate the folders in your FrontPage Web site. Clicking a folder in Folders view shows the folder's contents, along with valuable information about each file in the folder, such as its size, type, and title. Using Folders view is very similar to using Windows Explorer to examine files. When you double-click a filename in Folders view, the file opens in Page view. Amanda wants you to examine the files and folders that comprise the Web site, so you will change to Folders view.

To change to Folders view:

1. Click the **Close** button ☒ on the Internet Explorer title bar to close it.

2. If necessary, click the **Microsoft FrontPage** program button on the taskbar to return to FrontPage, and then click the **Normal** tab to return to Normal Page view.

3. Click **View** on the menu bar, and then click **Views Bar** to show the Views bar.

4. Click the **Folders** button 📁 on the Views bar to change to Folders view. The Web site is stored in a folder named SunnyMorningProducts, which contains two folders (_private and images), and 16 files. The **_private folder** contains the hidden files that make up a Web site. **Hidden files** are files that are not accessible to users of your Web site after it is published. You will learn more about hidden files in Tutorial 6. The **images folder** contains all of the picture and multimedia files that are included in a Web site.

Reports View

Reports view lets you analyze and summarize your Web site and generate reports that contain useful information about your Web site. For example, the **Site Summary report** contains statistical information to help you to manage your Web site, including information about the total number and size of the site's files, the number of pictures in the site, and the names of Web pages in the site that are slow to download (pages that take longer than a set number of seconds using a 28.8 bps modem; the default setting is 20 seconds). FrontPage generates a Site Summary report automatically when you change to Reports view, as you will see next.

To change to Reports view:

1. Click the **Reports** button 🗐 on the Views bar. Figure 1-26 shows a Site Summary report for the SunnyMorningProducts Web site. It is a good idea to run a Site Summary report periodically as you develop a Web site so that you can locate and correct problems as you work. Notice that you can use the Report list arrow on the Reporting toolbar to display different reports.

| Figure 1-26 | SITE SUMMARY REPORT IN REPORTS VIEW |

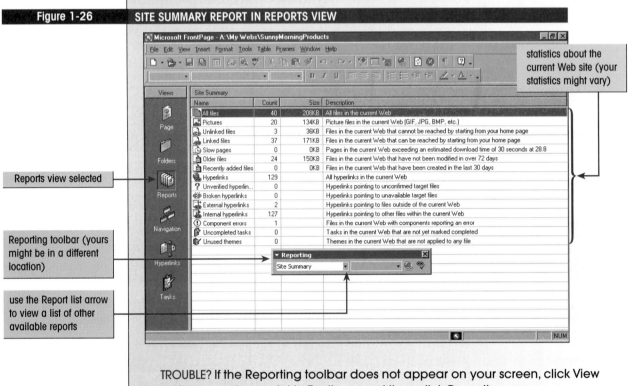

Reports view selected

Reporting toolbar (yours might be in a different location)

use the Report list arrow to view a list of other available reports

statistics about the current Web site (your statistics might vary)

TROUBLE? If the Reporting toolbar does not appear on your screen, click View on the menu bar, point to Toolbars, and then click Reporting.

TROUBLE? If the Reporting toolbar is blocking part of the Site Summary report, drag it to an open area of your screen so that you can see the entire Site Summary report.

TROUBLE? If you don't see the Site Summary report, click the Report list arrow on the Reporting toolbar, and then click Site Summary in the list.

Navigation View

Navigation view displays your Web site as a diagram that shows its navigation structure in a folder-like hierarchy that resembles an organization chart. This hierarchy allows you to drag and drop pages into your site structure to show how pages are related to each other. You can size Navigation view to fit the Contents pane to make it easier to examine this diagram. In addition, you can change the arrangement of the view to rotate the objects, and you can print Navigation view.

Amanda asks you to open the SunnyMorningProducts Web site in Navigation view so that you can examine its structure.

To explore a Web site in Navigation view:

1. Click the **Navigation** button 🖻 on the Views bar to change to Navigation view for the SunnyMorningProducts Web site.

2. If necessary, click the **Zoom** list arrow on the Navigation toolbar, and then click **Size To Fit** to size Navigation view to fit the Contents pane. See Figure 1-27.

| Figure 1-27 | NAVIGATION VIEW OF THE SUNNYMORNINGPRODUCTS WEB SITE |

TROUBLE? If the Navigation toolbar does not appear on your screen, click View on the menu bar, point to Toolbars, and then click Navigation.

TROUBLE? If the Navigation toolbar is blocking the diagram, drag it to an open area of your screen so that you can see all of the Web site's navigation structure.

Navigation view shows that the Home Page is the top-level page in the Web site. The top-level page in a Web site is called the **parent page**; normally a Web site's Home Page is its parent page. A page that appears below the parent page or another page in a Web site's structure is called a **child page**. Seven child pages are shown below the Home Page. One of those—the What's New Web page—is a child page of the Profile Web page. When you create a new Web site, only the Home Page is displayed in Navigation view. To add a page to Navigation view, you drag its filename from the Folder List and drop it into the correct position in the navigation structure. You use Navigation view when creating a **FrontPage navigation bar**, which is a group of hyperlinks to link the pages in the Web site; this type of navigation bar is created and updated automatically by FrontPage. You will learn more about Navigation view and FrontPage navigation bars in Tutorial 5.

Hyperlinks View

In **Hyperlinks view**, your Web site appears graphically as a hierarchical picture of the hyperlinks that connect its files, including multimedia files.

Amanda wants you to know how to view a Web site in Hyperlinks view so that you can see how the Web pages that make up the Web site are linked together. Hyperlinks view shows only part of the entire Web site at one time, so you must adjust the page in order to view its other areas.

To view a Web site in Hyperlinks view:

1. Click the **Hyperlinks** button 📷 on the Views bar, and then, if necessary, click **index.htm** in the Folder List to see the Hyperlinks view of the Home Page for the SunnyMorningProducts Web site. See Figure 1-28.

Figure 1-28   **HYPERLINKS VIEW OF THE HOME PAGE**

Home Page (index.htm)
selected

TROUBLE? You can customize Hyperlinks view to show page titles instead of page filenames, so your Hyperlinks view might show names different from those in Figure 1-28. To show the page titles or filenames, right-click the background in Hyperlinks view, and then click Show Page Titles on the shortcut menu to turn this feature on or off.

TROUBLE? As you switch among views in your Web site and examine its files and folders, you might find that names appear in uppercase letters, lowercase letters, or mixed-case letters. Each file and folder is uniquely identified by its name, regardless of the case of the letters.

In Figure 1-28, most of the hyperlinks end with an arrow, but one ends with a bullet. An arrow indicates a hyperlink to another Web page in your Web site; a bullet indicates a hyperlink to a sound or other type of file.

Switching Pages

Although the default Web page in Hyperlinks view is the Home Page (displayed in the Contents pane), you can easily switch to another page in the Web site. The selected page then becomes the focus of Hyperlinks view. When you maintain and create a Web site, you should use Hyperlinks view to examine the various pages that make up that Web site to ensure that you are linking them correctly. FrontPage makes it easy for you to follow the hyperlinks from one page to the next. Amanda asks you to change the focus of Hyperlinks view to the Products page, so you can examine its hyperlinks.

To switch pages:

1. Click **products.htm** in the Folder List. The Products page becomes the focus and its hyperlinks display in the Contents pane so that you can see the origin and destination of each hyperlink to and from the Products Web page.

2. Click **index.htm** in the Folder List to display this page again with the focus in the Contents pane.

Following a Hyperlink

You can follow the hyperlinks from one document to another by expanding (showing) or contracting (hiding) the hyperlinks displayed in Hyperlinks view. Expanding the hyperlinks lets you see how the pages in a Web site are connected to each other. Amanda asks you to follow the hyperlinks from the Products page.

To follow a hyperlink:

1. Click the **plus (+)** symbol in the products.htm icon to expand this hyperlink and display the pages used with the Products frames page.

2. Click the **plus (+)** symbol in the contents.htm icon to expand this hyperlink. The pages referenced by all of the hyperlinks in the content frame are included in the diagram.

3. Click the **plus (+)** symbol in the ordrinfo.htm icon to expand this hyperlink. See Figure 1-29. Now you can see how the hyperlinks extend from the Home Page to the ordrinfo.htm page, and beyond.

Figure 1-29	EXPANDED HYPERLINKS IN HYPERLINKS VIEW

arrows show how hyperlinks connect the Web pages

To contract the hyperlinks, you would click the minus (-) symbol for the desired page.

Displaying a Repeated Hyperlink

As you saw in Session 1.1, a Web page can contain more than one hyperlink to the same location in a page or in a Web site. A hyperlink to a location that already is the target of another hyperlink is called a **repeated hyperlink**. You can examine the repeated hyperlinks in a Web site in Hyperlinks view to help determine if you have defined all of the hyperlinks among the pages in your Web site. The Home Page contains two hyperlinks to the Products page—one in the navigation bar and another in the text in the page—as you will see next.

> ### To display the repeated hyperlinks in the Home Page:
>
> **1.** Right-click any open area in the Contents pane, and then click **Repeated Hyperlinks** on the shortcut menu. Hyperlinks view changes to show the repeated hyperlinks for the Home Page. See Figure 1-30.

Figure 1-30	REPEATED HYPERLINKS FOR THE HOME PAGE

> TROUBLE? If you see a check mark in front of the Repeated Hyperlinks command, then this feature is already turned on; clicking it will turn off the display of the repeated hyperlinks.
>
> **2.** Repeat Step 1 to return to Hyperlinks view without displaying the repeated hyperlinks.

Tasks View

One way to manage the development of a Web site is to use a **Tasks list**, which is a detailed listing of the necessary activities or items required to complete a Web site. It describes each task, indicates the person assigned to complete it, and specifies its priority. Once you have completed the initial design of your Web site, you can create a Tasks list that describes all of the pages you need to develop. You can add activities to it, modify task names, assign developers, and include descriptions. When a task is finished, you can mark it as completed and then archive or delete it from the Tasks list. To open the Tasks list, click the Tasks button 📋 on the Views bar. When many people are working on developing a new Web site, they can use Tasks view to manage the Web site's overall development. You will learn more about Tasks view in Tutorial 3.

Closing a Web Site and Exiting FrontPage

You can close a Web site before exiting FrontPage, or you can close FrontPage and any open Web site at the same time. FrontPage allows only one open Web site at a time, so Amanda wants you to learn how to close a Web site. Then you will exit FrontPage.

To close a Web site and exit FrontPage:

1. Click **File** on the menu bar, and then click **Close Web**. FrontPage closes the SunnyMorningProducts Web site.

   TROUBLE? If you do not see the Close Web command on the File menu, keep the File menu open for a few seconds, and then the menu will show the command.

2. Click the **Close** button ⊠ on the FrontPage program window to close this program.

In the next session, Amanda will review some basic HTML concepts with you. Although you will use FrontPage to create and edit your Web pages, it is important for you to understand the HTML code that FrontPage uses to create these pages.

Session 1.2 QUICK CHECK

1. What is the main advantage of using FrontPage to create and maintain a Web site?

2. You create, edit, and format the content of a Web page in _____ view.

3. The FrontPage view that lets you analyze and summarize your Web site is _____ view.

4. The FrontPage view that shows your Web site's hierarchy of parent and child pages is _____ view.

5. What is a repeated hyperlink?

6. You can use a(n) _____ to manage the development of a Web site and to coordinate the efforts of many people.

7. True or False: You can use Page view to see the HTML code that FrontPage used to create a Web page.

8. True or False: You can use Internet Explorer to determine the approximate time required to download a specific Web page using a Web browser.

SESSION 1.3

In this session, you will learn how HTML is used to define a Web page. You will use FrontPage and Internet Explorer to view the HTML code for a Web page. Finally, you will use the FrontPage Help system.

How HTML Works

Recall that HTML describes the appearance of a Web page that you create using FrontPage. The code in an HTML document specifies the appearance of text in terms of its font (such as Arial or Times Roman), its attributes (such as bold or italic), or its placement (such as a heading or a bulleted list). An HTML document also contains codes that specify the playing of sound files, the placement of pictures, and the appearance of the page's background, if these elements are used. A Web browser interprets the HTML codes in a Web page to determine how to display these elements on the page when the page is viewed by a client.

Even though HTML uses a standard character set to ensure that documents can be easily transferred and viewed by many different types of computers, not all Web browsers interpret these codes and display the requested HTML document in *exactly* the same way. For example, text that is formatted as bold might be displayed as bold text by one browser or as blue text by another browser. Even with this limitation, the use of HTML in storing, transferring, and viewing HTML documents among the many different computers that are connected to the Internet is the key element in providing a standard method for displaying information.

Understanding HTML Tags

The HTML document that creates a Web page contains codes, called **tags**, that the browser interprets when displaying the page. The name of an HTML tag is enclosed in angle brackets (< >). Most tags are **two-sided**; that is, they are used in pairs that consist of an opening tag and a closing tag. The **opening tag** is the first tag, which tells the browser to turn on a particular feature and apply it to the document content that follows the tag. The browser continues applying the feature until it encounters the **closing tag**, which is the indication to the browser to stop applying the feature. The forward slash character identifies a closing tag (/) in the tag name. For example, the pair of tags <BODY> and </BODY> specify the beginning and end of the body of an HTML document, and the tags <B> and </B> indicate the beginning and end of boldface text.

Most tags are two-sided, but some tags are **one-sided**, that is, they require only an opening tag. When a one-sided tag is used, the browser stops applying the formatting indicated by the one-sided tag when it encounters a new line.

Some common tags are described in Figure 1-31. The ellipsis (...) in the tags indicates the text information that is entered by the Web page creator, either between two-sided tags or to the right of a one-sided tag.

Figure 1-31 | **SELECTED HTML TAG DESCRIPTIONS**

HTML TAG	DESCRIPTION	USE
<! ... >	Creates a comment that is not displayed in the Web page.	To document HTML code and to insert comments. For example, a comment might indicate that a frames page may not be recognized by all Web browsers.
<A> ... </A>	Defines a hyperlink or an anchor.	Indicates an internal or external hyperlink and its target.
<B> ... </B>	Changes text to bold.	
<BGSOUND SRC=...>	Specifies a background sound.	Indicates the filename containing the sound.
<BLOCKQUOTE> ... </BLOCKQUOTE>	Indents text.	Sets off long quotations or for other text indention.
<BODY> ... </BODY>	Encloses the body of the HTML document.	
 	Forces a new line break on a page.	
<DD> ... </DD>	Specifies a definition within a glossary list.	Provides a heading line for a defined term.
<DL> ... </DL>	Specifies a definition or glossary list.	
<DT> ... </DT>	Specifies a definition term within a glossary list.	Provides font size and indentation for a defined term.
<EM> ... </EM>	Emphasizes text, usually with italic.	
<H1> ... </H1> <H2> ... </H2> <H3> ... </H3> <H4> ... </H4> <H5> ... </H5> <H6> ... </H6>	Specifies a heading and its level.	Indicates the font size of a heading. H1 has the largest size.
<HR>	Draws a horizontal line across the page.	Provides a visual break for sections of a page.
<HTML> ... </HTML>	Encloses the entire HTML document.	Identifies the file as one that contains HTML codes.
<I> ... </I>	Italicizes the text.	
<IMG> ... </IMG>	Specifies the appearance of a picture in a page.	Inserts a picture from a file into the HTML document.
<LI> ... </LI>	Specifies an individual element in a list.	
<OL> ... </OL>	Specifies an ordered list of elements.	Creates numbered elements in a list.
<P> ... </P>	Divides text into paragraphs.	
<PRE> ... </PRE>	Specifies preformatted text.	Keeps the spacing arrangement of text as entered in the document. Use for text that needs special indentations or column layouts.
<STRONG> ... </STRONG>	Strongly emphasizes text, usually with bold.	
<TABLE> ... </TABLE>	Specifies a table.	Organizes data in a row-and-column table arrangement.
<TD> ... </TD>	Defines the data contained in a table's cells.	
<TH> ... </TH>	Creates a row of headings in a table.	
<TITLE> ... </TITLE>	Defines the text that appears in the Web browser's title bar.	Creates the Web page's title.
<TR> ... </TR>	Indicates the beginning of a row in a table.	Provides rows that hold the data for each cell.
<TT> ... </TT>	Formats text in typewriter font, usually Courier.	Applies monospaced font; used with the <PRE> tag.
<UL> ... </UL>	Specifies an unordered list of elements.	Creates bulleted elements in a list.

Just as important as the tags themselves is the order of their placement. Tags often appear within each other; these tags are **nested tags**. The browser processes the tag on the outside, called the **outside tag**, first, and then it processes the tag on the inside, called the **inside tag**. When nesting tags, you must close the inside tag before closing the outside tag. When you create a nested list—for example, a bulleted list within a numbered list—in a Web page, FrontPage handles the opening and closing of each pair of tags automatically. You only need to be concerned with nesting the tags if you decide to make changes directly to your HTML code, which is not the recommended approach when using FrontPage. However, it is helpful to understand how a browser applies two different formats to a single text segment.

Many HTML tags require one or more **attributes**, or properties, that specify additional information about the tag. For example, an attribute might supply a sound's filename to an HTML tag which specifies that a sound plays on the Web page. Attributes are included within the brackets that enclose the tag. Figure 1-32 shows an example of some of the HTML tags for the Sunny Morning Products Home Page. (*Note*: For clarity, tag names are set in all capital letters in the text, even though they appear in lowercase letters in FrontPage.) The <BODY> tag specifies the beginning of the body of the HTML document. Included with this tag is the BACKGROUND attribute, which specifies the name of the file that contains the page's background picture. The <BGSOUND> tag indicates that a background sound is included. The source of this sound, which is a sound file, is indicated by the SRC (for "source") attribute. The LOOP attribute specifies how many times the browser should repeat the sound while the page is open.

Figure 1-32	HTML CODE IN PAGE VIEW

You can create an HTML document using a program other than FrontPage; for example, you can use a text editor, such as Notepad, or an HTML authoring program. Notepad does not insert any HTML codes into its document file. Instead you need to write and edit the codes yourself, and therefore, you need to know each tag's name and its attributes. Writing HTML code can be tedious when creating a complex Web page. FrontPage's ability to enter HTML codes automatically lets you create an HTML document without needing to learn HTML. Regardless of how a Web page was created, you can use FrontPage to open the Web page and make any revisions to it.

Viewing **HTML Code**

By viewing the HTML code for a Web page, you can see how a particular feature has been implemented using HMTL tags. In this book, you will create and edit Web pages using FrontPage. However, you will study the HTML code that FrontPage used to create the Web page to gain a better understanding of how HTML works. Some Web page authors find it easier to make changes directly to the HTML code, even when working in FrontPage. You can examine a Web page's HTML code by using FrontPage, a Web browser, or any text editor.

Viewing HTML Code Using FrontPage

When you view HTML code using FrontPage, the HTML codes appear in a different color (usually, blue) to distinguish between your page's content and the HTML tags that FrontPage automatically created for you. Amanda asks you to examine the HTML code for the Sunny Morning Products Home Page.

To view HTML code using FrontPage:

1. If necessary, start **FrontPage**, open the **SunnyMorningProducts** Web site in Folders view, and then open the **Home Page (index.htm)** in Page view.

2. Click the **HTML** tab at the bottom of the Contents pane to display the page's HTML code. Notice that the HTML tags appear in blue, and the content of the Web page (as entered by the page's creator) appears in black.

3. Inspect the HTML code to see if you can identify the tags that provide the formatting instructions that create the Home Page. As you work through the tutorials in this book, you will learn about the different HTML tags that specify the appearance of the Web pages for Sunny Morning Products.

4. Click the **Normal** tab to return to Page view.

Viewing HTML Code Using Internet Explorer

Another method of viewing HTML code is to use your Web browser, which is convenient when you want to inspect the HTML code for a Web page that was created by someone else and that you opened on the Web. Next, you will view the HTML code for the Home Page using Internet Explorer.

To view HTML code using Internet Explorer:

1. Click the **Preview in Browser** button 🔍 on the Standard toolbar. If necessary, maximize the Internet Explorer window. The Home Page opens in the browser.

2. Click **View** on the menu bar, and then click **Source**. Notepad starts automatically and displays the HTML document that created this Web page. When you view the HTML code in Notepad, it's a good idea to turn on the Word Wrap command so that the HTML code will fit in the window.

3. Click **Edit** on the Notepad menu bar, and then click **Word Wrap**. Now all of the HTML code fits in the Notepad window. Notice that the HTML code is the same as that displayed in Page view, except that the HTML codes do not appear in a different color.

   TROUBLE? If the Word Wrap command has a check mark in front of it, then the Word Wrap feature is already on. If you accidentally turned off the Word Wrap feature, repeat Step 3 to turn it back on.

4. Click the **Close** button ✕ on the Notepad program window. If you turned on the Word Wrap feature, a dialog box opens and asks if you want to save your changes. You didn't change the code, so do not need to save the file.

5. If necessary, click the **No** button to close the dialog box and Notepad.

6. Click ✕ on the Internet Explorer program window to close Internet Explorer.

Getting Help in FrontPage

The FrontPage Help system provides the same options as the Help systems in other Windows programs, including the Contents, the Answer Wizard, and the Index tabs. You also can obtain help while working on your Web pages by clicking the What's This? command on the Help menu. The What's This? command provides **context-sensitive Help**, which is Help that is specific to your current task. When you choose this command from the Help menu, the pointer changes to the Help pointer ⏳?. You then click any object or option on the screen to see its description.

To use Help:

1. Click **Help** on the menu bar, and then click **Microsoft FrontPage Help**. The Microsoft FrontPage Help window opens. Depending on your computer's settings, the Help window might open so that the FrontPage window remains visible on one side of the desktop, or it might open as a maximized window on the desktop.

2. If necessary, click the **Show** button 🔲 on the toolbar in the Help window to display the Contents, Answer Wizard, and Index tabs. See Figure 1-33.

| Figure 1-33 | MICROSOFT FRONTPAGE HELP WINDOW |

Show/Hide button

tabs are displayed

After you click the Show button, it changes to the Hide button, which you can click to hide the Contents, Answer Wizard, and Index tabs.

Amanda wants you to learn how to use FrontPage to print the HTML code for a Web page. The **Contents tab** lets you search for information that is organized into groups by subject, such as "Designing Webs" or "Authoring HTML." The **Answer Wizard tab** lets you find Help by asking a question. The Wizard provides hyperlinks to information that might answer your question. The **Index tab** lets you enter a specific term or phrase. Help then displays a list of hyperlinks that contain that term or phrase. You decide that the Answer Wizard is the best approach to use now.

3. Click the **Answer Wizard** tab to select it. The "Type your question here and then click Search" phrase is selected in the What would you like to do? text box.

4. Type **How do I print the HTML code for a Web page?** in the text box, and then click the **Search** button. See Figure 1-34. Help provides five topics that might answer your question. The first topic is automatically selected, and the text of that topic is displayed in the right frame of the Help window. Read the information so that you know how to print the HTML code for a Web page.

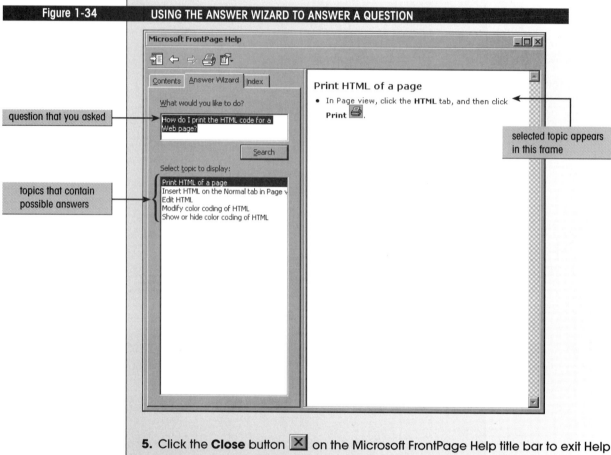

Figure 1-34   USING THE ANSWER WIZARD TO ANSWER A QUESTION

question that you asked

topics that contain possible answers

selected topic appears in this frame

5. Click the **Close** button ☒ on the Microsoft FrontPage Help title bar to exit Help and return to FrontPage.

6. Click ☒ on the FrontPage title bar to close it and the SunnyMorningProducts Web site.

Now that you have a better understanding of Microsoft FrontPage and are familiar with the Web site that Amanda created for Sunny Morning Products, you can proceed with the next part of your training. In Tutorial 2, you will learn the five-part process for developing a Web site.

Session 1.3 QUICK CHECK

1. Some HTML tags require _____ that contain additional information about an HTML document's appearance.

2. What are two methods for viewing the HTML code of a Web page?

3. Write a line of HTML code to italicize the words "Home Page" in a Web page.

4. The _____ tab in the Microsoft FrontPage Help window lets you find information that is organized into groups by subject.

5. True or False: You can use HTML to create a nested list in a Web page.

6. True or False: When viewing HTML code in Internet Explorer, the HTML tags and properties appear in different colors.

REVIEW ASSIGNMENTS

Amanda is pleased with the progress you are making in your training course. Before you continue with your training, however, she wants you to examine some additional Web page features to help you increase your understanding of Web pages and Web browsers. By practicing these related skills, you will be better prepared for developing future Web pages.

If necessary, start Internet Explorer, insert your Data Disk in the appropriate disk drive, and then do the following:

1. Type a:\My Webs\SunnyMorningProducts\index.htm in the Address bar, and then press the Enter key to open the Home Page for Sunny Morning Products.

Explore   2. Click View on the menu bar, and then click Full Screen to increase the size of the Internet Explorer window. Next click the Products hyperlink to open that Web page, and then examine each of the four alternatives available in the contents frame by selecting each hyperlink in turn to open the linked Web page. Note whether the page displayed in the main frame changes while the other pages displayed in the other frames remain the same.

3. Click anywhere in the banner frame, except on a hyperlink, to give this frame the focus. Print the Web page that is displayed in the banner frame by clicking the Print button on the Standard Buttons toolbar.

Explore   4. Use Internet Explorer to display the HTML code for the Products page. (*Hint*: Right-click the Web page to open the shortcut menu, but do not right-click a picture or a hyperlink, and then use a command on the shortcut menu to view the HTML code.) Describe the HTML code that opens in the Notepad window. Does the HTML code contain tags for the banner, contents, or the main frame's page, or for none of these pages? Close Notepad.

5. Right-click the page that appears in the main frame to open the shortcut menu, and then click View Source to display the HTML code. Note whether this is the same code you viewed in Step 4 or if it describes the page that is displayed in the main frame. Close Notepad.

6. If necessary, use a hyperlink in the contents frame to open the Order Information page in the main frame, and then scroll to the bottom of the page. Click the order form hyperlink to open the Order Form page in the main frame.

Explore   7. Fill out the order form with data that you make up, and then print the Order Form Web page.

Explore   8. Click the Send Order push button to simulate the action of submitting a completed order form. (*Hint*: If you do not enter a month number or a four-digit year number in the text boxes next to the Card Number, the submission will fail. You will need to change those values before the submission is accepted.) What happens after you submit the form, and why?

Explore   9. Return to the Order Form page, and then click the Clear Order push button to remove the data you entered from the order form. Display and print the HTML code for the Order Form Web page.

Explore   10. Review the printout of the Order Form Web page, and then circle the HTML code that creates the Send Order button on the printout. Close Notepad and Internet Explorer.

11. Start FrontPage and then open the **SunnyMorningProducts** Web site in Navigation view. Click the Print button on the Standard toolbar to print the view.

Explore   12. Use the Help system to learn how to produce a report of slow pages. Review the information that you find, and then print it. Close Help.

13. Change to Reports view. Run a Slow Pages report and find all the pages that take longer than 15 seconds to download. Which page(s), if any, did your report identify?

Explore   14. Change to Hyperlinks view and set the **contents.htm** page as the focus. Then print Hyperlinks view. (*Hint*: FrontPage does not have a feature to print Hyperlinks view, so you must print the screen. In Hyperlinks view, press the Print Screen key on the keyboard. Click the Start button on the taskbar, point to Programs, point to Accessories, and then click WordPad. Click the Paste button on the WordPad Standard toolbar to paste the image into the blank WordPad document. Then click File on the menu bar, click Page Setup, click the Landscape option button in the Orientation section, and then click the OK button. Click the Print button on the Standard toolbar to print the image. Close WordPad without saving changes.)

15. Close FrontPage.

CASE PROBLEMS

Case 1. Exploring the Web Site for the American Carpenters Society The American Carpenters Society (ACS) is a not-for-profit organization that enhances the skills of professional carpenters. ACS has a small headquarters staff of 15 people that supports its entire membership. Recently, Adi McDonald, ACS president, hired you to support all of the end-user computing activities at the ACS. Adi wants you to maintain the daily operations of the company's computers and of the ACS Web site. She had previously contracted EarthShare, its current ISP, to create and maintain the ACS Web site. However, she prefers to have the ongoing development of the Web site managed in-house so you can easily adapt it.

If necessary, start Internet Explorer, insert your Data Disk in the appropriate disk drive, and then do the following:

1. Open the Home Page for the ACS Web site on your Data Disk. (*Hint*: Type the following text into the appropriate location in Internet Explorer: a:\My Webs\Carpenter\index.htm and then press the Enter key.)

2. Click the Membership Benefits hyperlink at the top of the Web page to open the Membership Benefits Web page. Examine each of the four alternatives available in the Table of Contents by clicking a hyperlink and opening the linked Web page. Note if the page that opens in the main frame changes while the pages in the other frames remain the same.

3. Click anywhere in the banner frame, but do not click a hyperlink, to select the banner frame.

4. Print the page that appears in the banner frame, and then print the page that appears in the main frame.

Explore   5. Use Internet Explorer to display the HTML code for the Membership Benefits Web page, and then print it. What does the HTML code for this page describe? Close Notepad.

6. Right-click the main frame to open the shortcut menu, and then click View Source to display the HTML code for the page. Note whether this code describes the main frame or it is the same code you looked at in Step 5. Print the HTML code, and then close Notepad.

7. Click the Become A Member hyperlink in the banner frame to open that page. Does the Become A Member page replace the frames page, or does it appear in the main frame?

Explore 8. Complete the Become A Member form with data that you make up, and then print the completed form.

9. Click the Submit Form button to simulate the action of submitting a completed Become A Member form to the server. What happens after you submit the form?

Explore 10. In Internet Explorer, click the Back button on the Standard Buttons toolbar, click the Reset Form button to remove the data you entered in the Become A Member form, and then display and print the HTML code for the form. Review the HTML code, and circle the HTML code for the Submit Form button on the printout. Close Notepad.

11. Click the Who's Who hyperlink to open the Who's Who Web page. Does this page contain a table?

Explore 12. Display and print the HTML code for the Who's Who Web page. Review the printout of the HTML code, and locate and circle the tags that you think create the table in the Web page. Close Notepad and Internet Explorer.

Explore 13. Start FrontPage and open the ACS Web site from your Data Disk. Change to Hyperlinks view for the Home Page, and then print it. (*Hint*: FrontPage does not have a feature to print Hyperlinks view, so you must print the screen. In Hyperlinks view, press the Print Screen key on the keyboard. Click the Start button on the taskbar, point to Programs, point to Accessories, and then click WordPad. Click the Paste button on the WordPad Standard toolbar to paste the image into the blank WordPad document. Then click File on the menu bar, click Page Setup, click the Landscape option button in the Orientation section, and then click the OK button. Click the Print button on the Standard toolbar to print the image. Close WordPad without saving changes.)

14. Close FrontPage.

Case 2. *Examining Web Sites for Guardian Mutual Insurance* Guardian Mutual Insurance (GMI) is a large, national insurance company, which sells insurance to both individuals and businesses. GMI employs a staff of nearly 100 computer programmers and analysts who maintain and build its management information systems. Marcella Riley is the Human Resources manager at GMI. She recently hired Ollie Sherman as a systems analyst and assigned him to GMI's Web development team. Marcella wants you to help Ollie review some competitors' Web sites to obtain some ideas for developing GMI's Web site. (*Note*: You must have an Internet connection to complete this Case Problem.)

If necessary, start Internet Explorer, and then do the following:

Explore 1. Use your Web browser to connect to the Internet and then visit at least five business-oriented Web sites. Examine Web sites that provide corporate information, as well as sites designed for doing business on the Internet.

2. While looking at each site, analyze the amount and type of information provided, and note the site's overall appearance and ease of use.

3. Based on the standards described in the case introduction, identify the three Web sites that you feel are the best. Print the pages for each (print a maximum of 10 pages for any one site).

4. For each Web site, choose one Web page and print its HTML code. Note which pages contain at least one <TABLE> tag.

Explore ▷ 5. Draw a diagram similar to what might appear in Navigation view for one of the sites.

Explore ▷ 6. For each Web site, write a one-page report that describes its key features. Your report should include the following information: best and worst features, features that need improvement, suggestions for improvement, and commentary about ease of use and overall style.

7. Based on the reports you completed in Step 6, identify which sites you rated as the best and the worst. Defend your selections.

8. Close your Web browser and your Internet connection, if necessary.

QUICK | CHECK ANSWERS

Session 1.1

1. Internet
2. The Web browser requests and receives information for the client that is stored on the Web server.
3. start
4. Uniform Resource Locator (URL)
5. hyperlink (link)
6. disk-based Web files are obtained from a disk without the use of a server program; server-based Web files require a server for processing
7. True
8. True

Session 1.2

1. It creates all of the HTML code for you.
2. Page
3. Reports
4. Navigation
5. A hyperlink to a location in a page that already has a hyperlink to it.
6. Tasks list
7. True
8. False

Session 1.3

1. attributes (or properties)
2. Use the HTML tab in Page view, or use the Source command on the View menu in Internet Explorer.
3. <I> Home Page </I>
4. Contents
5. True
6. False

LAB ASSIGNMENTS

These Lab Assignments are designed to accompany the interactive Course Lab called Computer History Hypermedia. To start the Computer History Hypermedia Lab, click the Start button on the Windows taskbar, point to Programs, point to Course Labs, point to New Perspectives Applications, and then click Computer History Hypermedia. If you do not see Course Labs on your Programs menu, see your instructor or technical support person.

Computer History Hypermedia   The Computer History Hypermedia Lab is an example of a multimedia hypertext, or hypermedia that contains text, pictures, and recordings which trace the origins of computers. This Lab provides you with two benefits: first, you learn how to use hypermedia links, and second, you learn about some of the events that took place as the computer age dawned.

1. Click the Steps button to learn how to use the Computer History Hypermedia Lab. As you proceed through the Steps, answer all the Quick Check questions that appear. After you complete the Steps, you will see a Quick Check Summary Report. Follow the instructions on the screen to print this report.

   Click the Explore button. Find the name and date for each of the following:

   a. First automatic adding machine
   b. First electronic computer
   c. First fully electronic stored-program computer
   d. First widely used high-level programming language
   e. First microprocessor
   f. First microcomputer
   g. First word-processing program
   h. First spreadsheet program

2. Select one of the following computer pioneers and write a one-page paper about that person's contribution to the computer industry: Grace Hopper, Charles Babbage, Augusta Ada, Jack Kilby, Thomas Watson, or J. Presper Eckert.

3. Use this Lab to research the history of the computer. Based on your research, write a paper explaining how you would respond to the question, "Who invented the computer?"

These Lab Assignments are designed to accompany the interactive Course Lab called The Internet: World Wide Web. To start The Internet: World Wide Web Lab, click the Start button on the Windows taskbar, point to Programs, point to Course Labs, point to New Perspectives Applications, and then click The Internet: World Wide Web. If you do not see Course Labs on your Programs menu, see your instructor or technical support person.

The Internet: World Wide Web   One of the most popular services on the Internet is the World Wide Web. This Lab is a Web simulator that teaches you how to use Web browser software to find information. You can use this Lab whether or not your school provides you with Internet access.

1. Click the Steps button to learn how to use Web browser software. As you proceed through the Steps, answer all of the Quick Check questions that appear. After you complete the Steps, you will see a Quick Check Summary Report. Follow the instructions on the screen to print this report.

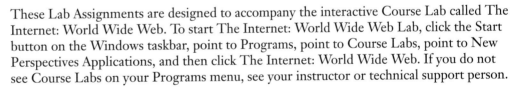

2. Click the Explore button on the Welcome screen. Use the Web browser to locate a weather map of the Caribbean Virgin Islands. What is its URL?

3. A SCUBA diver named Wadson Lachouffe has been searching for the fabled treasure of Greybeard the pirate. A link from the Adventure Travel Web site www.atour.com leads to Wadson's Web page called "Hidden Treasure." In Explore, locate the Hidden Treasure page and answer the following questions:

   a. What was the name of Greybeard's ship?
   b. What was Greybeard's favorite food?
   c. What does Wadson think happened to Greybeard's ship?

4. In the Steps, you found a graphic of Jupiter from the photo archives of the Jet Propulsion Laboratory. In the Explore section of the Lab, you can also find a graphic of Saturn. Suppose one of your friends wanted a picture of Saturn for an astronomy report. Make a list of the blue, underlined links your friend must click in the correct order to find the Saturn graphic. Assume that your friend will begin at the Web Trainer home page.

5. Enter the URL **http://www.atour.com** to jump to the Adventure Travel Web site. Write a one-page description of this site. In your paper, include a description of the information at the site, the number of pages the site contains, and a diagram of the links it contains.

6. Chris Thomson is a student at UVI and has his own Web pages. In Explore, look at the information Chris has included on his pages. Suppose you could create your own Web page. What would you include? Use word-processing software to design your own Web pages. Make sure you indicate the graphics and links you would use.

In this tutorial you will:

- Study the five-part process for developing a Web site

- Use FrontPage to create a Web site and a Web page

- Enter and spell check text in a Web page

- Save a Web page

- Format a Web page

- View a Web page in Internet Explorer

- Print a Web page

- Add a background picture and sound to a Web page

- Insert a picture, horizontal line, and marquee in a Web page

- Learn about the importance of META tags in promoting a Web site

CREATING AND REVISING A WEB PAGE

Developing the Home Page for Sunny Morning Products

Sunny Morning Products

Before Amanda Bay began developing the Web site for Sunny Morning Products, she visited many Web sites of the company's competitors. She compiled a list of six sites that had a Web presence similar to the one she envisioned for Sunny Morning Products. She then met with Andrew Towle and the Web site development team to review these sites and to clarify the requirements for the Web site for Sunny Morning Products. They discussed the Web site's overall design, as well as the specific design and content of its Home Page. They agreed that Amanda would develop the Home Page and Andrew would review it. Amanda then would incorporate Andrew's input into the development of the pages in the rest of the Web site.

In this tutorial, you continue your Web training course by studying Amanda's five-part process for developing and creating the Web site for Sunny Morning Products. You will create the Home Page for Sunny Morning Products and apply different formatting techniques to organize the information in the page. Then you will add a picture and a sound to the Home Page.

SESSION 2.1

In this session, you will study the five-part process for creating and developing a Web site. You will create a Web site, enter text, check its spelling, and create a navigation bar. Finally, you will close a Web page, a Web site, and FrontPage.

Developing a Web Site

A commercial Web site often results from the efforts of a development team consisting of a copy writer, an editor, a graphic designer, a programmer, a systems administrator, and a marketing representative, with a Web design director as the team's coordinator. Figure 2-1 shows the organization of this type of team and lists some of the general responsibilities of each member. Often, a single employee, called the **webmaster**, is assigned these responsibilities. Also, individuals who are not necessarily employees in large or small companies may also create and develop their own Web sites. Regardless of who is responsible for developing a Web site, FrontPage makes it easy to perform the various activities required to create and administer it.

Figure 2-1   WEB DEVELOPMENT TEAM

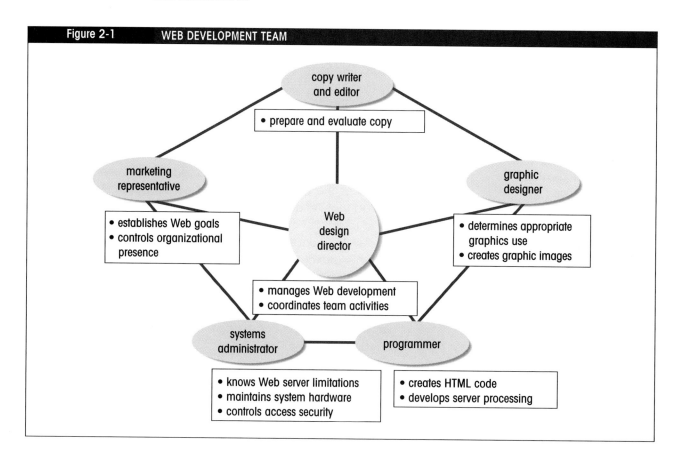

Developing a Web site is a multitask process that includes the following activities:

■ Define the goal and purpose of the Web site.

■ Determine and prepare the Web site's contents.

■ Design the Web site.

■ Build the Web site.

■ Test the Web site.

Amanda is ready to explain the first step in this process—defining the site's goal and purpose.

Defining the Site's Goal and Purpose

The first step in creating a professional-looking Web site is for the Web site development team to define its goal and purpose. What do you want to achieve with your site? What will a Web site help you accomplish that other marketing media cannot? Who is your target audience? Sunny Morning Products wants to develop a Web site that provides a corporate Web presence and that markets the items sold through the Sunshine Country Store.

After agreeing on the Web site's goal and purpose, the Web site development team at Sunny Morning Products discussed the Web site's requirements. Amanda then met with each of the company's department heads to obtain the preliminary information needed to begin developing the site. Specific factors to consider when planning a Web site include the following:

■ Primary intent. What is the purpose of the Web site?

■ Short- and long-term goals. What specific goals should the Web site meet? For example, do you want to market your company's products to increase sales or to increase the company's visibility?

■ Intended audience. Who do you want or expect to visit your Web site? The quality and level of the design and the information must meet the expectations of the intended audience.

Using this preliminary information, Amanda created a planning analysis sheet. A **planning analysis sheet** is a document that contains answers to the following questions:

1. What are the objectives of the Web site? For example, you might be taking advantage of an opportunity or responding to specific needs from customers.

2. What data do you need in order to create your Web pages? This information is your **input**.

3. What specific results are you seeking? This information describes your **output**, or the information that your Web site should provide.

4. How will you connect the Web pages in your Web site? Hyperlinks connect the Web pages to give users access to the information in your Web site.

Figure 2-2 shows Amanda's completed planning analysis sheet for the Web site.

Figure 2-2   **AMANDA'S PLANNING ANALYSIS SHEET FOR THE SUNNY WEB SITE**

Planning Analysis Sheet

Objective

Develop a marketing and corporate Web site that provides relevant company information and allows users to place orders from the Sunshine Country Store.

Requirements

Company description

Mission statement

List of product groups and individual product descriptions and prices

List of available positions and their job descriptions

Financial performance and stock information

Results

Web pages with the following information:

      Company description

      Current press releases

      Product descriptions and ordering information

      Employment information

      Investor information

      Customer feedback form

      Search capability for Web content

Determining and Preparing the Web Site's Contents

After preparing a planning analysis sheet, you are ready to begin preparing the Web site's content. You should gather relevant documents, workbooks, presentations, and other data that you might use or adapt for use in the Web site. As part of this step, you might need to revisit people who were involved in planning the Web site to see if they have material that you can use in your Web pages.

Content is the most fundamental aspect of Web design, because the success of a Web site ultimately depends on the quality of information in it. Streamlined, appropriate language is part of any well-designed site.

Designing the Web Site

Your next step in developing a Web site is to design the site. Good graphic design is crucial in the commercial and competitive realm of the World Wide Web. The overall layout and pictures in a Web page need to make it attractive and interesting to its users.

During this stage, you should ask and answer questions related to your company's organizational image. What message is your company trying to convey? What distinguishes your organization from its competitors? Should the Web site be environmental, classic, stylish, or contemporary?

When armed with the answers to these questions, you can sketch a design of the site, including its individual pages. In this way, you plan the relationships among Web pages before creating them and connecting them using hyperlinks. Figure 2-3 shows Amanda's plan for linking together the pages that will make up the Web site. The plan specifies which Web pages must be created and the likely hyperlinks that will connect the Web pages.

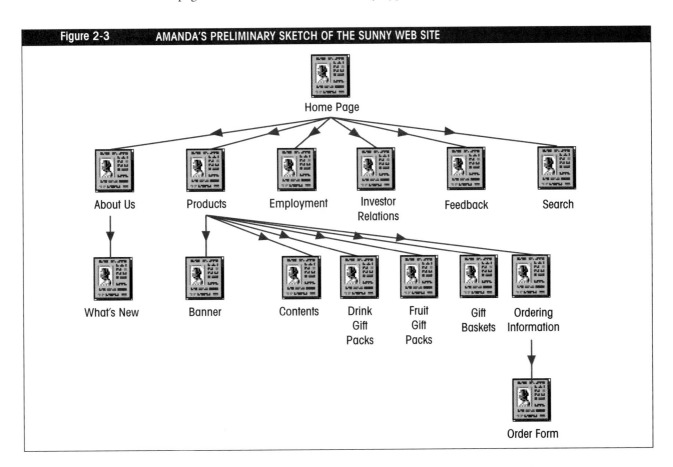

Figure 2-3   **AMANDA'S PRELIMINARY SKETCH OF THE SUNNY WEB SITE**

With your Web design plan in place, you can begin building the site. You will create all of the pages for Sunny Morning Products as you work through the tutorials in this book.

Building the Web Site

As you transform your Web site's plans into a FrontPage Web site, it is important to consider the fact that Internet Explorer and other popular Web browsers, such as Netscape Navigator, might display your pages in slightly different ways. When creating a Web site, you should always test your pages in different browsers to ensure that your pages are displayed correctly. Fortunately, FrontPage includes an option that you can set before developing any Web pages to ensure compatibility with certain browsers, servers, and Internet technologies. For example, you might choose to develop your Web site with the settings enabled for creating pages that are supported by both Internet Explorer and Netscape Navigator when you are certain that your Web site will be viewed using both browsers. When you set this option, FrontPage dims commands that are not supported by both browsers. To enable these settings, click Tools on the menu bar, click Page Options, and then click the Compatibility tab. In this book, you will use the default setting for FrontPage, which is to create a Web site that is supported by Internet Explorer 5.0.

Another important consideration during this phase is that the best Web sites are visually appealing, convey information correctly and succinctly, and download quickly. Consider the following guidelines when building a Web site:

- Know and adhere to the goals of the site as you decide how to present the site's information.

- Consider your audience's reaction to every piece of information and every picture to be included.

- Include components that download quickly. People often leave a site if downloading its pages takes too long. Large pictures can download slowly; if you must include them, provide an option to download them as separate Web pages.

- Make the site visually appealing. Strike a balance between a site design that is too simple and one that is chaotic. Make the text large enough for easy viewing, and use color and font variations to add interest and to draw attention to items. However, don't use every possible font, color, and feature on every page because excessive formatting is distracting.

- Organize your content into groups of related information. For example, if you are designing a Web site for a bookstore, arrange the material according to subject areas.

- Include appropriate navigation options, including a hyperlink in every page in the Web site to return to the Home Page. Make it easy for users to move around in your site.

Testing the Web Site

The final step in developing a Web site is to test it. This step includes verifying that hyperlinks work correctly and that all multimedia files are available. You should thoroughly test the Web site before publishing it to a Web server. In these tutorials, you will test Web pages using the Preview tab in Page view and also in Internet Explorer. It is also important to test your Web site for different browsers and their versions to ensure that all of your pages function correctly.

Creating **the Sunny Web Site**

Based on the five-part Web development process, Amanda helped you identify a clear vision of the Web site needed by Sunny Morning Products. After reviewing the planning analysis sheet for the Web site and its preliminary design, you are ready to begin creating the Web site.

When creating a new Web site, you must create the FrontPage Web that will contain the individual Web pages of the site. A **FrontPage Web** is a Windows folder, similar to a file folder that you use in other programs. The additional files and folders used by FrontPage—the FrontPage extensions—are saved in the FrontPage Web folder. You always use FrontPage to create the folder for your Web site.

Note: The Web site that you will create and use in these tutorials is named "Sunny." This Web site differs from the SunnyMorningProducts Web site that you explored in Tutorial 1. Always make sure that you are working in the correct Web site.

To create the Sunny Web site:

1. Make sure that your Data Disk is in the appropriate drive on your computer.

2. Start **Microsoft FrontPage**, and make sure that you are in Page view. If necessary, click **View** on the menu bar, and then click **Views Bar** to show the Views bar.

   TROUBLE? If a diallog box opens and asks if you would like to make FrontPage your default editor, click the No button.

3. Click **File** on the menu bar, point to **New**, and then click **Web**. The New dialog box opens. See Figure 2-4.

Figure 2-4	NEW DIALOG BOX

selected template

default location for new Web site (yours might be different)

description of selected template or Wizard

You can use the options in this dialog box to create a new FrontPage Web using one of five templates (see Figure 2-4). Or you can use one of three Wizards to answer questions about the FrontPage Web that you want to create, and FrontPage will create it for you. The description of the selected template or Wizard appears in the Description section. Figure 2-5 describes the different template and Wizard options in more detail.

Figure 2-5	OPTIONS FOR CREATING A NEW FRONTPAGE WEB SITE
WEB SITE NAME	**DESCRIPTION**
One Page Web	Creates a Web site that contains one blank page
Corporate Presence Wizard	Creates a Web site with professionally styled pages that a corporation might use
Customer Support Web	Creates a Web site that contains pages useful for companies providing customer support
Discussion Web Wizard	Creates a Web site that contains a table of contents, full-text searching capability, and threads organized around a specific discussion topic
Empty Web	Creates a Web site that has no pages
Import Web Wizard	Creates a Web site that contains pages you import from another location
Personal Web	Creates a Web site that an individual might use to publish pages about his or her interests and favorite Web sites
Project Web	Creates a Web site that contains a list of members, a schedule, a status, and a discussion archive related to a specific project

4. Click in the **Specify the location of the new web** text box to select the text in it. When you create a new Web site, you must specify the location in which to store the Web site's files and folders. In these tutorials, you will store your Web sites in the My Webs folder on your Data Disk.

5. Type **a:\My Webs\Sunny** in the text box.

TROUBLE? If you must store your Data Files on a different drive or in a different folder, your instructor might provide you with a location different from that specified in Step 5. Ask your instructor or technical support person for help if you are unsure where to create your FrontPage Webs.

6. Double-click the **One Page Web** icon to create the FrontPage Web using the One Page Web template.

TROUBLE? If a dialog box opens and indicates that FrontPage must convert this folder to a FrontPage Web, click the Yes button to continue. FrontPage then will convert your folder into a FrontPage Web.

During the next few minutes, FrontPage creates the new Sunny Web site and creates and saves the Web site's Home Page. FrontPage then displays a new, blank, unsaved page in Page view named new_page_1.htm. You could start entering text into this new page right away. However, in this tutorial, you will do your work in the Home Page.

7. Click the **Folders** button 📁 on the Views bar to change to Folders view. Notice that Folders view shows that your new Web site contains two folders (_private and images) and one file (index.htm).

When you used the One Page Web template to create the Sunny Web site, FrontPage created and saved the Sunny Web site's Home Page as **index.htm**. If you are creating your Web site on a Web server, rather than on disk, then the Home Page is named **default.htm**. A Web browser recognizes either of these files—index.htm or default.htm—as a Web site's Home Page.

Creating a Web Page

After creating a Web site, you create its individual Web pages. As the previous set of steps showed, FrontPage automatically creates and saves the index.htm (or default.htm) Home Page when you create a new FrontPage Web. It also opens a new, blank page that it does not automatically save. All other new Web pages that you create are included in the open Web site when you save them.

Entering Text in a Web Page

You will now begin adding content to the Home Page. As part of Amanda's Web development training program, you will prepare a Home Page for Sunny Morning Products that is similar to the one that you examined in Tutorial 1.

To enter text in a Web page:

1. Open the Sunny Web site's Home Page by double-clicking **index.htm** in the Contents pane. The blank Home Page, which FrontPage saved when you created the Web site, opens in Page view.

   TROUBLE? If you are using a server-based Web, double-click default.htm to open the Home Page.

2. Type the two paragraphs shown in Figure 2-6 *exactly* as displayed, including the misspelled word. As with any word-processing program, you do not need to press the Enter key at the end of each line. You press the Enter key only once when advancing to a new paragraph. Do not press the Enter key twice because FrontPage will automatically insert blank space above a new paragraph.

Figure 2-6	SUNNY MORNING PRODUCTS HOME PAGE TEXT

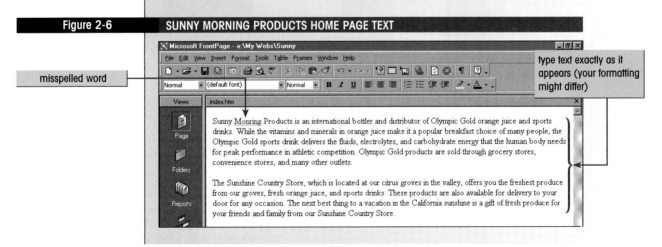

misspelled word

type text exactly as it appears (your formatting might differ)

Sunny Monring Products is an international bottler and distributor of Olympic Gold orange juice and sports drinks. While the vitamins and minerals in orange juice make it a popular breakfast choice of many people, the Olympic Gold sports drink delivers the fluids, electrolytes, and carbohydrate energy that the human body needs for peak performance in athletic competition. Olympic Gold products are sold through grocery stores, convenience stores, and many other outlets.

The Sunshine Country Store, which is located at our citrus groves in the valley, offers you the freshest produce from our groves, fresh orange juice, and sports drinks. These products are also available for delivery to your door for any occasion. The next best thing to a vacation in the California sunshine is a gift of fresh produce for your friends and family from our Sunshine Country Store.

Spell Checking a Web Page

Notice that a red, wavy underline appears under the word "Monring." Like Microsoft Word, FrontPage highlights misspelled words as you type them. You should always check the spelling in your Web pages as part of the development process.

REFERENCE   WINDOW   **RW**

Spell Checking a Web Page
- Click the Spelling button on the Standard toolbar to open the Spelling dialog box.
- As potentially misspelled words are displayed in the Spelling dialog box, click the correct suggestion, click the Ignore button to accept the spelling, or type the correct word in the Change To text box, and then click the Change button.
- Click the OK button to close the Spelling dialog box.

To check the spelling in a Web page:

1. Click the **Spelling** button on the Standard toolbar. The Spelling dialog box opens with the word "Monring" displayed in the Not in Dictionary text box. See Figure 2-7.

Figure 2-7   **SPELLING DIALOG BOX**

misspelled word

suggestions for correcting the misspelled word

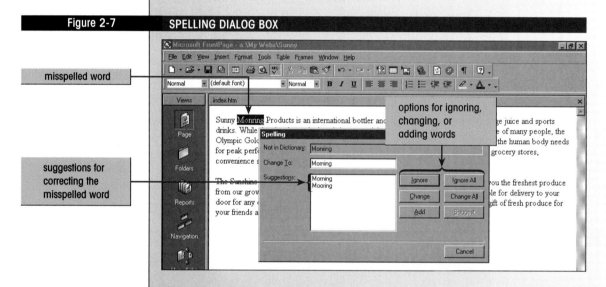

You can click one of the suggested corrections in the Suggestions list box to change the spelling of the selected word, and then click the Change button. Alternatively, you can type a new spelling in the Change To text box, and then click the Change button. If the selected word is spelled correctly, but not in the FrontPage dictionary, click the Ignore button. You also can click the Change All or Ignore All button to bypass checking the spelling of the same word again. If you want to add a word to FrontPage's dictionary, click the Add button. Normally, you only add words to the dictionary that you will use often, such as your name.

2. Click **Morning** in the Suggestions list box, and then click the **Change** button.

TROUBLE? If you do not encounter any misspelled words in your Web page, then the word "Monring" is in your dictionary or you typed it correctly. Click the OK button to close the Spelling dialog box and, if necessary, edit the word to change it to "Morning."

3. If necessary, correct any other misspellings that appear in the Spelling dialog box. When you are finished, click the **OK** button to continue.

Adding a Navigation Bar

Next, you add key features such as the navigation bar, which will contain hyperlinks that open other Web pages. Although you can add a navigation bar before including any text information, you will often find it helpful to see how the main body of your text appears in the page before creating a navigation bar.

With FrontPage, you can create a navigation bar in one of two ways. One way is to enter text, format it, and then create hyperlinks to create a **user-defined navigation bar**. Another way is to create a **FrontPage navigation bar**, which is a group of hyperlinks created and managed by FrontPage. In this tutorial, you will implement a user-defined navigation bar. You will learn more about creating FrontPage navigation bars in Tutorial 5 and about hyperlinks in Tutorial 3.

You create a user-defined navigation bar from text that you type just like any other text in your Web page. You separate the entries in your navigation bar using one of several options. One common option to separate entries is to use special characters, such as a vertical bar (|) or square brackets ([ ]), as the separators. Usually, a single vertical bar is placed between entries, whereas square brackets surround each entry.

For the Home Page of the Sunny Web site, you decide to place the navigation bar at the top of the page. You will use the vertical bar character (|) as the separator. With Amanda's assistance, you are ready to create the navigation bar at the top of the Home Page.

To create a navigation bar:

1. Click before the word **Sunny** at the beginning of the first line of the Home Page.

2. Press the **Enter** key to insert a line before the first paragraph, and then press the **up arrow** key ↑. The insertion point moves to the beginning of the new line, which is where you will type the text for the navigation bar for the Home Page.

3. Type the following navigation bar text *exactly* as it appears. Be sure to type the vertical bar and spacebar characters before the first entry. After each subsequent entry, press the **spacebar**, type the **vertical bar**, and then press the **spacebar** again. The text for the navigation bar should fit on one line.

   | Home | About Us | Products | Employment | Investor Relations | Feedback | Search |

   TROUBLE? The key for typing the vertical bar character (|) is located below or to the left of the Backspace key. You must press the Shift key to type it.

   Your completed navigation bar should match the one shown in Figure 2-8.

| Figure 2-8 | NAVIGATION BAR FOR THE HOME PAGE |

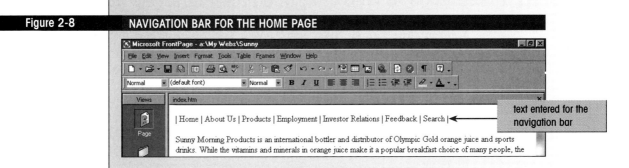

You are finished with your work on the Home Page for now, so you will save it.

Saving a Web Page

Saving your work on a regular basis is important. You use the Save command on the File menu or the Save button on the Standard toolbar to save a Web page. Keep in mind that using the Save command does not create a separate version of your old Web page, but rather, it replaces the old version with the new version. To save the original file and create a new file, save the file under a different filename by using the Save As command on the File menu.

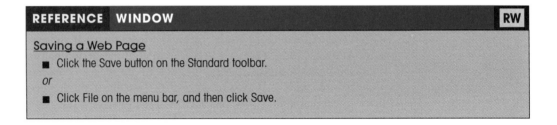

REFERENCE WINDOW   **RW**

Saving a Web Page
- Click the Save button on the Standard toolbar.
or
- Click File on the menu bar, and then click Save.

Amanda asks you to save the Sunny Web site's Home Page.

To save the Home Page:

1. Click the **Save** button 🖫 on the Standard toolbar to save the Home Page. The Home Page was assigned the filename index.htm when FrontPage created it, so the page is saved immediately without requesting a filename.

TROUBLE? If the Save dialog box opens, then you did your work in the new_page_1.htm page instead of the Home Page. Click the Cancel button. Then click File on the menu bar, click Save As, make sure that the My Webs folder on your Data Disk appears in the Look in list box, type index.htm in the File name text box (or default.htm if you are using a server-based Web), and then click the Save button. Click the Yes button to replace the current file.

You are done with your work on the Home Page, so Amanda asks you to close the page, the Sunny Web site, and FrontPage.

Closing a Web Page, a Web Site, and FrontPage

You can close a single Web page, a Web site, or FrontPage by choosing the appropriate Close button. When you close FrontPage, it automatically closes any open page or site. If you did not save your changes to an open Web page, FrontPage will prompt you to do so before closing the page. Next, you will close the Home Page, the Sunny Web site, and FrontPage.

To close a Web page, a Web site, and FrontPage:

1. Click the **Close** button ☒ on the Contents pane to close the Home Page. You have not made any changes since the last time you saved the page, so the Home Page closes and the Contents pane no longer displays a Web page.

TROUBLE? If you made changes to the Web page since you last saved it, a FrontPage message box opens and asks if you want to save the file. Click the Yes button to save your changes and to close the Home Page.

2. Click **File** on the menu bar, and then click **Close Web**. The Sunny Web site closes, and FrontPage remains open.

TROUBLE? If you do not see the Close Web command on the File menu, click the double arrows that appear at the bottom of the File menu. The rest of the menu will open and display the Close Web command so that you can click it.

3. Click ☒ on the FrontPage title bar to close FrontPage.

Amanda is pleased with your progress on creating the Home Page. In the next session, you will format the Home Page to make it more visually interesting.

Session 2.1 QUICK CHECK

1. List the five major tasks involved in developing a Web site.

2. When you create a new Web site on a server, FrontPage automatically creates a Home Page named _____.

3. Describe the two ways to create a navigation bar in a Web page.

4. True or False: You should test your Web pages in different browsers to make sure that your pages are displayed correctly.

5. True or False: FrontPage automatically saves your Web pages while you are working on them, so you do not need to save them periodically.

6. To close a FrontPage Web site, click File on the menu bar, and then click _____.

SESSION 2.2

In this session, you will format a Web page by changing the style and color of text and its alignment in a Web page and by inserting special characters. You will test the appearance of your Web page by viewing it in Internet Explorer. Finally, you will use FrontPage to print a Web page.

Formatting a Web Page

You can make your Web pages more interesting and visually appealing by formatting them to draw attention to important content. **Formatting** is the process of changing the appearance of text in a Web page; it does not alter the Web page's content. You must be in Page view to apply formatting. You can access the FrontPage formatting options three ways:

■ Use the Format menu command, which provides access to all formatting commands, ranging from revising paragraph organization to creating numbered lists.

■ Right-click the text or an object in your Web page to open the shortcut menu, which provides quick access to many formatting commands that you can use to apply formatting to specific characters, words, text, or pictures, such as fonts, numbered lists, or special effects.

■ Click the buttons on the Formatting toolbar. Figure 2-9 describes the Formatting toolbar buttons and their uses in more detail.

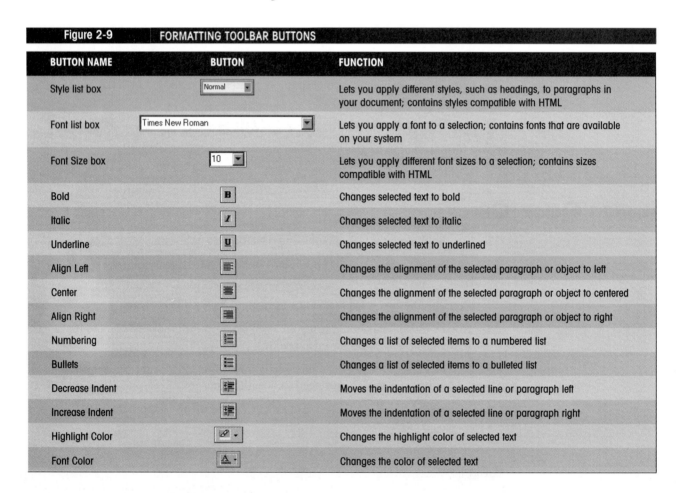

Figure 2-9	FORMATTING TOOLBAR BUTTONS	
BUTTON NAME	**BUTTON**	**FUNCTION**
Style list box	Normal	Lets you apply different styles, such as headings, to paragraphs in your document; contains styles compatible with HTML
Font list box	Times New Roman	Lets you apply a font to a selection; contains fonts that are available on your system
Font Size box	10	Lets you apply different font sizes to a selection; contains sizes compatible with HTML
Bold	**B**	Changes selected text to bold
Italic	*I*	Changes selected text to italic
Underline	U	Changes selected text to underlined
Align Left		Changes the alignment of the selected paragraph or object to left
Center		Changes the alignment of the selected paragraph or object to centered
Align Right		Changes the alignment of the selected paragraph or object to right
Numbering		Changes a list of selected items to a numbered list
Bullets		Changes a list of selected items to a bulleted list
Decrease Indent		Moves the indentation of a selected line or paragraph left
Increase Indent		Moves the indentation of a selected line or paragraph right
Highlight Color		Changes the highlight color of selected text
Font Color	A	Changes the color of selected text

Now that the Home Page of the Sunny Web site contains text and a navigation bar, Amanda asks you to continue developing it by formatting it.

Creating Headings

Headings in a Web page function like headings in other documents. The heading selections available for your Web page are limited to those defined by HTML tags. HTML provides six levels of headings, identified as H1, H2, and so on. H1 has the largest font; H6 has the smallest font. You can change the alignment of a heading before or after you enter the heading's text.

Next, you will create two headings in the Home Page—one at the top of the page that welcomes visitors to the site, and another at the bottom of the page that contains a slogan.

To open the Sunny Web site and create the headings:

1. Make sure that your Data Disk is in the appropriate drive, and then start **FrontPage**.

2. Click the list arrow for the **Open** button on the Standard toolbar, click **Open Web**, change to the drive or folder that contains your Data Disk, double-click the **My Webs** folder on your Data Disk, click the **Sunny** folder, and then click the **Open** button.

3. Click the **Folders** button on the Views bar to change to Folders view, and then double-click **index.htm** in the Contents pane to open the Home Page in Page view.

4. Click anywhere in the navigation bar, press the **End** key to move the insertion point to the end of the navigation bar, and then press the **Enter** key to insert a new line under the navigation bar.

5. Type **Welcome to the Sunny Morning Products Web Site!** on the new line as the text for your heading.

   Now you will apply a heading style to distinguish this text from the rest of the Web page.

6. Click the **Style** list arrow on the Formatting toolbar to display the list of available paragraph styles. These styles correspond to the HTML tags that you can use to define the various paragraphs in your Web page.

7. Click **Heading 3** to apply this style to the heading.

   Next you will add another heading at the bottom of the Home Page.

8. Press **Ctrl + End** to insert a new line below the last paragraph of the Web page, and then type **Brighten your day. Enjoy some of our sunshine!** as the heading.

9. Repeat Steps 6 and 7 to apply the **Heading 3** style to the heading you created in Step 8. The Home Page now contains two headings. See Figure 2-10.

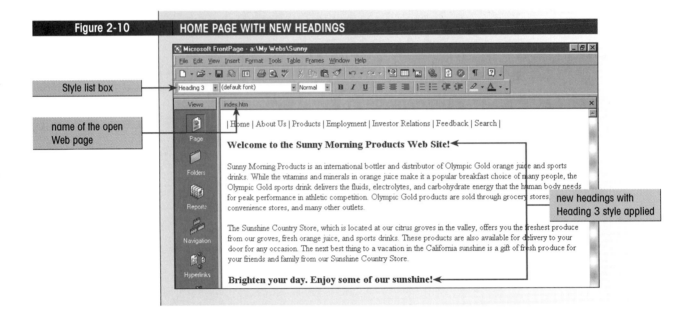

Figure 2-10 **HOME PAGE WITH NEW HEADINGS**

Style list box

name of the open Web page

new headings with Heading 3 style applied

Aligning Text

Like a word-processing program, FrontPage allows you to left-, center-, or right-align text in a Web page. The Web browser interprets the alignment tags based on the formatting you apply and displays the text accordingly.

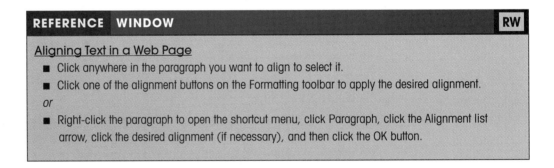

REFERENCE WINDOW   **RW**

<u>Aligning Text in a Web Page</u>
- Click anywhere in the paragraph you want to align to select it.
- Click one of the alignment buttons on the Formatting toolbar to apply the desired alignment.

or

- Right-click the paragraph to open the shortcut menu, click Paragraph, click the Alignment list arrow, click the desired alignment (if necessary), and then click the OK button.

Next, you'll center the heading at the bottom of the page. Then, to balance the Web page, you will center the navigation bar.

To center text in a Web page:

1. Click anywhere in the heading at the bottom of the page to select it.

2. Click the **Center** button 🔳 on the Formatting toolbar to center the heading.

3. Click anywhere in the navigation bar at the top of the page to select it.

4. Click 🔳 to center the navigation bar. See Figure 2-11.

| **Figure 2-11** | **CENTERING TEXT IN THE HOME PAGE** |

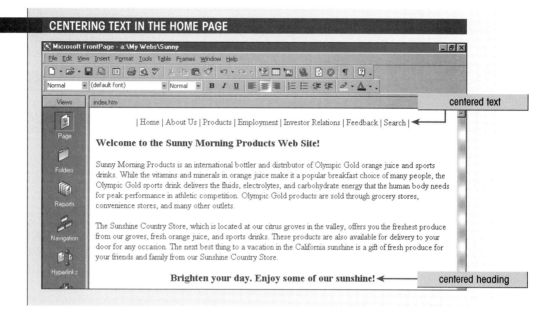

Using Fonts

A **font** is a set of letters, numbers, and symbols distinguished by their typeface, point size, and style. You can apply any of the following font styles to the text in your Web pages: regular, italic, bold, and bold italic. You also can apply underlining to any of these font styles. You can **toggle** the application of these styles to selected text. That is, if the style is not applied, then selecting the style applies it; if the style is applied, then selecting the style removes it.

In addition to including headings, Amanda asks you to insert a footer at the bottom of the Home Page that contains the company's copyright notice and the date that the page was last revised. You will apply italics to the footer in order to distinguish it from other text in the page.

To enter and format the footer text:

1. Press **Ctrl + End** to move to the bottom of the Home Page and to insert a new line after the last paragraph.

2. Type **Last updated May 31, 2001** as the first line of the footer.

3. Press **Shift + Enter** to advance to a new line without starting a new paragraph and without inserting a blank line between paragraphs.

4. Type **Copyright 2001 Sunny Morning Products. All rights reserved.** as the second line of the footer.

   Now that you've entered the footer information, you will format it by applying italics.

5. Select both lines of the footer, click the **Italic** button *I* on the Formatting toolbar, and then click anywhere in the selected text to deselect it. The completed footer information now appears italicized. See Figure 2-12.

Figure 2-12   **FORMATTED FOOTER**

Brighten your day. Enjoy some of our sunshine!

Last updated May 31, 2001
Copyright 2001 Sunny Morning Products. All rights reserved. } ← **italicized text**

Inserting Special Characters

You can insert special characters, such as the copyright symbol (©), in the text of a Web page to serve the same purposes that they do in other types of documents. In FrontPage, you insert special characters using the Symbol dialog box. Amanda asks you to add a copyright symbol after the word "Copyright" in the footer on the Home Page.

To insert a special character:

1. Click the insertion point to the right of the letter **t** in the word "Copyright" in the footer, and then press the **spacebar**. You will place the special character here.

2. Click **Insert** on the menu bar, and then click **Symbol** to open the Symbol dialog box.

3. Click the © symbol (fourth row, tenth character from the left), click the **Insert** button, and then click the **Close** button. The Symbol dialog box closes and the copyright symbol appears in the footer.

Changing Font Size

You also can change the size of text that appears in a Web page. You simply select the desired text and then change the text size by using the Font Size list arrow on the Formatting toolbar. When designing a Web page, you often will need to experiment with different font sizes to find the best one. Amanda instructs you to change the size of the footer text so that it is smaller than other text in the page.

To change text size:

1. Select both lines of the footer, and then click the **Font Size** list arrow on the Formatting toolbar to display the list of font sizes. See Figure 2-13.

Figure 2-13 **CHANGING THE FONT SIZE**

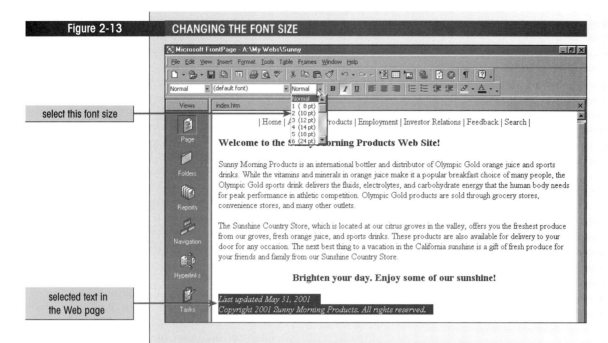

select this font size

selected text in
the Web page

Notice that the Font Size list includes only font sizes that are compatible with
HTML. You will select 2 as the font size, which is the equivalent of 10 points.

2. Click **2 (10 pt)** in the Font Size list to decrease the size of the text in the footer
   from 12 points to 10 points.

3. Click anywhere in the footer to deselect it.

Changing Text Color

As part of the Web page design, Amanda wants the occurrences of the text "Olympic Gold"
to have a more prominent appearance so as to distinguish this brand name from other text.
She thinks that the brand name will stand out more if it is formatted as bold, orange text.

To change text color:

1. Press **Ctrl + Home** to return to the top of the Home Page.

2. Select **Olympic Gold** in the first line of the first paragraph.

3. Click the **Bold** button **B** on the Formatting toolbar to change this text to bold.

4. Click the list arrow for the **Font Color** button **A** on the Formatting toolbar to
   open the color palette, and then click **More Colors** to open the More Colors
   dialog box. See Figure 2-14.

Figure 2-14	MORE COLORS DIALOG BOX

click to select
orange color

In the More Colors dialog box, you select an existing color by clicking the desired color on the color palette. Alternatively, you can create a custom color by clicking the Custom button. You need an orange color, which you can select from the palette.

5. Click the **orange** color (second to last row, third color from the left) to select it, and then click the **OK** button to close the More Colors dialog box and apply the orange color to the selected text.

6. Click anywhere in the first paragraph to deselect the Olympic Gold text.

TROUBLE? If the orange color on your screen doesn't match the exact shade of orange that you selected, don't worry. This difference reflects your hardware setup. The color should appear correctly when viewed in the browser.

Using the Format Painter

Amanda wants you to apply the bold, orange formatting to the other occurrences of the "Olympic Gold" text in the Home Page. You could select each occurrence of this text and apply the desired formatting changes to it. An easier way, however, is to use the Format Painter. The **Format Painter** lets you copy the format from existing formatted text and apply it to new text.

To use the Format Painter:

1. Click anywhere in the orange **Olympic Gold** text in the first line of the first paragraph.

If you click the Format Painter button once, you can copy the format of the selected text and apply it to any other text once. If you double-click the Format Painter button, you can apply the format to several locations until you click the button again to turn it off. You need to copy the format and apply it to the two other occurrences of the Olympic Gold text, so you will double-click the Format Painter button.

2. Double-click the **Format Painter** button 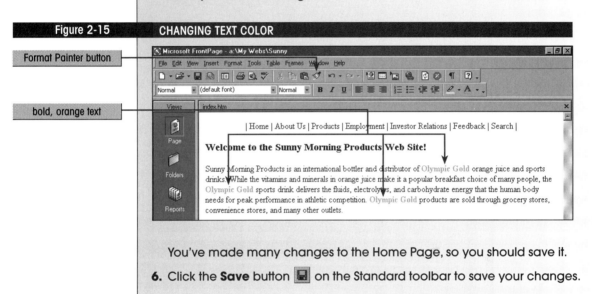 on the Standard toolbar to set the button to apply the format more than once.

3. Move the pointer, which changes to a 🖌️ shape, to the beginning of the third line in the first paragraph, and then select **Olympic Gold**. The text changes to bold, orange text.

4. Repeat Step 3 to change the **Olympic Gold** text in the next line to bold, orange text.

   TROUBLE? Depending on your monitor's resolution, the Olympic Gold text might be in different places on your screen. Just make sure that you find and apply the format to both additional occurrences of the Olympic Gold text.

5. Click 🖌️ to turn off the Format Painter, and then click in the selected text to deselect it. See Figure 2-15. Now the Olympic Gold brand name stands out clearly in the Home Page.

Figure 2-15	CHANGING TEXT COLOR

You've made many changes to the Home Page, so you should save it.

6. Click the **Save** button 💾 on the Standard toolbar to save your changes.

Now Amanda is ready for you to complete the final step in developing a Web page—testing it.

Testing a Web Page

For now, your testing is limited primarily to verifying that the appearance of the Home Page is the same in Internet Explorer and in Page view. Using the Preview tab to test the page lets you preview a Web page without actually opening the page in the browser. When you use the Preview in Browser button on the Standard toolbar to test a page, Internet Explorer starts and opens the page. You should check the page in your Web browser periodically to make sure that colors, fonts, and other elements are being positioned and applied correctly. As you add other features, such as hyperlinks, to your Web pages, you should confirm that they work correctly by testing them in the browser.

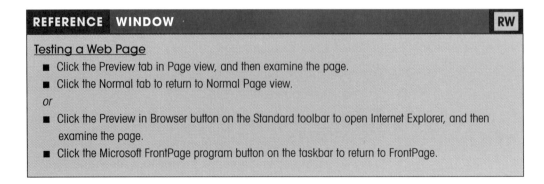

Testing a Web Page
- Click the Preview tab in Page view, and then examine the page.
- Click the Normal tab to return to Normal Page view.

or

- Click the Preview in Browser button on the Standard toolbar to open Internet Explorer, and then examine the page.
- Click the Microsoft FrontPage program button on the taskbar to return to FrontPage.

Now that you have completed your work on the Home Page for Amanda, you need to test it. First, you will use the Preview tab. Then you will view the Web page in the browser window.

To test the Web page and close Internet Explorer:

1. Click the **Preview** tab. The Home Page for the Sunny Web site is displayed as it will appear when viewed using a Web browser. Note that the "Olympic Gold" references appear as bold, orange text. The Web page appears as desired, so you are ready to test it in the browser.

2. Click the **Preview in Browser** button ⬚ on the Standard toolbar to start Internet Explorer and open the Home Page. If necessary, maximize the Internet Explorer program window. See Figure 2-16. The Home Page should look just as it did when you previewed it using the Preview tab. Your test was successful, so you can close the browser.

| Figure 2-16 | HOME PAGE DISPLAYED IN INTERNET EXPLORER |

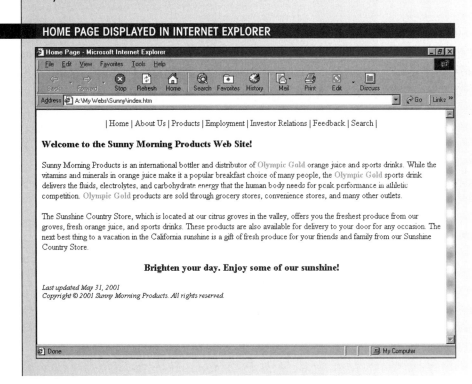

3. Click the **Close** button ☒ on the Internet Explorer title bar to close Internet Explorer.

4. If necessary, click the **Microsoft FrontPage** program button on the taskbar to return to FrontPage.

Printing a Web Page

Printing a Web page is helpful when you want to keep a paper copy to review later. Amanda wants you to print a copy of the Home Page for the Sunny Web site so that you can review your work with the rest of the Web site development team. After printing the page, you will close FrontPage.

To print a Web page and exit FrontPage:

1. Click the **Normal** tab to display the Home Page in Normal Page view, and then click the **Print** button 🖶 on the Standard toolbar to print the Home Page.

   TROUBLE? If the Home Page is displayed using the Preview tab, the Print button is dimmed and you are unable to print the Web page. Repeat Step 1.

   With the printed page in hand, you are ready to review your work with the Web site development team. Now that you have successfully created and printed the Home Page for Sunny Morning Products, you are ready to close this Web page.

2. Click the **Close** button ☒ on the FrontPage window title bar to close the Home Page, the Sunny Web site, and FrontPage.

In the next session, you will add a picture, a sound, and an active element called a marquee to the Home Page. You will also learn how to make your Web site available to Web search engines.

Session 2.2 QUICK CHECK

1. Describe the three different methods that you can use to access the formatting commands in Page view.

2. Which HTML tag identifies the largest font size available for use in headings?

3. A set of letters, numbers, and symbols that are distinguished by their typeface, point size, and style is called a(n) _____.

4. Describe how to use the Format Painter to apply the format of selected text to one other location in a Web page.

5. To print a Web page in FrontPage, you must be in _____ Page view.

6. True or False: It is important to test the appearance of a Web page periodically in the browser to make sure that it is being displayed correctly.

SESSION 2.3

In this session, you will revise a Web page by changing its background color and inserting a background picture and sound. You will save a Web page with embedded files. You also will add a picture, a horizontal line, and a marquee to a Web page. Finally, you will learn the significance of including META tags in a Web page so that Web search engines can index your Web site.

Revising a Web Page

After creating a Web page, you can add to, delete, or change its contents using the same text-editing features you used to create the page. In Sessions 2.1 and 2.2, you entered and formatted the basic content of the Home Page for Sunny Morning Products. The Web site development team is pleased with your progress, and now the team asks you to revise the Home Page by including picture and sound files to give it a more professional presentation. Figure 2-17 shows Amanda's planning analysis sheet with the team's recommendations for revising the Home Page.

Figure 2-17	AMANDA'S PLANNING ANALYSIS SHEET FOR THE HOME PAGE

Planning Analysis Sheet

Objective

Modify the Home Page to include the Sunny Morning Products logo, a background picture and sound, a marquee, and META tags.

Requirements

Picture file for the logo

File for background picture

File for background sound

Results

Home Page with the following enhancements:

       Background picture applied to it

       Logo added at the top of the page that displays alternative text

       Background sound that plays once

       Scrolling marquee

       META tags that identify the Web site's contents

With these suggestions in mind, you are ready to continue working on the Home Page.

Changing the Background Color of a Web Page

Like the other features of a Web page, the background color can make the Web page more attractive and easier to read. If you don't specify a background color, the default background color is white. You can change the background color to any available color. When choosing a background color for a Web page, make sure that it coordinates with the color of the page's text. You might need to try several colors before you find one that provides the desired appearance for your Web page.

FrontPage automatically applied the default background color of white to the Home Page. A white background usually provides a good contrast. However, changing it to another color is easy.

REFERENCE WINDOW   **RW**

<u>Changing the Background Color of a Web Page</u>
- Click Format on the menu bar, and then click Background to open the Page Properties dialog box.
or
- Right-click anywhere in the page to open the shortcut menu, click Page Properties, and then click the Background tab.
- In the Colors section, click the Background list arrow, and then click the desired color. If you want to use a color that is not listed, click More Colors, click a color on the color palette, and then click the OK button.
- Click the OK button to apply the new background color and to close the Page Properties dialog box.

Although Amanda feels that white is a good background color, she wants you to try another color to see if it might be more attractive for the Home Page.

To change the background color of a Web page:

1. Start **FrontPage**, open the **Sunny** Web site from your Data Disk (a:\My Webs\Sunny), change to Folders view, and then open the Home Page (**index.htm**) in Page view.

2. Click **Format** on the menu bar, and then click **Background** to open the Page Properties dialog box with the Background tab selected. See Figure 2-18. Notice that in the Colors section, the background color is currently set to Automatic (that is, the default, which is white).

Figure 2-18   BACKGROUND SETTINGS FOR THE HOME PAGE

Background tab
selected

Background list arrow

current background
color

white background

3. In the Colors section, click the **Background** list arrow to display the list of available standard colors, as well as the colors that are currently used in your Web page.

TROUBLE? If you don't see the same colors given in the steps, use a similar color. Your color selections might differ, depending on your system's color settings.

TROUBLE? If the list of available colors does not stay open when you click the list arrow, click and hold down the mouse button to display the list.

4. Point to the **Blue** color in the Standard colors section. After a few seconds, a ScreenTip identifies the color as Blue. See Figure 2-19.

Figure 2-19   BACKGROUND COLOR OPTIONS FOR THE HOME PAGE

current background
color

colors used in current
Web page

click to select a color
not listed here

available standard
colors

ScreenTip for the
Blue color

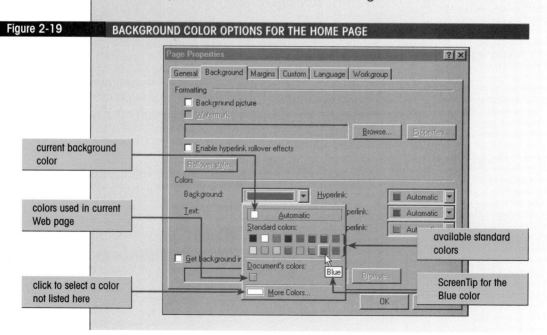

Sometimes FrontPage will use words such as "Blue" to describe a color. At other times, you might see a color indicated by values such as "RR,00,99." These values specify the amounts of red, green, and blue that are combined to create the selected color.

5. Click the **Blue** color to select it, and then click the **OK** button to close the Page Properties dialog box. The Home Page for Sunny Morning Products is displayed with a new blue background color. See Figure 2-20.

Figure 2-20   WEB PAGE WITH NEW BLUE BACKGROUND COLOR

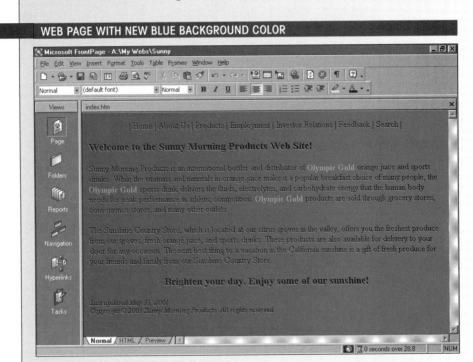

Although the blue background looks nice, it doesn't provide enough contrast with the black text. You could change the page's text to a lighter color to create a better contrast, or choose a more appropriate background color. Another option is to restore the default color. After discussing several other potential background colors with Amanda, you decide to reset the background color to the default (white).

To select the default background color:

1. Click **Format** on the menu bar, and then click **Background** to select those settings.

2. Click the **Background** list arrow, and then click **Automatic**.

3. Click the **OK** button. The Home Page appears again with the default background color of white.

Although the text in the Web page is much easier to read against the default background color, the page is not visually appealing. Amanda explains that there is another way to improve the appearance of a Web page—by inserting a background picture.

Inserting a Background Picture

A **background picture** can use almost any picture or texture file. FrontPage provides many files that you can use to create a background picture. You can use a photo or other picture as a background picture as well.

REFERENCE WINDOW   **RW**

Inserting a Background Picture in a Web Page

- Click Format on the menu bar, and then click Background to display those settings.

or

- Right-click anywhere in the page to open the shortcut menu, click Page Properties, and then click the Background tab.
- In the Formatting section, click the Background picture check box, and then click the Browse button to open the Select Background Picture dialog box.
- Click the Select a file on your computer button to open the Select File dialog box.
- Select the desired background picture.
- Click the OK button to return to the Page Properties dialog box, and then click the OK button to insert the background picture.

Amanda asks you to insert the background picture that she saved in the Tutorial.02 folder on your Data Disk to enhance the appearance of the Home Page.

To insert the background picture:

1. Click **Format** on the menu bar, and then click **Background** to open the Page Properties dialog box with the Background tab selected.

2. In the Formatting section, click the **Background picture** check box to select it, and then click the **Browse** button. The Select Background Picture dialog box opens. The buttons in the Select Background Picture dialog box let you select a background picture from the current Web site, from a file on your computer, or from the Clip Art Gallery. The Clip Art Gallery contains hundreds of pictures that you can use in your Web pages. You will use a file that already exists on your Data Disk.

3. Click the **Select a file on your computer** button 🔍 to open the Select File dialog box. You need to change to the Tutorial.02 folder on your Data Disk.

4. Click the **Look in** list arrow, select the drive or folder that contains your Data Disk, and then double-click the **Tutorial.02** folder to display its contents.

5. Double-click **WB00791** in the list box. The Page Properties dialog box reappears and shows that you are inserting a file from the Tutorial.02 folder as a background picture. See Figure 2-21.

Figure 2-21	BACKGROUND PICTURE SETTINGS

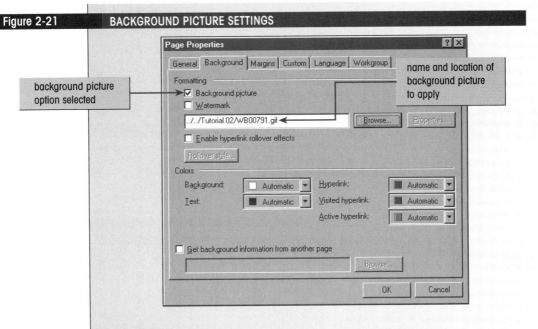

background picture option selected

name and location of background picture to apply

6. Click the **OK** button to close the Page Properties dialog box. The Home Page for Sunny Morning Products reappears with the background picture.

Saving an Embedded File in a Web Site

The new background picture is attractive, and the text in the Home Page is still easy to read. Before testing the Home Page in the browser, however, you need to save the Home Page. When you inserted the background picture in the Web page, you **embedded** it into your Web site. This embedded file is not part of your Web site until you save it in the Web site's images folder, which contains the picture and other multimedia files that are used in your FrontPage Web site. Saving the embedded background picture file in your Web site ensures that all of your Web site's files are saved within the Web site itself and that they will be accessible to all users.

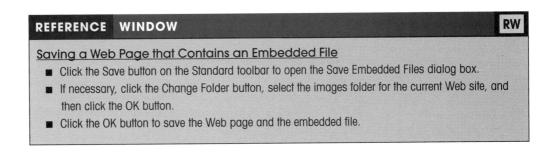

REFERENCE	WINDOW	RW

Saving a Web Page that Contains an Embedded File

■ Click the Save button on the Standard toolbar to open the Save Embedded Files dialog box.
■ If necessary, click the Change Folder button, select the images folder for the current Web site, and then click the OK button.
■ Click the OK button to save the Web page and the embedded file.

To save the Web page and the embedded picture file:

1. Click the **Save** button 🖫 on the Standard toolbar. The Save Embedded Files dialog box opens. You need to save the background picture file, WB00791.gif, in the Sunny Web site's images folder.

2. Click the **Change Folder** button to open the Change Folder dialog box, click the **images** folder to select it, and then click the **OK** button to return to the Save Embedded Files dialog box. See Figure 2-22.

TROUBLE? If the images folder is already selected in the Save Embedded Files dialog box, continue with Step 3.

Figure 2-22	SAVE EMBEDDED FILES DIALOG BOX

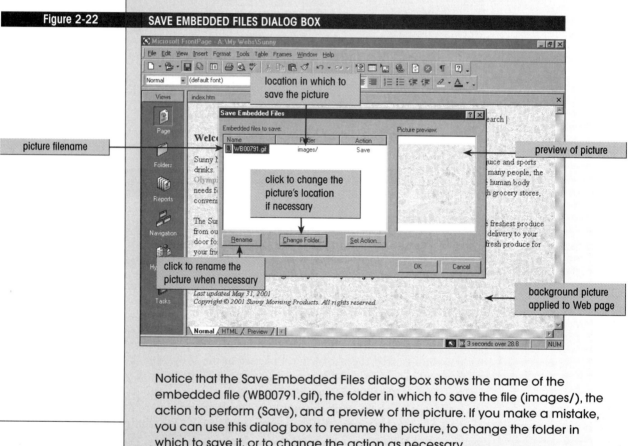

Notice that the Save Embedded Files dialog box shows the name of the embedded file (WB00791.gif), the folder in which to save the file (images/), the action to perform (Save), and a preview of the picture. If you make a mistake, you can use this dialog box to rename the picture, to change the folder in which to save it, or to change the action as necessary.

3. Click the **OK** button to save this file in the images folder and to save the Web page. After a few seconds, your Web site is updated.

Now that you have saved the Home Page, you need to test it using the browser.

To test a background picture using Internet Explorer:

1. Click the **Preview in Browser** button 🔍 on the Standard toolbar to start Internet Explorer and open the Home Page. The background picture adds visual interest to the page while maintaining the readability of the Web page's content. Your test is successful, so you can close the browser.

2. Click the **Close** button ☒ on the Internet Explorer title bar to close the browser.

3. If necessary, click the **Microsoft FrontPage** program button on the taskbar to return to FrontPage.

Your test of the background picture was a success—it improved the appearance of the Home Page. Now Amanda wants you to add the Sunny Morning Products logo to the page.

Adding a Picture to a Web Page

A **picture** is any file that contains a graphic image, such as a logo, photograph, or computer-generated image. You can use a picture as a background or to add visual interest to a Web page. You can also use a picture as a hyperlink that opens another Web page. Three of the most popular formats for picture files are the following:

- **GIF**, pronounced *jiff* or *giff* (with a hard "g"), which stands for **Graphics Interchange Format**. This format supports color and different screen resolutions, thereby making it suitable for scanned photos and pictures with smaller file sizes.
- **PNG**, pronounced *ping*, which stands for **Portable Network Graphics**. This new format is very similar to GIF. It differs from GIF in that certain aspects of GIF are patented, whereas PNG is patent- and license-free and therefore has no legal restrictions on its use.
- **JPG** (or **JPEG**), pronounced *jay-peg*, which stands for **Joint Photographic Experts Group**. This format is suitable for large pictures because it converts them to a format with smaller file sizes.

Most Web browsers will display pictures that are created using any of these picture file formats.

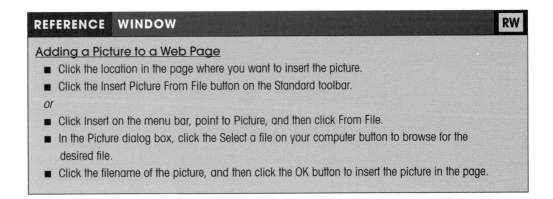

REFERENCE WINDOW   **RW**

Adding a Picture to a Web Page
- Click the location in the page where you want to insert the picture.
- Click the Insert Picture From File button on the Standard toolbar.

or
- Click Insert on the menu bar, point to Picture, and then click From File.
- In the Picture dialog box, click the Select a file on your computer button to browse for the desired file.
- Click the filename of the picture, and then click the OK button to insert the picture in the page.

Amanda already created the Sunny Morning Products logo, which she saved in the Tutorial.02 folder on your Data Disk. Amanda asks you to add this picture at the top of the Home Page.

To add a picture to a Web page:

1. Click anywhere in the navigation bar at the top of the page, press the **Home** key, press the **Enter** key to create a new line, and then press the **up arrow** key ↑ to move the insertion point to the new line. The insertion point now appears at the location where you want to add the picture. Notice that the Center button on the Standard toolbar is indented, which indicates that the new line is centered in the page.

2. Click the **Insert Picture From File** button 🖼 on the Standard toolbar to open the Picture dialog box, and then click the **Select a file on your computer** button 🔍 to open the Select File dialog box.

3. If necessary, click the **Look in** list arrow, change to the drive or folder that contains your Data Disk, and then double-click the **Tutorial.02** folder.

4. Double-click **smplogo** to insert the logo in the Web page, and then click the logo in the Web page to select it. See Figure 2-23.

Figure 2-23	PICTURE LOGO INSERTED IN THE HOME PAGE

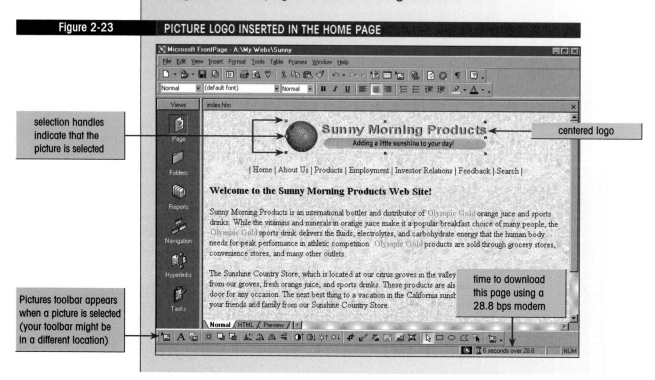

Notice that the current paragraph alignment—centered—is applied to the logo. Notice also the **selection handles**—eight small black squares around the logo—that you can use to resize the selected picture. The Pictures toolbar appears either as a floating or docked toolbar, depending on your system configuration. Finally, notice that the status bar indicates that the page with this picture inserted will take approximately 6 seconds to download using a 28.8 bps modem.

A picture might take some time to appear in a Web page. The length of the delay will depend on the transmission speed from the Web server to the client's browser. Often, while a picture is being transferred from the server to the client's browser window, an alternative text message appears. **Alternative text** is a descriptive message that identifies a picture in a Web page; it is an optional feature that you can include to identify a picture. Its primary purpose is to inform the user that a picture file is being transmitted to the browser but has not yet arrived. The message also appears when you point to the picture in the browser. Alternative text that you add to a picture in a Web page consists of HTML code.

Adding Alternative Text to a Picture
- Right-click the picture to open the shortcut menu, and then click Picture Properties.
- Make sure that the General tab is selected.
- Type the alternative text in the Text text box in the Alternative representations section, and then click the OK button.

Although the download time of approximately 6 seconds is acceptable, Amanda tells you that adding alternative text to the picture is good design practice. She asks you to include alternative text for the Sunny Morning Products logo.

To add alternative text for a picture and test it:

1. Right-click the **logo** to open the shortcut menu, and then click **Picture Properties** to open the Picture Properties dialog box.

2. If necessary, click the **General** tab to display those settings. See Figure 2-24. Notice that the GIF option button is selected in the Type section to indicate the selected picture's file format.

| Figure 2-24 | GENERAL SETTINGS FOR THE SELECTED PICTURE |

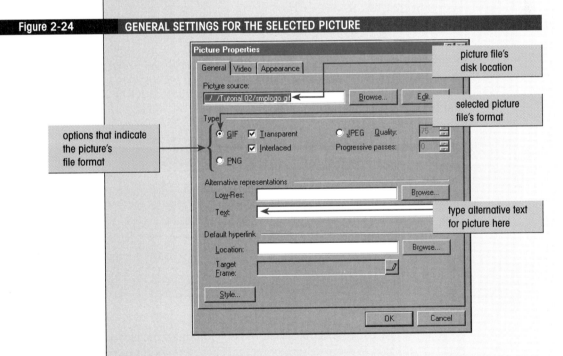

3. Click in the **Text** text box in the Alternative representations section, type **Sunny Morning Products Logo**, and then click the **OK** button. The Picture Properties dialog box closes, and the Home Page reappears.

   You can see the alternative text that you added by using the Preview tab or the browser. You will test the alternative text using the Preview tab.

4. Click the **Preview** tab. Point to the logo until the ScreenTip displays the alternative text that you added in Step 3. After a few seconds, the alternative text will disappear. Now if the picture fails to download from the server, or if it downloads slowly, the alternative text will be displayed.

5. Click the **Normal** tab to return to Normal Page view.

You added another picture to your Web site, so you need to save its file in the Sunny Web site's images folder.

To save the Home Page with the logo file:

1. Click the **Save** button 🖫 on the Standard toolbar. The Save Embedded Files dialog box opens and displays the name of the new embedded file (smplogo.gif), the folder in which it will be saved (images/), and the action to perform (Save). Notice that the Picture preview box shows a preview of the picture.

2. Click the **OK** button to save the embedded file in the Sunny Web site and to save the changes to the Home Page. After a few seconds, the file is saved and your Web site is updated.

Using **Horizontal Lines**

Sometimes you might want to emphasize the different parts of a Web page. One way to do this is to provide a visual break between sections of text by inserting a horizontal line. After inserting a horizontal line, you can change its characteristics by adjusting its length, width, and color.

REFERENCE WINDOW   **RW**

Inserting a Horizontal Line and Changing Its Properties
- Click at the beginning of the line directly below the location at which to insert the horizontal line.
- Click Insert on the menu bar, and then click Horizontal Line to insert a horizontal line.
- If necessary, right-click the horizontal line in the Web page, click Horizontal Line Properties on the shortcut menu, and then use the Horizontal Line Properties dialog box to change the line's characteristics.

To provide a visual break between the main body of the text and the footer information, Amanda asks you to insert a horizontal line above the footer in the Home Page.

To insert a horizontal line in a Web page:

1. Press **Ctrl + End** to scroll to the bottom of the Sunny Morning Products Home Page.

2. Click the insertion point before the word **Last** at the beginning of the first line of the footer. The insertion point is now positioned directly below the location at which to insert the horizontal line.

3. Click **Insert** on the menu bar, and then click **Horizontal Line**. A horizontal line is inserted above the footer.

Next, Amanda asks you to make the line stand out more in the Home Page by making it shorter and wider and by changing its color.

To change horizontal line settings:

1. Right-click the **horizontal line** to select it and to open the shortcut menu, and then click **Horizontal Line Properties** to open the Horizontal Line Properties dialog box. See Figure 2-25.

| Figure 2-25 | CHANGING THE PROPERTIES OF A HORIZONTAL LINE |

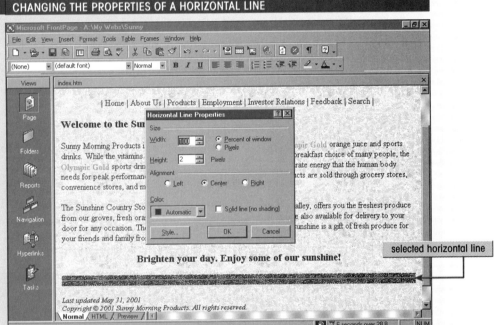

2. In the Size section, replace the selected text in the Width text box by typing **80**. This sets the line's width to 80% of the screen's width.

3. Click the **Height** up arrow until the value is set to **5**. This sets the height of the line to 5 pixels.

4. Click the **Color** list arrow, and then click the **orange** color in the Document's colors section. This is the same orange color that you applied to the Olympic Gold text in the Home Page in Session 2.2.

5. Click the **OK** button, and then click below the horizontal line to deselect it. The horizontal line is redisplayed as a centered, thicker, shorter, orange line. See Figure 2-26.

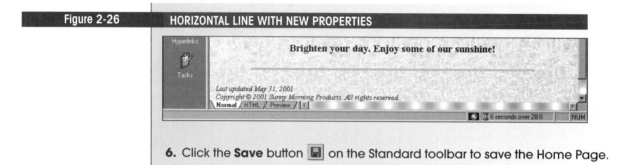

Figure 2-26   HORIZONTAL LINE WITH NEW PROPERTIES

6. Click the **Save** button on the Standard toolbar to save the Home Page.

Adding a Background Sound to a Web Page

The Sunny Morning Products logo that you added to the Home Page is an example of a multimedia file. You can add a variety of multimedia files to your Web site, including picture, video, and sound files. Sound files add interest to a page, but they also have a disadvantage: They often are very large and thus can take a long time to download. Two of the most popular sound file types for Web pages are the following:

- **WAV** (*.WAV), which is the standard file format for sound on personal computers.
- **MIDI** (*.MID), which stands for **Musical Instrument Digital Interface**. This format is used by the electronic music industry for controlling devices that emit music, such as synthesizers and sound cards.

A WAV file usually produces better quality sound than a MIDI file. By contrast, MIDI files are usually smaller than WAV files and therefore download from the Web server more quickly.

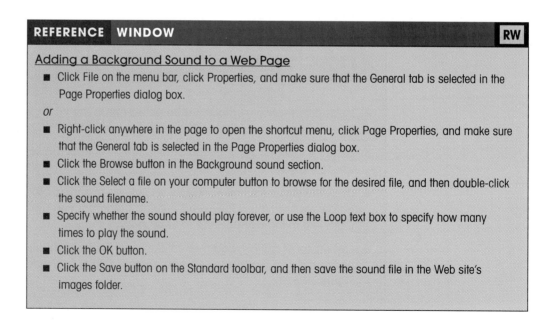

REFERENCE   WINDOW   RW

Adding a Background Sound to a Web Page

- Click File on the menu bar, click Properties, and make sure that the General tab is selected in the Page Properties dialog box.

or

- Right-click anywhere in the page to open the shortcut menu, click Page Properties, and make sure that the General tab is selected in the Page Properties dialog box.
- Click the Browse button in the Background sound section.
- Click the Select a file on your computer button to browse for the desired file, and then double-click the sound filename.
- Specify whether the sound should play forever, or use the Loop text box to specify how many times to play the sound.
- Click the OK button.
- Click the Save button on the Standard toolbar, and then save the sound file in the Web site's images folder.

Amanda asks you to add a sound file that will play once when the Home Page is opened or refreshed in the browser. She already saved a MIDI sound file, which plays a minuet, in the Tutorial.02 folder on your Data Disk.

To add a background sound to a Web page:

1. Click **File** on the menu bar, click **Properties** to open the Page Properties dialog box, and then make sure that the General tab is selected.

2. Click the **Browse** button in the Background sound section to open the Background Sound dialog box.

3. Click the **Select a file on your computer** button to open the Select File dialog box. The Tutorial.02 folder opens, displaying the sound (audio) files contained within it.

4. Double-click **minuet** to select it as the background sound and to return to the Page Properties dialog box. Notice that the minuet.mid file is listed in the Location text box in the Background sound section.

   TROUBLE? If you do not see the minuet file in the Select File dialog box, make sure that the Look in folder displays the Tutorial.02 folder on your Data Disk and that the Files of type list box is set to display "All Audios." If you still do not see the minuet file, ask your instructor or technical support person for help.

When you add a background sound to a Web page, the default is for the sound to play forever (or continuously) while the page that contains it is open in the browser. You can change this setting to specify a number of times for the sound to play while the page is open in the browser. Now that you've added the background sound to the Home Page, you will set it to play only once when the Home Page is opened or refreshed in the browser.

To adjust the loop setting for a background sound, and then save and test it:

1. In the Background sound section, click the **Forever** check box to deselect an infinite loop and to enable the Loop text box.

2. Click the **Loop** up arrow once to change the value to 1, and then click the **OK** button to close the Page Properties dialog box.

   Now you can save the minuet file in the Sunny Web site and then test it in the browser.

3. Click the **Save** button on the Standard toolbar to open the Save Embedded Files dialog box. If necessary, click the **Change Folder** button, click the **images** folder for the Sunny Web site, click the **OK** button, and then click the **OK** button to save the file.

   Next, test the page in Internet Explorer.

4. Click the **Preview in Browser** button on the Standard toolbar to open the Home Page in Internet Explorer. The background sound will play once and then stop.

> TROUBLE? If you do not hear the background sound, make sure that your computer is equipped with a sound card and that the speakers are turned on. If you still do not hear the sound, ask your instructor or technical support person for help.
>
> TROUBLE? If the music sounds like it is playing too slowly on your computer, don't worry. This performance reflects your hardware and software setups.

5. Click the **Refresh** button 🔄 on the Internet Explorer toolbar. When you **refresh** a Web page, it is reloaded in the Web browser. In this example, the background sound starts to play again.

6. Click the **Stop** button ⊗ on the Internet Explorer toolbar to stop the music.

7. Click the **Close** button ✕ on the Internet Explorer title bar to close Internet Explorer.

8. If necessary, click the **Microsoft FrontPage** program button on the taskbar to return to FrontPage.

Amanda is pleased with the enhancements you have made to the Home Page. She asks you to add one more feature to make the page more interesting: a marquee.

Using a Marquee

Another way to draw attention to information in a Web page is to scroll text across the page. A **marquee** is a text box in a Web page that displays a scrolling message. You can create a marquee by using existing text or by entering new text. You should use marquees sparingly, however, because they can easily overpower a Web page and distract users.

REFERENCE WINDOW   **RW**

Creating a Marquee in a Web Page
- Select the text in the Web page that is to appear in the marquee.
- Click the Insert Component button on the Standard toolbar, and then click Marquee to open the Marquee Properties dialog box.
- If necessary, enter or edit the text for the marquee in the Text text box.
- In the Behavior section, click the option button for the desired behavior of the marquee's text.
- Specify any other desired characteristics of the marquee, such as its alignment, and the direction, speed, size, and/or background color of its text, or accept the default settings for these characteristics.
- If necessary, click the Style button, click the Format button in the Modify Style dialog box, and then click an option in the list that opens to change the settings for the marquee's font, paragraph, border, bullets, and position.
- Click the OK button.

Amanda wants you to create a marquee that draws more attention to the sentences, "Brighten your day. Enjoy some of our sunshine!" Placing this text in a marquee will animate it when the Home Page is viewed using the Preview tab or the browser. When creating a marquee, keep in mind that the text in a marquee should fit on one line, and that shorter phrases or sentences work better than longer ones.

To create and test the marquee:

1. Select the text **Brighten your day. Enjoy some of our sunshine!** in the Home Page. This text will appear in your marquee.

2. Click the **Insert Component** button 🖾 on the Standard toolbar, and then click **Marquee** to open the Marquee Properties dialog box. See Figure 2-27. Notice that the text you selected appears in the Text text box automatically.

| Figure 2-27 | MARQUEE PROPERTIES DIALOG BOX |

text that will be used in the marquee

options for moving text across the screen

options for setting the number of times to scroll the text

options for the size of the marquee's text box

option to change the background color of the marquee's text box

TROUBLE? If a space appears after the exclamation point in the Text text box, you selected the hard return at the end of the paragraph in the Web page. Delete the space and continue with Step 3.

3. Click the **Alternate** option button in the Behavior section. Selecting this setting causes the marquee's text to move back and forth across your screen. The Scroll setting causes the text to move across the screen in only one direction, and the Slide setting causes the text to scroll across the screen and then stop.

4. In the Size section, click the **Width** check box to select it, select the value in the Width text box and type **90**, and then click the **In percent** option button to select that option. These settings limit the width of the marquee to 90% of the screen's width. Notice that you can set similar limits on the marquee's height or use pixels as your unit of measurement.

TROUBLE? If you accidentally close the Marquee Properties dialog box, right-click the marquee in the Web page and then click Marquee Properties on the shortcut menu to reopen the dialog box.

Amanda suggests that you use a different background color for the marquee's text box so that it will stand out in the page.

5. Click the **Background color** list arrow to open the list of available colors. See Figure 2-28.

Figure 2-28

CHANGING THE MARQUEE'S BACKGROUND COLOR

colors used in
the Web page

click to select a color
not listed here

select this color

6. Click the **Aqua** color in the Standard colors section (see Figure 2-28). This color has the ScreenTip "Aqua."

Notice that you can change other marquee options as well. For example, checking the Continuously check box in the Repeat section causes the marquee's text to remain animated indefinitely while the page is open. If you clear this check box, you can specify the number of times that the marquee's text will move across the screen. Other options let you set the text's direction of movement (Left or Right) and the alignment of other text in the page with the marquee (Top, Middle, or Bottom). You specify delay and speed parameters in the Speed section. In the Delay text box, you type the amount of time, in milliseconds, that the text should wait before it begins to move. In the Amount text box, you type the speed at which the text is to move in the marquee. The default settings for these options are acceptable, so you will close the dialog box.

7. Click the **OK** button. The Page Properties dialog box closes and an aqua marquee surrounds the heading in the Web page. No movement is shown, however. To test this feature, you must save the page and then use the Preview tab.

8. Click the **Save** button 🖫 on the Standard toolbar, and then click the **Preview** tab to preview the page. If necessary, scroll down the page to see the marquee. The text moves back and forth in the marquee.

9. Click the **Normal** tab to return to Normal Page view.

Amanda is pleased with the revised content and appearance of the Home Page. She wants you next to include information in the Home Page that will help people locate the Sunny Morning Products Web site.

Using **META Tags**

A Web site can be an effective marketing tool for a company only if people are aware that the site exists. One way to promote a Web site so that users can find it is indexing. **Indexing** is the process of listing a Web site in Web search engines. An **index** is a database that Web users search to find specific Web sites. Normally, you conduct searches using a **Web search engine**, which is a Web site that automatically gathers and maintains information about all of the Web sites on the Web. Each Web search engine uses a different method to index the Web, so your search results using different search engines might vary. In addition to using indexing, some search engines, such as Yahoo!, also list Web sites by category. Other search engines, such as AltaVista, Excite, and HotBot, search the Web for new sites and compile data about the information contained within each site.

Most search engines gather information about Web sites by collecting data based on HTML code entered into the HTML document by the Web page's developer. These keywords are called META tags. A **META tag** is an HTML tag that includes text which identifies how the Web page's developer wants to add the Web site to a search engine's index. For example, if a user enters the search terms "orange juice" in a Web search engine, Amanda wants the search engine to match the Sunny Morning Products Home Page. To accomplish this objective, you will add the keywords "orange juice" to the Home Page's META tag.

A META tag can include attributes that specify the page's subject, author, content, and description, as well as keywords that are used to identify the site. The description and keywords META tags are the most useful in providing information for indexing purposes. FrontPage automatically creates two META tags in all FrontPage-created documents: One indicates that the Web page was created using FrontPage, and the other indicates that the Web page is an "http" page and specifies the character set used by the page. FrontPage places all META tags at the beginning of the HTML document. META tags do not change the appearance of the Web page; only search engines use them for the purpose of updating their search indexes.

REFERENCE WINDOW   RW

Inserting META tags in a Web Page
- Right-click anywhere in the Web page to open the shortcut menu, click Page Properties, and then click the Custom tab.
- Click the Add button in the User variables section.
- Type the META tag name in the Name text box, and then press the Tab key.
- Type the desired text for the META tag in the Value text box.
- Click the OK button.
- Click the Add button, and then repeat the process to add additional META tags as necessary.
- Click the OK button.

To promote the Web site for Sunny Morning Products, Amanda wants you to include indexing information in the Home Page so that the site will be added automatically to the indexes of various Web search engines. You will add two META tags—description and keywords—to the Home Page.

To insert META tags:

1. Right-click anywhere in the Web page to open the shortcut menu, click **Page Properties** to open the Page Properties dialog box, and then click the **Custom** tab to display those settings.

2. In the User variables section, click the **Add** button to open the User Meta Variable dialog box.

TROUBLE? If you accidentally click the Add button in the System variables section, the System META Variable (HTTP-EQUIV) dialog box opens rather than the User Meta Variable dialog box. Click the Cancel button, and then click the Add button in the User variables section. Continue with Step 3. (Creating system variables is beyond the scope of this tutorial.)

3. Type **description** in the Name text box, and then press the **Tab** key to move the insertion point to the Value text box. You will use the description META tag to summarize your Web site's contents.

4. With the insertion point in the Value text box, type **Sunny Morning Products produces Olympic Gold brand orange juice and sports drink. Check out our Sunshine Country Store.** as the description. See Figure 2-29.

Figure 2-29 **DEFINING META TAGS FOR THE SUNNY WEB SITE**

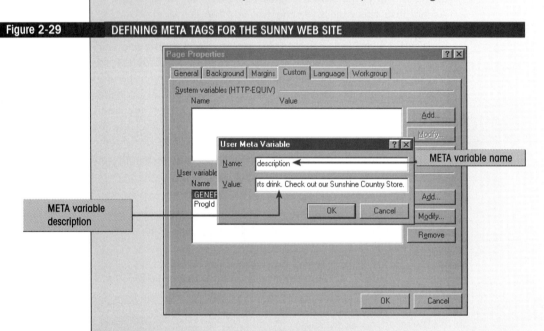

5. Click the **OK** button to return to the Page Properties dialog box. Notice that the text you just typed in the Name and Value text boxes appears under the Name and Value columns in the User variables section.

6. Click the **Add** button in the User variables section again, type **keywords** in the Name text box, and then press the **Tab** key to advance to the Value text box. Web search engines use the keywords META tag to catalog your Web site.

7. Type **orange juice, sports drink, citrus products, gifts, holiday gifts, oranges, grapefruit** in the Value text box as the desired keywords.

8. Click the **OK** button to return to the Page Properties dialog box, and then click the **OK** button to close it.

META tags do not appear in the Web page in FrontPage or Internet Explorer. Amanda wants you to view the META tags in the HTML code in order to better understand the exact information that search engines will add to their indexes. Viewing the tags also allows you to confirm that the entries were correctly inserted in the HTML code.

Viewing **HTML Code**

Recall from Tutorial 1 that FrontPage produces the HTML code for your Web page and that a Web browser interprets this code in order to display the page. In creating the Home Page for Sunny Morning Products, you used FrontPage to include many features that are represented by different HTML tags, including different paragraph styles, multimedia files, and a marquee. For example, BGSOUND specifies the background sound you inserted, and the ALIGN property of the P (paragraph) tag specifies the paragraph's alignment. The H3 tag specifies a heading and its style, and the MARQUEE tag specifies the use of a marquee in the page. FrontPage created each of these tags and their related properties as you created the Home Page. Even though FrontPage created the HTML code, it is important for a Web site developer to understand HTML code because it is the foundation of creating any Web page.

Amanda wants you to examine the HTML code for the Home Page to get a better understanding of the code that FrontPage created. As you learn more about HTML, you will gain confidence and be comfortable making changes to the Web page by editing the HTML code.

To view the HTML code and close FrontPage:

1. Press **Ctrl + Home** to scroll to the top of the Home Page.

2. Click the **HTML** tab to switch to that view and to display the HTML code for the Home Page. See Figure 2-30. Examine the HTML code that FrontPage created to insert the META tags, the background sound, and other features of the Home Page.

Figure 2-30	VIEWING THE FIRST PAGE OF HTML CODE FOR THE HOME PAGE

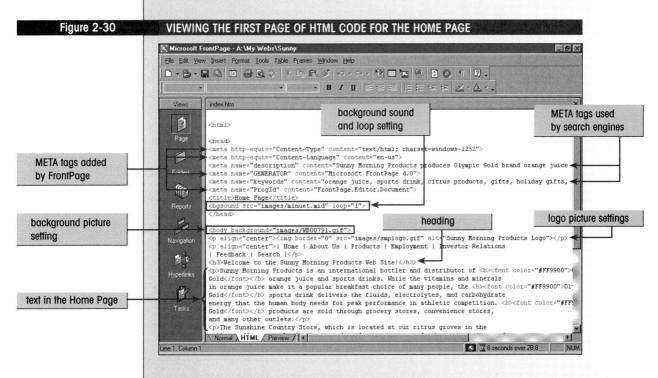

3. Press **Ctrl + End** to scroll to the end of the document. The remainder of the HTML code appears in your window. See Figure 2-31. Examine the HTML code that created the marquee, the footer, and other features of the Home Page.

Figure 2-31   **VIEWING THE SECOND PAGE OF THE HTML CODE FOR THE HOME PAGE**

4. Click the **Normal** tab to return to Normal Page view. Your work on the Home Page is complete for now, so you can close FrontPage.

5. Click the **Close** button ⊠ to close the Home Page, the Sunny Web site, and FrontPage. If FrontPage asks if you want to save your changes, click the **Yes** button.

With the Home Page created and its contents and features revised, you are well on your way to implementing the Web site design for Sunny Morning Products. You are confident that the Home Page design meets the requirements of the Web site development team. In Tutorial 3, you will create additional pages and link them to each other by using hyperlinks.

Session 2.3 QUICK CHECK

1. The default background color of a Web page when you first create it is _____.

2. What are three common picture file formats that are used in Web pages?

3. In addition to being a good design practice, why should you add alternative text to a picture that you use in your Web page?

4. A good way to separate sections in a Web page is to insert a(n) _____.

5. Describe two popular sound file formats that you can use in a Web page.

6. Text that is formatted to animate in a Web page when it is displayed in the browser appears in a(n) _____.

7. Describe the purpose of the images folder that is automatically created when you create a FrontPage Web.

8. To supply information that is used by a search engine to make your Web site available to Internet users, use a(n) _____.

REVIEW ASSIGNMENTS

Amanda is pleased with the progress you are making in her training course. She asks you to finish formatting the Home Page by inserting another horizontal line and changing the HTML code.

If necessary, start FrontPage and insert your Data Disk in the appropriate disk drive, and then do the following:

1. Open the **Sunny** Web site (that you created in the tutorial) from the My Webs folder on your Data Disk, change to Folders view, and then open the Home Page (**index.htm** or **default.htm**) in Page view.

2. Add a horizontal line between the "Welcome" heading and the first paragraph of the narrative text. If necessary, change the line to make it the same size and color as the line you added at the bottom of the page in the tutorial.

3. Center the "Welcome" heading in the Home Page.

Explore   4. Change to HTML Page view, and then locate the HTML tags that apply the Heading 3 style to the "Welcome" heading. Change the HTML code so that the "Welcome" heading uses the Heading 1 style. (*Hint*: You will need to change the opening and closing tags to use the Heading 1 style.) Save your changes to the Home Page, and then preview the page in the browser. Describe what happened to the "Welcome" heading.

Explore   5. Use Internet Explorer to print the HTML code for the Home Page, and then change the "Welcome" heading's style back to Heading 3. Save your changes, and then refresh the page.

6. Close Internet Explorer and FrontPage.

CASE PROBLEMS

Case 1. Preparing a Web Presence for Royal Hair Care Products Royal Hair Care Products, established in 1984, is a leader in hair care products for women, men, and children. Its current product line includes shampoos, conditioners, hair sprays, and styling gels. All products carry a satisfaction guarantee. The company's newest product is Quick Dry Solution, which when applied to wet hair, dries it quickly without the need for a hair dryer. Quick Dry Solution is available in either a gel form or a liquid spray. The easy-to-use product leaves hair feeling natural and manageable.

Recently, Valerie Suarez, the president of Royal Hair Care Products, hired Nathan Dubois as an information systems specialist and assigned him to Royal's Web site development team. Valerie wants Nathan to design Royal's Web site and then create a Home Page for the company. Valerie and Nathan met with the rest of the Web site development team members. In the meeting, all agreed that, in addition to the Home Page, the company needs six more pages with the following titles: (1) About Us, (2) News, (3) Employment, (4) Financial Info, (5) Feedback, and (6) Search. Valerie has asked you to assist Nathan with the development of the site and the Home Page.

If necessary, start FrontPage, insert your Data Disk in the appropriate disk drive, and then do the following:

1. Prepare a planning analysis sheet for the Royal Web site.

2. Prepare a Web site plan that shows the desired Web pages and the expected hyperlinks from the Home Page.

3. Create the Royal Web site using FrontPage. Title it **Royal** and save it in the My Webs folder on your Data Disk. (The location is a:\My Webs\Royal.) Use the One Page Web template to create the Web site.

4. Use Page view to enter, edit, and spell check the following two paragraphs of content for the Home Page of the Royal Web site:

   Royal Hair Care Products was established in 1984 and remains a leader in hair care products, including shampoos, conditioners, hair sprays, and styling gels. We are committed to offering quality products for women, men, and children. Our products carry a 100% satisfaction guarantee. If you are not satisfied for any reason, you can return your purchase for a full refund.

   Our newest product is Quick Dry Solution, which dries wet hair quickly. In the time it takes you to finish your morning cup of coffee, your hair is dry and you are on your way.

5. Create the heading "Welcome to the Royal Web Site. Join us in your quest for beautiful hair." Place the heading above the text you entered in Step 4. Change the style of this line to Heading 3, and then center it.

6. Create a navigation bar for the Home Page based on your design for the Web site. Limit the navigation bar to a single line, and center it in the Home Page. Change the text in the navigation bar to bold, and then change its color to blue.

Explore 7. Add a footer that includes a copyright symbol and the company name on the first line. On the next line, type "Last updated," and then add a field that automatically updates the date and time since you last changed the Web page. (*Hint*: To add the date and time field, click Insert on the menu bar, and then click Date and Time.) Format the date using the format *month day, year*—for example, "September 22, 2001"—and the time with the hour and minutes. Change the footer text to bold text and then change its color to blue.

8. Change the size of the footer text to 10 points.

9. Add a horizontal line to the Web page between the "Welcome" heading and the first paragraph. Change the line's color to blue.

10. Save your changes, and then test the Home Page by using the Preview tab. If necessary, return to Normal Page view to correct any errors.

11. Insert at the top of the Home Page the logo file for the company, **Royal01.gif**, from the Tutorial.02 folder on your Data Disk.

Explore 12. Enter "The professional look for modern living!" as the slogan for Royal Hair Care Products, and place it in a marquee that is centered in the page above the footer. Change the default settings of the marquee so that it is an alternate marquee that uses 90% of the page's width. Select an appropriate color for the text and background of the marquee to coordinate with the logo's colors. (*Hint*: Click the Style button in the Marquee Properties dialog box, and then click the Format button in the Modify Style dialog box to change the format of the text in the marquee.)

13. Add to the Home Page the **Quantum.mid** file from the Tutorial.02 folder as a background sound that plays three times when the Home Page is opened or refreshed in Internet Explorer.

Explore   14. Create appropriate META descriptions and keywords for the Home Page, and then save the Home Page. Save the page, and save all multimedia files in the Web site's images folder.

15. Test the Web page using the Preview tab. If necessary, return to Normal Page view to correct any errors. Print the page.

16. In FrontPage, print the HTML code for the Home Page. On the printout, circle the META tags for the description and keywords that you added and the tags for the background picture and sound.

17. Close FrontPage.

Case 2. Developing a Web Site for Buffalo Trading Post Buffalo Trading Post (BTP) is a regional retail clothing business that specializes in buying, selling, and trading used clothing. The company buys all of its merchandise from people who take the items to one of its trading post stores. Employees then sort the items based on style, size, fabric, and garment condition. BTP specializes in natural fabric clothing items, but it also carries a limited inventory of polyester, acetate, Lycra, and other manufactured fibers in order to follow current styles and trends. BTP accepts only good-condition clothing for resale and attracts a loyal following of fashion enthusiasts and bargain hunters.

Karla Perez was recently hired by the president of the company, Donna Vargas, as a systems analyst and was assigned to BTP's Web site development team. Donna wants Karla to prepare a plan for BTP's Web site and then create its Home Page. Karla and Donna met with the rest of the Web site development team. They agreed that, in addition to the Home Page, the site should include five more pages with the following titles: (1) Who, (2) How, (3) What, (4) Where, and (5) Contact. Donna has asked you to help Karla with the development of the site and of the Home Page.

If necessary, start FrontPage and insert your Data Disk in the appropriate disk drive, and then do the following:

1. Prepare a planning analysis sheet for BTP's Web site.

2. Prepare a Web site plan that shows the desired Web pages and the expected hyperlinks from the Home Page.

3. Create the Buffalo Web site using FrontPage. Title it **Buffalo**, and save it in the My Webs folder on your Data Disk. (The location is a:\My Webs\Buffalo.) Use the One Page Web template to create the Web site.

Explore   4. Use FrontPage to write, enter, edit, and spell check at least two paragraphs of content for the Home Page of the Buffalo Web site. You may use any available reference sources to help develop your content, including other Web sites.

5. Create a heading, determine the most appropriate style and alignment for it, and place it above the text you entered in Step 4.

6. Create a navigation bar for the Home Page, and then center it. Change the color of the navigation bar to one of your choice and its style to bold.

Explore   7. Add a footer that consists of the copyright symbol and the company name on the first line. On the next line, add the following text: BTP™ is a registered trademark of Buffalo Trading Post. (*Hint*: Use the symbol set to insert the trademark character.) Change the footer text to bold, 10-point, Arial font.

8. Add a horizontal line between the navigation bar and the heading that you created in Step 5. Change the line's color to match the one that you used for the navigation bar. Change the line's height to four pixels and its width to 90% of the window's width.

9. Format the first instance of the text "Buffalo Trading Post" in the page's narrative so that it is easily distinguished. Then use the Format Painter to change other text occurrences of "Buffalo Trading Post" to match.

10. Change the background color of the Home Page to one that complements the text that you entered in Step 6.

11. Insert the **Buffalo1.gif** picture from the Tutorial.02 folder on your Data Disk on a new, centered line below the heading at the top of the Web page. Add to the picture the alternative text "Buffalo Trading Post Logo."

Explore ▷ 12. Create a slogan for BTP and place it in a centered marquee above the footer. Select appropriate colors for the marquee's text and background. Format the text as 12-point Comic Sans MS font. (*Hint*: Click the Style button in the Marquee Properties dialog box, click the Format button in the Modify Style dialog box, and then click Font to change the marquee text color and style.)

13. Add the **Cheers.mid** file from the Tutorial.02 folder as a background sound that plays once when the Web page is opened or refreshed in the browser.

Explore ▷ 14. Create META descriptions and keywords and include them in the Home Page.

15. Save your changes to the Home Page, and save all multimedia files in the Web site's images folder. Test the Home Page using Internet Explorer. If necessary, return to FrontPage and correct any errors. Print the page in Internet Explorer, and then close Internet Explorer.

16. Use FrontPage to print the HTML code for the Home Page. On the printout, circle the META tags for the description and keywords and the tags for the horizontal line and navigation bar.

17. Close FrontPage.

Case 3. Creating a Web Site for Garden Grill   Garden Grill is a growing chain of casual, full-service restaurants. Its moderately priced menu features delicious dishes taken from various locations around the world. Garden Grill uses sophisticated consumer marketing research techniques to monitor customer satisfaction and evolving customer expectations. It strives to be a market leader in its segment by utilizing technology as a competitive advantage. Since 1976, management has used in-store computers to assist in the operation of the restaurants. Support is provided from the corporate office, 7 days a week, 24 hours a day. Management believes that these information systems have positioned the chain to handle both its current needs and future growth.

The corporate office has prepared a long-range information systems plan, which it reviews annually with all levels of management. Management's plan for the coming year includes the development of a Web site. Shannon Taylor just completed her management orientation at the corporate offices of Garden Grill and was assigned to work with Nolan Simmons, who manages the information systems department. Last week, Nolan's job responsibilities were increased to include managing the company's Web site development team. Nolan wants Shannon to help him prepare the Web design plan and create a Home Page for Garden Grill.

Nolan and Shannon just met with the rest of the Web site development team. All agreed that, in addition to the Home Page, the company's Web site should include six more pages with the following titles: (1) Company Profile, (2) Menu, (3) Franchise Info, (4) Employment Opportunities, (5) Feedback, and (6) Search. Nolan has asked you to assist Shannon with the design and development activities.

If necessary, start FrontPage and insert your Data Disk in the appropriate disk drive, and then do the following:

1. Prepare a planning analysis sheet for Garden Grill's Web site.

2. Prepare a Web site plan that shows the desired Web pages and the expected hyperlinks from the Home Page.

3. Create the Garden Web site using FrontPage. Title it **Garden**, and save it in the My Webs folder on your Data Disk. (The location is a:\My Webs\Garden.) Use the One Page Web template to create the Web site.

4. Use FrontPage to enter, edit, and spell check the following content for the Home Page for the Garden Web site:

   Value and variety are always on our menu! Where would you like to dine tonight? How about America, Mexico, or Italy? We've got delicious dishes cooking tonight just for you, no matter what your mood.

   Garden Grill is a premier casual, full-service restaurant. Our moderately priced menu features favorite entrees from many locations around the world that are sure to please you and your guests.

5. Create the heading "Welcome to Garden Grill. Join us for food and fun!" and place it above the text you entered in Step 4. Change the heading's style to Heading 3 and its font style to Arial. (*Hint*: Use the Font list arrow on the Formatting toolbar.) Then center the heading and change its color to red.

6. Create a navigation bar for the Home Page below the heading that you created in Step 5. Follow your Web site design plan, and limit the bar to a single line in the Web page. (*Hint:* You might need to reduce the font size of the navigation bar to make it fit on one line.) Use square brackets ([ ]) to enclose the navigation items. Change the color of the text in the navigation bar to purple, its style to bold, and its font to Century Gothic. Center the navigation bar.

7. Insert the **Garden01.gif** picture from the Tutorial.02 folder on a new line below the navigation bar and then center it.

Explore

8. Add a footer that consists of the copyright symbol and the company name on the first line. On the second line, add the text "Last updated" and a date field that indicates when the page was last edited. (*Hint*: To add the date field, click Insert on the menu bar, and then click Date and Time.) Format the date with the day of the week and the full date with the month spelled out.

9. Change the style of the footer you created in Step 8 to italic, 10-point, Arial font. Change the footer's color to match the color that you used for the navigation bar.

10. Apply to the Home Page the background picture file named **WB02245.gif** that is saved in the Tutorial.02 folder.

11. Add at least one horizontal line to the Web page whose length is half the width of the page and whose color complements the rest of the Web page.

Explore 12. Enter "Come to Garden Grill for food and fun!" as the slogan for Garden Grill on a new line above the footer and place it in a centered, sliding marquee that is 85% of the page's width. Change the marquee's text to white, 14-point, bold, Century Gothic font. (*Hint*: Click the Style button in the Marquee Properties dialog box, click the Format button, and then click Font to change the marquee text font color and style.) In the Marquee Properties dialog box, use the Background color list arrow to change the background color of the marquee to match the color of the navigation bar.

13. Add the **Casper.mid** file from the Tutorial.02 folder as a background sound that plays once when the Web page is opened or refreshed in the Internet Explorer.

Explore 14. Create META descriptions and keywords and include them in the Home Page. Save the Home Page, and save any multimedia files in the Garden Web site's images folder.

15. Test the Home Page using Internet Explorer. If necessary, return to FrontPage and correct any errors. Print the page in Internet Explorer, and then close Internet Explorer.

16. Use FrontPage to print the HTML code for the Home Page. Circle the META tags for all of the formatting changes that you made to the Home Page.

17. Close FrontPage.

Case 4. Producing a Web Site for Replay Music Factory Replay Music Factory (RMF) is a regional music store that specializes in buying, selling, and trading used compact discs (CDs). As the sale of new CDs expands, phenomenal growth is expected in the market for used CDs. Unlike records and tapes, used CDs offer quality that is comparable to that of new CDs, along with substantial savings. RMF buys used CDs from three sources: the Internet, customers, and brokers. This strategy allows RMF to offer a wide variety of music to the most discriminating listener. The company's quality control division has identified a defect rate of less than 1%, so all of its products are 100% guaranteed.

Alec Johnston was recently hired by RMF president, Charlene Fields, as a systems analyst and was assigned to RMF's Web site development team. Charlene wants you to help Alec to design the Web site and create a Home Page for it.

If necessary, start FrontPage and insert your Data Disk in the appropriate disk drive, and then do the following:

Explore 1. Prepare a planning analysis sheet for RMF's Web site. Determine which features and functions should be included in this Web site. If you have access to the Internet, reference three to five other Web sites that will be accessible from the RMF Home Page. If you do not have Internet access, use information that you know from other sources, such as magazine or newspaper articles that you have read or from televised news reports.

2. Prepare a Web site plan that shows the desired Web pages and the expected hyperlinks from the Home Page.

3. Create the Replay Web site using FrontPage. Title it **Replay**, and save it in the My Webs folder on your Data Disk. (The location is a:\My Webs\Replay.) Use the One Page Web template to create the Web site.

Explore 4. Use FrontPage to write, enter, edit, and spell check at least two paragraphs of content for the Home Page of the Replay Web site. Use any available reference sources to help develop your content, including other commercial Web sites.

5. Create a heading and place it above the text that you entered in Step 4. Apply an appropriate style, alignment, and color to the heading.

6. Create a navigation bar above the heading you created in Step 5 for the Home Page. Separate the navigation bar entries with a tilde (~). Change the text color in the navigation bar to match that of the heading, and apply an appropriate alignment to it.

Explore   7. Add a footer that includes the current date (in any format you choose), the copyright symbol, and the company name. (*Hint*: To add the date field, click Insert on the menu bar, and then click Date and Time.)

8. Use boldface, italics, and color to improve the appearance of your Web page. Save your changes to the Home Page.

Explore   9. Create a slogan for RMF and place it in a scrolling marquee on a new line above the footer. Select appropriate colors for the marquee text and background. (*Hint*: Click the Style button in the Marquee Properties dialog box, click the Format button in the Modify Style dialog box, and then click Font to change font style and color of the marquee text.)

Explore   10. Locate a MIDI or WAV file on your computer and include it as a background sound that plays twice when the Web page is opened or refreshed in the browser. (*Hint*: Sound files are usually saved in the Windows\Media folder on your computer. If you cannot find a MIDI or WAV file on your system, use any MIDI file in the Tutorial.02 folder on your Data Disk.)

11. Apply the background picture saved as **WB00760.gif** in the Tutorial.02 folder on your Data Disk to the Home Page. Save your changes, and save all multimedia files in the Web site's images folder.

Explore   12. Create a logo for RMF using an appropriate picture from the Clip Art Gallery supplied with FrontPage or from any other source, and then insert it in the Home Page. (*Hint*: To open the Clip Art Gallery, click Insert on the menu bar, click Picture, and then click Clip Art. Click the Pictures tab, and then click the categories to browse for an appropriate picture. To insert a picture, click it and then click the Insert clip button on the shortcut menu that opens.)

13. Add at least one horizontal line to the Web page that is five pixels in height and an appropriate color.

Explore   14. Create META descriptions and keywords and include them in the Home Page. Save the Home Page and all multimedia files in the Web site's images folder.

15. Test the Web page using Internet Explorer. If necessary, return to FrontPage and correct any errors. Print the page in Internet Explorer, and then close Internet Explorer.

Explore   16. Use FrontPage to print the HTML code for the Home Page. On the printout, circle the HTML tags that define the date field that you added in Step 7 and the logo that you added in Step 12.

17. Close FrontPage.

QUICK | CHECK ANSWERS

Session 2.1

1. Define the site's goal and purpose, determine and prepare the site's contents, design the site, build the site, test the site

2. default.htm

3. Enter text, separated by special characters such as a vertical bar or brackets, or use FrontPage to generate a navigation bar.

4. True

5. False

6. Close Web

Session 2.2

1. Format menu, shortcut menu, or Formatting toolbar buttons

2. H1

3. font

4. Select the text whose format you want to copy, click the Format Painter button on the Standard toolbar once, and then select the text to which you want to copy the format with the Format Painter pointer.

5. Normal

6. True

Session 2.3

1. white

2. GIF, JPG, PNG

3. Alternative text identifies the name of the file that is being downloaded so that the user knows that it is being transmitted to the browser but has not yet arrived.

4. horizontal line

5. WAV (*.WAV) is the standard for sound on personal computers; MIDI (*.MID) is used by the electronic music industry for controlling devices that emit music, such as synthesizers and sound cards.

6. marquee

7. The images folder is used to store all of the multimedia files used in the pages of the Web site.

8. META tag

OBJECTIVES

In this tutorial you will:

- Import an existing Web page into a Web site

- Insert a file created in another program in a Web page

- Create definition, bulleted, numbered, and nested lists

- Create bookmarks and hyperlinks to them in a Web page

- Create and test hyperlinks to other Web pages

- Create a hyperlink to an e-mail address

- Convert a JPEG picture to GIF format with a transparent background

- Create a hotspot in a picture and assign a hyperlink to it

- View and print Hyperlinks view for a Web site

- Use the Tasks list to add, complete, view, reassign, and delete tasks

LABS

Web Pages & HTML

USING
LISTS, HYPERLINKS, PICTURES, AND THE TASKS LIST

Creating the Employment Web Page

CASE

Sunny Morning Products

Amanda Bay created the design for the Sunny Morning Products Web site and for several Web pages, for which she received approval from the Web site development team. The navigation bar entries in the Home Page include hyperlinks that open pages with the following titles: About Us, Products, Employment, Investor Relations, Feedback, and Search. In addition to completing each of these pages, Amanda needs to add hyperlinks to link each page to the Home Page. At the request of Pilar Caballero, human resources manager at Sunny Morning Products, Amanda focused first on developing the Employment Web page, which provides information about current employment opportunities at Sunny Morning Products. She created a draft of this Web page and then met with Pilar to review the page's proposed design and content. For organizational purposes, Amanda captured the meeting results in a planning analysis sheet.

In this tutorial, you will continue developing the Sunny Web site by creating the Employment Web page. You will use lists, hyperlinks, pictures, and a Tasks list to turn a partially completed Web page into a finished one.

SESSION 3.1

In this session, you will import an existing Web page into a Web site and insert an Office 2000 document in a Web page. In addition, you will create definition, bulleted, numbered, and nested lists.

Importing a Web Page into a Web Site

You can easily place, or **import**, an existing Web page into the current Web site. Importing allows you to incorporate Web pages—even those created using a Web authoring program other than FrontPage—into your current Web site. In addition, you can import different types of files, such as Word documents and Excel workbooks, into a Web site and automatically convert them to HTML. Importing content into a Web site saves you the trouble of retyping the material.

Amanda already started developing the Employment Web page and now asks you to import her partially completed Web page into the Sunny Web site. Figure 3-1 shows Amanda's planning analysis sheet for the revisions to the Employment Web page.

| Figure 3-1 | AMANDA'S PLANNING ANALYSIS SHEET FOR THE EMPLOYMENT WEB PAGE |

Planning Analysis Sheet

Objective

Create an Employment Web page that includes a table of contents and descriptions for the position openings.

Requirements

Partially completed Employment Web page

Job descriptions for the MIS and Customer Support positions

Picture file for the page's logo

Results

Employment Web page with the following information:

> Table of contents
>
> Complete job descriptions
>
> Links from the table of contents to each job description
>
> E-mail hyperlink for contacting the human resources manager
>
> Logo that provides a corporate identity for the page

The Employment Web page that Amanda started is not saved in the Sunny Web site, so you will need to import it. First you will open the Sunny Web site, and then you will import Amanda's partially completed Employment Web page into it.

REFERENCE WINDOW   **RW**

Importing an Existing Web Page into a Web Site
- Open in Folders view the Web site into which you will import the existing Web page.
- Click File on the menu bar, click Import, and then click the Add File button in the Import dialog box to display a list of files.
- Locate the desired file, and then double-click it.
- Click the OK button to import the page.

After importing Amanda's Web page, you can modify it just like any other Web page.

To open the Sunny Web site and import an existing Web page into it:

1. Make sure your Data Disk is in the appropriate disk drive on your computer, start **FrontPage**, and then open the **Sunny** Web site (a:\My Webs\Sunny) from your Data Disk in Folders view.

2. Click **File** on the menu bar, and then click **Import** to open the Import dialog box.

3. Click the **Add File** button to open the Add File to Import List dialog box.

4. Click the **Look in** list arrow, change to the drive or folder that contains your Data Disk, and then double-click the **Tutorial.03** folder to display its contents.

5. Double-click **EmpPage** to select it and to return to the Import dialog box. The full path of the emppage.htm file appears in the Import dialog box. If you wanted to import another page at this time, you could click the Add File button and select another file.

   TROUBLE? If you selected the wrong file to import, make sure that the file you imported by mistake is selected, click the Remove button in the Import dialog box, and then repeat Steps 2 through 5 to select the correct file.

6. Click the **OK** button. The Employment Web page, emppage.htm, is now in the Sunny Web site. See Figure 3-2.

| Figure 3-2 | EMPLOYMENT WEB PAGE IMPORTED INTO THE SUNNY WEB SITE |

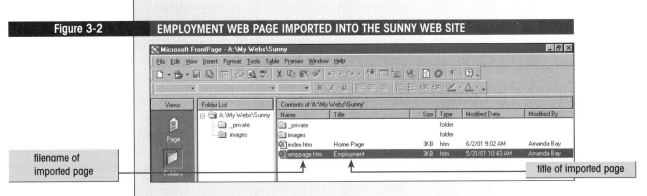

filename of imported page

title of imported page

Now that you've imported the Employment Web page into the Sunny Web site, you can open it just like any other Web page.

To open the imported Web page:

1. Double-click **emppage.htm** in the Contents pane to open the partially completed Web page in Page view. Notice that the Employment Web page appears with the default white background. See Figure 3-3.

| Figure 3-3 | PARTIALLY COMPLETED EMPLOYMENT WEB PAGE IN PAGE VIEW |

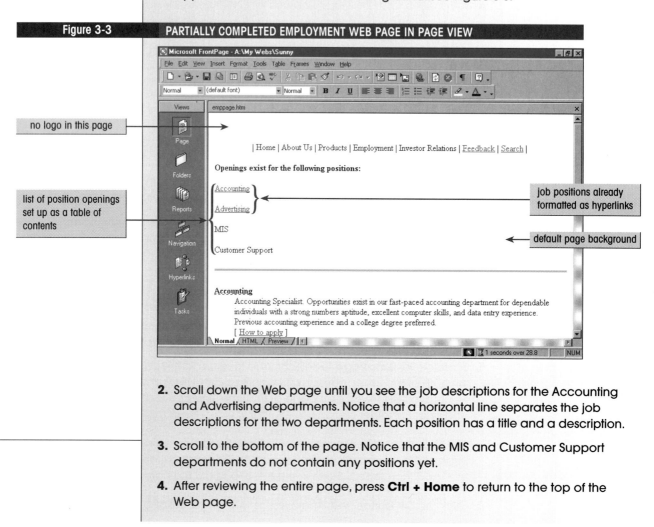

2. Scroll down the Web page until you see the job descriptions for the Accounting and Advertising departments. Notice that a horizontal line separates the job descriptions for the two departments. Each position has a title and a description.

3. Scroll to the bottom of the page. Notice that the MIS and Customer Support departments do not contain any positions yet.

4. After reviewing the entire page, press **Ctrl + Home** to return to the top of the Web page.

Before adding any new features or text to the Employment Web page, Amanda wants you to apply the background that you applied to the Home Page so that the Employment Web page has the same appearance.

Specifying a Common Background

A well-designed Web site usually uses the same design features—color, background, and so on—for all of its pages. This similarity provides a visual cue that the pages belong to the same Web site. To make the background the same for every Web page, you can use one of two methods. You can apply the same background to every Web page in the Web site, or you can specify that the background for a page uses the same one as another Web page. With the second method, for example, changing the background of the Home Page also changes the backgrounds of all of the pages that use the same background as the Home Page.

Amanda wants you to change the background of the Employment page to use the same one that you applied to the Home Page in Tutorial 2.

To specify a background from an existing Web page:

1. Click **Format** on the menu bar, and then click **Background** to display the background settings in the Page Properties dialog box.

2. Click the **Get background information from another page** check box, and then click the **Browse** button to open the Current Web dialog box.

   You want to use the Home Page as the source for applying the background of the Employment Web page.

3. Click **index.htm** to select the Home Page, and then click the **OK** button to return to the Page Properties dialog box. See Figure 3-4. Notice that index.htm now appears in the Get background information from another page text box.

Figure 3-4	SPECIFYING A COMMON BACKGROUND

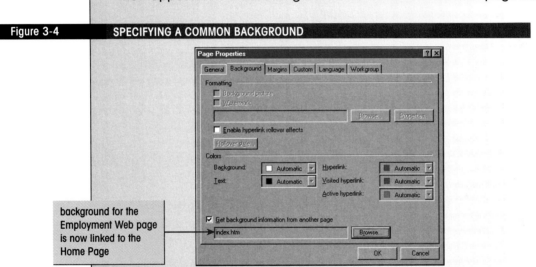

background for the Employment Web page is now linked to the Home Page

TROUBLE? If default.htm, rather than index.htm, appears in the file list, click default.htm.

4. Click the **OK** button. The Page Properties dialog box closes, and the Employment page redisplays with the same background that you applied to the Home Page, rather than the default background. See Figure 3-5.

Figure 3-5   **EMPLOYMENT WEB PAGE WITH THE NEW BACKGROUND**

5. Click the **Save** button 🖫 on the Standard toolbar to save the page. The background picture file is already stored in your Web site, so you don't have to save it as an embedded file.

Now that you have successfully updated the design of the Employment page by applying the new background, you are ready to add the information for the new positions in the Customer Support and MIS departments.

Inserting a File in a Web Page

You can enter new content for a Web page by typing all of the necessary text in the Web page in Page view. However, if this content already exists in another text-based file format or in an Office 2000 Word, Excel, or PowerPoint file, you can insert it directly into the page instead of retyping it. When you include content from another file in a Web page, FrontPage automatically converts the new content to HTML code. Being able to insert the contents of a file in a Web page makes it easy for members of a Web site development team to divide the tasks required to complete a Web page and to exchange information.

REFERENCE WINDOW   RW

Inserting a File in a Web Page
- Place the insertion point where you want the new content to appear.
- Click Insert on the menu bar, click File, change to the location that contains the desired file, click the Files of type list arrow, and then click All Files to display a list of available files.
- Double-click the desired file to insert its contents.

Pilar prepared the job description for the Customer Support position and saved it as a Word document, so you won't need to retype this information. She asks you to follow the design used for the Accounting and Advertising departments by placing the new job description below the Customer Support heading.

To include a Word file in a Web page:

1. Scroll down the Web page until you see the Customer Support heading that appears between two horizontal lines, and then click the blank line below the heading.

   TROUBLE? If the Customer Support heading does not have a horizontal line immediately above and below it, you are not in the job description area of the Web page. Repeat Step 1.

2. Click **Insert** on the menu bar, and then click **File**. The Select File dialog box opens.

3. If necessary, click the **Look in** list arrow, change to the drive or folder that contains your Data Disk, and then double-click the **Tutorial.03** folder to display its contents.

   By default, FrontPage displays only HTML files. You need to display Word files, however, to find Pilar's document.

4. Click the **Files of type** list arrow to display a list of available file types, and then click **Word 97-2000 (*.doc)** to display a list of Word files.

5. Double-click **Customer** to open the file and convert its content to HTML code. The Customer Support Representatives job title and its description appear in the Web page below the Customer Support heading. See Figure 3-6.

Figure 3-6	NEW CUSTOMER SUPPORT POSITION ADDED TO THE WEB PAGE

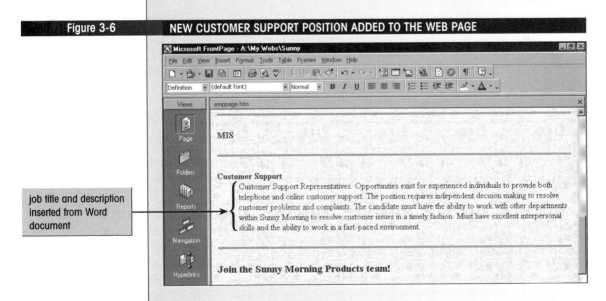

job title and description inserted from Word document

TROUBLE? If a Microsoft FrontPage dialog box opens and informs you that it can't import the specified format because it is not currently installed, insert your Microsoft Office 2000 CD into the correct drive, and then click the Yes button. If you do not have this CD, ask your instructor or technical support person for help.

Now that you have included the Customer Support position, Amanda asks you to add the MIS position in the page.

Creating Lists

A list is a convenient way to display a series of text items in a Web page. You can use FrontPage to create bulleted, numbered, and definition lists, as well as **nested lists**, which are lists within lists. You will use all of these list types to complete the Employment Web page.

Creating a Definition List

A **definition list** is a list that contains defined terms and their definitions. A **defined term** is the term that is being explained. Generally, you left-align a defined term with the page margin and indent its **definition**, or description, below it. For example, the list of jobs and their job descriptions in the Employment Web page is organized as a definition list. Notice in Figure 3-6 that the definition (the job description) is indented under the defined term (the Customer Support heading). When creating a definition list, you apply the Defined Term and the Definition styles to the items in the list. When you added the job description below the Customer Support heading, the text was formatted automatically using the Definition style because Amanda already applied that style to the line where you inserted the Word document.

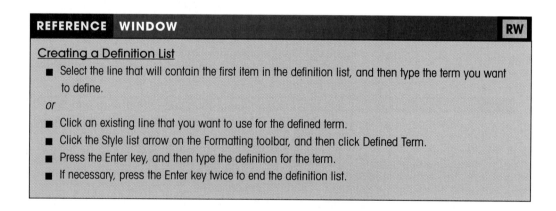

REFERENCE WINDOW   RW

Creating a Definition List
- Select the line that will contain the first item in the definition list, and then type the term you want to define.

or

- Click an existing line that you want to use for the defined term.
- Click the Style list arrow on the Formatting toolbar, and then click Defined Term.
- Press the Enter key, and then type the definition for the term.
- If necessary, press the Enter key twice to end the definition list.

When Amanda created the plan for the Employment Web page, she did not have the MIS position from Pilar. Amanda formatted the MIS heading as a normal paragraph. Amanda asks you to change the current line style to Defined Term and then to enter the MIS job title and description (the definition) to complete the definition list.

To add a defined term and definition to the list:

1. If necessary, scroll up the Employment Web page until you see the MIS heading that appears between two horizontal lines. Amanda already added horizontal lines above and below the MIS heading to set it off from the other positions.

2. Click immediately to the right of **MIS** to place the insertion point there. See Figure 3-7.

Figure 3-7	ADDING THE MIS JOB DESCRIPTION

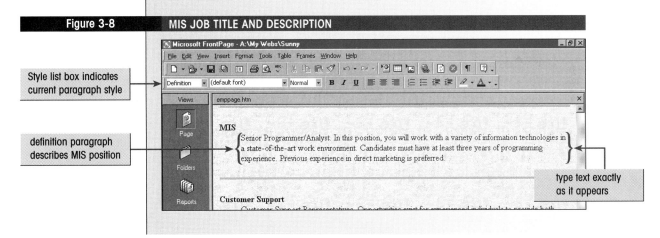

Style list arrow

defined term

insertion point

TROUBLE? If the MIS heading does not have a horizontal line immediately above and below it, you are not in the job description area of the Web page. Repeat Steps 1 and 2.

3. Click the **Style** list arrow on the Formatting toolbar to display the list of available formats, and then scroll down the list and click **Defined Term** as the desired paragraph format. Defined Term now appears in the Style list box, and the MIS heading changes to the Defined Term style.

4. Press the **Enter** key to create a new indented line below the MIS heading with the Definition style applied to it. When you press the Enter key on a line that has the Defined Term style applied to it, FrontPage automatically formats the next line with the Definition style.

5. Type the MIS job description exactly as it appears in Figure 3-8.

Figure 3-8	MIS JOB TITLE AND DESCRIPTION

Style list box indicates current paragraph style

definition paragraph describes MIS position

type text exactly as it appears

With the two new job titles and descriptions now added to the Employment Web page, Amanda asks you to create the table of contents using a bulleted list.

Creating a Bulleted List

A **bulleted list**, or an **unordered list**, is a list of items that are not sequentially organized. Each item in the list begins with a bullet character. You create a bulleted list either by clicking the Bullets button on the Formatting toolbar before typing the items in the list or by selecting existing text and then clicking the Bullets button.

REFERENCE WINDOW   **RW**

Creating a Bulleted List
- Select the line that will contain the first item in the bulleted list.
- Click the Bullets button on the Formatting toolbar.

or

- Click the Style list arrow, and then click Bulleted List.
- Type each item in the list, pressing the Enter key after each item.
- Press the Enter key twice to end the bulleted list.

Long Web pages usually include a table of contents at the top of the page that is formatted as a list. Amanda already entered the items that will form the table of contents for the page, as shown in Figure 3-9. The list contains the department names. Amanda asks you to format the list as a bulleted list.

To create a bulleted list:

1. Press **Ctrl + Home** to scroll to the top of the Web page, and then select the **Accounting**, **Advertising**, **MIS**, and **Customer Support** department names that form the table of contents. See Figure 3-9.

| Figure 3-9 | **CREATING THE TABLE OF CONTENTS** |

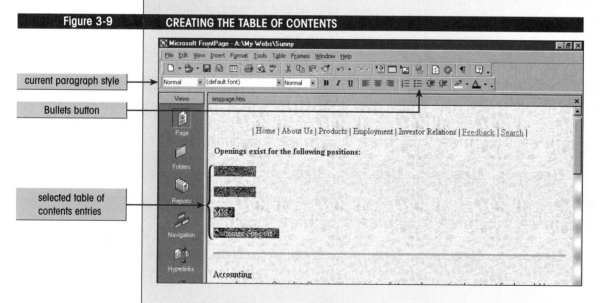

current paragraph style

Bullets button

selected table of contents entries

2. Click the **Bullets** button on the Formatting toolbar to format these lines as a bulleted list, and then click the first item in the list to deselect the bulleted list. See Figure 3-10.

| Figure 3-10 | TABLE OF CONTENTS FORMATTED AS A BULLETED LIST |

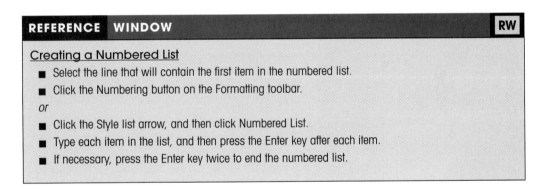

Next, Amanda asks you to format the two job openings in the Advertising department to be more prominent in the Web page.

Creating a Numbered, Nested List

A **numbered list**, or an **ordered list**, is a sequentially numbered or lettered list. A numbered list is the same as a bulleted list, except that each item begins with a number instead of a bullet. Amanda wants you to organize the Advertising department's job openings for a Production Manager and an Editorial Assistant as a numbered list. This will help to better differentiate between the two available positions in the Advertising department.

REFERENCE WINDOW   **RW**

Creating a Numbered List
- Select the line that will contain the first item in the numbered list.
- Click the Numbering button on the Formatting toolbar.

or
- Click the Style list arrow, and then click Numbered List.
- Type each item in the list, and then press the Enter key after each item.
- If necessary, press the Enter key twice to end the numbered list.

Amanda wants you to insert the numbered list as a nested list within the existing bulleted list of position openings.

REFERENCE WINDOW   **RW**

Creating a Nested List
- Within a numbered or bulleted list, insert another list item where you want the nested list to start.
- Click the Increase Indent button on the Formatting toolbar to nest the first item in the list.
- Click the Numbering button or the Bullets button on the Formatting toolbar to select the desired list type.
- Type each item in the list, pressing the Enter key after each item. Do not press the Enter key after typing the final item in the nested list.

To create a numbered, nested list:

1. Click to the right of the **Advertising** item in the bulleted list, and then press the **Enter** key to insert a new line with a bullet.

2. Click the **Increase Indent** button 🔲 on the Formatting toolbar to indent this paragraph and change its style to Normal. Notice that the top two bulleted items are now separated from the bottom two items by additional space.

3. Click the **Numbering** button 🔲 on the Formatting toolbar to insert the number 1. (You might need to click 🔲 again to see the number 1.)

   TROUBLE? If all of the items change to a numbered list, then you did not click the Increase Indent button before you clicked the Numbering button. Click the Bullets button, and then repeat Steps 2 and 3.

4. Type **Production Manager** as the first numbered list item, and then press the **Enter** key. FrontPage continues the nested list on the second line by inserting the number 2.

5. Type **Editorial Assistant** as the second numbered list item to complete the numbered list. See Figure 3-11.

Figure 3-11	TABLE OF CONTENTS WITH A NESTED, NUMBERED LIST

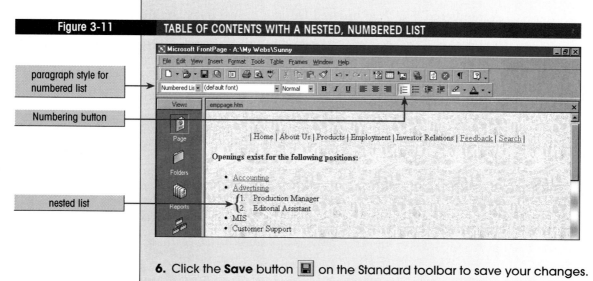

6. Click the **Save** button 🔲 on the Standard toolbar to save your changes.

You've formatted the table of contents as a bulleted list and organized the two advertising positions as a numbered, nested list. In the next session, you'll format the MIS and Customer Support items in the table of contents as hyperlinks so that users can link directly to the respective job descriptions.

Session 3.1 QUICK CHECK

1. True or False: The content of a Word document is converted to HTML when the file is inserted in a Web page.

2. True or False: You cannot import Web pages created by programs other than FrontPage into a FrontPage Web site.

3. A(n) _____ list is one that is not sequentially organized.

4. What is a nested list?

5. True or False: You press the Enter key twice to end a bulleted or numbered list.

6. To start a nested list, click the _____ button on the Formatting toolbar to create the first item in the list.

SESSION 3.2

In this session, you will create a bookmark, specify a hyperlink to a bookmark, and use different methods to create hyperlinks to other Web pages. You also will create a hyperlink that contains an e-mail address. Then you will convert a picture saved in JPEG format to GIF format, make a GIF picture transparent, and create a hotspot in a picture. Then you will test hyperlinks within a Web page, between Web pages, and to an e-mail hyperlink. Finally, you will view a Web site in Hyperlinks view and print it.

Creating Bookmarks and Hyperlinks to Bookmarks

A **bookmark** is a named location in a Web page that is the target of a hyperlink. A bookmark often consists of text as the location. For example, clicking a "Top of Page" hyperlink in a Web page automatically scrolls to the top of the Web page; in this case, the hyperlink is to a bookmark that was created at the top of the Web page. You can also create a bookmark to a location that is not based on text. You can place bookmarks anywhere in a Web page to make it easier for users to navigate. For example, the table of contents at the top of the Employment Web page is organized so that users can scroll to each department's job listings by clicking the relevant department name in the list.

Bookmarks viewed in Page view appear as dashed, underlined text. When you view a page with bookmarks using your browser, no underlining or other identification of the bookmark appears. When a bookmark is not based on text, the bookmark appears as an icon when viewed in Page view.

Each bookmark within a Web page must have a unique name. You can use the suggested name of the bookmark—which is taken from the text that you selected when you created it—or you can assign a new bookmark name. The bookmark's name serves to identify the bookmark's location in the Web page.

Creating a Text-Based Bookmark

Amanda designed the Employment Web page so that each department listed in the table of contents is associated with a bookmark in the Web page. She already created two text-based bookmarks—one each for the Accounting and Advertising departments.

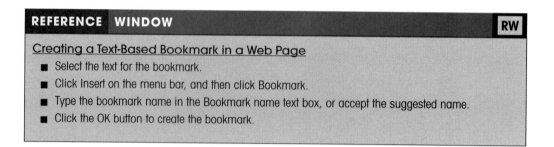

Creating a Text-Based Bookmark in a Web Page

■ Select the text for the bookmark.
■ Click Insert on the menu bar, and then click Bookmark.
■ Type the bookmark name in the Bookmark name text box, or accept the suggested name.
■ Click the OK button to create the bookmark.

Next you will create bookmarks for the MIS and Customer Support departments.

To create a text-based bookmark:

1. If you took a break after the last session, make sure that **FrontPage** is running, that your Data Disk is in the correct drive, and that the **Sunny** Web site (a:\My Webs\Sunny) is open. Change to Folders view, and then open the Employment Web page (**emppage.htm**) in Page view.

2. Scroll down the Employment Web page so you can see the MIS heading that appears between two horizontal lines.

3. Select the **MIS** heading, which will become the location of the new bookmark.

4. Click **Insert** on the menu bar, and then click **Bookmark** to open the Bookmark dialog box. See Figure 3-12.

| Figure 3-12 | BOOKMARK DIALOG BOX |

text for bookmark
selected in Web page

existing bookmarks
in the page

bookmark name taken
from selected text

Notice that "MIS" appears in the Bookmark name text box as the suggested name for this bookmark. This name was taken from the selected text—MIS—in the Employment Web page. Also notice that the Other bookmarks on this page list box shows the two bookmarks that Amanda already created. You can use MIS as the new bookmark's name.

5. Click the **OK** button to accept the suggested name for the bookmark, and then click the **MIS** heading in the Web page to deselect it. MIS now appears with a dashed underline, which indicates that it is a bookmark.

Next, you will create the bookmark for the Customer Support heading. You can use the word "Customer" as the bookmark, instead of using the entire heading.

6. Scroll down the Web page as necessary until you see the Customer Support heading, select **Customer** in the heading, and then repeat Steps 4 and 5 to create the bookmark for this location. See Figure 3-13.

Figure 3-13   **EMPLOYMENT WEB PAGE WITH NEW BOOKMARKS**

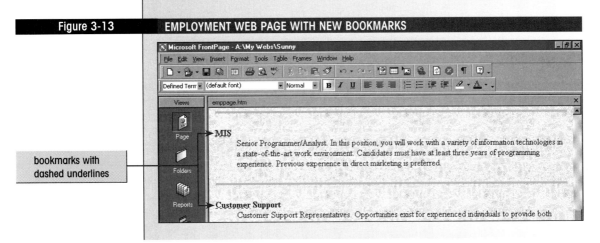

bookmarks with dashed underlines

Amanda explains that the next step is to link the bookmarks to their associated text by creating hyperlinks.

Creating a Hyperlink to a Bookmark

Amanda asks you to create hyperlinks from the MIS and Customer Support entries in the table of contents to their corresponding bookmarks. When a user clicks a hyperlink to a bookmark, the Web page scrolls to the bookmark's location in the Web page. Figure 3-14 illustrates how the bookmarks you created work.

Figure 3-14   **EMPLOYMENT WEB PAGE WITH BOOKMARKS**

REFERENCE WINDOW   **RW**

Creating a Hyperlink to a Bookmark

- Select the text for the hyperlink.
- Click the Hyperlink button on the Standard toolbar.
- Click the Bookmark list arrow in the Optional section to display the list of available bookmarks.
- Click the desired bookmark to select it, and then click the OK button.

Next you will create the hyperlinks from the MIS and Customer Support entries in the table of contents at the top of the page to the appropriate bookmarks in the body of the Web page.

To create the hyperlinks to the bookmarks:

1. Press **Ctrl + Home** to scroll to the top of the Web page.

   You begin by creating a hyperlink to the MIS bookmark.

2. Select **MIS** in the table of contents (the bulleted list) as the text of the hyperlink.

3. Click the **Hyperlink** button 🖻 on the Standard toolbar to open the Create Hyperlink dialog box.

4. In the Optional section, click the **Bookmark** list arrow to display a list of bookmarks in the Employment Web page. See Figure 3-15.

Figure 3-15	LIST OF AVAILABLE BOOKMARKS IN THE EMPLOYMENT WEB PAGE

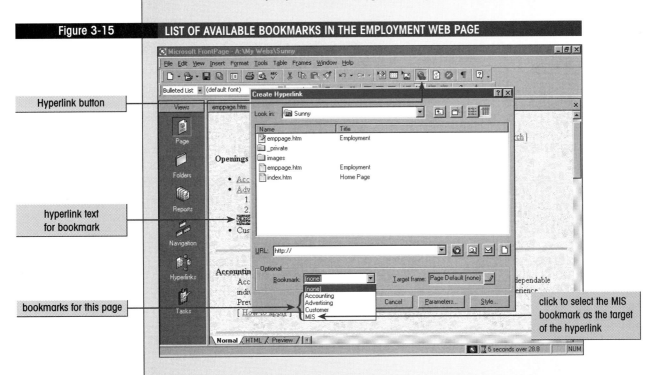

Hyperlink button

hyperlink text
for bookmark

bookmarks for this page

click to select the MIS
bookmark as the target
of the hyperlink

5. Click **MIS** in the Bookmark list box to select it. Notice that the URL text box changes to display the text #MIS, which identifies the location of the bookmark in the Web page. The pound sign (#) in the hyperlink indicates that its location is in the same Web page. This type of hyperlink is called an **internal hyperlink**.

6. Click the **OK** button to return to the Web page, and then click **MIS** to deselect it. MIS now appears as blue text with a solid underline, indicating that it is a hyperlink.

7. Select **Customer Support** in the table of contents as the next hyperlink, and then repeat Steps 3 through 6 using the **Customer** bookmark.

8. Point to the **Customer Support** hyperlink. Notice that the name of the hyperlink—#Customer—appears on the status bar and confirms the existence of the internal hyperlink to the bookmark that you created. See Figure 3-16.

| Figure 3-16 | COMPLETED TABLE OF CONTENTS WITH HYPERLINKS |

pointer over hyperlink

bookmark location appears on the status bar

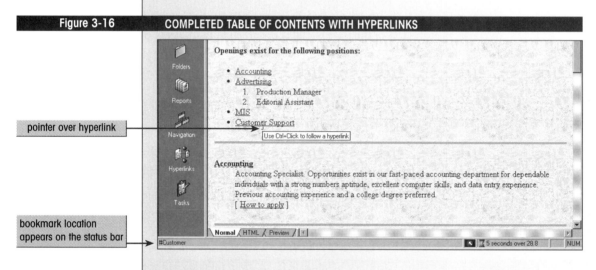

9. Click the **Save** button 🖫 on the Standard toolbar to save your changes.

Before continuing, you need to verify that the hyperlinks to the bookmarks work correctly. You will test the hyperlinks using the Preview tab.

To test an internal hyperlink using the Preview tab:

1. Click the **Preview** tab.

2. Point to the **MIS** hyperlink in the table of contents. The pointer changes to a 🖑 shape.

3. Click the **MIS** hyperlink. The Web page scrolls so that the bookmark location is at the top of the window. See Figure 3-17. Notice that the bookmarks do not have a dashed underline as they do when you view them in Normal Page view.

Figure 3-17	PREVIEW OF THE EMPLOYMENT WEB PAGE

bookmarks appear without dashed underlining

Your test was successful so you can return to Normal Page view.

4. Click the **Normal** tab to return to Normal Page view.

You have now completed the internal hyperlinks from the entries in the table of contents to their respective departments in the Employment Web page. Amanda now explains that job applicants need to be able to contact Sunny Morning Products. Regardless of the position in which applicants are interested, they need to access the same contact information to apply for the position. You can identify the location of the contact information with a single bookmark; in this case, you will create a bookmark that is not based on text. Then you will create the hyperlinks to that bookmark that will let applicants contact Sunny Morning Products.

Creating Nontext-Based Bookmarks

The bookmarks that you have created so far used text in the Web page to identify their location. You can also create a bookmark that is based not on text but on a specific spot in the page. In this case, an icon appears in Page view to show the bookmark's location. When you view the Web page in a browser, however, the icon is not visible.

Next, you will insert a nontext-based bookmark to the Sunny Morning Products contact information.

To create a nontext-based bookmark:

1. Scroll down the Web page until you see the phrase, "Join the Sunny Morning Products team!" This is the beginning line for the contact information.

2. Click to the left of the **J** in **Join** (but do *not* select the word "Join") to place the insertion point at the location of the new bookmark.

TROUBLE? If you selected the J in Join or the entire word "Join," repeat Step 2.

3. Click **Insert** on the menu bar, and then click **Bookmark** to open the Bookmark dialog box. Because you did not select any text, FrontPage does not suggest a name for the bookmark in the Bookmark name text box. When you create bookmark names, it is a good idea to select ones that are descriptive of the location in which the bookmark appears, so it is easy to recognize a bookmark in the page.

4. Type **To Apply** in the Bookmark name text box as the name for this new book-mark, click the **OK** button, and then press the **End** key to deselect the icon. A bookmark icon appears to the left of the word "Join." See Figure 3-18.

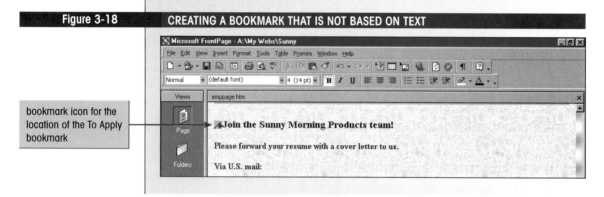

Figure 3-18   **CREATING A BOOKMARK THAT IS NOT BASED ON TEXT**

bookmark icon for the location of the To Apply bookmark

Next, you will create the hyperlinks from the job descriptions to this new bookmark, following the same process you used when creating hyperlinks earlier in this session.

Creating Multiple Hyperlinks to a Bookmark

A bookmark can have many hyperlinks to it from different locations within a Web page. For example, regardless of the position in which applicants are interested, they need to access the same contact information. You can create a single bookmark in the Web page and then set a hyperlink from each job description to that bookmark. When multiple hyperlinks reference a single bookmark, the bookmark has **multiple hyperlinks**, or **multiple references**, to it.

Amanda designed the Employment Web page to include a hyperlink from each job description to the nontext-based bookmark that is the contact information for Sunny Morning Products. She already created the hyperlinks from the Accounting and Advertising departments to the "To Apply" bookmark. You will create the hyperlinks from the other two departments—MIS and Customer Support—to the same "To Apply" bookmark.

To create multiple hyperlinks to the same bookmark:

1. Scroll up the Web page until you see the MIS heading.

2. Click to the right of the last line in the job description to place the insertion point there.

3. Press **Shift + Enter** to create a new line within the same paragraph.

Next, add the text for the new hyperlink.

4. Type **[How to apply]** (including the spaces after the opening bracket and before the closing bracket), and then select the text **How to apply** as the hyperlink text.

5. Click the **Hyperlink** button 🖼 on the Standard toolbar to open the Create Hyperlink dialog box, and then click the **Bookmark** list arrow to display the list of available bookmarks. See Figure 3-19.

Figure 3-19   **LIST OF AVAILABLE BOOKMARKS**

select this bookmark

6. Click **To Apply** in the Bookmark list box to select it, click the **OK** button to return to the Web page, and then click **How to apply** to deselect the text. The text is now blue and underlined, which indicates that you created a hyperlink.

7. If necessary, scroll down the Web page until you see the Customer Support heading, and then repeat Steps 2 through 6 to create a second How to apply hyperlink below the Customer Support Representatives job description to the To Apply bookmark.

8. Click the **Save** button 🖫 on the Standard toolbar to save the page.

You now have created several hyperlinks to the bookmarks in the Employment Web page. Next, Amanda wants you to create hyperlinks to other Web pages. When you are finished, you will test all of these hyperlinks in the browser to make sure that they are working correctly.

Linking **to Other Web Pages**

Web Pages & HTML

You can create hyperlinks that open other Web pages, not just other locations in the same Web page. These hyperlinks can connect to another page within the same Web site or to a page at a different Web site. You create a hyperlink to another Web page by selecting the location in the page where you want the link to appear and then specifying the target Web page. The **target** of a hyperlink is the page that opens when a user clicks the hyperlink. Usually, hyperlinks that open other Web pages within the same Web site appear in the navigation bar.

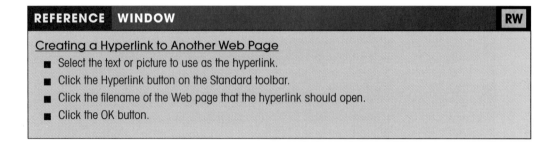

Creating a Hyperlink to Another Web Page
■ Select the text or picture to use as the hyperlink.
■ Click the Hyperlink button on the Standard toolbar.
■ Click the filename of the Web page that the hyperlink should open.
■ Click the OK button.

Amanda wants you to create a hyperlink from the Employment Web page to the Home Page and one from the Home Page to the Employment Web page. These hyperlinks will allow easy navigation between these Web pages. She already included the various Web page names in the navigation bar of the Employment Web page, but she did not create the hyperlinks to the pages.

To create a hyperlink to another Web page:

1. Press **Ctrl + Home** to scroll to the top of the Employment Web page.

2. Double-click the word **Home** in the navigation bar to select it. This text will become a hyperlink that opens the Home Page when clicked.

3. Click the **Hyperlink** button 🖼 on the Standard toolbar to open the Create Hyperlink dialog box. (You used the same dialog box to create the bookmarks.) See Figure 3-20. Notice that the file for the Employment Web page (emppage.htm) is listed twice—once at the top of the list, preceded by the 📝 icon, and again at the bottom of the list, preceded by the 📄 icon. The first emppage.htm icon indicates that this page is *open* in Page view; the second icon indicates that the file is *available* in your Web site. The file for the Home Page (index.htm) is not open, so it is listed only once, as an available page.

Figure 3-20   CREATE HYPERLINK DIALOG BOX

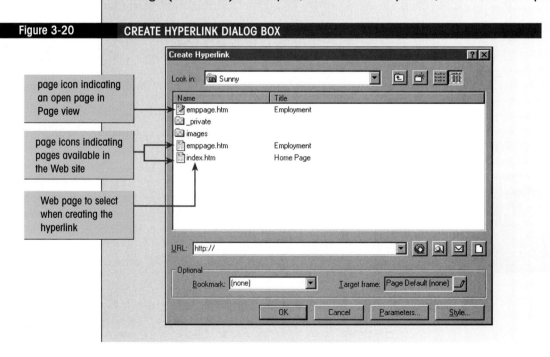

page icon indicating an open page in Page view

page icons indicating pages available in the Web site

Web page to select when creating the hyperlink

4. Double-click **index.htm** to select it as the target Web page for the hyperlink and to close the Create Hyperlink dialog box and return to the Web page.

TROUBLE? If your Web site contains the file default.htm rather than index.htm, click default.htm to select the Home Page.

5. Click **Home** in the navigation bar to deselect the new hyperlink. "Home" is now formatted as underlined, blue text. See Figure 3-21.

Figure 3-21	CREATING A HYPERLINK IN THE NAVIGATION BAR IN PAGE VIEW

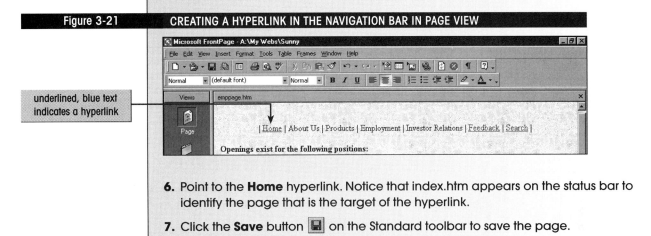

underlined, blue text indicates a hyperlink

6. Point to the **Home** hyperlink. Notice that index.htm appears on the status bar to identify the page that is the target of the hyperlink.

7. Click the **Save** button 🖫 on the Standard toolbar to save the page.

Now that you have successfully established the hyperlink from the Employment Web page to the Home Page, you must create the hyperlink from the Home Page to the Employment Web page. You could use the same method to create the return hyperlink, but Amanda wants to show you another method.

Creating a Hyperlink Using Drag and Drop

Another method to create a hyperlink between pages in a Web site is **drag and drop**. By default, the title of the linked page (the **target page**) becomes the text for the hyperlink in the Web page that contains the hyperlink (the **source page**). Therefore, you might want to consider a title for a Web page that can later be used as the text for its hyperlink.

To use drag and drop, you open the source page in Page view and then switch to Folders view. In Folders view, you select the filename of the target page and drag the pointer on top of the Page view button on the Views bar. After a pause, the source page will open in Page view. Then you place the pointer at the location where you want to insert the hyperlink and release the mouse button, which creates the hyperlink. The name of the hyperlink is the target page's title. You can use a different name for the hyperlink by editing it after placing the hyperlink in the Web page.

Next, Amanda wants you to use drag and drop to create the hyperlink from the Home Page to the Employment page. After you create this second hyperlink, you will test both hyperlinks in the browser.

To create a hyperlink using drag and drop:

1. In the Employment Web page, point to the **Home** hyperlink in the navigation bar, press and hold down the **Ctrl** key, and then click the **Home** hyperlink. The Home Page opens in Page view.

2. Click the **Folders** button [🗂] on the Views bar to change to Folders view.

3. Click **emppage.htm** (the target page) in the Contents pane to select it, and then hold down the left mouse button as you drag the pointer from the Contents pane to the Page view button [🗂] on the Views bar. The pointer changes to a ⊘ shape while you are moving the file—do *not* release the mouse button yet. The Home Page opens in Page view.

4. While still holding down the mouse button, move the pointer to the left of **Employment** in the navigation bar in the Home Page. The pointer changes to a ▨ shape. See Figure 3-22.

Figure 3-22	CREATING THE HYPERLINK TO THE EMPLOYMENT WEB PAGE

5. Release the mouse button to create the hyperlink, and then click **Employment** to deselect it. An Employment hyperlink is inserted in the navigation bar in the Home Page using the page title from the Employment Web page. See Figure 3-23. Notice that the text in the navigation bar is now "<u>Employment</u>Employment" because the page title was inserted in front of the text that already existed in the navigation bar.

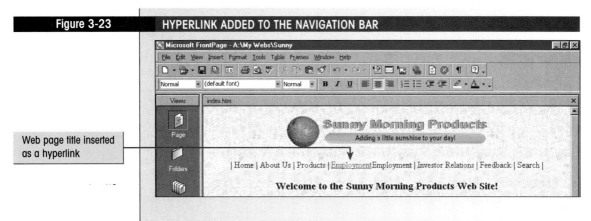

Figure 3-23 HYPERLINK ADDED TO THE NAVIGATION BAR

Web page title inserted as a hyperlink

Next, remove the extra text to create the desired entry in the navigation bar.

6. Select **Employment**, the word that is not underlined in the navigation bar, and then press the **Delete** key to remove it. The correct (underlined) Employment hyperlink remains in the navigation bar.

7. Click the **Save** button on the Standard toolbar to save the page.

Now, test the hyperlinks between the Home Page and the Employment Web page in Internet Explorer.

To test hyperlinks between Web pages using Internet Explorer:

1. Click the **Preview in Browser** button on the Standard toolbar to open the Home Page in Internet Explorer. Notice that the Employment entry in the navigation bar is underlined, which indicates that it is a hyperlink.

2. Point to the **Employment** hyperlink. Notice that "file:///A:/My Webs/Sunny/emppage.htm" appears in the status bar to confirm that this hyperlink connects to a different Web page.

   TROUBLE? If your files are stored in a different location or on a different drive, then your path will be different.

3. Click the **Employment** hyperlink in the navigation bar. The Employment Web page opens.

4. Click the **Home** hyperlink in the navigation bar of the Employment Web page to reopen the Home Page.

5. Click the **Close** button on the Internet Explorer title bar to close it, and then, if necessary, click the **Microsoft FrontPage** program button on the taskbar to return to FrontPage.

You have successfully completed the hyperlink test. You will create the remaining hyperlinks and their Web pages as you complete the tutorials in this book. Next, you need to establish a way for applicants to send an e-mail message to the human resources manager if they are interested in applying for a position listed in the Employment Web page.

Creating a Hyperlink to an E-mail Address

A **mailto** is a special hyperlink that contains an e-mail address. When a user clicks a mailto in a Web page, the mailto automatically starts the browser's default e-mail program and addresses a message to the address contained in the mailto. The user then can type the message and send it as usual.

When you add an e-mail address in a Web page in Page view, FrontPage automatically recognizes it as a mailto, creates the hyperlink, and changes the appearance of the address to that of a hyperlink.

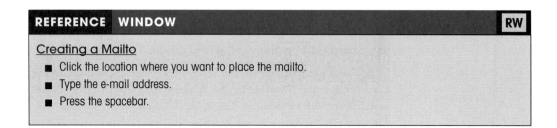

REFERENCE WINDOW   **RW**

<u>Creating a Mailto</u>
- Click the location where you want to place the mailto.
- Type the e-mail address.
- Press the spacebar.

Amanda wants to include Pilar's e-mail address in the Employment Web page so that potential applicants can send their resumes to her via e-mail.

To create a mailto:

1. Click **Window** on the menu bar, and then click **emppage.htm** to open the Employment Web page.

2. Press **Ctrl + End** to scroll to the bottom of the Employment Web page.

3. Click at the end of the **Via e-mail** heading to place the insertion point there.

4. Press the **Enter** key to insert a new line for the mailto, and then click the **Increase Indent** button 🔳 on the Formatting toolbar to indent the line by one tab stop. Notice that the Bold button 🅱 on the Formatting toolbar is indented, indicating that bold formatting is currently activated because it is carried over from the previous paragraph.

5. Type **pilar.caballero@admin.sunnymorning.com** and then press the **spacebar**. When you press the spacebar, FrontPage automatically recognizes the e-mail address as a mailto, creates a hyperlink for it, and changes it to underlined, blue text to indicate that it is a hyperlink. The red, wavy line under part of the mailto indicates a word that is not in the FrontPage dictionary.

6. Point to the **pilar.caballero@admin.sunnymorning.com** mailto. The description of the mailto appears on the status bar. See Figure 3-24.

Figure 3-24   **MAILTO IN THE EMPLOYMENT WEB PAGE**

mailto and its
e-mail address

mailto hyperlink

7. Click the **Save** button 🖫 on the Standard toolbar to save the page.

Pilar's e-mail address is now included in the Employment Web page. Next, you need to test this feature, so you will open the page in the browser.

To test a mailto using Internet Explorer:

1. Click the **Preview in Browser** button 🔍 on the Standard toolbar to open the Employment Web page in Internet Explorer, and then press **Ctrl + End** to scroll to the bottom of the page.

2. Click anywhere on the **pilar.caballero@admin.sunnymorning.com** mailto to start your default e-mail program and to open a new message. Figure 3-25 shows the New Message window for Microsoft Outlook Express (the default mail program for Internet Explorer 5).

Figure 3-25   **MICROSOFT OUTLOOK EXPRESS NEW MESSAGE WINDOW**

e-mail address
from mailto

TROUBLE? If a Microsoft FrontPage dialog box opens and asks if you want to specify a default e-mail program, click the No button.

TROUBLE? If your computer uses an e-mail program other than Microsoft Outlook Express, then your e-mail window will look different.

TROUBLE? If an Internet Connection Wizard dialog box opens, click the Cancel button, and then click the Yes button to close the dialog box.

TROUBLE? If a Microsoft Outlook dialog box opens and indicates that no e-mail client is specified for your computer, click the OK button to continue.

Because the Outlook Express mail program started when you clicked the mailto in the Web page, your test is complete. An applicant who wants to send a message to Pilar regarding any of the job positions would type a subject and a message and include an attachment, if necessary. Because you are just testing the mailto to see if it links to your Internet e-mail program, rather than actually sending a message to Pilar, you can exit the e-mail program now.

3. Click the **Close** button ☒ on the New Message window to return to the Employment Web page.

4. Click ☒ on the Internet Explorer title bar to close it.

Your successful test of the Employment Web page confirms that an applicant can examine the job descriptions and send a message to Pilar.

According to Amanda's plan for the Sunny Web site, each page should include the Sunny Morning Products logo at the top of the page. The logo for each page is slightly different, and the logos are stored in different file formats. The graphics designer who created the logos saved the one for the Employment Web page as a JPEG file. Amanda wants you to use a GIF file instead. She asks you to use FrontPage to convert the logo to another format, instead of asking the graphics designer to do the conversion.

Converting a Picture to a Different Format

In Tutorial 2, you learned about three popular file formats for pictures that are used in Web pages: GIF, JPEG, and PNG. FrontPage lets you convert a picture saved in one format to another without using a graphics program.

If you are working in a graphics program, such as Adobe Illustrator or Microsoft Image Composer, you can usually edit the characteristics of any picture file, such as changing the background color or adding special effects to the picture's edges. However, in FrontPage, you must convert a non-GIF picture to the GIF format in order to change these types of effects. For example, if you try to change the background of a JPEG or PNG file, FrontPage will open a dialog box and display a message that you *must* convert the picture to GIF format before you can change it.

The logo for the Employment Web page is saved as a JPEG file. Amanda wants you to convert the logo to GIF format to ensure that the file's size and download time are small. She also wants you to change the picture's appearance. For these reasons, you will need to convert the JPEG picture to GIF format. Before you can convert the file's format, you must insert it in the Employment Web page.

To insert a picture in a Web page:

1. Press **Ctrl + Home** to move the insertion point to the top of the Employment Web page. This is the location where you will insert the logo.

2. Click the **Insert Picture From File** button 🖼 on the Standard toolbar to open the Picture dialog box, and then click the **Select a file on your computer** button 🔍 to open the Select File dialog box.

3. Make sure the drive or folder that contains your Data Disk appears in the Look in text box, double-click the **Tutorial.03** folder, and then double-click **Employ**. The JPEG picture is inserted at the top of the page. Notice the subtitle for the picture is Employment Opportunities, which identifies the content of this Web page.

Next you will convert the logo from the JPEG format to the space-saving GIF format, which will decrease the picture's file size and prepare it for editing. Then you will save the picture file in the Sunny Web site.

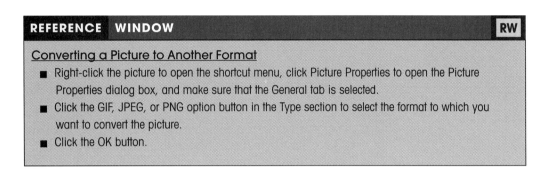

REFERENCE   WINDOW   **RW**

Converting a Picture to Another Format
- Right-click the picture to open the shortcut menu, click Picture Properties to open the Picture Properties dialog box, and make sure that the General tab is selected.
- Click the GIF, JPEG, or PNG option button in the Type section to select the format to which you want to convert the picture.
- Click the OK button.

To convert a picture from JPEG to GIF format and then save it:

1. Click the logo to select it. Notice that eight small squares appear as selection handles at the edges of the picture to indicate that it is selected, and the Pictures toolbar appears. See Figure 3-26.

| Figure 3-26 | JPEG PICTURE INSERTED IN THE EMPLOYMENT WEB PAGE |

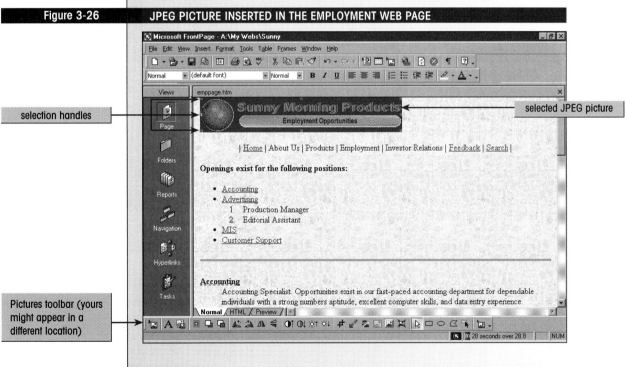

2. Right-click the logo to open the shortcut menu, click **Picture Properties** to open that dialog box, and then make sure that the General tab is selected.

3. In the Type section, click the **GIF** option button to select it.

When you convert a picture to GIF format, you can click the Interlaced check box to cause the picture to be displayed with increasing detail as it is being downloaded from the server. You also can make the background of a picture transparent, so that the background of the Web page will show through the picture, by checking the Transparent check box (when this option is enabled). The PNG and JPEG formats do not support transparency or interlacing, so these options are not enabled for these formats. For a JPEG picture, you can set the desired quality of it as a number from 1 to 100, with 100 being the best. You also can set the number of progressive passes, as a number from 0 to 100, with 100 being the most passes, that the browser should make to display the picture before it is completely downloaded from the server. For more information about editing pictures and setting their characteristics, consult FrontPage Help.

You will accept the default GIF settings. The Picture Properties dialog box is already open, so Amanda asks you to add the alternative text for the logo before closing the dialog box.

4. In the Alternative representations section, type **Employment Opportunities Logo** in the Text text box, and then click the **OK** button to return to the Employment Web page.

5. Click the **Save** button 🖫 on the Standard toolbar. The Save Embedded Files dialog box opens with the Employ.gif file in the Embedded files to save list box. The GIF file extension confirms that you converted the picture to GIF format.

6. Make sure that the picture will be saved in the Web site's images folder, and then click the **OK** button to save the Employ.gif file and the Employment Web page.

TROUBLE? If images/ is not selected as the destination folder in which to save the Employ.gif file, click the Change Folder button, click the images folder to select it as the destination for the file, and then click the OK button to return to the Save Embedded Files dialog box.

Notice that the background of the logo is blue. This logo's color doesn't match the one in the Home Page, so Amanda asks you to change the blue background to transparent.

Changing a Color in a Picture to Transparent

One way to enhance the appearance of a picture in a Web page is to change one of the picture's colors to transparent. A color that is set to transparent will not show in the picture, thereby allowing the page's background to show through.

REFERENCE WINDOW   **RW**

Changing a Color in a Picture to Transparent
- Click the picture to select it.
- Click the Set Transparent Color button on the Pictures toolbar.
- Click the color in the picture that you want to make transparent.

Amanda asks you to change the blue background of the logo to transparent so that it will be consistent with the logo in the Home Page.

To change a color in a picture to transparent:

1. Click the logo to select it. Selection handles appear at the edge of the picture to indicate that it is selected and the Pictures toolbar appears.

2. Click the **Set Transparent Color** button 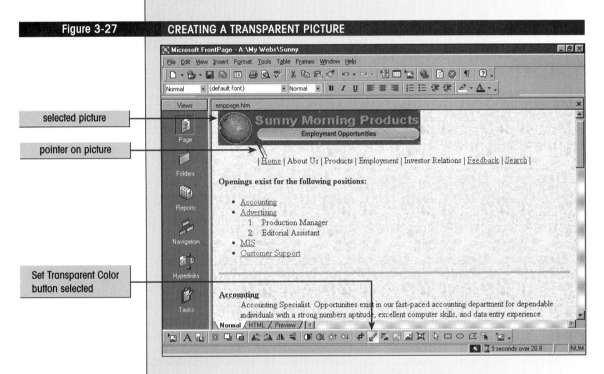 on the Pictures toolbar.

3. Point to the logo. The pointer changes to a ✎ shape. See Figure 3-27.

Figure 3-27	CREATING A TRANSPARENT PICTURE

4. Make sure that the small arrow of the pointer points to the blue color that you want to make transparent, and then click the blue color. The blue background of the picture becomes transparent, thereby allowing the background of the Web page to show through.

   TROUBLE? If you change the wrong color to be transparent, click the Undo button ↶ on the Standard toolbar, and then repeat Steps 1 through 4.

5. Click the **Save** button 🖫 on the Standard toolbar. The Save Embedded Files dialog box opens so you can overwrite the current version of this picture with the new version.

6. Make sure that the Employ.gif file will be saved in the Web site's images folder, and then click the **OK** button to save the GIF file with the transparent background.

7. Click anywhere outside of the picture to deselect it.

The Employment Opportunities logo in the Web page looks more attractive with its new transparent background. Next, Amanda wants you to create a special hyperlink using the orange that appears in the logo.

Creating Picture Hotspots

Pictures not only add visual interest to your Web pages; they also can serve a functional purpose. For example, you can use a picture to link to a bookmark or to another Web page by creating one or more hotspots on it. A **hotspot** is an area of a picture that, when clicked, activates a hyperlink. The shape of a hotspot may be rectangular, circular, or polygonal.

REFERENCE WINDOW   **RW**

Creating a Picture Hotspot
- Click the picture in which to create a hotspot to select it.
- Click the button for the desired hotspot shape on the Pictures toolbar.
- Click and hold down the mouse button while you drag the pointer to specify the desired size of the hotspot, and then release the mouse button. The Create Hyperlink dialog box opens.
- Specify the hyperlink in the Create Hyperlink dialog box.
- Click the OK button.

Amanda wants the orange in the Employment Opportunities logo to be a hotspot with a hyperlink to the Home Page. You will create this hotspot as a circle.

To create a hotspot:

1. Click the logo to select it and to display the Pictures toolbar.

2. Click the **Circular Hotspot** button ⬭ on the Pictures toolbar, and then place the pointer in the middle of the orange in the logo. The pointer changes to a ✏ shape when it is pointing to the picture. See Figure 3-28.

Figure 3-28	CREATING A PICTURE HOTSPOT

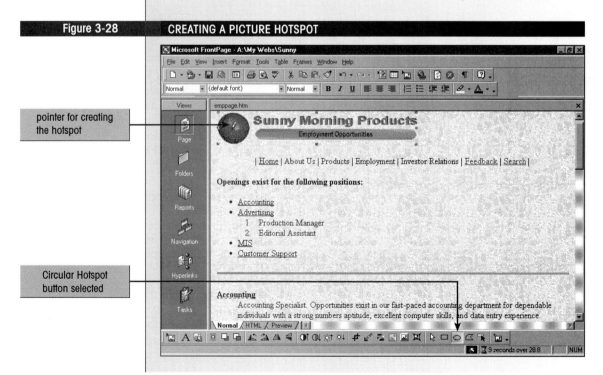

pointer for creating the hotspot

Circular Hotspot button selected

3. Hold down the mouse button and drag the pointer in any direction until you reach the edge of the orange. Notice that as you drag the pointer, a circle appears to specify the size and location of the hotspot.

4. Release the mouse button. The Create Hyperlink dialog box opens. See Figure 3-29.

Figure 3-29   CREATING THE HYPERLINK FOR THE HOTSPOT

5. Double-click the second **index.htm** file in the list to select the Home Page as the target page and to close the Create Hyperlink dialog box. Notice that the circle in the picture indicates the hotspot.

   TROUBLE? If your hotspot appears somewhere other than on top of the orange, press the Delete key to remove it, and then repeat Steps 1 through 5.

6. Click the **Save** button 🖫 on the Standard toolbar to save the page.

You successfully created the hotspot and specified its hyperlink to the Home Page. Now, users of the Sunny Web site can click either the orange in the logo or Home in the navigation bar to link to the Home Page.

Highlighting Hotspots

When you create a hotspot, you can see its shape. However, depending on the picture, it might be difficult to see its hotspots. By highlighting hotspots, you can see their location more clearly and confirm their placement.

Highlighting Hotspots on a Picture
- Click the picture that contains the hotspot(s).
- Click the Highlight Hotspots button on the Pictures toolbar.
- Click anywhere in the page, except in the picture, to turn off the hotspot highlights.

Next, you will check the location of the hotspot on the logo and verify its placement.

To highlight hotspots:

1. Make sure that the picture is still selected, and then click the **Highlight Hotspots** button ⬛ on the Pictures toolbar. The hotspot in the logo is displayed as a black circle in a white picture. See Figure 3-30.

| Figure 3-30 | HIGHLIGHTING A HOTSPOT IN A PICTURE |

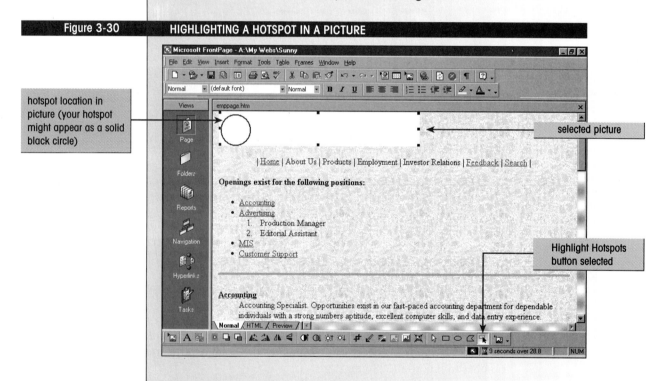

hotspot location in picture (your hotspot might appear as a solid black circle)

selected picture

Highlight Hotspots button selected

2. Click anywhere outside of the logo to turn off the hotspot highlights.

3. Point to the orange, which is the hotspot. Notice that the filename for this hyperlink—index.htm—appears in the status bar to confirm that it is a hyperlink.

Next, test the hotspot in the browser to make sure that it works correctly.

To test a hotspot using Internet Explorer:

1. Click the **Preview in Browser** button 🔍 on the Standard toolbar to open the Employment Web page in Internet Explorer. The Employment Opportunities logo appears with its transparent background.

2. Point to the orange in the logo. The pointer changes to a 👆 shape and the file-name for the hyperlink appears in the status bar, both of which indicate that the orange is a hyperlink. See Figure 3-31. Notice that the alternative text that you added to the logo displays as a ScreenTip and then disappears.

| Figure 3-31 | TESTING THE HOTSPOT IN INTERNET EXPLORER |

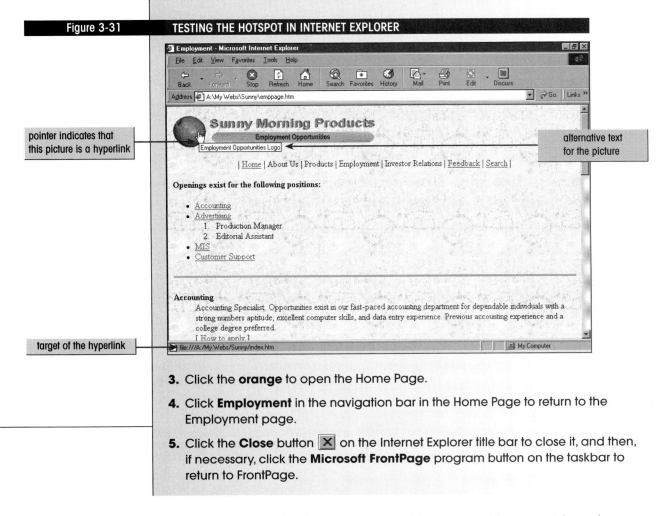

pointer indicates that this picture is a hyperlink

alternative text for the picture

target of the hyperlink

3. Click the **orange** to open the Home Page.

4. Click **Employment** in the navigation bar in the Home Page to return to the Employment page.

5. Click the **Close** button ⊠ on the Internet Explorer title bar to close it, and then, if necessary, click the **Microsoft FrontPage** program button on the taskbar to return to FrontPage.

The hotspot in the Employment Opportunities logo provides users with another way to link to the Home Page. You have made many changes to the Sunny Web site. Amanda wants you to check Hyperlinks view to ensure that there are no missing or broken hyperlinks.

Viewing **Hyperlinks**

As you develop a Web site, you can get an overview of it by using Hyperlinks view to examine the hyperlinks that connect the site's pages. It is a good idea to check Hyperlinks view periodically to make sure that your links are set up the way you want them. It is easier to check your site's hyperlinks after you add some hyperlinks to its pages, so you can check smaller parts of the Web site as you go, instead of waiting until the Web site is completed. A completed Web site might contain hundreds of hyperlinks, so checking them as you go ensures that they are set up as desired.

To view hyperlinks between Web pages:

1. Click the **Hyperlinks** button ▣ on the Views bar. The Employment Web page is displayed as the center focus of Hyperlinks view with hyperlinks to and from the Home Page and to the mailto address.

2. If necessary, use the horizontal scroll bar to scroll the hyperlinks diagram in the Contents pane to the right so that the diagram is centered in the window. See Figure 3-32.

Figure 3-32	HYPERLINKS VIEW FOR THE EMPLOYMENT WEB PAGE

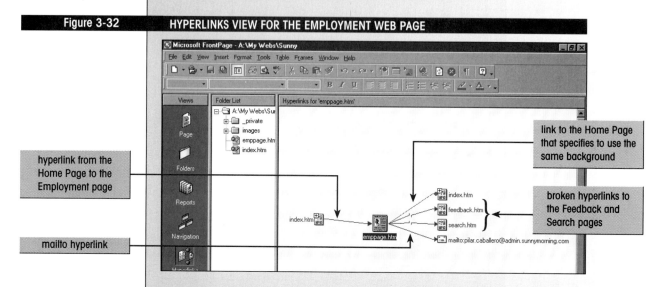

TROUBLE? If you see repeated hyperlinks or hyperlinks to pictures, right-click an empty area of the Contents pane to open the shortcut menu, and then click either the Repeated Links or the Hyperlinks to Picture option as needed to turn off the feature.

Notice that the Employment Web page shows a hyperlink from the Home Page, a hyperlink to the Home Page, and a hyperlink to the mailto that you created. Amanda created the hyperlinks to the Feedback and Search Web pages, but because these Web pages do not exist in the current Sunny Web site, their links are broken. Now, check the hyperlinks in the Home Page.

3. Click **index.htm** in the Folder List to display the hyperlinks for that page. See Figure 3-33. There are hyperlinks to and from the Employment Web page, as shown in Hyperlinks view. This confirms that you have created the hyperlinks for navigating between these two pages. There is also a link to the minuet background sound that you added in Tutorial 2.

Figure 3-33	HYPERLINKS VIEW FOR THE HOME PAGE

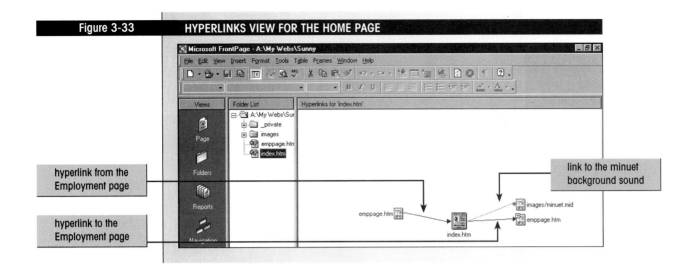

hyperlink from the
Employment page

hyperlink to the
Employment page

link to the minuet
background sound

Two of the hyperlinks in Figure 3-33 end with an arrow, whereas one ends with a bullet. An arrow indicates a hyperlink to another Web page in your Web site; a bullet indicates a hyperlink to a sound file or other type of multimedia file.

Notice also the plus (+) symbol in the upper-left corner of the right emppage.htm filename. Recall from Tutorial 1 that an icon with a plus or minus sign means that you can expand or collapse the hyperlinks to and from that page.

There are actually two hyperlinks from the Employment Web page to the Home Page—one from Home in the navigation bar and the other is a hotspot from the Employment Web page logo—these are repeated hyperlinks. You can display and verify repeated hyperlinks in Hyperlinks view. You also can display and verify the hyperlinks to picture files inserted in your Web pages. Amanda wants you to verify all of the hyperlinks you created to ensure that they are the ones desired and that none have been missed.

To display repeated and picture hyperlinks:

1. Click **emppage.htm** in the Folder List to select this page as the center focus of Hyperlinks view. If necessary, use the horizontal scroll bar to center the hyperlinks diagram in the Contents pane.

2. Right-click any empty area in the Contents pane to open the shortcut menu, and then click **Repeated Hyperlinks** to display the repeated hyperlinks for this page. Notice that three hyperlinks appear from the Employment Web page to the Home Page. The hyperlink that ends with a bullet is an included style link that specifies to use the same background as the Home Page. The other two hyperlinks end with an arrow; one represents the hyperlink in the navigation bar and the other represents the hotspot.

3. Point to the **index.htm icon** to the right of the emppage.htm icon (the one that ends with a bullet and not an arrow). An Included Style ScreenTip appears to indicate the use of the background properties from the Home Page. See Figure 3-34.

   TROUBLE? Your icons might appear in a different order, depending on how FrontPage created the view. Just make sure that all of the filenames are displayed.

Figure 3-34	REPEATED HYPERLINKS FOR THE EMPLOYMENT WEB PAGE

You can also show hyperlinks to pictures to check the pictures that you inserted in the page.

4. Right-click any empty area in the Contents pane, and then click **Hyperlinks to Pictures** to add these hyperlinks to the current Hyperlinks view of the Employment Web page. There are two pictures—one for the background picture (WB00791.gif) and one for the logo (Employ.gif).

Printing **Hyperlinks View**

Because you use Hyperlinks view interactively, FrontPage does not have a Print command that allows you to print the view. To print Hyperlinks view, however, as a reference or a resource, you can copy it to the Windows Clipboard and then print it using WordPad or another word-processing program. Amanda asks you to bring the hyperlinks diagram with you to the next meeting of the Web site development team, so you need to print the view.

To print Hyperlinks view:

1. With the Employment Web page still displayed in Hyperlinks view, press the **Print Screen** key to copy the picture of the screen to the Windows Clipboard.

2. Click the **Start** button on the taskbar, point to **Programs**, point to **Accessories**, and then click **WordPad** to start WordPad and to open a new document. If necessary, maximize the WordPad program window.

3. Press **Ctrl + V** to paste your Hyperlinks view screen into the document. See Figure 3-35.

Figure 3-35	WORDPAD PROGRAM WINDOW

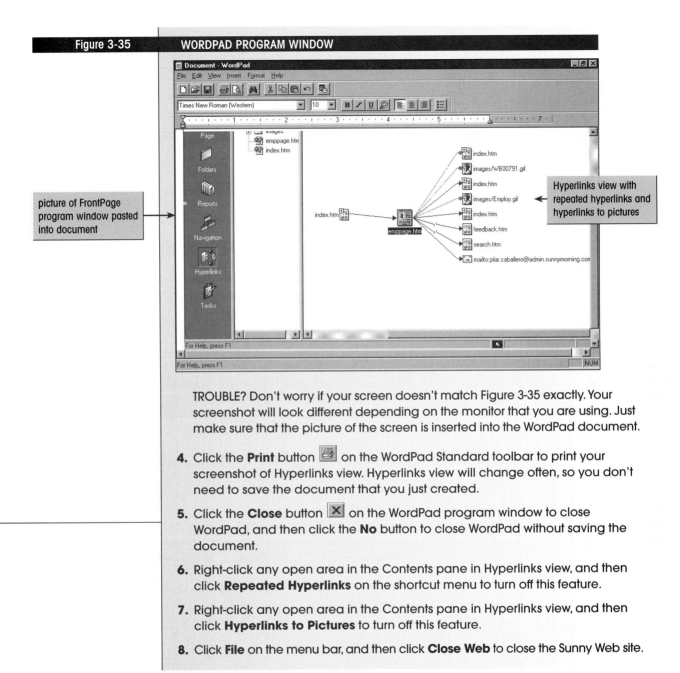

picture of FrontPage program window pasted into document

Hyperlinks view with repeated hyperlinks and hyperlinks to pictures

TROUBLE? Don't worry if your screen doesn't match Figure 3-35 exactly. Your screenshot will look different depending on the monitor that you are using. Just make sure that the picture of the screen is inserted into the WordPad document.

4. Click the **Print** button on the WordPad Standard toolbar to print your screenshot of Hyperlinks view. Hyperlinks view will change often, so you don't need to save the document that you just created.

5. Click the **Close** button on the WordPad program window to close WordPad, and then click the **No** button to close WordPad without saving the document.

6. Right-click any open area in the Contents pane in Hyperlinks view, and then click **Repeated Hyperlinks** on the shortcut menu to turn off this feature.

7. Right-click any open area in the Contents pane in Hyperlinks view, and then click **Hyperlinks to Pictures** to turn off this feature.

8. Click **File** on the menu bar, and then click **Close Web** to close the Sunny Web site.

With a printed copy of Hyperlinks view of the Employment Web page in hand, you can demonstrate to the Web site development team how the Web pages and files in the Sunny Web site are linked together. In the next session, you will use the Tasks list to organize the team's work on the Web site.

Session 3.2 QUICK CHECK

1. A(n) _____ is a named location in a Web page that identifies its position in the page.

2. If a bookmark is not associated with a text selection, then a(n) _____ appears in Page view to specify the bookmark's location.

3. Describe how to create a hyperlink to a bookmark in a Web page.

4. What does a pound sign (#) in a hyperlink indicate?

5. True or False: When using FrontPage to change a picture's background to transparent, you must convert the picture to GIF format.

6. A(n) _____ is an area of a picture that you can click to activate a hyperlink.

7. What are the three shapes that you can use to create a hotspot?

8. Describe how to include an e-mail address in a Web page.

9. True or False: FrontPage includes a Print command for printing Hyperlinks view.

SESSION 3.3

In this session, you will use the Tasks list to manage a Web site's development. You will add, modify, reassign, complete, and delete tasks. Finally, you will view the HTML code that implements the features of the Employment Web page.

Managing a Web Site's Development Using a Tasks List

In your meeting with the Web site development team, you presented your printout of Hyperlinks view for the Employment Web page. The team was pleased with the current structure and content of the Web site. Every team member is busy working on his or her contribution to the site, and you realize that building and testing a Web site is a big task. At the meeting, Amanda suggests that you use a Tasks list to track the tasks that are needed to complete the Web site.

Recall from Tutorial 1 that a Tasks list is an organized, detailed listing of the necessary activities or items required to complete a Web site. The Tasks list describes each task, indicates the person assigned to complete it, and specifies its priority. Once you have completed the initial design of your Web site, you can create a Tasks list that describes all of the pages you need to develop. You can add activities to a Tasks list, modify task names, assign developers, include descriptions, and remove a task from the list. When a task is finished, you can mark it as completed and then archive or delete it from the Tasks list. If the Web page that you need to create does not already exist, you can add the task of preparing the page and add a blank page to the Web site at the same time. When a task is linked to a page in this way, you can open the page in Page view directly from the Tasks list.

Adding a Task to the Tasks List

You can add a task to the Tasks list either in Tasks view or as you create hyperlinks to new pages in the Web site. Amanda asks you first to create the hyperlinks to the pages that are listed in the navigation bar of the Home Page. With the exception of the Employment Web page that you created in this tutorial, none of these pages have been created yet. For each new page, you will create the hyperlink, a new page, and the task to complete the page all at the same time.

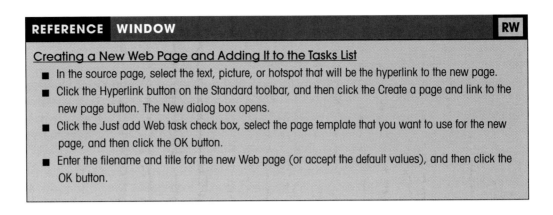

REFERENCE WINDOW   **RW**

Creating a New Web Page and Adding It to the Tasks List
- In the source page, select the text, picture, or hotspot that will be the hyperlink to the new page.
- Click the Hyperlink button on the Standard toolbar, and then click the Create a page and link to the new page button. The New dialog box opens.
- Click the Just add Web task check box, select the page template that you want to use for the new page, and then click the OK button.
- Enter the filename and title for the new Web page (or accept the default values), and then click the OK button.

The navigation bar in the Home Page contains several entries that you need to link to other Web pages. You will create the hyperlinks and the new pages at the same time.

To create a hyperlink to a new Web page and add its task to the Tasks list:

1. Start **FrontPage**, make sure your Data Disk is in the correct drive, open the **Sunny** Web site (a:\My Webs\Sunny) from your Data Disk in Folders view, and then open the Home Page (**index.htm**) in Page view.

2. Select **Products** in the navigation bar as the text for the hyperlink.

3. Click the **Hyperlink** button 🔳 on the Standard toolbar to open the Create Hyperlink dialog box, and then click the **Create a page and link to the new page** button 🗋 to open the New dialog box. See Figure 3-36.

| Figure 3-36 | NEW DIALOG BOX |

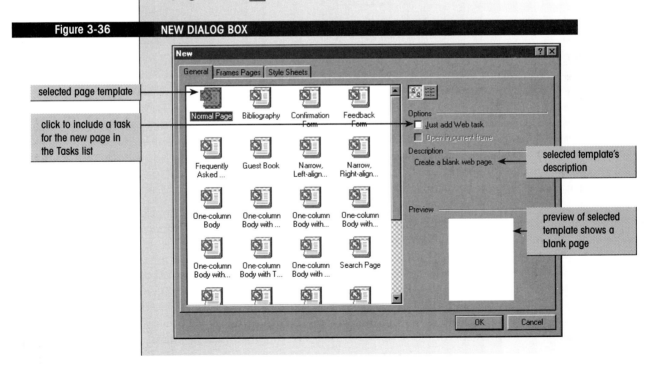

You can use the General tab to create a Web page based on a template. A specific template is not required, so the Normal Page template that is already selected is appropriate for this new page.

4. Click the **Just add Web task** check box in the Options section to select it, and then click the **OK** button. The Save As dialog box opens with a default filename of "new_page_1" and a default page title of "New Page 1." You will change both values to be consistent with the naming of other pages in the Sunny Web site, so that you can identify each page's contents by its filename and title.

5. Type **Products** to replace the default filename in the File name text box. FrontPage will add the htm extension automatically. Next, change the default page title.

6. Click the **Change** button to open the Set Page Title dialog box, type **Products** in the Page title text box, and then click the **OK** button to return to the Save As dialog box. See Figure 3-37.

Figure 3-37	SAVE AS DIALOG BOX

Web site in which to save the new page

new page title

page's filename

7. Click the **Save** button. The Save As and Create Hyperlink dialog boxes close. FrontPage creates the new Products Web page, saves it in the Sunny Web site, and creates a hyperlink in the navigation bar in the Home Page that opens the new Products Web page. FrontPage also adds a task to complete the Products page to the Tasks list.

8. Click the **Products** hyperlink in the navigation bar to deselect it, and then point to the **Products** hyperlink. The target of the hyperlink—Products.htm—is displayed on the status bar.

TROUBLE? If "unsaved:///new_page_1.htm" is displayed on the status bar, right-click the Products hyperlink in the navigation bar to open the shortcut menu, click Hyperlink Properties to open the Edit Hyperlink dialog box, and then double-click Products.htm in the file list. Click the Save button 🖫 on the Standard toolbar to save the Home Page, and then repeat Step 8.

When creating a new page, you can specify a title that differs from the hyperlink text. In Amanda's design of the Web site for Sunny Morning Products, the "About Us" hyperlink opens the Company Profile page, and the "Investor Relations" hyperlink opens the Investor page. Next, you will create the hyperlinks to these new pages and add them as tasks.

To create a new page with a different title and add a new task:

1. Select **About Us** in the navigation bar in the Home Page as the hyperlink text.

2. Click the **Hyperlink** button on the Standard toolbar to open the Create Hyperlink dialog box, and then click the **Create a page and link to the new page** button to open the New dialog box.

3. Click the **Just add Web task** check box, click the **OK** button to open the Save As dialog box, type **Company** to replace the default filename, click the **Change** button and enter the page title **Company Profile**, and then click the **OK** button.

4. Click the **Save** button to close the Save As and Create Hyperlink dialog boxes. FrontPage creates the new Company Profile Web page and its hyperlink in the Home Page, and adds a task to the Tasks list.

5. Repeat Steps 2 through 4 to create the hyperlink in the navigation bar using the **Investor Relations** entry. The page's name is **Investor** and its title is **Investor Relations**.

6. Point to the **About Us** and **Investor Relations** hyperlinks in the navigation bar and confirm that their hyperlinks were created correctly by examining the named hyperlink target in the status bar. If necessary, use the TROUBLE? paragraph in the previous set of steps to correct any FrontPage errors that occurred while creating the hyperlinks.

7. Click the **Save** button on the Standard toolbar to save the Home Page.

You created three new pages—Products, Investor Relations, and Company Profile—in the Web site, added tasks for completing these pages to the Tasks list, and created the hyperlinks to these pages in the Home Page. The Web site also will have two more Web pages—one each for Feedback and Search. Amanda doesn't want you to create these new pages using the Normal Page template, so you will just add their tasks.

REFERENCE WINDOW   **RW**

Adding a Task in Tasks View
- Click the Tasks button on the Views bar.
- Click the list arrow for the New Page button on the Standard toolbar, and then click Task in the list to open the New Task dialog box.
- Enter the information for the task.
- Click the OK button to add the task to the list.

For now Amanda asks you to use Tasks view to add tasks for creating these pages, but you will not create the pages.

To add a task in Tasks view:

1. Click the **Tasks** button 📝 on the Views bar to change to Tasks view. The three tasks for the three Web pages that you just created appear in the list.

2. Click the list arrow for the **New Page** button 🗋 on the Standard toolbar, and then click **Task** in the list. The New Task dialog box opens.

3. Type **Create Feedback Web page** in the Task name text box, and then press the **Tab** key to move to the Assigned to list box. You don't know who will be responsible for this task, so you will assign it to "Team Member."

4. Type **Team Member** in the Assigned to list box, and then press the **Tab** key to move to the Description text box.

5. Type **Create a Web page that contains a form** in the Description text box.

   When you create a new task in Tasks view, the default priority is medium. When you create a hyperlink to a new Web page and add it to the Tasks list, FrontPage gives the task a high priority. Assigning priority to a task is up to the Web site developer; you might want to prioritize tasks or just accept the defaults. You will accept the default priority of medium, so you are ready to close the dialog box.

6. Click the **OK** button to add the task for creating the Feedback Web page to the Tasks list.

7. Repeat Steps 2 through 6 to add the second task to the Tasks list based on the following information:

   Task name: **Create Search Web page**

   Assigned to: **Team Member**

   Description: **Create a Web page that searches the Sunny Web site**

   Your Tasks list should look like Figure 3-38.

Figure 3-38	REVISED TASKS LIST

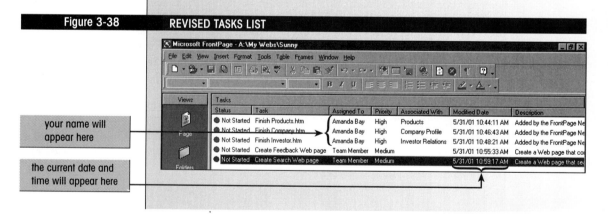

your name will appear here

the current date and time will appear here

You have finished entering new tasks to the Tasks list. Next, Amanda wants to show you how to sort and edit tasks.

Sorting and Changing Tasks

A Tasks list might contain hundreds of tasks, so it is important to keep it organized. You can sort tasks by clicking the column heading that you want to sort. For example, clicking the Task column heading sorts the list in ascending alphabetical order by task; clicking the Task column heading again sorts the list in descending alphabetical order. Amanda wants you to sort and change tasks now, while the list is still small, so you can practice this skill. As development of the Sunny Web site continues, you will most likely add many more tasks to the list.

To sort a Tasks list and change a task:

1. Click the **Task** column heading to sort the tasks alphabetically by task name.

2. Click the **Task** column heading again to sort the tasks in descending alphabetical order.

   You can double-click any task to see its details.

3. Double-click the **Finish Company.htm** task to open the Task Details dialog box. See Figure 3-39. In the Task Details dialog box, you can change the status of a task, its description, its priority, or the person assigned to complete it. Notice the current description of this task in the Description text box shows that this task was added when you used the New dialog box to create the task and the page.

| Figure 3-39 | TASK DETAILS DIALOG BOX |

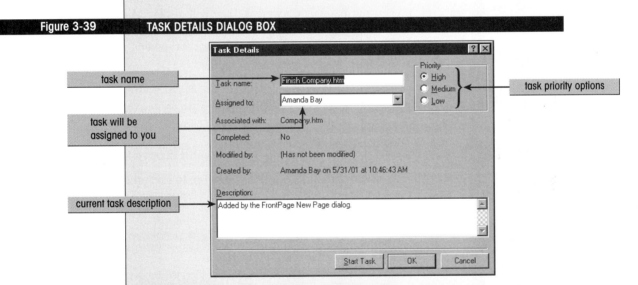

4. Type **Finish Company Profile Web page** in the Task name text box to provide a more descriptive name for the task.

5. In the Priority section, click the **Medium** option button to change the priority of this task. High priority is the default when you create a task in the Tasks list by adding a new page.

6. Select the current name in the Assigned to text box, and then type **Team Member** to reassign this task to the Web site development team.

7. Select the current description in the Description text box, and then replace it by typing **This page has been created and is ready to be imported into the Web site** as the new description.

> You could click the Start Task button to have FrontPage open the page associated with this task in Page view (Company.htm), so you can begin working on the page. However, you will close the Task Details dialog box for now.
>
> 8. Click the **OK** button to update the Tasks list.

Now that you've finished making changes to one of the tasks in the Tasks list, you can complete one of the tasks in the list. The process of completing a task in the Tasks list can mean anything from importing a new page to updating a hyperlink in an existing page. Next, you will import the Company Profile Web page into the Sunny Web site as part of completing the Finish Company Profile Web page task that you just modified.

Importing a Web Page and Checking It for Broken Links

Amanda received the Company Profile Web page, Company.htm, from the development team member who created it, and then she sent it to you using the company intranet. You saved this page in the Tutorial.03 folder on your Data Disk. Now you need to import this page into the Sunny Web site. This page will replace the Company Profile Web page that you created with the About Us hyperlink in the Home Page.

This page's developer included some pictures in the page. When you import a page into a FrontPage Web site, you import only the page's HTML document. If the page's developer included pictures in the HTML document, they will display as empty boxes until you add their files to the current Web site. As part of completing the task for the Company Profile Web page, you will import the page and then check it for missing pictures.

> *To import the Company Profile Web page into the Sunny Web site:*
>
> 1. Click the **Folders** button 📁 on the Views bar.
>
> 2. Click **File** on the menu bar, and then click **Import** to open the Import dialog box.
>
> 3. Click the **Add File** button to open the Add File to Import List dialog box. If necessary, change to the drive or folder that contains your Data Disk, and then double-click the **Tutorial.03** folder.
>
> 4. Double-click **Company** to return to the Import dialog box, and then click the **OK** button.
>
> The Confirm Save dialog box opens, indicating that the page already exists in the Web site. You created this page when you added its task to the Tasks list. You will replace the existing page with the completed Company Profile page.
>
> 5. Click the **Yes** button. The page is replaced, and you return to Folders view.

Next, you will check the page that you just imported for broken hyperlinks. A **broken hyperlink**, or a **broken link**, is one that references a bookmark, Web page, or multimedia file that does not exist in the current Web site.

To check the Web site for broken hyperlinks:

1. Click the **Hyperlinks** button 🖳 on the Views bar, and then click **Company.htm** in the Folder List to make that file the center focus of Hyperlinks view.

2. Right-click an empty area in the Contents pane to open the shortcut menu, and then click **Hyperlinks to Pictures**. Hyperlinks view now includes hyperlinks to pictures. See Figure 3-40.

Figure 3-40	HYPERLINKS VIEW FOR THE COMPANY PROFILE WEB PAGE

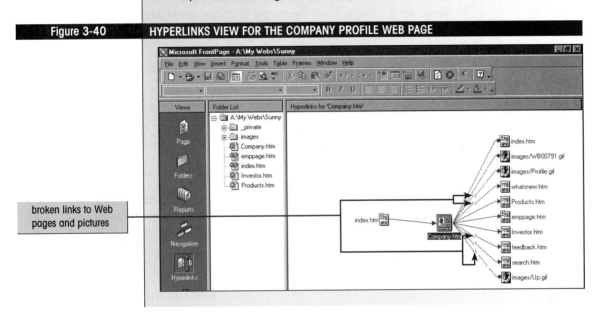

broken links to Web pages and pictures

Two of the broken links in Figure 3-40 are to the feedback.htm and search.htm pages. You added these tasks to the Tasks list, but you chose not to create these pages yet, so these broken links are fine for now. There is also a broken link to the whatsnew.htm page. You don't have any information about this page right now, so you will discuss this page with the Web site development team at your next meeting.

There are three pictures used in this page: WB00791.gif, which is the background picture; and Profile.gif and Up.gif, which are pictures that the developer inserted in the page. These last two pictures are displaying as broken links, so you will need to insert them in your page. These files are stored in the Tutorial.03 folder on your Data Disk. To complete the Company Profile page, you will use Tasks view to open it.

Opening a Web Page from Tasks View

You can use the Tasks list to open a Web page that is associated with a task. Amanda asks you to complete the necessary work to finish the Finish Company Profile task. After you are finished, you will mark this page as completed.

To access a Web page from the Tasks list:

1. Click the **Tasks** button 📝 on the Views bar to switch to Tasks view, and then right-click the **Finish Company Profile Web page** task to select it and open the shortcut menu.

2. Click **Start Task**. The Company Profile page opens in Page view. A broken link icon ☒ appears in a box at the top of the Web page. Amanda tells you that you will need to insert this picture in the page.

3. Right-click ☒ to open the shortcut menu, and then click **Picture Properties** to open the Picture Properties dialog box. The Picture source text box contains the filename of the picture that the developer used in this location, Profile.gif, and its expected location, which is the images folder of the current Web site. The Profile.gif file is missing from the Sunny Web site's images folder, but it is saved on your Data Disk.

4. Click the **Browse** button to the right of the Picture source text box to open the Picture dialog box, and then click the **Select a file on your computer** button ☒ to open the Select File dialog box.

5. Make sure the drive or folder that contains your Data Disk appears in the Look in text box, double-click the **Tutorial.03** folder, and then double-click **Profile**. The Picture Properties dialog box reappears with the correct path for the Profile.gif file.

6. Click the **OK** button. The picture now appears at the top of the Company Profile Web page, where the broken link previously was displayed. Next, you will fix the broken link to the Up.gif picture that you discovered while viewing this page in Hyperlinks view.

7. Press **Ctrl + End** to scroll to the bottom of the Web page. Notice the broken link to the picture that should be displayed to the left of the "Top of Page" hyperlink.

8. Repeat Steps 3 through 6 to insert the Up.gif picture at the location of the broken link. The Up.gif file is stored in the Tutorial.03 folder on your Data Disk.

   You need to save the Company Profile Web page and its embedded files in the Sunny Web site.

9. Click the **Save** button ☐ on the Standard toolbar. A Microsoft FrontPage dialog box opens and asks if you want to mark the task as completed. Click the **No** button for now. The Save Embedded Files dialog box opens with the files Profile.gif and Up.gif listed.

10. Make sure that the images folder is selected in the Save Embedded Files dialog box, and then click the **OK** button to save the Web page and to save the embedded GIF files in the images folder of the Sunny Web site.

After reviewing the page, you decide that it is finished, so you can mark its task as completed in the Tasks list.

Marking a Task as Completed

After finishing a task in your Tasks list, you can mark it as completed and it will remain in the Tasks list.

REFERENCE WINDOW	RW

Marking a Task as Completed
- Click the Tasks button on the Views bar to display the Tasks list.
- Right-click the desired task to open the shortcut menu, and then click Mark as Completed.

Now you can mark the Finish Company Profile task as completed in your Tasks list. After marking this task as completed, you will set the Tasks list to show the task history.

To mark a task as completed and show the task history:

1. Click the **Tasks** button [icon] on the Views bar to display the Tasks list. The Finish Company Profile Web page task currently shows a status of "In Progress," because you are working on it in Page view.

2. Right-click the **Finish Company Profile Web page** task to open the shortcut menu, and then click **Mark as Completed**. After a few seconds, the status of this task changes from "In Progress" to "Completed" and its status symbol changes from a red dot to a green dot.

   When you mark a task as completed, it remains visible in the Tasks list. However, after you refresh the view, the task is not visible unless you set the list to show the task history.

3. Click the **Refresh** button [icon] on the Standard toolbar. Notice that the Finish Company Profile Web page task no longer appears in the Tasks list. To display the list of completed tasks, you need to show the task history.

4. Right-click any blank area in the Tasks pane, and then click **Show Task History** on the shortcut menu. The Tasks list is updated to reflect the unfinished tasks and the ones marked as completed. See Figure 3-41.

Figure 3-41	UPDATED TASKS LIST

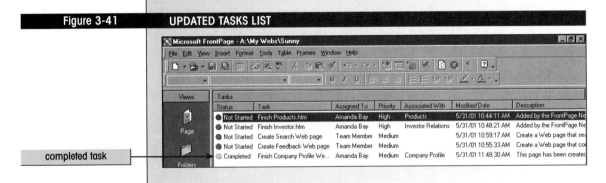

Deleting a Task from the Tasks List

You can delete a task marked for completion from the Tasks list. Deleting a task is a permanent action.

REFERENCE WINDOW   **RW**

Deleting a Task from the Tasks List
- Click the Tasks button on the Views bar to display the Tasks list.
- Right-click the task that you want to delete to open the shortcut menu, and then click Delete.
- Click the Yes button in the Confirm Delete dialog box to delete the page.

Because you have completed the Finish Company Profile Web page task, Amanda asks you to delete it from the Tasks list.

To delete a completed task from a Tasks list:

1. Right-click the **Finish Company Profile Web page** task to open the shortcut menu, and then click **Delete**. The Confirm Delete dialog box opens.

2. Click the **Yes** button to remove this task from the Tasks list.

3. Right-click any blank area in the Tasks pane, and then click **Show Task History** on the shortcut menu to turn off the task history. Because there are no completed tasks in the list any longer, the list continues to display four tasks, all of which have a status of "Not Started."

You have finished working with the Tasks list. Amanda asks you to view the HTML code for the work that you've done in the Employment Web page.

Viewing HTML Code

You changed the Employment Web page by including the background from the Home Page, adding bookmarks and internal hyperlinks, creating a hotspot, and including a mailto. Different HTML tags implement each of these features. For example, an HREF property of the A tag (the A indicates an anchor, which implements the hyperlinks) uses a pound sign (#), such as #MIS, to specify an internal hyperlink, whereas the NAME property uses a pound sign to specify a bookmark location in a Web page, such as #To Apply. The MAP tags were created by a FrontPage component to implement the hotspot in the logo. Amanda wants you to view the HTML code for the Employment Web page to gain a better understanding of the code FrontPage created to build this page.

To view HTML code of the Employment page and close FrontPage:

1. Click the **Folders** button 🗐 on the Views bar to change to Folders view, and then double-click **emppage.htm** in the Contents pane to open the Employment Web page in Page view.

2. Click the **HTML** tab to switch to HTML view and display the HTML code, and then scroll down the page until the BODY STYLESRC tag is at the top of the screen. See Figure 3-42. Notice the tags and code associated various tasks, such as including a common background, implementing a hotspot, and creating a bulleted and numbered list.

Figure 3-42	HTML CODE FOR THE EMPLOYMENT WEB PAGE

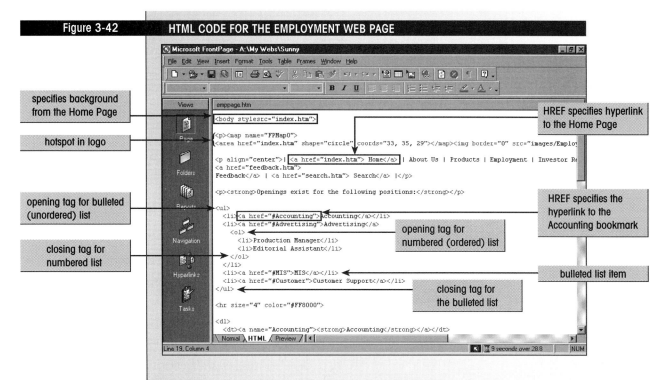

3. Press the **Page Down** key to move down one page, and then scroll down the page so that the opening DL tag for the Accounting defined term appears at the top of the screen. See Figure 3-43. Notice the tags and code associated with creating a definition list and a defined term.

Figure 3-43	HTML CODE FOR THE EMPLOYMENT WEB PAGE (CONTINUED)

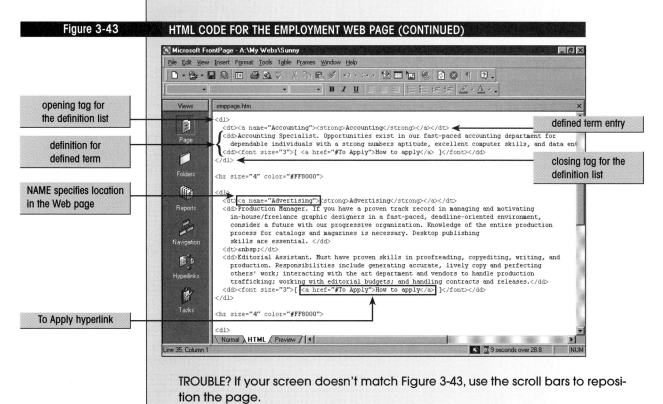

TROUBLE? If your screen doesn't match Figure 3-43, use the scroll bars to reposition the page.

> **4.** Scroll down the page, and examine the remaining tags that you created in this tutorial, including the mailto.
>
> **5.** Click the **Normal** tab to return to Normal Page view.
>
> **6.** Click the **Close** button [X] on the FrontPage title bar to close the open Web pages, the Sunny Web site, and FrontPage.

Amanda and Pilar are pleased with the Employment Web page. In the next tutorial, you will create Web pages that contain tables and frames.

Session 3.3 QUICK CHECK

1. A(n) _____ is a record of the details necessary for completing a Web site.

2. In the New dialog box, selecting the _____ check box lets you add a task to the Tasks list when you create a new page.

3. To add a new task in Tasks view, click the list arrow on the _____ button on the Standard toolbar, and then click _____ in the list.

4. True or False: You can sort a Tasks list based on the values in any column in Tasks view.

5. To show a "Completed" status for a task, right-click the task in Tasks view, and then click _____ on the shortcut menu.

6. True or False: Deleting a task from the Tasks list deletes it permanently from the list.

7. True or False: You can reassign a task to another member of the Web site development team.

REVIEW ASSIGNMENTS

After reviewing the Employment Web page, Amanda and Pilar ask you to add a new department and job position. After completing the Employment Web page, you will import the What's New page to the Sunny Web site and update the hyperlinks in the navigation bar in the Company Profile Web page.

If necessary, insert your Data Disk in the appropriate disk drive, start FrontPage, and then do the following:

1. Open the **Sunny** Web site (a:\My Webs\Sunny) from your Data Disk, and then open the Employment Web page (**emppage.htm**) in Page view.

2. Create the bookmarks and hyperlinks for the items in the nested list in the table of contents at the top of the page.

Explore

3. Create another position in the Employment Web page for which you determine the department name, the job title, and the job description. Enter the new department's heading and the job's title and description below the horizontal line for the Customer Support department. Format the heading as a defined term and the description as a definition. Use the same format and organization as used for the other departments, but do *not* create the How to apply hyperlink. Copy and paste a horizontal line from another department below the new one that you created.

4. Add the department name for the position you created in Step 3 to the table of contents at the top of the page as a new bulleted item. Create the hyperlink from the new entry to the department heading in the body of the Web page. (*Hint*: Create a bookmark first.)

5. Create a bookmark named "Top" to the left of the logo at the top of the Employment Web page. Do not select any text or the logo for the Top bookmark.

6. Add the text "Top of Page" on a new line immediately above the last updated date at the bottom of the Web page. Create a hyperlink from the Top of Page text to the Top bookmark you created in Step 5.

Explore 7. Insert the **Up.gif** picture from the Web site's images folder to the left of the Top of Page hyperlink that you created in Step 6, with one space separating the picture and the hyperlink. Create a hyperlink from the **Up.gif** picture to the Top bookmark. (*Hint*: To create a hyperlink using a picture, select the picture, and then use the Hyperlink button on the Standard toolbar.)

8. Save the Employment Web page, and then use the Preview tab to test the bookmarks and hyperlinks in the page.

Explore 9. Use the HTML tab to create the "How to apply" hyperlink below the new job description that you added. (*Hint*: Type the HTML equivalent for creating a new line, <br>, type an opening bracket and a space before the hyperlink text and a space and a closing bracket after it. Review the other How to apply hyperlinks in the page to see how they are formatted.) Save the page, and then use the Preview tab to verify that the hyperlink works correctly.

Explore 10. Open the Company Profile Web page (**Company.htm**) in Page view. The navigation bar in this page includes the What's New entry, which is already formatted as a hyperlink. However, this page does not exist in the Sunny Web site yet. Use Tasks view to add a new entry to the Tasks list for creating the What's New Web page, but do not create the new page. Include a description for this task to import the What's New page into the Sunny Web site, assign the task to Team Member, and then sort the Tasks list in ascending alphabetical order by task.

Explore 11. Complete the task you added to the Tasks list in Step 10 by importing into the Sunny Web site the What's New Web page (**whatsnew.htm**) from the Tutorial.03 folder. Add its logo (**WhatLogo.gif**) where the broken hyperlink appears. Save the page, and save the picture file in the Sunny Web site's images folder.

12. Use the Preview tab to test the hyperlinks between the What's New page and the Company Profile page, mark the task for the What's New page as completed in the Tasks list, make sure the task history is on, and then print the list. (*Hint*: You will need to copy the screen and print it using WordPad.) Close WordPad without saving changes, and then turn off the task history.

13. Display the What's New Web page as the center focus page in Hyperlinks view. If necessary, center the hyperlinks diagram in the Contents pane. Display the repeated hyperlinks and the hyperlinks to pictures, and then print Hyperlinks view using WordPad. Close WordPad without saving changes. Turn off the display of the repeated hyperlinks and the hyperlinks to pictures.

14. Update the navigation bar in the Employment Web page so that each entry, with the exception of the Employment entry, contains a hyperlink that opens the correct page. Use the HTML tab to print the HTML code for the Employment Web page. On the printout, circle the HTML code for the Top bookmark, the Top of Page and Up button hyperlinks, and the new job heading, description, and How to apply hyperlink that you added.

15. Close FrontPage.

CASE PROBLEMS

Case 1. Preparing an Information Page for Royal Hair Care Products The product launch for Quick Dry Solution at Royal Hair Care Products is well underway. Valerie Suarez met with Sharon Brock, the Quick Dry product manager, to discuss the support the company might provide through its Web site. Together, Valerie and Sharon determined that they could use the planned Company Information Web page to provide distributors and retailers with information about the product and its promotion. Valerie and Nathan Dubois, the information systems specialist, then met with Sharon and her staff to finalize their ideas on the Web page content. They agreed that the page should contain four sections: distribution, promotion, packaging, and legal. Sharon agreed to write a draft of the distribution information and provide Nathan with a copy of that file for use in the Company Profile page. Nathan has started developing the Company Information page, and Valerie wants you to help him complete this task.

If necessary, start FrontPage, insert your Data Disk in the appropriate disk drive, and then do the following:

1. Read all of the questions for this case problem, and then prepare a planning analysis sheet for the revisions to the Royal Web site.

2. Open the **Royal** Web site (a:\My Webs\Royal) that you created in Tutorial 2 in Folders view. (If you did not create this Web site in Tutorial 2, ask your instructor for assistance.)

3. Import the partially completed Company Information (**Rcompany.htm**) page from the Tutorial.03 folder on your Data Disk into the Royal Web site, and then open this page in Page view. Review the page and locate the navigation bar, the items listed as a table of contents below the navigation bar, and the four content areas of the page that are separated by horizontal lines. If necessary, change the entries in the navigation bar in the Home Page that you created in Tutorial 2 to match the navigation bar in the Company Information page.

4. Insert the **Royal02.gif** picture from the Tutorial.03 folder at the top of the page above the navigation bar.

5. Change the dark gray, outer background color of the **Royal02.gif** picture to transparent.

6. Insert the text from the **Distrib.doc** file in the Tutorial.03 folder as a definition under the Distribution heading that appears between two horizontal lines.

7. Format the list containing the Distribution, Promotion, Packaging, and Legal section titles that make up the table of contents (located below the navigation bar) as a numbered list. Create a bookmark for each of these items where they are described in the body of the Web page. Then create a hyperlink from each of the table of contents items to its respective bookmark.

8. Include your e-mail address at the bottom of the Web page below the "For additional information contact us:" line. If you don't have an e-mail address, create one or use one your instructor provides.

9. Create a bookmark named "Top" to the left of the **Royal02.gif** picture at the top of the page. Do not select any text or the logo for the Top bookmark.

10. Place the text "Top of Page" on a new line below the mailto that you added in Step 8. Create a hyperlink from the Top of Page text to the Top bookmark.

Explore ▶ 11. Insert the **Up.gif** picture from the Tutorial.03 folder to the left of the Top of Page hyperlink with one space separating the picture and the hyperlink. Create a hyperlink from the **Up.gif** picture to the Top bookmark.

12. Save the Web page, and save the picture files in the Royal Web site's images folder. Use the browser to test the internal hyperlinks.

13. Return to the Company Information page in Normal Page view. Create a hyperlink in the navigation bar to the Home Page, and then create a hyperlink in the navigation bar from the Home Page to the Company Information page. Save the Home Page.

14. Use the navigation bar in the Company Information (**rcompany.htm**) page to create the following hyperlinks and new Web pages based on the Normal Page template. Add a task for creating each page in the Tasks list. Use the News entry in the navigation bar to create the **RNews** page with the title "What's New," use the Feedback entry in the navigation bar to create the **RFeedbak** page with the title "Feedback," and use the Employment entry in the navigation bar to create the **REmploy** page with the title "Employment." Save the Company Information page.

15. Open the Tasks list, and then change the Finish task for the What's New page to "Import," add an appropriate description, assign the task to yourself (if necessary), and assign it medium priority. Then change the Finish task for the Feedback page to "Create," add an appropriate description, assign the task to yourself (if necessary), and assign it medium priority.

16. Import the What's New page (**RNews.htm**) from the Tutorial.03 folder into the Royal Web site, replacing the current page. Insert the **Royal01.gif** file from the Royal Web site's images folder at the top of the page, press the spacebar, and then insert the **RNewsLog.gif** picture from the Tutorial.03 folder on the same line and to the right of the **Royal01.gif** picture. Save the page and save the picture files in the Web site's images folder.

17. Use drag and drop to create the hyperlink from the What's New (**RNews.htm**) page to the Home Page. Then use drag and drop to create the hyperlink from the Home Page to the What's New page. Edit the Home entry in the navigation bar so that it displays only the underlined text, "Home." Save the What's New page. Save the Home Page. Test the new hyperlinks in Internet Explorer, and then close Internet Explorer.

18. Mark the task for the What's New page as completed in the Tasks list. Add a new task for creating the Search page to the Tasks list, but do not add this page to the Web site. Give the task an appropriate title, a medium priority, a description, and assign the task to yourself.

19. Display the Company Information (**rcompany.htm**) page as the center focus page in Hyperlinks view. If necessary, center the hyperlinks diagram in the Contents pane. Display the repeated hyperlinks and the hyperlinks to pictures. Use WordPad to print Hyperlinks view, and then close WordPad without saving any changes. Turn off the display of the repeated hyperlinks and the hyperlinks to pictures.

Explore ▷ 20. Print the Company Information (**rcompany.htm**) page from Page view. Print the HTML code for this page, and then on the printout, circle the HTML code for the hyperlinks and bookmarks that you created.

21. Close FrontPage.

Case 2. Developing the Web Pages for Buffalo Trading Post   The recycling business at Buffalo Trading Post remains strong. Donna Vargas and the sales staff receive approximately 50 phone calls each day from potential customers. As a result, Donna wants to add a page to the Buffalo Web site that provides customers with information about the company's recycling process. Donna, Karla Perez, and the sales staff agree that the page should contain sections entitled "Frequently Asked Questions" and "How It Works" to describe the process of buying and selling clothing. They also want a "Choose To Re-Use" section that will describe Buffalo's overall commitment to recycling. Karla began the process of creating this page, while Donna wrote the text for the How It Works section. Karla asks you to help her complete the remaining Web development activities.

If necessary, start FrontPage, insert your Data Disk in the appropriate disk drive, and then do the following:

1. Read all of the questions for this case problem, and then prepare a planning analysis sheet for the revisions to the Buffalo Web site.

2. Open the **Buffalo** Web site (a:\My Webs\Buffalo) that you created in Tutorial 2 in Folders view. (If you did not create this Web site in Tutorial 2, ask your instructor for assistance.)

3. Import the partially completed How (**Bhow.htm**) page in the Tutorial.03 folder into the Web site, and then open the How page in Page view. Review the page, locating the navigation bar, the items listed as a table of contents below the navigation bar, and the three content areas of the page that are separated by horizontal lines. If necessary, change the entries in the navigation bar in the Home Page that you created in Tutorial 2 to match the navigation bar in the How page.

4. Insert the **BHowLogo.jpg** picture from the Tutorial.03 folder at the top of the page above the navigation bar, and then center it.

5. Convert the JPG picture that you added in Step 4 to GIF format.

Explore   6. Use the **BWMark.gif** file from the Tutorial.03 folder as the background picture for the How page. Change the background picture to a watermark.

7. Insert the **HowWorks.doc** file in the Tutorial.03 folder as a definition below the How It Works heading that appears between two horizontal lines in the body of the How page.

Explore   8. Format the How It Works, Frequently Asked Questions, and Choose To Re-Use list that make up the table of contents (below the navigation bar) as a bulleted list with square bullet characters. (*Hint*: Select the items in the list, click Format on the menu bar, and then click Bullets and Numbering. On the Plain Bullets tab, select the square bullet character. If the square bullet character is not available, select any other bullet character that is not a small circle.)

9. Create a bookmark for each of the table of contents items where they are described in the body of the Web page, and then create a hyperlink from each of the bulleted list items in the table of contents to its respective bookmark.

10. Include your e-mail address at the bottom of the Web page below the "For additional information please contact us:" line. If you don't have an e-mail address, create one or use one your instructor provides. Change the style of your e-mail address to the Address style. Save the How page, and save its picture files in the Buffalo Web site's images folder.

11. Create a bookmark named "Top" to the left of the logo at the top of the page.

12. Place the text "Top of Page" on a new line formatted with the Normal style below the mailto that you added in Step 10. Create a hyperlink from the Top of Page text to the Top bookmark.

Explore   13. Insert an appropriate picture from the Clip Art Gallery that users can click to scroll to the top of the How page. Place it to the left of the Top of Page hyperlink that you added in Step 12. (*Hint*: To open the Clip Art Gallery, place the insertion point where you want to add the picture, click Insert on the menu bar, point to Picture, and then click Clip Art. Browse the categories. To insert a picture, select it to open the shortcut menu, and then click the Insert clip button.) Insert one space between the picture and the text. If necessary, use the sizing handles on the picture to reduce the picture's size. If necessary, convert the picture to GIF format.

Explore   14. Create a hyperlink from the picture you added in Step 13 to the Top bookmark. Save the Web page, and save its pictures in the Buffalo Web site's images folder. Rename the clip art picture that you added in Step 13 to **Up.gif**. Test all of the internal hyperlinks using the browser.

15. Use drag and drop to create a hyperlink in the navigation bar from the How page to the Home Page, and then create a hyperlink in the navigation bar from the Home Page to the How page. Save the Home Page.

Explore   16. Create a rectangular hotspot that encloses the "Buffalo Trading Post" text in the logo at the top of the How page. Link this hotspot to the Home Page.

17. Select "What" in the navigation bar of the How page, add a normal page to the Buffalo Web site with the filename **BWhat.htm** and the title "What," and add this page as a task in the Web site's Tasks list.

18. Import the Who page (**BWho.htm**) from the Tutorial.03 folder into the Buffalo Web site. Insert the **BWhoLogo.gif** picture from the Tutorial.03 folder at the top of the page, and then center it. Save the page, and save the picture in the Buffalo Web site's images folder.

19. Use drag and drop to create the hyperlinks between the Home, How, and Who pages so that each page has an active hyperlink to the other two pages. Save each page after creating its hyperlinks. Use the Preview tab to test these hyperlinks.

20. Use Tasks view to add a task to create the Where page to the Tasks list, but do not add this page to the Web site. Assign the task to yourself, add an appropriate description and task name, and assign a medium priority.

Explore   21. Change to Folders view. Change the title of the Home Page to "Buffalo Trading Post Home Page." (*Hint*: Click index.htm in the Contents pane, click the page's title to display the insertion point, and then type the new title and press the Enter key.) Preview the Home Page in Internet Explorer, and notice that the title bar in the browser displays the new name. Use the Source command on the View menu in Internet Explorer to access the page's source HTML code and then change the title in the HTML code back to "Home Page." (*Hint*: Look for the TITLE tags in the HTML code.) Close Notepad, save your changes, and then refresh the Home Page. Notice that the title bar in Internet Explorer now displays the title "Home Page." Close Internet Explorer, return to Folders view, click the Refresh button on the Standard toolbar, and then confirm that the title of the Home Page is correct in FrontPage.

22. Display the How (**bhow.htm**) page as the center focus page in Hyperlinks view. If necessary, center the hyperlinks diagram in the Contents pane. Display the hyperlinks within the page, and then use WordPad to print Hyperlinks view. Close WordPad without saving changes. Turn off the display of hyperlinks within the page.

23. Use FrontPage to display the HTML code for the How (**bhow.htm**) page, and then print it. On the printout, circle the HTML code for the pictures that you added to the page.

24. Close FrontPage.

Case 3. Completing the Employment Page for Garden Grill Hiring and retaining the best possible staff is key to the continued growth of Garden Grill. Nolan Simmons and Shannon Taylor met with the corporate human resources director to discuss the content of the planned Employment Opportunities Web page. They want the page to emphasize that Garden Grill is a fun place to work and that employees are rewarded well. They agreed that the Employment Opportunities page should include information about both management and staff associate positions. The human resources director promised to create a Word document that contains a description of the manager's position and then to send that file to Shannon the next day. Shannon started developing the Employment Opportunities page based on the detailed requirements from the meeting. Nolan wants you to help Shannon complete the development and testing of this Web page.

If necessary, start FrontPage, insert your Data Disk in the appropriate disk drive, and then do the following:

1. Read all of the questions for this case problem, and then prepare a planning analysis sheet for the revisions to the Garden Web site.

2. Open the **Garden** Web site (a:\My Webs\Garden) that you created in Tutorial 2 in Folders view. (If you did not create this Web site in Tutorial 2, ask your instructor for assistance.)

3. Import the partially completed Employment Opportunities page (**GEmploy.htm**) from the Tutorial.03 folder on your Data Disk into the Web site, and then open it in Page view. Review the page, locating the items listed as a table of contents at the top of the page and the two content areas of the page that are separated by horizontal lines.

4. Insert the **Garden01.gif** picture from the Garden Web site's images folder on a new centered line above the broken picture link at the top of the Web page. Insert the **GNavBar.gif** picture from the Tutorial.03 folder in place of the broken link at the top of the page.

5. Specify the same background for this Web page that you used for the Home Page.

6. Insert the **Manager.doc** file from the Tutorial.03 folder on the blank line below the Managers heading that appears between two horizontal lines in the body of the Web page. Select the list of five items that appear under the description that you just added, and change them to a bulleted list. Use the Increase Indent button on the Formatting toolbar to indent the list one additional tab stop.

Explore ▶ 7. Change the format of the bullets in the bulleted list that you created in Step 6 to pictures of something that is appropriate for a restaurant (such as food or an interesting shape). (*Hint*: Select the bulleted list, click Format on the menu bar, and then click Bullets and Numbering. Click the Picture Bullets tab, click the Specify picture option button, click the Browse button, and then click the Clip Art button in the Select Picture dialog box to open the Clip Art Gallery. Select an option from the Buttons & Icons category.) Save the page, and save the picture file for the bullet characters and the navigation bar picture in the images folder.

Explore ▶ 8. Select the bulleted list in the Staff Associates section, and then apply the same bullets that you added in Step 7 to the list. (*Hint*: Select the bulleted list, click Format on the menu bar, click Bullets and Numbering, and then apply the bullet picture that you saved in the Web site's images folder.)

9. Format as a numbered list the Managers and Staff Associates entries that make up the table of contents at the top of the page. Create a bookmark for each of these entries where they are described later in the Web page. Then create a hyperlink from each of the entries in the table of contents to its respective bookmark.

10. Include your e-mail address at the bottom of the Web page below the "For additional information contact us:" paragraph. If you don't have an e-mail address, create one or use one your instructor provides.

11. Create a bookmark named "Top" to the left of the Garden Grill logo at the top of the page.

12. Place the text "Top of Page" on a new line below the mailto that you added in Step 10. Create a hyperlink from the Top of Page text to the Top bookmark.

Explore ▸   13. Insert the **Up.gif** picture from the Tutorial.03 folder to the left of the Top of Page hyperlink with one space between the picture and the hyperlink. Create a hyperlink from the **Up.gif** picture to the Top bookmark. Save the Employment Opportunities page, and save all pictures in the Garden Web site's images folder.

14. Create a hotspot in the navigation bar of the Employment Opportunities page that opens the Home Page.

Explore ▸   15. Replace your text navigation bar in the Home Page with the **GNavBar.gif** picture that is saved in the Garden Web site's images folder. Then create a hotspot in the navigation bar in the Home Page that opens the Employment Opportunities page. Save the Home Page.

Explore ▸   16. Use the navigation bar in the Home Page to create the following hotspots and new Web pages based on the Normal Page template. Add a task for creating each page in the Tasks list. Use the About Us entry in the navigation bar to create the **GAbout** page with the title "Company Profile," and use the Feedback entry in the navigation bar to create the **GFeedbak** page with the title "Feedback." Save the Home Page.

17. Import the Company Profile page (**GAbout.htm**) from the Tutorial.03 folder into the Garden Web site, replacing the page that you created in Step 16. Open the page in Page view. Insert the **Garden01.gif** picture at the top of the page. Create hotspots to open the Home Page, the Jobs page, and the Feedback page. Save the Company Profile (**GAbout.htm**) page.

18. Mark the task for the Company Profile page as completed in the Tasks list. Then add a new task for creating the Search page, but do not add this page to the Web site. Assign the task to yourself with medium priority, and create an appropriate task name and description.

19. Use Hyperlinks view to check your Web site for broken hyperlinks. Make sure that each page contains the appropriate hyperlinks between them, adding any that are needed and correcting any errors.

20. Display the Company Profile (**GAbout.htm**) page as the focus page in Hyperlinks view. If necessary, center the hyperlinks diagram in the Contents pane. Display the repeated hyperlinks and the hyperlinks to pictures. Use WordPad to print Hyperlinks view, and then close WordPad without saving changes. Turn off the display of the repeated hyperlinks and hyperlinks to pictures.

Explore ▸   21. Open the Employment Opportunities (**GEmploy.htm**) page in Page view, and then print it. Then use FrontPage to print the HTML code for this page. On the printout, circle the code that specifies the hotspots that you added in the navigation bar, and the code that adds the background picture to the page.

22. Close FrontPage.

Case 4. Creating a New Page for Replay Music Factory   Business has been brisk at the Replay Music Factory. One frequently asked question (FAQ) concerns how the exchange process works for buying, selling, and trading compact discs (CDs). Charlene Fields and Alec Johnston met with the marketing manager to see how they might use the company's Web site to provide information to customers. They are convinced that expanding the Web site to include this information will translate into fewer phone calls from people asking for information about the exchange process. This in turn might help delay the need to hire additional sales associates to handle those calls. Charlene and Alec decide to create a new Web page to describe the exchange process. In addition, they also want you to create new, blank pages for the planned pages in the Web site. Charlene asks you to assist Alec with this enhancement of the company's Web site.

If necessary, start FrontPage, insert your Data Disk in the appropriate disk drive, and then do the following:

1. Read all of the steps for this case problem, and then prepare a planning analysis sheet for the revisions to the Replay Web site.

2. Open the **Replay** Web site (a:\My Webs\Replay) that you created in Tutorial 2. (If you did not create this Web site in Tutorial 2, ask your instructor for assistance.)

3. Open the Home Page in Page view. Use the navigation bar that you created in Tutorial 2 to create hyperlinks to the planned pages in the Web site and add them to the Tasks list. Add blank, normal pages to the Web site as necessary to create the hyperlinks.

Explore ▶ 4. Design the new Web page that describes Replay's process for buying, selling, and trading used CDs. Include a table of contents with at least two entries, at least one bulleted list or numbered list, at least two defined terms and their associated definitions, internal hyperlinks from the table of contents to the detailed information for each table of contents entry in the document, a mailto, a navigation bar, at least one picture, and a hyperlink from the bottom of the page to a nontext-based bookmark at the top of the page. You may use any available sources to help you develop your content, including accessing several commercial Web sites.

5. Open the Web page that you created in Step 4 from Tasks view. This page will describe the exchange process at Replay Music Factory. Create the page using your plan from Step 4. Use the background from the Home Page for this page.

Explore ▶ 6. Create a logo for this page using any graphics program. (If you do not have a graphics program, skip to Step 7.) Save your logo as a GIF file in the Tutorial.03 folder on your Data Disk.

7. Insert the GIF file you created in Step 6 at the top of the page. If you do not have access to a graphics program, use the **Deal.gif** file in the Tutorial.03 folder.

8. Save the Web page, and save all of the page's pictures in the images folder of the Replay Web site.

9. Use drag and drop to update the navigation bar in the page that you created in Step 5 to include hyperlinks to the other pages in the Web site that you added in Step 3.

10. Create a hotspot in the logo at the top of the page that you created in Step 5 that opens the Home Page. Save the Home Page, and then save the new page. Use Internet Explorer to test the hyperlinks and bookmarks that you created, and then close the browser.

11. Mark the task for creating the page that describes the exchange process as completed in the Tasks list, but do not delete the task.

12. Display your new page as the focus page in Hyperlinks view. If necessary, center the hyperlinks diagram in the Contents pane. Display the repeated hyperlinks and the hyperlinks to pictures, and then print Hyperlinks view using WordPad without saving changes. Close WordPad, and then turn off the display of the repeated hyperlinks and hyperlinks to pictures.

13. In FrontPage, print your new page. Then print its HTML code. On the printout, circle and label the HTML code entries that create the hyperlinks, bookmarks, background picture, and hotspot that you created.

14. Close FrontPage.

Quick | Check answers

Session 3.1

1. True
2. False
3. bulleted (unordered)
4. A list within another list
5. True
6. Increase Indent

Session 3.2

1. bookmark

2. icon

3. Create the bookmark in the page by selecting the text or location for it, clicking Insert on the menu bar, and then clicking Bookmark. Accept the default bookmark name or provide a name, and then click the OK button. Then select the text or location in the page that will contain the hyperlink to the bookmark, click the Hyperlink button on the Standard toolbar, click the Bookmark list arrow, select the bookmark, and then click the OK button.

4. A hyperlink to a location in the same Web page (an internal hyperlink)

5. True

6. hotspot

7. circle, rectangle, and polygon

8. Type it and then press the spacebar

9. False

Session 3.3

1. Tasks list

2. Just add Web task

3. New Page, Task

4. True

5. Mark as Completed

6. True

7. True

LAB ASSIGNMENTS

Web Pages & HTML

These Lab Assignments are designed to accompany the interactive Course Lab called Web Pages and HTML. To start the Web Pages and HTML Lab, click the Start button on the Windows taskbar, point to Programs, point to Course Labs, point to New Perspectives Applications, and then click Web Pages & HTML. If you do not see Course Labs on your Programs menu, see your instructor or technical support person.

Web Pages and HTML It's easy to create your own Web pages. As you learned in Tutorials 2 and 3, there are many software tools to help you become a Web author. In this Lab, you'll experiment with a Web authoring Wizard that automates the process of creating a Web page. You'll also try your hand at working directly with HTML code.

1. Click the Steps button to activate the Web authoring Wizard and learn how to create a basic Web page. As you proceed through the Steps, answer all of the Quick Check questions. After you complete the Steps, you will see a Quick Check summary Report. Follow the instructions on the screen to print this report.

2. In Explore, click the File menu, and then click New to start working on a new Web page. Use the Wizard to create a Home Page for a veterinarian who offers dog day-care and boarding services. After you create the page, save it on drive A or C, and print the HTML code. Your site must have the following characteristics:

   a. Title: Dr. Dave's Dog Domain
   b. Background color: Gold
   c. Picture: Dog.jpg
   d. Body text: Your dog will have the best care day and night at Dr. Dave's Dog Domain. Fine accommodations, good food, play time, and snacks are all provided. You can board your pet by the day or week. Grooming services also available.
   e. Text link: "Reasonable rates" links to **www.cciw.com/np3/rates.htm**
   f. E-mail link: "For more information:" links to **daveassist@drdave.com**

3. In Explore, use the File menu to open the HTML document called Politics.htm. After you use the HTML window (not the Wizard) to make the following changes, save the revised page on drive A or C, and then print the HTML code. Refer to the following table for a list of HTML tags you can use.

   a. Change the title to Politics 2000.
   b. Center the page heading.
   c. Change the background color to FFE7C6 and the text color to 000000.
   d. Add a line break before the sentence "What's next?".
   e. Add a bold tag to "Additional links on this topic:".
   f. Add one more link to the "Additional links" list. The link should go to the site **http://www.elections.ca** and the clickable link should read "Elections Canada".
   g. Change the last image to display the picture "next.gif".

4. In Explore, use the Web authoring Wizard and the HTML window to create a Home Page about yourself. You should include at least a screenful of text, a picture, an external link, and an e-mail link. Save the page on drive A, and then print the HTML code. Turn in your disk and printout.

HTML TAGS	MEANING AND LOCATION
<HTML></HTML>	States that the file is an HTML document. Opening tag begins the page; closing tag ends the page (required).
<HEAD></HEAD>	States that the enclosed text is the header of the page. Appears immediately after the opening HTML tag (required).
<TITLE></TITLE>	States that the enclosed text is the title of the page. Must appear within the opening and closing HEAD tags (required).
<BODY></BODY>	States that the enclosed material (all the text, pictures, and tags in the rest of the document) is the body of the document (required).
<H1></H1>	States that the enclosed text is a heading.
 	Inserts a line break. Can be used to control line spacing and breaks in lines.
<UL></UL> <OL></OL>	Indicates an unordered list (list items are preceded by bullets) or an ordered list (list items are preceded by numbers or letters).
<LI>	Indicates a list item. Precedes all items in unordered or ordered lists.
<CENTER></CENTER>	Indicates that the enclosed text should be centered across the width of the page.
<B></B>	Indicates that the enclosed text should be bold.
<I></I>	Indicates that the enclosed text should be italic.
<A HREF=" "> </A>	Indicates that the enclosed text is a hypertext link; the URL of the linked material must appear within the quotation marks after the equals sign.
<IMG SRC=" ">	Inserts picture into the document. The URL of the picture appears within the quotation marks following the SRC=" " attribute.
<HR>	Inserts a horizontal line.

OBJECTIVES

In this tutorial you will:

- Save a Web page from a World Wide Web site in a FrontPage Web

- Create a table in a Web page

- Modify a table's appearance and properties

- Split and merge cells in a table

- Enter data in a table

- Create a nested table

- Insert a picture in a table

- Create and edit a frames page

- Specify target frames in a frames page

- Print a frames page

- View the HTML code for a frames page

CREATING
TABLES AND FRAMES
IN A WEB PAGE

Completing the Investor Relations and Products Web Pages

CASE

Sunny Morning Products

During the design phase of the Sunny Morning Products Web site, Andrew Towle gave detailed requirements to Amanda Bay, who is heading the Web site development team. Andrew described his vision of the Investor Relations and Products pages. He wants the Investor Relations page to include the company's financial performance information and the Products page to include information about the products available from the Sunshine Country Store. Based on this feedback, Amanda prepared sketches of these Web pages and asked Andrew to approve them before starting their development.

In this tutorial, you will create the Investor Relations and Products pages for Sunny Morning Products. You will import and use Amanda's partially completed Web pages. As you develop each page, you will review Amanda's design notes and documentation to familiarize yourself with the necessary planning activities. Your main activities in completing these Web pages include adding a table to the Investor Relations page and creating frames for the Products page. As a management intern in the marketing department, you are especially interested in the Products page, because it will be used to accept online orders from the Sunshine Country Store.

SESSION 4.1

In this session, you will create and format a table in a Web page. You will change the alignment of a table and its cells; insert, select, and delete rows and columns; split and merge cells; resize table cells; enter data in a table; create a nested table; insert a picture in a cell; add a caption; and change a table's background color. Finally, you will test the table in the browser and examine its HTML code.

Reviewing the Tasks List

After your meeting with the Web site development team, Amanda asks you to review the Tasks list you created in Tutorial 3, which contains the tasks necessary to complete the Sunny Web site. After you review the list, Amanda wants you to meet with her to discuss the Investor Relations Web page, which you will create first.

To open the Sunny Web site and review the Tasks list:

1. Make sure your Data Disk is in the appropriate disk drive on your computer, start **FrontPage**, and then open the **Sunny** Web site (a:\My Webs\Sunny) from your Data Disk in Folders view.

2. Click the **Tasks** button 📝 on the Views bar to open the Tasks list.

3. If necessary, click the **Task** column heading to sort the revised list in ascending alphabetical order. See Figure 4-1.

Figure 4-1	CURRENT TASKS FOR THE SUNNY WEB SITE

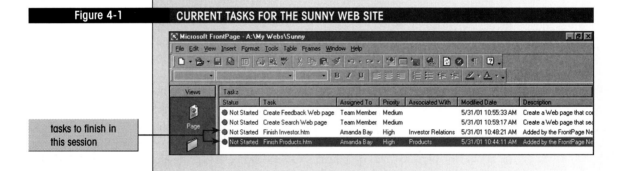

tasks to finish in
this session

The two Finish tasks show that you need to finish the Investor Relations and Products Web pages. You meet with Amanda, who asks you to finish her partially completed Investor Relations page first. Amanda stored her Web page on the World Wide Web site for Sunny Morning Products. You will retrieve her page from the site using a Web browser.

Saving a Web Page from a World Wide Web Site

In Tutorial 3, you learned how to import an HTML document stored on your Data Disk into a disk-based Web site. You can also import a Web page from a World Wide Web site into a FrontPage Web by opening the page in your browser and then using the Edit button on the Internet Explorer toolbar to open the page in FrontPage so you can save the page as part of your disk-based Web.

Amanda saved her partially completed Investor Relations Web page on the Web server for Sunny Morning Products. She asks you to replace the current, blank Investor Relations Web page that you created as part of the Tasks list in Tutorial 3 with the one that she stored on the company's Web server. When you replace a Web page, FrontPage overwrites the original Web page with the new one.

Regardless of the explicit copyrights placed on a Web page, you should *never* copy or revise a Web page without permission from the site's owner. A **copyright** is a right granted by law to an author or other entity to control the reproduction, publication, or distribution of the author's or entity's original work. Amanda tells you that reproducing a Web page from a Web site from which you do not have permission is a violation of copyright law. However, in this case, Sunny Morning Products owns the page that you will save, so you are not violating a copyright.

REFERENCE WINDOW   **RW**

Saving a Web Page from a World Wide Web Site
- Connect to the Internet and then use Internet Explorer to navigate to the Web page that you want to save.
- After the page has loaded, click the Edit button on the Standard Buttons toolbar. The Web page opens in FrontPage in Page view.
- Click File on the menu bar, and then click Save As. Use the Save As dialog box to save the Web page in the desired location on your computer.
- Click the Save button.

Note: You must be able to connect to the Internet to complete the next set of steps. In these tutorials, you will navigate to the Course Technology Web site to simulate using the Web server for Sunny Morning Products.

To save a Web page from a World Wide Web site:

1. Click the **Start** button on the taskbar, point to **Programs**, and then click **Internet Explorer** to start the browser. If necessary, click the **Connect** button to connect to the Internet through your Internet service provider.

   TROUBLE? If you are not using Internet Explorer as your browser, start the correct browser. The steps that you will complete might be slightly different; if necessary, ask your instructor or technical support person for help.

   TROUBLE? If you cannot connect to the Internet, click the Cancel button in the Dial-up Connection dialog box, and then click the Work Offline button to close it. You will use the Investor Relations page that is saved on your Data Disk to simulate saving a page from a Web site. In the browser, type a:\Tutorial.04\Investor.htm in the Address bar, and then press the Enter key to load the Investor.htm page that is stored on your Data Disk. Continue with Step 4.

2. Select the current URL in the Address bar, type **http://course.com/downloads/ newperspectives/fp2000/investor.htm**, and then press the **Enter** key. The Investor Relations page opens in the browser. See Figure 4-2.

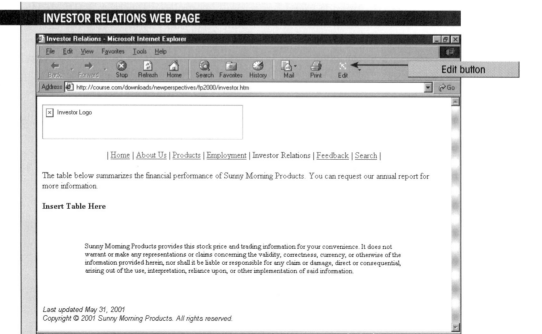

Figure 4-2   INVESTOR RELATIONS WEB PAGE

3. Click the **Edit** button on the Standard Buttons toolbar. After a moment, FrontPage becomes the active program, and the investor.htm page from the Web site opens in Page view.

   TROUBLE? If you do not see on the Standard Buttons toolbar, click the button on the right side of the Standard Buttons toolbar, and then click in the list.

   TROUBLE? If Notepad or Microsoft Word starts and opens the investor.htm page, then your copy of Internet Explorer is configured to use one of these programs as its default Web page editor. Click the Close button to close Notepad or Word, and then, if necessary, click the Internet Explorer program button on the taskbar to return to Internet Explorer. Click the list arrow for , and then click Edit with Microsoft FrontPage in the list to start FrontPage and open the investor.htm page. Continue with Step 4.

   TROUBLE? If your Edit button does not have an option to open the page in FrontPage, close Internet Explorer, and then return to FrontPage. In Folders view, use the Import command on the File menu to import the investor.htm file from the Tutorial.04 folder on your Data Disk into the Sunny Web site. Click the Yes button to overwrite the existing file and then skip to Step 6.

   TROUBLE? If the page background is white, instead of the same as the Home Page background, click Format on the menu bar, click Background, click the Get background information from another page check box, click the Browse button and double-click index.htm, and then click the OK button.

   If you have the necessary permission, you could edit the Investor Relations page and then send the revised file back to the Web server to update it. However, Amanda asks you to save the Investor Relations page in the Sunny Web site, so you can edit it as part of your disk-based Web. In Tutorial 6, you will publish your Web site to a Web server, which will update the site's contents.

4. In FrontPage, click **File** on the menu bar, and then click **Save As**. The Save As dialog box opens. You need to specify the Sunny Web site on your Data Disk as the location in which to save the Web page.

5. Click the **Look in** list arrow, change to the drive or folder that contains your Data Disk, double-click the **My Webs** folder, and then double-click the **Sunny** folder. Make sure that the File name text box displays the filename "Investor," and then click the **Save** button. A dialog box opens and asks if you want to replace the investor.htm page that you added with the Tasks list in Tutorial 3. Click the **Yes** button to continue.

   Now the Investor Relations Web page is saved in the Sunny Web site on your Data Disk. However, you must add the logo to the page and save it in the Sunny Web site before continuing.

6. Right-click the broken link at the top of the page to open the shortcut menu, click **Picture Properties** to open that dialog box, and click the **Browse** button to the right of the Picture source text box. Click the **Select a file on your computer** button 🔍 in the Picture dialog box, open the **Tutorial.04** folder on your Data Disk, and then double-click **Invest**. Click the **OK** button in the Picture Properties dialog box to close it.

   The logo now appears at the top of the Investor Relations page. Next, save the Web page with the embedded picture.

7. Click the **Save** button 💾 on the Standard toolbar. The Save Embedded Files dialog box opens. Make sure that the location to save the file is the Sunny Web site's images folder, and then click the **OK** button.

8. Click the **Internet Explorer** program button on the taskbar to reopen that program, and then click the **Close** button ❌ on the title bar to close it. If necessary, close your dial-up connection, as well.

The partially completed Investor Relations Web page contains all the desired content, except for a table that summarizes the company's financial performance over the past two years. Next, Amanda wants you to add this table to the Web page.

Understanding **Tables**

A **table** consists of one or more rows of cells that organize and arrange data. A **cell** is the smallest component of a table. You can place text or a picture in a table cell. You can also create a **nested table**, which is a table within a table cell.

If your Web site development plan includes a Web page with a table, you should sketch on paper how you want the table to appear before you create it using FrontPage. Sketching a table first helps you plan how many rows and columns you will need. You can add or delete columns after creating the table, but it is easier to create the table correctly from the start.

The steps you take to create a table using FrontPage are similar to those you would use to create a table with Microsoft Word. For smaller-sized tables, you use the **Insert Table button grid**—a toolbar button that displays a miniature table four rows high by five columns wide—to specify the table's size. If your table is relatively small (fewer than four rows by five columns), you can click a cell in the lower-right corner of the grid to specify the desired table size. If you need to create a table that is larger than four rows by five columns, you can click and drag the last cell in the grid to create a table with the desired number of rows and columns.

When creating a table in FrontPage, you must specify table properties, such as the size of the border, the cell padding, the cell spacing, and the table width. A **border** is a line that surrounds each cell and the entire table. **Cell padding** is the distance between the contents of a cell and the inside edge of the cell, measured in pixels. **Cell spacing** is the distance between table cells, also measured in pixels. Increasing the cell spacing increases the distance between the borders that surround each cell.

You can specify the table width as a percentage of the width of the screen or as a fixed width in pixels. Remember that HTML documents will be displayed by a variety of computers that have monitors with different resolutions. Most developers set column widths for a table as a percentage of the page's width (such as 85%), rather than as a fixed measurement (such as 100 pixels wide). You need to specify these types of settings to ensure that all users of your Web page—regardless of their monitors, computers, or Web browsers—will be able to view your tables correctly.

When you use FrontPage to create a table, each cell in the table is specified by individual HTML tags. A simple three-row and three-column table can generate 20 or more lines of HTML code.

Figure 4-3 shows Amanda's sketch of the summary of financial performance table that you will create in the Investor Relations Web page. Amanda shows you the left, center, and right alignments used for the column headings and numbers in the table. Although her sketch is complete for now, Amanda tells you that you might need to revise the table's design and appearance as you complete your work. Changes are a normal part of the evolution of any Web page.

Figure 4-3   SKETCH OF THE SUMMARY OF FINANCIAL PERFORMANCE TABLE

After you review the table, Amanda asks you to also review the planning analysis sheet, shown in Figure 4-4, which she created when planning the development of the Investor Relations Web page.

Figure 4-4	AMANDA'S PLANNING ANALYSIS SHEET FOR THE INVESTOR RELATIONS WEB PAGE

Planning Analysis Sheet

Objective

Create an Investor Relations Web page that contains a table of financial performance information.

Requirements

Partially completed Investor Relations Web page

Financial performance information for the past two fiscal years, including sales
            revenue, net income, price per share, and earnings per share

Approval of table layout sketch

Logo for the first table cell

Results

Investor Relations Web page with the following information:

            Company logo and navigation bar

            Introductory paragraph

            Financial performance information in a table format

            Common background with the Home Page

Creating a Table in a Web Page

After sketching your table and securing the necessary approval from the Web site development team, you are ready to create it in the desired location in the Web page.

When Amanda prepared the Investor Relations page, she typed a placeholder in the page indicating the intended location of the table. With the Investor Relations page now included in the Sunny Web site, you are ready to create the summary of financial performance table.

To insert the table:

1. With the Investor Relations Web page still displayed in Page view, select the **Insert Table Here** text. This is where you will insert the table.

2. Click the **Insert Table** button 🖽 on the Standard toolbar to open the Insert Table button grid. You might notice that this is the same Insert Table button grid that Word uses.

3. Click and hold down the mouse button on the cell in the lower-right corner of the grid, and then hold down the mouse button while you drag the grid down and to the right to expand it to a size of 5 rows and 9 columns. See Figure 4-5.

Figure 4-5	INSERT TABLE BUTTON GRID

use button grid to specify the table's size

drag pointer to here and release the mouse button to create a table with five rows and nine columns

table will be created here

4. Release the mouse button. A table that contains five rows and nine columns replaces the "Insert Table Here" text that you selected in the Web page. The insertion point is blinking in the first cell of the table.

TROUBLE? If you clicked the cell in the lower-right corner of the grid and did not hold down the mouse button, a 4-row by 5-column table is inserted. Click the Undo button 🖴 on the Standard toolbar, and then repeat Steps 1 through 4.

5. Right-click anywhere in the table that you just inserted to open the shortcut menu, and then click **Table Properties** to open the Table Properties dialog box. See Figure 4-6. This dialog box lets you specify the table's properties and characteristics.

Figure 4-6 | **TABLE PROPERTIES DIALOG BOX**

options for changing cell spacing and padding

option for changing the border size between cells

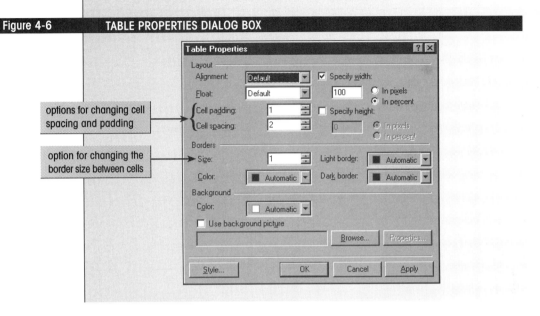

Amanda's sketch of the table (see Figure 4-3) indicates centered column headings and split and merged cells. The first cell in the table is not split. The row headings are left-aligned, and the numbers in the cells are right-aligned. The values in the table are fairly close together, which indicates lower padding and spacing values. You will format the table to Amanda's design specifications next. To help position the insertion point correctly, you will turn on the display of nonprinting characters. **Nonprinting characters** are symbols in a Web page, such as paragraph marks.

To format the table and turn on the nonprinting characters:

1. In the Borders section, click the **Size up** arrow to change the border size to **2**.

2. In the Layout section, click the **Cell padding up** arrow to change the cell padding to **4**, and then click the **Cell spacing up** arrow to change the cell spacing to **3**. These settings will increase the spacing between cells in the table, which will make the table's contents easier to read.

3. Make sure that the Specify width check box in the Layout section is selected (that is, it contains a check mark). Select **100** or the current value in the Specify width text box and type **95**, and then make sure that the In percent option button is selected. This setting specifies that your table will be displayed at 95% of the browser's window size.

4. Click the **OK** button. The Table Properties dialog box closes, and the new table properties are applied to it.

5. If necessary, scroll down the page so you see the entire table. The table contains empty cells.

   Amanda explains that tables are easier to work with when you can see the nonprinting characters. She asks you to turn on this feature next.

6. Click the **Show All** button ¶ on the Standard toolbar to turn on the display of nonprinting characters. See Figure 4-7. Notice that the cells have a left alignment, as indicated by the paragraph marks appearing in the left side of each cell.

Figure 4-7	INVESTOR RELATIONS PAGE WITH TABLE INSERTED

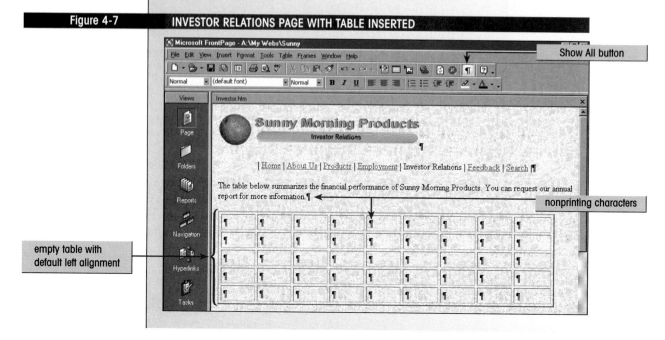

You inserted the table in the correct location in the page. Amanda thinks that the table will look better if it is centered in the page.

Aligning a Table

A table's alignment in a Web page is different from the alignment of the data in the table's cells. A table can have only one alignment, whereas the cells in the table can have different alignments. The alignment of a table and the alignment of a table's cells are specified using different HTML tags. To specify a different alignment for the entire table, you need to change the table's properties.

REFERENCE WINDOW   **RW**

Aligning a Table in a Web Page
- Right-click anywhere in the table to select it and to open the shortcut menu, and then click Table Properties.
or
- Click anywhere in the table to select it, click Table on the menu bar, point to Properties, and then click Table.
- In the Table Properties dialog box, click the Alignment list arrow in the Layout section, click the desired alignment, and then click the OK button.

The table you inserted in the Investor Relations Web page is left-aligned, which is the default alignment. Amanda wants this table to be center-aligned to give it a more balanced appearance when viewed in the browser. She asks you to center the table next.

To align a table in a Web page:

1. Right-click anywhere in the table to open the shortcut menu, and then click **Table Properties** to open that dialog box.

2. In the Layout section, click the **Alignment** list arrow, and then click **Center**. Selecting this option will center-align the table (but not the data in the table's cells) in the page.

3. Click the **OK** button. The Table Properties dialog box closes and the table's alignment changes to centered. See Figure 4-8.

| Figure 4-8 | CENTERED TABLE IN THE WEB PAGE |

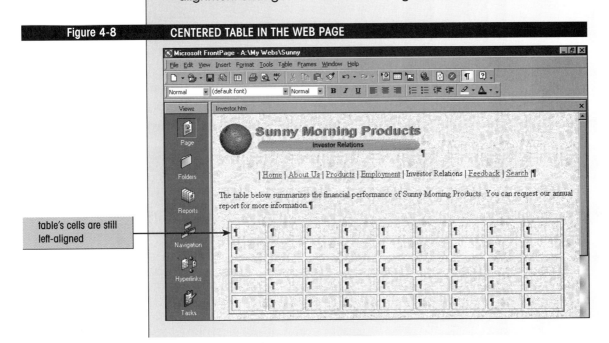

table's cells are still left-aligned

Inserting Rows and Columns in a Table

After creating a table, you can insert additional rows and columns as needed—either before or after entering data in the table's cells. After approving the table's initial design, Andrew wants to include another row and column to contain data about the average annual return for earnings. Amanda asks you to accommodate this change by inserting one row and one column in the table. First Amanda asks you to display the **Tables toolbar**, which provides tools specific to creating and formatting tables. Then you will insert the new row and column.

To display the Tables toolbar:

1. Click **View** on the menu bar, point to **Toolbars**, and then click **Tables**. The Tables toolbar opens. Depending on your system configuration, the toolbar might display as a docked or floating toolbar anywhere in Page view.

   TROUBLE? If a check mark already appeared in front of the Tables command on the Toolbars menu, then the toolbar was already selected and displayed. When you clicked Tables, you hid the toolbar. Repeat Step 1 to display it again.

2. If necessary, drag the Tables toolbar to the top of the Contents pane so it does not block the table. See Figure 4-9.

Figure 4-9	DISPLAYING THE TABLES TOOLBAR

Tables toolbar (yours might appear in a different location)

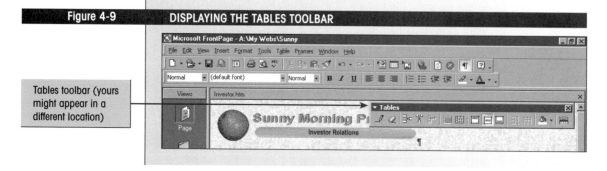

Figure 4-10 describes the tools available on the Tables toolbar.

Figure 4-10	TABLES TOOLBAR BUTTONS AND THEIR DESCRIPTIONS	
BUTTON NAME	**BUTTON**	**FUNCTION**
Draw Table		Lets you draw a new table using the pointer, which changes to a pencil shape, or modify an existing table by drawing lines to indicate rows and columns
Eraser		Lets you use the pointer, which changes to an eraser shape, to erase a row or column in an existing table or to merge cells
Insert Rows		Inserts a new row in a table above the selected row
Insert Columns		Inserts a new column in a table to the left of the selected column
Delete Cells		Deletes the selected cells
Merge Cells		Merges the selected cells into one larger cell
Split Cells		Splits the selected cell into one or more cells
Align Top		Vertically aligns the data in the selected cells at the top of the cells
Center Vertically		Vertically centers the data in the selected cells
Align Bottom		Vertically aligns the data in the selected cells at the bottom of the cells
Distribute Rows Evenly		Changes the height of the selected rows to equal measurements
Distribute Columns Evenly		Changes the width of the selected columns to equal measurements
Fill Color		Lets you change the background color of the selected cells to a standard or custom color
AutoFit		Changes the width of the selected columns in a table to best fit the data they contain

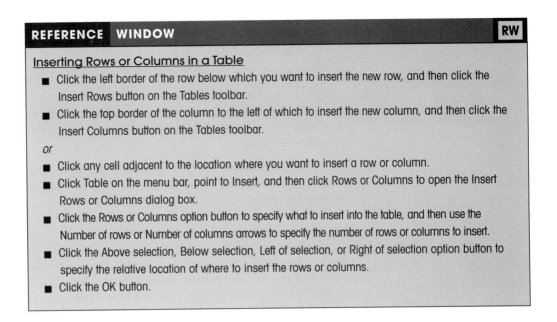

Inserting Rows or Columns in a Table

- Click the left border of the row below which you want to insert the new row, and then click the Insert Rows button on the Tables toolbar.
- Click the top border of the column to the left of which to insert the new column, and then click the Insert Columns button on the Tables toolbar.

or

- Click any cell adjacent to the location where you want to insert a row or column.
- Click Table on the menu bar, point to Insert, and then click Rows or Columns to open the Insert Rows or Columns dialog box.
- Click the Rows or Columns option button to specify what to insert into the table, and then use the Number of rows or Number of columns arrows to specify the number of rows or columns to insert.
- Click the Above selection, Below selection, Left of selection, or Right of selection option button to specify the relative location of where to insert the rows or columns.
- Click the OK button.

With the Tables toolbar displayed, you can insert the new row and column. Because your table is empty, you could insert the new row and column anywhere in the table. You will insert a new fourth row and a new second-to-last column so that you will gain experience in adding rows and columns in different locations in the table.

To insert a row and a column in the table:

1. Move the pointer to the left border of the third row in the table so the pointer changes to a ➡ shape, and then click the left border to select the third row of the table. See Figure 4-11. When you insert the new row, it will appear above the selected row.

Figure 4-11	SELECTING AND INSERTING A ROW IN A TABLE

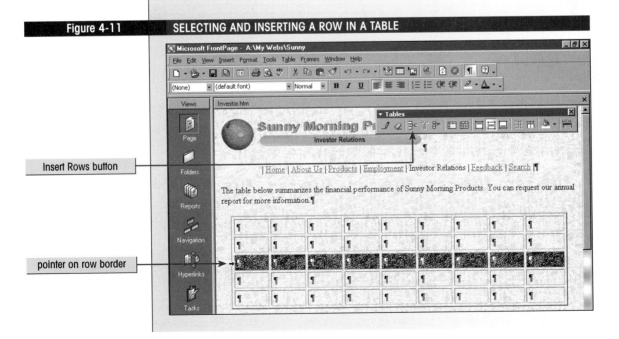

Insert Rows button

pointer on row border

2. Click the **Insert Rows** button ⊞ on the Tables toolbar. A new row is inserted above the selected row.

Next, insert a column before the last column in the table.

3. Move the pointer to the top border of the last column in the table so the pointer changes to a ↓ shape, and then click the top border to select the last column in the table. When you insert the new column, it will appear to the left of the selected column.

4. Click the **Insert Columns** button 🗗 on the Tables toolbar to insert the new column, and then click the cell in row 1, column 1 to deselect the new column. Your table now contains six rows and 10 columns.

With the addition of the new row and column to the table, Amanda is concerned about the readability of the table for users who have monitors with lower screen resolutions. She asks you to delete the row and column that you just added. You could click the Undo button on the Standard toolbar twice to cancel the insertion of the column and the row, but Amanda wants you to learn how to select and delete rows and columns as part of your training.

Selecting and Deleting Rows or Columns

Even when you sketch a table before inserting it in a Web page, you sometimes might need to add or delete rows and columns to create the right table to contain your data. The process of deleting rows or columns is straightforward. First, you select the table row or column that you want to delete, or drag the pointer over a group of cells in several rows and columns. If you need to select more than one row or column at a time, hold down the Ctrl key while you select the other rows or columns. These selection methods are similar to those you use when selecting table cells in Word. After selecting the cells, rows, or columns to delete, click the Delete Cells button on the Tables toolbar.

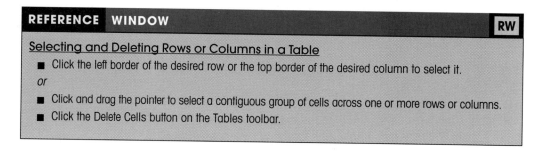

REFERENCE WINDOW **RW**

Selecting and Deleting Rows or Columns in a Table
- Click the left border of the desired row or the top border of the desired column to select it.
or
- Click and drag the pointer to select a contiguous group of cells across one or more rows or columns.
- Click the Delete Cells button on the Tables toolbar.

Amanda wants you to delete the third row and the second-to-last column from the table.

To select and delete a row and column from a table:

1. Click ➡ on the left border of the third row in the table to select the row. Amanda wants you to select the fourth row in the table, as well, to practice selecting multiple rows.

2. Hold down the **Ctrl** key, click ➡ on the border for the fourth row, and then release the **Ctrl** key. Now the third and fourth rows are selected.

3. Click ➡ on the third row. Only the third row is selected now.

4. Click the **Delete Cells** button 🔳 on the Tables toolbar. The third row is deleted from the table.

5. Click ⬇ on the top border of the second-to-last column in the table to select it, and then click 🔳 to delete it. Now your table contains five rows and nine columns.

Next Amanda asks you to create the column headings for the summary of financial performance table.

Splitting **and Merging Table Cells**

There are many ways to arrange the information in a table. One popular method is to include column headings to identify the data displayed in each column. You can arrange the cells in a row or column by splitting and merging cells. **Splitting cells** is the process of dividing a single cell into two or more rows or columns, whereas **merging cells** is the process of combining two or more cells in a row or column to form a single cell.

Splitting Table Cells

For the summary of financial performance table, Amanda wants you to split the cells in the eight columns that will contain the column headings for each quarter. You will not split the first cell in the first column because you will insert a picture in this cell later.

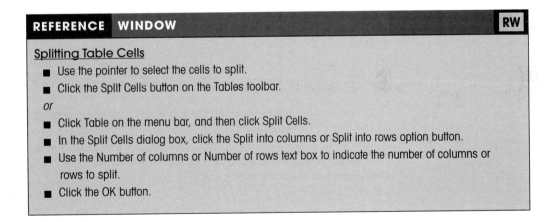

REFERENCE   WINDOW   **RW**

Splitting Table Cells
- Use the pointer to select the cells to split.
- Click the Split Cells button on the Tables toolbar.

or

- Click Table on the menu bar, and then click Split Cells.
- In the Split Cells dialog box, click the Split into columns or Split into rows option button.
- Use the Number of columns or Number of rows text box to indicate the number of columns or rows to split.
- Click the OK button.

Next, split the cells that will contain the column headings for the table.

To split cells:

1. Click the left border of the first row in the table to select it, press and hold down the **Ctrl** key, and then click the cell in row 1, column 1 to deselect it so this cell will not be split. Now cells 2 through 9 in the first row are selected.

2. Click the **Split Cells** button 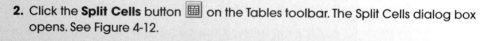 on the Tables toolbar. The Split Cells dialog box opens. See Figure 4-12.

Figure 4-12	SPLIT CELLS DIALOG BOX

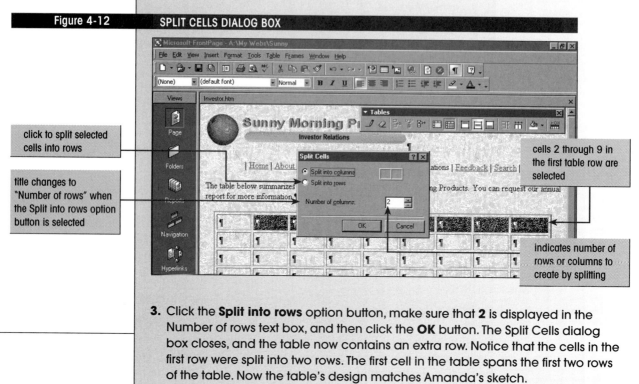

click to split selected cells into rows

title changes to "Number of rows" when the Split into rows option button is selected

cells 2 through 9 in the first table row are selected

indicates number of rows or columns to create by splitting

3. Click the **Split into rows** option button, make sure that **2** is displayed in the Number of rows text box, and then click the **OK** button. The Split Cells dialog box closes, and the table now contains an extra row. Notice that the cells in the first row were split into two rows. The first cell in the table spans the first two rows of the table. Now the table's design matches Amanda's sketch.

Now that you have split the cells, you are ready to create the cells that will contain the year column headings in the table.

Merging Table Cells

According to Amanda's sketch of the table, the cells containing the year headings will appear at the top of the columns that contain the information for their respective four quarters. Unlike some spreadsheet programs, HTML does not provide tags to center text across several columns, so you need to merge the cells that will span multiple rows or columns. To create the headings for each year, you need to merge each set of four cells in the first row into single cells.

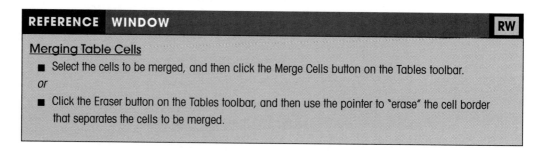

REFERENCE WINDOW   **RW**

Merging Table Cells
- Select the cells to be merged, and then click the Merge Cells button on the Tables toolbar.
or
- Click the Eraser button on the Tables toolbar, and then use the pointer to "erase" the cell border that separates the cells to be merged.

Amanda next asks you to merge the cells for the year headings.

To merge cells:

1. Click the cell in row 1, column 2, press and hold down the **Shift** key, click the cell in row 1, column 5, and then release the mouse button and the **Shift** key to select cells 2 through 5 in row 1. See Figure 4-13.

Figure 4-13   **TABLE WITH SELECTED CELLS**

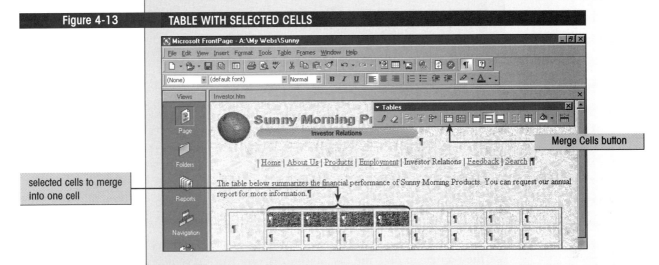

2. Click the **Merge Cells** button on the Tables toolbar. Click the cell in row 1, column 1 to deselect the merged cell, which is now one long cell in the row that spans the four columns below it. You will enter the column heading "Fiscal Year 1999" in this merged cell later. Now you can merge the cells for the "Fiscal Year 2000" column heading. Amanda wants you to use the Eraser to merge the second set of cells.

3. Click the **Eraser** button on the Tables toolbar to select this tool.

4. Move the pointer over the border between the cells in row 1 and columns 6 and 7. As you move the pointer back and forth across the border, the pointer changes from a ↔ shape to a ✐ shape. See Figure 4-14.

Figure 4-14   **USING THE ERASER TO MERGE CELLS**

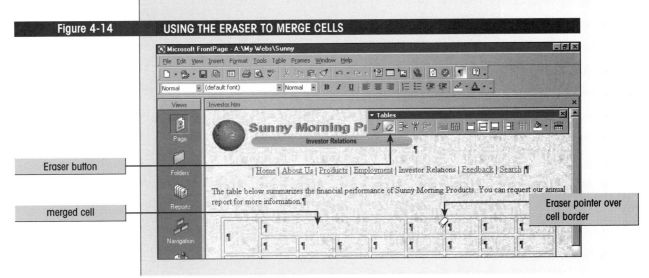

5. Press and hold down the mouse button, and then drag the pointer across the border between the cells in row 1, columns 6 and 7. The border turns red to show that you are erasing it. Release the mouse button to merge these cells.

TROUBLE? If you erase the wrong border, click the Undo button on the Standard toolbar to undo your change.

6. Repeat Step 5 to erase the borders between the cells in row 1, columns 7 and 8, and in row 1, columns 8 and 9. Now the first row contains two merged cells that will serve as your column headings.

7. Click on the Tables toolbar to turn off the Eraser.

The table organization is complete: You have split and merged the appropriate cells to match Amanda's table design.

Resizing **Rows and Columns**

Your next task is to widen the first column to make room for the headings that Amanda designed for these rows. The easiest way to resize a column is by using the pointer—you just click and drag the column's right border to the left to decrease the column's width, or click and drag the column's right border to the right to increase the column's width. You can also use the pointer to drag the bottom border of a row up to decrease its height or down to increase its height.

REFERENCE WINDOW   **RW**

Resizing a Row or Column in a Table
- Select the row or column that you want to resize.
- For a row, click and drag the bottom border down to increase the row's height, or click and drag the bottom border up to decrease the row's height.

or
- For a column, click and drag the right border to the left to decrease the column's width, or click and drag the right border to the right to increase the column's width.
- Release the mouse button when the column or row is the desired size.

Amanda's table design shows that the first column is wider than the other columns. The other columns in the table should have equal widths.

To resize a column in a table:

1. Click ⬇ on the top border of the first column to select it.

2. Click and drag the right border of the selected column to the right. When the dotted vertical line is positioned as shown in Figure 4-15, release the mouse button.

| Figure 4-15 | RESIZING A COLUMN'S WIDTH |

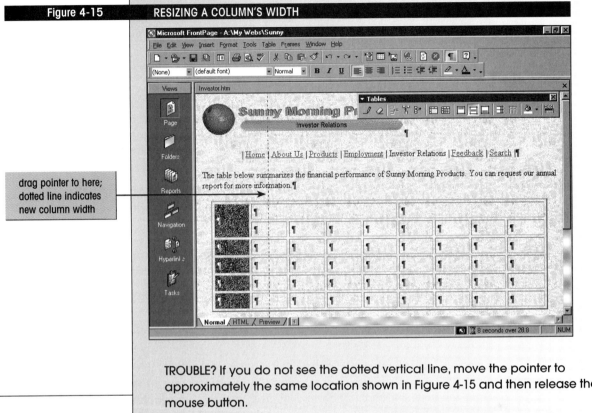

drag pointer to here; dotted line indicates new column width

TROUBLE? If you do not see the dotted vertical line, move the pointer to approximately the same location shown in Figure 4-15 and then release the mouse button.

3. Click the cell in row 1, column 1 to deselect the first column.

Notice that the width of the second column decreased by more than half of its original size when you resized the first column. You could increase the size of each column in columns 2 through 9 individually, but a faster and more accurate way of resizing columns is to select them as a group and use the Distribute Columns Evenly button on the Tables toolbar.

To distribute the columns evenly:

1. Click the cell in row 2, column 2, press and hold down the **Shift** key, click the cell in row 6, column 9, and then release the mouse button and the **Shift** key. The cells are selected. See Figure 4-16.

Figure 4-16   SELECTING A GROUP OF CELLS

2. Click the **Distribute Columns Evenly** button [icon] on the Tables toolbar. Notice that the cells' widths are not exactly equal; the widths of the cells in columns 2 through 5 are equal, and the widths of the cells in columns 6 through 9 are equal. To make the widths of the cells in columns 2 through 9 equal, you need to click [icon] again.

3. Click [icon] again. Now all of the selected cells have approximately the same width. Click the cell in row 1, column 1 to deselect the cells.

You can select rows and use the Distribute Rows Evenly button on the Tables toolbar to change the heights of a group of selected rows to the same measurement, as well. Now you can enter the data into the table.

Entering Data in a Table

Entering data in a table in a Web page is similar to entering table data in a Word document or in an Excel worksheet. You position the insertion point in the cell where you want to enter the data, and then type the data. You move the insertion point into a cell either by clicking in the cell or by pressing the appropriate arrow keys or the Tab key. Begin by adding the text for the column headings.

To enter data in a table:

1. Click the cell in row 1, column 2, and then type **Fiscal Year 1999**.

TROUBLE? If you aren't sure where to enter the column heading in the table, refer to the table's sketch in Figure 4-3.

2. Press the **Tab** key to move to the next column, and then type **Fiscal Year 2000**.

3. Enter the data shown in Figure 4-17 in the table. Press the **Tab** key after typing the data in a cell to move the insertion point to the next cell or row. Do not press the Tab key after typing the data in the last cell in the table or you will create a new row. The automatic line wrap feature expands the cells containing the row headings (Sales revenue, Net income, Price per share, and Earnings per share) so that all the text fits in one cell. Your completed table should look like Figure 4-17.

Figure 4-17   **COMPLETED TABLE WITH DATA ENTERED**

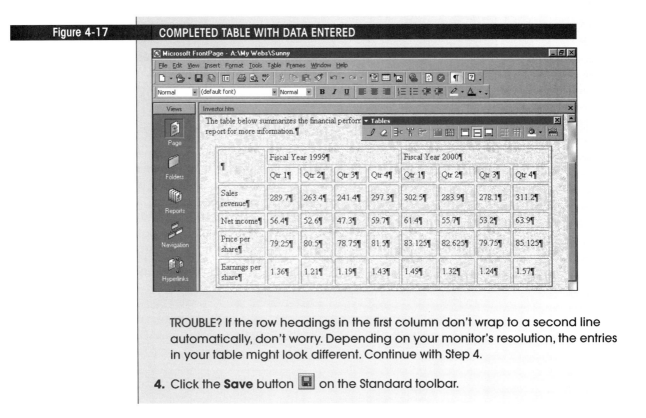

TROUBLE? If the row headings in the first column don't wrap to a second line automatically, don't worry. Depending on your monitor's resolution, the entries in your table might look different. Continue with Step 4.

4. Click the **Save** button 🖫 on the Standard toolbar.

Andrew still wants to include the average earnings per share amount for each year's data in the table. Amanda explains that adding the row and column to the table might compromise the table's readability, and she suggests an alternative to adding the new columns. She asks you to create a nested table to store the new data.

Creating a Nested Table

When you need to add additional data in a cell, but not to an entire table, you can use a nested table to hold the new data. A nested table is a separate table in the cell that contains it in the main table.

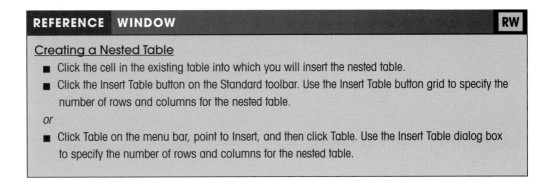

REFERENCE WINDOW   **RW**

Creating a Nested Table
- Click the cell in the existing table into which you will insert the nested table.
- Click the Insert Table button on the Standard toolbar. Use the Insert Table button grid to specify the number of rows and columns for the nested table.

or
- Click Table on the menu bar, point to Insert, and then click Table. Use the Insert Table dialog box to specify the number of rows and columns for the nested table.

Amanda asks you to create two nested tables—one for each year—in the current table.

To create the nested tables:

1. Click the cell in row 6, column 5 to select it, and then press the **End** key to position the insertion point at the end of the data in this cell.

2. Click the **Insert Table** button 🖾 on the Standard toolbar, and then click the first cell in the second row in the Insert Table button grid (a 2 by 1 table). A table with two rows and one column appears in the selected cell below the current cell value.

3. Click the first cell of the nested table, and then type **Average Return**.

4. Press the **Tab** key, and then type **1.2975**.

5. Click the last cell in the last row of the table, press the **End** key, and then repeat Step 2 to create a nested table with two rows and one column. Type **Average Return** in the first cell of the nested table, press the **Tab** key, and then type **1.405** in the second cell of the nested table. See Figure 4-18.

| Figure 4-18 | TABLE WITH TWO NESTED TABLES |

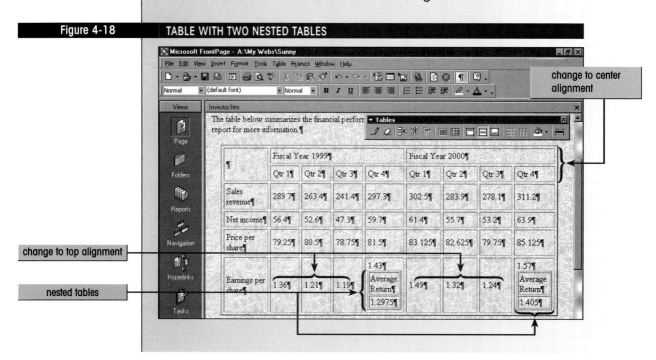

The data that you entered in the table's cells is left-aligned, which is the default alignment for cells. However, Amanda's sketch of the table shows that this data should be right-aligned. You also need to center-align the table's headings. The nested tables that you added to the main table cause the fourth quarter earnings per share amounts to display higher in the cells than the values for the other quarters. You will correct all of these problems next.

Aligning **Cell Contents**

In addition to the horizontal alignment of left, center, and right, you can also select a vertical alignment of top, middle, or bottom for cells. These two different alignments—horizontal and vertical—are specified using different HTML tags. Middle is the default vertical alignment, and left is the default horizontal alignment.

You align cell contents by selecting the cells and specifying the desired alignment. You specify a selected cell's horizontal alignment using the alignment buttons on the Formatting toolbar. You specify a selected cell's vertical alignment using the alignment buttons on the Tables toolbar.

To align table data:

1. Use the pointer to select rows 1 and 2 at the top of the table, containing the year and quarter number column headings and the empty cell in row 1, column 1.

2. Click the **Center** button ▦ on the Formatting toolbar to center the data horizontally in these cells. The default vertical alignment for cells is middle (centered), so these cells are correctly aligned. Next you will top-align the cells that contain the earnings per share data for quarters 1 through 3 for fiscal year 1999.

3. Click the cell in row 6, column 2 (which contains the data 1.36), press and hold down the **Shift** key, click the cell in row 6, column 4 (which contains the data 1.19), release the mouse button and the **Shift** key, and then click the **Align Top** button 🔲 on the Tables toolbar. The cells that contain the earnings per share data for quarters 1 through 3 of fiscal year 1999 now have a top vertical alignment to match the earnings per share data for quarter 4 of fiscal year 1999. The cells that contain the nested tables already appear to have the top alignment, so you don't need to change their alignments to top.

4. Select cells 6 through 8 in the last row (which contain the data 1.49, 1.32, and 1.24), and then click 🔲 to apply the top alignment to these cells. Click the cell in row 1, column 1 to deselect the cells. Now the values in the Earnings per share row are easier to read. See Figure 4-19.

| Figure 4-19 | TABLE WITH TOP-ALIGNED CELLS IN LAST ROW |

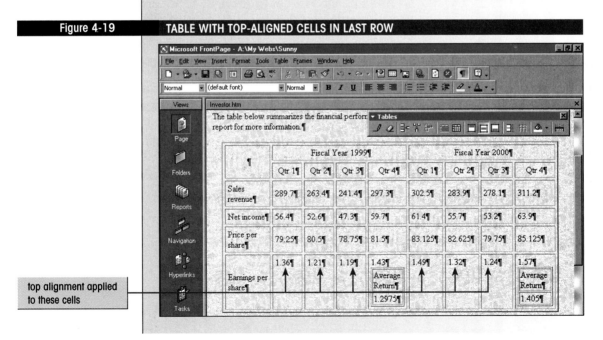

top alignment applied to these cells

Next, Amanda wants you to change the horizontal alignment of the numeric data in the table to right. Right-aligning financial data is the standard when including currency amounts in a financial document.

> *To right-align numeric data in a table:*
>
> **1.** Select the cells in rows 3 through 6 and columns 2 through 9.
>
> **2.** Click the **Align Right** button 🔲 on the Formatting toolbar to right-align the data in these cells.
>
> **3.** Click the cell in row 1, column 1 to deselect the cells.
>
> **4.** Click the **Save** button 🔲 on the Standard toolbar.

Inserting **a Picture in a Table**

You can insert a picture in any table cell. If the picture is larger than the cell that holds it, FrontPage adjusts the size of the cell automatically to accommodate the picture's size. You follow the same process for inserting a picture in a cell as when inserting a picture elsewhere in a Web page. The only difference is that you select a cell as the location for the picture, instead of selecting a line in the Web page. Amanda already created a logo file that she wants you to include as a picture in the first cell of the table.

> *To insert a picture in a table cell:*
>
> **1.** With the insertion point in the cell in row 1, column 1, click the **Insert Picture From File** button 🔲 on the Standard toolbar to open the Picture dialog box, and then click the **Select a file on your computer** button 🔍 to open the Select File dialog box.
>
> **2.** Make sure the drive or folder that contains your Data Disk appears in the Look in list box, double-click the **Tutorial.04** folder (if necessary), and then double-click **Finperf**. The Select File and Picture dialog boxes close, and the logo appears in the first cell of the table. Notice that the cell's size adjusts automatically to accommodate the picture. See Figure 4-20.

| Figure 4-20 | LOGO INSERTED IN THE FIRST TABLE CELL |

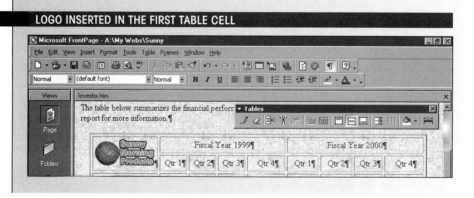

Amanda also wants you to add a caption to the table to identify its contents.

Adding **a Table Caption**

A **table caption** is a title that appears either above or below a table. The table caption can contain one or more lines of text. Although the table caption appears to be a part of the table, a caption actually resides outside of the table's border and is created by a separate HTML tag. When you insert a caption, its default location is above the table. However, you can relocate a caption by clicking the Caption Properties command on the table's shortcut menu.

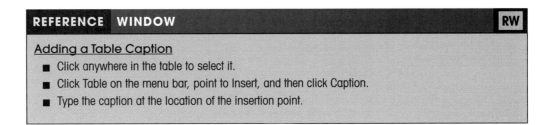

REFERENCE WINDOW | **RW**

Adding a Table Caption
- Click anywhere in the table to select it.
- Click Table on the menu bar, point to Insert, and then click Caption.
- Type the caption at the location of the insertion point.

Amanda asks you to add a caption at the top of the table.

To add a table caption:

1. Click anywhere in the table to select it.

2. Click **Table** on the menu bar, point to **Insert**, and then click **Caption**. A new line appears above the table, and the insertion point moves to the new line automatically. This new line is the table's caption. Although the caption *looks* like any other line in Page view, the caption is formatted as an HTML caption and not as a new line.

3. Type **Summary of Financial Performance**.

4. Select the **Summary of Financial Performance** caption, and then click the **Bold** button B on the Formatting toolbar to change the caption to bold text.

5. Click anywhere in the Summary of Financial Performance caption to deselect it.

After adding a caption to a table, you can change its properties. For example, you might want to set the caption on two lines, or you might want to place one or more blank lines between the caption and the table. You can press Shift + Enter to create a new line in your caption. Another way to change an existing caption's properties is to use the settings in the Caption Properties dialog box.

Amanda wants you to move the caption to below the table to see if this looks better.

To change caption properties and save the Web page:

1. Right-click the **Summary of Financial Performance** caption to open the shortcut menu, and then click **Caption Properties** to open that dialog box. See Figure 4-21.

Figure 4-21   **CAPTION PROPERTIES DIALOG BOX**

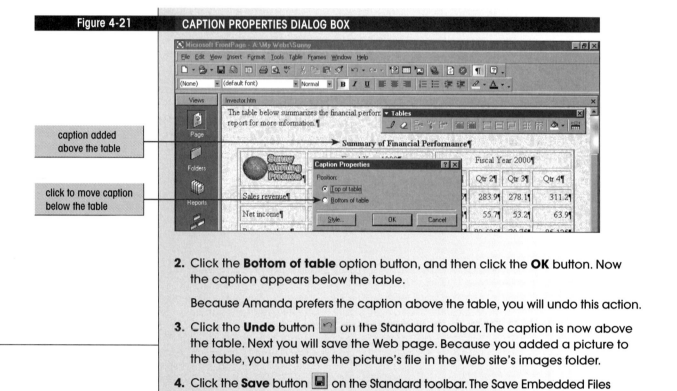

caption added
above the table

click to move caption
below the table

2. Click the **Bottom of table** option button, and then click the **OK** button. Now the caption appears below the table.

Because Amanda prefers the caption above the table, you will undo this action.

3. Click the **Undo** button on the Standard toolbar. The caption is now above the table. Next you will save the Web page. Because you added a picture to the table, you must save the picture's file in the Web site's images folder.

4. Click the **Save** button 🖫 on the Standard toolbar. The Save Embedded Files dialog box opens with the Finperf.gif file in the Embedded Files to save text box.

5. Make sure that the file will be saved in the Sunny Web site's images folder, and then click the **OK** button to save the picture file and the Investor Relations Web page.

You are almost finished completing the table. However, Amanda has some additional table properties that she wants you to set to enhance the table's appearance.

Setting **Table Properties**

FrontPage includes many tools that let you specify additional properties to create sophisticated tables. In addition to the layout and width properties that you set using the Table Properties dialog box, you also can use background and border colors and pictures. A table's background is separate from the background specified for the Web page that contains the table. When you change a table's background color, you can either select from a list of common colors or open the More Colors dialog box and choose from a wide color spectrum.

REFERENCE   WINDOW   **RW**

Changing a Table's Background Color

■ Right-click anywhere in the table to select it and to open the shortcut menu, and then click Table Properties.

■ Click the Color list arrow in the Background section to select a background color.

or

■ Click the Use background picture check box, and then click the Browse button to select a file to use as the table's background picture.

Amanda wants you to change the current background color of the table to white.

To change the table's background color:

1. Right-click anywhere in the table to open the shortcut menu, and then click **Table Properties** to open that dialog box.

2. In the Background section, click the **Color** list arrow to display a list of available colors, and then click the **White** color.

3. Click the **Apply** button. The white background is applied to the table. Notice that the Web page still uses a background picture.

Next you will change the color of the table's border.

REFERENCE WINDOW   **RW**

Changing a Table's Border Color
- Right-click anywhere in the table to select it and to open the shortcut menu, and then click Table Properties.
- Click the Color list arrow in the Borders section to select a border color.
or
- Click the Light border list arrow and select a color for the bottom and right borders of each cell, and then click the Dark border list arrow and select a color for the top and left borders of each cell to create a three-dimensional appearance.
- Click the OK button.

Amanda wants you to change the border color of the table to dark blue. She thinks this will make the table more attractive to visitors of the Investors Relations Web page.

To change the border color, close the Tables toolbar, and turn off the display of nonprinting characters:

1. In the Borders section, click the **Color** list arrow to display a list of available colors, and then click **More Colors**. The More Colors dialog box opens.

2. Click the **dark blue** color (the last color in the first row), click the **OK** button to close the More Colors dialog box, and then click the **OK** button to close the Table Properties dialog box. The main table and the picture are displayed with a white background and each cell in the table has a dark blue border. See Figure 4-22. Notice that the two nested tables do not use the same border color, but they do use the same background color.

| Figure 4-22 | BACKGROUND AND COLORED BORDER ADDED TO TABLE |

dark blue cell borders

new white background

nested tables use the main table's background color, but not the cell border color

3. Click the **Save** button 🖫 on the Standard toolbar. You are finished working with tables, so you can close the Tables toolbar.

4. Click the **Close** button ✕ on the Tables toolbar to hide it.

5. Click the **Show All** button ¶ on the Standard toolbar to turn off the display of nonprinting characters.

Now that you've completed these table property changes, you are finished creating the table. However, your task is not complete until you test the appearance of the table in the browser.

Testing a Table Using Internet Explorer

Like other Web pages, the Investor Relations page should be tested in the browser to make sure that the table appears exactly as specified. In this case, testing is especially important because you formatted the table to occupy a percentage of the page's width.

To test a table using Internet Explorer:

1. Click the **Preview in Browser** button 🔍 on the Standard toolbar. Internet Explorer starts and opens the Investor Relations Web page. If necessary, maximize the Internet Explorer window and scroll down the page to review the table's appearance. Make sure the data is displayed as desired and that the caption, background, and picture all match your specifications.

2. Click the **Close** button 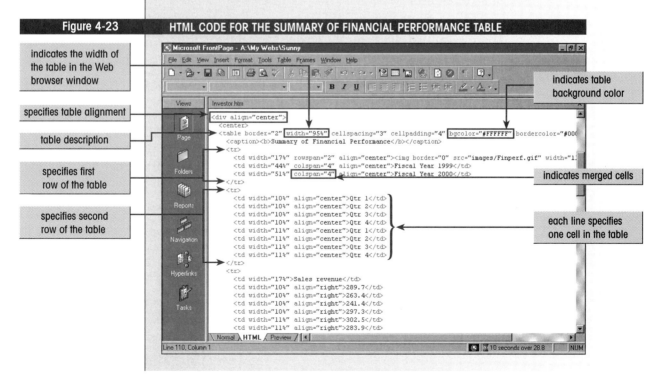 on the Internet Explorer title bar to close it.

3. If necessary, click the **Microsoft FrontPage** program button on the taskbar to return to FrontPage.

If you are more comfortable creating a table using a spreadsheet program (such as Excel) or a word processor (such as Word), you can create a table in another format and then insert the file in the Web page. FrontPage recognizes the table and translates it to HTML code. The HTML code that FrontPage creates for a table you created in another program is the same, and you can use the tools in FrontPage to edit the inserted table as if you created it using FrontPage.

Viewing **HTML Tags for a Table**

When you create a table—either by using FrontPage or another program—you create a complex HTML document. For example, the <TABLE> and </TABLE> tags specify the beginning and end of the table. The <TR> and </TR> tags indicate the beginning and end of one row in the table, whereas individual <TD> and </TD> tags indicate the beginning and end of each cell. FrontPage generates a separate line for each cell in a table. The <DIV> and <CENTER> tags cause the table to be center-aligned in the page.

So that you can gain a better understanding of the HTML code that FrontPage used to create the Investor Relations page, Amanda asks you to view the page's HTML code.

To view the HTML code for a table and close FrontPage:

1. Click the **HTML** tab to switch to HTML Page view, and then scroll up until the <DIV ALIGN="CENTER"> tag is at the top of the window. See Figure 4-23.

| Figure 4-23 | HTML CODE FOR THE SUMMARY OF FINANCIAL PERFORMANCE TABLE |

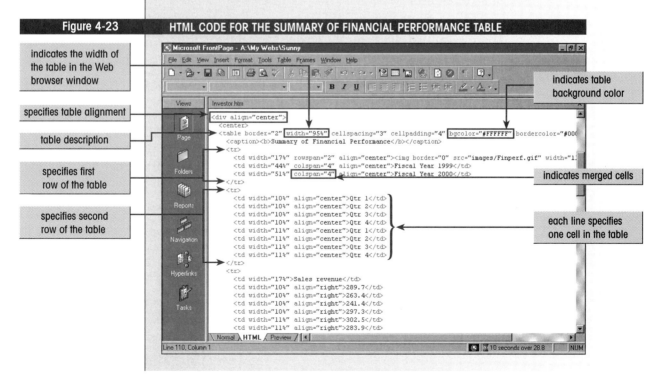

TROUBLE? If your tags are slightly different than those shown in the figure, don't worry. Examine the code so that you understand how the tags create the table.

The <DIV> tag defines a section in a page that serves as a container for page elements. The <DIV ALIGN="CENTER"> form of the tag is a more recent version of this tag that is designed to replace the <CENTER> tag. FrontPage inserts both of these tags in the page so it will be rendered correctly on both older and new releases of Web browser programs. Also notice the use of the COLSPAN property, which was inserted when you merged the cells that contain the year headings.

2. Scroll to the bottom of the page and examine the HTML code that specifies the elements in the table.

3. Click the **Normal** tab to return to that view.

4. Click the **Close** button ☒ on the FrontPage title bar to close the Investor Relations Web page, the Sunny Web site, and FrontPage.

The Web site development team is happy with your progress. Your next assignment is to create a frames page in which to display the navigation bar, table of contents, and individual product Web pages.

Session 4.1 QUICK CHECK

1. Describe what happens when a Web page is displayed in the browser and you click the Edit button.

2. What is the smallest component of a table?

3. Why should you create a table using a percentage of the window size, instead of using fixed measurements such as inches or pixels?

4. _____ is the distance between the contents of a cell and its inside edge.

5. True or False: If you select a table cell and then click the Align Left button on the Formatting toolbar, you will left-align the cell's contents.

6. True or False: Clicking the Center button on the Formatting toolbar will center-align a table in a Web page.

7. When you insert a row in a table using the Tables toolbar, the new row appears _____ the selected row.

8. Describe two ways to merge two adjacent cells into a single cell.

9. The default location for a table's caption is _____ the table.

SESSION 4.2

In this session, you will create a new frames page using a template, import Web pages into the Sunny Web site to use in the frames page, and then specify the pages to open in the frames page. You will specify target frames for pages displayed in the frames page and use predefined frame names. Finally, you will test the frames page in the browser and examine its HTML code.

Understanding Frames

In Tutorial 1, you examined the Products Web page, which is an example of a Web page that contains frames. A **frames page**, or a **frameset**, is a single Web page that divides the browser window into two or more windows, each of which can contain a separate, scrollable page. It is important to understand that the frames page itself does not contain any *content*—it contains only the empty frames.

You use a frames page when you want the contents of one frame in the browser window to remain unchanged while the contents of other frames change. For example, one frame might display a set of hyperlinks (such as a table of contents), while a second frame displays the target pages of the hyperlinks.

The Products Web page (Products.htm) is a frames page that contains three frames: banner, contents, and main. The Products Web page itself is just a set of empty frames; its HTML code contains the code that specifies each frame's name and size specifications. Amanda created a Web page that contains a navigation bar to open in the banner frame and a Web page that contains a table of contents with hyperlinks to open in the contents frame. The target pages of the hyperlinks in the contents frame will open in the main frame.

When you open a frames page in a browser, the browser first displays the frames page and then opens the pages that are specified to load into the individual frames. If the frames page contains three frames, your browser is really displaying *four* separate Web pages—the frames page and one page each in the three frames. Figure 4-24 shows the Products frames page and describes how it works.

Figure 4-24	PRODUCTS FRAMES PAGE ACTIONS

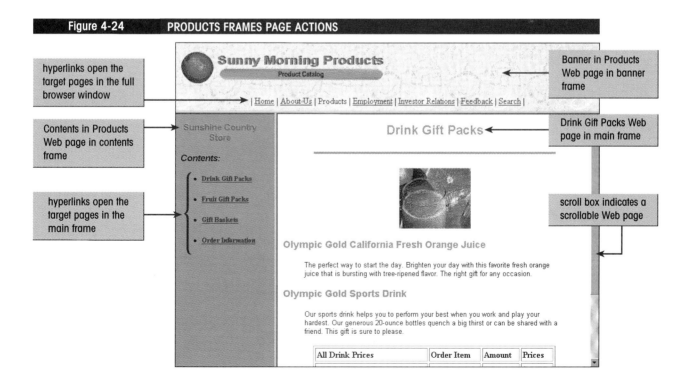

Frames provide Web site developers with a means to display two or more Web pages at once. An advantage of displaying multiple Web pages is that a navigation bar or table of contents is always visible, making it easier to navigate the site. However, keep in mind that using a frames page has some disadvantages, as well. Some browsers cannot display Web pages that contain frames, which means that some of your Web site's users might not see the frames page with the different Web pages. Therefore, you should use frames only when you are certain that your Web site's users will be able to display them. Another concern of using a frames page is that the page displayed in the main frame is displayed in a smaller window than when it is displayed in the full browser window. If the page in the main frame contains a lot of text, the user will need to scroll the page frequently to read its contents, which can be very distracting.

Creating a Frames Page

FrontPage contains many different frames page templates that you can use to create a frameset. A **frames page template** is a Web page that contains the specifications for the individual locations and sizes of the frames in a frames page. When you create a frames page using a template, FrontPage assigns each frame a default name. You can resize any of the frames in the frames page after creating them.

Figure 4-25 shows Amanda's sketch of the Products Web page. Products.htm is the frames page, Banner.htm is the Web page that contains the navigation bar, Contents.htm is the Web page that contains the table of contents, and Drink.htm will open in the main frame.

Figure 4-25	SKETCH OF THE PRODUCTS FRAMES PAGE

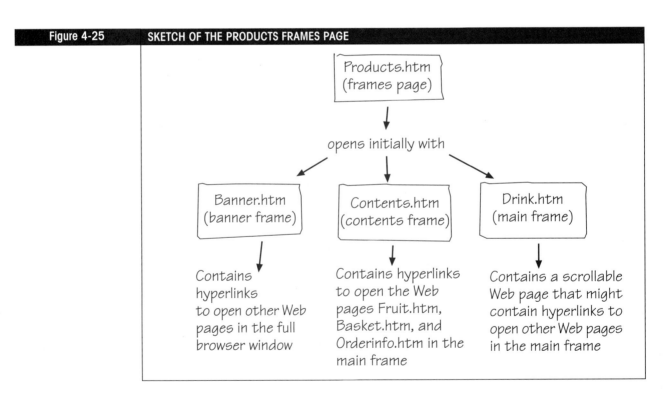

Figure 4-26 shows Amanda's planning analysis sheet for the development of the Products Web page.

Figure 4-26   AMANDA'S PLANNING ANALYSIS SHEET FOR THE PRODUCTS WEB PAGE

Planning Analysis Sheet

Objective

Create a frames page for displaying product information and accepting online

orders. The page should include a navigation bar with hyperlinks to other Web pages

in the Sunny Web site, a table of contents with hyperlinks that open Web pages

in the main frame, and the individual product pages.

Requirements

Page for banner frame

Page for contents frame

Pages for main frame—one for each hyperlink in the contents frame

Picture files

Results

Products Web page with three frames: the banner frame will contain links to other

Sunny Web pages, the contents frame will contain links that open pages

in the main frame, and the main frame will display pages with product

information

Clicking a hyperlink in the contents frame will open the target page in the main

frame

Clicking a hyperlink in the banner frame will open the target page in the full browser

window, replacing the frames page

Amanda wants you to create the Products Web page. She already created some of the
pages that will open in the main frame.

REFERENCE WINDOW   **RW**

Creating a Frames Page
- In Page view, click File on the menu bar, point to New, and then click Page.
- In the New dialog box, click the Frames Pages tab.
- Click a template to see its preview and description.
- Double-click a template icon to close the New dialog box and create the new frames page.

You will create the Products Web page using a frames page template.

To create a frames page:

1. Start **FrontPage**, insert your Data Disk in the appropriate drive, and then open the **Sunny** Web site (a:\My Webs\Sunny).

2. If necessary, click the **Page** button 🗐 on the Views bar to change to Page view.

   TROUBLE? If the Tables toolbar is displayed in Page view, click View on the menu bar, point to Toolbars, and then click Tables to close it. If the Show All button ¶ is indented on the Standard toolbar, click ¶ to turn off the display of non-printing characters.

3. Click **File** on the menu bar, point to **New**, and then click **Page**. The New dialog box opens.

4. Click the **Frames Pages** tab to display the list of available frames page templates.

   You can preview a template to see its description and appearance before using it.

5. If necessary, click the **Banner and Contents** icon. A preview and description of the selected template appear on the right side of the New dialog box. See Figure 4-27.

Figure 4-27	NEW DIALOG BOX

6. Select other templates and examine their previews and descriptions.

   The plan you reviewed with Amanda most closely matches the Banner and Contents template. This template has a banner frame, a contents frame, and a main frame.

7. Double-click the **Banner and Contents** icon to close the New dialog box and to create a new page. The new frames page opens in Page view using the title new_page_2.htm. (Your page might use a different number in the filename.) See Figure 4-28.

Figure 4-28   NEW FRAMES PAGE IN NORMAL PAGE VIEW

dark blue inside border indicates a selected frame

click to set an existing Web page as the page that opens in this frame when the frames page opens

additional tabs for working with frames

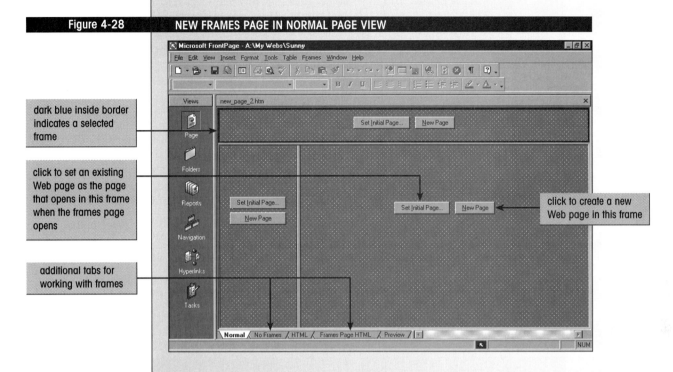

click to create a new Web page in this frame

Amanda asks you to save the new page.

8. Click the **Save** button on the Standard toolbar to open the Save As dialog box. You will change the settings in the Save As dialog box to change the page's title and filename.

9. Type **Products** as the filename, click the **Change** button to open the Set Page Title dialog box, type **Products** in the Page title text box, click the **OK** button, make sure that the Save in list box displays the Sunny folder, and then click the **Save** button in the Save As dialog box. A dialog box opens to inform you that the Products.htm file already exists. Amanda reminds you that you added a page to the Web site in Tutorial 3 when you added the associated task to the Tasks list. The existing Products.htm file is blank, so you can replace the page.

10. Click the **Yes** button to replace the existing page. The frames page is saved in the Web site using the filename Products.htm.

Examining the HTML Code for a Frames Page

The Products Web page that you just created is only a single Web page with no content, which contains three frames. Notice that two new tabs—No Frames and Frames Page HTML—appear at the bottom of the Contents pane. Amanda wants you to examine the HTML code that created the frames page to help you understand more about frames pages.

To examine the No Frames page and the HTML code for a frames page:

1. Click the **No Frames** tab at the bottom of the Contents pane. A new page opens in Page view and completely replaces the frames page. This page contains the text, "This page uses frames, but your browser doesn't support them." FrontPage created this page automatically with your frames page. If a Web browser that cannot display frames tries to open a frames page, this page will open in its place. Amanda explains that you could change the content of this page to include hyperlinks to pages that would otherwise be available in the frames page. Because you expect the Sunny Web site users to have current releases of browsers that support frames, you will not modify this No Frames page.

2. Click the **HTML** tab. The same frames page that was displayed in Normal Page view appears in HTML view. Notice that the banner frame is selected, as indicated by its dark blue inside border. If you already set a Web page to appear in the banner frame, the HTML code for the displayed page would appear in the frame. However, the frame is empty, so there is no HTML code to show.

3. Click the main frame to select it, and then click the outside border of the frames page to select the frameset. You can click any frame in the frameset. The outside frame on the page that you just selected holds the inside frames.

4. Click the **Frames Page HTML** tab. The HTML code for the Products.htm page—the frameset—appears in this view and is selected. See Figure 4-29. Notice that the FRAME NAME tags identify the three frames—banner, contents, and main. Also notice that the title of the page, as specified by the TITLE tags, is Products.

Figure 4-29	HTML CODE FOR THE FRAMES PAGE

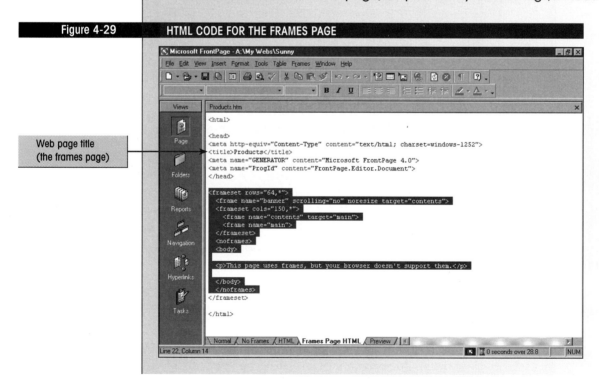

Web page title (the frames page)

> TROUBLE? If your screen contains selected text different from that shown in Figure 4-29, then you did not select the outside frame in Step 3 before clicking the Frames Page HTML tab. This difference is not a problem; your code is the same.
>
> 5. Click the **Normal** tab to return to Normal Page view.

Your next task is to set the page that opens in each frame when the Products Web page is opened in the browser. Amanda already created these pages for you. You can import them into the Sunny Web site and use them in the Products Web page.

Importing Web Pages for Use in a Frames Page

Before you can use Amanda's existing pages in the Products frames page, you must change to Folders view and import them into the Sunny Web site. Then you will set these pages to open in the frames page.

> *To import pages for a frames page:*
>
> 1. Click the **Folders** button [icon] on the Views bar to change to Folders view.
>
> 2. Click **File** on the menu bar, and then click **Import** to open the Import dialog box.
>
> 3. Click the **Add File** button to open the Add File to Import List dialog box. If necessary, click the **Look in** list arrow and change to the drive or folder that contains your Data Disk. Double-click the **Tutorial.04** folder, and then click **Banner** in the file list.
>
>   Rather than import the rest of the files from the list one at a time, you can select the remainder of the files to import all seven files at once.
>
> 4. Press and hold down the **Ctrl** key, click the following files: **Basket**, **Contents**, **Drink**, **Fruit**, **Ordrform**, and **Ordrinfo**, and then release the **Ctrl** key. All seven files are selected.
>
> 5. Click the **Open** button to close the Add File to Import List dialog box and to return to the Import dialog box. The seven files you selected in Steps 3 and 4 are displayed and selected in the Import dialog box.
>
> 6. Click the **OK** button to import the files into the Sunny Web site.
>
>   TROUBLE? If you are storing your Web site on a floppy disk, it might take a few minutes to import these pages.

The pages that will open in the Products frames page now are saved in the Sunny Web site.

Setting Initial Pages for Frames

When you created the frames page, it displayed three frames, each containing a Set Initial Page button and a New Page button. Clicking the Set Initial Page button lets you specify an existing Web page (from the current Web site or from another location) as the page that opens in the selected frame. Clicking the New Page button lets you create a new blank page in the Web site and open it in the frame so you can enter its content. Creating a new page for use in any of the frames in the frames page is the same as creating a new Web page in Page view—the only difference is that you are creating and editing the new page in a frame. Because you already imported the Web pages for use with the frames page, they exist in the Sunny Web site. Creating the pages outside of the frames page is usually the easiest way to specify the Web pages that open in the frames page.

Amanda wants you to specify, or set, the initial page to open for each frame in the Products Web page.

To set the initial pages for a frames page:

1. Double-click **Products.htm** in the Contents pane to open the Products Web page in Page view.

2. Click the **Set Initial Page** button in the banner frame. The Create Hyperlink dialog box opens. When you set the page, you are really creating a hyperlink to it.

3. Double-click **banner.htm**. The Create Hyperlink dialog box closes and the banner.htm page (Banner in Products) appears in the banner frame. Notice that the page contains a broken link, and that you cannot see the page's content. You will fix these problems later.

   TROUBLE? If you accidentally set the wrong page to open in a frame, right-click in the frame to select it and open the shortcut menu, click Frame Properties, click the Browse button to the right of the Initial page text box to browse for and select the correct file, click the OK button, and then click the OK button again.

4. Repeat Steps 2 and 3 to set the **contents.htm** page (Contents in Products) to open in the contents frame on the left side of the frames page.

5. Repeat Steps 2 and 3 to select the **drink.htm** page (Drink Gift Packs) to open in the main frame on the right side of the frames page. Notice that a broken link to a picture appears in the Drink Gift Packs Web page. See Figure 4-30.

Figure 4-30	INITIAL PAGES DISPLAYED IN THE FRAMES PAGE

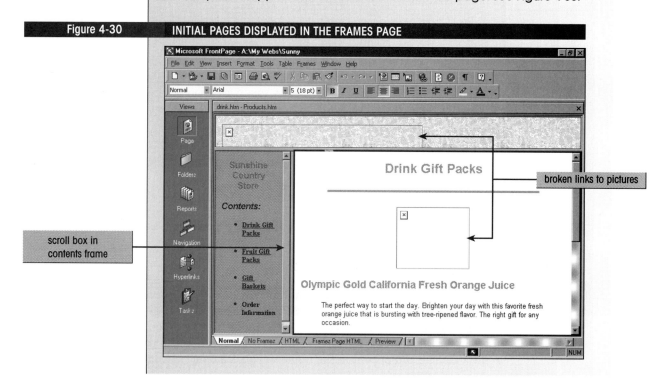

Editing the Frames in a Frames Page

The Web pages that you imported into the Sunny Web site and then set to open in the frames contain some problems that you must fix. First, the pages in the banner and main frames contain broken links to pictures, so you will need to add these picture files to the Web site. The page in the banner frame is not visible, so you will need to increase its height to see the page correctly. Finally, depending on your screen resolution, the page in the contents frame contains a vertical scroll bar and possibly a horizontal scroll bar. Although users can use the scroll bars to scroll the contents of the page, the frame would be easier to view if they did not need to scroll the page, so you will resize the contents frame as well.

First, you will edit the frames to display the Web pages correctly.

To edit the frames:

1. Click in the banner frame to select it. A dark blue border appears inside the banner frame to indicate that it is selected.

2. Move the pointer to the bottom frame border of the banner frame until the pointer changes to a $\updownarrow$ shape. Click and hold down the mouse button on the bottom frame border, drag the frame border down about an inch, and then release the mouse button. After you release the mouse button, the navigation bar should be visible. (See Figure 4-31.)

   Next, resize the contents frame.

3. Click in the contents frame to select it, and then click and drag its right border to the right about one-half inch so that each hyperlink is displayed on a single line. Now the horizontal scroll bar disappears and it is easier to view the hyperlinks in the contents frame. See Figure 4-31.

| Figure 4-31 | FRAMES PAGE AFTER RESIZING THE BANNER AND CONTENTS FRAMES |

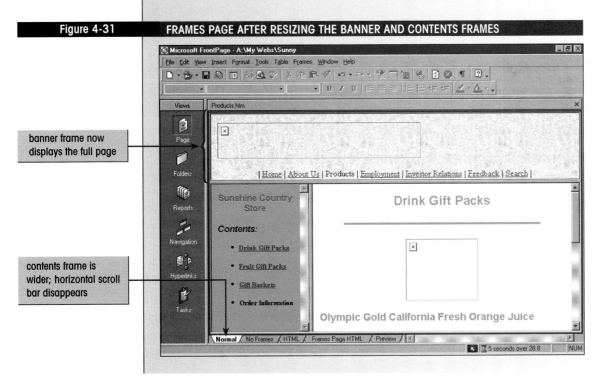

banner frame now displays the full page

contents frame is wider; horizontal scroll bar disappears

When you changed the sizes of the frames, you changed the HTML document that contains information about the frames. When you display a frames page in Page view, clicking the Save button saves the changes that you made to the pages in the frameset or to the frameset itself.

4. Click the **Save** button 🖫 on the Standard toolbar to save the frames page with these initial page settings.

Next, you need to include the two missing picture files from the Banner in Products and Drink Gift Packs Web pages in the Sunny Web site. You learned in Tutorial 3 that when you import an existing Web page into a Web site, its embedded picture files are not imported with the pages.

To embed pictures in the imported Web pages:

1. Right-click the broken picture link in the banner frame page to select it and open the shortcut menu, and then click **Picture Properties**. The Picture Properties dialog box opens.

2. In the Picture source section, click the **Browse** button to open the Picture dialog box, and then click the **Select a file on your computer** button 🔍 to open the Select File dialog box.

3. If necessary, click the **Look in** list arrow and change to the drive or folder that contains your Data Disk, and then double-click the **Tutorial.04** folder to display its contents.

4. Double-click **Catalog** in the list to close the Select File and Picture dialog boxes and to return to the Picture Properties dialog box.

5. Click the **OK** button to close the Picture Properties dialog box and to insert the picture in the Banner in Products page.

6. Click the **Save** button 🖫 on the Standard toolbar to open the Save Embedded Files dialog box, make sure that the Catalog.gif file will be saved in the Sunny Web site's images folder, and then click the **OK** button in the Save Embedded Files dialog box to save the picture.

   Next, insert the missing picture in the Drink Gift Packs page.

7. Repeat Steps 1 through 6 to add the **Juice** picture from the Tutorial.04 folder to the Drink Gift Packs Web page and to save the file in the images folder.

Now that you have updated and saved the pages that open in the frames page, Amanda asks you to specify the other pages that open in the main frame.

Specifying the Target Frame

A **target frame** is the designated frame in a frames page where a hyperlinked page opens. For example, the target frame for the Drink Gift Packs Web page is the main frame of the Products Web page. When Amanda created the contents.htm page, she specified the hyperlinks, including their target frames, except for the Ordering Information page. Amanda wants you to modify the Contents page to include the hyperlink that opens the Ordering Information page in the main frame of the Products Web page.

To specify the target frame for a Web page:

1. In the contents frame, select **Order Information** as the text for the hyperlink, and then click the **Hyperlink** button 🖼️ on the Standard toolbar to open the Create Hyperlink dialog box.

2. Scroll down the list of files until you see ordrinfo.htm, and then click **ordrinfo.htm** to select the Ordering Information page.

3. Look at the Target frame text box and verify that "Page Default (main)" is specified as the frame where the Ordering Information page will open. When you specify a hyperlink, the default target frame is for the linked document to open in the main frame. See Figure 4-32.

Figure 4-32	CREATE HYPERLINK DIALOG BOX

target page selected

target page will open in the main frame

4. Click the **OK** button to close the Create Hyperlink dialog box and to create the hyperlink. Click **Order Information** in the contents frame to deselect it; "Order Information" now appears as a hyperlink.

5. Click the **Save** button 💾 on the Standard toolbar to save the Contents in Products page.

Examining a Frame's Properties

After creating a frames page, you can verify that the pages will open in the correct frames by checking the values in the Target frame text box. Amanda wants you to verify that the Drink Gift Packs page was specified as the default target page that opens in the main frame when the Products Web page is opened in the browser.

To examine a frame's properties:

1. Right-click in the main frame to select it and open the shortcut menu, and then click **Frame Properties**. The Frame Properties dialog box opens. See Figure 4-33.

Figure 4-33 | **FRAME PROPERTIES DIALOG BOX**

page that opens when the frames page is opened

settings for the target frame's size

settings for the target frame's margins

options for changing the frame's properties

target frame name

click to browse for a different initial page if the specified page is incorrect

Figure 4-34 describes the changes that you can make to a selected frame using this dialog box.

Figure 4-34 | **OPTIONS IN THE FRAME PROPERTIES DIALOG BOX AND THEIR DESCRIPTIONS**

OPTION	DESCRIPTION
Name	The name of the selected frame in the frames page.
Initial page	The filename of the page that opens in the named frame when the frames page is opened in the browser. Click the Browse button to change or set the page that opens initially.
Width (Frame size)	The frame's width. Use the list box to specify the frame's width relative to other frames, to set the width as a percentage of the browser window's size, or to set the width as a fixed number of pixels. The default width is 1 with relative sizing.
Row Height (Frame size)	The frame's height. Use the list box to specify the frame's height relative to other frames, to set the height as a percentage of the browser window's size, or to set the height as a fixed number of pixels. The default height is 1 with relative sizing.
Width (Margins)	The frame's margin width (in pixels), which indicates the amount of left and right space to indent the content in the frame from the inside frame border.
Height (Margins)	The frame's margin height (in pixels), which indicates the amount of top and bottom space to indent the content in the frame from the inside frame border.
Resizable in Browser check box	Select this check box to let users resize the current frame using a Web browser. Clear this check box to prevent users from resizing the frame.
Frames Page button	Opens the Frame Properties dialog box so you can change frame properties, such as the spacing between frames or to turn on or off the display of frame borders.
Show scrollbars list box	Lets you specify whether to display scroll bars as needed for longer pages or to always or never display scroll bars.
Style button	Lets you change the style of the frames in the page; this topic is beyond the scope of this tutorial.

2. Verify that the Name text box displays the value "main" and that the Initial page text box has the value "drink.htm." These values were set automatically when you set the Drink Gift Packs page to open in the main frame of the frames page.

If you needed to revise any of these values, you could. However, for the Products frames page, they are acceptable.

3. Click the **OK** button to close the dialog box and to return to the Products frames page.

Now that you have specified all of the pages, you can test the frames page in the browser.

To test a frames page using Internet Explorer:

1. Click the **Preview in Browser** button 🔍 on the Standard toolbar. The Products Web page opens in the browser and displays the Web pages that you specified in each frame.

   TROUBLE? If a dialog box opens and asks you to save your changes, click the Yes button.

2. Click the **Order Information** hyperlink in the contents frame. The Ordering Information page opens in the main frame.

3. Click the **Home** hyperlink in the navigation bar in the banner frame. The Home Page opens in the contents frame, which indicates that there is a problem with the target frame for this page. See Figure 4-35.

Figure 4-35	PRODUCTS FRAMES PAGE AFTER CLICKING THE HOME HYPERLINK

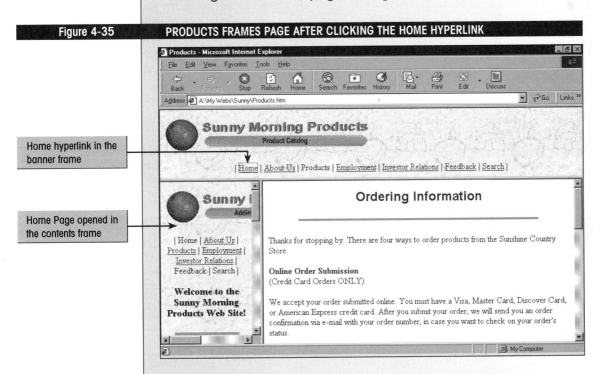

Home hyperlink in the banner frame

Home Page opened in the contents frame

4. Click the **Employment** hyperlink in the navigation bar in the banner frame. The Employment page replaces the entire Products Web page and opens in the full browser window. This action is the one that you want to occur when any page is opened from the navigation bar in the banner frame.

> **5.** Click the **Products** hyperlink in the navigation bar. The Products Web page reopens and replaces the Employment page in the browser window.
>
> **6.** Click the **Close** button ☒ on the Internet Explorer title bar to close it.

When you clicked the link to the Home Page in the navigation bar in the banner frame, the page did not completely replace the Products frames page. Instead, the Home Page opened in the contents frame. You need to change the target frame for the Home Page by modifying its hyperlink in the navigation bar in the Banner in Products page so the frames page closes before the Home Page opens. In other words, the target of the hyperlink should open in the full browser window without any frames.

Using **Predefined Frame Names**

When you use a FrontPage frames page template to create a frames page, the navigation between frames is already set up for you. For example, the Banner and Contents frames page template specifies that pages opened using hyperlinks in the contents frame will open in the main frame. For the Products frames page, you imported the pages that open into each frame into the Web site—including their existing hyperlinks—into each frame, instead of creating them as new pages from within the frames page. Sometimes you might find that you need to change the target frame for a hyperlink. For example, your testing in the previous section revealed that the Home hyperlink in the Banner in Products page did not open the Home Page correctly.

There are four predefined frame names that tell a Web browser where to open hyperlinked pages in a frames page. A **predefined frame name** is an HTML value that specifies which Web page to open and in which frame to open it. Figure 4-36 describes the four predefined frame names that you can use to specify target frames.

Figure 4-36	PREDEFINED FRAME NAMES	
HTML CODE	**PREDEFINED FRAME NAME**	**DESCRIPTION**
_self	Same Frame	The target of a hyperlink opens in the same frame as the page containing the hyperlink.
_top	Whole Page	The target of the hyperlink replaces all frames pages and opens in the full browser window.
_blank or _new	New Window	The target of the hyperlink opens in a new window. A new window means that a second instance of the browser starts and displays the page. Use this option to open a page that is related to the frames page's contents, but is not part of the frames page. For example, a page that displays information about eyeglasses might contain a hyperlink related to diseases of the eye that opens a new browser window.
_parent	Parent Frame	The target of the hyperlink opens a page that replaces the entire frameset that defines the frame containing the hyperlink.

The default target frame for a hyperlink is Page Default (*frame name*), where *frame name* is the name of the frame in which the page will open. For example, if you create a hyperlink in a page that appears in the contents frame, the default target frame for the hyperlinked page would be Page Default (main). If you do not specify a predefined frame name when creating a hyperlink, the target of the hyperlink will open in the main frame.

When Amanda created the navigation bar in the Banner in Products page, she specified the _top target frame for every hyperlink, except for the Home hyperlink. In your testing, you confirmed this problem: The Home Page opened in the contents frame, whereas the

Employment page opened correctly in the full browser window. Amanda wants you to learn how to change the target frame of a hyperlink, so she asks you to specify the _top target frame for the hyperlink to the Home Page.

To change the target frame for a hyperlink and test it in the browser:

1. If necessary, click the **Microsoft FrontPage** program button on the taskbar to return to FrontPage.

2. Right-click the **Home** hyperlink in the navigation bar in the banner frame to open the shortcut menu, and then click **Hyperlink Properties** to open the Edit Hyperlink dialog box. The index.htm filename, which represents the Home Page, appears selected in the URL text box, and "Page Default (contents)" appears in the Target frame list box.

3. Click the **Change Target Frame** button [icon] next to the Target frame list box to open the Target Frame dialog box. The current target frame—Page Default (contents)—is selected in the Common targets list box, and the Target setting text box is empty. You need to change the target frame so that the Home Page opens in the full browser window, replacing the entire frames page. To do this, you must specify the Whole Page (_top) target setting.

4. Click **Whole Page** in the Common targets list box. FrontPage adds the HTML equivalent, _top, to the Target setting text box. See Figure 4-37.

Figure 4-37	TARGET FRAME DIALOG BOX

FrontPage equivalent for the full browser window

HTML equivalent for the full browser window

5. Click the **OK** button to close the Target Frame dialog box and to return to the Edit Hyperlink dialog box. Notice that the Target frame text box now displays the target frame named "Whole Page."

6. Click the **OK** button to close the Edit Hyperlink dialog box, and then click the **Save** button [icon] on the Standard toolbar to save your changes.

7. Click the **Preview in Browser** button [icon] on the Standard toolbar to open the revised Products frames page in Internet Explorer.

   Now test the page again to make sure that it works correctly.

8. Click the **Home** hyperlink in the navigation bar in the banner frame. The Home Page replaces the entire Products frames page in the browser. Your test is successful, so you can close the browser.

9. Click the **Close** button ☒ on the Internet Explorer title bar to close the browser.

You will need to change a target frame only when the desired target frame is not set correctly when you created your frames pages. Creating hyperlinks that open pages in frames can be a complicated chore, so it is important for you to test your frames pages thoroughly to ensure that all of the hyperlinked pages open correctly. You can also use Hyperlinks view to examine all of the hyperlinks to and from a frames page, and use Reports view to search for broken links.

Adding a New Frame to an Existing Frames Page

After creating a frames page, you can add a new frame to it by dividing an existing frame into two separate frames. To divide one existing frame into two frames within the same frames page, you hold down the Ctrl key while dragging the border of the existing frame that you want to divide to create a new frame. After adding the new frame, you can specify the Web page to open in the new frame using the same procedure you followed for creating the other pages in the frames page.

REFERENCE WINDOW   **RW**

Adding a New Frame to an Existing Frames Page
- Open the frames page in Page view.
- Press and hold down the Ctrl key, and then click and drag the border of an existing frame that you want to split to the desired location.
- Release the Ctrl key.
- Use the Set Initial Page button to specify an existing page to open in the new frame, or use the New Page button to create a new page.

Amanda wants to add a sales slogan in a new frame in the Products frames page. She asks you to split the current main frame into two frames.

To add a new frame to an existing frames page:

1. Press and hold down the **Ctrl** key, and then click the bottom border of the main frame. The pointer changes to a ↕ shape.

2. While still holding down the Ctrl key, drag the bottom frame border up about one inch, and then release the mouse button and the **Ctrl** key. A new frame is created, containing the Set Initial Page and New Page buttons. See Figure 4-38.

Figure 4-38   **CREATING A NEW FRAME IN A FRAMES PAGE**

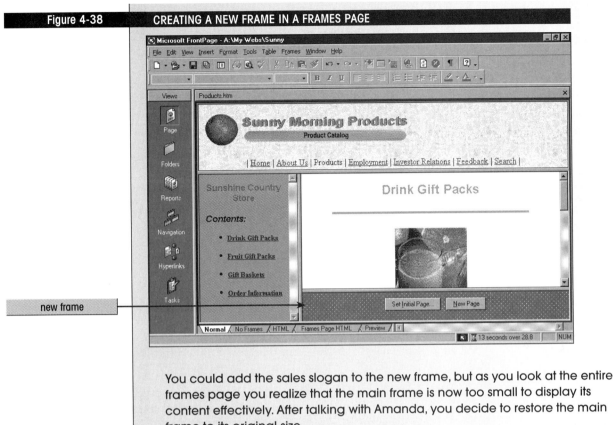

new frame

You could add the sales slogan to the new frame, but as you look at the entire frames page you realize that the main frame is now too small to display its content effectively. After talking with Amanda, you decide to restore the main frame to its original size.

3. Click the **Undo** button 🔄 on the Standard toolbar to delete the new frame and to restore the main frame to its original size.

4. Click the **Save** button 💾 on the Standard toolbar to save your changes.

FrontPage lets you subdivide existing frames within a frames page easily and quickly to provide the best presentation for your Web pages. However, you need to exercise care so that you do not make a frame too small to be useful.

Now the Products frames page and its accompanying Web pages are complete. You will test all of the pages in the frameset in the Review Assignments.

Printing a Frames Page

Printing a frames page is not as straightforward as printing a Web page that does not contain frames. In FrontPage, you can print the individual Web pages that appear in each frame in a frames page, but you cannot print the frames page itself. For example, if you select the outer border for the frames page, the Print button on the Standard toolbar and the Print command on the File menu become disabled. However, if you select an individual frame in the frames page, you can use either of these methods to print the page that appears in that frame.

When you view a frames page in the browser, you have more options for printing the frames page. If you click File on the menu bar, and then click Print, you can use the Print dialog box to select what to print. Figure 4-39 shows the Print dialog box in Internet Explorer.

Figure 4-39   PRINT DIALOG BOX IN INTERNET EXPLORER

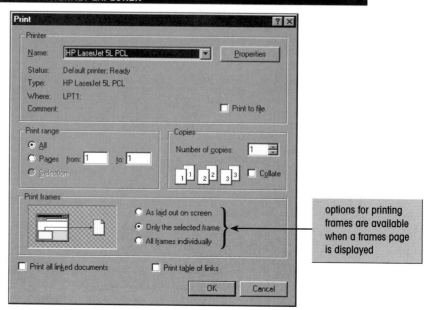

options for printing frames are available when a frames page is displayed

When a frames page is displayed in the browser, the Print frames section displays three options:

■ The As laid out on screen option prints the frames page as it appears on the screen (in other words, this option prints the full content of the pages that you see in the browser window).

■ The Only the selected frame option prints the active frame. This is the default option; when you click the Print button on the Standard Buttons toolbar, the selected frame prints automatically.

■ The All frames individually option prints the full content of each page displayed in the frames page on a separate sheet of paper.

Amanda wants you to print the frames page, and not just the individual pages contained within the frames page, so you will use Internet Explorer to print.

To print the frames page:

1. Click the **Preview in Browser** button 🔍 to open the Products Web page in the browser.

2. Click **File** on the menu bar, and then click **Print**. The Print dialog box opens.

3. Click the **As laid out on screen** option button in the Print frames section, and then click the **OK** button. Internet Explorer prints the contents of each page contained in the frames page and their layout on the screen.

4. Click the **Close** button ⊠ on the title bar to close Internet Explorer.

Viewing **HTML Tags for Frames Pages**

Earlier in this session when you viewed the HTML code for the frames page, you saw only the HTML code that created the frames page. Now Amanda wants you to examine the HTML code for the frames page again, so you can see the HTML code that FrontPage created to display the Web pages in the frames page. FRAMESET tags indicate the beginning and end of the frameset and specify each frame in the frames page. Within the FRAME tag, the SRC property indicates the filename for the target page, and the NAME property identifies the frame name in which to display the target page. The ROWS and COLUMNS properties of the FRAMESET tag indicate the layout of the frames as a percentage of the size of the page when it is displayed in the browser.

To view the HTML code for a frames page and the pages within it, and then close FrontPage:

1. Click the **Frames Page HTML** tab to display the HTML code for the Products frames page, and then click the **<html>** line at the top of the Contents pane to deselect any selected text. See Figure 4-40. For each frame in your frames page, the HTML code specifies the frame's name (FRAME NAME), the page to open initially (SRC), and the size of the frame (FRAMESET COLS).

Figure 4-40	HTML CODE FOR THE PRODUCTS FRAMES PAGE

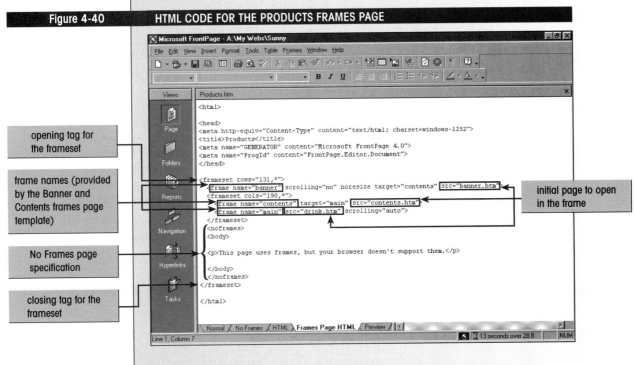

2. Click the **HTML** tab. The HTML code for each page that is displayed in the frames page appears in each frame. See Figure 4-41. Notice that the hyperlinks in each page show the target frame in which to open the hyperlinked page.

Figure 4-41   HTML CODE FOR THE INDIVIDUAL WEB PAGES DISPLAYED IN THE FRAMES PAGE

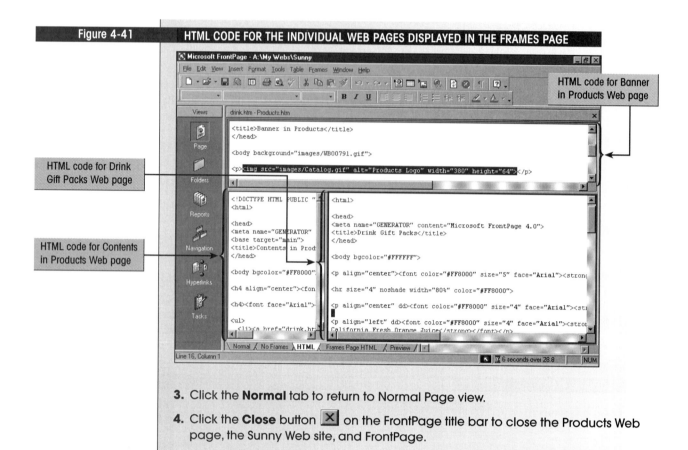

HTML code for Banner in Products Web page

HTML code for Drink Gift Packs Web page

HTML code for Contents in Products Web page

3. Click the **Normal** tab to return to Normal Page view.

4. Click the **Close** button ☒ on the FrontPage title bar to close the Products Web page, the Sunny Web site, and FrontPage.

With the Investor Relations and Products pages complete, you review your progress with Amanda and the rest of the Sunny Morning Products Web site development team. The summary of financial performance table adds key information to the Investor Relations page in an organized and attractive format. The Products frames page lets customers examine the different categories of products available from the Sunshine Country Store easily. In the next tutorial, you will learn how to enhance the appearance of the Web site by applying a Web theme.

Session 4.2 QUICK CHECK

1. True or False: A frames page does not contain any content; it contains only the specifications that define the empty frames.

2. A frames page that displays two frames will display _____ Web pages when it is opened in the browser window.

3. True or False: You can use a frames page without hesitation because all browsers can display frames.

4. Click the _____ tab in Page view to examine the HTML code for a frames page.

5. Click the _____ button in an empty frame to specify an existing Web page to open when the browser loads the frames page.

6. Which predefined frame name causes the browser to remove all loaded frames pages before displaying the target of a selected hyperlink?

7. The HTML tag that specifies the beginning of a frames page is _____.

REVIEW ASSIGNMENTS

During your meeting with the Web site development team, you received feedback on how to improve the Investor Relations and Products Web pages. The team suggests adding two additional tables of information to the Investor Relations page. They also suggest creating a new Web page for the company's new clothing line, which includes T-shirts, tote bags, and other items. You will create the Clothing Web page and set it to open in the main frame of the Products Web page.

If necessary, insert your Data Disk in the appropriate disk drive, start FrontPage, and then do the following:

1. Open the **Sunny** Web site (a:\My Webs\Sunny) from your Data Disk in Folders view.

Explore   2. Open the Investor Relations page (**Investor.htm**) in Page view, and then display the Tables toolbar and nonprinting characters. Insert a new row at the bottom of the summary of financial performance table. (*Hint*: Use the Table menu to insert the new row below the existing last row in the table.) Use the Eraser to merge all of the cells in the new row into a single cell.

3. Add the following text to the cell you created in Step 2: "Note: All amounts in millions, except per share amounts, which are in dollars." Center the text in the cell, decrease the font size to 10 points, and then change the text color to red.

4. Add the table of stock trading information shown in Figure 4-42 below the summary of financial performance table. Separate the two tables on the page with one blank line. Use the same settings for the new table as the summary of financial performance table. (*Hint*: Use the Table Properties and Cell Properties dialog boxes to examine the format of the summary of financial performance table.) Add the caption "Stock Trading Information" at the top of the table, and then change it to bold.

Figure 4-42

SUNNY MORNING PRODUCTS (SMP)
NEW YORK STOCK EXCHANGE (NYSE)

Last Traded at	85.125	Date/Time	May 31 15:54:00
$ Change	2.125	% Change	2.59
Volume (000)	84.7	# of Trades	104
Open	82.5	Previous Close	81.875
Day Low	82.25	Day High	83.25
52-Week Low	73.25	52-Week High	87.25

Explore   5. Create a custom background color of your choice and apply it to the first row of the table that you created in Step 4. (*Hint*: Right-click the cell, click Cell Properties on the shortcut menu, click the Color list arrow in the Background section, and then click More Colors to open the More Colors dialog box. Click the Custom button to open the Color dialog box. Click any color in the Basic colors section to open the Color dialog box, and then click in the color spectrum and look at the Color|Solid preview boxes to see the color. When you find a color that you like, and one that will not interfere with the readability of the text in the cell, click the Add to Custom Colors button, and then click the OK button. Close the remaining dialog boxes.)

Explore   6. Apply the custom background color that you created in Step 5 to the nested tables in the summary of financial performance table. (*Hint*: Select both nested tables, right-click one of the tables, click Cell Properties on the shortcut menu, click the Color list arrow in the Background section, and then use the Custom Color palette to apply the custom color.) Save the Investor Relations Web page.

7. Use a word processor or spreadsheet program to create a third table in the Investor Relations page. Your table should include the following information about shareholders: Fiscal Year 1999: 251,215 shareholders, 74,512,255 shares transacted, 16% increase; and Fiscal Year 2000: 352,584 shareholders, 84,752,922 shares transacted, 29% increase. Determine the best way to present this information using a table. If you use a word processor to create the table, make sure that you use the program's table commands. Save the file as **Table** in the Tutorial.04 folder on your Data Disk with the default file extension, and then close your word processor or spreadsheet program.

Explore   8. Insert two blank lines after the stock trading information table, and then place the insertion point on the second blank line. Use the Insert menu to insert the **Table** file that you created in Step 7 in the Investor Relations Web page. Add an appropriate caption at the top of the table, and then change it to bold. Make any other changes to your table so that the three tables in this page have the same appearance.

9. Save the Investor Relations Web page, and then close the Tables toolbar and turn off the display of nonprinting characters in your document. Preview the page in the browser, and then use the browser to print the page and its HTML code. Close Internet Explorer.

Explore   10. Return to FrontPage, and then design and create a new Web page named and titled **Clothing** to introduce the company's new product line of T-shirts, sweatshirts, and tote bags. Write the content of the page based on the writing style, format, and content of other pages in the Products frames page. Save your changes to the Clothing Web page.

11. Open the Products Web page (**Products.htm**) in Page view, and then create a new entry in the bulleted list in the contents frame page with a hyperlink to open the Clothing Web page in the main frame. (*Hint*: Click below the Order Information bullet to place the insertion point there, and then change that line to the Bulleted List style. Otherwise, the spacing between items will not be equal.) If necessary, change the font and style of the new hyperlink to match the other hyperlinks in the contents frame. Save your changes.

12. Open the Products Web page in the browser and test all of the hyperlinks that appear in its pages. If necessary, return to FrontPage and correct any problems that you discover, including fixing broken links to picture files. Specify the **Orngback.jpg** file as the background picture for the Ordering Information page (**Ordrinfo.htm**). Save your changes after revising each page, and save the picture files in the Web site's images folder. (*Hint*: The picture files are saved in the Tutorial.04 folder on your Data Disk.)

Explore   13. Revise the Banner in Products page in the Products frames page by creating a table that contains each of the navigation entries. (*Hint*: Rather than using the vertical bar to separate navigation choices, display them in a table with a single row. Use the Help system to learn more about the Convert Text to Table command on the Table menu. Use the vertical bar symbol as the Other separator value.) Separate each of the entries using dark blue borders around each cell. If any extra cells are created when you convert the text to a table, delete them. If necessary, adjust the banner frame's size so that the navigation bar is completely visible. Save your changes, and then test the revised frames page in the browser. Open the Clothing page in the main frame, and then use Internet Explorer to print the entire frames page as it appears in the browser window. Close Internet Explorer.

14. Return to FrontPage. Open the Tasks list and mark the Finish Investor.htm and Finish Products.htm tasks as completed.

Explore   15. Open the Products Web page in Page view, and then print the HTML code for the individual Web pages displayed by the frameset. (*Hint*: Select a frame, and then click the Print button on the Standard toolbar. Print the HTML code for each frame separately.)

16. Close FrontPage.

CASE PROBLEMS

Case 1. Building an Investors Page for Royal Hair Care Products Sales of Quick Dry Solution have enhanced the profitability of Royal Hair Care Products' operations. Valerie Suarez met with the company's senior managers to present an update on the company's Web site. The management team asked Valerie to expand the Web site to include information required by the company's investors, such as information on the company's financial performance and current stock performance. After the meeting, Valerie revised her Web site plan to include a new Web page and collected the necessary information for its content from the appropriate individuals. She asked Nathan Dubois to sketch and create a Web page of the stock market performance information. Valerie wants you to help Nathan complete the financial information page.

If necessary, start FrontPage, insert your Data Disk in the appropriate disk drive, and then do the following:

1. Read all the questions for this case problem, and then prepare a planning analysis sheet for the changes to the Royal Web site.

2. Open the **Royal** Web site (a:\My Webs\Royal) from your Data Disk in Page view. (If you did not create this Web site in Tutorial 2 and change it in Tutorial 3, ask your instructor for assistance.)

Explore   3. Create a frames page using the Banner and Contents template. Save the frames page with the filename **RInvest.htm** and the title "Financial Information."

4. Create the new Financial Performance Web page in the main frame, and then save it using the filename **RFinInfo.htm** and the title "Financial Performance." Display the Tables toolbar and nonprinting characters. Create the table shown in Figure 4-43 in the page. Add the caption "Financial Performance Information" above the table, and then change it to bold.

Figure 4-43

	FISCAL YEAR 2000			
	Qtr 1	Qtr 2	Qtr 3	Qtr 4
Sales revenue	421.3	474.2	508.1	480.3
Net income	14.0	14.1	14.5	14.2
Price per share	34.250	33.625	36.125	32.250
Earnings per share	2.20	2.19	2.30	2.01
Note: All amounts in thousands, except per share amounts, which are in dollars.				

Explore   5. Specify a custom color for the table's background that you created in Step 4, and then choose appropriate light and dark border colors for the table and its cells. (*Hint*: To select a custom color, right-click the cell, click Table Properties on the shortcut menu, click the Color list arrow in the Background section, and then click More Colors to open the More

Colors dialog box. Click the Custom button to open the Color dialog box. Click any color in the Basic colors section, and then click in the color spectrum and look at the Color|Solid preview boxes to see the color. When you find a color that you like, and one that will not interfere with the readability of the text in the table, click the Add to Custom Colors button, and then click the OK button. Close the remaining dialog boxes.) Make sure that you use complementary colors that maintain the readability of the table's data.

6. Import the **RStock.htm** file from your Data Disk into the Web site. This page contains the stock performance information and will open in the main frame of the frames page.

Explore

7. Create a new page in the banner frame named and titled **Banner**. Insert a user-defined navigation bar that contains the same entries as the navigation bar on the Home Page. (*Hint*: Use the Windows Clipboard to copy the navigation bar from the Home Page and paste it into the Banner page. You will create the hyperlink to the Home Page in the next step.) Change the navigation bar to use a table with a single row. (*Hint*: Use the Help system to learn more about the Convert Text to Table command on the Table menu.) Delete any extra cells that are created after the conversion. When a user clicks a hyperlink in the navigation bar in the banner frame, the target page should replace the frames page and open in the full browser window. (*Hint*: Use the Edit Hyperlink dialog box to check the target frame of any existing hyperlinks in the navigation bar.) The navigation bar should have active hyperlinks to the following pages: **rcompany.htm**, **RNews.htm**, **REmploy.htm** and **RFeedback.htm**.

Explore

8. Create a hyperlink to the Home Page that opens the Home Page in the full browser window. Save your changes.

9. Create a new page in the contents frame named and titled **Contents**. The entries in the table of contents should appear on separate lines in the contents frame. Create hyperlinks to the pages that will open in the main frame (**RFinInfo.htm** and **Rstock.htm**).

10. Verify that the **RFinInfo.htm** page is the default page that opens in the main frame when the frames page is opened in the browser. Save your changes.

Explore

11. Use the browser to test the frames page to make sure each of the hyperlinks results in the appropriate action. If necessary, return to FrontPage to create new hyperlinks in the navigation bars in other pages in the Web site to open the new **RInvest.htm** frames page. Save your changes to each page. Then use the browser to print all three pages individually in the frames page with the Financial Performance Web page displayed in the main frame. Close Internet Explorer.

12. Use FrontPage to print the HTML code for the frames page (**RInvest.htm**) and the Banner page (**Banner.htm**).

13. Display the **RInvest.htm** page as the center focus in Hyperlinks view, expand the hyperlinks for the Contents page, and then print Hyperlinks view using WordPad.

14. Close FrontPage.

Case 2. Creating a "What" Page for Buffalo Trading Post   Retail-clothing customers usually want to know which items are the current best sellers. At Buffalo Trading Post, Donna Vargas and Karla Perez decided that a list of the current top 10 hot items would be a great addition to their Web site. As you discuss this concept with a sales associate, you conclude that there are three main areas of interest: women's clothing, children's clothing, and accessories. Karla asks you to help her create the "What" page for the company's Web site.

If necessary, start FrontPage, insert your Data Disk in the appropriate disk drive, and then do the following:

1. Read all the questions for this case problem, and then prepare a planning analysis sheet for the changes to the Buffalo Web site.

2. Open the **Buffalo** Web site (a:\My Webs\Buffalo) from your Data Disk in Page view. (If you did not create this Web site in Tutorial 2 and change it in Tutorial 3, ask your instructor for assistance.)

3. Donna wants you to use a frames page to implement the top 10 list of hot items by category with a separate Web page for each of the following categories: women's clothing, children's clothing, and accessories. Use the Banner and Contents frames page template to create a new frames page with the filename **BWhat.htm** and the title "What." Replace the existing **BWhat.htm** file that you created with the Tasks list in Tutorial 3.

Explore   4. Create a new Web page in the banner frame with the filename and title **Banner**. Design and create a table that will contain the entries for the navigation bar. Your table design should include a cell with a picture for each of the following navigation choices: Home, Who, How, Where, and Contact.

Explore   5. Change the color of the table's background, light border, and dark border to white so that the table's borders are not displayed. Insert the **BWhatLog.gif** picture as a centered logo in this page, and then insert the following pictures in the appropriate cells in the table that you created in Step 4: **BNavHome.gif**, **BNavWho.gif**, **BNavHow.gif**, **BNavWhre.gif**, and **BNavCtct.gif**. (*Hint*: The picture files are saved in the Tutorial.04 folder on your Data Disk.) Add appropriate alternative text to each of the pictures. Change the height of the banner frame so that the logo and table contents are visible. Save the page and save the embedded picture files in the Web site's images folder.

6. Create the hyperlinks for the Home, Who, and How pictures to open the appropriate pages in the full browser window.

7. Create a new table of contents page in the contents frame with the filename and title **Contents**. Create hyperlinks for each of the pages that will open in the main frame, and then format the list of hyperlinks as a bulleted list.

Explore   8. Design one table for the hot items list for each category. Each table should include the name of the item, a brief description, and a current price range. Then create separate Web pages to open in the main frame of the frames page for each of these tables, using appropriate filenames and titles for each page. Use the cell width percentage option to adjust the width of the cells, if necessary. Set the page for the women's list to open as the default page in the main frame when the frames page is opened in the browser. Save each page.

9. If necessary, create the hyperlink from the Home Page to the What page, from the How page to the What page, and from the Who page to the What page, saving each page.

Explore   10. Test the frames page using Internet Explorer and make sure that each of the hyperlinks results in the appropriate action. If you encounter any problems during testing, return to FrontPage and correct them. Then use the browser to print the frames page as it appears in the browser window with the Accessories page displayed in the main frame. Close Internet Explorer.

Explore   11. Use FrontPage to print the HTML code for the frames page. Circle the FRAME tags that specify the name of each default page that opens in a frame and the name of the frame in which the page opens.

Explore   12. Display the What page (**BWhat.htm**) as the center focus in Hyperlinks view, expand the hyperlinks from the Contents page, and then print Hyperlinks view using WordPad.

Explore   13. Run a Site Summary report to discover any broken hyperlinks, and then correct the problems. (*Hint*: Display the Reporting toolbar, and then use the list arrow to display the correct report.)

14. Close FrontPage.

Case 3. Developing the Menu Pages for Garden Grill   Nolan Simmons and Shannon Taylor, members of the Web site development team at Garden Grill, just returned from a meeting with Amy Gotcher, who runs the marketing department. During the meeting, Amy described her vision of the restaurant menu Web pages so that Garden Grill can remain competitive in the casual, full-service restaurant industry. Her goal is for customers to be able to view the menu from their homes or offices before coming to the restaurant. There will be four separate pages—one each for appetizers, sandwiches, entrees, and desserts. Amy wants to use a table to arrange the entries in each menu. She asks you to help Shannon develop these Web pages.

If necessary, start FrontPage, insert your Data Disk in the appropriate disk drive, and then do the following:

1. Read all the questions for this case problem, and then prepare a planning analysis sheet for this enhancement to the Garden Web site.

2. Open the **Garden** Web site (a:\My Webs\Garden) from your Data Disk in Page view. (If you did not create this Web site in Tutorial 2 and change it in Tutorial 3, ask your instructor for assistance.)

3. Use the Contents frames page template to create the menu as a frames page. Save the page with the filename **GMenu.htm** and the title "Menu."

4. Sketch the design and contents of each table that will contain the menu items in each menu category. Each table should include at least three menu choices. The table should include cells for the item's name, description, and price.

5. Create the four Web pages according to the design you prepared in Step 4. Create appropriate filenames and titles for each of the pages.

6. Insert the **Garden01.gif** picture from the Garden Web site's images folder as a logo at the top of each page that you created in Step 5. Save each page as you complete it.

7. Create a new page to open in the contents frame with the filename and title **Contents**. The Contents Web page should include hyperlinks to each of the menu pages with the main frame as the target for the four menu category pages and an appropriate target for the Home Page so that it replaces the entire frames page and opens in the full browser window.

8. Edit the frames page so that the Appetizers Web page opens first when the Menu frames page is opened in the browser.

Explore   9. Apply complementary background and border colors to the table in each of the menu category pages. Then change the background color of the Contents page to use the same background as the Home Page. (*Hint*: The picture for the background is stored in the Web site's images folder.) Save each page as you finish it.

10. Create a hyperlink from the Home Page to the Menu Web page. Make sure that each of the Web pages in the Web site contains active hyperlinks to the other Web pages in the site. Then test each of the hyperlinks in the frames page using the browser. If you encounter any problems during testing, return to FrontPage and correct them.

Explore   11. Create a new frame by splitting the contents frame. Drag the bottom border of the contents frame up approximately two inches to create the new frame. Then create a new Web page in the new frame with the filename **Contact.htm** and the title "Contact Us." Apply the same background to the Contact Us Web page that you applied to the Home Page, and then enter the following text: "Didn't find your favorites? Send your menu suggestions to" and then press the spacebar and create a mailto with your e-mail address. (Don't worry if your e-mail address is longer than the frame's width.) Save the page.

12. Test the frames page in Internet Explorer. Then use the browser to print the frames page as it appears in the browser window with the Desserts Web page displayed in the main frame. Close Internet Explorer.

Explore ➤ 13. Use FrontPage to print the HTML code for the frames page. Circle the FRAME tags that specify the name of each default page that opens in a frame and the name of the frame in which the page opens.

14. Display the Menu Web page (**GMenu.htm**) as the center focus in Hyperlinks view, expand the hyperlinks for the Contents Web page, and then print Hyperlinks view using WordPad.

Explore ➤ 15. Run a Site Summary report to discover any broken hyperlinks, and then correct the problems. (*Hint*: Display the Reporting toolbar, and then use the list arrow to display the correct report.)

16. Close FrontPage.

Case 4. Preparing a Specials Page for Replay Music Factory Charlene Fields is pleased with your progress in assisting Alec Johnston with the development of the company's Web site. During a recent management meeting, Charlene presented the content of the current Replay Web site and received feedback from members of Replay's senior management team. Cassady Spruiell, senior marketing manager, suggested including a Specials Web page in the Web site that would contain a list of the CDs for which Replay wants to provide additional exposure. Cassady wants to use the Specials page to promote several different music categories. She approved a design using a frames page in which the contents page would display the selection of music types and the main page would display the available specials for that music type. Furthermore, Cassady wants you to arrange the specials for each music type as a table so that the information in each page is easy to read. Charlene asks you to assist Alec with this Web revision.

If necessary, start FrontPage, insert your Data Disk in the appropriate disk drive, and then do the following:

1. Read all the questions for this case problem, and then prepare a planning analysis sheet for this enhancement to the Replay Web site.

2. Open the **Replay** Web site (a:\My Webs\Replay) from your Data Disk in Page view. (If you did not create this Web site in Tutorial 2 and change it in Tutorial 3, ask your instructor for assistance.)

3. Sketch the appearance of the Specials frames page. Your frames page should include at least one frame for the table of contents with each of the types of music and one frame to display the individual page with the details of each type of music. At least one of the tables should contain a nested table.

4. Create a new frames page using a template that closely matches your design. (*Hint*: If you do not find a frames page template that matches your design, adjust your design to match an existing template.) Save the frames page with the filename **MSpecial.htm** and the title "Specials" in the Replay Web site.

5. Sketch the design of each of the tables that you will use on each music category page. Include a minimum of three different music types of your choice. Each special music offering should include information that indicates the artist, title, identification number, and current price.

6. Create all the Web pages for your design using real or fictitious data. (*Hint*: Recall that you need at least one page for each of the frames in your frames page.) The user should be able to return to the Home Page from a hyperlink displayed in one of the frames.

7. Specify the hyperlinks for displaying each of the pages for the type of music in a main frame. Adjust the sizes of the frames in the frames page as necessary to accommodate the text that they contain.

8. Using either the Contents Web page or a page displayed in another frame, specify the hyperlinks for all the other pages that are opened from this frames page. For any page that is not part of the frames page, that page should replace the entire frames page and open in the full browser window.

9. Display one of the music type pages as the initial page in the main frame when the frames page is opened in the browser window.

10. Use the browser to test the frames page to make sure each of the hyperlinks results in the appropriate action. If you discover any problems during testing, return to FrontPage and correct them. Close Internet Explorer.

11. Use FrontPage to print each of the pages that opens in your frames page.

12. Display the Specials Web page (**MSpecial.htm**) as the center focus in Hyperlinks view, expand the hyperlinks from the Contents page, and then print Hyperlinks view using WordPad.

Explore   13. Run a Site Summary report to discover any broken links, and then correct the problems. (*Hint*: Display the Reporting toolbar, and then use the list arrow to display the correct report.)

14. Close FrontPage.

QUICK CHECK ANSWERS

Session 4.1

1. The Web page opens in Page view in FrontPage (or in Notepad or Microsoft Word, depending your system's settings) so you can edit the page and save it on disk or republish it to the Web server on which it is stored.

2. One cell

3. Creating a table using percentages ensures that all users will see the table correctly, regardless of their computer's monitor size and resolution.

4. Cell padding

5. True

6. False

7. above

8. Select the cells, and then click the Merge Cells button; or click the Eraser button, and then use the pointer to erase the border between the cells to merge.

9. above

Session 4.2

1. True

2. three

3. False

4. Frames Page HTML

5. Set Initial Page

6. _top (Whole Page)

7. FRAMESET

CREATING A WEB SITE WITH SHARED BORDERS AND A THEME

Creating the New Recipes Web Site

CASE

Sunny Morning Products

The Web site development team is pleased with how the Sunny Web site looks. The basic content for the Web site is complete, and now it is time to focus on its appearance. Amanda Bay wants you to change the appearance of pictures that you include in the Sunny Web site, not only to add visual interest, but also to use them as hyperlinks that open other pages. You will make other changes to the Home Page as well to add interest to the page by adding hover buttons, a page transition, and animation. These special effects are created using dynamic HTML code that FrontPage adds to your page automatically.

David Harrah manages the marketing department at Sunny Morning Products. In the past, he has successfully used print advertisements and telephone sales to promote the Sunshine Country Store. The store generates a large profit from sales conducted at the store and through telemarketing. The store receives many calls from customers who need directions to it, so David suggests including a picture of a directional map in the Sunny Morning Products Home Page. He already created the map and saved it on your Data Disk so you can insert it into the Sunny Web site.

David also reports that many customers have requested recipes for some of the products sold at the store, such as cakes, pies, and baked breads. At the weekly meeting of the Web site development team, David suggested including a few recipes for popular products in the Web site. David wants to add several recipes to the Web site initially and then add new recipes each month to increase the overall number of recipes slowly. David created several pages with recipes and then stored them on the company's Web server. David wants the pages for the recipes to have a different appearance from other pages in the Sunny Web site. Amanda suggests creating a separate Web site and linking it to the existing Sunny Web site to give the marketing department separate control over the site's appearance. Fortunately, you can link Web sites together easily using FrontPage.

In this tutorial, you will include the map in the Sunny Web site and then create and format the new Recipes Web site. When you are finished, patrons can use the Web site to obtain directions to the Sunshine Country Store and to print recipes for the store's products.

SESSION 5.1

In this session, you will create a thumbnail picture in a Web page, change its appearance, and add text to it. You will create a hover button with a hyperlink to the Home Page. Finally, you will add a page transition and animate text in a Web page.

Creating a Thumbnail Picture

So far in this book, you have included pictures in your Web pages and formatted some of them with transparent backgrounds and hotspots. You can use FrontPage to change a picture's appearance in other ways, as well. For example, you can create a smaller version of a picture, a picture with washed-out colors, or a picture with an enhanced border. In addition, you can change the way that a picture behaves in a Web page by applying special effects to it, such as changing the picture's color when the user points to it. Amanda wants you to enhance the appearance of the Home Page by adding a picture with some of these effects applied to it.

A **thumbnail picture** is a small version of a larger picture that contains a hyperlink to the larger picture. Using a thumbnail picture helps reduce the time it takes to download a page that contains the larger version of the thumbnail picture. Using a thumbnail picture is appropriate when some of your page's users might not need the larger version. Users who want to view the larger picture can click the thumbnail picture, which contains a hyperlink to open a new Web page that contains the larger picture. The hyperlink might be to a picture file or to an HTML document that contains the picture and some text. When the thumbnail opens a picture file, only the picture is displayed in the browser. The user must click the browser's Back button to return to the previous Web page. If the hyperlink opens an HTML document that contains the larger picture, the page can include hyperlinks to other Web pages, just like any other HTML document. When you create a thumbnail of a larger picture, FrontPage automatically creates the thumbnail picture, inserts it in place of the larger picture, and then creates a hyperlink from the thumbnail picture to the larger picture.

In response to David's request for a map in the Home Page, Amanda asks you to create a thumbnail of the map that he provided with a hyperlink to the full-sized map. Using a thumbnail in the Home Page—instead of the full-sized picture—ensures that the page will download quickly. To help plan your work, Amanda asks you to review the planning analysis sheet shown in Figure 5-1 that she prepared after meeting with David.

| Figure 5-1 | AMANDA'S PLANNING ANALYSIS SHEET FOR THE SUNSHINE COUNTRY STORE WEB PAGE |

Planning Analysis Sheet

Objective

Create a new Web page that identifies the location of the Sunshine Country Store and uses special effects to enhance the page's appearance.

Requirements

Map picture showing the location of the Sunshine Country Store

Sunshine Country Store Map Web page to import into the Web site

Results

A Web page that includes the following elements:

      A map picture with directions for locating the Sunshine Country Store

      A hover button with a hyperlink to return to the Home Page

      A page transition that occurs when the page is opened

      Animated text

The Sunshine Country Store Map Web page will open when the user clicks a thumbnail picture of the map in the Home Page.

REFERENCE   WINDOW   **RW**

Creating a Thumbnail Picture
- If necessary, insert the full-sized picture in the Web page in the desired location.
- Select the picture.
- Click the Auto Thumbnail button on the Pictures toolbar.

Amanda asks you to create the thumbnail picture in the Home Page. First, you will open the Sunny Web site.

To open the Sunny Web site and the Home Page, and to create the thumbnail:

1. Make sure your Data Disk is in the appropriate disk drive on your computer, start **FrontPage**, open the **Sunny** Web site (a:\My Webs\Sunny) from your Data Disk in Folders view, and then open the Home Page (**index.htm**) in Page view.

   TROUBLE? If you are storing your Data Files on drive A, you might not have enough disk space to complete this tutorial. To create more space on your Data Disk, open your Data Disk in Windows Explorer, and then delete the Tutorial.02, Tutorial.03, and Tutorial.04 folders and their contents from your Data Disk. If you are storing your Data Files on a hard drive or a network, then no action is necessary.

2. Press **Ctrl + End** to scroll to the bottom of the Home Page, click anywhere in the last line in the paragraph above the marquee, press the **End** key to position the insertion point at the end of the line, press the **Enter** key to insert a new line in which to place the picture, and then click the **Center** button 🔲 on the Formatting toolbar to center the line.

   Now you are ready to import the map picture that shows the Sunshine Country Store's location.

3. Click the **Insert Picture From File** button 🔲 on the Standard toolbar, and then click the **Select a file on your computer** button 🔲 to open the Select File dialog box. Make sure the drive or folder that contains your Data Disk appears in the Look in text box, double-click the **Tutorial.05** folder to open it, and then double-click **Map**. The map that David created is inserted at the location of the insertion point.

4. If necessary, scroll down the Home Page so that you can see the entire map, and then click the map picture to select it and to display the Pictures toolbar.

5. Click the **Auto Thumbnail** button 🔲 on the Pictures toolbar to create the thumbnail picture. See Figure 5-2.

Figure 5-2	HOME PAGE WITH THUMBNAIL MAP PICTURE

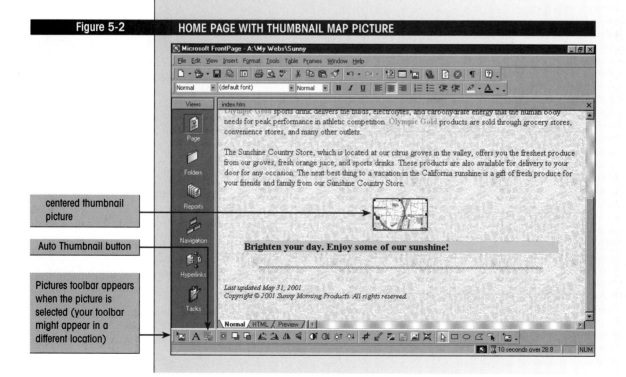

centered thumbnail picture

Auto Thumbnail button

Pictures toolbar appears when the picture is selected (your toolbar might appear in a different location)

The thumbnail picture replaced the full-sized picture in the Home Page. FrontPage created a hyperlink from the thumbnail to the Map.gif file in the Tutorial.05 folder on your Data Disk, which is the location of the original, full-sized picture from which the thumbnail was created. When you save the Home Page, you will need to save this smaller picture in the Sunny Web site. Before you save the picture, however, Amanda wants you to change its characteristics.

Changing **Picture Characteristics**

You can use FrontPage to change many picture characteristics. For example, you can convert a picture to black and white, rotate it, change its contrast, change its brightness level, add a beveled edge to the picture's frame, or wash out a picture. When you **wash out** a picture, you reduce its brightness and contrast to create a faded appearance.

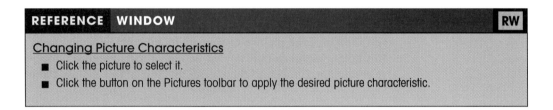

REFERENCE WINDOW · RW

Changing Picture Characteristics
- Click the picture to select it.
- Click the button on the Pictures toolbar to apply the desired picture characteristic.

Amanda wants you to make several changes to the thumbnail picture. You could make the same types of changes to the Map.gif file or to any other GIF picture. However, for now you will concentrate on the appearance of the thumbnail picture.

To change picture characteristics:

1. With the thumbnail picture still selected, click the **Black and White** button ▨ on the Pictures toolbar to apply that effect. The picture changes to a black-and-white image.

2. Click ▨ again to restore the colors to the thumbnail picture.

3. Click the **Rotate Left** button ▨ on the Pictures toolbar. The picture flips on its left side. Click the **Rotate Right** button ▨ to return the picture to its original orientation.

4. Click the **Wash Out** button ▨ on the Pictures toolbar. Notice that the colors become faded in the picture, but the picture still contains colors.

5. Click the **Restore** button ▨ on the Pictures toolbar to remove the wash-out effect and restore the picture to its original state. Clicking the Restore button removes all previously applied, unsaved picture effects.

   Amanda feels that the wash-out effect provides the best appearance for the thumbnail picture, so she wants you to use it. Then you will apply a new effect to the picture's edges.

6. Click the **Undo** button ▨ on the Standard toolbar to return to the thumbnail picture with the wash-out effect.

7. Click the **Bevel** button ▨ on the Pictures toolbar. Notice that the edges of the picture change to include a raised effect. The picture now has a wash-out effect and a beveled edge. Amanda asks you to save the page.

8. Click the **Save** button 🖫 on the Standard toolbar to open the Save Embedded Files dialog box. You need to save the original picture file, Map.gif, as well as the thumbnail picture to which FrontPage assigned the name Map_small.gif, in the images folder of the Sunny Web site. FrontPage automatically generates the name for the thumbnail by appending "_small" to the filename of the full-sized picture.

9. Make sure that the files will be saved in the Sunny Web site's images folder, and then click the **OK** button. The picture files are saved in the Sunny Web site.

Amanda asks you to add another enhancement to the thumbnail picture. You will add text over it so that users can easily identify its function.

Adding Text Over a Picture

When you insert a GIF picture in a Web page, a good design practice is to add descriptive text on top of the picture to identify its function. For pictures that are used as hyperlinks, this text is useful to indicate the action of the hyperlink. You place text over a picture by selecting the picture and then using the Text button on the Pictures toolbar to add the text.

REFERENCE WINDOW   **RW**

Adding Text Over a Picture
- In Page view, click the picture to select it.
- Click the Text button on the Pictures toolbar to open a text box on top of the selected picture.
- Type the desired text. If necessary, press the Enter key to start a new line.
- Click anywhere in the Web page to finish entering the text.

To continue enhancing the Home Page, Amanda wants you to place text on the thumbnail picture to indicate that it opens a map to the Sunshine Country Store.

To add text to a picture:

1. Click the **thumbnail picture** to select it and to display the Pictures toolbar.

2. Click the **Text** button 🅰 on the Pictures toolbar to open a text box on top of the picture.

3. Type **Store**, press the **Enter** key to start a new line, and then type **Map**. This text will appear on top of the picture.

   Next, change the color of the text that you added to the picture to the same orange color that you used for the "Olympic Gold" text in the Home Page.

4. Select the **Store Map** text, click the list arrow for the **Font Color** button 🅰 on the Formatting toolbar to open the color palette, and then click the **orange** color in the Document's Colors section. The text that you added on top of the thumbnail picture changes to orange.

5. Click outside the picture to deselect it and the text, and then click the **Save** button 🖫 on the Standard toolbar to save the picture with this change.

You created the thumbnail picture, changed several of its characteristics, and added text over it. Amanda wants you to test the thumbnail picture to make sure the hyperlink works correctly by opening the full-sized map picture.

To test the thumbnail picture:

1. Click the **Preview in Browser** button 🔍 on the Standard toolbar to open the Home Page in the browser, and then scroll to the bottom of the page so you can see the thumbnail picture.

2. Point to the thumbnail picture. The pointer changes to a 👆 shape. The path-name listed in the status bar indicates that this picture contains a hyperlink to the Map.gif file.

3. Click the **thumbnail picture**. The Map.gif file opens as a separate Web page in the browser window. The URL in the Address bar indicates that this page is a GIF file and not an HTML document. A GIF file cannot contain hyperlinks, so you will need to use the browser's Back button to return to the Home Page.

4. Click the **Back** button ⬅ on the Standard Buttons toolbar to return to the Home Page, and then click the **Close** button ❌ on the Internet Explorer title bar to close it.

To return to the previous Web page, you had to click the Back button on the toolbar. Some Web users might not know to do this, so Amanda asks you to provide navigation options for returning to the Home Page. To do this, you need to include the full-sized map picture in an HTML document. David created a Web page that contains the map picture, so you need only to import that page in the Sunny Web site and then set up the hyperlinks.

To import the Web page for the full-sized picture:

1. If necessary, click the **Microsoft FrontPage** program button on the taskbar to return to FrontPage, and then click the **Folders** button 📁 on the Views bar to change to Folders view.

2. Click **File** on the menu bar, and then click **Import** to open the Import dialog box.

3. Click the **Add File** button to open the Add File to Import List dialog box, and make sure the drive or folder that contains your Data Disk appears in the Look in text box. Double-click the **Tutorial.05** folder, and then double-click **MapPage**. The MapPage.htm file is listed in the Import dialog box.

4. Click the **OK** button to import the Web page into the Sunny Web site.

With the Web page for the map imported into the Sunny Web site, you are ready to add the link back to the Home Page. First, you'll change the link from the Home Page to the imported Sunshine Country Store Map page (mappage.htm). Then you'll create the link from the Map page to the Home Page.

To edit the hyperlink for the thumbnail picture:

1. Double-click **index.htm** in the Contents pane to open the Home Page in Page view.

2. Right-click the **thumbnail picture** (not the "Store Map" text) to select it and open the shortcut menu, and then click **Hyperlink Properties**. The Edit Hyperlink dialog box opens. Notice that the URL text box displays the current hyperlink to the Map.gif file in the Web site's images folder.

   TROUBLE? If the Create Hyperlink dialog box opens and the URL text box displays the text "http://," you right-clicked the picture's text box in Step 2. Click the Cancel button, and then repeat Step 2.

3. Scroll down the list box until you see mappage.htm. Double-click **mappage.htm** to change the thumbnail picture's hyperlink to this new Web page and to close the Edit Hyperlink dialog box.

4. Click the **Save** button 🔲 on the Standard toolbar to save your changes.

With this revision to the hyperlink to the Map page, you need to test the page to make sure that the hyperlink from the thumbnail picture opens the correct Web page.

To test the hyperlink from the thumbnail picture:

1. Click the **Preview in Browser** button 🔍 on the Standard toolbar. The Home Page opens in the browser window.

2. Scroll down the Home Page until you see the thumbnail picture, and then click the **Store Map** picture to open the Sunshine Country Store Map page. Notice that the URL in the Address bar is to the mappage.htm Web page, and not to the Map.gif file. David inserted the Map.gif picture in this page, but he did not include the link to return to the Home Page.

3. Click the **Edit** button 🔲 on the Standard Buttons toolbar. The Sunshine Country Store Map page opens in Page view in FrontPage and the browser remains open.

   TROUBLE? If your Edit button does not look like 🔲, click the Microsoft FrontPage program button on the taskbar, change to Folders view, and then double-click mappage.htm in the Contents pane to open the Web page in Page view.

You successfully created the link from the Home Page to the Sunshine Country Store Map page. Now you need to complete the link in the other direction from the Sunshine Country Store Map page back to the Home Page. A fun way to do this is to use a hover button.

Creating a Hover Button

A **hover button** is a special button that contains a hyperlink. A hover button is just like any other button that appears in a Web page, except that you can add animation and special effects to it. You can set an effect from a list of available effects, or you can use the custom option to create a picture that changes on mouse over. **Mouse over**, or **mouse fly over**, is the act of moving the pointer over a hover button or a picture. When you point to a hover button, the appearance of the button changes to match the specified mouse-over effect.

Amanda wants you to create a hover button in the Sunshine Country Store Map page that changes on mouse over and contains a hyperlink that opens the Home Page.

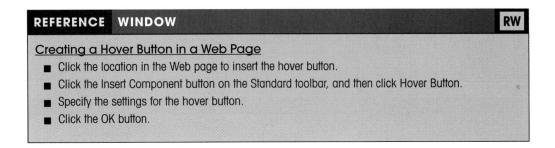

REFERENCE	WINDOW	RW

Creating a Hover Button in a Web Page
- Click the location in the Web page to insert the hover button.
- Click the Insert Component button on the Standard toolbar, and then click Hover Button.
- Specify the settings for the hover button.
- Click the OK button.

Amanda explains that there are many options for creating hover buttons. She asks you to create a hover button that displays the text "Return to Home Page," contains a hyperlink to open the Home Page, and has coordinated colors for the hover button's effects.

To create a hover button:

1. If necessary, scroll to the bottom of the Sunshine Country Store Map page. Notice that the table below the map contains two empty cells. You could not see this table when you viewed it in the browser because the table's cells do not have colored borders.

2. Click in the left cell of the table to select it. You will insert the hover button in this cell.

3. Click the **Insert Component** button [icon] on the Standard toolbar, and then click **Hover Button** to open the Hover Button Properties dialog box with the value in the Button text text box selected. See Figure 5-3. The text that appears in this text box will be displayed on the hover button. You need to enter text to indicate that clicking this button opens the Home Page. Amanda wants you to change the default font, size, style, and color of the text, as well.

Figure 5-3	HOVER BUTTON PROPERTIES DIALOG BOX

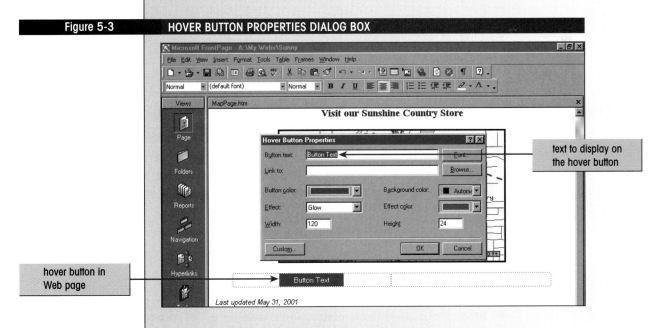

4. Type **Return to Home Page** as the Button text, and then click the **Font** button in the dialog box to open the Font dialog box.

5. Click the **Font** list arrow and then click **Arial**. Click the **Font style** list arrow and then click **Bold**. Click the **Size up** arrow four times to change the size to **18**, and then click the **Color** list arrow and click the **Yellow** color in the Standard colors section. See Figure 5-4.

Figure 5-4   COMPLETED FONT DIALOG BOX

6. Click the **OK** button to close the Font dialog box and return to the Hover Button Properties dialog box.

Next, choose the target page for the hyperlink. In this case, you will select the file for the Home Page.

7. Click the **Browse** button to open the Select Hover Button Hyperlink dialog box. Make sure that the folder for the Sunny Web site appears in the Look in list box, and then scroll down (if necessary) and double-click **index.htm** to select the Home Page and to return to the Hover Button Properties dialog box. The Link to text box now displays the filename for the Home Page.

Next, specify the colors and effect to use for the hover button.

8. Click the **Button color** list arrow, and then click the **Green** color in the Standard colors section.

9. Click the **Effect** list arrow, and then click **Reverse glow**.

10. Click the **Effect color** list arrow, click **More Colors** to open the More Colors dialog box, click the **orange** color (second to last row, third color from the left), and then click the **OK** button to close the More Colors dialog box. See Figure 5-5.

Figure 5-5   COMPLETED HOVER BUTTON PROPERTIES DIALOG BOX

FrontPage specified a default width and height for your hover button and displayed these measurements, in pixels, in the Width and Height text boxes. Usually, it is easiest to accept the default measurements and then to resize the button using the pointer, if necessary, in Page view.

11. Click the **OK** button to create the hover button. The button appears in the table, but some of its text is not visible. See Figure 5-6.

| Figure 5-6 | HOVER BUTTON IN THE WEB PAGE |

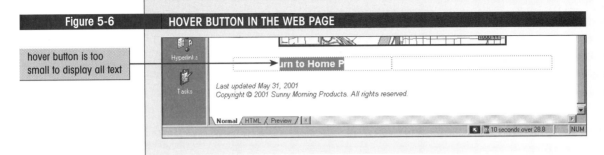

hover button is too small to display all text

The default size of the hover button is too small for the text that you set to be displayed on the button. You can resize the button so that all the text is displayed by selecting the button and dragging one of its corners until it is the desired size. Amanda asks you to increase the size of the hover button and then to test it in the browser.

To resize a hover button and test it in the browser:

1. Click the **hover button** to select it. Sizing handles appear around the button.

2. Click and drag any one of the corner sizing handles to increase the size of the hover button so all of the text appears. See Figure 5-7. The hover button does not need to fill the table cell in which it appears, because the table's borders will not be displayed in the browser.

| Figure 5-7 | RESIZED HOVER BUTTON IN THE WEB PAGE |

all text appears on the hover button

3. Click the **Save** button 🔲 on the Standard toolbar to save the revised page. Now you are ready to test the hover button.

4. Click the **Preview in Browser** button 🔍 on the Standard toolbar to reload the page in the browser, and then scroll to the bottom of the Web page.

5. Point to the **Return to Home Page** button and watch the reverse glow effect from the mouse over. See Figure 5-8. Notice that the status bar indicates a hyperlink to the index.htm file on mouse over.

Figure 5-8   **REVERSE GLOW EFFECT OF THE HOVER BUTTON**

hover button displays specified effect on mouse over

status bar indicates target page of the hover button's hyperlink

6. Click the **Microsoft FrontPage** program button on the taskbar to return to Page view.

The hover button provides an attractive, animated way of creating a hyperlink to another Web page. The hover button effect helps draw the user's attention to the button for selecting the hyperlink.

Changing FrontPage Component Properties

A hover button is created using a Java applet that is one of several components built into FrontPage. A **Java applet** is a short program written in the Java programming language that is attached to a Web page and executed by the user's browser. Java applets provide dynamic features in a Web page, including the hover button's animation effects. After creating a hover button or other component, you can modify its action or appearance by changing its properties.

Amanda asks you to change the properties of the hover button by revising the button's background color.

To change a FrontPage component property and test it in the browser:

1. Right-click the **Return to Home Page** hover button to open the shortcut menu, and then click **Hover Button Properties** to open the Hover Button Properties dialog box.

2. Click the **Button color** list arrow, and then click the **Maroon** color in the Standard colors section.

3. Click the **Effect** list arrow, and then click **Glow**.

4. Click the **OK** button to close the dialog box, and then click the **Save** button 🔲 on the Standard toolbar to save the Web page. Notice that the hover button is now maroon.

5. Click the **Preview in Browser** 🔍 button on the Standard toolbar, and then scroll down the page and point to the hover button. The orange glow now appears with the maroon background.

Amanda feels that this color combination is more appealing. Next, she asks you to test the action of the hover button in the browser.

6. Click the **Return to Home Page** button. The Home Page opens in the browser. Now test the link to the Sunshine Country Store Map page.

7. Scroll to the bottom of the Home Page, and then click the **Store Map** picture. The Sunshine Country Store Map page opens in the browser.

The hover button provides the desired effect of increased attention when the pointer moves over the button. As with other Web page features, you should apply these effects carefully to avoid overwhelming users.

Using **Dynamic HTML**

Dynamic HTML gives you the ability to control the display of elements in a Web page. When a dynamic HTML command is applied to text or to a picture, Internet Explorer 5 (and other Web browsers that support this feature) will animate the text or picture (or apply other effects that you specify) by executing the HTML code that creates the effect. Because dynamic HTML does not require additional information from the Web server that stores the Web page, it is very efficient and presents the user with a lively, interesting page without requiring time-consuming network activity. Page transitions and animations are two methods of making a Web page more interesting. You will apply each of these features to enhance the Sunshine Country Store Map page when it is opened in the browser.

Creating a Page Transition

A **page transition** is an optional animated effect that you can apply to one or more Web pages in a Web site. When a page with a transition is opened in the browser, the specified transition animates while the page is being opened. You can specify a closing transition for a page, as well. Amanda tells you to use transitions sparingly because too many can overwhelm users and make opening and closing pages occur much slower than when no transitions are used.

REFERENCE WINDOW   **RW**

Applying a Page Transition
- With the desired page open in Page view, click Format on the menu bar, and then click Page Transition to open the Page Transitions dialog box.
- Click the Event list arrow, and then click the desired event.
- Enter a value (in seconds) for the duration in the Duration (seconds) text box.
- Click the desired Transition effect, and then click the OK button.

Amanda asks you to apply the Vertical blinds transition effect to the Sunshine Country Store Map page.

To add a page transition:

1. Click the **Microsoft FrontPage** program button on the taskbar to return to the Sunshine Country Store Map page in Page view.

2. Click **Format** on the menu bar, and then click **Page Transition** to open the Page Transitions dialog box. See Figure 5-9.

Figure 5-9	PAGE TRANSITIONS DIALOG BOX

event that causes the transition to occur

enter the number of seconds for the transition to occur here

available transition effects (your list might differ)

The default Event is **Page Enter**, which means that the transition will occur when the page is opened or refreshed in the browser. The other options are **Page Exit**, which applies the transition when the user leaves the page; **Site Enter**, which applies the transition when the user opens any page in the Web site; and **Site Exit**, which applies the transition when the user leaves the Web site by going to a new Web server. You want the transition to occur when the page is opened, so the Event is correctly set.

3. Click in the **Duration (seconds)** text box, and then type **5** as the value for the duration.

4. In the Transition effect list box, click **Vertical blinds** to select that effect, and then click the **OK** button to complete the page transition specifications.

TROUBLE? If you do not have the Vertical blinds transition installed, select another transition effect.

In addition to page transitions, you also can control the manner in which individual objects, such as text or pictures, are displayed in a Web page.

Creating Animated Text in a Web Page

You can apply animation to selected page elements. **Animation** is an effect that causes an element to "fly" into view from a corner or side of the page or in some other eye-catching way, such as using a spiraling motion. You can apply animation to either text or pictures.

REFERENCE   WINDOW   RW

Creating Animated Text or Pictures in a Web Page
- Select the text or picture that you want to animate.
- Click Format on the menu bar, and then click Dynamic HTML Effects to open the DHTML Effects toolbar.
- Click the On list arrow, and then select the time at which you want the effect to occur.
- Click the Apply list arrow, and then select the effect that you want to apply.
- Click the Effect list arrow, when it is active, to apply the direction in which to apply the effect.

Amanda wants you to apply animation to the text that appears above the map for additional emphasis.

To add text animation:

1. Scroll to the top of the page, and then select the text **Visit our Sunshine Country Store**. Amanda wants this text to bounce into view from the right side of the screen when the page is opened or refreshed in the browser.

2. Click **Format** on the menu bar, and then click **Dynamic HTML Effects**. The DHTML Effects toolbar opens in the Contents pane, as either a docked or floating toolbar. If necessary, drag the DHTML Effects toolbar down to the bottom of the Contents pane, as shown in Figure 5-10, so the toolbar does not block the text that you selected in Step 1. Then make sure that the Highlight Dynamic HTML Effects button 📇 on the DHTML Effects toolbar is indented to indicate that this feature is turned on, so that the DHTML element is highlighted in Page view, making it easy to locate. Next, specify the effects for the selected text.

Figure 5-10	CREATING ANIMATED TEXT

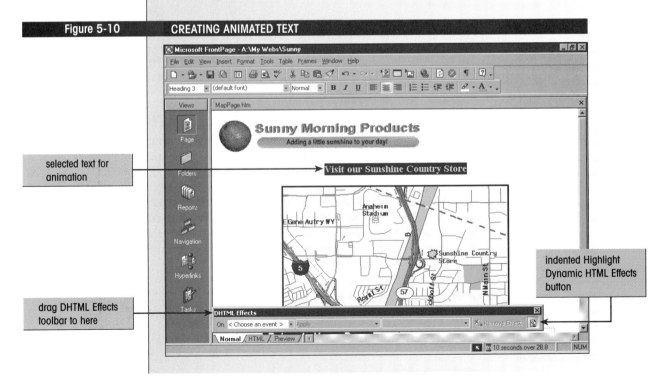

selected text for animation

indented Highlight Dynamic HTML Effects button

drag DHTML Effects toolbar to here

3. Click the **On** list arrow on the DHTML Effects toolbar, and then click **Page load**. This setting will apply the effect when the page is opened or refreshed in the browser. The effects that you can specify for pictures are **Click**, which causes the animation to occur when the element is clicked; **Double click**, which causes the animation to occur when the element is double-clicked; and **Mouse over**, which causes the animation to occur on mouse over.

4. Click the **Apply** list arrow on the DHTML Effects toolbar, and then click **Elastic**. This setting will cause the selected text to bounce into place. When you select certain effects, you must also indicate the direction from which to apply the effect.

5. Click the **Effect** list arrow on the DHTML Effects toolbar, which displays the text "< Choose Settings >" when it is active, and then click **From right**. This setting indicates that the specified effect will occur from the right side of the window. Notice that the DHTML element in your Web page is highlighted with a light blue background. This background will not be displayed in the browser.

You are finished setting the text animation. Amanda asks you to leave the DHTML Effects toolbar open for now so it is available should you need to change any settings.

6. Click the **Save** button 🖫 on the Standard toolbar to save the page.

Amanda asks you to open the Sunshine Country Store Map page from the Home Page so you can see the full effect in the browser. Recall that these effects only work in Internet Explorer 5.0 or later versions. If a browser is not capable of handling these effects, then it ignores them and opens the page. To make sure these effects work correctly, Amanda asks you to test the page transition and text animation that you created for the Sunshine Country Store Map page.

To test the page transition and text animation:

1. Click **Window** on the menu bar, and then click **index.htm** to open the Home Page in Page view, so this page will open in the browser.

2. Click the **Preview in Browser** button 🔍 on the Standard toolbar to open the Home Page in the browser, and then scroll down the page until you see the map.

3. Click the **Store Map** picture, and observe the Vertical blinds page transition and the Elastic animation. Keep in mind that you must have Internet Explorer 5.0 or higher in order to see these special effects.

TROUBLE? If you do not see the text animation in the page, click the Refresh button 🔄 on the Standard Buttons toolbar. When you store a Web site's file on a floppy disk, the files load slower than when the Web site's files are stored on a hard drive or on a Web server, and sometimes you cannot see the effects.

You successfully included several animation effects in the Web page. Amanda asks you to view the HTML code that FrontPage used to create these effects.

Viewing HTML Code for FrontPage Components

When you created these animations in the Sunshine Country Store Map page, FrontPage created a Java applet and inserted it into the HTML document. The hover button, page transition, and text animation were implemented with Java scripts using the APPLET and SCRIPT tags. An applet uses a series of parameters that specify an object's behavior. A **script** is code that is included in the Web page and executed by the Web browser. Amanda asks you to examine the HTML code for the hover button that is implemented using an applet.

To view the HTML for a Java applet:

1. Click the **Edit** button 🔄 on the Standard Buttons toolbar to open the Sunshine Country Store Map page in Page view. You don't need to change any of the animations, so you can close the DHTML Effects toolbar.

2. Click the **Close** button ⊠ on the DHTML Effects toolbar to close it, and then click the **HTML** tab to switch to that view.

3. Press **Ctrl + End** to view the code at the bottom of the page. See Figure 5-11. Notice the parameters for the text value and the effect value.

Figure 5-11	HTML CODE FOR THE SUNSHINE COUNTRY STORE MAP PAGE

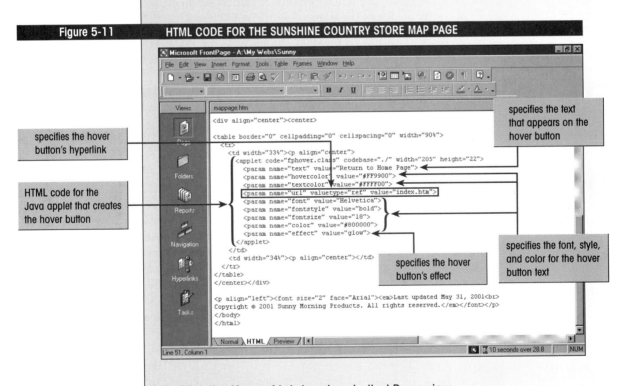

4. Click the **Normal** tab to return to that Page view.

   You are finished with your work, so you can close FrontPage and Internet Explorer.

5. Click the **Close** button ⊠ on the FrontPage title bar to close FrontPage and the Sunny Web site, and then click ⊠ on the Internet Explorer title bar to close the browser.

Amanda and David are pleased with the changes that you made to the Home Page. These changes will make the Home Page easier for patrons to use. In the next session, you will create the new Recipes Web site, which will include shared borders, FrontPage navigation bars, and a Web theme.

Session 5.1 QUICK CHECK

1. When you create a thumbnail picture in a Web page, FrontPage automatically creates a(n) _____ to the full-sized picture that was used to create the thumbnail.

2. List three effects that you can apply to a picture using the Pictures toolbar.

3. Describe the process for adding text over a picture in a Web page.

4. Moving the pointer over a hover button is called _____.

5. True or False: A Java applet creates a hover button in a Web page.

6. True or False: You can add a page transition to only one page in a Web site.

7. True or False: Animation is an effect that causes an element to "fly" into view from a corner or side of the page.

8. What are two actions that you can perform in a Web page using dynamic HTML?

SESSION 5.2

In this session, you will create a new Web site and import pages into it. You will create shared borders and navigation bars for the new Web site. You will apply a theme to the entire Web site and then customize the existing theme.

Using a Wizard to Create a New Web Site

David has created the Web pages that you can use to create the new Recipes Web site. He saved these pages in the Tutorial.05 folder on your Data Disk. Amanda wants you to import these pages from your Data Disk to create a new disk-based FrontPage Web. In Tutorial 3, you learned how to import a Web page into a Web site. When you use the Import Web Wizard to create a new FrontPage Web, you create the site and import the pages at once. You will import David's recipe pages to create the new Recipes Web site.

Figure 5-12 shows Amanda's planning analysis sheet for the new Recipes Web site that you will create.

Figure 5-12   AMANDA'S PLANNING ANALYSIS SHEET FOR THE RECIPES WEB SITE

Planning Analysis Sheet

Objective

Create a new Web site that includes recipes for items sold by the Sunshine Country Store. The Web site will include shared borders with navigation bars created by FrontPage. The Web site will use a theme to add visual interest to the pages.

Requirements

Files for the Web pages for the Home Page and the individual pages that contain the recipes

Results

A Home Page that includes an introduction and hyperlinks to the recipes pages

Navigation bars with links to same-level and child pages and the Home Page;
FrontPage should update the navigation bars automatically as new recipe pages are added to the Web site

Each recipe should appear in its own Web page, with links to related recipes

A Web site that uses a customized Web theme

REFERENCE WINDOW   **RW**

Using the Import Web Wizard to Create a New Web Site

- Start FrontPage, and then change to Folders view. If necessary, close any open Web site or Web page.
- Click File on the menu bar, point to New, and then click Web.
- In the New dialog box, click in the Specify the location of the new web text box, and then type the location in which to store the new Web site.
- Double-click the Import Web Wizard icon to create the new Web site and to start the Wizard.
- Select the location from which to import the existing Web pages, and then click the Next button.
- Select any files to exclude from the specified location, and then click the Exclude button.
- Click the Next button, and then click the Finish button.

Next, you will create the Recipes Web site using David's existing files.

To create a new Web site using the Import Web Wizard:

1. Start **FrontPage**, make sure that your Data Disk is in the correct drive, and then change to Folders view. If necessary, close any open Web site or Web page.

2. Click **File** on the menu bar, point to **New**, and then click **Web** to open the New dialog box. Recall from Tutorial 2 that you can use the templates and Wizards in this dialog box to create a new FrontPage Web.

3. Click in the **Specify the location of the new web** text box, and then type **a:\My Webs\Recipes**. This path will create a new Web site named Recipes in the My Webs folder on your Data Disk. If you are using a different drive or folder for your Data Disk, use the appropriate path for your Data Disk.

4. Double-click the **Import Web Wizard** icon to create the Recipes Web site. After a few moments, the Web site is created on your Data Disk, and the Wizard starts and opens the Import Web Wizard – Choose Source dialog box, in which you specify the location from which to import your existing files. You can import the files from a disk location or from a World Wide Web site. You will import the files from your Data Disk.

5. Click the **From a source directory of files on a local computer or network** option button, select the text in the Location text box, and then type **a:\Tutorial.05**. (If you are storing your Data Files in a different location, type the path to the Tutorial.05 folder on your Data Disk.)

6. Click the **Next** button. The Import Web Wizard – Edit File List dialog box opens, in which you can choose to import all files from the location that you just speci- fied, or exclude files that you don't need. The Tutorial.05 folder on your Data Disk includes files that you used in Session 5.1 and the files that you will use in the end-of-tutorial exercises. You don't need to include these files in the Recipes Web site, so you will exclude them.

7. Press and hold down the **Ctrl** key, click the files **Map.gif**, **Up.gif**, **MapPage.htm**, **Beach.gif**, and **BD14530_.GIF** to select them, and then release the **Ctrl** key. Click the **Exclude** button to display the list of five files that you will import, and then click the **Next** button.

   TROUBLE? If necessary, exclude any other files so that only the files Bread.htm, Cake.htm, Icing.htm, Pie.htm, and Recipes.htm are imported.

8. Click the **Finish** button in the Import Web Wizard – Finish dialog box to import the specified pages into the Recipes Web site. After a few moments, the pages are imported into the Recipes Web site.

9. If necessary, click the **Folders** button 🗀 on the Views bar to display the files that you imported in Folders view.

David did not create a Home Page for the Web site. When a Web browser opens a Web site, it searches for a page named index.htm or default.htm to open as the site's Home Page. Amanda asks you to rename the Recipes.htm page to index.htm so that a Web browser will open this page as the site's Home Page automatically. Then she wants you to change this page's title to "Country Recipes." You can change a page's filename and title in Folders view or Navigation view. Amanda asks you to complete these tasks in Folders view.

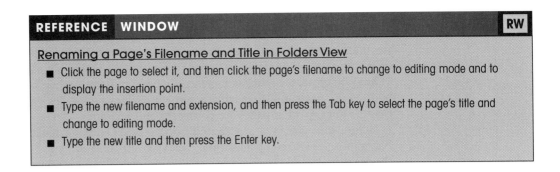

Renaming a Page's Filename and Title in Folders View
- Click the page to select it, and then click the page's filename to change to editing mode and to display the insertion point.
- Type the new filename and extension, and then press the Tab key to select the page's title and change to editing mode.
- Type the new title and then press the Enter key.

To rename a page's filename and title in Folders view:

1. If necessary, click **Recipes.htm** in the Contents pane to select it, and then click **Recipes.htm** again to change to editing mode. The filename is selected, a text box appears around the filename, and the insertion point is blinking in the text box. You can just type the new name to change the page's filename. Amanda asks you to rename this page to index.htm so that browsers will recognize this page as the first page to open in the Recipes Web site.

2. Type **index.htm** and then press the **Tab** key. The Rename dialog box opens while FrontPage changes the page's filename to index.htm. Then FrontPage selects the page's title and adds the text box with an insertion point in it.

   Amanda wants you to change the page's title to "Country Recipes."

3. Press the **Home** key to place the insertion point before the "R" in Recipes.

4. Type **Country**, press the **spacebar**, and then press the **Enter** key. The page's title is renamed to Country Recipes. See Figure 5-13.

Figure 5-13	CHANGING A FILENAME AND PAGE TITLE IN FOLDERS VIEW

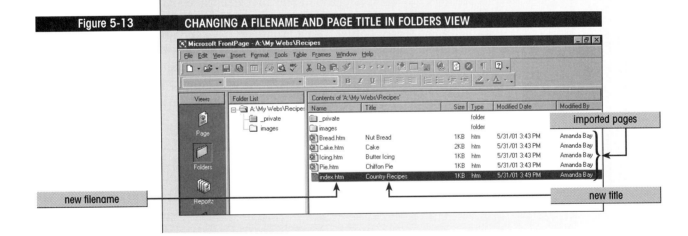

Understanding **Shared Borders and Navigation Bars**

When your Web site contains many pages, you can use shared borders and a FrontPage navigation bar to ensure a consistent appearance for all pages. A **shared border** presents information common to all Web pages in a consistent manner across selected Web pages or the entire Web site.

In Tutorials 2 and 3, you entered and formatted a user-defined navigation bar for the pages in the Sunny Web site. Creating a user-defined navigation bar is easy and useful, but *you* must ensure that all changes made to the navigation structure, including adding and deleting pages, are updated in every Web page that includes a user-defined navigation bar. When you create a FrontPage navigation bar, on the other hand, FrontPage maintains and updates the navigation bar entries automatically, which saves you some time and ensures that the links to other pages are consistent and accurate.

Before you can create a shared border or FrontPage navigation bar, you must use Navigation view to add pages from your Web site in a navigation structure, which identifies the pages in your Web site and how they are related to each other. The navigation structure resembles an organization chart; usually, the Home Page appears at the top level of the Web site, with some pages below it, and then additional levels of pages below them, and so on. In this context, the Home Page is the parent page, the pages under the Home Page are child pages of the Home Page, and so on. You can add any Web page from the Web site to its navigation structure. However, usually some pages that appear in a frames page, such as a banner or contents page, are not included in the navigation structure, because these pages are relevant only to the frameset.

After creating the navigation structure and turning on the shared borders, you add the content of the shared border(s) to your Web site by opening any page in Page view that uses the border and entering the content in the border. A shared border appears with a dotted outline in Page view to indicate its location in a Web page. This outline is not displayed in the browser.

Shared borders usually appear in every Web page in a Web site. FrontPage lets you set top, bottom, left, and right borders, or any two or more borders, for the entire Web site. A shared border often includes button or text hyperlinks to other pages in the Web site, as well as other text or pictures you want to appear in every page in the site.

When you edit the content of a shared border in a single Web page, your changes apply to all pages in the Web site that use the same shared border. For example, adding a company name and logo to a top shared border in one Web page will cause all other pages in the Web site that use the top shared border to display the same name and logo in the same location in the shared border.

You could add a shared border with a FrontPage navigation bar to the Sunny Web site, but Amanda doesn't feel that this change is necessary because all of the hyperlinks in the navigation bar are in place and active. However, Amanda does feel that the new Recipes Web site that you created for the marketing department is an excellent candidate for shared borders. You will set the Home Page as the parent for the Recipes Web site, with child pages that include recipes for cakes, pies, and breads. Then those child pages will have child pages to icings, crusts, and butters. This structure will ensure that when a recipe for a cake is displayed in the browser, the page containing a recipe for an icing for that cake will be included as a hyperlink in the page with the recipe.

Now you are ready to create the navigation structure for the Web site. The Country Recipes page will be the top-level page in the Recipes Web site. You will add the Nut Bread, Cake, and Chiffon Pie pages as child pages of the Country Recipes Web page. Then you will add the Butter Icing page as a child of the Cake page.

Creating a Navigation Structure

After you import or create Web pages in a Web site, they are available for use in the Web site's navigation structure. You add a file to the navigation structure by dragging its filename from the Folder List to the Navigation pane and positioning the page icon so that the connector specifies the desired level and order for the page in the structure. Amanda wants you to create the navigation structure for the Recipes Web site next.

To add existing Web files to the navigation structure:

1. Click the **Navigation** button on the Views bar to change to Navigation view. If necessary, turn on the Navigation toolbar by clicking **View** on the menu bar, pointing to **Toolbars**, and then clicking **Navigation**.

   TROUBLE? If the Navigation toolbar is blocking the navigation structure, drag it to the top of the Navigation pane to move it out of the way.

   TROUBLE? If necessary, click the Folder List button on the Standard toolbar to display the Folder List.

   The Web site's current navigation structure includes only the top-level page in the Web site, Country Recipes (index.htm). To create the navigation structure, drag a filename from the Folder List to the Navigation pane, and release the mouse button when the page is in the correct position.

2. Click **Pie.htm** in the Folder List, and then drag it to the Navigation pane. Position the Pie.htm page so that it is below the Country Recipes page (see Figure 5-14). When the page is correctly positioned, release the mouse button.

Figure 5-14	CREATING A WEB SITE'S NAVIGATION STRUCTURE

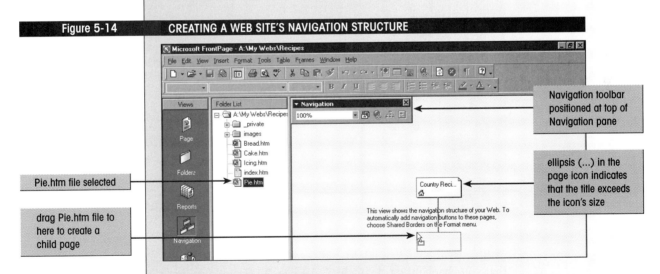

3. Repeat Step 2 to add the **Bread.htm** and **Cake.htm** pages to the Navigation pane as child pages of the Country Recipes page, and then click anywhere in a blank area of the Navigation pane to deselect the pages. See Figure 5-15.

Figure 5-15	NAVIGATION STRUCTURE WITH THREE CHILD PAGES

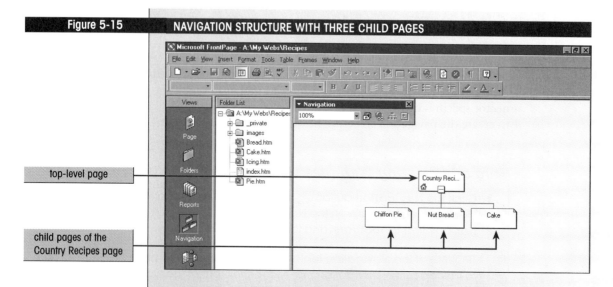

TROUBLE? If you drop a page in the wrong position, click the page that you need to fix and drag it into the correct position so your Navigation pane looks like Figure 5-15.

4. Drag the **Icing.htm** page from the Folder List into the Navigation pane and position it as a child page of the Cake page, and then release the mouse button. See Figure 5-16.

Figure 5-16	COMPLETED NAVIGATION STRUCTURE

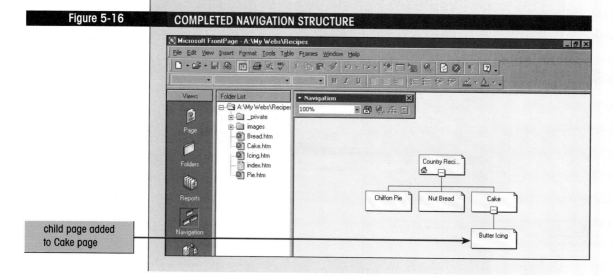

Because the kitchen might add several recipes for different cakes, Amanda recommends that you change the title of the Cake page to something that is more descriptive. She asks you to change the page's title to "Chiffon Cake." Because Navigation view is currently displayed, you will change the title in Navigation view.

REFERENCE   WINDOW   RW

Renaming a Page's Title in Navigation View
- Right-click the page icon in the Navigation pane that you want to change to open the shortcut menu, and then click Rename.
- Type the new page title, and then press the Enter key.

To rename a page's title in Navigation view:

1. Right-click the **Cake** page icon in the Navigation pane to select it and open the shortcut menu, click **Rename**, and then type **Chiffon Cake**. You are changing the title of the Web page, but not the filename, which is still Cake.htm.

2. Press the **Enter** key to rename the page. This title change will also be displayed in Folders view and when the page is viewed with a Web browser.

Now that you have created the navigation structure, you can turn on the shared borders for the Web site and start creating the FrontPage navigation bars.

Creating a Shared Border with Navigation Buttons

When you created the navigation structure, you were really telling FrontPage about the relationships between the Web pages in your Web site. For example, without creating the navigation structure, FrontPage would not know that the Butter Icing page is a child page of the Chiffon Cake page. The reason for creating the navigation structure is to identify these relationships so that FrontPage will create the correct navigation bar in the shared border for each page that uses one.

REFERENCE   WINDOW   RW

Turning on Shared Borders for a Web Site
- If necessary, create the navigation structure for the Web site in Navigation view.
- In Navigation view, click Format on the menu bar, and then click Shared Borders.
- Select the option button for applying the shared border to all or selected pages, select the shared border(s) to add, select the option to include navigation buttons if desired, and then click the OK button.

Your next task is to turn on the shared borders for the Recipes Web site. Amanda's planning analysis sheet indicates that the pages in the Recipes Web site will have two shared borders: a top shared border, containing the page's title and a navigation bar with links to pages at the same level, the Home Page, and the parent page; and a left shared border, containing a navigation bar with links to child pages. All pages in the Recipes Web site will share the same borders, so you can turn on the shared borders with any page selected in the Navigation pane.

To turn on the shared borders:

1. Click **Format** on the menu bar, and then click **Shared Borders**. The Shared Borders dialog box opens and displays a blank sample page. You have not added any shared borders to the Recipes Web site yet, so no options are selected.

2. If necessary, click the **All pages** option button to indicate that the shared borders you will select should be applied to all pages that appear in the Navigation pane. It is important to note that you must add a page to the Navigation pane in order to create a shared border in that page. If you select the All pages option button, but do not add a particular Web page to the navigation structure, then that page will display an error message in Page view indicating that you must add the page to the navigation structure for it to be able to use the shared border.

3. Click the **Top** check box to select it, and then click the **Include navigation buttons** check box, which becomes active after you click the Top check box. This change adds a top shared border with a navigation bar to every page in the navigation structure.

4. Click the **Left** check box to select it, and then click the **Include navigation buttons** check box to add the left shared border with a navigation bar to every page in the navigation structure. See Figure 5-17.

Figure 5-17	SHARED BORDERS DIALOG BOX

shared borders will be applied to all pages in the Web site's navigation structure

option to turn off shared borders for the selected page

left shared border with navigation buttons

top shared border with navigation buttons

5. Click the **OK** button to close the Shared Borders dialog box and to create the top and left shared borders. The status bar will display some messages indicating that the Web site's shared borders are being created. This process will take a few seconds if you are storing your Data Files on a floppy disk.

FrontPage creates the shared borders, but you can't see them in your Web site in Navigation view. However, when you open any page that appears in the navigation structure in Page view, you will see the borders, which are indicated by dashed outlines. Next, open the Chiffon Cake page to see the shared borders.

To open the Chiffon Cake page in Page view:

1. Double-click the **Chiffon Cake** page icon to open that page in Page view. See Figure 5-18.

| Figure 5-18 | CHIFFON CAKE PAGE WITH SHARED BORDERS |

TROUBLE? If the Chiffon Cake page does not open in Page view, repeat Step 1 and double-click the icon, not the page title.

Notice the shared borders at the top and on the left side of the page. The top shared border includes the page's title, Chiffon Cake, and the navigation options for the top-level page (Home) and the pages at the same level as the Chiffon Cake page (Chiffon Pie, Nut Bread, and Chiffon Cake). The option for including the Home Page was automatically selected for the top shared border. When this option is selected, FrontPage inserts the link named "Home" in the navigation bar and creates a link to the page named index.htm.

The Chiffon Cake page is the only child page in the Web site with a child page, and the link to that page (Butter Icing) appears automatically in the left shared border. For pages without links in any border, a message appears indicating that you can click the border to add content to it. The Country Recipes page does not contain any links in the top shared border, as you will see next.

To examine the shared borders for the Country Recipes page:

1. Click the **Navigation** button 🖼 on the Views bar to change to Navigation view.

2. Double-click the **Country Recipes** page icon to open this page in Page view. See Figure 5-19.

| Figure 5-19 | COUNTRY RECIPES PAGE WITH SHARED BORDERS |

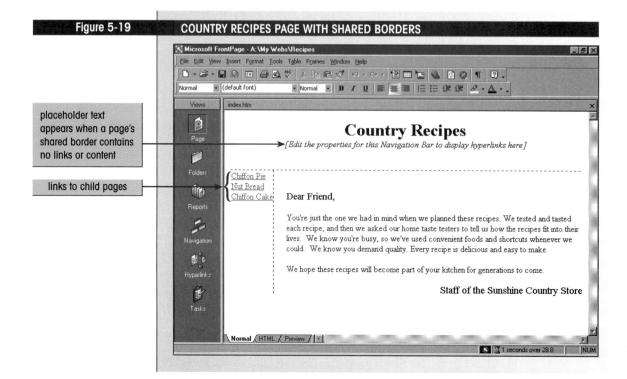

placeholder text appears when a page's shared border contains no links or content

links to child pages

The top shared border displays the page's title and a message. The top shared border does not contain a navigation bar because the Country Recipes page is the top-level page in the Web site and there are no "higher" pages to display. The left shared border contains links to the child pages of the Country Recipes Web page.

Next, Amanda wants you to explore the shared borders in the browser.

To test the shared borders and navigation bars in the browser:

1. Click the **Preview in Browser** button [icon] on the Standard toolbar, and then if necessary, click the **Yes** button to save your changes to the shared borders. The Country Recipes page opens in the browser. The top shared border displays the page's title, and the left shared border displays the links to this page's child pages. See Figure 5-20.

| Figure 5-20 | COUNTRY RECIPES PAGE IN INTERNET EXPLORER |

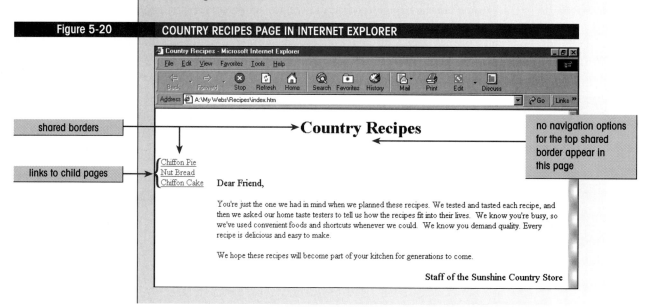

shared borders

links to child pages

no navigation options for the top shared border appear in this page

2. Click the **Chiffon Cake** link to open that page. The top shared border includes the page's title, and links to the Home Page and to the pages at the same level as the Chiffon Cake page. The left shared border includes a link to the Chiffon Cake's child page, Butter Icing.

3. Click the **Butter Icing** link to open that page. The left shared border does not appear because this page has no child pages. The top shared border includes links to "Home" and "Up." Clicking the Home link will open the Country Recipes page, and clicking the Up link will open the parent page, which is the Chiffon Cake page. See Figure 5-21.

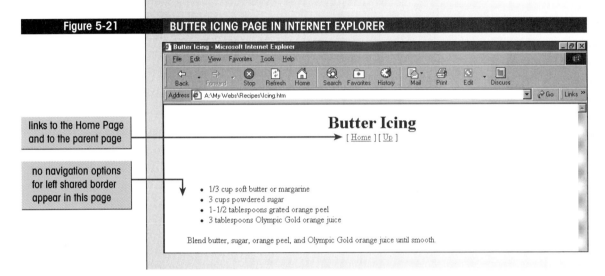

| Figure 5-21 | BUTTER ICING PAGE IN INTERNET EXPLORER |

links to the Home Page and to the parent page

no navigation options for left shared border appear in this page

As you examine the pages in the browser, you decide to add a horizontal line in the top shared border to separate the navigation bar from the recipes. You can make this change by editing the top shared border.

Editing a Shared Border

After creating a shared border, you can modify it by opening in Page view any page that uses the shared border and making the desired changes. Remember that all of the Web pages that you include in the Web site's navigation structure use the *same* shared borders, so any changes that you make to any single shared border are automatically applied to all pages that use it. You select the border that you want to change by clicking anywhere in the border's outline. Then you make changes to the content of the shared border in the same manner that you would use to revise any other Web page in Page view.

Amanda wants you to add a horizontal line at the bottom of the top shared border to separate the border from the actual page content. You will make this change in Page view for the Country Recipes page, but you could make this change using any page in the Web site because all pages use the same top shared border.

To edit a shared border:

1. Click the **Microsoft FrontPage** program button on the taskbar to return to the Country Recipes page in Page view.

2. Click anywhere in the top shared border to select the top and left shared borders in the page. The dashed outline changes to a solid outline to indicate that the borders are selected.

3. Click the **navigation bar placeholder text** (the text that appears in square brackets and begins "Edit the properties") in the top shared border to select it. Notice that the pointer changes to the component pointer when you point to the navigation bar placeholder text. Press the **down arrow** key ↓ on the keyboard to position the insertion point on the next line, and then press the **Delete** key to remove this line.

4. Click at the end of the navigation bar placeholder text in the top shared border, click **Insert** on the menu bar, and then click **Horizontal Line**. A horizontal line appears in the shared border below the navigation bar placeholder text.

5. Click the **Save** button on the Standard toolbar to save the changes to the top shared border.

6. Click **Window** on the menu bar, and then click **Cake.htm** to open the Chiffon Cake page in Page view. Notice that the horizontal line appears in the top shared border for this page as well.

Changes to any of the other shared borders are made in the same manner. However, the default navigation bars could provide better choices for the user. Amanda asks you to review the navigation bars to see if you can improve them.

Revising a Navigation Bar

After you create a FrontPage navigation bar, you might need to revise it occasionally to change the pages to display as navigation options or to change the format to use for the links (text or buttons). Amanda asks you to check the current navigation bar properties next.

To change a navigation bar:

1. Click the **navigation bar** in the top shared border to select it. The pointer changes to the component pointer when you point to the navigation bar.

2. Right-click the **navigation bar** to open the shortcut menu, and then click **Navigation Bar Properties** to open the Navigation Bar Properties dialog box. See Figure 5-22. Notice that in the Hyperlinks to add to page section, most of the choices are option buttons, so only one selection is permitted.

Figure 5-22	NAVIGATION BAR PROPERTIES DIALOG BOX

select only one option from this option group

diagram indicates the current settings for the navigation bar

legend for interpreting the diagram

sample diagram of the navigation bar settings for this page

Navigation Bar Properties

Hyperlinks to add to page
- Parent level
- Same level
- Back and next
- Child level
- Top level
- Child pages under Home

Additional pages:
- ☑ Home page
- ☑ Parent page

select either, both, or no option in this check box group

- ☐ Page navigation bars will appear on
- ■ Pages navigation bars will link to
- ⌂ Home page
- ☐ Other pages

Orientation and appearance
- ● Horizontal
- ○ Vertical
- ● Buttons
- ○ Text

OK   Cancel

select one option button from each group

Figure 5-23 describes the settings in the Navigation Bar Properties dialog box and provides an example of how these settings would apply to the Chiffon Cake page. When you change an option in this dialog box, the sample diagram changes to reflect the new links. Make sure that you study these settings and understand how they work before continuing.

Figure 5-23	NAVIGATION BAR PROPERTY DESCRIPTIONS AND EXAMPLES

OPTION	DESCRIPTION	EXAMPLE FOR THE CHIFFON CAKE PAGE IN THE RECIPES WEB SITE
Hyperlinks to add to page section: Select one option button and one or both check boxes.		
Parent level option button	All pages will include a link to the parent-level page.	Home link only (the parent page)
Same level option button	All pages will include links to pages at the same level as the currently displayed page.	Links to Nut Bread, Chiffon Cake, and Chiffon Pie
Back and next option button	All pages will include links to the page to the left and right of the currently displayed page, based on how the pages were added to the navigation structure.	Back and Next links, which open the Nut Bread and Chiffon Pie pages, respectively
Child level option button	All pages will include a link to the currently displayed page's child pages, if applicable.	Link to the Butter Icing page
Top level option button	All pages will include a link to the top-level page in the Web site.	Home link only (the top-level page in Navigation view)
Child pages under Home option button	All pages will include links to the child pages of the Home Page.	Links to Nut Bread, Chiffon Cake, and Chiffon Pie
Home page check box	All pages will include a link to the Home Page, regardless of what other options are selected.	Home link, plus any other links included by the option button selected in the Hyperlinks to add to page section
Parent page check box	All pages will include a link to the page's parent-level page, regardless of what other options are selected.	Home link (which is the Chiffon Cake's parent page), plus any other links included by the option button selected in the Hyperlinks to add to page section

Figure 5-23	NAVIGATION BAR PROPERTY DESCRIPTIONS AND EXAMPLES (CON'T)	
OPTION	**DESCRIPTION**	**EXAMPLE FOR THE CHIFFON CAKE PAGE IN THE RECIPES WEB SITE**
Orientation and appearance section: Select either the Horizontal or Vertical option button and either the Buttons or Text option button.		
Horizontal option button	Displays buttons or text in a horizontal list.	Displays the top shared border navigation options on a single line
Vertical option button	Displays buttons or text in a vertical list.	Displays the left shared border navigation options in a single column
Buttons option button	Displays buttons containing hyperlinks for navigation options.	Displays buttons in the navigation bar
Text option button	Displays text hyperlinks for navigation options.	Displays text hyperlinks in the navigation bar

3. Click the **Back and next** option button to select it. The Home page and Parent page check boxes are still selected. Notice that the diagram in the dialog box changes, indicating these changes to the hyperlinks included in the navigation bar.

4. Click the **Same level** option button to select it and to return to the original configuration.

5. If necessary, click the **Buttons** option button in the Orientation and appearance section. Notice that the sample page shows buttons, instead of text, in the top shared border.

6. Click the **Text** option button in the Orientation and appearance section to select text hyperlinks in the top shared border.

7. Click the **OK** button to close the Navigation Bar Properties dialog box for the top shared border. You can make the same types of changes to the left shared border, as well.

8. Click the **navigation bar** in the left shared border (the Butter Icing hyperlink) to select it, right-click the **navigation bar** to open the shortcut menu, and then click **Navigation Bar Properties** to open the Navigation Bar Properties dialog box. Make sure that the Child level, Vertical, and Buttons option buttons are selected, and the Home page and Parent page check boxes do not contain check marks. The top shared border will include a link to the Home page, so you don't need to repeat that link in the left shared border.

9. Click the **OK** button to close the Navigation Bar Properties dialog box for the left shared border, and then click the **Save** button 🖫 on the Standard toolbar to save your changes.

These changes to the shared borders will appear in every page in the Web site that uses them. Even though you specified to use buttons, and not text, for the navigation bar in the left shared border, the hyperlink in the left shared border still appears as text. The hyperlinks in the left shared border will display as text until you apply a theme to the Web site later in this session, because the buttons are supplied by a Web theme.

Revising the Navigation Structure

After creating the navigation structure, turning on shared borders, and changing the navigation bar's properties, you might need to revise the navigation structure. You can delete or add pages to the navigation structure, or change the existing page titles. You can also drag and drop the page icons in the Navigation pane to rearrange them in the structure.

Deleting a Page from the Navigation Structure

When you use Navigation view to delete a page from the Web site, you can delete the page from the navigation structure only, or delete the page from the entire Web site. If you delete the page from the navigation structure only, then the page is deleted from the structure and from any FrontPage navigation bars, but the page remains in the Web site. Deleting the page from the Web site removes the page permanently from the navigation structure, from the FrontPage navigation bars, and from the Web site.

REFERENCE WINDOW   **RW**

Deleting a Page from the Navigation Structure
- In Navigation view, right-click the page icon in the Navigation pane that you want to delete to select the page and open the shortcut menu.
- Click Delete to open the Delete Page dialog box.
- Click the Remove this page from all navigation bars option button to delete the page from the navigation structure, or click the Delete this page from the Web option button to delete the page from the Web site.
- Click the OK button.

David wants to prepare the butter recipe that complements the Nut Bread recipe, so he doesn't want the Nut Bread recipe link to appear in the shared borders right now. To meet David's needs, Amanda asks you to delete the Nut Bread page from the navigation structure, but not from the Web site.

To delete a page from the navigation structure:

1. Click the **Navigation** button ⊞ on the Views bar to return to Navigation view.

2. Right-click the **Nut Bread** page icon to open the shortcut menu, and then click **Delete** to open the Delete Page dialog box.

3. If necessary, click the **Remove this page from all navigation bars** option button to select it, and then click the **OK** button. The Nut Bread Web page is deleted from the navigation structure, but the Bread.htm page still appears in the Folder List, indicating that the Web page still exists in the Web site.

In place of the Nut Bread recipe that you just added, David wants you to create a new Web page for a recipe that the kitchen is preparing. The recipe is for Cranberry Bread. You will create the new page in Navigation view and add it to the navigation structure, which will automatically update the Web site's navigation bars. David will send you the recipe later.

Adding a New Web Page in Navigation View

When you use Navigation view to create a new Web page, you add it to the navigation structure and to the Web site at the same time. Next, you will add a blank page to the Web site as a child page of the Country Recipes Web page. You already set the Web site to include shared borders and a FrontPage navigation bar, so FrontPage will automatically update the hyperlinks to this new page and include the top and left shared borders in it.

REFERENCE WINDOW   **RW**

Adding a New Page in Navigation View
- Click the page icon that is the parent for the new page.
- Click the New Page button on the Standard toolbar to add the page as a child of the selected parent page and to assign the new page a default title and filename.
- Right-click the new page icon to open the shortcut menu, click Rename, enter the page's title, and then press the Enter key.

After adding the new page to the navigation structure, you will rename the page. FrontPage automatically assigns a filename that is the same as the title you enter, with the exception of changing any spaces in your Web page's title to underscore characters

To add a new page to the Web site and change its title:

1. Click the **Country Recipes** page icon in the Navigation pane to select it. When you add a new page, you must first select the parent of the page that you want to add.

   TROUBLE? If the navigation structure collapses when you click the Country Recipes page icon, then you clicked the minus box on the page icon. Click the plus box on the Country Recipes page icon to expand the navigation structure, and then repeat Step 1.

2. Click the **New Page** button [icon] on the Standard toolbar. A new page with the default title "New Page 1" and the temporary filename new_page_1.htm is added to the Web site.

   TROUBLE? If your default page title includes another number, don't worry. Just make sure that a new page was created.

   Next, rename the new page.

3. Right-click the **New Page 1** page icon to open the shortcut menu, and then click **Rename**.

4. Type **Cranberry Bread** as the page's title, and then press the **Enter** key. The new page does not appear in the Folder List until you open it in Page view or change to Folders view.

5. Double-click the **Cranberry Bread** page icon to open the page in Page view. "Saving navigation changes..." is displayed in the status bar, and then the page opens in Page view, which creates the file in the Recipes Web site. Notice the shared borders at the top and left of the Web page. See Figure 5-24. These are the same shared borders that you set for all pages in the Web site. Also notice that FrontPage corrected the top shared border to reflect the deletion of the Nut Bread page and the addition of the Cranberry Bread page.

Figure 5-24	NEW CRANBERRY BREAD PAGE IN PAGE VIEW

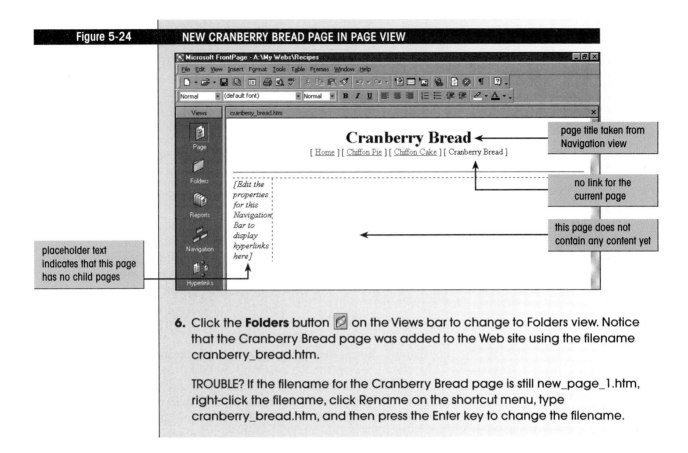

placeholder text indicates that this page has no child pages

page title taken from Navigation view

no link for the current page

this page does not contain any content yet

6. Click the **Folders** button 🗀 on the Views bar to change to Folders view. Notice that the Cranberry Bread page was added to the Web site using the filename cranberry_bread.htm.

TROUBLE? If the filename for the Cranberry Bread page is still new_page_1.htm, right-click the filename, click Rename on the shortcut menu, type cranberry_bread.htm, and then press the Enter key to change the filename.

Turning Off Shared Borders for a Single Page

If the content of a shared border is not appropriate for a single Web page, you can turn off its display in that Web page. The Country Recipes Web page does not include any links in the top shared border, because it is the top-level page in the Web site, and your top shared border is set to include links to the top-level and same-level pages. Because the top border of the Country Recipes page does not contain any links, Amanda asks you to turn it off. She asks you to turn off the left shared border, as well.

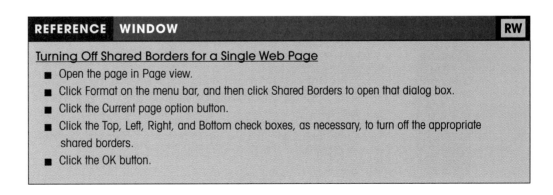

REFERENCE WINDOW	RW

Turning Off Shared Borders for a Single Web Page
- Open the page in Page view.
- Click Format on the menu bar, and then click Shared Borders to open that dialog box.
- Click the Current page option button.
- Click the Top, Left, Right, and Bottom check boxes, as necessary, to turn off the appropriate shared borders.
- Click the OK button.

To turn off shared borders for a single Web page:

1. Click **Window** on the menu bar, and then click **index.htm** to open the Country Recipes page in Page view.

2. Click **Format** on the menu bar, and then click **Shared Borders** to open the Shared Borders dialog box.

3. Click the **Current page** option button to select it, and then click the **Top** and **Left** check boxes to deselect them. The sample page changes to show that this page does not contain any shared borders.

4. Click the **OK** button to close the Shared Borders dialog box and to turn off the top and left shared borders for this page.

   TROUBLE? If a dialog box opens and warns you that changing the settings for the shared borders will overwrite any content that you have added to these borders, then you did not click the Current page option button in Step 3. Click the No button to return to the Shared Borders dialog box, and then repeat Steps 3 and 4.

Without any shared borders, there is no page title or navigation bar for the Country Recipes page. The other pages in the Recipes Web site use FrontPage navigation bars and include their titles in the top and left shared borders. You could enter and format a user-defined navigation bar for this page. However, an easier way to manage the navigation bar for this page is to create a new FrontPage navigation bar that will appear only in this page.

Adding a FrontPage Navigation Bar to a Web Page

You can add a FrontPage navigation bar to any Web page, not just to a shared border. Amanda wants you to include a FrontPage navigation bar in the Country Recipes page that includes links to the recipes (child pages) in the Web site. Using a separate FrontPage navigation bar for the Country Recipes page will permit more space for recipes that are added to the Recipes Web site in the future. In addition, you can use a different arrangement of hyperlinks than what is available in the shared borders. You could create a user-defined navigation bar to accomplish the same objective, but it would require more work to maintain than using a FrontPage navigation bar, which is automatically created and maintained by FrontPage.

To add a FrontPage navigation bar to a Web page:

1. Press **Ctrl + End** to move the insertion point to the last line of the Country Recipes Web page, and then click the **Align Left** button 🔳 on the Formatting toolbar to left-align this line. This is where you will insert the FrontPage navigation bar.

2. Click **Insert** on the menu bar, and then click **Navigation Bar** to open the Navigation Bar Properties dialog box.

3. If necessary, click the **Child level** option button to select it. If the Home page and Parent page check boxes contain check marks, click these check boxes to deselect them.

4. In the Orientation and appearance section, if necessary, click the **Horizontal** option button to select it. Click the **Buttons** option button to select it, and then click the **OK** button to finish specifying the navigation bar. The hyperlinks for the child pages of the Country Recipes page appear at the bottom of the Web page. Again, although you specified buttons, the hyperlinks appear as text, because this page doesn't use a theme yet.

5. Click the **Save** button 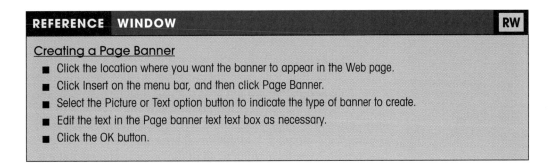 on the Standard toolbar to save your changes.

You added a FrontPage navigation bar to the Country Recipes page, but not to the other Web pages in the Recipes Web site. When the marketing department adds new pages to the Recipes Web site, FrontPage will update this navigation bar automatically to include hyperlinks to the new pages after the new pages are added to the Web site's navigation structure.

When you turned off the top shared border for this page, you deleted the page's title from the page. You want the page to include a title, but not a shared border. Amanda explains that you can add a page banner to the page to identify its content.

Creating a Page Banner

A **banner** is a text or picture object that usually appears at the top of each page in a Web site. You can add a page banner to any page. However, you must include the page in the Web site's navigation structure before you can add a page banner to it.

REFERENCE WINDOW   **RW**

Creating a Page Banner

■ Click the location where you want the banner to appear in the Web page.
■ Click Insert on the menu bar, and then click Page Banner.
■ Select the Picture or Text option button to indicate the type of banner to create.
■ Edit the text in the Page banner text text box as necessary.
■ Click the OK button.

You already created a navigation structure, so you will create a FrontPage page banner next.

To add a page banner to a Web page:

1. Press **Ctrl + Home** to position the insertion point at the top of the Country Recipes page. This is where you will add the page banner.

2. Click **Insert** on the menu bar, and then click **Page Banner**. The Page Banner Properties dialog box opens. See Figure 5-25.

| Figure 5-25 | PAGE BANNER PROPERTIES DIALOG BOX |

adds a picture banner with the page's title →

adds a text-only banner with the page's title

accept default page title or type a new title

Page Banner Properties

Properties

○ Picture
○ Text

Page banner text

Country Recipes ◄

OK   Cancel

3. Make sure that the Picture option button is selected and "Country Recipes" appears in the Page banner text text box, and then click the **OK** button to insert the page banner in the page. Now, if you update the Country Recipes Web page's title in Folders or Navigation view, FrontPage will automatically update the page's title in the page banner, as well. If you changed the page's title in the Page Banner Properties dialog box, FrontPage would automatically update the page title in Navigation and Folders view, too.

4. Click the **Save** button 🖫 on the Standard toolbar to save your changes. The page banner, Country Recipes, appears at the top of the Web page. You ask Amanda why the page banner displays as regular text, even though you selected the picture option. Amanda tells you that you could use the Formatting toolbar to change the appearance of the page banner, but an easier way is to apply a Web theme that automatically formats the entire page—including the page banner—using predefined pictures and fonts.

The work that you have done so far in this session—creating shared borders and a FrontPage navigation bar, and adding a page banner—have all made the Web site easy to navigate. However, remember that David wants the Web site to have a fun, interesting appearance. You could add a background picture and change the format of text that appears in each page in the Web site to add this visual interest. However, Amanda explains that an easier way to apply the same formatting to all of the pages in the Web site is to use a Web theme.

Applying a Theme to a Web Site

A **theme** is a collection of design elements, such as bullets, backgrounds, table borders, fonts, and pictures, that you can apply to an entire Web site or to a single Web page. A Web site with a theme applied to it has a consistent, professional appearance. Everything in the page—from its bullets to its background picture—is professionally designed to fit together. When you insert new bullets, horizontal lines, page banners, navigation bars, and other graphical elements in a page that uses a theme, these elements automatically match the theme. Also, if you add a new page to a Web site that has a theme applied to it, the new page will use the same theme automatically. FrontPage has over 50 built-in themes in a range of styles from conservative to flashy. (Not all of these themes are installed by default, however.) When you apply a theme, you can change it to use vivid colors, active graphics, or a background picture. You can even modify a theme to customize it for your needs.

REFERENCE WINDOW   **RW**

Applying a Theme to a Web Site

- In Page view, Folders view, or Navigation view, click Format on the menu bar, and then click Theme.
- In the Themes dialog box, click the All pages option button.
- Click the theme names and examine the Sample of Theme box to find the one that you like.
- Click the Vivid colors, Active graphics, or Background picture check box to select or deselect these options.
- Click the OK button.
- Click the Yes button to apply the theme to the current Web site.

FrontPage has many themes from which to select. Amanda reminds you that David wants the site to be fun, so you will look for a theme that adds a lot of color and visual interest.

To apply a theme to a Web site:

1. Click **Format** on the menu bar, and then click **Theme**. The Themes dialog box opens. The selected theme is "(No Theme)" to indicate that this Web site does not use themes.

2. If necessary, click the **All pages** option button to indicate a site-wide change.

3. Click some of the themes in the list. Notice that the theme's name might indicate its contents. For example, the Automotive theme displays a speedometer and a dashboard for page elements.

   TROUBLE? Depending on your installation of FrontPage and other Microsoft Office 2000 programs, you might have a different list of themes than those identified in the text. If you don't have a theme, select another appropriate theme.

   TROUBLE? If you see a message in the Sample of Theme box that tells you the theme needs to be installed, either insert your Microsoft Office 2000 CD into the correct drive and click the Install button, or select another theme in the list box until you find one that is already installed.

4. Scroll down the list of available themes until you see Citrus Punch, and then click **Citrus Punch** to preview it in the Sample of Theme box. If necessary, select the **Active graphics** and **Background picture** check boxes, and clear the **Vivid colors** and **Apply using CSS** check boxes. See Figure 5-26. You can change the theme to use vivid colors, active graphics, a background picture, and a cascading style sheet (CSS), which defines the styles used in your document (such as those used in headings).

Figure 5-26	THEMES DIALOG BOX

applies the theme to all pages in the Web site →

applies the theme only to the current page →

Citrus Punch theme selected →

options for changing the theme's general appearance →

Themes

Apply Theme to:
- ● All pages
- ○ Selected page(s)

Blocks
Blueprint
Bold Stripes
Bubbles
Cactus
Canvas
Capsules
Chalkboard
Citrus Punch
Classic
Clear Day

- ☐ Vivid colors
- ☑ Active graphics
- ☑ Background picture
- ☐ Apply using CSS

Sample of Theme:

Banner

Button)(Button)(Button

Heading 1 Style

■ Bullet 1
  ■ Bullet 2
    ■ Bullet 3

Heading 2 Style

preview of the selected theme ←

click to customize the selected theme

Delete   Modify ±   OK   Cancel

5. Click the **Background picture** check box to preview the theme without the background picture. Notice that the page's background is now white. You may have previewed some sample themes in Step 3 that used dark background colors. In these cases, you could use the theme without the background picture if the text in your page will not be readable after applying the theme.

6. Click the **Vivid colors** check box to select it. The white background changes to green. The green color is part of this theme's vivid color settings.

7. Click the **OK** button. A Microsoft FrontPage dialog box opens and indicates that this action will replace some of the existing formatting information permanently.

8. Click the **Yes** button to apply the theme to the Recipes Web site. Several messages are displayed in the status bar while this action is being performed—uploading, applying theme, and loading web. After the theme has been applied, the Country Recipes page is displayed in Page view. See Figure 5-27. Notice that the style of the headings, page banner, background, and FrontPage navigation bar have changed to match the new theme.

Figure 5-27	COUNTRY RECIPES PAGE WITH THEME APPLIED

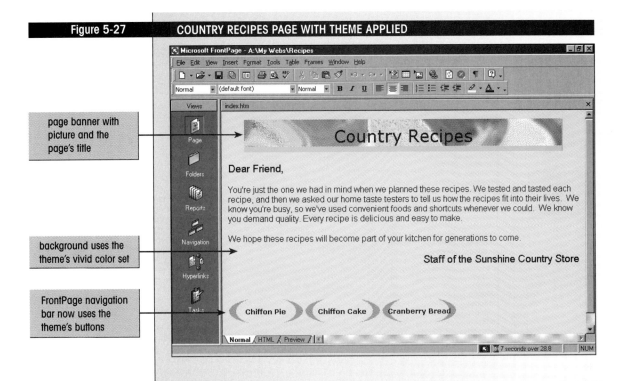

page banner with picture and the page's title

background uses the theme's vivid color set

FrontPage navigation bar now uses the theme's buttons

TROUBLE? It might take several minutes to apply the theme if your Data Files are saved on a floppy disk.

Next, open the Country Recipes page in the browser, and test the FrontPage navigation bar.

To view the page in the browser:

1. Click the **Save** button 🖫 on the Standard toolbar to save your changes.

2. Click the **Preview in Browser** button 🔍 on the Standard toolbar to open the page in the browser, and then, if necessary, scroll down the page to display the buttons for the FrontPage navigation bar.

3. Click the **Chiffon Cake** button in the navigation bar at the bottom of the page to open that Web page. See Figure 5-28. Notice that the navigation bar in the left shared border now uses a button that matches the theme, rather than the text hyperlink. Additionally, the page contains a page banner and a horizontal line that match the theme. These are the settings that you selected when you created the navigation bar in the left shared border and the page banner.

Figure 5-28   **CHIFFON CAKE PAGE WITH THEME APPLIED**

top shared border includes the page banner, text hyperlinks, and a horizontal line

left shared border includes a button hyperlink

page banner includes the page's title and a picture

Amanda likes the theme but feels that the page would look better with a picture background, instead of the green color. To make this modification, you need to change the theme's attributes.

Changing a Theme's Attributes

You can change a theme's attributes using the Themes dialog box. You will apply the Citrus Punch theme's background picture next.

To change a theme's attributes:

1. Click the **Microsoft FrontPage** program button on the taskbar to return to Page view for the Country Recipes page.

2. Click **Format** on the menu bar, and then click **Theme**. The Themes dialog box opens again. Notice that this time, the selected theme is "(Default) Citrus Punch."

3. Click the **Background picture** check box to select that option. The theme's background picture is applied to the theme's preview.

4. Click the **OK** button to apply the background picture to the theme. If you are storing your Web site on a hard drive, themes are applied and saved much faster than when you create your Web site on a floppy drive. The Country Recipes page is displayed using the theme's background picture. See Figure 5-29.

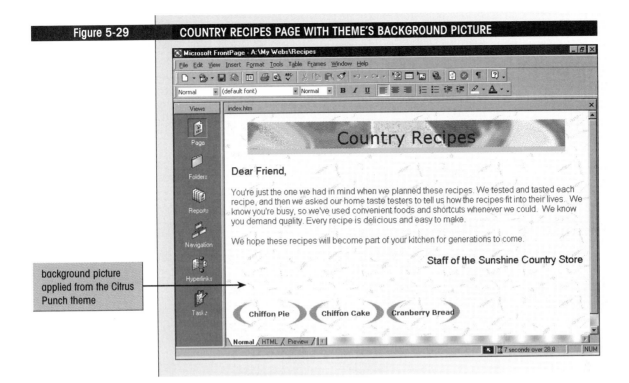

Figure 5-29 | **COUNTRY RECIPES PAGE WITH THEME'S BACKGROUND PICTURE**

background picture applied from the Citrus Punch theme

The revised theme is applied to the entire Recipes Web site. You ask David to visit your office to see if the theme is appropriate. After reviewing the Web pages, David is concerned that the Arial font used in the Web page's body text is difficult to read for the recipes. He asks you to change the font to Book Antiqua to see if the recipes are easier to read. After discussing this change with Amanda, she tells you that David's change requires you to customize the existing theme.

Customizing a Theme

After selecting a theme, you might find that you need to make some changes to it to better suit your needs. You could select and change the font in the body of every Web page to meet David's request, but an easier way is to customize the existing theme so that all existing and future Web pages will include the revised font.

To customize the Citrus Punch theme:

1. Click **Format** on the menu bar, and then click **Theme**. The Themes dialog box opens.

2. Click the **Modify** button in the dialog box. The dialog box changes to add the "What would you like to modify?" section, which includes buttons to change the theme's colors, graphics, and text. Also notice the Save and Save As buttons, which let you save a customized Web theme with a new name for future use. You need to change the font that the theme uses, so you will click the Text button to open a dialog box that lets you change the text options.

3. Click the **Text** button. The Modify Theme dialog box opens and displays the preview of the current theme, an Item list arrow, and a list of fonts available on your system. You need to change the style of the Body text, so the Item list arrow is already set for you. You could click the list arrow and change the style of headings used in the theme as well.

4. Make sure that the Item list box displays the Body option, click **Book Antiqua** in the Font list box, and then preview the change in the Sample of Theme box. See Figure 5-30.

   TROUBLE? If you do not have the Book Antiqua font on your system, select another font that looks similar to it.

Figure 5-30	MODIFY THEME DIALOG BOX

click to select the text item to modify

Font list (your fonts might differ)

preview includes the selected font

5. Click the **OK** button to close the Modify Theme dialog box. The Themes dialog box redisplays.

   TROUBLE? If you do not see the OK button in the dialog box, click the Modify Theme dialog box's title bar and drag up the dialog box until you see the OK button.

6. Click the **OK** button to close the Themes dialog box. A dialog box opens and asks if you want to save the changes to the Citrus Punch theme. Click the **Yes** button, and then click the **OK** button to accept "Copy of Citrus Punch" as the new theme name. The Themes dialog box closes, and after a few minutes, the new Book Antiqua font is applied to the body text in the pages in the Recipes Web site. See Figure 5-31.

TROUBLE? If a dialog box opens and tells you that the Copy of Citrus Punch theme already exists, click the OK button, change the theme's name to Copy of Citrus Punch 1, and then click the OK button.

Figure 5-31	COUNTRY RECIPES PAGE WITH MODIFIED THEME APPLIED

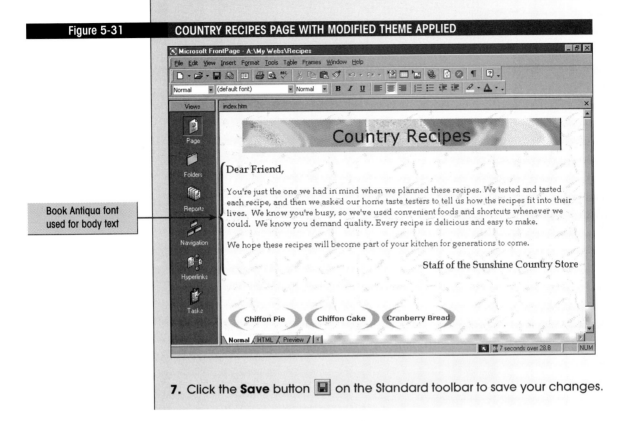

Book Antiqua font used for body text

7. Click the **Save** button on the Standard toolbar to save your changes.

The new theme is attractive and the text in the Web page is easier to read. Amanda wants you to view the HTML code that FrontPage used to implement your changes.

Viewing HTML Code for FrontPage Components and Themes

FrontPage hides most of the HTML code for shared borders, navigation bars, and themes in hidden folders and files that it automatically creates. The _borders and _themes folders are the primary folders where the theme's shared border and theme files are stored. FrontPage does not let you see these folders in Folders view unless you configure it to do so. However, you can see these folders and the files they contain using Windows Explorer.

Shared borders and themes are implemented in FrontPage using META tags, as described in Tutorial 2. These META tags are created automatically by FrontPage and inserted in each page in the Web site. FrontPage then uses these META tags to display the desired arrangement of borders and themes, using the files that are stored in the theme's and border's hidden folders. For the Recipes Web site, FrontPage created the top and left shared borders as Web pages in the _borders folder. The banners and navigation bars were created using FrontPage components, which are identified in each page's HTML document using a comment tag (<!-- ... -->). If a Web browser that does not support a FrontPage component opens a Web page that contains a component, the browser will ignore the components that it cannot process and display. When you use the HTML tab to view the HTML code for a Web page that contains components, FrontPage displays the component's HTML code in a different color to distinguish it.

To view the HTML code for themes and FrontPage components:

1. Make sure that the Country Recipes Web page appears in Page view, click the **HTML** tab, and then press **Ctrl + Home** to scroll to the top of the page. See Figure 5-32. Examine the code in the page and identify the changes that you made in this session.

Figure 5-32	HTML CODE FOR THE COUNTRY RECIPES PAGE

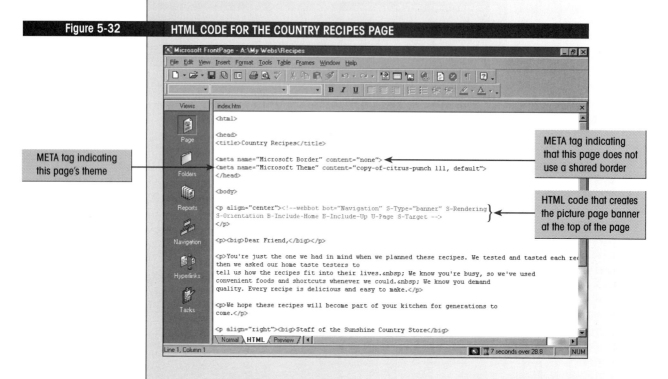

META tag indicating this page's theme

META tag indicating that this page does not use a shared border

HTML code that creates the picture page banner at the top of the page

2. Press the **Page Down** key to scroll to the bottom of the page. See Figure 5-33. The code that implements the FrontPage navigation bar in the Country Recipes page appears as gray text.

Figure 5-33	HTML CODE FOR THE COUNTRY RECIPES PAGE, CONTINUED

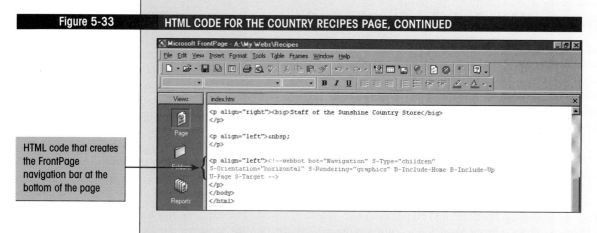

HTML code that creates the FrontPage navigation bar at the bottom of the page

Next, close FrontPage and Internet Explorer.

3. Click the **Close** button ☒ on the FrontPage title bar. If necessary, click the **Yes** button to save changes to any files.

> **TROUBLE?** If the Confirm Save dialog box opens and asks if you want to replace a shared border file, click the Yes button. FrontPage saves the shared borders in a Web site as separate files, so you must save these files after modifying them.
>
> 4. Click ☒ on the Internet Explorer title bar to close it.

David is pleased with the new Recipes Web site and feels that the FrontPage shared borders and navigation bars will make it easy to maintain and update the site as new recipes are added to it. In Tutorial 6, you will publish the Sunny Web site to a Web server and create pages that use FrontPage components for processing.

Session 5.2 QUICK CHECK

1. How many shared borders can you add to a Web site?
2. What information does a top shared border usually contain?
3. What is the advantage of using a FrontPage navigation bar instead of a user-defined navigation bar?
4. In which views can you change a page's filename and title?
5. How does FrontPage use the navigation structure to create a FrontPage navigation bar?
6. You can edit a shared border in _____ view.
7. A hyperlink named _____ in a FrontPage navigation bar will open the parent page for the current page.
8. To change a theme, click the _____ button in the Themes dialog box.
9. True or False: You must apply the same theme to every page in a Web site.

REVIEW ASSIGNMENTS

After examining the Recipes Web site and gathering input from other members of the marketing department, David asks you to make some changes to improve the site's functionality. He asks you to create two new recipe pages as placeholders in the Web site until he obtains the final recipes from the kitchen. Amanda also asks you to modify the Sunny Web site to link it to the Recipes Web site. You will also enhance the Clothing Web page you created in Tutorial 4 to add a picture.

If necessary, insert your Data Disk in the appropriate disk drive, start FrontPage, and then do the following:

1. Open the **Sunny** Web site (a:\My Webs\Sunny) from your Data Disk in Folders view.
2. Open the **Clothing.htm** Web page that you created in Tutorial 4 in Page view. Add a centered hover button with the text "Return to Home Page" on a new line above the footer that contains a hyperlink that opens the Home Page. Select colors of your choice and an appropriate mouse over effect for the hover button, and then, if necessary, change the hover button's size so that the text is displayed correctly.
3. Insert the **Beach.gif** picture from the Tutorial.05 folder on your Data Disk in the Clothing Web page on a new centered line below the hover button that you added in Step 2. If necessary, resize the picture to an appropriate size, and then apply a beveled edge to the picture's border. Save the page and save the picture in the Web site's images folder. Then preview the page in Internet Explorer and print it. Test your hover button to make sure that it links to the Home Page.

Explore

4. Return to FrontPage and then open the Sunshine Country Store Map page (**mappage.htm**) in Page view. Create a second hover button with your choice of colors and mouse over effect in the Sunshine Country Store Map page in the right cell of the table that appears below the map picture. Use the text "Go To Recipes Web Site" on the hover button and format it using 18-point, bold, Arial font. Then create a hyperlink to the Country Recipes page in the Recipes Web site (**a:\My Webs\Recipes\index.htm**) on your Data Disk. If necessary, change the size of the hover button to accommodate its text. Save your changes, and then test the new hover button in Internet Explorer to make sure that it opens the Recipes Web site. Use the browser's Back button to return to the Sunshine Country Store Map page, and then print it.

Explore

5. Use the hover button in the Sunshine Country Store Map to open the Sunny Morning Products Home Page, use a hyperlink to open the Investor Relations page, and then click the Edit button on the Standard Buttons toolbar to edit the Investor Relations page in FrontPage. Apply a page exit transition of your choice to the Investor Relations page that has a duration of four seconds, save the page, and then test the transition in the browser. (*Hint*: You must leave the page to test the transition.)

Explore

6. Animate the navigation bar in the Investor Relations page so that the words in the navigation bar fly across the screen from the left side. Save the page, and then test the animation in the browser. (*Hint*: You might need to refresh the page to see the text animation.)

7. Return to FrontPage, close the DHTML Effects toolbar, close the Sunny Web site, and then open the **Recipes** Web site (a:\My Webs\Recipes) from your Data Disk.

Explore

8. Use Navigation view to create two new pages in the Recipes Web site (you will create the pages, but you will not enter the recipes). The first page is for a recipe for Hard Candy. Add this page at the same level as the Chiffon Cake page. Then create another new page for a recipe for Christmas Candy. Add this page as a child page to the Hard Candy page. Open the Christmas Candy Web page in Page view, and then apply the Sweets theme to *only* this page. Choose the options to use vivid colors, active graphics, and a background picture. After applying the theme, save the Christmas Candy page.

9. Modify the FrontPage navigation bars in the top and left shared borders for all pages except the Country Recipes page. The top shared border should contain horizontal buttons for the back and next pages, and links to the Home Page and the parent page. The left shared border should contain vertical text hyperlinks for only the child-level pages. Save your changes, and then test these changes using the browser.

Explore

10. Add a bottom shared border to all pages in the Recipes Web site, except for the Country Recipes Web page, containing the text "To order items from Sunny Morning Products, click" and then type a space and add a hover button at the end of the sentence that includes the text "here". The hover button should include a link to the appropriate page in the Sunny Web site. Select colors and a mouse over effect of your choice. Save and test your changes in Internet Explorer.

Explore

11. Print Navigation view for the Recipes Web site. (*Hint*: Use a toolbar button.) Then use FrontPage to print the Christmas Candy page and its HTML code.

12. Close Internet Explorer and FrontPage.

CASE PROBLEMS

Case 1. Changing the Appearance of the Royal Hair Care Products Web Site Valerie Suarez is pleased with the financial performance and current stock market activities tables that you added to the Royal Web site in Tutorial 4. Now that the Web site includes many different pages of information, Valerie asks you to work on its appearance to ensure that it is visually interesting and easy to use. First, you will change the user-defined navigation bar to include hover buttons. Then you will change the appearance of the pages that open in the main frame of the frames page. After you have finished making these changes, Valerie will meet with the rest of the Web site development team to test the site and gather feedback.

If necessary, start FrontPage, insert your Data Disk in the appropriate disk drive, and then do the following:

1. Read all the questions for this case problem, and then prepare a planning analysis sheet for the changes to the Royal Web site.

2. Open the **Royal** Web site (a:\My Webs\Royal) from your Data Disk in Folders view. (If you did not create this Web site in Tutorial 2 and change it in Tutorials 3 and 4, ask your instructor for assistance.)

3. Open the Financial Information Web page (**RInvest.htm**) that you created in Tutorial 4 in Page view.

Explore   4. In the upper-left cell of the table in the Financial Performance page, which opens in the main frame, create a thumbnail of the **Royal01.gif** picture that is saved in the Web site's images folder. Change the picture to use a beveled edge. Then create a hyperlink from the thumbnail picture to the Royal Hair Care Products Home Page so that the Home Page opens and replaces the frames page in the browser. Add appropriate alternative text to the picture. Save your changes and save the picture in the site's images folder. Then test the page in the browser.

Explore   5. Change the user-defined navigation bar in the banner frame to include an appropriately sized hover button for each item in the navigation bar and links to the corresponding pages. Use the default hover button settings for each button, and create hyperlinks that open the pages in the full browser window, replacing the frames page. (*Hint*: There is no Search page in the Web site. When you create the hyperlink for the Search hover button, enter the filename **RSearch.htm** as the hyperlink, even though this page does not yet exist. You will create this page in Tutorial 6.) Save your changes, and then test the navigation bar in Internet Explorer. Return to FrontPage, and then print the HTML code for the page that is displayed in the banner frame.

6. Animate the words in the contents frame with an animation of your choice. Experiment with the different effects, and then select the one that you like the best.

7. Add a page transition of your choice to the Home Page. The transition should occur when the user enters the page and should have a duration of five seconds. Preview the Financial Information page in the browser to test the animation that you applied in Step 6, and then click the Home hyperlink in the banner frame to test the transition that you applied to the Home Page.

8. Apply an appropriate theme to the entire Web site. Before applying the theme, make sure that it includes vivid colors, active graphics, and a background picture.

9. Save your changes, and then test the Web site using Internet Explorer. If necessary, return to FrontPage and make any necessary corrections.

10. Close Internet Explorer and FrontPage.

Case 2. Adding Shared Borders and a Theme to the Buffalo Trading Post Web Site

Donna Vargas and Karla Perez realize that as business at the Buffalo Trading Post (BTP) continues to grow, they will be adding more Web pages to the Web site. They are pleased with the appearance of the site so far. Donna wants to make sure that it is easy to update the site when new pages are added, so she asks you to change the existing navigation bars to ones generated by FrontPage so that they are updated automatically when new pages are added to the site. Also, Karla wants you to add a theme to the pages to present a consistent appearance.

If necessary, start FrontPage, insert your Data Disk in the appropriate disk drive, and then do the following:

1. Read all the questions for this case problem, and then prepare a planning analysis sheet for the changes to the BTP Web site.

2. Open the **Buffalo** Web site (a:\My Webs\Buffalo) from your Data Disk in Navigation view. (If you did not create this Web site in Tutorial 2 and change it in Tutorials 3 and 4, ask your instructor for assistance.)

Explore ▶ 3. Create a navigation structure for the Web site using the existing pages. The Home Page should be the top-level page; the What, How, and Who pages should be children of the Home Page; and the Accessories, Women's Clothing, and Children's Clothing pages should be children of the What page. After creating the navigation structure, print Navigation view. (*Hint*: To print Navigation view, use a toolbar button.)

4. Open the Home Page in Page view, and then add a bottom shared border to all pages in the Web site.

5. Select both lines of the footer that appear at the bottom of the Home Page. Cut the footer from the page, select the comment placeholder text that appears in the bottom shared border, and then paste the footer into the bottom shared border. There should be one blank line at the top of the bottom shared border. Save your changes.

Explore ▶ 6. Use FrontPage Help to learn how to add a comment to the Home Page in Page view (insert a normal text comment, and *not* an HTML comment). Then insert the following comment at the top of the page, on a new line above the navigation bar, as a reminder to add the new company logo to the Web page: "Update the BTP logo when the new one is available next week." Save the Home Page, and then test your comment in Internet Explorer to make sure that it is not displayed in the browser.

Explore ▶ 7. Apply a customized version of the Sunflower theme to the entire Web site. The theme should use vivid colors, active graphics, and a background picture. Before applying the theme, click the Graphics button and use the Modify Theme dialog box to change the bullet list picture for List Bullet 1 to use the **BD14530_.gif** file that is stored in the Tutorial.05 folder on your Data Disk. Save the new theme using the default name. (*Hint*: Click the Item list arrow to change the bullet list picture.)

8. Open the Who page in Page view, and scroll to the bottom of the page. Change the numbered list that appears under the line "Why are we here?" to a bulleted list. Make sure that the bullets use the picture that you set in Step 7. Save the Who page, and save the picture for the bullet character in the Web site's images folder.

Explore ▶ 9. Open the Home Page in Page view. Change the heading that you created for the Home Page to a page banner. (*Hint*: First, select the heading, and then click the Cut button on the Standard toolbar. Next, create a new, centered line under the comment that you created in Step 6 as the location in which to insert the page banner. Click Insert on the menu bar, and then click Page Banner. Select the text that appears in the Page banner text text box, and then press Ctrl + V to paste the heading. Click the OK button.) If necessary, edit your banner text to make it fit on a single line. Save the Home Page, and then view it using Internet Explorer. Test the links throughout the Web site to ensure that they work correctly. Close Internet Explorer.

Explore ▶ 10. Use FrontPage to print the Home Page, and then print the HTML code for the Home Page. Circle the HTML code that implements the comment, page banner, and bottom shared border on the printout.

11. Close FrontPage and save your changes when prompted to do so.

Case 3. Enhancing the Appearance of the Menu Pages for Garden Grill Nolan Simmons and Shannon Taylor want to make sure that the new menu pages that you added to the Web site in Tutorial 4 are easy and fun to read. Nolan wants the menu pages to be similar in appearance to the restaurant's menus that are provided to patrons. Nolan asks you to use FrontPage to add logos and themes to the menu pages so they have the same professional appearance as the menus provided at the restaurant.

If necessary, start FrontPage, insert your Data Disk in the appropriate disk drive, and then do the following:

1. Read all the questions for this case problem, and then prepare a planning analysis sheet for the changes to the Garden Grill Web site.

2. Open the **Garden** Web site (a:\My Webs\Garden) from your Data Disk in Folders view. (If you did not create this Web site in Tutorial 2 and change it in Tutorials 3 and 4, ask your instructor for assistance.)

Explore ▷ 3. Change the **Garden01.gif** picture that appears at the top of the Appetizers page that you created in Tutorial 4 to have a beveled edge. Save the page and overwrite the existing **Garden01.gif** file in the Web site's images folder. Open the Home Page in Page view. Why does the logo in this page now have a beveled edge?

Explore ▷ 4. Change to Folders view and create a new Specials page that lists the daily restaurant specials. (*Hint*: Click the New Page button on the Standard toolbar, and then change the new page's filename to **GSpecial.htm** and its page title to "Specials.") Change to Page view, and then write the content of this page. Insert the **Garden01.gif** picture from the Web site's images folder in the Specials page. Apply a customized theme of your choice to the Specials page only, and then save the Specials page.

5. Create a centered hover button below the marquee in the Home Page that includes the text "Go to Specials Page" and that contains a hyperlink to the Specials page that you created in Step 4. Use 18-point, bold and italic, Arial font on the hover button, and colors and a mouse over effect of your choice. Save the Home Page.

6. Create a centered hover button in the Specials page that includes the text "Return to Home Page" and that contains a hyperlink to the Home Page. Use 18-point, bold and italic, Arial font on the hover button, and colors and a mouse over effect of your choice. Save the Specials page.

7. Select and apply a page transition and a text animation of your choice to the Specials page.

Explore ▷ 8. Change the **Garden01.gif** picture that you inserted in the Specials page to use a fly in from bottom animation effect. (*Hint*: Select the picture, and then use the DHTML Effects toolbar to create the effect.) Save the Specials page, and then test the Specials page and its link to the Home Page in the browser.

Explore ▷ 9. Use Internet Explorer to print the Specials page and then print its HTML code. On the printout, circle the HTML code that creates the text animation, the picture animation, the page transition, and the hover button. Close Notepad and Internet Explorer.

10. Close FrontPage and save your changes when prompted to do so.

Case 4. Enhancing the Replay Music Factory Web Charlene Fields and Alec Johnston are pleased with the Specials page that you added to the Replay Music Factory Web site. Based on feedback from the marketing department, Charlene asks you to add a picture to the Specials page and then create hover buttons with hyperlinks to navigate the Web site. Next, she wants you to create a navigation structure to make it easier for her to add pages based on current market trends in the industry.

If necessary, start FrontPage, insert your Data Disk in the appropriate disk drive, and then do the following:

1. Read all the questions for this case problem, and then prepare a planning analysis sheet for the changes to the Replay Web site.

2. Open the **Replay** Web site (a:\My Webs\Replay) from your Data Disk in Folders view. (If you did not create this Web site in Tutorial 2 and change it in Tutorials 3 and 4, ask your instructor for assistance.)

3. Open the **MSpecial.htm** page in Page view, and then apply a theme of your choice to each page that opens in the frames page, but not to the entire Web site. Set the theme's options to ensure that the text in the music type pages is readable.

4. Create a hover button in the Home Page that contains a hyperlink to the Specials page. Then create another hover button in the Contents page that returns the user to the Home Page. Save your changes, and then test the hover buttons in Internet Explorer.

Explore   5. Create a navigation structure that contains the Home Page and its child pages, including any child pages of the children of the Home Page. Print the navigation structure. (*Hint*: Use a toolbar button to print Navigation view. If necessary, update the page titles in Navigation view to make the banners fit correctly.)

Explore   6. Change the headings in the three music type pages to use page banners with pictures and the page title, instead of regular text headings. (*Hint*: Replace the existing page heading by selecting it and then inserting the page banner in its place.)

Explore   7. Replace the existing navigation bar in the Home Page with a FrontPage navigation bar that includes text hyperlinks to child pages. Apply a text animation of your choice to the FrontPage navigation bar. Save the page.

Explore   8. Replace the existing navigation bar in the page that you created in Tutorial 3 that describes Replay's process for buying, selling, and trading used CDs with a FrontPage navigation bar that includes text hyperlinks to pages at the same level and to the Home Page. Save the page.

9. Use Internet Explorer to test the Web site, making sure that your hyperlinks work correctly. Print the HTML code for the Home Page, and then close Notepad and Internet Explorer.

Explore   10. Use FrontPage to print the HTML code for one of the music type pages that opens in the Specials frames page. On the printout, circle the HMTL code that identifies the theme you applied to this page.

11. Close FrontPage and save your changes when prompted to do so.

QUICK CHECK ANSWERS

Session 5.1

1. hyperlink
2. Any three of: add text over a picture; create a thumbnail; rotate, increase or decrease contrast or brightness; crop; set transparent color; change to black and white; wash out; bevel the edges; create a hotspot; or restore
3. Select the picture, click the Text button on the Pictures toolbar, type the text, click anywhere outside the picture.
4. mouse over or mouse fly over
5. True
6. False
7. True
8. Create a page transition, or animated text and pictures

Session 5.2

1. Any number from zero to four
2. A top shared border usually contains a page banner and hyperlinks to same-level pages, along with a link to the Home Page and to the parent page.
3. When you use a user-defined navigation bar, you must create and maintain it. When you use a FrontPage navigation bar, FrontPage automatically creates and maintains the navigation bar, which is usually a more accurate and efficient method.
4. Navigation view and Folders view
5. FrontPage uses the information you provide in the navigation structure to establish the relationships of Web pages to each other.
6. Page
7. Up
8. Modify
9. False

In this tutorial you will:

- Create a new Web page using a template

- Change the properties of the search component

- Add a form component to a Web page

- Add form fields to a form and set their properties

- Validate form fields

- Use a form handler

- Open an Office 2000 document from a Web site

- Use a Personal Web Server

- Publish a Web site

- Process Web pages on a server

- Create a hit counter and a banner ad in a Web page

- Drag and drop files in a Web site

- Use the Find and Replace commands

- Recalculate and verify hyperlinks in a Web site

- Set permissions for a Web site

PUBLISHING A WEB SITE

Preparing the Search and Feedback Web Pages

CASE

Sunny Morning Products

In her design of the user-defined navigation bar for the Sunny Web site, Amanda Bay included a hyperlink to a Search Web page that you will create in this tutorial. The Web site development team requested this page so that users can easily search the entire Web site for information about specific products or employment positions.

Because the Web site is a new way of marketing Sunny Morning Products, Andrew Towle wants to collect as much data as possible about the people who use it. In response to Andrew's request, Amanda's Web site plan includes a Feedback Web page that will let users enter information into a form and submit it to Sunny Morning Products. This form will ask for the user's name and e-mail address and provide options for commenting on the Web site, products, and services of Sunny Morning Products. The marketing department will use this information to make decisions about expanding and updating the site.

The Search and Feedback Web pages that you will create in this tutorial will require a Web server for processing. You will create these pages and then publish the Sunny Web site to your computer's Personal Web Server. After publishing the Web site, you will enhance it by adding other server-based functions to it that analyze, update, and monitor the completed Web site. When you are finished with this tutorial, you will have finished the Web site that Sunny Morning Products will publish on its Web server so that Internet users can use it. In addition, you will be fully trained in creating, maintaining, and updating a Web site for the management department at Sunny Morning Products.

SESSION 6.1

In this session, you will use a template to create a new Web page that contains a search component. You also will add a form component to a Web page and add form fields to it.

Reviewing the Tasks List

In this week's meeting with the members of the Web site development team, you received a preliminary outline of the features that the team wants to include in the Search and Feedback Web pages. Before beginning these tasks, Amanda asks you to open the Sunny Web site and to assign the tasks for completing these pages to yourself.

To open the Sunny Web site and update the Tasks list:

1. Start **FrontPage**, insert your Data Disk in the appropriate disk drive, and then open the **Sunny** Web site (a:\My Webs\Sunny) from your Data Disk.

2. Click the **Tasks** button 🗒 on the Views bar to open the Tasks list. There are two tasks in the Tasks list—one each for creating the Feedback and Search Web pages.

3. Double-click the **Create Feedback Web page** task. The Task Details dialog box opens. You assigned this task to "Team Member" when you created it in Tutorial 3.

4. Click in the **Assigned to** text box to select the current entry, type your first and last names separated by a space, and then click the **OK** button. The Task Details dialog box closes, and the Tasks list is revised to show that this task is assigned to you.

5. Repeat Steps 3 and 4 to assign the Create Search Web page task to yourself.

Figure 6-1 shows Amanda's planning analysis sheet for creating the Search Web page, which you will create first.

| Figure 6-1 | AMANDA'S PLANNING ANALYSIS SHEET FOR THE SEARCH WEB PAGE |

Planning Analysis Sheet

Objective

Create a Search Web page that accepts text entered by the user, and then is processed by the server to return a list of hyperlinks to pages in the Web site that contain that text.

Requirements

Template for creating a Search Web page

Picture file for the logo

Results

A Search Web page that contains a search component that the server uses to process requests for information in the Sunny Web site. The page should include the Sunny Morning Products logo and a title.

Creating the Search Web Page Using a Template

In Tutorial 3, you used the Normal Page template to create new Web pages that did not contain any specific formatting or text. Recall that a Web page template is a Web page that contains formatting and content related to a specific type of page. When creating a new Web page, you can base it on a template that matches or approximates the content that you need. For example, if you are creating a Web page into which users will enter personal information, you might create your page using the Guest Book template. The Guest Book template includes FrontPage components and sample text that are commonly found in a printed guest book. After creating a new Web page that is based on a template, you can edit it just like any other Web page. Figure 6-2 describes several FrontPage templates that you can use to create new Web pages.

| Figure 6-2 | SELECTED TEMPLATE WEB PAGES AND WIZARDS AND THEIR DESCRIPTIONS |

NAME	DESCRIPTION
Confirmation Form	A page that confirms the receipt of information from a user of a form, discussion, or registration page
Feedback Form	A page that collects data entered by a user, such as comments and personal information
Form Page Wizard	A Wizard that creates a Web page which contains a form with appropriate data fields for the information that you need to collect
Frequently Asked Questions	A page that lists common questions about a topic and their answers
Search Page	A page that accepts keywords entered by a user and then returns a list of hyperlinks to pages with matching entries

Amanda asks you to preview the Search Page template to determine if its content is appropriate for the Search Web page that you will create for the Sunny Web site. To use a template for creating a new Web page, you must be in Page view.

To create a Web page using a template:

1. Click the **Page** button 📄 on the Views bar to change to Page view. A blank page is displayed in the Contents pane.

2. Click **File** on the menu bar, point to **New**, and then click **Page**. The New dialog box opens. If necessary, click the **General** tab to select it. The General tab contains a scrollable list of icons that represent different types of pages and Wizards that you can use to create a new Web page.

3. Scroll down the template list until you see the Search Page icon, and then click the **Search Page** icon to select it. See Figure 6-3. The description and preview indicate that this page will provide the capability for searching the entire Web site, so it is the correct template to use.

Figure 6-3	NEW DIALOG BOX

templates (your list might be different)

Search Page template description

selected Search Page template

preview of the selected template

4. Click the **OK** button to create a new Web page based on the Search Page template. A new page opens in the Contents pane. See Figure 6-4.

| Figure 6-4 | NEW WEB PAGE CREATED USING THE SEARCH PAGE TEMPLATE |

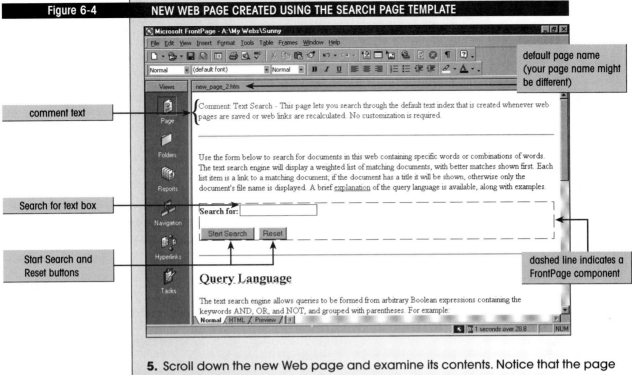

5. Scroll down the new Web page and examine its contents. Notice that the page contains a comment at the top of the page, text that describes how to use the page, a FrontPage component that contains a Search for text box and the Start Search and Reset buttons, and an "explanation" hyperlink that links to a Query Language section describing how to use the page in more detail. The bottom of the page contains a "Back to Top" hyperlink to a bookmark at the top of the page and a footer with sample copyright information.

6. Press **Ctrl + Home** to scroll to the top of the page.

The overall design and content of the new page is very similar to the page that the Web site development team requested. However, you need to make some minor changes to convert this generic Search page into the specific Search Web page you need. You need to remove the comment from the top of the page, include the same background that is used in the Home Page, insert the Sunny Morning Products logo at the top of the page, and then change the title of the page and the page's filename to "Search."

To revise a Web page created using a template:

1. Point to the purple **"Comment: Text Search - This page..."** text at the top of the page. The pointer changes to the FrontPage component pointer 📄 to identify the location of a FrontPage component in the Web page. The comment is a FrontPage component that inserts text you can see in Page view, but not in a Web browser.

2. Right-click the purple comment text to select it and open the shortcut menu, and then click **Cut** to delete the comment. The comment is deleted, and a blank line appears above the horizontal line at the top of the page. Next enter the page's title and then format it as a heading.

3. Type **Search** on the blank line at the top of the page, click the **Style** list arrow on the Formatting toolbar, and then click **Heading 2**.

Next, change the page to use the same background as the Home Page.

4. Click **Format** on the menu bar, click **Background**, click the **Get background information from another page** check box to select it, and then click the **Browse** button to open the Current Web dialog box.

5. Double-click **index.htm** in the list of files to select the Home Page and return to the Page Properties dialog box, and then the **OK** button. The Page Properties dialog box closes and the Web page displays the background picture.

Next, insert the Sunny Morning Products logo at the top of the page.

6. Press **Ctrl + Home** to move the insertion point to the top of the page, press the **Enter** key to insert a new line, and then press the **Up** arrow key ↑. The insertion point moves to the blank line that you created, which is where you will insert the logo.

7. Click the **Insert Picture From File** button 🖼 on the Standard toolbar to open the Picture dialog box, click the **Select a file on your computer** button 🔍 to open the Select File dialog box, click the **Look in** list arrow and select the drive or folder that contains your Data Disk, double-click the **Tutorial.06** folder, and then double-click **Search**. The Select File and Picture dialog boxes close and the logo is inserted at the top of the page.

Finally, save the page using the new filename and title, and save the logo file in the Web site's images folder.

8. Click the **Save** button 💾 on the Standard toolbar to open the Save As dialog box, make sure that the Sunny folder appears in the Save in text box, that the Page title is "Search," and that the filename is "search," and then click the **Save** button. The Save As dialog box closes. Because you added a picture to the page, the Save Embedded Files dialog box opens.

   TROUBLE? If the Sunny folder does not appear in the Look in text box, click the Look in list arrow, and then locate and click the Sunny folder on your Data Disk to select it.

9. Make sure that the Search.gif file will be saved in the Web site's images folder, and then click the **OK** button. The picture is saved in the Web site's images folder.

Changing the Search Component's Properties

When you created the Search page from the template, FrontPage automatically included a search component that searches for information in the Web site using keywords entered by the user. You can also add a search component to an existing page by clicking the Insert Component button on the Standard toolbar and then clicking Search Form. Regardless of how you create the search component, you can view the search component's properties and change them as necessary.

Amanda wants you to increase the size of the text box into which users type the text they want to search for, so you will change the search component's properties.

To change the properties of the search component:

1. If necessary, scroll down the Search page until you see the Search for text box and the Start Search and Reset buttons, and then place the pointer anywhere in the dashed-line box that contains these objects. The pointer changes to a 🖼 shape to indicate the location of a FrontPage component in the Web page.

2. Right-click anywhere in the search component to select the component and to open the shortcut menu, and then click **Search Form Properties** to open the Search Form Properties dialog box. See Figure 6-5.

| Figure 6-5 | SEARCH FORM PROPERTIES DIALOG BOX |

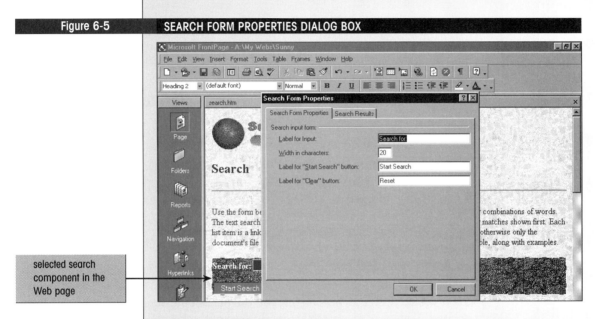

selected search
component in the
Web page

The Search Form Properties tab includes options for changing the defaults for the text box's label and its width, and the labels for the two buttons that are created by the page's template. You can accept these defaults or change them, when necessary, to match your requirements. You will change the width of the Search for text box so that users can enter more characters.

3. Select the current value in the Width in characters text box, and then type **24** to increase the size of the Search for text box. The other default settings are acceptable, so you can close the dialog box.

4. Click the **OK** button to close the dialog box and return to the Search Web page, and then click anywhere in the paragraph above the search component to deselect it. Notice that the size of the Search for text box increased to 24 characters.

Next, change the default footer text at the bottom of the page to match the content of other page footers in the Sunny Web site. Instead of typing this information, you will copy and paste it from the Home Page.

5. Click the **Folders** button 📁 on the Views bar to change to Folders view, double-click **index.htm** to open the Home Page in Page view, press **Ctrl + End** to scroll to the bottom of the Home Page, select both lines of the footer, and then click the **Copy** button 📋 on the Standard toolbar.

6. Click **Window** on the menu bar, click **search.htm**, press **Ctrl + End** to scroll to the bottom of the Search page, and then select the three lines in the existing footer. Click the **Paste** button 📋 on the Standard toolbar to paste the footer from the Home Page in the correct location in the Search page.

7. Click the **Save** button 🖫 on the Standard toolbar to save your changes.

With all the properties specified, Amanda asks you to test the Web page using the browser. Because you are using a disk-based Web, instead of a server-based Web, the search component will not work, but you can still examine the page's overall appearance.

To preview the Search Web page in the browser:

1. Click the **Preview in Browser** button 🔍 on the Standard toolbar. A dialog box opens to remind you that this page needs to be published to preview correctly.

2. Click the **OK** button in the dialog box to close it. The Search page opens in Internet Explorer.

3. Click in the **Search for** text box, and then type **MIS**.

4. Click the **Start Search** button. The FrontPage Run-Time Component Page opens in the browser to advise you that a Web server is required for the page to function correctly. You will use a Web server to process this page later in this tutorial.

5. Click the **Back** button ⇐ on the Standard Buttons toolbar to return to the Search page, and then click the **Reset** button to clear the MIS text from the Search for text box.

Your test was successful. In Session 6.3, you will publish the Sunny Web site on a server and use the Search Web page to search the site. Instead of the FrontPage Run-Time Component Page, you will see a list of hyperlinks to pages that contain the text for which you are searching. Now that the Search Web page is complete, you are ready to work on the Feedback Web page.

Creating a Web Page That Contains a Form

Next you will prepare the Feedback Web page, which will contain a form. A **form** is a collection of form fields in a Web page that gathers information. A **form field** is a data-entry field in a form, such as a text box or a radio button. A user enters data into the form by typing text directly into a text box, by selecting a radio button or a check box, or by selecting a value from a drop-down menu. After completing the form, the user submits it to the server, where a form handler processes it. A **form handler** is a program that collects and processes the form's data in a predetermined manner. For example, you might select a form handler to save the form's data as an HTML file or to send the form's data to an e-mail address. FrontPage includes many form handlers to process common requests, or you can design your own form handlers to handle your individual needs.

During your meeting with the Web site development team, the team members indicated a desire to collect information about the site's users and their impressions about the Web site, the company, and the company's products. The team wants users to be able to enter their names and e-mail addresses and have an option to ask for a response after submitting the form. In addition, users should be able to enter brief, open-ended comments. Finally, the team wants to ask users the number of times that they have visited the Sunshine Country Store. This information will help the marketing department gather information about who is visiting the site, as well as obtain positive and negative feedback in several categories. Figure 6-6 shows a sketch of the Feedback Web page that the team needs you to create.

Figure 6-6	DESIGN SKETCH OF THE FEEDBACK WEB PAGE

There are two ways to create a form. You can use the **Form Page Wizard**, which asks questions about the type of form that you want to create and lets you select the form's options to create a new Web page containing the form with the fields you specified using the Wizard. To use this option, double-click the Form Page Wizard icon in the New dialog box. You can use this method when you want to create a standard type of form, for example, a form that contains billing and shipping addresses or information about products such as quantity ordered.

The second way to create a form is to create a new Web page using the Normal Page template and then to insert a form component in the page. The form component appears as a box with a dashed outline in Page view. Then you use the Form command on the Insert menu to insert the form's fields in the form. After adding a form field, you can accept its default settings or change its properties.

Regardless of how you create the form, you edit it in the same way as any other Web page. For example, if you click to the left of a form field and start typing the text to serve as its label, the form field moves to the right to make room for the text. Pressing the Enter key to the left of a form field inserts a new paragraph, which causes the form field to appear at the beginning of the next line. You can cut or copy form fields to the Windows Clipboard and paste them into a form. Although a single Web page can contain more than one form, the most common situation is to create a single form in a Web page. You will create a single form in the Feedback Web page.

In addition to the sketch provided by the Web site development team, it is important to define other steps that you will use to create the new form. The sketch should identify which form fields you want to use and their approximate locations in the form component. Amanda's planning analysis sheet, shown in Figure 6-7, specifies how to validate the form fields, collect data from the form, and confirm the form's submission to the server for the user. You will learn more about the information shown in the planning analysis sheet as you complete this tutorial.

Figure 6-7	AMANDA'S PLANNING ANALYSIS SHEET FOR THE FEEDBACK WEB PAGE

Planning Analysis Sheet

Objective

Create a Feedback Web page that contains a form with form fields for collecting user feedback and contact information.

Requirements

Sketch of the page's planned appearance from the Web site development team, including the form fields to use to collect the desired data

Feedback logo to include in the page

Radio button group with only one selection permitted

Drop-down menu that shows three categories with only one selection permitted

Scrolling text box that is 50 characters wide and five lines high

One-line text boxes that are 35 characters wide for the user's name and e-mail address

A one-line text box that stores only integers from zero to 100

A check box to request a response

Submit Form and Clear Form buttons to submit and reset the form, respectively

Results

A Feedback Web page that includes the Sunny Morning Products logo, a title, and form fields that collect the desired data from users. The user's data is stored in a results file on the server, which the marketing department will use to collect positive feedback and to respond to problems. The results file will also be sent to the general e-mail address for the marketing department.

Before adding form fields to a form, you need to create a Web page that contains a form component. Rather than asking you to create a new blank page and type all the necessary text, Amanda created the Feedback Web page and entered some of the form's text for you. First, you will import Amanda's existing page into the Sunny Web site. Then you will create the necessary form fields and change their properties, as needed, to match Amanda's plan.

To import the Feedback Web page into the Sunny Web site:

1. Click the **Microsoft FrontPage** program button on the taskbar to return to FrontPage, and then click the **Folders** button 🔲 on the Views bar to change to Folders view.

2. Click **File** on the menu bar, and then click **Import**. The Import dialog box opens.

3. Click the **Add File** button to open the Add File to Import List dialog box, make sure the drive or folder that contains your Data Disk appears in the Look in text box, double-click the **Tutorial.06** folder, and then double-click **Feedback**. The path to the Feedback.htm file on your Data Disk appears in the Import dialog box.

4. Click the **OK** button to import the Feedback page into the Sunny Web site.

5. Double-click **feedback.htm** in the Contents pane to open the Feedback page in Page view. Notice that the page Amanda created contains a broken link to a picture at the top of the page. You need to insert the picture in the page and then save it in the Web site's images folder. The file for the logo is saved in the Tutorial.06 folder on your Data Disk.

6. Right-click the broken link at the top of the page, click **Picture Properties** on the shortcut menu, click the **Browse** button to the right of the Picture source text box, click the **Select a file on your computer** button 🔲 to open the Select File dialog box, make sure that the Look in list box displays the drive or folder that contains your Data Disk, double-click the **Tutorial.06** folder, and then double-click **FormLogo**. You return to the Picture Properties dialog box.

7. Click the **OK** button to close the Picture Properties dialog box. The logo is inserted at the top of the page.

8. Click the **Save** button 🔲 on the Standard toolbar. Save the FormLogo.gif file in the Sunny Web site's images folder.

Now you are ready to modify the Feedback Web page to add a form component. Then you will insert the form fields into it and modify their properties, as necessary, to meet Amanda's specifications.

Adding a Form Component to a Web Page

Before adding a form field to the Web page, you must add the form component that will contain the form field. If you used the Form Page Wizard to create your Web page, then FrontPage added the form component to the page automatically. Amanda's Feedback Web page does not yet contain a form. When you add a form component to a page, FrontPage creates the component and inserts the Submit and Reset buttons in it automatically.

Creating a Form Component and Adding Form Fields to It
- Position the insertion point where you want to insert the form.
- Click Insert on the menu bar, point to Form, and then click Form.
- Place the insertion point inside the form component where you want the first form field to appear.
- Click Insert on the menu bar, point to Form, and then click the desired form field to add it to the form.
- Right-click the form field object, and then click Form Field Properties on the shortcut menu to open the form field's Properties dialog box.
- Enter the appropriate values for the form field's properties.
- Click the OK button.

Amanda already created some of the content for the form. After you add the form component to the page, you will need to cut her content from the page and then paste it into the form component. The form handler on the server will only process form fields that are contained in the form component.

To insert the form component in the Feedback Web page:

1. Click to the left of the word "Tell" in the paragraph that appears under the horizontal line to position the insertion point there. This is the first line of the text that will appear in the form.

2. Click **Insert** on the menu bar, point to **Form**, and then click **Form**. FrontPage inserts a form component on a new line below the horizontal line. The form component contains the Submit and Reset buttons.

   You will cut the text that Amanda created for the form and then paste it into the form component. The insertion point is currently blinking to the left of the Submit button in the form component, which is where you will paste the existing text.

3. Use the pointer to select all of the lines of text beginning with "Tell us…" and ending with "Please contact me about my comments."

4. Click the **Cut** button ✂ on the Standard toolbar to cut the selected text from the page.

5. Click to the left of the Submit button, but inside the form component, to place the insertion point there. This is where you will paste the text that you just cut.

   TROUBLE? If you see selection handles around the Submit button, then you selected the button instead of the space between the form component and the Submit button. Repeat Step 5 to position the insertion point correctly.

6. Click the **Paste** button 📋 on the Standard toolbar to paste the text into the form component. The form component now contains the text that Amanda created. See Figure 6-8.

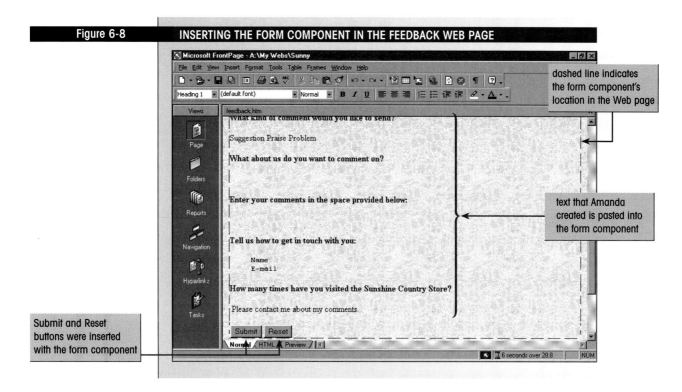

Figure 6-8   INSERTING THE FORM COMPONENT IN THE FEEDBACK WEB PAGE

Now you are ready to add fields to the form.

Adding Radio Buttons to a Form

Radio buttons, or **option buttons**, are usually arranged in a form in groups. A **group name** identifies a related set of radio buttons. Within a group of radio buttons, only one button can be selected at a time—selecting a radio button deselects a selected radio button. You create labels for radio buttons by typing the appropriate text next to the button. For example, a form might have a section with the group name "Age" that contains corresponding radio buttons with the labels "Under 25," "25-40," "41-65," and "Over 65." Radio buttons are appropriate to use when only a few choices are available, such as when specifying age groups. A form can contain more than one radio button group. In addition, the first radio button you add to a form will be selected automatically when you open the form in the browser, unless you change the default settings. Therefore, the first button should be the most common response, so users won't need to select it if it is their choice.

When you create radio button groups in a form, consider the following design suggestions:

- Use radio buttons when you want to limit the user to one of a few related and mutually exclusive choices.

- The minimum number of radio buttons in a group is two, and the recommended maximum is seven.

- Clearly label each radio button in a group so that users can easily determine the button to select when making a choice.

- Use a heading or easily distinguishable text to identify the group name for the radio buttons.

Amanda already included the labels for each radio button and asks you to insert the radio button form fields to the left of the labels. If necessary, refer to Figure 6-6 while creating the form to determine where to place the form fields.

To add a radio button to a form:

1. If necessary, scroll the Feedback Web page so you can see the "Suggestion Praise Problem" text. These words will be the labels for the radio buttons.

2. Click to the left of the word "Suggestion" to place the insertion point where you will insert the first radio button.

3. Click **Insert** on the menu bar, point to **Form**, and then click **Radio Button** to insert the first radio button in the form to the left of the "Suggestion" label. Notice that the radio button is selected, as indicated by the black dot that appears within the white circle. See Figure 6-9.

| Figure 6-9 | RADIO BUTTON FORM FIELD INSERTED IN THE FORM |

TROUBLE? If you insert the radio button in the wrong location or if you insert the wrong form field, click the Undo button 🔄 on the Standard toolbar to remove the form field, and then repeat the steps to insert the correct form field.

Next, include the radio buttons for the "Praise" and "Problem" labels to create the rest of the radio button group.

4. Click to the left of "P" in the word "Praise" to position the insertion point, and then repeat Step 3 to insert the radio button for this selection. Notice that this second radio button does not appear selected, as indicated by the solid white circle.

5. Click to the left of "P" in the word "Problem" to position the insertion point, and then repeat Step 3 to insert the radio button for this selection. This radio button is not selected.

6. Click the **Save** button 💾 on the Standard toolbar to save your changes.

The Suggestion, Praise, and Problem radio buttons now belong to a group that appears below the "What kind of comment would you like to send?" heading. Within any radio button group, the user can select only one radio button.

After placing a form field in the form, you can change its properties when necessary to more closely match your needs. For example, FrontPage assigned the group name R1 to the radio button group, the value V1 to the Suggestion radio button, the value V2 to the Praise radio button, and the value V3 to the Problem radio button. You could accept these default values for the group and button names, but Amanda suggests that you change the current radio button properties by changing the group name to MessageType and the button names to match their labels. Using more meaningful names will make the buttons easier to examine and locate in the HTML code. When creating names for groups and form fields, you may want to apply the common standard of omitting spaces between words so it is easier to determine the beginning and end of each name in the HTML code.

To change radio button properties:

1. Right-click the **radio button** to the left of the Suggestion label to select it and open the shortcut menu, and then click **Form Field Properties** to open the Radio Button Properties dialog box. You will change the group name and the value name for the radio button.

2. Type **MessageType** in the Group name text box, press the **Tab** key to select the value in the Value text box, and then type **Suggestion**. Now the radio button group is named MessageType, and the radio button form field is named Suggestion. See Figure 6-10. Notice that in the Initial state section, the Selected option button is selected, indicating that this radio button appears selected when the Feedback Web page is opened in the browser. You will learn more about the other options in this dialog box later in this tutorial.

| Figure 6-10 | COMPLETED RADIO BUTTON PROPERTIES DIALOG BOX |

selected radio button form field

indicates that this radio button will be selected in the form as its default value

radio button group in the form

new group name

selected radio button's name

3. Click the **OK** button to complete the changes to the radio button's properties and to close the dialog box.

    Next, change the properties for the other two radio buttons and assign them to the same group as the Suggestion radio button.

4. Right-click the **radio button** to the left of "Praise," and then click **Form Field Properties** to open the Radio Button Properties dialog box for this radio button. The default for the Praise radio button is "Not selected" because only one radio button can be selected in a group at a time.

5. Type **MessageType** in the Group name text box, press the **Tab** key, type **Praise**, and then click the **OK** button.

6. Right-click the **radio button** to the left of "Problem," click **Form Field Properties** to open the Radio Button Properties dialog box for this radio button, type **MessageType** in the Group name text box, press the **Tab** key, type **Problem**, and then click the **OK** button.

7. Click the **Save** button ▣ on the Standard toolbar to save the page.

You specified the MessageType radio button group to include each of the three radio button form fields you placed in the form. Next you will add another type of form field—a drop-down menu.

Adding a Drop-Down Menu to a Form

Radio buttons are useful when you want a user to select from only a few choices. When you want to present several choices in a single form field, a **drop-down menu** is a better choice because a drop-down menu saves space by organizing choices in a list. The user can select the correct choice from a scrollable list. Although a user could select one or more choices from a drop-down menu, usually only one selection is permitted from the list.

When you create drop-down menus in a form, consider the following design suggestions:

- Use a drop-down menu when you want the user to select a choice from a list.
- Drop-down menus should contain a minimum of three choices.
- Arrange items in the list so that the most commonly selected entries appear first, or arrange items in ascending order alphabetically, numerically, or chronologically.
- The default selection in a drop-down menu should be either the most used choice or the first choice in the list.

Amanda wants you to insert a drop-down menu form field in the form to provide a list of categories from which the user can select when sending comments to Sunny Morning Products. The marketing department supplied the following list of categories for the list: Web Site, Company, and Products.

To add a drop-down menu to a form:

1. Click the line immediately below the "What about us do you want to comment on?" heading to place the insertion point in the correct location for the drop-down menu.

2. Click **Insert** on the menu bar, point to **Form**, and then click **Drop-Down Menu** to insert the drop-down menu form field.

FrontPage creates a drop-down menu that displays only two characters. Amanda wants you to change the default settings to increase the width of the drop-down menu, to insert the menu items, and to change the default form field names.

To add choices to a drop-down menu and change its properties:

1. Right-click the **drop-down menu** to select it and open the shortcut menu, and then click **Form Field Properties**. The Drop-Down Menu Properties dialog box opens. FrontPage assigned the name D1 to the drop-down menu. The dialog box shows that there are no choices for the drop-down menu's list and that multiple selections are not permitted. You will rename the drop-down menu's name, and then you will create the choices that will appear in the list.

2. Type **Subject** in the Name text box. The drop-down menu form field now has the name Subject.

3. Click the **Add** button to open the Add Choice dialog box. You use this dialog box to create entries in the list. First, you supply the item's name, or choice, which is how the item will appear in the list. Then you supply the item's value, which is the name of the list item in the HTML code. Finally, you indicate whether the item is selected or not selected in the drop-down menu.

4. Type **Web Site** in the Choice text box, and then click the **Specify Value** check box to select it. FrontPage automatically adds the value "Web Site" to the Specify Value text box.

5. Click to the left of the letter "S" in the Specify Value text box, press the **Backspace** key to delete the space, and then in the Initial state section, click the **Selected** option button to select it. See Figure 6-11.

Figure 6-11	COMPLETED ADD CHOICE DIALOG BOX

selected drop-down menu form field in the form

indicates that this choice will be selected in the drop-down menu as the default

text to appear in the drop-down menu list

HTML name for this choice

6. Click the **OK** button to finish adding this choice to the drop-down menu and to close the Add Choice dialog box. The other two choices, Company and Products, will have the same choice name and value, so you will not need to check the Specify Value check box. FrontPage will use the choice name as the value.

7. Click the **Add** button in the Drop-Down Menu Properties dialog box, type **Company** in the Choice text box, make sure that the **Not selected** option button is selected, and then click the **OK** button to close the Add Choice dialog box.

8. Click the **Add** button in the Drop-Down Menu Properties dialog box, type **Products** in the Choice text box, make sure that the **Not selected** option button is selected, and then click the **OK** button to close the Add Choice dialog box. See Figure 6-12.

Figure 6-12   **COMPLETED DROP-DOWN MENU PROPERTIES DIALOG BOX**

name of drop-down menu form field

these choices will appear in the drop-down menu list

drop-down menu will display one choice when the list is not selected

users can select only one item in the list

click to add a new choice

click to change the selected choice

options for moving the choices up or down in the list

9. Click the **OK** button to close the Drop-Down Menu Properties dialog box. The drop-down menu appears in the form with "Web Site" displayed as the default choice.

10. Click the **Save** button 🖫 on the Standard toolbar to save the page.

If you click the list arrow on the drop-down menu in Page view, you will select the form field instead of displaying the list. To see the list, you must open the page in the browser or use the Preview tab and then click the list arrow. You will test all of the form fields in the browser after completing the form. Next Amanda asks you to add a one-line text box form field to the form.

Adding a One-Line Text Box to a Form

When you need a user to supply short information in a form field that is unique or uncommon, such as a phone number or an e-mail address, you can use a text box to collect the data. A **one-line text box** accepts a single line of typed information. You can also use a one-line text box form field to permit users to enter a password, in which case the password appears with asterisks to conceal it while it is being typed.

When you create one-line text boxes in a form, consider the following design suggestions:

■ Use a one-line text box when you want the user to enter a small amount of unique information.

■ A one-line text box limits the number of characters that a user can enter.

■ A one-line text box can be used as a password field.

In addition to being unique, a user's name and e-mail address usually are short so they are suitable candidates for one-line text box form fields.

To add a one-line text box to a form:

1. Press **Ctrl + End** to scroll down the Feedback Web page so you can see the "Tell us how to get in touch with you:" heading and the Name and E-mail labels for the one-line text boxes that you will create.

2. Click anywhere in the **Name** label, and then press the **End** key to place the insertion point a few spaces to the right of this text where Amanda inserted a tab stop.

3. Click **Insert** on the menu bar, point to **Form**, and then click **One-Line Text Box**. FrontPage places a one-line text box form field in the form.

4. Click in the **E-mail** label, press the **End** key, and then repeat Step 3 to add a one-line text box a few spaces to the right of the E-mail label.

5. Click the **Save** button on the Standard toolbar to save the page.

Now that you've added the text boxes to the form, you need to set their widths. Amanda wants you to adjust their current properties so that each text box holds a maximum of 35 characters, rather than the default setting of 20 characters. Another way of opening the properties dialog box for a form field is to double-click it, as you will see next.

To change the properties of a one-line text box:

1. Double-click the **one-line text box** for the Name label to open the Text Box Properties dialog box. FrontPage assigned the name T1 to the text box. If you want a default value to appear in the text box when the form is opened in the browser, you can set it by entering a value in the Initial value text box. You can also change the width of the text box (using a measurement indicating the maximum number of characters the text box will hold), change the text box to one that accepts a password, or change the order in which the user selects text boxes in the form by pressing the Tab key. Amanda wants you to rename the text box and then increase its width.

2. Type **UserName** in the Name text box, press the **Tab** key twice to select the value in the Width in characters text box, and then type **35** to set the text box to accept a maximum of 35 characters. See Figure 6-13.

| Figure 6-13 | COMPLETED TEXT BOX PROPERTIES DIALOG BOX |

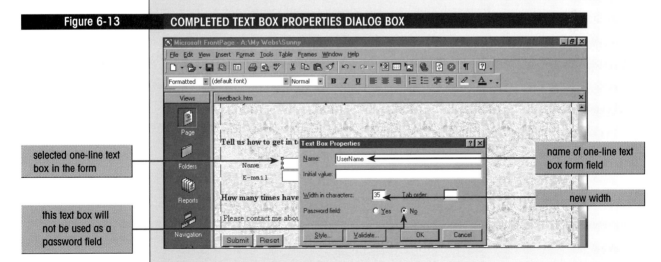

selected one-line text box in the form

this text box will not be used as a password field

name of one-line text box form field

new width

3. Click the **OK** button. The Name text box increases to a width of 35 characters.

4. Repeat Steps 1 through 3 to set the E-mail text box properties to have the name **UserEmail** and a width of **35** characters.

5. Click the **Save** button on the Standard toolbar to save the page.

The one-line text boxes will let a user enter a name and e-mail address with up to 35 characters each. Some text information, such as user comments or problem descriptions, requires more space. When you need to accept unique passages of longer text, you can use a scrolling text box form field.

Adding a Scrolling Text Box to a Form

A **scrolling text box** has the same characteristics as a one-line text box, except that it accepts multiple lines of text information and it cannot be used as a password field. A scrolling text box is an effective form field to use when asking a user to provide open-ended feedback about a particular product or service.

When you create a scrolling text box in a form, consider the following design suggestions:

- Use a scrolling text box when you want a user to supply information that might include more than one line.
- A scrolling text box accepts and displays multiple lines of text entered by the user. The size of the scrolling text box should be large enough to display several lines of text at a time.

Amanda's design of the Feedback Web page includes a scrolling text box form field that allows users to enter multiple lines of text. You will add this form field next.

To add a scrolling text box to a form:

1. Scroll up the Feedback Web page until the heading "Enter your comments in the space provided below:" is at the top of the Contents pane, and then click the blank line below the heading. You will insert the scrolling text box here.

2. Click **Insert** on the menu bar, point to **Form**, and then click **Scrolling Text Box**. FrontPage inserts a scrolling text box in the form.

To match the Web site development team's form design, you will change the default properties for the scrolling text box from 20 characters wide with two lines to 50 characters wide with five lines.

To change the properties of a scrolling text box:

1. Double-click the **scrolling text box** to open the Scrolling Text Box Properties dialog box. FrontPage assigned the name S1 to the scrolling text box. Notice that you can specify an initial value for the scrolling text box; if you leave this text box empty, then the scrolling text box will be empty when the Web page that contains it is opened in the browser. You can also set the properties for a scrolling text box to change its width and the number of lines of text to display in the box. If the user enters more text than is displayed in the scrolling text box, the form field will scroll the lines automatically. You will change the default name to be more descriptive of the scrolling text box, and then you will change the form field's size.

2. Type **Comments** in the Name text box; press the **Tab** key twice to move to the Width in characters text box and type **50**, and then press the **Tab** key twice to move to the Number of lines text box and type **5**. See Figure 6-14.

| Figure 6-14 | COMPLETED SCROLLING TEXT BOX PROPERTIES DIALOG BOX |

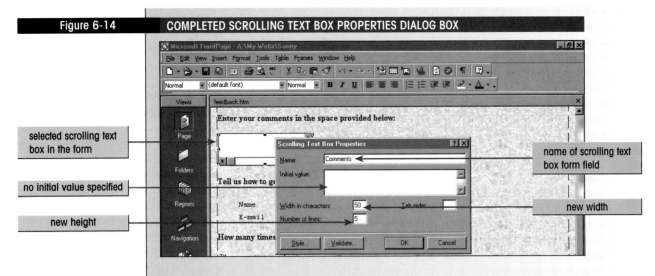

selected scrolling text box in the form

no initial value specified

new height

name of scrolling text box form field

new width

3. Click the **OK** button. The scrolling text box is displayed with the new properties—it is five lines high and 50 characters wide.

4. Click the **Save** button 🖫 on the Standard toolbar to save the page.

Next you will preview the Feedback page in the browser. After testing the page, you will mark the tasks for the Feedback and Search pages as completed.

To preview the Feedback page and complete the tasks:

1. Click the **Preview in Browser** button 🔍 on the Standard toolbar, and then click the **OK** button to close the dialog box. The Feedback Web page opens in the browser and displays the form.

TROUBLE? If Internet Explorer doesn't open, click its button on the taskbar.

2. Click the **Praise** radio button in the form to select it.

3. Scroll down the page as necessary, click the **list arrow** for the drop-down menu, and then click **Company** in the list.

4. Click in the **scrolling text box**, and then type **This is a test.**

5. Click in the **Name** text box, type your first and last names separated by a space, press the **Tab** key, and then type your e-mail address in the E-mail text box.

6. Scroll down the page as necessary, and then click the **Submit** button. The FrontPage Run-Time Component Page opens in the browser because you are working in a disk-based Web.

Your test of the form is successful, so you can mark the tasks for the Feedback and Search pages as complete.

To mark the tasks as completed and close FrontPage:

1. Click the **Close** button ⊠ on the Internet Explorer title bar to close Internet Explorer and return to FrontPage.

2. Click the **Tasks** button 🖋 on the Views bar to change to Tasks view.

3. Right-click the **Create Feedback Web page** task to open the shortcut menu, and then click **Mark as Completed**.

4. Right-click the **Create Search Web page** task to open the shortcut menu, and then click **Mark as Completed**.

5. Click ⊠ on the FrontPage title bar to close FrontPage.

In the next session, you will create the rules that FrontPage will use to verify that the form's fields accept the correct data from users.

Session 6.1 QUICK | CHECK

1. True or False: When you use a template to create a new Web page, FrontPage automatically enters content and components that are relevant to the page.

2. What two methods can you use to determine the location of a FrontPage component in a Web page?

3. True or False: You cannot change the properties of a component that is created in a Web page by a template.

4. What is a form field?

5. Before adding a form field to a Web page, you must first create a(n) _____ in the Web page that will contain the form field.

6. What is a form handler?

7. Why is it a good idea to change the default group name and value for a radio button group?

8. You are designing a Web page for a Canadian company that includes a list of the Canadian provinces. What form field would you use to collect the data, what properties would you assign to the form field, and which option would be the default selection? Defend your selections.

SESSION 6.2

In this session, you will validate form fields to verify data entered by a user. You will add a check box form field and push buttons to a form and change their default properties. You will specify and configure a form handler to process the form and test the form on a client. You will open an Office 2000 document from a Web site and create a hyperlink to it. Finally, you will view the HTML code for a Web page that contains a form.

Validating Form Fields

The one-line text boxes and scrolling text box that you added to the Feedback Web page in Session 6.1 accept unique text information entered by a user. In some situations, you might want to edit or validate the information a user enters into these form fields. For example, you might set the properties of a text box so that it must contain a minimum or maximum number of characters that must be numeric.

The process of checking the information entered by a user into one or more form fields to verify that the information is acceptable is called **validation**. If the data entered by a user fails the validation test, then the user must change it before the form handler on the server will accept the form for processing. You specify data validation criteria using the form field's Properties dialog box.

The sketch of the Feedback Web page (see Figure 6-6) shows that the Web site development team wants users to enter into a one-line text box the number of times that they have visited the Sunshine Country Store. The team wants to ensure that users can enter only a whole, positive number (or an **integer**) into this form field. In other words, a user shouldn't be able to enter a negative number, a number with a decimal, or letters into this form field. Amanda wants you to set this form field so that it must accept an integer that is in the range zero to 100. To ensure that users will not inadvertently skip this form field, you will also validate this form field so that it must contain an acceptable value. In other words, users cannot submit the form if this form field is empty.

To create the one-line text box and change its properties:

1. Start **FrontPage**, insert your Data Disk in the appropriate drive, and then open the **Sunny** Web site (a:\My Webs\Sunny) from your Data Disk in Folders view.

2. Double-click **feedback.htm** in the Contents pane to open the Feedback Web page in Page view.

3. Scroll down the Web page until you see the "How many times have you visited the Sunshine Country Store?" heading, click in the heading, and then press the **End** key. Now the insertion point is positioned in the correct location for the one-line text box.

4. Click **Insert** on the menu bar, point to **Form**, and then click **One-Line Text Box**. A one-line text box is added to the form. You will change the form field's settings to name it "Visits" and to change its width to 3 characters.

5. Double-click the **one-line text box** that you created in Step 4 to open the Text Box Properties dialog box, type **Visits** in the Name text box, press the **Tab** key twice to move to the Width in characters text box and type **3**, and then click the **OK** button. The dialog box closes and the one-line text box is displayed with the new properties.

Next you will set the validation criteria for the Visits text box.

To validate a one-line text box in a form:

1. Right-click the **Visits** text box to open the shortcut menu, and then click **Form Field Validation**. The Text Box Validation dialog box opens. (You can also open this dialog box by clicking the Validate button in the Text Box Properties dialog box.) Currently, there are no validation criteria placed on the data entered into the Visits text box, as indicated by the "No Constraints" setting in the Data type list box.

2. Click the **Data type** list arrow. Notice that you can select Text, Integer, or Number as the data type to validate. You want to make sure that this form field accepts whole numbers, so you will select Integer as the data type.

3. Click **Integer** to specify that data type. Notice that the settings in the Numeric format section become active.

4. In the Numeric format section, click the **None** option button in the Grouping category, because the data will not need to contain a comma or a period. You use this option when you want to change a number to include a comma or a period, such as changing the value 1000 to 1,000.

5. In the Data length section, click the **Required** check box to select it, press the **Tab** key to move to the Min length text box and type **1**, and then press the **Tab** key to move to the Max length text box and type **3**. You specified 1 as the minimum number of integers and 3 as the maximum number of integers that a user can enter into this form field. Selecting the Required check box means that a user must enter a value—even zero—into this form field before the server will accept the form for processing.

6. In the Data value section, click the **Field must be** check box to select it, click the **Field must be** list arrow and, if necessary, click **Greater than or equal to**, press the **Tab** key to move to the Value text box, and then type **0** (the number zero, and not the capital letter "O"). These settings specify that the integer must be greater than or equal to zero.

7. In the Data value section, click the **And must be** check box to select it, click the **And must be** list arrow and, if necessary, click **Less than or equal to**, press the **Tab** key to move to the Value text box, and then type **100**. These settings specify that the integer must be less than or equal to 100. See Figure 6-15.

Figure 6-15   **COMPLETED TEXT BOX VALIDATION DIALOG BOX**

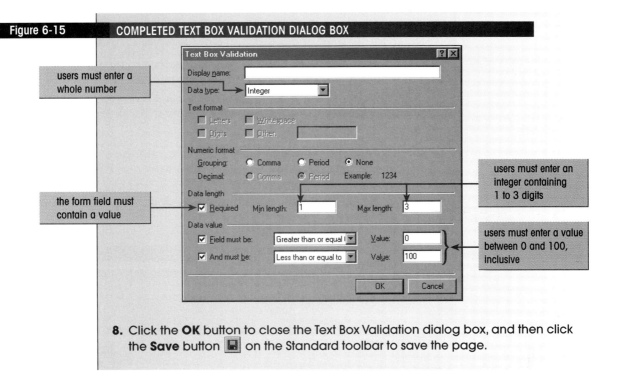

8. Click the **OK** button to close the Text Box Validation dialog box, and then click the **Save** button 🖫 on the Standard toolbar to save the page.

Now users must enter an integer between zero and 100 in the Visits text box before the server will process the form. Next Amanda wants you to add a form field that will alert the Web site development team when a user requests a response to his or her submission.

Adding a Check Box to a Form

You can use a **check box** by itself to indicate a yes/no response to a question, or you can use check boxes in a group to let users answer yes or no to more than one option. Unlike radio button groups, selecting one check box in a check box group does not deselect another check box. You can set the properties of each check box so it is selected or not selected when the form is opened in the browser.

When you create check boxes in a form, consider the following design suggestions:

- Use check boxes when you want a user to select from a group of one or more independent and nonexclusive choices.
- Set the default selection to the most frequently occurring selection.
- Clearly label each check box in a group.
- When necessary, use a heading or easily distinguishable text to identify the subject of the check box group.

You will add a check box to the form that lets a user request a response from Sunny Morning Products.

To add a check box to a form and change its properties:

1. Click anywhere in the text "Please contact me about my comments," and then press the **Home** key to place the insertion point at the beginning of the line. You will add the check box to the left of the text that describes it.

2. Click **Insert** on the menu bar, point to **Form**, and then click **Check Box**. FrontPage inserts a check box that is not selected at the beginning of the line.

3. Double-click the **check box** to open the Check Box Properties dialog box. You will change the default name and value of this form field. The default value that is stored in the results file when the check box is selected is "ON." You will change this value to "Yes" so it is easy to determine that a "Yes" value in the results file means the user requested a response.

4. Type **ContactMe** in the Name text box, press the **Tab** key to move to the Value text box, and then type **Yes**. See Figure 6-16. Notice that in the Initial state section the Not checked option button is selected, indicating that this check box will not contain a check mark when the Feedback Web page is opened in the Web browser.

Figure 6-16	COMPLETED CHECK BOX PROPERTIES DIALOG BOX

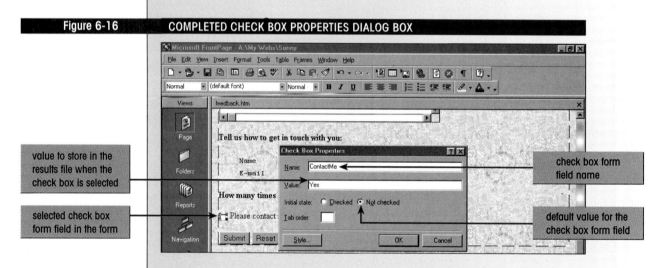

value to store in the results file when the check box is selected

selected check box form field in the form

check box form field name

default value for the check box form field

5. Click the **OK** button to close the Check Box Properties dialog box. The check box form field looks the same, because changing the Name property did not affect this form field's appearance in Page view. Your changes affected only how the server will process this form field.

You have finished adding all of the form fields that collect data from the user. To complete the development of this form, you need to supply the user with a way of sending the Web page to the server for processing.

Adding Push Buttons

Push buttons, or **command buttons**, are used to submit a form to the server or to clear the form's fields. You can create three types of push buttons in a form; each type implements a different processing action. You use a **Submit push button** to let a user submit a form to the server for processing. Clicking a **Reset push button** clears any previously entered data from the form, and clicking a **Normal push button** initiates a user-defined script (which is an advanced Web page feature that is beyond the scope of this tutorial). When you create a form, FrontPage automatically creates and programs the Submit and Reset push buttons for you. The Submit push button automatically is associated with the FrontPage form handler that processes the submitted form results on the Web server. Because these two buttons are automatically included in the form, you can either accept their default values or edit them to suit your needs. If you add a new push button to a form, FrontPage automatically creates a

Normal push button with the value "Button." You must change the properties of the new button to change its name and function.

Amanda wants you to edit the Submit and Reset push buttons in the form. Clicking the Submit push button will send the form to the server for processing; clicking the Reset push button clears the form's fields. To match the sketch shown in Figure 6-6, you will change the label for the Submit push button to "Submit Form" and the label of the Reset push button to "Clear Form."

To change the properties of the Submit push button:

1. Double-click the **Submit** push button to open the Push Button Properties dialog box.

2. Type **Submit** in the Name text box, press the **Tab** key to move to the Value/label text box, press the **End** key, press the **spacebar**, and then type **Form**. Notice in the Button type section that the Submit option button is selected, indicating that this button submits the form's data to the Web server. See Figure 6-17.

Figure 6-17	COMPLETED PUSH BUTTON PROPERTIES DIALOG BOX

3. Click the **OK** button to close the Push Button Properties dialog box. The Submit button now displays the label "Submit Form." Notice that FrontPage automatically resized the push button to accommodate the new label.

Next you will change the default settings for the Reset push button to change its name to "Clear" and its label to "Clear Form."

To change the properties of the Reset push button:

1. Double-click the **Reset** push button to open the Push Button Properties dialog box.

2. Type **Clear** in the Name text box, press the **Tab** key to move to the Value/label text box, and then type **Clear Form**. Notice that the Reset option button is selected in the Button type section, indicating that this button resets the values in the form's fields to their default settings.

3. Click the **OK** button to close the Push Button Properties dialog box. The Reset push button now displays the label "Clear Form."

4. Click the **Save** button 🖫 on the Standard toolbar to save the page.

You have finished placing all the form fields that collect data in the form and provided a means for the user to submit the form to the server for processing. When you submit a form to the server for processing, you must tell the server how to process it. Next you will specify the form handler to use for processing the form.

Using a Form Handler

Recall that a form handler is a program on a Web server that communicates with a browser to process form data received from the browser. FrontPage installs several form handlers with the FrontPage Server Extensions that reside on the Web server. You select a form handler based on how you want to process the data collected in your form. For the Feedback Web page, you will use the FrontPage Save Results component, which is a form handler that collects and saves form data.

The **FrontPage Save Results component** is a general data-collecting form handler that obtains data from a browser and stores that data in a desired format on the server. You have the option of sending the results to an e-mail address in addition to storing the results in a file on the server. The data entered by the user in the form, or the **form results**, is stored on the server in a format that you specify. The two most popular methods of storing form results are as a text file with one line for each form that was submitted to the server or as an HTML file with a line for each form field name and its value (known as a **field name-data value pair**). In the text file method, the first entry, or row, in the table contains the names of the form fields from which the data was obtained. In the HTML file method, each form field name is included as a field name-data value pair, where the name is repeated with the data from each form submission. When using either of these formats to store form results, most developers will set the results file to add the form results from each form submitted to the server at the end of the file.

In addition to storing the results in a file on the Web server, you can send the results to an e-mail address. In order to send the form results as an e-mail message, the FrontPage Server Extensions must be configured to deliver e-mail messages from the server. Normally, the Web site's administrator, or webmaster, configures the FrontPage Server Extensions for this type of processing. Check with your instructor or technical support person to determine if your FrontPage installation is enabled to send form results to an e-mail address.

When you configure the Save Results component, you must specify a format for your results file. You can use a text file to collect the data in each form field, along with optional information, such as the date the form was submitted and Internet Protocol (IP) address of the user. If you collect data in a text file, the file is stored in the _private folder of your FrontPage Web site, where it is hidden from Internet users. Data collected in an HTML file is also hidden from Internet users.

Amanda wants you to use the Save Results component to specify the processing method for the form data collected by the Feedback Web page.

To configure the Save Results component:

1. Right-click anywhere in the form component to open the shortcut menu, and then click **Form Properties**. The Form Properties dialog box opens. See Figure 6-18.

Figure 6-18	FORM PROPERTIES DIALOG BOX

Save Results component selected

enter the filename and path of the results file here

enter the optional e-mail address to which to send the form's result here

when this text box is empty, FrontPage will generate a default confirmation page

click to change the form handler's options

The settings in this dialog box let you choose the filename in which to store your results file and the optional e-mail address to which to send the results file. Notice that you can send your form results to a database or to a location defined by a script. You use the Form properties section to supply the page's filename that will serve as your confirmation page; you will learn more about confirmation pages later in this session. To change the options for any of these settings, click the Options button.

Amanda's planning analysis sheet shows that the form results will be stored in a text file and sent to an e-mail address at Sunny Morning Products. You will establish these settings next.

2. In the Where to store results section, verify that the **Send to** option button is selected. Select the default value in the File name text box, and then type **_private/feedback.txt**. You will store your results file in a file named feedback.txt in the _private folder of the Sunny Web site.

3. Press the **Tab** key twice to move to the E-mail address text box, and then type **results@sunnymorning.com**. The form results will also be sent to this e-mail address.

4. Click the **Options** button to open the Options for Saving Results of Form dialog box. See Figure 6-19. Make sure that "Text database using comma as a separator" appears in the File format list box and that the Include field names check box contains a check mark. When you select the option to use a comma as the data separator, a comma will separate the data entered into each form field. This format is also known as **comma-delimited text**, and it is a popular format for storing data because many different programs can read and use it.

TROUBLE? If "Text database using comma as a separator" does not appear in the File format list box, click the File format list arrow and then click this option to select it.

Figure 6-19 | FILE RESULTS SETTINGS

filename and path of the results file

data will be stored in a comma-delimited format

the results file will contain form field names

Options for Saving Results of Form

File Results | E-mail Results | Confirmation Page | Saved Fields

File name:
_private/feedback.txt   Browse...

File format:
Text database using comma as a separator

☑ Include field names   ☑ Latest results at end

Optional second file:

File name:
                              Browse...

File Format:
HTML

☑ Include field names   ☑ Latest results at end

OK   Cancel

5. Click the **Saved Fields** tab to display those settings. See Figure 6-20. In the Additional information to save section, click the **Remote computer name** check box to select it. This setting will save the user's IP address in the results file using the field name "Remote Name." Notice that the Form fields to save list box displays a list of all the form fields that you created in the Feedback Web page. The form fields are easy to distinguish because you gave them meaningful names instead of accepting the defaults names of V1, S1, etc. These form fields will be saved to the results file.

Figure 6-20 | SAVED FIELDS SETTINGS

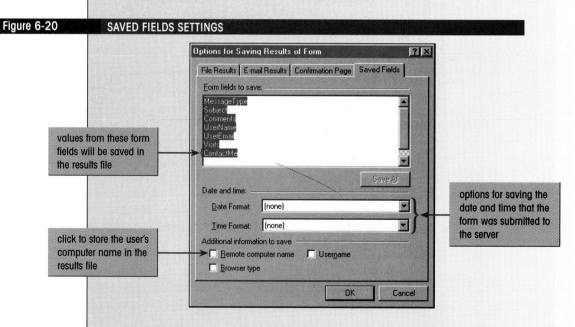

values from these form fields will be saved in the results file

click to store the user's computer name in the results file

Options for Saving Results of Form

File Results | E-mail Results | Confirmation Page | Saved Fields

Form fields to save:
MessageType
Subject
Comments
UserName
UserEmail
Visits
ContactMe

Save All

Date and time:

Date Format: (none)

Time Format: (none)

Additional information to save:
☐ Remote computer name   ☐ Username
☐ Browser type

OK   Cancel

options for saving the date and time that the form was submitted to the server

6. Click the **OK** button to return to the Form Properties dialog box, and then verify that the Form name text box is empty. When there is no form name specified, FrontPage automatically generates a default confirmation page, which is the action you want.

TROUBLE? If any value appears in the Form name text box, select it and then press the Delete key to remove it.

7. Click the **OK** button. A Microsoft FrontPage dialog box opens and displays a message indicating that you are creating the form in a disk-based Web. For now, you will delete the e-mail address. Your disk-based Web does not have the required FrontPage Server Extensions for sending e-mail messages.

8. Click the **Yes** button to display the E-mail Results tab, press the **Delete** key to delete the e-mail address that you entered in Step 3, and then click the **OK** button. The dialog boxes close and you return to the form.

9. Click the **Save** button 🖫 on the Standard toolbar to save the page.

Now that you identified the form handler, including specifying the file where you want the results stored on the server, you need to test the form.

Testing a Form on the Client

Unlike other Web pages, you need to test a page that contains a form on the client *and* on the server. When testing the form on a client, you need to test each form field by entering data into it. For example, you can enter text in text boxes or use drop-down menus to ensure that they display the choices you specified. Also, you can clear all the data from the form and then reenter it. However, any form fields that use data validation, such as the Visits text box, require a server for verification. Therefore, you cannot test form fields that are validated until you can submit the form to a server for processing.

At this point in the development of the form, Amanda wants you to test it on the client. Your test of the form will include reviewing the layout of form fields in the form and testing their operation. You will finish testing the form in the next session after publishing the Web site on a server.

To test a form on the client using Internet Explorer:

1. Click the **Preview in Browser** button 🔍 on the Standard toolbar, and then, if necessary, click the **OK** button in the message box that reminds you that some form elements won't work in a disk-based Web. The Feedback Web page opens in the browser.

2. Scroll down the page until you see the form fields, and then click the **Praise** option button under the "What kind of comment would you like to send?" heading to select it.

3. Click the **What about us do you want to comment on?** list arrow, and then click **Products**.

4. Click in the **Enter your comments in the space provided below** scrolling text box, and then type **This is a test**.

5. Press the **Tab** key to move to the Name text box, type your first and last names separated by a space, press the **Tab** key to move to the E-mail text box, and then type your e-mail address.

6. Press the **Tab** key to move to the Visits text box, and then type **200**.

7. Click the **Please contact me about my comments** check box to select it. Now you can submit the form to the server.

8. Click the **Submit Form** button. The FrontPage Run-Time Component Page opens in the browser to advise you that a Web server is required for the page to function correctly. You will test the page using a Web server later in this tutorial.

9. Click the **Back** button ⬅ on the Standard Buttons toolbar to return to the Feedback Web page, and then click the **Clear Form** button. The data you previously entered is cleared from the form; this action does not require a server. Your test of the form on the client is successful.

Although the browser performs data validation, a server is required to generate the error messages that appear when the Visits text box contains an invalid entry.

Opening an Office 2000 Document from a Web Site

The Web site development team wants to make sure that people who cannot submit forms to the server—for whatever reason—will be able to submit feedback to Sunny Morning Products. You could ask users to print the Feedback Web page and fill in the form, but then the default radio buttons would be selected and users would have no way to indicate their comment type because they cannot use a list arrow on a paper form. In response to the team's request, Amanda saved the form as a Microsoft Word 2000 document and then modified it to make the form easier to complete by hand. She asks you to create a link to the paper document and to open it. First, you will import the file into the Sunny Web site.

To import the Word document into the Sunny Web site:

1. Click the **Microsoft FrontPage** program button on the taskbar, and then click the **Folders** button 📁 on the Views bar to change to Folders view.

2. Click **File** on the menu bar, click **Import**, click the **Add File** button, click the **Look in** list arrow and change to the drive or folder that contains your Data Disk, double-click the **Tutorial.06** folder, and then double-click **Form** to select the document. Click the **OK** button in the Import dialog box to import the file.

3. Double-click **form.doc** in the Contents pane. Microsoft Word starts and opens the document. Amanda wants to give users some additional space in which to enter comments, so she asks you to increase the size of the scrolling text box.

   TROUBLE? If Microsoft Word does not open, your installation of FrontPage is not configured to open Office 2000 documents in the program that created them. If necessary, close the program that opened and return to FrontPage. Click Tools on the menu bar, click Options, and then click the Configure Editors tab to display those settings. Select the Open web pages in the Office application that created them check box, and then click the OK button. Repeat Step 3.

4. Scroll down the document, click the **scrolling text box** to select it, and then drag the middle-right resize handle to the right to enlarge the scrolling text box to approximately the same size shown in Figure 6-21.

Figure 6-21   WORD DOCUMENT OPENED FROM THE SUNNY WEB SITE

radio button group changed to a check box group

drop-down menu changed to a check box group

enlarged scrolling text box

5. Click the **Save** button 🖫 on the Standard toolbar to save the Word document, and then click the **Close** button ✕ on the Word title bar to close Word.

Next, create the hyperlink to the Word document.

To create a hyperlink to a Word document:

1. If necessary, click the **Microsoft FrontPage** program button on the taskbar to return to FrontPage, and then double-click **feedback.htm** in the Contents pane to open the Feedback Web page in Page view.

2. Scroll to the top of the page, and then double-click the word **here** in the third sentence of the paragraph that appears below the horizontal line.

3. Click the **Hyperlink** button 🖳 on the Standard toolbar to open the Create Hyperlink dialog box, scroll down the list of files in the Sunny Web site, and then double-click **form.doc**. The Create Hyperlink dialog box closes and the "here" text now contains a link to the Word document. The "here" link will not work in Internet Explorer because a server is required to open the Word document. However, you can test the link in Page view after saving the page.

4. Click the **here** hyperlink to deselect it, and then click the **Save** button 🖫 on the Standard toolbar to save the page.

5. Press and hold down the **Ctrl** key, and then click the **here** link. Microsoft Word starts and opens the document. Amanda wants you to print the form so that the Web site development team can examine its contents.

6. Click the **Print** button 🖨 on the Standard toolbar in Word to print the document.

7. Click the **Close** button ✕ on the Microsoft Word title bar to close it, and then, if necessary, click the **No** button when asked to save changes.

In the next session, you will publish the Sunny Web site to a server and then test the Feedback and Search Web pages again. Next Amanda wants you to examine the HTML code for the Feedback Web page.

Viewing HTML Code for a Form

Creating a form using HTML code is a complicated chore. All of the form fields are nested within the FORM tags that specify the beginning and end of the form in the Web page. The POST value for the METHOD property specifies that the data in the form will be processed by or posted to the server. The WEBBOT tag specifies the properties for the Save Results form handler. The radio button, one-line text box, and check box form fields are implemented using the INPUT tag. The drop-down menu form field is implemented using the SELECT tag, and the scrolling text box form field is implemented using the TEXTAREA tag. Each of these tags includes properties that specify the appearance of the form field in the form and its settings.

To view the HTML code for the Feedback Web page:

1. Click the **HTML** tab to display the HTML code for the Feedback Web page.

2. Scroll the page until the FORM tag appears at the top of the Contents pane. See Figure 6-22.

Figure 6-22	HTML CODE FOR THE FEEDBACK WEB PAGE

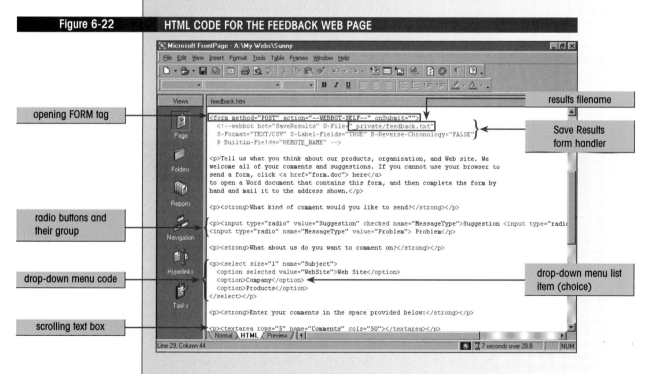

3. Press **Ctrl + End** to scroll to the end of the page. See Figure 6-23. Notice the amount of code that is required to validate the Visits text box.

| Figure 6-23 | HTML CODE FOR THE FEEDBACK WEB PAGE (CONTINUED) |

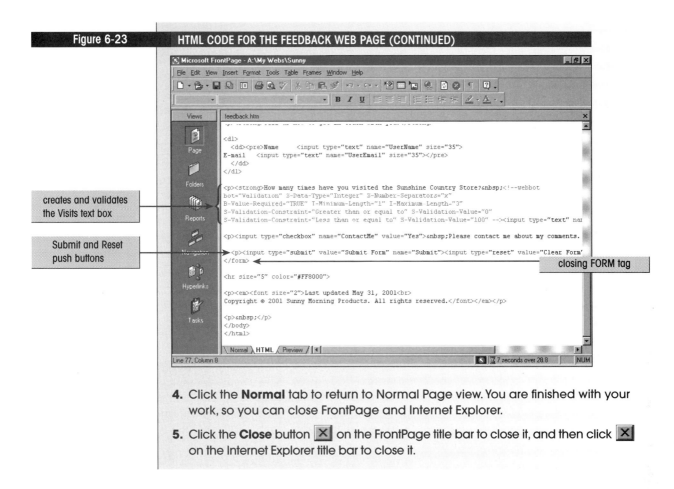

creates and validates
the Visits text box

Submit and Reset
push buttons

closing FORM tag

4. Click the **Normal** tab to return to Normal Page view. You are finished with your work, so you can close FrontPage and Internet Explorer.

5. Click the **Close** button ☒ on the FrontPage title bar to close it, and then click ☒ on the Internet Explorer title bar to close it.

In the next session, you will publish the Sunny Web site to a server and make sure that the server processes requests correctly. Then you will enhance the Web site by adding additional FrontPage components that require a server for processing.

Session 6.2 QUICK CHECK

1. True or False: When validating a form field, you can set the field to accept only numbers, integers, or letters as valid values.

2. To ensure that users will enter data into a form field, click the _____ check box in the form field's Validation dialog box.

3. Name and describe three validation criteria you can set for a form field that will contain integers.

4. Name and describe the three types of push buttons that you can create in a form.

5. The name and value of a form field in an HTML results file is known as a(n) _____.

6. A Web site's administrator is called a(n) _____.

7. The choices in a drop-down menu list are specified in HTML using the _____ tag.

SESSION 6.3

In this session, you will publish a disk-based Web to a server, process forms using a server, and examine form results stored on a server. You will create a hit counter, include a banner ad, move files using drag and drop, use the Find and Replace commands, and recalculate and verify hyperlinks. Finally, you will learn about using permissions to restrict access in a Web site.

Using a Personal Web Server

To function as a Web server, a computer requires a Web server program, which is special software that works with the computer's operating system to receive and execute requests for Web pages. The steps in this tutorial use the **Microsoft Personal Web Server 4.0**, or **PWS**, that is installed using the Windows 98 CD. Your computer might use a different Web server, such as the Microsoft FrontPage Personal Web Server or the Microsoft Internet Information Server (IIS). You can usually tell if the Microsoft PWS is running on your computer by the Web server icon 🐾 that is displayed on the Windows taskbar. Sometimes the PWS is running, but its icon on the taskbar is hidden. You can set the PWS to run when Windows starts or use the Programs menu to start it. The default is to display the icon and run the Web server when Windows 98 starts. If the Web server is not running, you can usually start it by using a Programs menu item or a desktop icon.

To access a local Web server, such as a PWS, you do not need to use the "www" prefix or the server type suffix in the URL; instead, you use the computer name or the default name of **localhost**. Most Web developers use a PWS to develop and test a Web site before publishing it on a Web server and making the site available to Internet users. Because the specifications for using a PWS vary from one computer to another, it is important to work with your instructor or technical support person to determine the correct configuration for your computer. Your instructor will advise you of any differences that you might encounter as you complete the steps in this session.

Figure 6-24 shows the differences between using a disk-based Web and a server-based Web to access your Web pages. With a disk-based Web, the Web browser opens each Web page by obtaining it directly from the file stored on disk. With a server-based Web, the Web browser uses the TCP/IP network software to send the request for a Web page to the server. The server obtains a copy of the file stored on disk and sends it back to the browser by way of the TCP/IP network connection, and then the browser opens the file. Thus, with a local Web server, the TCP/IP network software uses the same network processing to obtain the requested files as if it were connecting to a World Wide Web server.

Figure 6-24   **FILE TRANSFER COMPARISON OF A DISK-BASED AND SERVER-BASED WEB**

disk-based Web

Web browser — disk-based Web files

server-based Web

TCP/IP — ISP connection to WWW — PWS — Personal Web Server

Web browser — server-based Web files

The technical support person at Sunny Morning Products installed and configured the Microsoft PWS and FrontPage 2000 Server Extensions on Amanda's computer. The technical support person assigned the name "localhost" to Amanda's computer (your computer's name might be different). You will test your PWS to make sure that it is installed and operating correctly and that you can access it using your Web browser. Your instructor or technical support person will inform you of any differences that you will encounter in the lab. These steps assume a default installation of the PWS and a default URL of localhost to access it.

To test the PWS installation:

1. Make sure that the PWS is running by confirming that the PWS icon appears on the taskbar.

   TROUBLE? If the PWS icon has an "X" on it, then it is stopped. Right-click 🐾 on the taskbar, and then click Start Service to start the PWS.

   TROUBLE? If you do not see the PWS icon on the taskbar, click the Start button on the taskbar, point to Programs, point to Internet Explorer, point to Personal Web Server, and then click Personal Web Manager. In the Personal Web Manager dialog box, click the Start button to start the PWS, and then click the Close button ✕ to close the dialog box. If you do not see a Start button in the Personal Web Manager dialog box, then the PWS is already running. Close the dialog box.

2. Start **Internet Explorer**, but do not connect to the Internet. You do not need an Internet connection to complete these steps.

TROUBLE? If a Dial-up Connection dialog box opens, if necessary click the Cancel button, and then click the Work Offline button. You do not need to connect to your ISP to run the PWS.

3. Click in the **Address bar**, make sure any URL that appears is selected, type **localhost** (or the name or IP address provided by your instructor), and then press the **Enter** key. The Home Page that was created for your PWS or the default Home Page that installs with the PWS (see Figure 6-25) opens in Internet Explorer, confirming that the PWS or another Web server is installed and functioning.

Figure 6-25	DEFAULT HOME PAGE FOR THE MICROSOFT PWS 4.0

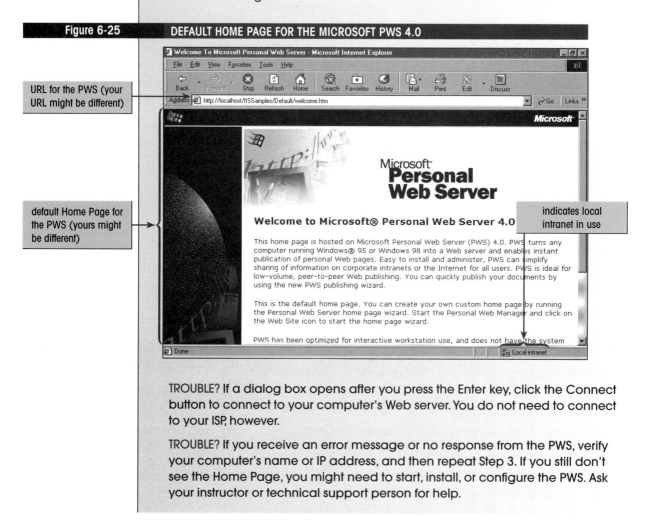

URL for the PWS (your URL might be different)

default Home Page for the PWS (yours might be different)

indicates local intranet in use

TROUBLE? If a dialog box opens after you press the Enter key, click the Connect button to connect to your computer's Web server. You do not need to connect to your ISP, however.

TROUBLE? If you receive an error message or no response from the PWS, verify your computer's name or IP address, and then repeat Step 3. If you still don't see the Home Page, you might need to start, install, or configure the PWS. Ask your instructor or technical support person for help.

You need to place your disk-based Web on the server so you can continue testing the Sunny Web site.

Publishing a Web Site

You **publish** a Web site by copying the Web site's files and folders to a PWS or to a Web server that is connected to the Internet. When you publish a Web site to the PWS, the default server-based folder for the PWS is c:\Inetpub\wwwroot; any Web sites that are published to the PWS are stored as subfolders, or subwebs, in this path. You will need to know how your computer is organized before publishing your Web site to ensure that the server-based Web folder contains the FrontPage 2000 Server Extensions. Your instructor will inform you of any differences that you might encounter in the lab.

REFERENCE WINDOW   **RW**

Publishing a Web Site to Your Computer's Server
- Open the Web site in Folders view.
- Click File on the menu bar, and then click Publish Web to open the Publish Web dialog box.
- Click in the Specify the location to publish your web to text box, and then type http://localhost/ and the name of the folder in which to store the Web site's files and folders.
- Click the Publish button.

You can publish a disk-based Web site to your computer's server using the same Web site name. Before publishing a Web site, check with the server's administrator to see if you need to use any special naming conventions, such as using only lowercase letters. Even though a disk-based and a server-based Web site can have the same name, you access a disk-based Web using a path to a folder on a floppy or hard drive. For a server-based Web, you use the http protocol, the server name (in this case, localhost), and the name of the Web site, such as http://localhost/Sunny.

When you publish a Web site to the PWS, the site is added as a subfolder in the c:\Inetpub\wwwroot folder on your hard drive. If you are publishing changes to an existing server-based Web site, you can click the Publish button on the Standard toolbar and FrontPage will automatically publish the changes to the correct Web site on the server without opening the Publish Web dialog box.

Amanda wants you to publish the Sunny Web site to the PWS to create a server-based Web.

Note: You must be able to publish files to your computer's hard drive or network drive to complete Session 6.3. If you cannot access one of these drives, read Session 6.3 without completing the steps at the computer so you know how to publish a Web site.

To publish a disk-based Web to the PWS:

1. Start **FrontPage**, and then open the **Sunny** Web site (a:\My Webs\Sunny) from your Data Disk in Folders view. Confirm that the PWS is running by verifying that the PWS icon 🐾 is displayed on the Windows taskbar.

2. Click **File** on the menu bar, and then click **Publish Web**. The Publish Web dialog box opens.

3. If necessary, click the **Options** button to expand the dialog box to match Figure 6-26.

Figure 6-26	PUBLISH WEB DIALOG BOX

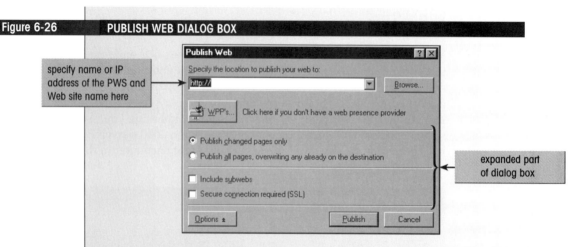

specify name or IP address of the PWS and Web site name here

expanded part of dialog box

You are publishing the entire Web site for the first time, so you will select the Publish all pages option button; you select the Publish changed pages only option button when you are updating the files for a previously published Web site. If your Web site contains subwebs or sensitive information, you can select the Include subwebs and/or the Secure connection required (SSL) check boxes to enable these options. Clicking the WPP's button connects you to a default Web site that provides options for establishing a connection to an ISP if you need to do so.

The default location for your PWS should be selected in the Specify the location to publish your web to text box. You will change this default location and then publish the Web site. To replace the default location, you can just type the new one.

4. Type **http://localhost/Sunny** in the Specify the location to publish your web to text box.

   TROUBLE? If your instructor provides you with a different path or computer name, or an IP address for publishing your Web site, use that path and computer name instead of the one in Step 4. If you are connected to a network server and your computer's name contains a period, then use the IP address and *not* the computer's name in Step 4.

5. If necessary, click the **Publish all pages, overwriting any already on the destination** option button.

6. Click the **Publish** button. The Publish Web dialog box closes, and FrontPage begins publishing the disk-based Web to the PWS. Several messages appear on the status bar and in the dialog box while FrontPage publishes your disk-based Web to the PWS. A "Web site published successfully!" message will appear in a dialog box when the publishing process is complete. See Figure 6-27.

Figure 6-27	DIALOG BOX THAT OPENS AFTER SUCCESSFULLY PUBLISHING A WEB SITE

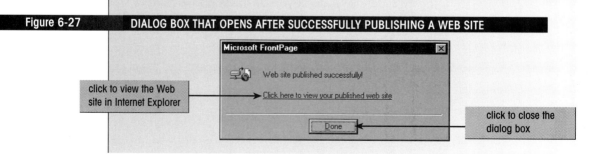

click to view the Web site in Internet Explorer

click to close the dialog box

TROUBLE? If a Microsoft FrontPage dialog opens and asks you to uncheck the File menu's Work Offline item, click the Internet Explorer program button on the taskbar, click File on the menu bar, and then click Work Offline. Then click the Microsoft FrontPage program button on the taskbar, and click the OK button in the dialog box to close it. Repeat Step 6.

TROUBLE? If a dialog box opens and tells you that FrontPage cannot locate the FrontPage Server Extensions, then you either typed the wrong computer name in Step 4 or the Server Extensions are not configured correctly. Ask your instructor or technical support person for help.

While publishing your Web site to the PWS, FrontPage automatically changed the filename of your disk-based Home Page from index.htm to Default.htm. FrontPage also updated any links to the file named index.htm to Default.htm. This renaming convention also works in reverse. If you publish a Web site from the PWS to a disk-based Web, then the file Default.htm is renamed to index.htm. Some developers publish a server-based Web to a folder on a hard drive to create a backup copy of the Web site because all of the FrontPage Server Extensions and the Web site's contents are copied to the disk.

Now that you have published the Sunny Web site to the PWS, you can open it using the hyperlink created by FrontPage.

7. Click the **Click here to view your published web site** hyperlink in the Microsoft FrontPage dialog box. The Home Page opens from the server-based Web in Internet Explorer. See Figure 6-28.

| Figure 6-28 | HOME PAGE FOR SERVER-BASED WEB |

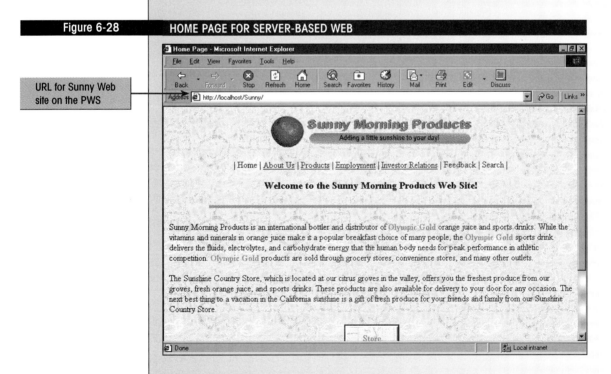

URL for Sunny Web site on the PWS

TROUBLE? If the logo in the Home Page does not appear, click the Refresh button on the Standard Buttons toolbar to reload the page.

Notice that the URL of the Home Page is now http://localhost/Sunny/. The http protocol in the URL indicates that your Web browser is communicating with a server to process requests instead of opening files directly from your computer's disk drive. The server is opening the files from the c:\Inetpub\wwwroot\Sunny folder on your hard drive. You can perform the same activities using this server-based Web as you did with the disk-based Web. In addition, when you open a server-based Web in FrontPage, you can edit pages, update hyperlinks, and do other tasks just as you did in the disk-based Web. The main difference between the two different Web sites, however, is that the server-based Web will process several key elements of the Web site, including the form that you created earlier in this tutorial.

Publishing Changes to Pages in a Web Site

Your disk-based Web site is still open in FrontPage. Amanda reminds you that you did not create the hyperlinks in the Home Page to open the Feedback and Search Web pages that you created. So that you can practice publishing changes to pages, you will update the Home Page using the disk-based Sunny Web and then publish the changes to the server-based Sunny Web. When you make changes to a server-based Web, you usually don't need to take the extra step of publishing your changes because your changes are made directly to the server-based Web. Some changes, however, must be published to work correctly, even if you make them in a server-based Web.

REFERENCE WINDOW   **RW**

Publishing Changes to a Server-Based Web Site
- Open in Page view the Web page that you need to edit, make the changes, and then save the page.
- Edit and save other Web pages, as necessary.
- Click the Publish Web button on the Standard toolbar.

To update the navigation bar in the Home Page and publish the changes:

1. Click the **Microsoft FrontPage** program button on the taskbar, and then click the **Done** button in the dialog box to close it. The disk-based Sunny Web site is still open in FrontPage, as indicated by the path A:\My Webs\Sunny in the title bar.

2. Double-click **index.htm** in the Contents pane to open the Home Page in Page view.

3. Double-click **Feedback** in the navigation bar, click the **Hyperlink** button 🖳 on the Standard toolbar to open the Create Hyperlink dialog box, and then scroll down the list of files and double-click **feedback.htm**.

4. Repeat Step 3 to create the **Search** hyperlink in the navigation bar to open the **search.htm** page.

5. Click the **Save** button 🖫 on the Standard toolbar to save the Home Page. You need to publish the Home Page to the server to update your changes in the server-based Web.

6. Click the **Publish Web** button 🖹 on the Standard toolbar. A Microsoft FrontPage dialog box opens and processes the updates to the Sunny Web site. After a few moments, the "Web site published successfully!" message appears again.

7. Click the **Click here to view your published web site** hyperlink to open the Home Page of your server-based Web site in Internet Explorer, and then click the **Refresh** button 🖹 on the Standard Buttons toolbar to load the new version of the Home Page. The Feedback and Search hyperlinks in the navigation bar are now active.

Processing **Web Pages on a Server**

When a server processes a Web page that contains a form, it usually returns a confirmation page to the browser that sent the page. A **confirmation page** is a Web page that contains a copy of the data entered by the user and often is used for verification purposes. FrontPage can return a default confirmation page or you can create, save, and specify a custom confirmation page. When you specify a custom confirmation page, FrontPage automatically inserts the data entered by the user in the correct locations in the confirmation page and then returns the confirmation page to the browser. You will not create a custom confirmation page in this tutorial, but you can search for the topic "Create a confirmation page and assign it to a form" in the FrontPage Help system to learn more about creating a custom confirmation page.

Next you will test the Search and Feedback Web pages to make sure that the PWS processes these pages correctly.

To test the Search Web page using Internet Explorer:

1. Click the **Search** hyperlink in the navigation bar in the Home Page. The Search page opens in the browser. Notice that the page's URL references the page in the server-based Web.

2. Click in the **Search for** text box, type **MIS**, and then click the **Start Search** button. The PWS processes your request and returns a new Web page with your search results. Depending on your computer's speed, the new page might appear so quickly that you won't notice it. However, you can see that the URL in the Address bar has changed. The Search page that is displayed in the browser is the page that the server generated to contain your search results.

   TROUBLE? If an Internet Explorer dialog box opens and says that you are sending information to the local intranet, click the Yes button and continue.

3. Scroll down the Search page until the Search for text box is at the top of the window. See Figure 6-29. This is the revised version of the Search page—the confirmation page—that the PWS generated. The Search Results table contains one entry that is formatted as a hyperlink. The Employment Web page contains the search text that you specified. Pages identified in the search results are hyperlinks that you can click to open each page.

Figure 6-29   SEARCH WEB PAGE WITH SEARCH RESULTS

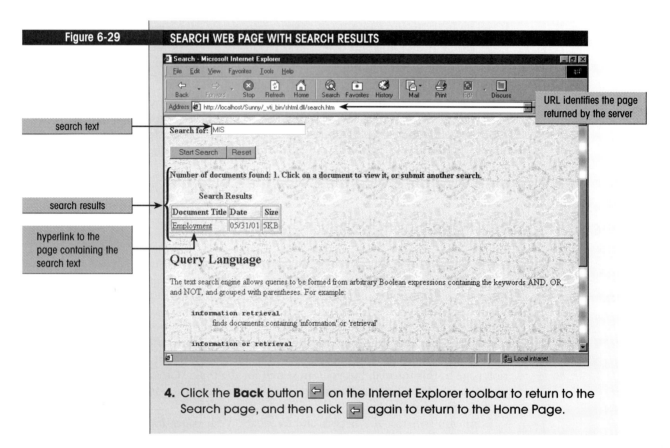

4. Click the **Back** button ⬅ on the Internet Explorer toolbar to return to the Search page, and then click ⬅ again to return to the Home Page.

Now you can test the Feedback Web page, which contains the form that must be processed by a server.

To test the Feedback Web page using Internet Explorer:

1. Click the **Feedback** hyperlink in the navigation bar in the Home Page to open the Feedback page.

2. Click the **Praise** option button, select **Company** in the drop-down menu list, type **This is a test** in the scrolling text box, type your name and e-mail address into the one-line text boxes, type **155** in the Visits text box, and then click the **Please contact me about my comments** check box to select it.

3. Click the **Submit Form** button. The form validation error message box opens to indicate that this data does not meet the validation condition. See Figure 6-30.

Figure 6-30   ERROR MESSAGE FOR THE VISITS TEXT BOX

4. Click the **OK** button, select **155** in the Visits text box and type **15**, and then click the **Submit Form** button. The Form Confirmation page opens with a copy of the data you entered into the form. The PWS generated this page automatically. See Figure 6-31.

Figure 6-31	FORM CONFIRMATION PAGE

URL identifies the page returned by the server

field name-value pairs for each form field

hyperlink to return to the Feedback Web page

your name and e-mail address will appear here

5. Click the **Return to the form** hyperlink at the bottom of the confirmation page to return to the Feedback Web page. The form fields are automatically restored to their default settings because a valid form was submitted to and accepted by the server. Your test of the form is successful. The page accepts your input, produces a confirmation page, and resets the form correctly.

When the confirmation page opened in the browser, the form's results were written to the feedback.txt file that you specified when you created the form. The feedback.txt file is stored in the Web site's _private folder, which is a hidden file that you can examine from FrontPage. It is a good practice to examine the data collected by a form to help you improve customer service or to identify problems. For example, you might select the "problem" information as a separate report to discuss with the customer service manager.

Examining a Form Results File

When you set the Save Results component to store the form's results, you specified a comma-delimited text file format. In a **comma-delimited text file**, the name of each form field appears in the first line of the file. The form results from each form submission are added to a new line at the end of the file. Unless you submitted your form more than once, the results file that you specified for the Save Results component contains only two lines—one containing the form field names and another containing the form results from your single submission. You can examine the contents of the results file at any time on the server computer. Amanda asks you to review this file to increase your understanding of how the data submitted to the server is stored. First, however, you must close the disk-based Sunny Web and open the server-based Sunny Web.

To open a server-based Web:

1. Click the **Microsoft FrontPage** program button on the taskbar, and then click the **Done** button to close the dialog box. Notice that the title bar indicates that the current Web site is the one that is stored on your Data Disk. You will close this Web site and then open the published Web site.

2. Click **File** on the menu bar, and then click **Close Web**. The disk-based Web closes.

3. Click the list arrow for the **Open** button 🗁 on the Standard toolbar, and then click **Open Web** in the list. The Open Web dialog box opens. You need to change to the folder on your computer that contains server-based Webs.

4. Click the **Web Folders** button in the Look in column, and then double-click the **localhost** folder to open it. See Figure 6-32.

   TROUBLE? If you do not see "localhost" or your server's name in the list box, don't worry. Just make sure that the Sunny Web folder or the Sunny on localhost folder appears in the list box.

Figure 6-32	WEB FOLDERS AVAILABLE ON LOCALHOST

your server name might be different

Sunny Web site folder (yours might appear as "Sunny on localhost")

your list of folders might be different

Web Folders button

5. Click the **Sunny** folder (or the **Sunny on localhost** folder) to select it, and then click the **Open** button. If necessary, change to Folders view. Notice that the Web site contains the file Default.htm instead of index.htm, which is the Home Page in a server-based Web.

Now that the server-based Web is open, you can examine the file that contains the form results.

To examine stored results:

1. Click the **_private** folder in the Folder List, and then double-click **feedback.txt** in the Contents pane. The file opens in Notepad or the default text editor for your installation of FrontPage. The form results for one form appear in the file. Each value in quotation marks represents the value from one form field in the form. See Figure 6-33.

Figure 6-33	FORM RESULTS TEXT FILE

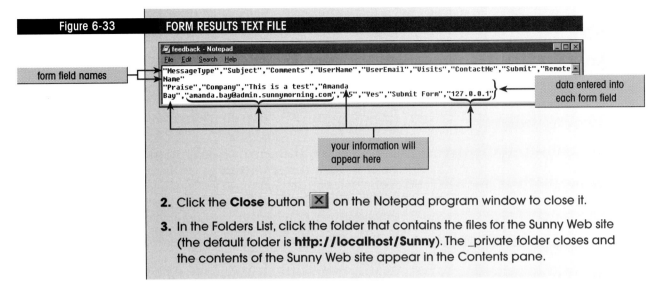

form field names

"MessageType","Subject","Comments","UserName","UserEmail","Visits","ContactMe","Submit","Remote Name"
"Praise","Company","This is a test","Amanda Bay","amanda.bay@admin.sunnymorning.com","5","Yes","Submit Form","127.0.0.1"

data entered into each form field

your information will appear here

2. Click the **Close** button ⊠ on the Notepad program window to close it.

3. In the Folders List, click the folder that contains the files for the Sunny Web site (the default folder is **http://localhost/Sunny**). The _private folder closes and the contents of the Sunny Web site appear in the Contents pane.

You verified that the forms results were collected correctly and stored in the feedback.txt file in the _private folder of the server-based Sunny Web site. The data in this file is arranged using the information that you specified when you created the form.

Amanda wants you to add the remaining features to the Web site before preparing the site for publication on the Web server for Sunny Morning Products.

Using a Hit Counter

The Web site development team is interested in counting the number of visitors to the site. A **hit counter** is a FrontPage component that counts the number of times that a page in a Web site has been opened or refreshed using a Web browser. Usually a hit counter appears in the Web site's Home Page, although you can set hit counters to appear in other pages, as well. A hit counter requires a server for processing, so you can test it only in a server-based Web. Because a hit counter is a built-in FrontPage component, you just need to insert it in the appropriate location in a Web page, and FrontPage will create its complex HTML code. You can accept the default settings for the hit counter or change the counter style and other properties if desired. The counter style is implemented using a default or custom-designed GIF picture that contains the digits zero through nine. The counter displays the number of times that the page containing the counter has been opened or refreshed in the browser.

REFERENCE WINDOW | **RW**

Creating a Hit Counter in a Web Page
- Click the location in the Web page where you want to insert the hit counter.
- Click the Insert Component button on the Standard toolbar, and then click Hit Counter to open the Hit Counter Properties dialog box.
- Click the option button for the desired counter style.
- Set the options to reset the counter or to display a fixed number of digits as needed.
- Click the OK button to insert the hit counter.

Amanda asks you to insert a hit counter in the Home Page. The hit counter will begin at 1000 and display six digits. Because the hit counter will work only in a server-based Web, you will create it in the Home Page for the server-based Web.

To create a hit counter in a Web page:

1. Double-click **Default.htm** in the Contents pane to open the Home Page in Page view. You will insert the hit counter above the footer.

2. Press **Ctrl + End** to scroll to the bottom of the Home Page, click to the left of the "L" in the first line of the footer, press the **Enter** key to create a new line above the footer, press the **Up** arrow key ↑ to move to the new line, click the **Center** button 🔳 on the Formatting toolbar, and then click the **Bold** button 🄱 on the Formatting toolbar to center the new line and change it to bold.

3. Type **You are visitor number** as text that precedes the hit counter, and then press the **spacebar**.

4. Click the **Insert Component** button 🔲 on the Standard toolbar, and then click **Hit Counter**. The Hit Counter Properties dialog box opens. See Figure 6-34.

Figure 6-34	HIT COUNTER PROPERTIES DIALOG BOX

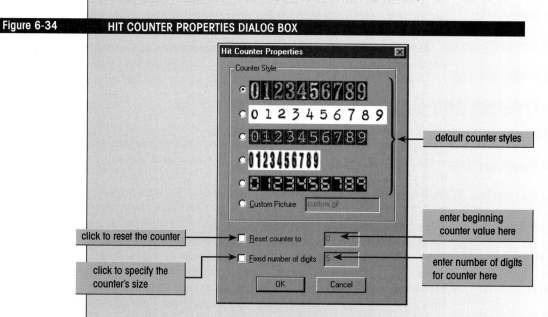

5. In the Counter Style section, click the third option button to select it.

6. Click the **Reset counter to** check box to select it, press the **Tab** key to move to its text box, and then type **1000**. The hit counter will start at 1000, instead of at zero. Starting the hit counter at 1000 is a common practice on the Internet.

7. Click the **Fixed number of digits** check box to select it, press the **Tab** key to move to its text box, and then type **6**. The counter will display six digits.

8. Click the **OK** button to close the Hit Counter Properties dialog box and to insert the hit counter. The placeholder **[Hit Counter]** indicates the hit counter's location in the Web page. Next, complete the rest of the sentence that contains the hit counter.

9. Press the **spacebar**, and then type **to our Web site.** as the text that follows the hit counter.

10. Click the **Save** button 🖫 on the Standard toolbar to save your changes.

Now you can test the hit counter. Adding a hit counter to a server-based Web page does not require you to publish the page again, so you can preview the page immediately.

To test the hit counter:

1. Click the **Preview in Browser** button 🔍 on the Standard toolbar to open the Home Page in Internet Explorer.

2. Press **Ctrl + End** to scroll to the bottom of the Home Page to see the hit counter. You are visitor number 1001.

3. Click the **Refresh** button 🔄 on the Standard Buttons toolbar to refresh the page, and then scroll to the bottom of the Web page. Now you are visitor number 1002. Each time the page is opened or refreshed, the hit counter is incremented by one. See Figure 6-35.

 Figure 6-35   **HIT COUNTER IN THE HOME PAGE**

4. Click the **Close** button ❌ on the Internet Explorer title bar to close it.

The hit counter will count the number of visitors to the Web site. By measuring this Web traffic, the Web site development team will have a better idea for future commitments to enhancing the Sunny Web site.

Your next task is to include a banner ad manager in the Home Page.

Using **the Banner Ad Manager**

Banner ads are dynamic billboards that display a series of images, such as pictures of products or the text for a company slogan. As each new image in the series appears, the Web browser applies a visual transition effect so the transition from one image to the next is not noticeable. If desired, you can associate a hyperlink with a banner ad.

The **Banner Ad Manager** is a Java applet that controls the continuous display of images in the Web page. For the Banner Ad Manager to work correctly, you need to test it using a server-based Web.

Before creating a banner ad, you need to create the GIF files that you will use in it. You can use Microsoft Image Composer as an image-editing program to create these images, or you can obtain them from some other source. (Creating images using Image Composer is beyond the scope of this tutorial.)

REFERENCE WINDOW   **RW**

<u>Creating a Banner Ad</u>

- Click the location where you want to insert the banner ad.
- Click the Insert Component button on the Standard toolbar, and then click Banner Ad Manager.
- Type the desired values, in pixels, for the width and height of the banner ad.
- Click the Transition effect list arrow to select the desired transition effect.
- Enter the number of seconds to show each picture in the Show each picture for (seconds) text box.
- Click the Add button, select the file for the first image, and then click the Add button and select the rest of the images for the banner.
- If creating a hyperlink, click the Browse button to locate and select the target page.
- Click the OK button.

Amanda asks you to replace the current Sunny Morning Products logo in the Home Page with a banner ad. The page that contains a banner ad must be published for FrontPage to add the necessary components that control the display of the images in the page. Therefore, you will create the banner ad in the server-based Web site that is stored on the hard drive, instead of making this change directly on the server.

To include a banner ad in the Home Page:

1. If necessary, click the **Microsoft FrontPage** program button on the taskbar to return to FrontPage.

2. Click **File** on the menu bar, and then click **Close Web**. The server-based Sunny Web site closes.

3. Click the list arrow for the **Open** button 📂 on the Standard toolbar, and then click **Open Web**. Browse to the Inetpub folder on your hard drive, and then double-click the **Inetpub** folder to open it. Double-click the **wwwroot** folder, click the **Sunny** folder, and then click the **Open** button. The server-based Sunny Web site opens from your hard drive.

4. Change to Folders view, double-click **Default.htm** to open the Home Page, click the **Sunny Morning Products** logo to select it, and then press the **Delete** key. The logo is deleted. You will insert the banner ad in its place.

5. Click the **Insert Component** button 🖳 on the Standard toolbar, and then click **Banner Ad Manager**. The Banner Ad Manager Properties dialog box opens. See Figure 6-36.

Figure 6-36   **BANNER AD MANAGER PROPERTIES DIALOG BOX**

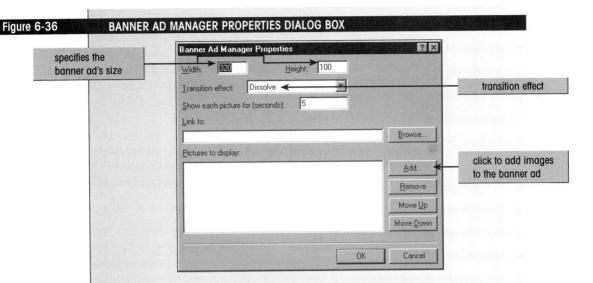

specifies the
banner ad's size

transition effect

click to add images
to the banner ad

Amanda gave you the dimensions for the pictures that will be displayed by the Banner Ad Manager so you can set them. The default value is selected in the Width text box, so you can just type the new value.

6. Type **380** in the Width text box, press the **Tab** key to move to the Height text box, and then type **65**. You will accept the default transition values, which are a Dissolve transition and to display each picture for five seconds. The banner ad will not serve as a hyperlink, so you will leave the Link to text box empty.

Next, specify the picture files for the banner ad.

7. Click the **Add** button to open the Add Picture for Banner Ad dialog box, click the **Select a file on your computer** button ▣ to open the Select File dialog box, make sure the drive or folder that contains your Data Disk appears in the Look in text box, double-click the **Tutorial.06** folder, and then double-click **Banner1**. The Select File dialog box closes and the Banner1.gif file appears in the Pictures to display list box.

8. Repeat Step 7 to select the **Banner2** file as the second file. Now both filenames appear in the Pictures to display list box.

9. Click the **OK** button. Only the first picture that you specified is displayed in Page view. The pictures that Amanda created for use in the banner ad have a white background. She explains that after inserting a picture into a banner ad, you cannot change the picture's characteristics. If you want the pictures to have a certain appearance, such as a transparent background, you need to make the desired changes before inserting the file in the Banner Ad Manager.

10. Click the **Save** button 🖫 on the Standard toolbar. The Save Embedded Files dialog box opens and displays the two files used in the Banner Ad Manager. The two banner ad pictures—Banner1.gif and Banner2.gif—do not have a folder location specified, which means that they will be saved in the root folder of the Sunny Web site. Amanda wants you to save the files for the banner ad in the root folder of the Sunny Web site, instead of in the site's images folder, so click the **OK** button to save the files and the page.

> TROUBLE? If images/ or any folder name appears in the Folder column for the Banner1.gif and Banner2.gif files, click Banner1.gif, press and hold down the Ctrl key, press Banner2.gif and release the Ctrl key to select both files, click the Change Folder button, click the Sunny folder that appears in the Look in list box, and then click the OK button to return to the Save Embedded Files dialog box. Click the OK button to save the files in the root folder.

With the banner ad included in the Home Page, you are ready to test it to make sure that it operates correctly. Before previewing it, however, you must publish the revised Home Page to the server so that FrontPage can create the hidden files that run the Banner Ad Manager on the server.

To test the Banner Ad Manager:

1. Click the **Publish Web** button 🗐 on the Standard toolbar to publish the revised Home Page to the server.

   TROUBLE? If the Publish Web dialog box opens, type http://localhost/sunny (or the URL for your Web server) in the specify the location to publish your Web to list box, and then click the Publish button.

   TROUBLE? If a Do you want to overwrite this file? dialog box opens, click the Yes to All button to continue.

   TROUBLE? If a Publishing Web Structure dialog box opens, click the Let FrontPage merge the changes option button, and then click the Continue button.

2. Click the **Click here to view your published web site** hyperlink to open the Home Page in the browser. Watch the logo as the picture changes every five seconds. See Figure 6-37.

Figure 6-37	BANNER AD IN THE HOME PAGE

3. Click the **Close** button ✖ on the Internet Explorer title bar to close it.

This banner ad should increase the visual impact of the Home Page, as Andrew had anticipated.

Moving a File Using Drag and Drop

In Tutorial 5, you learned how to use drag and drop to arrange the pages in your Web site in a navigation structure. You can also use drag and drop to move files in your Web site from one folder to another. Drag and drop is useful when you need to move one or more files to another folder. When you use drag and drop, FrontPage automatically updates any pages that contain hyperlinks to the files that you move. Amanda wants you to use drag and drop to move the files used in the banner ad into the Web site's images folder, so they will be in the same folder as other multimedia files in the Web site. After moving the files, you will confirm that FrontPage updated the location of the files.

To use drag and drop to move files:

1. If necessary, click the **Microsoft FrontPage** program button on the taskbar to return to FrontPage, and then click the **Done** button to close the dialog box.

2. Click the **Folders** button 🗋 on the Views bar to change to Folders view. Make sure that the Folder List is displayed.

3. Click the **Refresh** button 🔄 on the Standard toolbar to refresh the file listing in the Contents pane.

4. Click **Banner1.gif** in the Contents pane to select that file, and then press and hold down the **Shift** key and click **Banner2.gif** to select both files.

5. Point to the file icon for the Banner1.gif file, press and hold down the left mouse button, and then move the pointer to the images folder in the Folder List. The pointer changes to a 🔲 shape when you point to the images folder.

6. Release the mouse button. The Rename dialog box opens, and then the files are moved to the images folder. FrontPage automatically updates the references in the Banner Ad Manager, as you will see next.

7. Double-click **Default.htm** in the Contents pane to open the Home Page in Page view, and then double-click the **banner ad** in the page. The Banner Ad Manager Properties dialog box opens. Notice that the Pictures to display list box shows that the pictures for the banner ad are now stored in the images folder.

8. Click the **Cancel** button to close the Banner Ad Manager Properties dialog box.

Although drag and drop is similar to moving files in Windows Explorer, it is important to note that moving the files using Windows Explorer will not automatically update the hyperlinks to those files. You should only use FrontPage to move files to ensure that your hyperlinks are updated using the files' new location.

Global **Find and Replace**

When you need to find a specific occurrence of text in a Web page or make a site-wide change, you can use the Find and Replace commands on the Edit menu to search each page in the Web site for the text. When you use the Replace command, you can tell FrontPage to find and replace text with text that you specify. The Find and Replace commands search only for text in a Web page; you cannot use them to search for specific settings in dialog boxes, such as searching for a page's title. The options in the Find and Replace dialog box let you search only the current page or the entire Web site, set the direction to search from the current location of the insertion point (up or down), and specify options for finding the text, such as matching the case of letters in the word ("Letter" instead of "letter") and to locate only whole words ("pencil" but not words that contain "pen").

After reviewing the published Web site, the Web site development team suggests changing the "About Us" text in the user-defined navigation bar in each Web page to "Company

Profile." The team feels that renaming the hyperlink for the Company.htm page will make it easier to identify the page. You can make this change using the Replace command, instead of changing it manually in every page in the Web site.

To use the Replace command to replace text in the Web site:

1. Click **Edit** on the menu bar, and then click **Replace**. The Replace dialog box opens.

2. If necessary, click in the **Find what** text box, and then type **About Us**.

3. Press the **Tab** key to move to the Replace with text box, and then type **Company Profile**.

4. In the Search options section, make sure that the All pages and the Down option buttons are selected; and then click the **Match case** check box to select this option. See Figure 6-38.

Figure 6-38   REPLACE DIALOG BOX

5. Click the **Find In Web** button. After a few moments, FrontPage lists the pages in the Sunny Web site that contain at least one occurrence of the "About Us" text. Notice that the bottom of the dialog box indicates that FrontPage found six occurrences of the About Us text in six Web pages, and 17 Web pages total were searched. See Figure 6-39.

Figure 6-39   REPLACE DIALOG BOX WITH DETAILS

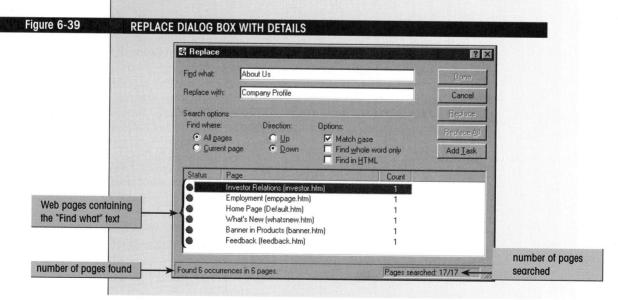

In other Office 2000 programs, such as Microsoft Word, when you use the Replace command, you can tell the program to replace text automatically. However, the Replace command in FrontPage only locates the pages that contain the text for which you are searching. To replace the text, you need to open the listed Web pages and click the Replace button in the dialog box that opens to finish the replace task.

6. Double-click the first page in the list. The Replace dialog box is still open, and FrontPage opens the first page in the list (investor.htm). Click the **Replace** button to replace the "About Us" text in this page. The Continue with next document? dialog box opens. See Figure 6-40. FrontPage replaced the "About Us" text in this Web page. You can click the Next Document button to continue searching the other pages in the list, or you can click the Cancel button to close the dialog box. You will continue checking the pages.

Figure 6-40	CONTINUE WITH NEXT DOCUMENT? DIALOG BOX

7. Click the **Next Document** button to check the next page in the list. Continue clicking the **Replace** and **Next Document** buttons until you have opened all the pages that contain occurrences of the text "About Us" and replaced the text. The Replace dialog box reappears. The Status column now shows that the pages identified by the Replace command have been edited. See Figure 6-41.

TROUBLE? If a dialog box opens and asks if you would like to save and close the current document, click the OK button.

Figure 6-41	COMPLETED REPLACE DIALOG BOX

status shows that all pages have been edited

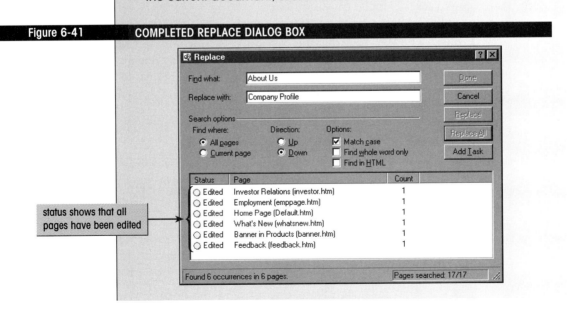

8. Click the **Cancel** button to close the Replace dialog box. You can check the Home Page to verify that FrontPage made your change correctly. FrontPage saved and closed the Home Page when you used the Replace command, so you need to reopen the page.

9. Click the **Folders** button 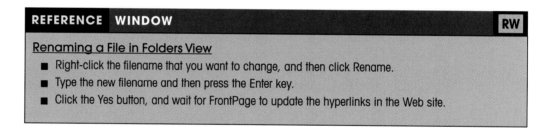 on the Views bar to change to Folders view, and then double-click **Default.htm** to open the Home Page in Page view. The navigation bar now contains a hyperlink named "Company Profile," indicating that FrontPage correctly replaced the "About Us" text in this page.

10. Point to the **Company Profile** hyperlink in the navigation bar. Notice that the status bar displays the file named Company.htm, indicating that the hyperlink still references the correct file.

Changing a Filename in Folders View

After creating your Web pages, you might want to change the page filenames to have more meaningful descriptions. Because filenames are used as hyperlinks throughout the Web site, it would be a tedious and error-prone activity for you to search each hyperlink and change the filename manually. When you use Folders view to change a page's filename, FrontPage automatically updates the links to that page to use the new filename.

REFERENCE WINDOW   **RW**

Renaming a File in Folders View
- Right-click the filename that you want to change, and then click Rename.
- Type the new filename and then press the Enter key.
- Click the Yes button, and wait for FrontPage to update the hyperlinks in the Web site.

You have already changed the hyperlink text for the "About Us" hyperlink to "Company Profile." The Web page that this hyperlink references is the Company.htm file with a page title of "Company Profile." Amanda would like you to rename the Company.htm file to Profile.htm so that the filename matches the page title, similar to the manner in which other files are named in the Sunny Web site.

To rename a file in Folders view:

1. Click the **Folders** button 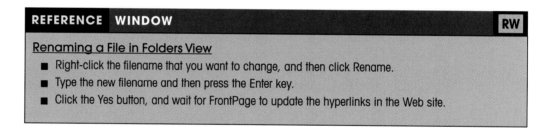 on the Views bar to change to Folders view.

2. Right-click **Company.htm** in the Contents pane to open the shortcut menu, and then click **Rename**. The filename changes to editing mode. To change the filename, just type a new one.

3. Type **Profile.htm** as the new filename, and then press the **Enter** key. The Rename dialog box opens and asks if you want to update the hyperlinks in six pages that contain hyperlinks to the Company Profile Web page.

4. Click the **Yes** button. FrontPage renames the page and updates the hyperlinks to it.

> Amanda wants you to verify this update by checking the hyperlink in the Home Page.
>
> **5.** Double-click **Default.htm** to open the Home Page in Page view, and then point to the **Company Profile** hyperlink in the navigation bar. The filename Profile.htm appears in the status bar, confirming the update of the hyperlink.

You confirmed that the hyperlink to the Company Profile Web page was updated. Amanda thinks that now is a good time to see if there are any problems with any of the other hyperlinks in the Web site.

Recalculating **and Verifying Hyperlinks**

When you are working on a Web site, it is a good idea to recalculate the hyperlinks contained in it periodically. **Recalculating hyperlinks** is the process of updating the display of all views of the Web site in which you are working, including updating the text index created by a FrontPage search component (when one is used) and deleting files for unused themes. If any hyperlink in the Web site is invalid, it will appear as a broken hyperlink in Hyperlinks view after you recalculate the hyperlinks. You can recalculate the hyperlinks of a disk-based Web or a server-based Web. However, when recalculating the hyperlinks in a server-based Web, FrontPage updates the index that it maintains for the search component, as well.

Verifying hyperlinks is the process of checking all of the hyperlinks in a Web site to identify any internal or external broken hyperlinks. An **external hyperlink** is a hyperlink to a location that is not in the current Web site, such as a hyperlink to a URL on a different Web server. Any broken hyperlinks will be listed in Reports view so you can repair them.

You can use the Recalculate Hyperlinks and Verify Hyperlinks commands to help you detect and repair broken hyperlinks. One of the primary differences between these two commands is how broken hyperlinks are displayed. Both commands list broken hyperlinks, but the Verify Hyperlinks command provides a report of all the broken hyperlinks, both internal and external. Both commands provide information that is useful in locating and correcting hyperlink problems.

Recalculating Hyperlinks

First Amanda asks you to recalculate the hyperlinks in the server-based Sunny Web site.

To recalculate hyperlinks:

1. Click the **Hyperlinks** button [icon] on the Views bar, and then click **Default.htm** in the Folder List to make this page the center focus.

2. Click **Tools** on the menu bar, and then click **Recalculate Hyperlinks**. The Recalculate Hyperlinks dialog box opens and describes the actions that will occur after clicking the Yes button. See Figure 6-42.

Figure 6-42   **RECALCULATE HYPERLINKS DIALOG BOX**

Recalculate Hyperlinks

? The Recalculate Hyperlinks command does the following:

· Repairs all hyperlinks in your web
· Updates information for all FrontPage-based components, including shared borders and navigation bars
· Synchronizes web data, database information, and categories

This process may take several minutes. Do you wish to continue?

Yes   No

3. Click the **Yes** button. The "Updating hyperlinks and text indices..." message appears on the status bar. After a few seconds, Hyperlinks view is refreshed with the Home Page as the center focus in the right pane, and all the hyperlinks are updated. FrontPage also deleted any unnecessary files in the Sunny Web site.

The hyperlinks are recalculated, and their display is updated if there were any changes. No broken links are visible for the Home Page.

Verifying Hyperlinks

When you recalculated the hyperlinks for the Sunny Web site, only the selected page—the Home Page—was visible in Hyperlinks view. To see the hyperlinks for the remaining pages in the Sunny Web site, you would need to select and examine each page in Hyperlinks view. A better way of identifying broken links in a Web site is to use Reports view. When you click the Verify Hyperlinks button on the Reporting toolbar, FrontPage checks each Web page for missing or broken hyperlinks and then displays a report of its findings.

Amanda wants you to verify the hyperlinks in the Sunny Web site to look for problems, so you can fix them.

To verify hyperlinks:

1. Click the **Reports** button 📖 on the Views bar to change to Reports view. If necessary, click **View** on the menu bar, point to **Toolbars**, and then click **Reporting** to display the Reporting toolbar.

TROUBLE? If the Reporting toolbar is blocking the report that is displayed in Reports view, drag it to another location on your screen.

2. Click the **Verify Hyperlinks** button 🔍 on the Reporting toolbar. The Verify Hyperlinks dialog box opens. Make sure that the Verify all hyperlinks option button is selected, and then click the **Start** button. See Figure 6-43. A broken hyperlink—to the Home Page in the Recipes Web site—is listed because the Recipes Web site does not exist in the expected location. You haven't published this Web site yet, so this error is fine. However, to remind you to publish the Recipes Web site to the Sunny Morning Products Web server, you will add this problem to the Web site's Tasks list.

| Figure 6-43 | BROKEN HYPERLINKS REPORT IN REPORTS VIEW |

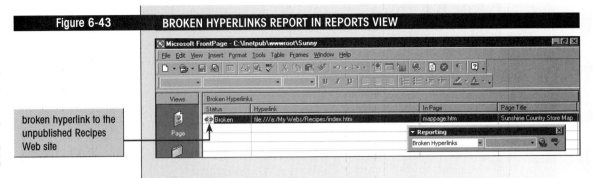

broken hyperlink to the unpublished Recipes Web site

TROUBLE? If your list differs from Figure 6-43, then you probably introduced some errors while working on the Review Assignments for Tutorials 2 through 5. To edit a page and correct an error, double-click the page in the list. The page will open in Page view so you can correct the error. Save the page and then return to Reports view. Repeat this process to correct any other errors in your Sunny Web site.

TROUBLE? If you stored your Data Files for the Recipes Web site in a different location from drive A, the path to your broken link will be different.

3. Right-click the broken hyperlink to open the shortcut menu, and then click **Add Task**. The New Task dialog box opens.

4. Change the task name to **Publish Recipes Web site**, assign the task to yourself, and then click the **OK** button. Notice that the status changes to "Added task."

5. Click the **Close** button ☒ on the FrontPage title bar to close it.

Recalculating and verifying hyperlinks helped you isolate a broken hyperlink, and possibly other problems in your Web site.

Setting Permissions for a Web Site

Permissions allow a Web site developer to control who can browse, author, or administer a Web site after it is published. When the Web server is properly configured for using permissions, you use FrontPage to administer the permissions for a Web site. There are three types of permissions: browsing, authoring, and administering. **Browsing permissions** authorize a user to browse (open) the pages in a Web site, but the user cannot make changes to the pages. **Authoring permissions** allow a user to browse and change a site's pages by opening them in Page view. Finally, **administering permissions** allow a user to browse and change a site's pages and to set other users' permissions. For example, if you do not want a user to be able to change the content of a Web site, you would set that user's permission to browsing only. Permissions are hierarchical; for example, a user with administering permissions also has authoring and browsing rights, whereas authoring permissions give a user browsing rights but not administering rights.

If you are using the Microsoft PWS version 4.0 on a computer running Windows 98, you cannot set the permissions for a Web site because PWS 4.0 does not support security features. In this case, all users on the network or computer on which the PWS and Web site are installed have browsing access. Authoring and administering rights are available only on the individual computer on which the PWS resides. In other words, if the Web site is stored on the PWS on your computer, then *anyone* using your computer can create and update pages and administer the site.

If the Web server is a Windows NT server running Microsoft Internet Information Server (IIS), users and groups are set up and maintained in Windows NT and cannot be created in FrontPage. In this case, the system administrator determines the users and groups who can set security for Web sites that reside on that server. You will be able to set permissions for a Web site only if you have the necessary permissions to do so for the network on which the IIS server resides.

If the server allows permissions, the permissions are established for the root Web and are inherited by all other Web sites, unless these settings have been changed. The Sunny Web site that you published to the PWS is a subweb in the FrontPage root Web, which is c:\Inetput\wwwroot. In other words, any permissions that were set for the root Web are also in effect for the Sunny Web site that you published.

You create and update the permissions for an individual Web site by opening the site in FrontPage, clicking Tools on the menu bar, pointing to Security, and then clicking Permissions. If the Security command on the Tools menu is dimmed, then you cannot set the permissions for the Web site. (For more information about setting permissions for Web sites on computers in your lab, ask your instructor or technical support person for help.) You use the Permissions dialog box to create or change the Web site's permissions, to add users and groups to the Web site, and to set and change permissions for individual users and for groups. For example, at Sunny Morning Products, Amanda and other members of the Web site development team would have administering permissions, whereas employees who are not involved in the development of the Web site might only have browsing permissions.

Going Live

Going live is the process of publishing your Web site on a Web server to make it accessible to other users. In this tutorial, you published a disk-based Web to your computer's PWS and tested it to ensure that its features work as expected. Before publishing a Web site on a World Wide Web server, most commercial Web site developers will also test the Web site using different Web browsers, screen resolutions, and connection speeds to make sure that the Web site works consistently for the many ways in which people will access it. After thoroughly testing the site, the developer or administrator publishes it on the World Wide Web server.

You published the Sunny Web site to the Web server on your computer. After thorough testing and analysis, you will be ready to publish the Web site to the Web server for Sunny Morning Products. You use the Publish Web button on the Standard toolbar in FrontPage to publish your Sunny Web site from the PWS on your computer to the Web server for Sunny Morning Products. To publish the site to a World Wide Web server, you need the URL for the Web server and you must have the correct permission to do so.

Generally, an individual designated as its administrator manages a Web server. The administrator is responsible for the overall management of the server, including the management of user access to it. The administrator determines how and where a Web site will be located on the server based on the procedures that have been established for the Web server by the company or ISP that owns and operates the server. The procedures for publishing a Web site on an Internet Web server vary.

Acceptable Use Policies

Most companies and ISPs maintain an **acceptable use policy (AUP)**. An AUP is usually a published or online document that an ISP or company creates to indicate the acceptable activities permitted on the Web server. For example, an AUP for an educational institution might prohibit users from using the network to engage in commercial activities, or an AUP for an ISP might prohibit users from creating Web sites on the network that include pornographic material. It is the responsibility of the Web site's administrator to verify that the Web site will be acceptable.

FrontPage 2000 Server Extensions

You learned in this tutorial that the FrontPage 2000 Server Extensions must be installed and properly configured for certain features of the Sunny Web site, such as the hit counter and the form processing, to work correctly. Some ISPs do not accept Web sites with server extensions because, in some cases, the extensions can compromise the security of the Web server on which they reside. Before creating your Web site, it is important to learn about any restrictions imposed by the operator of the Web server on which your Web site will ultimately reside. You might learn that the ISP will not accept server extensions. In this case, you can either search for another ISP to host your Web site, or you can set your installation of FrontPage to disable features that the ISP will not allow. In this case, after creating the Web site and before creating any of its pages, click Tools on the menu bar, click Page Options, and then click the Compatibility tab. You can use this tab to disable the server extensions and other Web elements, as necessary.

Fortunately, most ISPs have a technical support staff available to answer questions about publishing a Web site on its Web server. Your best course of action is to find and communicate with an ISP before creating your Web site to gather information about the ISP's AUP and policy for accepting Web sites that contain server extensions. In most cases, the ISP will be ready to answer your questions and provide alternative means for creating pages in the event that the server cannot accept server extensions.

Now that you have finished your Web site development-training course, you are ready to return to the marketing department to help create, manage, and update its Web site.

Session 6.3 QUICK CHECK

1. The default name of the PWS is _____.

2. True or False: To connect to your computer's PWS, you must also connect to your ISP.

3. What is the default directory in which FrontPage publishes Web sites?

4. After publishing a disk-based Web site, FrontPage automatically renames the filename for the Home Page to _____.

5. What is a confirmation page?

6. A text file that contains form results where the first line contains form field names and subsequent lines contain data submitted by each form is called a(n) _____ file.

7. True or False: You can include only one hit counter in a Web site.

8. How do you update the text index used by a FrontPage search component?

9. What is the primary difference between recalculating and verifying the hyperlinks in a Web site?

10. What are the three types of permissions that you can set for a FrontPage Web?

REVIEW ASSIGNMENTS

Before preparing the Sunny Web site for publication on the Sunny Morning Products Web server, Amanda asks you to test the pages again and to make any necessary adjustments.

If necessary, start FrontPage, insert your Data Disk in the appropriate disk drive, and then do the following:

1. Open the **Sunny** Web site that you published to your computer's PWS (c:\Inetpub\wwwroot\Sunny) in Folders view, and then open the Search Web page (**search.htm**) in Page view.

2. Add a navigation bar below the page's logo to the Search Web page. (*Hint*: Copy the navigation bar from the Home Page, paste it into the Search Web page, and then update the navigation bar to include a link to the Home Page and to disable the link to the Search page.) Save the Search Web page.

3. Open the Feedback Web page (**Feedback.htm**) in Page view. Change the Subject drop-down menu form field to include two new choices: Employee and Other. These new choices should not be selected and their choice and value names should be the same. Then change the drop-down menu form field so that two items are displayed in the browser. Save the Feedback Web page, and then use the Preview tab to check the page's appearance.

Explore ▷ 4. Start Microsoft Excel, and then open the **feedback.txt** file from the _private folder of the Web site. (You will need to select the "All Files" option in the Files of type list box to find the file.) This file contains the stored results from the Feedback Web page. When the Text Import Wizard dialog box opens, click the Delimited option button, click the Next button, click the Comma check box and clear the Tab check box in the Delimiters section, and then click the Finish button. The data is displayed in the worksheet using the form field names as the column headings. Print the worksheet in landscape orientation, and then close Excel without saving changes.

Explore ▷ 5. Modify the banner ad that you created for the Home Page by adding the **Banner3.gif** file as its third image. (This file is saved in the Tutorial.06 folder on your Data Disk.) Then change the time that images are displayed to three seconds each. After inserting the new image, save the Home Page and save the new GIF file in the Web site's images folder. Publish the changes, use the browser to test the banner ad, and then close the browser.

Explore ▷ 6. Use FrontPage to print the HTML code for the Home Page. On the printout, circle the code that adds the image to the Banner Ad Manager and changes the duration time for each image.

7. Recalculate and verify the hyperlinks in the Web site and correct any problems. (Do not correct the broken link to the Recipes Web site that you identified in the tutorial.) When you are finished, run a Site Summary report and then use WordPad to print it. Close WordPad without saving changes.

8. Close FrontPage and Internet Explorer.

CASE PROBLEMS

Case 1. Constructing Search and Feedback Pages for Royal Hair Care Products

Customer response to Quick Dry Solution has exceeded company expectations. Many customers wrote letters to Royal Hair Care Products to praise the product. Valerie Suarez met with Nathan Dubois to share this information and to discuss the Feedback Web page that they will include in the Web site. They decide to design this page to gather specific information from customers on how well the product works, how often customers use it, and so forth. They also need to create a Search Web page that lets users search the entire Royal Web site. Valerie asks you to help Nathan complete the necessary design and development activities for the Feedback and Search Web pages.

If necessary, start FrontPage, insert your Data Disk in the appropriate disk drive, and then do the following:

1. Read all the questions for this case problem, and then prepare a planning analysis sheet for the enhancements to the Royal Web site.

2. Open the **Royal** Web site (a:\My Webs\Royal) from your Data Disk. (If you did not create this Web site in Tutorial 2 and change it in Tutorials 3, 4, and 5, ask your instructor for assistance.)

3. Create the Search Web page using the Search Page template. Delete the comment at the top of the page, and then insert the **Royal01.gif** file from the Web site's images folder in its place. Copy the navigation bar from the Home Page, and then paste it below the logo. Change the navigation bar to include the links to the Home Page and to the Feedback page. Save the page using the filename **RSearch.htm** and the title "Search."

Explore 4. Open the Feedback Web page (**RFeedbak.htm**) that you created with the Tasks list in Tutorial 3 in Page view. Insert the **Royal01.gif** file at the top of the page, copy and paste a navigation bar in the page, and then revise the navigation bar so that it includes active links to the other pages in the Web site. Write and enter an appropriate introduction below the navigation bar. Insert a form component in the page, and then create and design the Feedback page using the following information:

- There are three types of comments and feedback: Testimonial, Suggestion, and Problem.

- The customer should be able to indicate the average weekly number of applications of Quick Dry Solution. Apply criteria to this field so that it will not accept values higher than 15 or inappropriate values.

- The customer should be able to indicate where the product is purchased most often from the following choices: Drug Store, Discount Store, Department Store, Salon, Supermarket, or Other. If the response is "Other," ask the customer to enter the location into a separate one-line text box.

- The customer should be able to enter up to five optional lines of comments and feedback.

- The customer should provide his or her name, e-mail address, and home phone number.

- The customer should be able to give or deny permission to use his or her comments in company advertisements.

- The customer should be able to send the form to the server or clear the form's fields.

Save the form's results as comma-delimited text in the **RFeedbak.txt** file in the _private folder of the Web site. Save the Feedback Web page, test it using the browser, and then use the browser to print its HTML code.

5. Examine each page in the Web site and update the navigation bar to ensure that all links are active and created properly. Save your changes.

6. Use the Publish Web command on the File menu to publish the Royal Web to your computer's PWS with the same name, and then use the hyperlink created by FrontPage to open the published Web site in Internet Explorer. Test the Search and Feedback Web pages that you created. Print the results page and the confirmation page that you receive from the server. If necessary, return to your disk-based Web (a:\My Webs\Royal), make any necessary corrections, and then republish the Web site to the PWS, replacing any necessary pages.

Explore ▶ 7. Close your disk-based Web and then open the Royal Web site (c:\Inetpub\wwwroot\Royal) from your hard drive. Recalculate the hyperlinks in the Web site, and then verify all hyperlinks. If you identify any broken links to existing pages, edit the page to correct the error. If you identify any links to missing pages, add an appropriate task to the Tasks list to identify the problem and assign the task to yourself.

8. Mark the tasks for creating the Search and Feedback Web pages as completed.

9. Add a hit counter to the Home Page with your choice of specifications, location, and style.

10. Find and replace all occurrences of the hyperlink name that you used for the **RInvest.htm** page with "Performance."

11. Thoroughly test the Web site in the browser, and then publish only the changed pages. If necessary, return to the server-based Web site and make any necessary corrections. Then use FrontPage to print the Home Page and its HTML code.

12. Close FrontPage and Internet Explorer.

Case 2. Preparing a Contact Page for Buffalo Trading Post Many Buffalo Trading Post (BTP) customers have told their sales associates that they would like to be able to use the BTP Web site to request additional information and to be added to a mailing list. During a recent Web site development meeting, the sales associates encouraged Donna Vargas to develop a Contact Web page for customers. The sales associates agreed that the page's design should include a way for customers to provide their contact information and be added to the company's mailing list. Customers should also be able to send comments directly to BTP about items they would like to buy or sell using the categories of women's clothing, children's clothing, and accessories. The sales associates also were interested in finding out how many times a customer visited a BTP retail store. Donna organized the ideas from the meeting and then met with Karla Perez to review the Contact page requirements. Donna asks you to help Karla make these enhancements to the BTP Web site.

If necessary, start FrontPage, insert your Data Disk in the appropriate disk drive, and then do the following:

1. Read all the questions in this case problem, and then prepare a planning analysis sheet for the BTP Web site enhancements.

2. Open the **Buffalo** Web site (a:\My Webs\Buffalo) from your Data Disk. (If you did not create this Web site in Tutorial 2 and change it in Tutorials 3, 4, and 5, ask your instructor for assistance.)

3. Create the Contact page using the information supplied in the Case Problem description. Use form fields as necessary to create the form and define any necessary validation

criteria to ensure that data is correctly input. Insert the **B_contac.gif** picture from the Tutorial.06 folder on your Data Disk at the top of the page, copy and paste a navigation bar in the page, and then revise the navigation bar so that it includes active links to the other pages in the Web site. Write and enter an appropriate introduction below the navigation bar. Save the results collected from this form as comma-delimited text in the **Contact.txt** file in the _private folder of the Web site. Save the page using the filename **Contact.htm** and the title "Contact." Save the **B_contac.gif** file in the Web site's images folder.

4. Use FrontPage to print the Contact page and its HTML code. On the printout, circle the code that implements the FrontPage Save Results component.

5. Examine each page in the Web site, and update the navigation bar to ensure that all links are active and created properly. Save your changes.

6. Use the Publish Web command on the File menu to publish the Buffalo Web to your computer's PWS with the same name, and then use the hyperlink created by FrontPage to open the published Web site in Internet Explorer. Test the Contact Web page that you created, and then print the confirmation page that you receive from the server. If necessary, return to your disk-based Web (a:\My Webs\Buffalo), make any necessary corrections, and then republish the Web site to the PWS, replacing any necessary pages.

7. Close your disk-based Web and then open the Buffalo Web site (c:\Inetpub\wwwroot\Buffalo) from your hard drive. Recalculate the hyperlinks in the Web site, and then verify all hyperlinks. If you identify any broken links to existing pages, edit the page to correct the error.

Explore 8. Use the Help system to find information about creating a custom confirmation page. (*Hint*: Ask the Answer Wizard the following question: How do I create a confirmation form?) Use the information you find in the Help system to create a new Web page using the Confirmation Form template. You will use this new Web page, instead of a default confirmation page, to confirm data submitted by the Contact Web page. Modify the form using the appropriate form field names in the form. Make any other appearance-related revisions to the form. Save the Web page using the filename **Confirm.htm** and the page title "Confirmation" in the _private folder of the Buffalo Web site. Return to the Contact Web page, and then open the Form Properties dialog box. Click the Options button, and then click the Confirmation Page tab. Type **_private/Confirm.htm** in the URL of confirmation page (optional) text box to use the new Confirmation page with the form. Publish the changes to the Buffalo Web site, test the Confirmation page by submitting the Contact Web page to the server, and then print the Confirmation page in Internet Explorer.

9. Design and create a new Web page using the filename and title "Where." This page will provide information on the nearest BTP store location. Insert the **B_where.gif** picture from the Tutorial.06 folder on your Data Disk as the page's logo and save it in the Web site's images folder. The page should also include a navigation bar with links to the other pages in the Buffalo Web site. Update the navigation bars in the other pages in the Web site to activate the hyperlink to the Where page. Publish the changes to the PWS, and then use the browser to print the Where page.

10. Close FrontPage and Internet Explorer.

Case 3. Developing Search and Feedback Pages for Garden Grill
Nolan Simmons is pleased with Shannon Taylor's progress on the Garden Grill Web site. The team's next priorities are creating the Feedback and Search Web pages. After a meeting with Beau Walker, who directs the company's marketing department, Nolan directs Shannon to create a new Web page to gather customer information and customer feedback about their eating habits and impressions about the restaurant's menu, prices, service, and Web site. Nolan also asks Shannon to use a template to create a Search Web page.

If necessary, start FrontPage, insert your Data Disk in the appropriate disk drive, and then do the following:

1. Read all the questions for this case problem, and then prepare a planning analysis sheet for these revisions to the Garden Web site.

2. Open the **Garden** Web site (a:\My Webs\Garden) from your Data Disk. (If you did not create this Web site in Tutorial 2 and change it in Tutorials 3, 4, and 5, ask your instructor for assistance.)

3. Create a Search Web page using a template. After creating the page, delete the comment component, and then insert the **Garden01.gif** picture from the Web site's images folder as the logo for this page. Copy the navigation bar from the Home Page, and then paste it in approximately the same location as the one in the Home Page. Update the hyperlinks in the navigation bar in the Search Web page to include active links to other pages in the Web site and an inactive link to the Search Web page. Set the page to use the same background as the Home Page. Save the page using the filename and title "Search."

Explore 4. Design and create the Feedback Web page for Garden Grill using the information provided in the Case Problem description. Use different form fields and validation as necessary to gather and test the data. Insert the **Garden01.gif** picture as the logo for this page and create a user-defined navigation bar. Save the form results as comma-delimited text in the **Feedback.txt** file in the _private folder of the Web site. Save the page using the title "Feedback" and the filename **GFeedbak.htm** (replace the existing file with the same name, if necessary).

5. Use FrontPage to print the HTML code for the Feedback page. On the printout, circle the FORM, SELECT, and INPUT tags and the code that implements the FrontPage Save Results component.

6. Examine each page in the Web site and update the navigation bar to ensure that all links are active and created properly. Save your changes.

7. Use the Publish Web command on the File menu to publish the Garden Web site to your computer's PWS with the same name, and then use the hyperlink created by FrontPage to open the published Web site in Internet Explorer. Test the Feedback and Search Web pages that you created, and print the confirmation and the search results pages that you receive from the server. If necessary, return to your disk-based Web (a:\My Webs\Garden), make any necessary corrections, and then republish the Web site to the PWS, replacing any necessary pages.

Explore 8. Close your disk-based Web and then open the Garden Web site (c:\Inetpub\wwwroot\Garden) from your hard drive. Recalculate the hyperlinks in the Web site, and then verify all hyperlinks. If you identify any broken links to existing pages, edit the page to correct the error. If you identify any links to missing pages, add an appropriate task to the Tasks list to identify the problem and assign the task to yourself.

Explore 9. Modify the Feedback Web page so that the Save Results component also stores the results in an HTML file named **Feedback.htm** in the _private folder of the Web site. (*Hint*: Specify the second results file using the Options button.) Publish the changed pages to the PWS, and then open the Web site from the server.

Explore 10. Use Internet Explorer to test the Feedback Web page using realistic data that you create. Enter data for three different users. Then return to FrontPage and print the **Feedback.htm** page that contains the form results.

Explore 11. Design and create the Franchise Information page that provides information about applying for and managing a Garden Grill franchise. This page should include a navigation bar with links to the other pages in the Web site. Insert the **Garden01.gif** picture from the Web site's images folder as the logo for the page. Save the page using the filename **FranInfo.htm** and the title "Franchise Information." Update the links in the rest of the Web site to activate the Franchise link. Save your changes to each page, publish the changed pages to the PWS, and then use Internet Explorer to print the page.

Explore 12. Start Microsoft Excel, and then open the **Feedback.txt** file from the folder c:\Inetpub\wwwroot\Garden_private on your hard drive. (You will need to select the "All Files" option in the Files of type list box to find the file.) This file contains the stored results from the Feedback Web page. When the Text Import Wizard dialog box opens, click the Delimited option button, click the Next button, click the Comma check box and clear the Tab check box in the Delimiters section, and then click the Finish button. The data is displayed in the worksheet using the form field names as the row headings. Print the worksheet in landscape orientation, and then close Excel without saving changes.

13. Close FrontPage and Internet Explorer.

Case 4. Producing Search and Feedback Pages for Replay Music Factory   Many of Replay Music Factory's satisfied customers have swapped their old CDs for different ones. Based on the success of the Specials Web page, Charlene Fields asked to meet with Alec Johnston to review the current Web site. Charlene described her plans to include a Search Web page and a form that collects data to help the company make sound marketing decisions. Charlene is particularly interested in gathering information about CDs that Replay does not currently stock. This information should include different categories of music and performers, as well as specific titles of interest. Charlene asks you to help Alec make these enhancements to the Web site.

If necessary, start FrontPage, insert your Data Disk in the appropriate disk drive, and then do the following:

1. Read all the questions for this case problem, and then prepare a planning analysis sheet for the modifications to the Replay Web site.

2. Open the **Replay** Web site (a:\My Webs\Replay) from your Data Disk. (If you did not create this Web site in Tutorial 2 and change it in Tutorials 3, 4, and 5, ask your instructor for assistance.)

Explore 3. Create a new Web page in Page view. Include an appropriate page heading and logo and create a FrontPage navigation bar. Then use the Insert Component button to insert a Search Form in the page with a "Search for" text box that holds 30 characters, and two push buttons with the labels "Search Now" and "Clear Fields." Save the page using the filename and title "Search."

Explore 4. Design and create the Feedback Web page based on information you determine the user will provide. Use appropriate form fields and validation criteria to collect the desired data. Include a page heading and logo in this page, and create a FrontPage navigation bar. Save the form results as comma-delimited text in the **Feedback.txt** file and also as **Feedback.htm** in the _private folder of the Web site. Save the page using the filename and title "Feedback."

5. Use FrontPage to print the HTML code for the Feedback page. On the printout, circle the FORM, SELECT, and INPUT tags and the code that implements the FrontPage Save Results component.

6. Examine each page in the Web site, and update the navigation bar to ensure that all links are active and created properly. Save your changes.

7. Use the Publish Web command on the File menu to publish the Replay Web site to your computer's PWS with the same name, and then use the hyperlink created by FrontPage to open the published Web site in Internet Explorer. Test the Feedback and Search Web pages that you created and print the confirmation and the search results pages that you receive from the server. If necessary, return to your disk-based Web (a:\My Webs\Replay), make any necessary corrections, and then republish the Web site to the PWS, replacing any necessary pages.

Explore   8. Close your disk-based Web and then open the Replay Web site (c:\Inetpub\wwwroot\Replay) from your hard drive. Recalculate the hyperlinks in the Web site, and then verify all hyperlinks. If you identify any broken links to existing pages, edit the page to correct the error. If you identify any links to missing pages, add an appropriate task to the Tasks list to identify the problem and assign the task to yourself.

Explore   9. Use the Help system to learn about creating a custom confirmation page. (*Hint*: Ask the Answer Wizard the following question: How do I create a confirmation form?) Use the information you find in the Help system to create a new Web page using the Confirmation Form template. You will use this new Web page, instead of a default confirmation page, to confirm data submitted by the Feedback Web page. Modify the form using the appropriate form field names in the form. Make any other appearance-related revisions to the form. Save the Web page using the filename **Confirm.htm** and the page title "Confirmation" in the _private folder of the Replay Web site. Return to the Feedback Web page, and then open the Form Properties dialog box. Click the Options button, and then click the Confirmation Page tab. Type _private/Confirm.htm in the URL of confirmation page (optional) text box to use the new Confirmation page with the form.

Explore   10. Use the Frequently Asked Questions template to create a new page in the Web site. Include several questions that Replay customers might ask. Make the pages similar to the other pages in the Replay Web site. Save the page using the filename and title "FAQ."

Explore   11. Design and create a banner ad using the Banner Ad Manager in an appropriate page in the Web site. If possible, create the GIF files that you will use in the banner ad. (If you cannot create the files, use the Clip Art Gallery to locate appropriate GIF files.) The banner ad should use at least three images. Save the images in the Web site's images folder.

Explore   12. Perform a spell check of the entire Web site and correct any misspellings. Save any pages in which you make corrections, and then republish all changed pages to the PWS. Use the browser to print the FAQ page and its HTML code, the confirmation page returned by the Feedback Web page, and the HTML code for the page in which you created the banner ad.

13. Close FrontPage and Internet Explorer.

QUICK CHECK ANSWERS

Session 6.1

1. True
2. The pointer changes to the Component pointer when you point to the component, and a dashed outline surrounds the component.
3. False
4. A data-entry field in a form, such as a text box or radio button, that is used to collect data from a user.
5. form component
6. A program on a Web server that collects and processes a form's data in a predetermined manner.
7. So that the group name and the button values are easy to locate in the HTML code.
8. Use a drop-down menu with the name "Province" and assign each value in the list a name that is equivalent to the province's name. The reason for using a drop-down menu is that there are several mutually exclusive choices. The option that should be selected in the drop-down menu would be the most populated province, or the province that is closest to the company's location.

Session 6.2

1. True
2. Required
3. Grouping, which edits the value to insert a comma or period; data length, which specifies the minimum and maximum number of integers that the form field can contain; and data value, which lets you specify that the entered value must be greater than, equal to, or less than, or in a certain range based on a predetermined value.
4. Submit, which lets a user send the form to the server for processing; Reset, which clears the form's fields of any previously entered data; and Normal, which initiates a user-defined script.
5. field name-data value pair
6. webmaster
7. OPTION

Session 6.3

1. localhost
2. False
3. c:\Inetpub\wwwroot
4. Default.htm
5. A Web page that contains a copy of the data entered into a form that the server sends to the browser to confirm a form's submission.
6. comma-delimited text
7. False
8. Recalculate the Web site's hyperlinks by clicking Tools on the menu bar and then clicking Recalculate Hyperlinks from Hyperlinks view.
9. Verifying hyperlinks checks for broken external and internal links and presents findings as a report in Reports view, making it easy to identify all broken links quickly and easily.
10. Browsing permissions allow a user to browse (open) pages in a Web site. Authoring permissions allow a user to browse and change a site's pages by opening them in Page view. Administering permissions allow a user to browse and change a site's pages and set other users' permissions.

New Perspectives on

MICROSOFT®

FRONTPAGE® 2000

Read This Before You Begin

To the Student

Data Disks

To complete the Level II Tutorials, Review Assignments, Case Problems, and Additional Cases in this book, you need three Data Disks. Your instructor will either provide you with the Data Disks or ask you to make your own.

If you are making your own Data Disks, you will need three blank, formatted high-density disks. You will need to copy a set of folders from a file server or standalone computer or the Web onto your disks. Your instructor will tell you which computer, drive letter, and folders contain the files you need. You could also download the files by going to www.course.com, clicking Data Disk Files, and following the instructions on the screen.

The following list shows you which folders go on your disks:

Data Disk 1

Write this on the disk label:
Data Disk 1: Level II Tutorials 7-9

Put these folders on the disk:
Tutorial.07
Tutorial.08
Tutorial.09

Data Disk 2

Write this on the disk label:
Data Disk 2: Level II Tutorials, Additional Case Problems 1 and 2

Put these folders on the disk:
AddCase1
AddCase2

Data Disk 3

Write this on the disk label:
Data Disk 3: Level II Tutorials, Additional Case Problem 3

Put this folder on the disk:
AddCase3

Hard Drive Disk Structure

For these tutorials, you must be able to create FrontPage Web sites on your computer's Personal Web Server (PWS). The default path for storing Web sites on the PWS is c:\Inetpub\wwwroot\ plus the Web site folder name. Your instructor must install the starting Data Files for Case

Problems 1 through 4 before you can begin working on them. If you are using your own computer, ask your instructor for these files and their installation instructions.

When you begin each tutorial, be sure you are using the correct Data Disk. See the inside front or inside back cover of this book for more information on Data Disk files, or ask your instructor or technical support person for assistance.

Using Your Own Computer

If you are going to work through this book using your own computer, you need:

- **Computer System** Microsoft FrontPage 2000, Internet Explorer 5, Windows 98, and Microsoft Personal Web Server 4.0 or higher must be installed on your computer. You also must have the FrontPage 2000 Server Extensions installed and configured for the PWS 4.0. This book assumes a complete installation of FrontPage 2000.

- **Data Disks** You will not be able to complete the tutorials or exercises in this book using your own computer until you have Data Disks.

- **Course Lab** See your instructor or technical support person to obtain the Course Lab software for use on your own computer.

Course Lab

The Level II tutorials in this book feature two interactive Course Labs to help you understand Database and Spreadsheet concepts. There are Lab Assignments at the end of Tutorials 8 and 9 that relate to these Labs.

To start a Lab, click the **Start** button on the Windows taskbar, point to **Programs**, point to **Course Labs**, point to **New Perspectives Applications**, and click the appropriate lab.

Visit Our World Wide Web Site

Additional materials designed especially for you are available on the World Wide Web. Go to http://www.course.com.

To the Instructor

The Data Files and lab are available on the Instructor's Resource Kit for this title. Students will create the Web site used in the Tutorials and Review Assignments. The instructor must install the starting Data Files for Case Problems 1 through 4 on the PWS. Follow the instructions in the Help file on the CD-ROM to install the programs to your network or standalone computer. For information on creating the Data Disk, see the "To the Student" section above.

You are granted a license to copy the Data Files and lab to any computer or computer network used by students who have purchased this book.

OBJECTIVES

In this tutorial you will:

- Use the Import Web Wizard to import a Web site from a URL
- Change a Web site's settings
- Create a site map
- Assign Web pages to categories and use the categories component
- Use source control
- Create a shared template
- Use absolute positioning to place text and pictures in a Web page
- Use a Wizard to create a discussion group
- Post, reply to, and search for messages in a discussion group
- Display and examine the hidden folders in a Web site
- Change the properties of a discussion group

CREATING

A NEW WEB SITE ON A WEB SERVER

Creating the Recipes Web Site and a Discussion Group

CASE

Sunny Morning Products

Microsoft FrontPage, or simply **FrontPage**, is a program that lets you develop, maintain, and publish a Web site. Using this program, you can create, view, and edit your Web pages; insert and edit text and pictures; import and export files; and add, test, and repair hyperlinks to and within your pages.

Amanda Bay is a marketing manager at Sunny Morning Products, a California-based international bottler and distributor of Olympic Gold brand fresh orange juice and thirst-quencher sports drinks. Olympic Gold products are sold in grocery stores, convenience stores, and many other outlets. In addition to selling Olympic Gold products, Sunny Morning Products sells its fresh produce, such as oranges and grapefruits, through the Sunshine Country Store located at its California groves and through the company's Web site. At the request of the company's president, Andrew Towle, Amanda created a Web site development-training course to teach people in the different departments at Sunny Morning Products how to use the Internet and the company's Web site to increase sales and improve communication with customers.

In addition to selling fresh produce and Olympic Gold products, the Sunshine Country Store specializes in baked goods, such as cakes, breads, and pies. To help promote the store and its products, David Harrah, another marketing manager, created a Web site to share recipes for the store's products. Initial customer reaction to the recipes Web site has been very favorable. Andrew gave David his permission to expand the site to include additional recipes, a discussion forum, and the capability for the marketing department to manage the site as needed.

In this tutorial, you will import the recipes Web site from a World Wide Web server to your computer's Personal Web Server (PWS) and then help the marketing department set up and enhance the site.

In this session, you will use the Import Web Wizard to import a Web site from a URL and then change the new Web site's settings to make it compatible with different browsers and servers. You will enable source control for the new Web site to restrict access to the site's pages to one author at a time. Finally, you will create a template for the Web site to ensure a consistent appearance for its pages.

Using the Import Web Wizard to Import a Web Site

When you use the Import Web Wizard to create a new Web site, you can simultaneously create a new Web site and import pages into it from a file location or from a World Wide Web server. David published the existing recipes Web site on the Sunny Morning Products Web server, but he needs you to change the Web site to include additional features. You will import his pages and create a new FrontPage Web site on your computer's PWS.

Note: The steps in this tutorial assume that you are running Windows 98 and Personal Web Server version 4.0. To complete this tutorial, you must have an Internet connection, and you must be able to publish Web pages to your computer's hard drive or network drive using the PWS. If you are using a different Web server, ask your instructor or technical support person for help.

To create the new Web site and import pages from a URL:

1. Start **FrontPage** and then change to Folders view. If necessary, close any open Web page or Web site.

2. Click **File** on the menu bar, point to **New**, and then click **Web**. The New dialog box opens and displays a list of Web sites that you can create.

3. Click the **Import Web Wizard** icon to select it. Notice that the Description section changes to identify the use of this Wizard.

4. Click in the **Specify the location of the new web** list box to select its current entry, and then type **http://localhost/recipes**, where *localhost* is the name of your computer or your computer's IP address. If you are using a different computer name, enter that name instead. This Web site name will create a new Web site named "recipes" on your computer's PWS.

   Normally a Web site's name will appear in all lowercase letters, with no spaces or other punctuation marks, so that it is a legal folder name on any operating system on which it might reside. The PWS will accept "Recipes" as a legal filename, but you will use all lowercase letters to ensure that the Web site name is permissible on other servers.

5. Click the **OK** button. The Create New Web dialog box opens and FrontPage creates the new Web site on the server. After a moment, the Import Web Wizard - Choose Source dialog box opens. You will import files from a World Wide Web site. For this tutorial, you will use the Course Technology Web site to simulate using the Sunny Morning Products Web site.

6. If necessary, click the **From a World Wide Web site** option button to select it, click in the **Location** text box to select the current entry, and then type **http://course.com/downloads/newperspectives/fp2000/recipes**

7. Click the **Next** button. The Import Web Wizard - Choose Download Amount dialog box opens. See Figure 7-1. You can use this dialog box to limit the number and size of the pages to download. You can also limit the download to only text and image files.

IMPORT WEB WIZARD – CHOOSE DOWNLOAD AMOUNT DIALOG BOX

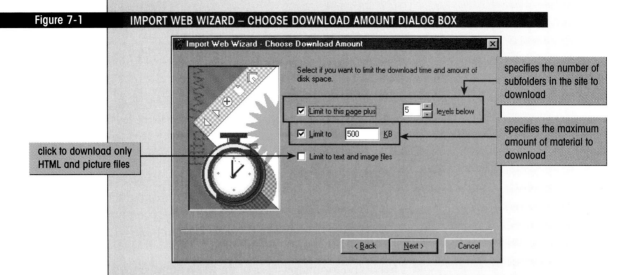

click to download only
HTML and picture files

specifies the number of
subfolders in the site to
download

specifies the maximum
amount of material to
download

8. Click the **Limit to this page plus** and **Limit to** check boxes to clear them, as you will not need to enforce any restrictions on what to download.

9. Click the **Next** button to display the final dialog box of the Import Web Wizard, and then click the **Finish** button. The Import Web Progress dialog box opens while FrontPage imports the files from the Web site into the new recipes Web site on the PWS. Depending on the speed of your Internet connection, this process will take from a few seconds to several minutes. After the import process is finished, the files are displayed in Folders view. See Figure 7-2.

Figure 7-2   **FOLDERS VIEW OF THE RECIPES WEB SITE**

recipes Web site
on the PWS

imported pages from a
URL (your modified
dates will be different)

TROUBLE? If a Dial-up Connection dialog box opens, click the Connect button. You must have an Internet connection to import the pages.

TROUBLE? If a dialog box opens and warns you that the Web site must use the current themes and elements, click the Yes button to continue.

You created the new Web site directly on the PWS using the http protocol, so you won't need to publish the Web site's pages to the server using the Publish Web command on the File menu as you do when you create a disk-based Web. When you access a FrontPage Web using the http protocol, all changes to the Web site are made on the server automatically.

Modifying the New Web Site

After creating a new Web site, you can begin formatting and adding pages to it immediately. However, before starting your work on the pages, David wants to change some of the default Web settings to ensure that the Web site is properly configured. During his testing of the recipes Web site on the Sunny Morning Products Web server, David encountered the following problems that he would like you to address:

- The site's pages have different appearances when viewed using older browser versions.

- Users currently have no method for isolating recipes in the different categories. For example, if a user wants a list of recipes for cakes, he or she will need to use the page titles to infer the pages' contents.

- There is no limitation on the number of authors revising any single Web page at one time.

- There is no forum for users of the Web site to discuss cooking techniques, to submit recipes, or to recommend changes or enhancements to existing recipes.

With these problems in mind, David created the planning analysis sheet shown in Figure 7-3. You will solve these problems for David as you complete this tutorial.

Figure 7-3   DAVID'S PLANNING ANALYSIS SHEET FOR THE RECIPES WEB SITE

Planning Analysis Sheet

Objective

Create a new FrontPage Web site on the PWS using files available on the Sunny Morning Products server. Set the Web site to function for specific browsers and servers and to enable the FrontPage Server Extensions and certain Internet technologies. Create a site map and a discussion group. The Web site should use source control. The pages in the Web site will feature recipes with pictures of popular products at the Sunshine Country Store.

Requirements

Files for current Web pages on the Sunny Morning Products server

Categories to use in the site map

Picture files to use in the recipes pages

Results

A new Web site that has the following characteristics:

      Pages for recipes, with pictures

      An index for locating the site's recipes

      Source control

      FrontPage navigation bars in all pages

      A theme

      A discussion group that is accessible to all site visitors

Specifying a Browser Version

As part of the recipe Web site's initial development and testing, David tested the site's pages using computers with different browser versions and operating systems. He also collected data from the site's current users and determined that most of them have Windows 98 and either Internet Explorer or Netscape Navigator version 4.0 or higher. The Sunny Morning Products Web server is a Microsoft Internet Information Server version 4.0; this is the only Web site that will store the site's pages. In addition, the Sunny Morning Products Web server is enabled with the FrontPage Server Extensions and can run programs and scripts.

With these criteria in mind, David asks you to set the recipes Web site to match these settings. When you change the default settings for a single Web site, FrontPage will use those settings for all future Web sites. Therefore, it is a good idea to check these settings for all new Web sites that you create to ensure their accuracy.

To change the settings of a FrontPage Web:

1. In Folders view, click **Tools** on the menu bar, and then click **Page Options**. The Page Options dialog box opens.

2. Click the **Compatibility** tab to display those settings.

3. Click the **Browsers** list arrow, and then click **Both Internet Explorer and Navigator**.

4. Click the **Browser versions** list arrow, and then click **4.0 browsers and later**.

5. Click the **Servers** list arrow, and then click **Microsoft Internet Information Server 3.0 and later**.

6. If necessary, click the **Enabled with Microsoft FrontPage Server Extensions** check box to select it, and then make sure that every check box *except* for the ActiveX controls and VBScript check boxes in the Technologies section contain a check mark. See Figure 7-4. When you selected the browsers and their versions, FrontPage automatically deselected the ActiveX controls and VBScript check boxes because the browsers that you selected do not support these technologies.

Figure 7-4	SETTING THE WEB SITE'S COMPATIBILITY OPTIONS

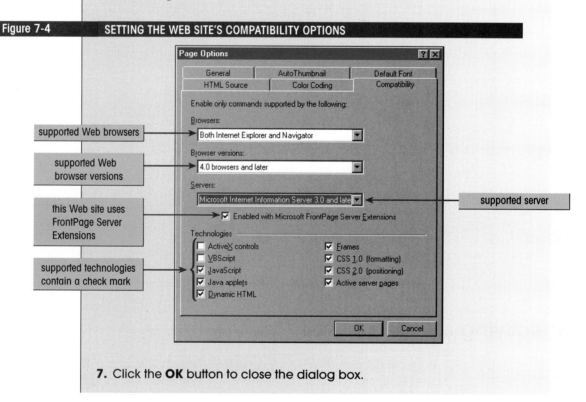

7. Click the **OK** button to close the dialog box.

Next David asks you to create a site map so users can more easily locate specific recipes.

Creating a Site Map

If you have surfed the Web, you may have noticed that some Web sites include a hyperlink to a site map. A **site map** is a list of hyperlinks that shows how the pages in the site are related to each other or organizes them in some meaningful way. In a small Web site, the site map might contain a list of hyperlinks to pages. In a large Web site, the site map might contain hyperlinks to subcategories and to other Web pages.

Assigning Web Pages to Categories

Before you can create a site map Web page, you must decide how to organize the Web pages in the Web site. For example, David wants to group recipes using categories such as cakes, icings, and pies. You create categories to identify the topic of each Web page in your Web site. Then you can use the FrontPage categories component to tell FrontPage how to organize the Web pages to include in the site map. FrontPage supplies a variety of categories that you can use, or you can create your own categories. You can also delete the default categories or categories that you do not use, as necessary.

REFERENCE WINDOW   **RW**

<u>Creating Categories and Assigning Pages to Them</u>
- In Folders view, right-click any Web page filename in the Contents pane to open the shortcut menu, and then click Properties.
- Click the Workgroup tab, and then click the Categories button.
- In the Master Category List dialog box, type the name of the new category in the New category text box, and then click the Add button.
- Repeat the process to add the remaining categories for the entire Web site, as needed, and then click the OK button.
- Click the check box for the appropriate category for the page that you selected. (The selected page's name appears in the title bar of the Properties dialog box.)
- If desired, click the Assigned to list arrow and select the team member to whom the page is assigned, or click the Names button to enter a new name.
- If desired, click the Review status list arrow and select a review status for the page, or click the Statuses button to enter a new status.
- Click the OK button in the Properties dialog box to close it.
- To assign other pages in the Web site to categories, right-click the page's filename in Folders view to open the shortcut menu, click Properties, click the Workgroup tab, and then click the check box for the appropriate category in the Available categories list box.
- Click the OK button.

First you will create all of the categories for the recipes Web site. David suggests that you use the categories Cakes, Pies, Breads, Icings, Butters, and New Recipes. After creating the categories, you will assign each existing page in the Web site to one of these categories. After creating the categories, you will use a FrontPage component to create the site map.

To create the categories:

1. Right-click **nut_bread.htm** in the Contents pane to open the shortcut menu, and then click **Properties**. The nut_bread.htm Properties dialog box opens.

2. Click the **Workgroup** tab. See Figure 7-5. FrontPage contains several default categories that appear in the Available categories list box. You could select one of these default categories; however, David wants you to create new

categories to use in this Web site. When you add or delete categories, your changes are made only in the current Web site and do not affect the default categories supplied by FrontPage.

Figure 7-5	WORKGROUP TAB

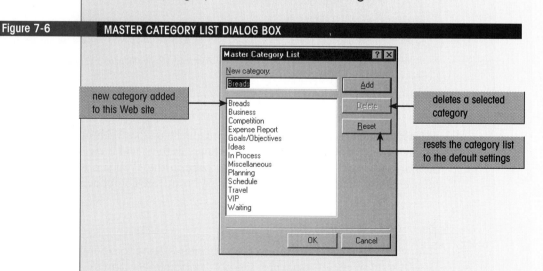

TROUBLE? If your Properties dialog box does not contain a Workgroup tab, then the FrontPage 2000 Server Extensions are not installed and properly config- ured on your computer's server. Ask your instructor or technical support person for help.

3. Click the **Categories** button. The Master Category List dialog box opens.

4. Type **Breads** in the New category text box, and then press the **Enter** key. The Breads category is added to the list. See Figure 7-6.

Figure 7-6	MASTER CATEGORY LIST DIALOG BOX

To add the next category, simply type its name and then press the Enter key.

5. Type **Pies** and then press the **Enter** key. The Pies category is added to the list.

6. Repeat Step 5 to add the following categories to the list: **Cakes, Icings, Butters,** and **New Recipes**. After pressing the Enter key for the New Recipes category, click the **OK** button. You return to the Properties dialog box for the nut_bread.htm file. Before closing the dialog box, you need to assign the nut_bread.htm page to a category. You will not assign this page to any member of the Web site development team, nor will you select a review status. A **review status** is a way to select the type of review or approval that the page needs before being considered final. For example, if the page contains legal material that requires verification by an attorney, you might select the "Legal Review" category.

7. Click the **Breads** check box in the Available categories list box to select it, and then click the **OK** button. The Properties dialog box closes, and the nut_bread.htm page is now assigned to the Breads category.

You created all of the categories. The next step is to assign the other pages in the Web site to the appropriate category. You won't assign a category to the site_map.htm page or to the Default.htm page. You don't need to assign every page in the Web site to a category.

To assign pages to categories:

1. Right-click **chiffon_cake.htm** in the Contents pane to open the shortcut menu, click **Properties**, and then click the **Workgroup** tab.

2. Click the **Cakes** check box in the Available categories list, and then click the **OK** button.

3. Repeat Steps 1 and 2 to assign the following pages to the following categories:

   chiffon_pie.htm, Pies

   butter_icing.htm, Icings

You can use Reports view to check the categories of the pages in the Web site to make sure that you assigned the pages to categories correctly.

To run a Categories report:

1. Click the **Reports** button 🗔 on the Views bar. If necessary, turn on the Reporting toolbar by clicking **View** on the menu bar, pointing to **Toolbars**, and then clicking **Reporting**.

   TROUBLE? If the Reporting toolbar is blocking the report, drag it out of the way.

2. Click the **Report** list arrow on the Reporting toolbar, scroll down the list, and then click **Categories**. The Categories report appears in Reports view. You can sort the list using any of the column headings, just as you sorted the Tasks list.

3. Click the **Category** column heading to sort the Categories list by category name. Notice that the Home Page (Default.htm) and the Recipe Index page (site_map.htm) are not assigned to categories.

Using the Categories Component

Now that you have created categories and assigned the pages to them, you are ready to add the FrontPage categories component to David's page. When you add new Web pages to the Web site, you will need to assign them to the appropriate categories or create new categories when necessary. Then, as when using other FrontPage components, FrontPage will automatically update the site map Web page and display the new Web pages in the correct categories.

REFERENCE WINDOW   RW

Creating a Site Map
- Create or open the page that will contain the site map in Page view. If necessary, enter text and format the page.
- Click the Insert Component button on the Standard toolbar, and then click Categories.
- Click the check box for the appropriate category in the Choose categories to list files by list box.
- Click the OK button.
- Repeat the steps to add additional categories to the page as necessary.

You will add the component for each category to David's existing Web page. The site_map.htm page will include a page banner, so you will need to add the page to the Web site's navigation structure.

To create the site map:

1. Click the **Folders** button ▱ on the Views bar to change to Folders view.

2. Double-click **site_map.htm** in the Contents pane to open the page in Page view. The message in the top shared border reminds you to add this page to the navigation structure to use the page banner.

3. Click the **Navigation** button ▱ on the Views bar, and then drag the file **site_map.htm** from the Folder List to the navigation structure to make it a child of the Home Page.

4. Double-click the **Recipe Index** icon in the navigation structure to open the page in Page view. See Figure 7-7. Now the page has a centered page banner and a navigation bar at the top of the page. Notice that David already created bookmarks to each category and inserted a blank line after each category heading. You will insert the categories component for each category on the blank line following its heading.

Figure 7-7   RECIPE INDEX WEB PAGE IN PAGE VIEW

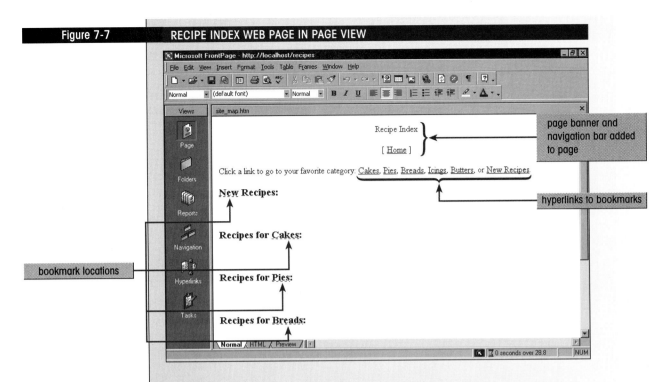

5. Click the blank line under the New Recipes heading, click the **Insert Component** button on the Standard toolbar, and then click **Categories**. The Categories Properties dialog box opens.

   TROUBLE? If the Categories component is dimmed in the list, then your PWS does not have the FrontPage 2000 Server Extensions installed on it. Ask your instructor or technical support person for help.

6. Scroll down the list of available categories, click the **New Recipes** check box to select it, and then click the **OK** button. The Recipe Index page now displays three "Page in Category" placeholders for the New Recipes category. The categories component always displays three placeholders; they do not indicate the number of Web pages that are currently in the category. To see the Web pages in this category, you must open the page in the browser.

   TROUBLE? If you do not see the three "Page in Category" placeholders, then you did not check the New Recipes check box. Repeat Steps 5 and 6.

7. Repeat Steps 5 and 6 to insert the appropriate categories component under each heading in the page.

8. Click the **Save** button on the Standard toolbar, and then click the **Preview in Browser** button on the Standard toolbar. See Figure 7-8. The correct hyperlinks for each category are added by the categories component. There are no recipes in the Butters and New Recipes categories, so there are no hyperlinks under this heading.

| Figure 7-8 | RECIPE INDEX WEB PAGE IN THE BROWSER |

there are no recipes
in the New Recipes
category

FrontPage categories
component inserts
hyperlinks based on the
page's category

9. Click the **Close** button ☒ on the Internet Explorer title bar to close it, and then if neccessary, click the **Microsoft FrontPage** program button on the taskbar to return to FrontPage.

As the marketing department adds new pages to the Web site and assigns them to categories, the categories component will update the site map to keep it current.

Using Source Control to Manage Multiple Users

David is concerned about the way that pages are updated in the recipes Web site. Because more than one person will contribute to the work required to complete each page, he wants to make sure that only one person can work on each page at a time. For example, he doesn't want the person who is coordinating the product pictures to work on a page at the same time as the person who enters the actual recipe, because one person's changes to the Web page could be lost.

Fortunately, FrontPage has a built-in source control feature in Web sites that are enabled with FrontPage 2000 Server Extensions. **Source control** lets you ensure that only one copy of a Web page can be edited at a time. Normally, a Web site that is developed by multiple developers is stored on an intranet, making it accessible to all developers. When an author checks out a page to edit it, other authors can open the page, but they cannot edit it. When a page is checked out to the current author, a check mark appears to the left of the page's filename in Folders view. Other authors will see a padlock icon, which indicates that the page is in use. A green asterisk icon indicates a page that is available for editing.

REFERENCE WINDOW   RW

Enabling Source Control for a Web Site
- Close all open pages in the Web site that you are going to enable with source control.
- In Folders view, click Tools on the menu bar, and then click Web Settings.
- If necessary, click the General tab.
- Click the Use document check-in and check-out check box to select it.
- Click the OK button, and then click the Yes button.
- To check out a page, double-click it in Folders view, and then click the Yes button. Edit and save the page as usual.
- To check in a page, close it in Page view, change to Folders view, right-click the filename to open the shortcut menu, and then click Check In.

David asks you to enable source control for the recipes Web site to ensure that only one author can edit a page at a time.

To enable source control for the recipes Web site:

1. Click the **Close** button ☒ on the Contents pane to close the Recipe Index page (site_map.htm). You must close all Web pages in the Web site to enable source control; otherwise, the open pages will not be enabled.

2. Click the **Folders** button ▯ on the Views bar to change to Folders view.

3. Click **Tools** on the menu bar, click **Web Settings**, and then make sure that the General tab is selected.

4. Click the **Use document check-in and check-out** check box to select it, and then click the **OK** button. A dialog box opens and tells you that you have changed the source control for this Web site and that FrontPage must recalculate the Web site to proceed.

5. Click the **Yes** button. The dialog box closes. Now the pages in the Web site have a green asterisk to the left of their filenames. See Figure 7-9. Any new pages added to the Web site will also use source control.

| Figure 7-9 | WEB SITE ENABLED WITH SOURCE CONTROL |

green asterisks indicate pages that are not in use

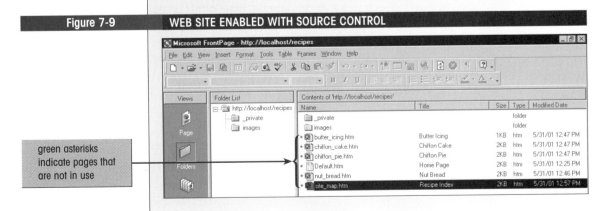

The green asterisks to the left of the filenames indicate that the pages are not in use by you or any other author. To check out a page so that you can edit it, double-click it.

To check out a Web page:

1. Double-click **site_map.htm** in the Contents pane. A dialog box opens to tell you that this page uses source control. See Figure 7-10.

Figure 7-10   **MICROSOFT FRONTPAGE DIALOG BOX**

message indicates the page's filename and status

2. Click the **Yes** button to check out the page. The page opens in Page view. You could edit the page now just like any other page.

3. Click the **Folders** button 📁 on the Views bar. Notice that a red check mark appears to the left of the site_map.htm page, indicating that this page is in use. If another user was logged on to your computer, the user would see a padlock icon to the left of the page's filename, indicating that the file is locked.

Next you will close the page and check it in.

To check in a Web page:

1. Click the **Page** button 📄 on the Views bar to return to the Recipe Index page in Page view.

2. Click the **Close** button ❌ on the Contents pane to close the page.

3. Click the **Folders** button 📁 on the Views bar to change to Folders view. You closed the page, but it is still checked out to you. If you close the Web site without checking in the page, you will lock the page so that no other user can edit it.

4. Right-click **site_map.htm** in the Contents pane to open the shortcut menu, and then click **Check In**. FrontPage checks in the page, releases the lock, and changes the check mark to an asterisk. Now other users can edit the page.

To disable source control for a Web site, return to the Web Settings dialog box, and then clear the Use document check-in and check-out check box on the General tab. Usually, a site's administrator is the only person who can enable and disable source control for a Web site. However, when you are using a PWS, you can enable source control without needing permission to do so.

Creating a Shared Template

David wants to make sure that all of the recipes in the recipes Web site have a common presentation. One way to accomplish this objective is to apply a theme to the entire Web site. However, the theme changes only the appearance of a Web site's pages; it does not ensure that every page has a heading, footer, and other elements in common.

You have learned that FrontPage includes a variety of templates you can use to create new Web pages. You can also create your own template and save it in the Web site so that other authors can use it to create new pages. When you create a template and make it available to other users, it is called a **shared template**.

The template that David wants you to create will have a page banner, a FrontPage navigation bar, an introductory paragraph, a bulleted list of the recipe's ingredients, a photo of the finished product, a description for making the recipe, and a page footer. David already started work on the page and saved it in the Tutorial.07 folder on your Data Disk. You will import this page into the recipes Web site, open the page in Page view, make some changes to it, and then save it as a shared template.

To import the page and add page components to it:

1. Click **File** on the menu bar, click **Import**, click the **Add File** button, click the **Look in** list arrow and change to the drive or folder that contains your Data Disk, double-click the **Tutorial.07** folder, and then double-click **style**. Click the **OK** button to import the style.htm page into the Web site. Notice that this page automatically is enabled with source control, as indicated by the green asterisk to the left of its filename.

2. Double-click **style.htm** in the Contents pane, and then click the **Yes** button to check out the page and open it in Page view. See Figure 7-11. David wants the template to include a page banner and a navigation bar. The page already contains placeholder text that tells users how to enter information into the page.

Figure 7-11	STYLE.HTM PAGE THAT WILL BECOME A SHARED TEMPLATE

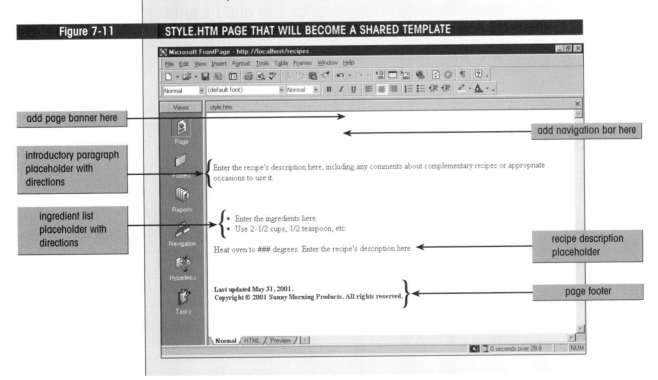

3. Click the first blank, centered line at the top of the page, click **Insert** on the menu bar, and then click **Page Banner**. The default settings for the page banner are correct, so click the **OK** button. Because this page is not part of the Web site's navigation structure, a placeholder appears for the page banner. When authors create new pages using the template, the placeholder will remind them to add the page to the navigation structure for this element to work correctly.

4. Press the **down** arrow key ↓ to move to the next blank, centered line, click **Insert** on the menu bar, and then click **Navigation Bar**. The Navigation Bar Properties dialog box opens.

5. Click the **Same level** option button, click the **Home page** check box to select it, click the **Parent page** check box to select it, click the **Horizontal** option button, click the **Text** option button, and then click the **OK** button. The Navigation Bar Properties dialog box closes and the navigation bar placeholder appears in the page.

Before you save the page as a template, David asks you to format the page to create an area in which to insert a photo of the finished product. For example, a recipe for a cake should include a picture of the finished cake. The marketing department will coordinate with the kitchen staff to obtain these product shots.

Using Absolute Positioning for Text and Pictures

So far in these tutorials, you have used the insertion point to position text and pictures in a location in an existing page. Using **absolute positioning**, or simply **positioning**, lets you place text or a picture in an exact location in a page without regard to a blank or existing line. You can use positioning to place text or a picture anywhere in a page, including placing it in front of or behind other elements. When you use absolute positioning, you can format text that surrounds the positioned text or object to flow on top of or behind the object.

REFERENCE WINDOW	RW

Inserting Text or a Picture in a Web Page Using Absolute Positioning

- Enter the text or insert the picture that you want to position in the page.
- Select the text or picture that you inserted.
- Click View on the menu bar, point to Toolbars, and then click Positioning to display the Positioning toolbar.
- Click the Position Absolutely button on the Positioning toolbar.
- Use the move pointer to drag the selected text or picture to the exact location in the page; use a sizing handle to resize the selected text or picture to the correct size. Then release the mouse button.

David's planning analysis sheet shows that each recipe's picture should appear to the right of the bulleted list that contains the recipe's ingredients. You will use positioning to place a text box with instructions in this location. When an author creates a new page using the template, he or she can replace the text with the recipe's picture.

To insert text using absolute positioning:

1. Click **View** on the menu bar, point to **Toolbars**, and then click **Positioning**. The Positioning toolbar opens. If necessary, drag the Positioning toolbar so that it is not blocking the Web page.

2. Click the blank line that appears between the "Enter the recipe's description..." paragraph and the first bulleted item in the bulleted list. When using absolute positioning, you can insert the text or picture anywhere in the page; the location is not important. Usually, however, it is easiest to insert the text or picture on a blank line to make it easier to select the text or picture later.

3. Type **Replace this text with the product shot and resize it, if necessary.** This text is a placeholder to remind authors to insert the photo in the correct location in the page. See Figure 7-12.

Figure 7-12	USING ABSOLUTE POSITIONING

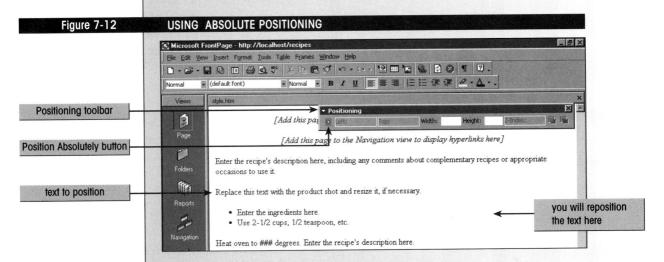

4. Select the text that you typed in Step 3, and then click the **Position Absolutely** button on the Positioning toolbar. See Figure 7-13. FrontPage places a position box with sizing handles around the selected text. The text will correct its awkward appearance after you resize the position box.

Figure 7-13	POSITION BOX AROUND THE SELECTED TEXT

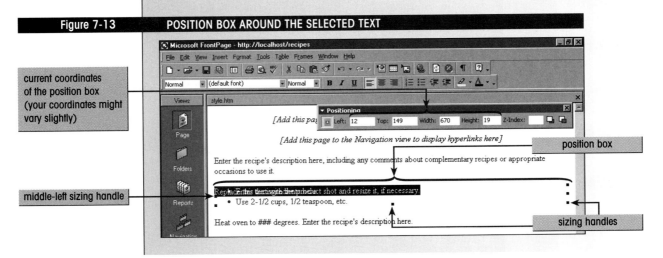

5. Point to the middle-left resize handle so that the pointer changes to a ↔ shape, and then click and drag the pointer to the right until the position box is the same size as the one shown in Figure 7-14. Release the mouse button. If necessary, use the pointer to resize the position box so it has approximately the same coordinates shown on the Positioning toolbar in Figure 7-14.

| Figure 7-14 | RESIZED POSITION BOX |

new coordinates of the position box

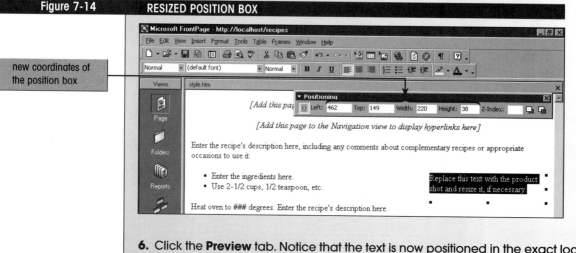

6. Click the **Preview** tab. Notice that the text is now positioned in the exact location in the page. When the page's author uses the position box, he or she will need to verify that the position box is in the correct location when the Web page is viewed using different browsers and monitors. However, it is easy to resize and move the position box as necessary using a sizing handle or the pointer.

7. Click the **Normal** tab to return to Normal Page view, and then click the **Close** button ✖ on the Positioning toolbar to close it.

8. Click the **Save** button 🖫 on the Standard toolbar to save the Web page.

Now that you have finished formatting the page, you can save it as a shared template.

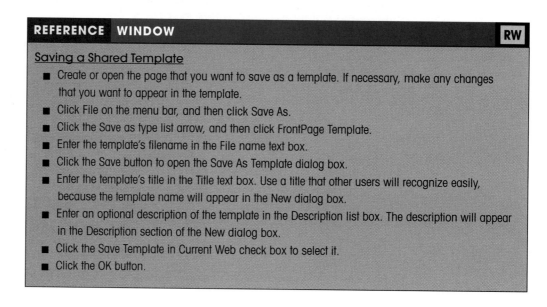

| REFERENCE | WINDOW | RW |

Saving a Shared Template

- Create or open the page that you want to save as a template. If necessary, make any changes that you want to appear in the template.
- Click File on the menu bar, and then click Save As.
- Click the Save as type list arrow, and then click FrontPage Template.
- Enter the template's filename in the File name text box.
- Click the Save button to open the Save As Template dialog box.
- Enter the template's title in the Title text box. Use a title that other users will recognize easily, because the template name will appear in the New dialog box.
- Enter an optional description of the template in the Description list box. The description will appear in the Description section of the New dialog box.
- Click the Save Template in Current Web check box to select it.
- Click the OK button.

You will save the shared template in the recipes Web site.

To save the shared template:

1. Click **File** on the menu bar, and then click **Save As**. The Save As dialog box opens.

2. Click the **Save as type** list arrow, and then click **FrontPage Template**.

3. Click the **Save** button. The Save As Template dialog box opens.

4. Type **Style Page** in the Title text box. This is the name of the template that you will create. This name differs from the value in the Name text box, which is the filename of the template.

5. Press the **Tab** key three times to move to the Description list box, and then type **Use this template to create a new recipe page.**

6. Click the **Save Template in Current Web** check box to select it. See Figure 7-15.

Figure 7-15	COMPLETED SAVE AS TEMPLATE DIALOG BOX

template's title → Title: Style Page

template's filename → Name: style

template's description → Description: Use this template to create a new recipe page.

saves this template in the current Web site → ☑ Save Template in Current Web

7. Click the **OK** button. FrontPage creates the template in the Web site in a hidden folder named _sharedtemplates. The next time you open the New dialog box you will see the Style Page icon in the list.

8. Click the **Close** button ⊠ on the Contents pane to close the style.htm page. Because source control is enabled for this page, you must check it in.

9. Click the **Folders** button 📁 on the Views bar to change to Folders view, right-click **style.htm** in the Contents pane to open the shortcut menu, and then click **Check In**.

You can verify that you created the template correctly by creating a new Web page.

To use the Style Page template to create a new Web page:

1. Click the **Page** button 📄 on the Views bar to change to Page view.

2. Click **File** on the menu bar, point to **New**, and then click **Page**. The New dialog box opens.

3. Scroll down the list of icons until you see the Style Page icon, and then click the **Style Page** icon. See Figure 7-16.

Figure 7-16   **NEW DIALOG BOX**

4. Click the **OK** button. A new page named new_page_1.htm is created using the Style Page template. An author would replace the existing text in this page to create a new recipe, add the page to the navigation structure, and then save the page in the recipes Web site. You don't need to save this page, so you will close it without saving changes.

5. Click the **Close** button ☒ on the Contents pane to close the page without saving it.

6. Click the **Close** button ☒ on the FrontPage title bar to close the recipes Web site and FrontPage.

In the next session, you will create a discussion group for the recipes Web site.

Session 7.1 QUICK CHECK

1. True or False: When developing a Web site using FrontPage, you must use the FrontPage Server Extensions.

2. True or False: You can set a FrontPage Web to disable certain Internet technologies, such as Java applets or ActiveX controls.

3. A Web page that shows how the pages in a Web site are related to each other and provides hyperlinks to these pages is called a(n) _____.

4. Why must you create categories for Web pages and assign the site's pages to categories before creating a site map?

5. Suppose that you are creating a personal Web site on your computer's PWS. Would you enable source control for that Web site? Why or why not?

6. When a Web page that is enabled with source control is checked out to another user, you will see a(n) _____ icon to the left of the page's filename in Folders view.

7. How do you check in a Web page that is enabled with source control?

8. You can use _____ to precisely position text or pictures in a Web page.

SESSION 7.2

In this session, you will use a Wizard to create a discussion group for a Web site. You will post messages to the site, reply to messages, and search for a message. You will display and examine a Web site's hidden folders. You will change the properties of a discussion group. Finally, you will view the HTML code for the discussion group's table of contents.

Setting Up a Discussion Group

In his planning analysis sheet for the recipes Web site (see Figure 7-3), David wanted to create a way for users of the Web site to exchange ideas and information. A **discussion group** is a specialized Web site, which can be separate or part of an existing Web site, that accepts messages from users, catalogs and indexes the information in these messages, and lets users reply to messages. The discussion group can be open to everyone or protected so that only registered users can read and post messages.

When you use the Discussion Web Wizard to create a discussion group, the Wizard asks you a series of questions and then creates the discussion group and its pages for you. Figure 7-17 describes the pages that the Wizard creates. In the following sections, you will create a discussion group for the recipes Web site and learn about each page in more detail.

Figure 7-17	PAGES CREATED BY THE DISCUSSION WEB WIZARD	
PAGE NAME	**DESCRIPTION**	**REQUIRED?**
Confirmation	A confirmation page containing a message that the server received a new message posted using a Submission Form.	No. You do not need to provide confirmation of receipt of a visitor's submission.
Frameset	A frames page that contains the TOC and Welcome pages in the Web site.	No. You can set an option using the Wizard to use frames all the time, when the visitor's browser supports them, or not at all.
Search Form	A page containing a search form that site visitors can use to search for keywords in messages posted to the site.	No. However, including a search form in a discussion group makes it easier to locate messages related to a specific topic.
Submission Form	The form that site visitors use to submit comments to the discussion group.	Yes. A discussion Web site must have a Submission Form.
TOC (Table of Contents)	A page that serves as a site index. FrontPage creates hyperlinks to every message in the discussion group. Clicking a hyperlink opens the message.	No. However, it is suggested that you include this page in your discussion group. Without it, users have no way to view the contents of the site.
Welcome	The discussion Web site's Home Page. This page contains default instructions for using the site and hyperlinks to the Submission Form and the Search Form Web pages.	No. You can set an option using the Wizard to use an existing Home Page, or you can ask FrontPage to create the Welcome page for you. The site can contain only one Home Page.

Planning a Discussion Group

Before you create a discussion group, it is a good idea to consider how visitors will use the site and any special requirements that you need to implement. For example, when using the Discussion Web Wizard to create a new discussion group, you have the option of creating a new Web site or adding the discussion group to the current Web site. You will add the new discussion group to the recipes Web site. Regardless of whether the discussion group is part of an existing Web site, the Wizard lets you create the Web pages described in Figure 7-17 and a hidden folder in which to store the discussion group's content. You will learn more about this hidden folder after you create the discussion group.

Another consideration during the planning phase is to consider how you will manage the content of the discussion group. The site's administrator should not delete messages submitted to a discussion group because doing so will interfere with the hyperlinks that link together the site's messages. In addition, there isn't a method for validating the comments submitted to the discussion group to check them for inappropriate content. For example, if the discussion group is open to all visitors, there is no way to automatically delete messages that contain inappropriate language or content. In some cases, the site's administrator can read the messages and replace the content of inappropriate messages with a "Deleted Content" message, but this process puts a heavy burden on the site's administrator, who must read each message and determine its usefulness and appropriateness to the site.

To ensure quality, some discussion groups are secure Web sites in which visitors must have a valid logon and a password to participate. Usually the site's administrator sets up accounts with logons and passwords for qualified visitors. When you create a secure discussion group, the risk of inappropriate content is less than having an open discussion group.

Using a Wizard to Create a Discussion Group

Although you could create a discussion group by developing the individual Web pages that are required by the site, it is far easier to let the Discussion Web Wizard do the work for you. Most of the files that actually run and administer the discussion group are hidden files that contain FrontPage components. The FrontPage Server Extensions do most of the work of maintaining the discussion group, so the FrontPage 2000 Server Extensions must be installed and properly configured on the Web server on which the discussion group is created and published.

REFERENCE WINDOW   **RW**

Using the Discussion Web Wizard to Create a Discussion Group

- Open the Web site to which you will add the discussion group in Folders view. If you want to create a new Web site for the discussion group, close any open Web pages or Web sites, and then change to Folders view.
- Click File on the menu bar, point to New, and then click Web.
- If you are creating a new Web site, click in the Specify the location of the new web list box, and then type http://localhost/ and the name of the Web site, where *localhost* is the name or IP address of the Web server.
- If you are adding the discussion group to an existing Web site, click the Add to current Web check box to add the discussion group to the current Web site.
- If necessary, click the Secure connection required (SSL) check box if you are creating the discussion group on a Web server that requires Secure Socket Layer (SSL) communication.
- Double-click the Discussion Web Wizard icon. FrontPage starts the Discussion Web Wizard. Use the dialog boxes to specify the pages to create, a title for the discussion group, a name for the discussion folder, the input fields to create in the Submission Form, the site's security status (open versus closed), the sort order for the index (oldest to newest or newest to oldest), whether the Contents page should also be the discussion group's Home Page, the information that the Search Form should supply with hyperlinks to matching pages, an optional Web theme, and the frames page options.
- Click the Finish button to create the discussion group.

David asks you to create the discussion group using the title "Recipe Discussion" and the name "_disc." The Recipe Discussion will be an open site; any visitor can read and submit messages. David wants you to create all of the default pages suggested by the Wizard. The Submission Form will contain the Subject, Category, and Comments fields; the table of contents will be sorted with the newest message listed first; you will not create a new Home Page; the Search Form will supply hyperlinks to matching pages with each message's subject, size, and date; and you will create a frames page. Because you are adding the discussion group to an existing Web site, the Wizard will not prompt you to select a theme. However, you can apply a theme later.

After creating the initial discussion group, you can format its pages just like any other Web page. However, it is very important to maintain certain aspects created by the Wizard. For example, you should not move pages or hidden files or rename any form fields created in the Submission Form or the Search Form. These types of changes will cause the discussion group to stop functioning correctly. However, formatting the pages by adding pictures, themes, and other visual interest is appropriate—and suggested—because the Wizard creates only the basic content for you with minimal formatting.

Before creating the discussion group, you need to open the recipes Web site from the PWS.

To open the recipes Web site from the PWS:

1. Start **FrontPage** and change to Folders view.

2. Click the list arrow for the **Open** button 📂 on the Standard toolbar, and then click **Open Web**. The Open Web dialog box opens.

3. Click the **Web Folders** button in the Open Web dialog box. See Figure 7-18.

Figure 7-18	OPENING A WEB SITE FROM THE PWS

PWS name or name of your server (your PWS name might be different)

Web Folders button

4. Double-click the name of your Web server. The default name is **localhost**.

   TROUBLE? If you see a "recipes on localhost" folder instead of the localhost folder, click the recipes on localhost folder to select it, click the Open button, and then skip Step 5.

5. Click the **recipes** folder, and then click the **Open** button. The recipes Web site opens in Folders view. Notice that your files still use source control, as indicated by the green asterisks to the left of each filename.

> TROUBLE? If your Web site does not open in Folders view, click the Folders button
> on the Views bar.

Now that the recipes Web site is open, you can create the discussion group. The pages for the discussion group will use source control automatically.

To create the discussion group:

1. Click **File** on the menu bar, point to **New**, and then click **Web**. The New dialog box opens.

2. Click the **Add to current Web** check box to select it. FrontPage dims the Specify the location of the new web list box.

   TROUBLE? If the Web server you are using requires SSL communication, check the Secure connection required (SSL) check box to select it. Usually you do not need to select this option when creating Web sites on the PWS. If you are unsure about the need for SSL communication, ask your instructor or technical support person for help.

3. Double-click the **Discussion Web Wizard** icon. FrontPage starts the Discussion Web Wizard and opens the first dialog box. Read the information provided in the first dialog box.

4. Click the **Next** button. The second dialog box opens. See Figure 7-19. You use this dialog box to select the pages and features that you want to create in the discussion group. You already learned about the Submission Form, Table of Contents, Search Form, and Confirmation pages (see Figure 7-17). Selecting the Threaded Replies option enables the site to index messages based on their topics and replies, where the original message appears flush with the left margin, and replies to that message appear indented on a new line below the original message. If you do not select this option, then all messages in the discussion group will be listed in chronological order using the sort order you specified in the Wizard.

| Figure 7-19 | SELECTING THE DISCUSSION GROUP PAGES AND FEATURES |

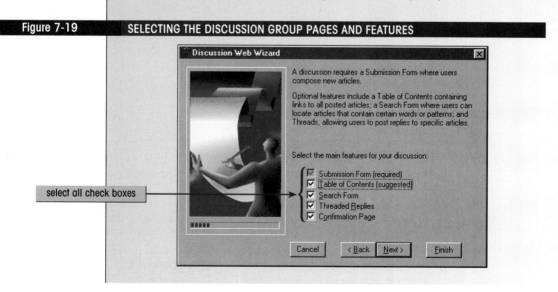

5. If necessary, click any empty check box to select it, and then click the **Next** button. The next dialog box asks you to enter a title and name for the discussion group. Type **Recipe Discussion** in the Enter a descriptive title for this discussion text box, press the **Tab** key to move to the Enter the name for the discussion folder text box, and then type **_disc**. See Figure 7-20. Notice that the note in the dialog box reminds you that the discussion folder's name must begin with an underscore character for FrontPage to index the messages submitted to the discussion group. Folders that have an underscore as the first character are hidden.

Figure 7-20	ENTERING THE TITLE AND NAME OF THE DISCUSSION GROUP

discussion group title

discussion group folder name

note regarding hidden folders

6. Click the **Next** button. If necessary, click the **Subject, Category, Comments** option button to select it and to create these form fields in the Submission Form, and then click the **Next** button. The next dialog box asks if your discussion group is protected. See Figure 7-21.

Figure 7-21	SETTING SECURITY FOR A DISCUSSION GROUP

select this option

7. If necessary, click the **No, anyone can post articles** option button to select it, and then click the **Next** button. The next dialog box asks how you want to sort the messages listed in the table of contents.

8. If necessary, click the **Newest to oldest** option button to select it, and then click the **Next** button. The next dialog box asks if you want to create a new Home Page. See Figure 7-22. Your recipes Web site already has a page named Default.htm, so you will select the No option button.

Figure 7-22   **SELECTING THE HOME PAGE FOR THE DISCUSSION GROUP**

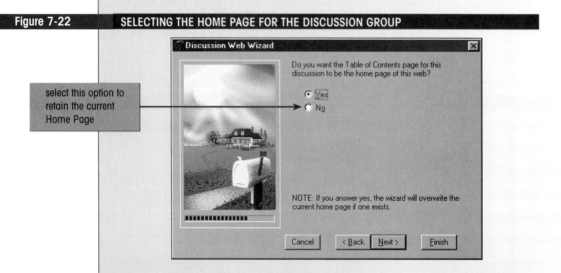

select this option to retain the current Home Page

9. If necessary, click the **No** option button, and then click the **Next** button. The next dialog box asks you to select the information that will appear with the search results created by the Search Form.

10. If necessary, click the **Subject, Size, Date** option button to select it, and then click the **Next** button. The next dialog box asks you to specify a frame option. See Figure 7-23. Notice that a preview of the selected frame option appears on the left side of the dialog box. The best option to use is the dual interface. This option will create a frames page when the browser can display frames, and normal pages if the browser cannot display frames.

Figure 7-23   **SELECTING A FRAME OPTION**

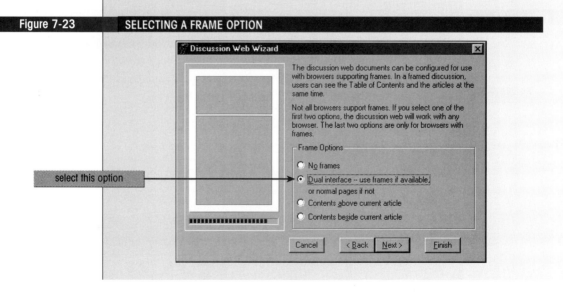

select this option

11. If necessary, click the **Dual interface - use frames if available, or normal pages if not** option button to select it, and then click the **Next** button. The final dialog box of the Discussion Web Wizard tells you how to display the Web site's hidden files and reviews the main pages that you selected. See Figure 7-24. If you need to change any options, you can click the Back button to return to a previous dialog box.

Figure 7-24	FINAL DIALOG BOX OF THE DISCUSSION WEB WIZARD

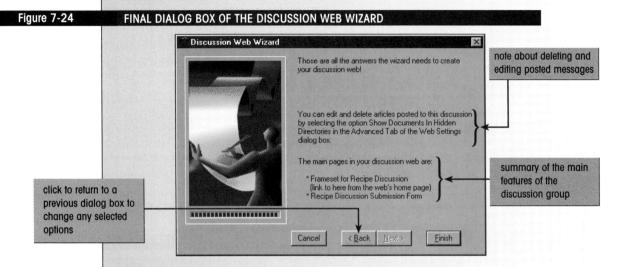

note about deleting and editing posted messages

summary of the main features of the discussion group

click to return to a previous dialog box to change any selected options

12. Click the **Finish** button. FrontPage creates the pages in the discussion group and the hidden folder and files that will maintain and run it. Notice that the default Web pages created by the Discussion Web Wizard have the prefix "Recipe Discussion" and the default page title. The Wizard appended the default page titles to include the discussion group's name that you entered in the Wizard.

The discussion group that you created is very easy to use. Most pages contain instructions for using the page. To learn how to use the discussion group, you will post and reply to a message to simulate how the site's visitors would use the forum. Keep in mind, however, that an active discussion group can receive hundreds of messages a day. These messages require processing resources and space on the server on which the discussion group is published. Before you create a discussion group on a Web server, it is important to make sure that the server has the necessary resources to maintain and store the site.

Posting a Message

When you **post** a message, or article, to a discussion group, you are submitting a form to a server for processing. The FrontPage Server Extensions process the form and store its contents in the discussion group's hidden folder in the Web site. The Discussion Web Wizard creates and programs all of the default forms that are required to run the discussion group, so the discussion group is ready to use right away. You could start your work by formatting the pages created by the Wizard. However, you will begin by using the discussion group so that you understand how it works. Your practice work will also give you an opportunity to examine the pages created by the Wizard and to consider ways to improve on the Wizard's work.

REFERENCE WINDOW   RW

Posting a Message to a Discussion Group
- Open or link to the Submission Form Web page using the Web browser.
- Use the form fields to enter the content of the message.
- Click the Post Article button.

You will post a message to the discussion group by opening the site's Welcome page and navigating to the Submission Form page. You must use the browser to post a message to the discussion group.

To post a message to the discussion group:

1. Click the **Recipe Discussion Welcome** page (disc_welc.htm) in the Contents pane to select it, and then click the **Preview in Browser** button 🔍 on the Standard toolbar. The Welcome page opens in the browser. See Figure 7-25. Notice that the page created by the Wizard contains only the basic content of the page. The page does not include any special formatting.

| Figure 7-25 | WELCOME PAGE IN THE BROWSER |

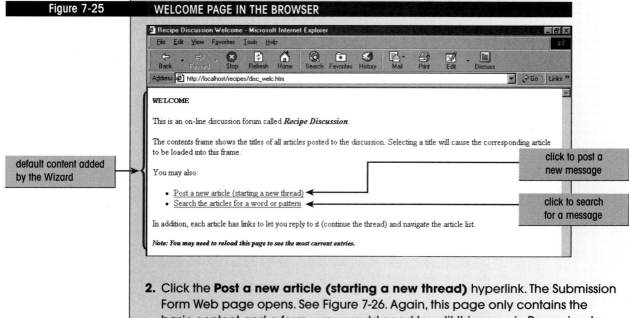

default content added by the Wizard

click to post a new message

click to search for a message

2. Click the **Post a new article (starting a new thread)** hyperlink. The Submission Form Web page opens. See Figure 7-26. Again, this page only contains the basic content and a form—you would need to edit this page in Page view to change the categories supplied in the drop-down menu form field and to customize the other form fields to more closely match your needs. You also would need to apply any special formatting to the page, such as adding pictures, a page background, and hyperlinks to other pages in the recipes Web site.

Figure 7-26 **POSTING A NEW MESSAGE**

default top shared border created by the Wizard

default form created by the Wizard

3. Click in the **Subject** text box, and then type **Test Message**.

4. Press the **Tab** key to move to the From text box, and then type **David Harrah**.

5. Click the **Category** list arrow, and then click **Category 3**. You can see that you will need to change this drop-down menu form field in Page view to create appropriate choices for the recipes Web site in the list. For example, you might change the choices to "Recipe Enhancement," "Recipe Correction," "Recipe Comments," and "Other."

6. Click in the **Comments** text box, and then type **This is a test.**

7. Scroll down the page as necessary, and then click the **Post Article** button. The Confirmation page is displayed in the browser, acknowledging that the server received your message. See Figure 7-27. Notice that the page includes a message to remind you to refresh the main page (Contents) to see your message in the list.

Figure 7-27	CONFIRMATION PAGE

default shared border created by the Wizard

default content created by the Wizard

a FrontPage component added your message title here

Recipe Discussion

[Home | Contents | Search | Post]

CONFIRMATION

Your article, titled **Test Message**, has been submitted to the discussion group *Recipe Discussion*.

If you refresh the main page you should see your new article appear in the list.

Last changed: May 31, 2001

8. Click the **Contents** hyperlink at the top of the page. The Contents page opens in the browser. A link to your test message—with the current date—appears at the top of the list. Notice that the Contents and Welcome pages are now displayed in a frames page. You set this option using the Wizard. See Figure 7-28.

Figure 7-28	FRAMES PAGE

Contents page in the contents frame

Welcome page in the main frame

your Test Message will display the current date

CONTENTS

Test Message *David Harrah 5/31/01*

WELCOME

This is an on-line discussion forum called *Recipe Discussion*.

The contents frame shows the titles of all articles posted to the discussion. Selecting a title will cause the corresponding article to be loaded into this frame.

You may also:

- Post a new article (starting a new thread)
- Search the articles for a word or pattern

In addition, each article has links to let you reply to it (continue the thread) and navigate the article list.

Note: You may need to reload this page to see the most current entries.

Now your discussion group contains one message. You can reply to that message to see how threads work. A **thread** is a series of messages on a related topic and their replies.

Replying to a Message

The Test Message that you created in the previous set of steps is now stored in the recipes Web site. Notice that the Test Message is formatted as a hyperlink in the Contents frame. To reply to a message, you click its hyperlink to open it. Then you use a hyperlink to select the Reply option.

REFERENCE   WINDOW   RW

Replying to a Message
- Click the hyperlink in the contents frame for the message that you want to reply to.
- Click the Reply hyperlink in the main frame.
- Complete the Submission Form to reply to the message.
- Click the Post Article button.

To simulate replying to a message, you will reply using the name "Amanda Bay."

To reply to a message:

1. Click the **Test Message** hyperlink in the contents frame. The main frame changes to display a page with the contents and details of the Test Message that you submitted. See Figure 7-29.

Figure 7-29   REPLYING TO A MESSAGE

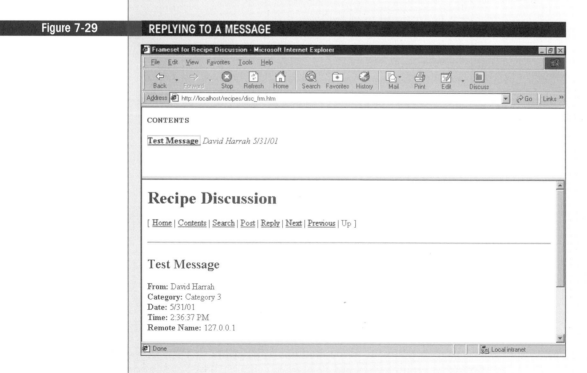

2. Click the **Reply** hyperlink in the main frame. A blank Submission Form opens. This is the same Submission Form that you used to post your original message. However, notice that the Subject text box contains the text "Re: Test Message." This text indicates that you are replying to a message that was entitled "Test Message."

3. Click in the **From** text box, and then type **Amanda Bay**.

4. Click the **Category** list arrow, and then click **Category 3**.

5. Click in the **Comments** text box, and then type **I am replying to your test message.**

6. Scroll down the page as necessary, and then click the **Post Article** button. The Confirmation page opens in the browser.

7. Click the **Contents** hyperlink to return to the frames page. See Figure 7-30. Your reply is now indented below the original message. This indentation indicates a threaded reply, or a message with the same topic.

| Figure 7-30 | THREADED REPLY IN THE CONTENTS PAGE |

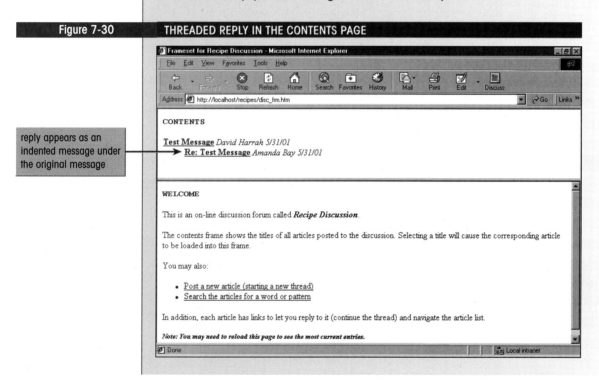

reply appears as an indented message under the original message

Now the discussion group contains two messages. To help you understand the Search Form, you will search for your messages.

Searching a Discussion Group

The page in the main frame contains a hyperlink that lets you search the messages in the discussion group for a word or pattern (phrase). The Search Form page contains the same FrontPage search component that you would use to search a Web site.

REFERENCE   WINDOW   **RW**

Searching a Discussion Group
- Click the Search the articles for a word or pattern hyperlink in the Welcome page to open the Search Form page.
- Click in the Search for text box, and then type the word or phrase that you want to search for.
- Click the Start Search button.
- Click a hyperlink in the results page to open the page(s) that contain your search text.

You will search for the word "test." The search component should find this word in both of your messages.

To search a discussion group:

1. Click the **Search the articles for a word or pattern** hyperlink in the main frame. The Search Form Web page opens in the main frame.

2. Click in the **Search for** text box, and then type **test**.

3. Click the **Start Search** button. Scroll down the page as necessary to see the search results area, which shows that both of your messages contain the text.

4. Click the **Test Message** hyperlink in the search results to open that message. Notice that the hyperlinks at the top of the page include one named "Next." Clicking this hyperlink will open the next message, which in this case is the reply from Amanda Bay. The "next" message is not always a reply; it is just the next message in the list.

5. Click the **Next** hyperlink. The Re: Test Message message opens.

6. Click the **Microsoft FrontPage** program button on the taskbar to return to FrontPage.

David wants to make sure that you are able to view and, if necessary, edit the messages in the discussion group.

Displaying and Examining a Web Site's Hidden Folders

To see the hidden folders and files for the discussion group, you need to change the Web site to display hidden folders.

REFERENCE   WINDOW   **RW**

Displaying a Web Site's Hidden Folders
- In Folders view, click Tools on the menu bar, and then click Web Settings.
- Click the Advanced tab.
- Click the Show documents in hidden directories check box to select it.
- Click the OK button, and then click the Yes button.

David asks you to display the hidden folders in the recipes Web site. You will see the hidden folder created by the Discussion Web Wizard, along with the _sharedtemplates folder that you created with your shared template in Session 7.1.

To display the Web site's hidden folders:

1. Click **Tools** on the menu bar, and then click **Web Settings**. The Web Settings dialog box opens.

2. Click the **Advanced** tab to display those settings.

3. Click the **Show documents in hidden directories** check box to select it, and then click the **OK** button. The Web Settings dialog box closes and a Microsoft FrontPage dialog box opens. See Figure 7-31.

| Figure 7-31 | DIALOG BOX ASKING TO REFRESH THE WEB SITE |

4. Click the **Yes** button. Folders view is refreshed and all of the site's files and folders are displayed in Folders view. See Figure 7-32.

| Figure 7-32 | FOLDERS VIEW WITH THE HIDDEN FOLDERS DISPLAYED |

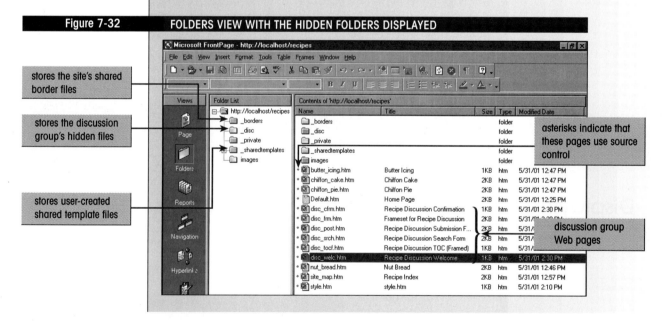

To hide the Web site's hidden folders again, clear the Show documents in hidden directories check box on the Advanced tab.

When you post a message to a discussion group, FrontPage names the HTML document using a sequential filename. For example, the Test Message has the filename 00000001.htm. The reply to the Test Message has the filename 00000002.htm. As additional messages are submitted to the discussion group, they will have sequential filenames. You can open the HTML documents that contain the posted messages by double-clicking them.

David asks you to open the Test Message and to edit its content, to simulate how you might handle a message that contains inappropriate content.

To open a posted message and the table of contents in FrontPage:

1. Click the **_disc** folder in the Folder List to open it. The contents of this folder appear in the Contents pane. Unless you submitted additional messages, you should see your Test Message, your reply to the Test Message, and a file named tocproto.htm. See Figure 7-33.

Figure 7-33	CONTENTS OF THE _DISC HIDDEN FOLDER

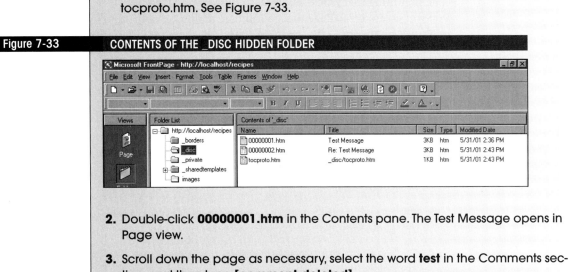

2. Double-click **00000001.htm** in the Contents pane. The Test Message opens in Page view.

3. Scroll down the page as necessary, select the word **test** in the Comments section, and then type **[comment deleted]**.

4. Click the **Save** button 🖫 on the Standard toolbar.

   Now view the page in the browser.

5. Click the **Internet Explorer** program button on the taskbar, click the **Test Message** hyperlink in the contents frame, and then click the **Refresh** button 🔁 on the Standard Buttons toolbar. Scroll down the page as necessary. Notice that the update you made to the Test Message is displayed.

   You can also edit the discussion group's table of contents by opening the tocproto.htm file in Page view.

6. Click the **Microsoft FrontPage** program button on the taskbar, and then click the **Folders** button 📂 on the Views bar to return to Folders view.

7. Double-click **tocproto.htm** in the Contents pane. The Contents page opens in Page view. You can edit the content of this page, as well. However, be careful not to delete any hyperlinks, as this change will affect the way that messages are linked together.

8. Delete the word **Message** in the Test Message hyperlink so it is just "Test."

9. Click 🖫, click the **Internet Explorer** program button on the taskbar, and then click 🔁. The hyperlink for the Test Message is now just "Test."

10. Click the **Test** hyperlink in the contents frame. The Test Message appears in the main frame. Your changes are displayed in the contents frame, but the hyperlink to the Test Message still works. Normally, you would not need to make this type of change, but you can do so when necessary.

You have posted and replied to a message, searched the discussion group, and edited a message. The discussion group works correctly and should serve your needs. However, as with most Web sites created using a Wizard, you can always improve their content and format by adding your own elements. David asks you to change some of the default pages to make them easier to use and to apply a Web theme to the entire recipes Web site.

Changing the Properties of a Discussion Group

The first thing that David asks you to do is to add the site's pages to Navigation view. Then you will create FrontPage navigation bars and page banners in every page. Finally, you will apply a Web theme to the entire Web site. Because you are the only user for the PWS, you will disable source control to make your work go faster.

To disable source control:

1. Click the **Microsoft FrontPage** program button on the taskbar to return to FrontPage.

2. Click the **Close** button ⊠ on the Contents pane as necessary to close all open pages, and then click the **Folders** button 🗁 on the Views bar to change to Folders view.

3. Click **Tools** on the menu bar, and then click **Web Settings**. If necessary, click the **General** tab to display those settings.

4. Click the **Use document check-in and check-out** check box to clear it, and then click the **OK** button.

5. Click the **Yes** button to recalculate the Web site. The files in the Web site do not have green asterisks to the left of their filenames any longer, and the source control for this Web site is disabled.

Next you will add the site's pages to the navigation structure.

To add the pages to the navigation structure:

1. Click the **Navigation** button 🗁 on the Views bar. The navigation structure currently contains the Home Page (Default.htm) and the Recipe Index page (site_map.htm) that you added in Session 7.1.

2. Drag the pages from the Folder List and drop them into the navigation structure so that it looks like Figure 7-34.

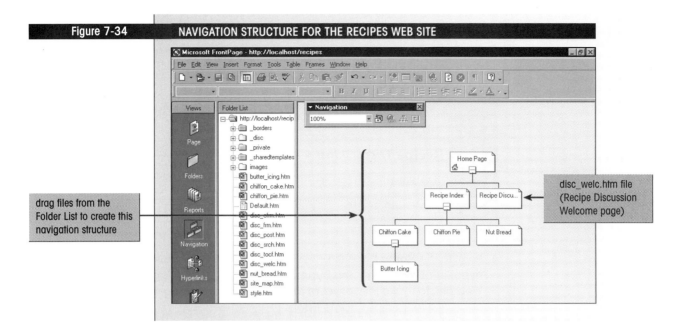

Figure 7-34   NAVIGATION STRUCTURE FOR THE RECIPES WEB SITE

Changing the Discussion Group's Shared Borders

You might have noticed that the pages in the discussion group use a page banner with text and a FrontPage navigation bar with text hyperlinks to the discussion group's pages and to the Home Page. When you create a discussion group, FrontPage creates a shared border that only the discussion group Web pages use. Hyperlinks to the pages in the discussion group are automatically added to the shared border. If you need to rename or add a hyperlink to the discussion group's shared border, you can edit it just like any other shared border.

David thinks that the top shared border for the discussion group pages would be more effective if it contained hyperlinks to the Welcome page and to the Home Page of the recipes Web site. These changes will make it easier for the site's visitors to navigate the Web site.

To edit a discussion group's shared border:

1. Click the **Folders** button 📁 on the Views bar to change to Folders view.

2. Click the **_borders** folder in the Folder List. There are several files in this folder. The disc_aftr.htm file is the footer for pages that display messages, the disc_ahdr.htm file is the header for pages that display messages (with the page banner and hyperlinks), disc_foot.htm is the footer for pages that do not display messages, and disc_head.htm is the header for pages that do not display messages.

3. Double-click **disc_head.htm** in the Contents pane to open it in Page view. See Figure 7-35. To make David's suggested changes, you will need to change the hyperlinks.

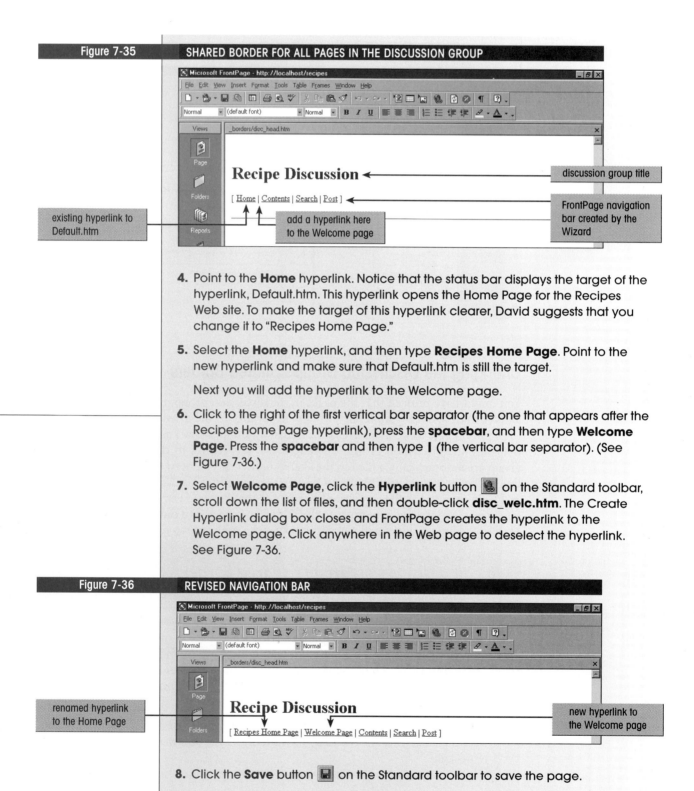

Figure 7-35   SHARED BORDER FOR ALL PAGES IN THE DISCUSSION GROUP

discussion group title

FrontPage navigation bar created by the Wizard

existing hyperlink to Default.htm

add a hyperlink here to the Welcome page

4. Point to the **Home** hyperlink. Notice that the status bar displays the target of the hyperlink, Default.htm. This hyperlink opens the Home Page for the Recipes Web site. To make the target of this hyperlink clearer, David suggests that you change it to "Recipes Home Page."

5. Select the **Home** hyperlink, and then type **Recipes Home Page**. Point to the new hyperlink and make sure that Default.htm is still the target.

   Next you will add the hyperlink to the Welcome page.

6. Click to the right of the first vertical bar separator (the one that appears after the Recipes Home Page hyperlink), press the **spacebar**, and then type **Welcome Page**. Press the **spacebar** and then type **|** (the vertical bar separator). (See Figure 7-36.)

7. Select **Welcome Page**, click the **Hyperlink** button 🔲 on the Standard toolbar, scroll down the list of files, and then double-click **disc_welc.htm**. The Create Hyperlink dialog box closes and FrontPage creates the hyperlink to the Welcome page. Click anywhere in the Web page to deselect the hyperlink. See Figure 7-36.

Figure 7-36   REVISED NAVIGATION BAR

renamed hyperlink to the Home Page

new hyperlink to the Welcome page

8. Click the **Save** button 🔲 on the Standard toolbar to save the page.

You made this change to the top shared border for the pages that do not contain messages. You can test this change in the browser.

To test the shared border in the browser:

1. Click the **Internet Explorer** program button on the taskbar, and then the **Post a new article (starting a new thread)** hyperlink in the main frame. If necessary, click the **Refresh** button on the Standard Buttons toolbar to reload the page. The page now displays the changes that you made to the navigation bar in the main frame.

2. Click the **Close** button on the Internet Explorer title bar to close it.

3. If necessary, click the **Microsoft FrontPage** program button on the taskbar to return to FrontPage.

Adding a Page Banner and Navigation Bar to the Welcome Page

David suggests that you change the discussion pages to include page banners, instead of the default page headings, and to add a FrontPage navigation bar to the Welcome page. These changes will make it easier for users to navigate the site. After making these changes, you will apply a theme to the Web site to create some visual interest.

To include a page banner and a FrontPage navigation bar in the Welcome page:

1. Press and hold down the **Ctrl** key, click the **Welcome Page** hyperlink that you created in the disc_head.htm page, and then release the **Ctrl** key. The Welcome page opens in Page view.

2. Select the **WELCOME** heading at the top of the Welcome page, click **Insert** on the menu bar, and then click **Page Banner**. Click the **OK** button to insert the page banner with the default settings.

3. Click the **Center** button on the Standard toolbar to center the page banner.

4. Press the **Enter** key to create a new centered line.

5. Click **Insert** on the menu bar, and then click **Navigation Bar**. The Navigation Bar Properties dialog box opens.

6. Click the **Same level** option button, click the **Home page** check box to select it, click the **Parent page** check box to select it, click the **Horizontal** option button, click the **Text** option button, and then click the **OK** button. A navigation bar appears below the page banner.

7. Click the **Save** button on the Standard toolbar to save the page.

Applying a Theme to the Recipes Web Site

Your Web site's navigation structure is complete, so you are ready to select a theme.

To apply a Web theme:

1. Click **Format** on the menu bar, and then click **Theme**. The Themes dialog box opens.

2. Scroll down the list of themes, and then click **Loose Gesture**.

TROUBLE? If you do not have the Loose Gesture theme installed on your computer, select another theme. If you select another theme, your Web pages will look different from the ones shown in the steps. However, the pages' contents will be the same.

3. If necessary, click the **Vivid colors**, **Active graphics**, and **Background picture** check boxes to select them, and then click the **OK** button.

4. Click the **Yes** button to apply the theme. After a few moments, the Welcome page is displayed using the new settings. See Figure 7-37.

Figure 7-37   RECIPE DISCUSSION WELCOME PAGE WITH THE LOOSE GESTURE THEME APPLIED

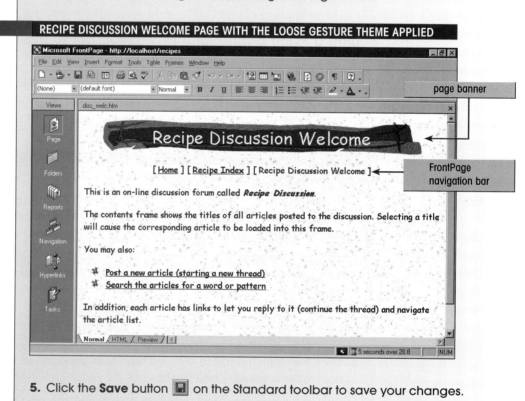

5. Click the **Save** button 🖫 on the Standard toolbar to save your changes.

Now the Web site is visually interesting and easier to use. You will finish revising the discussion pages in the Review Assignments.

David wants you to examine the HTML code for the Contents page that the Wizard created to see how messages are added to the discussion group's table of contents.

Viewing HTML Code for a Contents Page

The Discussion Web Wizard created several Web pages, a hidden folder, and hidden files, all of which maintain and run the discussion group. Many of these pages contain HTML elements with which you are familiar. For example, the discussion group contains a frames page, a page with a form component, and a page with a search component.

The Contents page is a new type of HTML document that you have not used. This page contains a FrontPage component that inserts the results of a form in the Contents page and creates a hyperlink to the form (message). In addition, the FrontPage component also names the form (message) sequentially as the server receives forms and then stores them in the _disc folder of the Web site.

David wants you to examine the HTML code for the Contents page.

To view the HTML code for the Contents Web page and then close FrontPage:

1. Click the **Folders** button 🗀 on the Views bar to change to Folders view, click the **_disc** folder in the Folder List, and then double-click **tocproto.htm** in the Contents pane. The Contents page opens in Page view.

2. Click the **HTML** tab to display the HTML code for the Contents page.

3. Scroll the page until the DL tag appears at the top of the Contents pane. See Figure 7-38. The FrontPage components that create the content of this page appear as gray text.

Figure 7-38	HTML CODE FOR THE CONTENTS PAGE

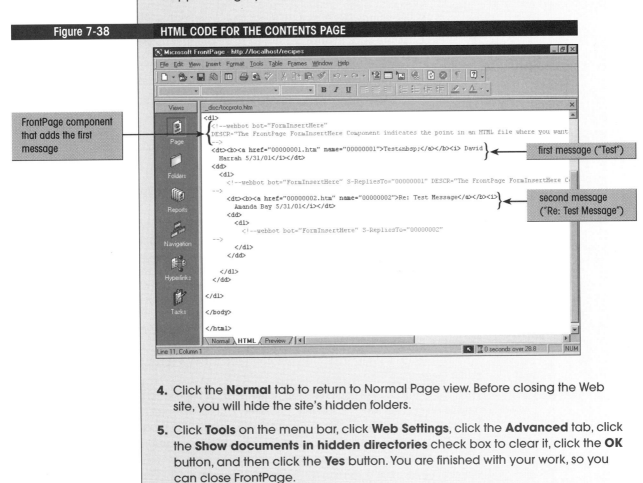

4. Click the **Normal** tab to return to Normal Page view. Before closing the Web site, you will hide the site's hidden folders.

5. Click **Tools** on the menu bar, click **Web Settings**, click the **Advanced** tab, click the **Show documents in hidden directories** check box to clear it, click the **OK** button, and then click the **Yes** button. You are finished with your work, so you can close FrontPage.

6. Click the **Close** button ☒ on the FrontPage title bar to close it.

In the next tutorial, you will create a Web page that stores information about the recipes Web site's visitors in an Access database.

Session 7.2 QUICK CHECK

1. Suppose you are creating a discussion group for benefits administrators affiliated with a statewide agency. Would you use a protected Web for the discussion group? Why or why not?

2. True or False: You must install and configure the FrontPage 2000 Server Extensions to publish a discussion group on a server.

3. The easiest way to create a discussion group in FrontPage is to use the
   _____.

4. Which page created by the Discussion Web Wizard is not optional?

5. In FrontPage, how can you identify folders that are hidden?

6. How do you display a FrontPage Web's hidden folders?

7. True or False: You can post a message to a discussion group from FrontPage.

8. What filename does FrontPage use to store the first message posted to a new discussion group?

9. What is the filename of the top shared border for a discussion group Web page that does not display a message?

REVIEW ASSIGNMENTS

David asks you to enhance the recipes Web site by making several changes. First, you will use absolute positioning to add the product shots to some of the pages that contain recipes. David just received several new pages for inclusion in the Web site, so you will import these pages from your Data Disk and then assign them to the appropriate categories. First, you will change the Wizard's default term of "article" to "message." Then you will change the Submission Form to include appropriate content for accepting information from users regarding cooking and the site's recipes. You will customize the Wizard's default confirmation page to personalize it for visitors.

If necessary, start FrontPage, insert your Data Disk in the appropriate disk drive, and then do the following:

1. Open the **recipes** Web site from your computer's PWS (http://localhost/recipes) in Folders view.

Explore

2. Open the Chiffon Cake page (**chiffon_cake.htm**) in Page view. Use absolute positioning to place the picture saved as **CCake.gif** in the Tutorial.07 folder on your Data Disk to the right of the ingredients list. (*Hint*: Insert the picture anywhere in the page, display the Positioning toolbar, click the Position Absolutely button, and then place the picture in the correct location. You might need to resize the picture to make it fit correctly. Save your changes and save the picture in the Web site's images folder. Then preview the page in the browser. If necessary, return to the Chiffon Cake page and make any adjustments. When you are finished, close the page and the Positioning toolbar.

3. Change to Folders view, and then import the following pages from the Tutorial.07 folder on your Data Disk into the Web site: **orange_pecan_bread**, **orange_cake**, and **orange_icing**. Change to Navigation view and then add the new pages to the site's navigation structure. The Orange Pecan Bread and the Orange Cake pages should be children of the Recipe Index page, and the Orange Icing page should be a child of the Orange Cake page.

4. Open each new page that you imported into the Web site in Step 3 in Page view, and adjust the position text box as necessary to place it to the right of the bulleted ingredient list. For the Orange Cake page, change the Orange Icing ingredient to a hyperlink to the Orange Icing page (**orange_icing.htm**) in the Web site. Then insert the picture saved as **orange_ck.jpg** in the Tutorial.07 folder and absolutely position the picture to the right of the ingredient list in the Orange Cake page. (*Hint*: Select the text in the position box, and then insert the picture. With the picture selected, click the Position Absolutely button on the Pictures toolbar. Resize and move the picture as necessary to place it correctly.) Save each page, and save the **orange_ck.jpg** file in the Web site's images folder. (You will not insert pictures in the Orange Icing and Orange Pecan Bread Web pages.)

5. Assign the three pages that you imported in Step 3 to the New Recipes category. Open the Recipe Index page (**site_map.htm**) in Page view, and then preview the page in the browser. If necessary, refresh the page to display the new version. Make sure that the categories component correctly added the three new recipes under the New Recipes heading.

 6. Return to FrontPage and use the Replace command to search all pages in the Web site to find all occurrences of the word "article" and replace them with the word "message." (*Hint*: Do not select the Match case check box. Some pages might have more than one occurrence of the word "article"; use the Replace dialog box to determine how many occurrences to replace in each page. Click the Replace button to replace each occurrence individually.)

7. Open the Submission Form Web page (**disc_post.htm**) in Page view. Change the "POST MESSAGE" heading to the Heading 1 style. Delete the comment component that appears in the form.

Explore ▸ 8. Make the following changes to the form component in the Submission Form Web page:
   a. Change the label for the Subject one-line text box to "Message Subject:". (Do not change the name of the one-line text box form field.) Then change the width of the Subject one-line text box form field to 65 characters.
   b. Change the label for the From one-line text box to "From (please enter your first and last names):". (Do not change the name of the one-line text box form field.) Change the width of the From one-line text box form field to 65 characters and validate this form field so that it must contain a text entry.
   c. Enter the following label to the left of the drop-down menu form field: "Select a category for your comments:" and then change this label to bold text. Press the spacebar twice to insert two spaces. Then change the properties of the drop-down menu form field to include the following choices: Recipe Enhancement, Recipe Correction, Recipe Comments, General Cooking, and Other. The value for each choice should be the same as its choice name with any spaces omitted. The Recipe Enhancement choice should be the default selection. The drop-down menu form field should have a height of one and should not allow multiple selections.
   d. Change the width of the Comments scrolling text box to 65 characters.
   e. Change the default value/label of the form's Submit button to "Post Message."
   f. Save your changes to the Submission Form Web page, and then preview the page using the browser. (*Hint*: You might need to refresh the page in the browser to see your changes.) Use Internet Explorer to print the form's HTML code, and then close the browser. On the printout, circle the HTML code that implemented the changes you made in Step 8.

Explore ▸ 9. Return to FrontPage and examine the form properties for the form in the Submission Form Web page. What is the name of the form handler that processes this form? Click the Cancel button to close the dialog box without making any changes.

10. Open the Confirmation Web page (**disc_cfrm.htm**) in Page view. Change the "CONFIRMATION" heading to the Heading 1 style. Press the End key to reposition the insertion point, and then press the Enter key to insert a new line. On the new line, type "Dear", press the spacebar, and then insert a confirmation field that uses the name entered in the From form field in the Submission Form. (*Hint*: Insert a confirmation field component using the Insert Component button on the Standard toolbar.

The confirmation field's name is From.) Type a comma after the confirmation field component. Save the Confirmation Web page.

11. Open the Search Form Web page (**disc_srch.htm**) in Page view. Change the "SEARCH FOR MESSAGE" heading to the Heading 1 style. Change the width of the Search for text box to 65 characters. Save the Search Form page.

12. Change the user-defined navigation bar in the Home Page (**Default.htm**) to a FrontPage navigation bar with horizontal text hyperlinks to child pages. Save the Home Page. Preview the Home Page in the browser. Make sure that all pages are working correctly. Use the browser to print the Submission Form Web page.

13. Close Internet Explorer and FrontPage.

CASE PROBLEMS

Case 1. Creating a Discussion Group for Royal Hair Care Products   Royal Hair Care Products, established in 1984, is a leader in hair care products for women, men, and children. Its current product line includes shampoos, conditioners, hair sprays, and styling gels. The company's newest product is Quick Dry Solution, which when applied to wet hair, dries it quickly without the need for a hair dryer. Quick Dry Solution is available in either a gel form or a liquid spray. The easy-to-use product leaves hair feeling natural and manageable.

Valerie Suarez, president of Royal Hair Care Products, and Nathan Dubois, an information systems specialist, are responsible for creating and maintaining the Web site for Royal Hair Care Products. The current Web site includes the following main pages: a Home Page; an About Us page with distribution, promotion, packaging, and legal information; a Financial Information page with information about the company's financial performance and stock; a What's New page with information about Quick Dry Solution; a Feedback page that contains a form for commenting about Royal Hair Care Products; and a Search page that lets users search the Web site using a keyword or phrase.

Valerie wants to expand the Web site to include a discussion group where consumers can comment about Royal Hair Care products and industry trends. As a progressive company, Royal Hair Care Products is always looking for new product ideas that save people time and money and keep them looking their best.

If necessary, start FrontPage, insert your Data Disk in the appropriate disk drive, and then do the following:

1. Read all the questions for this case problem, and then prepare a planning analysis sheet for the enhancements to the royal Web site.

2. Open the **royal** Web site from your computer's PWS. The default location is http://localhost/royal. Your instructor will advise you of any differences you will encounter in the lab.

3. Use the Discussion Web Wizard to add a discussion group to the royal Web site. The discussion group should have the following features:

   a. Include all of the main features (Submission Form, Table of Contents, Search Form, Threaded Replies, and a Confirmation Page).
   b. The title of the discussion group is Royal Discussion. The discussion folder name is _disc2.
   c. Choose the Subject, Product, and Comments input fields for the Submission Form.
   d. The discussion group is not protected.
   e. Sort the messages in order from newest to oldest.
   f. Do not replace the existing Home Page in the royal Web site.

g. The Search Form should report only the Subject for matching documents.

h. Use a dual interface frames page.

4. Open the Submission Form Web page (**disc2_post.htm**) in Page view. Change the form component as follows:

a. Enter the following label to the left of the drop-down menu form field: "Select a category for your comments:" and then change this label to bold text. Press the spacebar twice to insert two spaces. Then change the properties of the drop-down menu form field to include the following choices: Suggestion, Feedback, Quick Dry Solution, Shampoo, Conditioner, Hair Spray, and Styling Gel. The default selected entry should be Suggestion. The value for each choice should be the same as its choice name with any spaces omitted. The drop-down menu form field should have a height of one and should not allow multiple selections.

b. Delete the comment component from the form component.

c. Change the width of the scrolling text box to 75 characters.

d. Validate the From text box so that it must contain a text value.

e. Save the page.

5. Add the Royal Discussion Welcome page (**disc2_welc.htm**) for the discussion group to the navigation structure as a child page of the Home Page. Position the Royal Discussion Welcome page to the right of the Search page.

6. Open the Royal Discussion Welcome page in Page view, and then change the existing "WELCOME" heading to a centered page banner. Insert a new, centered line below the page banner, and then enter a FrontPage navigation bar with links to back and next pages and the Home Page. The links should have a horizontal orientation and a button appearance.

7. Place the insertion point at the end of the first line of text in the Royal Discussion Welcome page ("This is an on-line discussion forum called Royal Discussion."). Press the spacebar, and then insert the following text: "We encourage you to use this discussion group to comment on Royal Hair Care Products, to offer your suggestions, and to ask questions about product usage. Other users can reply to your comments to share their experiences. Please use the Search option to find topics of interest." Save the page.

Explore

8. Modify the header for all pages in the discussion group to change the existing heading to "Royal Hair Care Products" and to add a hyperlink to the Royal Discussion Welcome page. Change the existing Home hyperlink to "Royal Home Page." (*Hint*: To access the header files for the discussion Web pages, display the Web site's hidden folders. You will need to make this change in both header files for the discussion group pages.) Save your changes.

9. Open the Home Page (**Default.htm**) in Internet Explorer. Use the navigation bar to open the Royal Discussion Welcome page, and then print it.

10. Use a hyperlink in the Royal Discussion Welcome page to post a new article using data that you make up. Before posting the article, print the Submission Form Web page. Click the link in the Confirmation page to refresh the main page.

11. Post a new message to the discussion group (do not reply to the message that you posted in Step 10). Refresh the main page, and then print only the Contents page. Close Internet Explorer.

12. Return to FrontPage. Print the HTML code for the Submission Form page. On the printout, circle the code for the changes that you made to this page.

13. Close FrontPage.

Case 2. Creating an Online Forum for Buffalo Trading Post   Buffalo Trading Post (BTP) is a regional retail clothing business that specializes in buying, selling, and trading used clothing. The company buys all of its merchandise from people who take items to one of BTP's trading post stores. BTP accepts only good-condition clothing for resale and attracts a loyal following of fashion enthusiasts and bargain hunters.

Donna Vargas, BTP's president, and Karla Perez, a systems analyst, are the primary developers of the BTP Web site. The current Web site includes the following main pages: a Home Page; a "What" page that lists the top 10 selling items in different categories; a "How" page that describes how BTP buys and sells merchandise; a "Who" page that describes the history of BTP; a "Where" page that provides a toll-free number for locating a BTP store; and a "Contact" page that includes a form component for submitting comments and feedback to BTP.

Donna and Karla met with a group of sales representatives from different stores and learned that many clothing genres have a distinct customer following. In response to these followings, Donna proposed creating an online forum in the BTP Web site that would permit customers to interact with each other. In addition to providing a service to customers, BTP would benefit from the free nature of the comments and could use this information to spot emerging fashion trends.

If necessary, start FrontPage, insert your Data Disk in the appropriate disk drive, and then do the following:

1. Read all the questions for this case problem, and then prepare a planning analysis sheet for the enhancements to the buffalo Web site.

2. Open the **buffalo** Web site from your computer's PWS. The default location is http://localhost/buffalo. Your instructor will advise you of any differences you will encounter in the lab.

3. Use the Discussion Web Wizard to add a discussion group to the buffalo Web site. The discussion group should have the following features:

   a. Include all of the main features (Submission Form, Table of Contents, Search Form, Threaded Replies, and a Confirmation Page).
   b. The title of the discussion group is Fashion Trends. The discussion folder name is _disc3.
   c. Choose the Subject, Category, and Comments input fields for the Submission Form.
   d. The discussion group is not protected.
   e. Sort the messages in order from newest to oldest.
   f. Do not replace the existing Home Page in the buffalo Web site.
   g. The Search Form should report only the Subject for matching documents.
   h. Use a dual interface frames page.

Explore

4. Open the Submission Form Web page (**disc3_post.htm**) in Page view. Change the form component as follows:

   a. Enter the following label to the left of the drop-down menu form field: "Select a category for your comments:" and then change this label to bold text. Press the spacebar twice to insert two spaces. Then change the properties of the drop-down menu form field to include the following choices: The Sixties, The Seventies, The Eighties, The Nineties, and Wanted Items. The default selected entry should be The Sixties. The value for each choice should be the same as its choice name with any spaces omitted. The drop-down menu form field should have a height of one and should not allow multiple selections.
   b. Delete the comment component.
   c. Change the width of the scrolling text box to 70 characters and five lines.
   d. Validate the From text box so that it must contain a text value.
   e. Change the properties of the Discussion Form handler so that it collects the date and time that the message was posted and the user name that posted the form. (*Hint*: Right-click the form component to open the shortcut menu, click Form Properties, and then click the Options button.)
   f. Save the page.

5. Add the Fashion Trends Welcome page (**disc3_welc.htm**) for the discussion group to the navigation structure as a child page of the Home Page. Position the Fashion Trends Welcome page to the right of the Contact page.

6. Open the Fashion Trends Welcome page in Page view, and then change the existing "WELCOME" heading to a centered page banner. Insert a new, centered line below the page banner, and then insert a FrontPage navigation bar with links to same-level pages and the Home Page. The links should have a horizontal orientation and a button appearance. Return to Navigation view and then change the page title for the Fashion Trends Welcome page to "Fashion Forum." Then change to Folders view and, if necessary, change the title of the **disc3_welc.htm** page to "Fashion Forum."

7. Rewrite the default content in the Fashion Forum page that the Wizard created to make it more closely match Donna's vision of how visitors might use this page. Do not change the default hyperlinks. Save the page.

8. Open the Fashion Forum Web page (**disc3_welc.htm**) in Internet Explorer, and then print the page.

9. Post a new article to the discussion group using data that you make up. Before posting the article, print the page. Click the link in the Confirmation page to refresh the main page.

Explore   10. Reply to the message that you posted in Step 9. Return to FrontPage and open the Contents page (**tocproto.htm**) in Page view and print its HTML code. (*Hint*: To access the Contents page, display the Web site's hidden folders.) On the printout, circle the HTML code that inserted the message you posted in Step 9.

11. Close FrontPage and Internet Explorer.

Case 3. Creating a Site Map for Garden Grill   Garden Grill is a national chain of casual, full-service restaurants. Its moderately priced menu features delicious dishes taken from various locations around the world. Shannon Taylor and Nolan Simmons manage the company's Web site. The current Web site includes the following main pages: a Home Page, a Menu page with sample menu items, a Specials page with today's special entree, a Franchise Information page with a toll-free number to call for information about opening a new restaurant, a Company Profile page with information about the restaurant, a Career Opportunities page with information about current employment opportunities, a Feedback page for customers to use to comment on the restaurant, and a Search page that customers can use to search the site.

Nolan wants to add several new pages to the Web site featuring new entrees at the restaurant. After adding these pages, Nolan wants to create a site map to make it easier for the Web site's visitors to locate new pages. Finally, Nolan wants to include pictures of the new entrees with their descriptions.

If necessary, start FrontPage, insert your Data Disk in the appropriate disk drive, and then do the following:

1. Read all the questions for this case problem, and then prepare a planning analysis sheet for the enhancements to the garden Web site.

2. Open the **garden** Web site from your computer's PWS in Folders view. The default location is http://localhost/garden. Your instructor will advise you of any differences you will encounter in the lab.

3. Import the files **GAngel.htm**, **GPasta.htm**, **GPudding.htm**, and **GPecan.htm** from the Tutorial.07 folder on your Data Disk into the garden Web site.

Explore   4. Create the following categories in the Web site: Appetizers, Desserts, Entrees, Specials, Sandwiches, and New Menu Items. Then delete all other default categories from the Web site. (*Hint*: Click the Yes button when asked to remove a category.)

5. Examine each page in the Web site and assign it to an appropriate category. Categorize the pages that you imported in Step 3 as new menu items. (*Note*: Some pages in the Web site will not fit into these categories. In these cases, do not assign the page to a category. Do not assign the frames page to a category.)

6. Run a report to check the pages in the Web site to make sure that you assigned the correct pages to the correct category.

Explore

7. Add each page that you imported in Step 3 (**gpecan.htm**, **gangel.htm**, **gpuddng.htm**, and **gpasta.htm**) to the Web site's navigation structure as child pages of the Menu page. Then use absolute positioning to center each photo below the text in the Web page. Use the photos **GPiePic**, **GAnglPic**, **GPuddPic**, and **GPastPic** in the Pecan Pie, Angel Food Cake, Banana Pudding, and Pasta Salad Web pages, respectively. These picture files are saved in the Tutorial.07 folder on your Data Disk. After positioning each picture, save the picture in the Web site's images folder.

8. In Page view, add a new Normal page to the Web site with the filename **site_map.htm** and the title "Menu Options." After saving the page, add it to the Web site's navigation structure as a child page of the Home Page. Position the page to the left of the Menu page in the navigation structure.

9. Create the content of the Menu Options page using the categories that you created in Step 4. Use any design that you like; however, the new menu items must appear at the top of the page. Use the appropriate FrontPage component to insert the pages into the proper categories. When you are finished, save the page, preview it in the browser, and then print it. Use a hyperlink in the Menu Options page to open the Pasta Salad Web page in the browser. Print the HTML code for the page. On the printout, circle the HTML code that identifies this page's category and the code that absolutely positions the picture in this page.

10. Close FrontPage and Internet Explorer.

Case 4. *Creating a Discussion Group for Replay Music Factory*   Replay Music Factory (RMF) is a regional music store that specializes in buying, selling, and trading used compact discs (CDs). RMF buys used CDs from three sources: the Internet, customers, and brokers. This strategy allows RMF to offer a wide variety of music to the most discriminating listener. The company's quality control division has identified a defect rate of less than 1%, so all of its products are 100% guaranteed.

Charlene Fields, the company's president, and Alec Johnston, a systems analyst, are in charge of the content and development of RMF's Web site. The current Web site includes the following main pages: a Home Page; a Specials page with special deals for CDs in the categories country & western, classic rock, and contemporary music; a frequently asked questions page; a page explaining how RMF conducts business; a feedback page with a form for submitting comments to RMF; and a search page that lets users search the site using key terms.

Charlene wants to expand the current Web site by creating a discussion group that will enable RMF to monitor current trends in the music industry.

If necessary, start FrontPage, insert your Data Disk in the appropriate disk drive, and then do the following:

1. Read all the questions for this case problem, and then prepare a planning analysis sheet for the enhancements to the replay Web site.

2. Open the **replay** Web site from your computer's PWS. The default location is http://localhost/replay. Your instructor will advise you of any differences you will encounter in the lab.

3. Use the Discussion Web Wizard to add a discussion group to the replay Web site. The discussion group should have the following features:
    a. Include all of the main features except for Threaded Replies.
    b. The title of the discussion group is Music Trends. The discussion folder name is _disc4.
    c. Choose the Subject, Category, and Comments input fields for the Submission Form.
    d. The discussion group is not protected.

    e. Sort the messages in order from newest to oldest.

    f. Do not replace the existing Home Page in the replay Web site.

    g. The Search Form should report only the Subject for matching documents.

    h. Use a dual interface frames page.

Explore

4. Open the Submission Form Web page (**disc4_post.htm**) in Page view. Change the form component as follows:

    a. Enter the following label to the left of the drop-down menu form field: "Select a category:" and then change this label to bold text. Press the spacebar twice to insert two spaces. Then change the properties of the drop-down menu form field to include the following choices: Purchase, Trade, Sell, and Other. The default selected entry should be Sell. The value for each choice should be the same as its choice name. The drop-down menu form field should have a height of one and should not allow multiple selections.

    b. Delete the comment component.

    c. Change the width of the scrolling text box to 75 characters and four lines.

    d. Validate the From text box so that it must contain a text value.

    e. Change the properties of the Discussion Form handler so that it collects the date and time that the message was posted and the user name that posted the form. (*Hint*: Right-click the form component to open the shortcut menu, click Form Properties, and then click the Options button.)

    f. Save the page.

5. Add the Music Trends Welcome Web page (**disc4_welc.htm**) to the navigation structure as a child page of the Home Page. Position the Welcome page to the right of the Search page. Then open the Music Trends Welcome Web page in Page view and add a centered page banner and a centered FrontPage navigation bar at the top of the page. The navigation bar should include horizontal button links to same-level pages and to the Home Page.

6. Rename the Music Trends Welcome Web page (**disc4_welc.htm**) to "Music Trends" in Folders view and in Navigation view.

7. Rewrite the default content in the Music Trends Web page that the Wizard created to make the text more closely match how visitors might use this page. Do not change the default hyperlinks. Save the page.

8. For each page created by the Discussion Web Wizard, change the page's title (which appears in all uppercase letters) to centered with the Heading 1 style. Save each page.

9. Open the Music Trends Web page in Internet Explorer, and then print the page.

10. Post a new article to the discussion group using data that you make up. Before posting the article, print the page. Click the link in the Confirmation page to refresh the main page.

Explore

11. Why can't you reply to the article that you posted in Step 10?

12. Close FrontPage and Internet Explorer.

Quick | Check answers

Session 7.1

1. False
2. True
3. site map
4. FrontPage uses the categories to insert hyperlinks to appropriate pages in the correct location in the Web page that contains the FrontPage categories component (the site map).
5. If you are the only user of the site, then you do not need to enable source control for the site because no other user will be working on pages.
6. padlock
7. Close and save the page, right-click the filename in the Contents pane of Folders view, and then click Check In on the shortcut menu.
8. absolute positioning

Session 7.2

1. Answers will vary. However, you probably would want to secure the site to keep the discussion focused on topics that apply to benefits administrators.
2. True
3. Discussion Web Wizard
4. Submission Form
5. The names of hidden folders begin with an underscore character.
6. Click Tools on the menu bar, click Web Settings, click the Advanced tab, click the Show documents in hidden directories check box to select it, click the OK button, and then click the Yes button.
7. False
8. 00000001.htm
9. disc_head.htm

OBJECTIVES

In this tutorial you will:

■ Start Access and open and examine a database

■ Import an Access database into a FrontPage Web

■ Verify a database connection and set a Web site to run scripts

■ Insert a Database Results region in a Web page

■ Use a Web page to query a database

■ Create a form that sends data to an Access database

■ Create and use a data access page

LABS

Databases

INTEGRATING A DATABASE WITH A FRONTPAGE WEB

Using Web Pages to View and Store Data in an Access Database

CASE

Sunny Morning Products

David Harrah is pleased with your progress in developing the recipes Web site. The process of adding new recipes to the site should be an easy one because FrontPage will automatically update the navigation bars in every page. New pages will use the same theme and be consistent because of the shared template that you created.

David's next expansion of the Web site is to compile an electronic guest book, which is similar to a guest book that you might find at a wedding reception or an open house. David wants to collect information from people who use the recipes Web site so that he can create an electronic mailing list for people who want to receive promotional materials and notice of new recipes. David realizes that direct marketing using e-mail addresses is much less expensive than using printed materials. In addition, David believes that the e-mail mailing list will be directed to a much more specific target audience, because the recipients have already used the Web site and expressed an interest in receiving additional materials.

To collect the information that David needs, you will need to use a Web page to collect the user's information. Instead of storing this information in a text file in the _private folder of the Web site, you will store this information in an Access database in the Web site. Data stored in a database is easily sorted, retrieved, and printed. The marketing department will use this data for many purposes, including the e-mail mailing list. To make it easier to view the data from the database, you will also create a Web page that displays database data and lets the user update, add, delete, and sort records.

SESSION 8.1

In this session, you will learn about databases. You will start Access and open and examine a database. You will import a database into a Web site and use it in a Web page. Finally, you will use a Web page to query a database.

Understanding Databases

Databases

A **database**, or a **relational database**, is a collection of related **tables** that store data about an object. Each table is made up of fields. A **field** is a single characteristic about an object. For example, at Sunny Morning Products, a database maintains data about each salable item at the Sunshine Country Store. The Product table contains the fields ProductID, Name, Description, and Size. The Price table contains the fields ProductID, Cost, and RetailPrice. The information in these tables stores each salable item's product description, characteristics, cost, and selling price.

The tables in a single database can be linked together—or *related*—using a common field. A **common field** is a field that appears in two tables in the database. For example, the Product and Price tables are linked together using a common field that identifies each item's product number. Figure 8-1 shows the Product and Price tables and how they are related.

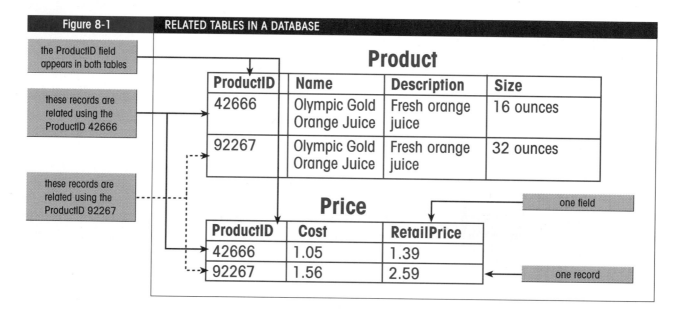

Figure 8-1	RELATED TABLES IN A DATABASE

the ProductID field appears in both tables

these records are related using the ProductID 42666

these records are related using the ProductID 92267

Product

ProductID	Name	Description	Size
42666	Olympic Gold Orange Juice	Fresh orange juice	16 ounces
92267	Olympic Gold Orange Juice	Fresh orange juice	32 ounces

Price

one field

ProductID	Cost	RetailPrice
42666	1.05	1.39
92267	1.56	2.59

one record

Microsoft Access 2000, or simply **Access**, is a relational database that you can use to store data. By creating a connection between a FrontPage Web and an Access database, you can display and query the data from the database in a Web page. A **database connection** specifies the name, location, and type of database that you want to access. There are four kinds of database connections that you can make using a FrontPage Web and an Access database:

- A **file-based connection** is made when you import an Access database into a FrontPage Web. FrontPage creates the database connection automatically when you import a database into it.

- A **System DSN** (or **System Data Source Name**) connection is made when you connect a database that is stored on a Web server to a FrontPage Web.

■ A **network connection** is made to a database server, which is a server that is dedicated to managing a database. Microsoft SQL Server is one example of a database server. (Database servers are beyond the scope of this tutorial.)

■ A **custom connection** is one in which you use a file that contains the commands to define the necessary connection information between the database and the FrontPage Web. (Creating a custom connection is beyond the scope of this tutorial.)

David created the Recipes database from data collected using the Feedback Web page in the Sunny Web site. This Web page collected each customer's first and last names, e-mail address, and comments about Sunny Morning Products. David's staff was assigned the task of inputting information collected in the feedback.txt file in the _private folder of the Sunny Web site into the Access database. The information could not be easily imported directly from the feedback.txt file because it was not stored in the correct format. For example, David's database stores the customer's name in two fields—FirstName and LastName— whereas the feedback form stored the customer's name in one field, with the names separated by a space. David's table design for the Customers table appears in Figure 8-2.

Figure 8-2	CUSTOMERS TABLE DESIGN IN THE RECIPES DATABASE		
FIELD NAME	**DATA TYPE**	**FIELD SIZE**	**DESCRIPTION**
CustomerID	AutoNumber	Long Integer	An AutoNumber field that is created by Access adds the CustomerID. CustomerIDs are assigned sequentially as new records are added to the table.
FirstName	Text	30	The customer's first name.
LastName	Text	50	The customer's last name.
EmailAddress	Text	30	The customer's e-mail address.
PhoneNum	Text	30	The customer's telephone number, which is entered in the format ##########; an input mask formats and stores the value in the format (###) ###-#### in the database.
Category	Text	50	A lookup field that selects the following values from the Category table: Web Site, Company, or Products.
Subject	Text	50	A lookup field that selects the following values from the Subject table: Suggestion, Praise, or Problem.

David's planning analysis sheet for the incorporation of a database into the recipes Web site appears in Figure 8-3.

Figure 8-3	DAVID'S PLANNING ANALYSIS SHEET FOR INCORPORATING A DATABASE

Planning Analysis Sheet

Objective

Create two database connections and new Web pages with the following capabilities: display records from the Customer Query in the Recipes database, filter the records in the Customer Query in the Recipes database using information supplied by the user, accept data entered in a form from a Web page and store it in the Guest database, and display records from the Results table in the Guest database.

Requirements

Access file for the Recipes database

Access file for the Guest database

Web page that contains the form

Results

A Web page that connects to a database and allows the marketing department to see who is using the Sunny Web site.

A separate Web page stored in the recipes Web site into which users can enter their names, e-mail addresses, phone numbers, and areas of interest. The marketing department will use this information to target advertising to the appropriate individuals and to plan future enhancements to the Web site.

A new database that contains data about people who use the recipes Web site. The form will collect the user's name, address, city, state, Zip code, phone number, and e-mail address and store it in a database.

A data access page that displays records from the Guest database and that permits authorized users to view, add, delete, sort, filter, and update records using a Web page.

Starting Access and Opening an Existing Database

David wants you to open the Recipes database to make sure that you are familiar with its contents and organization.

REFERENCE WINDOW   **RW**

Starting Access and Opening an Existing Database

- Click the Start button on the taskbar, point to Programs, and then click Microsoft Access.
- Click the Open an existing file option button, click the More Files option in the list box, and then click the OK button.
- In the Open dialog box, click the Look in list arrow, click the drive or folder that contains the database, and then double-click the database to open it.

The Recipes database is saved in the Tutorial.08 folder on your Data Disk.

To start Access and open the Recipes database:

1. Click the **Start** button on the taskbar, point to **Programs**, and then click **Microsoft Access**. The Access 2000 startup screen opens for a moment, and then the Microsoft Access dialog box opens.

2. If necessary, click the **Open an existing file** option button and click the **More Files** option in the list box, and then click the **OK** button. The Open dialog box opens.

3. Click the **Look in** list arrow, change to the folder or drive that contains your Data Disk, double-click the **Tutorial.08** folder, and then double-click **Recipes**. The Recipes database opens in the Access program window.

4. If necessary, click the **Maximize** button ☐ on the Database window to maximize it. See Figure 8-4.

| Figure 8-4 | DATABASE WINDOW FOR THE RECIPES DATABASE |

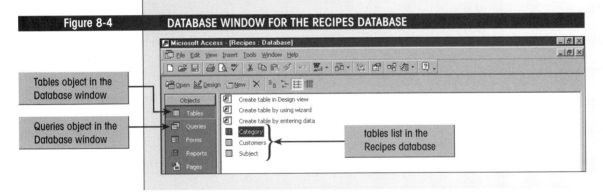

Tables object in the Database window

Queries object in the Database window

tables list in the Recipes database

The Recipes database contains three tables named Category, Customers, and Subject, and one query named Customer Query. A **query** is a database object that displays data to answer a question. For example, you might ask a question such as "Which records in the Customers table have the value 'Praise' in the Subject field?" When you run this query, Access will select the records and fields that answer your question.

The Category and Subject tables contain values that Access uses to look up the values in the Category and Subject fields in the Customers table. You will examine the Customers table and the Customer Query objects next.

To open the table and query:

1. If necessary, click the **Tables** object in the Database window to display the tables list.

2. Double-click **Customers** in the tables list. The Customers table opens in Table Datasheet view. See Figure 8-5. The Customers table contains 20 records. The AutoNumber field provides a value that uniquely identifies each table record. In the Customers table, each record must contain a unique value in the CustomerID field to ensure that no two records have duplicate CustomerID values. The field that uniquely identifies each table record is called its **primary key**.

Figure 8-5	CUSTOMERS TABLE IN TABLE DATASHEET VIEW

3. Click the **Close** button ☒ for the Table window to close it. The Database window for the Recipes database reappears.

4. Click the **Queries** object in the Database window to display the queries list, and then double-click **Customer Query** in the queries list to open the query in the Query window. Notice that the query displays all records in the Customers table in ascending order by LastName. The CustomerID values do not appear in the query results because the CustomerID field is not included in the query design. See Figure 8-6.

Figure 8-6	CUSTOMER QUERY IN THE QUERY WINDOW

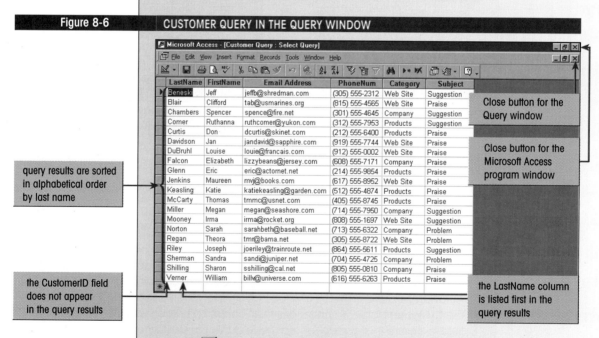

5. Click ☒ on the Query window title bar to close the Query window.

6. Click ☒ on the Access program window to close the Recipes database and Access.

Now that you have examined the Access database, you are ready to import it into the recipes Web site.

Importing an Access Database into a FrontPage Web

You can import an existing database into a FrontPage Web by copying the database file in Windows Explorer and then pasting it into the open FrontPage Web. This is the easiest way to integrate an existing database into a Web site because FrontPage creates the database connection for you.

When you paste a database into the FrontPage Web, the Add Database Connection dialog box opens and requests a name for the new database. After you provide a connection name and click the Yes button to continue, a Microsoft FrontPage dialog box opens and asks where to store your database files. When you import a database, FrontPage creates a folder named **fpdb** (for FrontPage database) and automatically configures this folder so that it is inaccessible to people browsing your published Web site. FrontPage recommends that you save your database files in this folder, which is also the recommended method in this book, so you will click the Yes button. The Importing Files dialog box closes when the database has been successfully imported into your FrontPage Web and is stored in the fpdb folder.

REFERENCE WINDOW   **RW**

Importing an Access Database into a FrontPage Web
- Click the Start button on the taskbar, point to Programs, and then click Windows Explorer.
- Locate the database that you want to import into the FrontPage Web, right-click it to open the shortcut menu, and then click Copy. Close Windows Explorer.
- Start FrontPage and open the Web site in Folders view.
- Right-click the Folder List to open the shortcut menu, and then click Paste.

David asks you to import the Recipes database into the recipes Web site. First you will copy the Recipes database, and then you will start FrontPage, open the recipes Web site, and paste the database into it.

To import an existing database into a FrontPage Web:

1. Click the **Start** button on the taskbar, point to **Programs**, and then click **Windows Explorer**. Windows Explorer opens and displays the files and folders on your computer.

2. If necessary, click the **3½ Floppy (A:)** drive in the Folders list to display the contents of your Data Disk.

   TROUBLE? If you are storing your Data Files in another location, click that location to display the contents of your Data Disk. This tutorial assumes that you are storing your Data Files on drive A.

3. Open the **Tutorial.08** folder to display its contents.

4. Right-click **Recipes** (or **Recipes.mdb** if Windows is configured to show filename extensions) to open its shortcut menu, and then click **Copy**. A copy of the Recipes database is stored on the Windows Clipboard. You will close Windows Explorer before starting FrontPage.

5. Click the **Close** button ⊠ on the Windows Explorer title bar to close it.

6. Start **FrontPage** and open the **recipes** Web site from your computer's PWS. If necessary, change to Folders view.

7. Right-click any empty area in the **Folder List** to open the shortcut menu, and then click **Paste**. The Importing Files dialog box opens, and then the Add Database Connection dialog box opens on top of it. See Figure 8-7. You use the Add Database Connection dialog box to provide a name for the database connection. The URL of the database is its Windows filename. You can use the same connection name and URL for a database.

Figure 8-7   **ADD DATABASE CONNECTION DIALOG BOX**

8. Type **Recipes** in the Name text box, and then click the **Yes** button. The Importing Files dialog box appears again and the status bar indicates that FrontPage is creating the fpdb folder in which to store the database files. After a few seconds, a dialog box opens and asks if you want to store your database files in the fpdb folder.

   TROUBLE? If a Microsoft FrontPage dialog box opens and tells you that the database name must be unique, then a database connection named Recipes already exists in your FrontPage Web. Click the OK button to continue, and then change the database connection name to Recipes1. Click the Yes button to continue.

9. Click the **Yes** button. After a few seconds, the Importing Files dialog box closes. Folders view now shows the fpdb folder that was created. Notice that a new page named global.asa appears in the Contents pane. This file stores the VBScript that connects the Web site to the Recipes database. A **VBScript** is a program written in the Visual Basic programming language that contains programming instructions for a Web page. The VBScript is embedded into the HTML document in which it resides so that Web browsers can read and execute its commands.

   TROUBLE? If you do not see the fpdb folder in the Folder List, click Tools on the menu bar, click Web Settings, click the Advanced tab, click the Show documents in hidden directories check box to select it, click the OK button, and then click the Yes button.

10. Click the **fpdb** folder in the Folder List to display its contents. The Access file for the Recipes database is stored in this folder.

11. Click the folder for the recipes Web site (the default folder is **http://localhost/recipes**) in the Folder List to display its contents.

Verifying a Database Connection

After importing the database, you can verify the database connection by using the Web Settings dialog box.

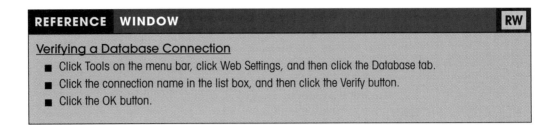

REFERENCE WINDOW   **RW**

Verifying a Database Connection
- Click Tools on the menu bar, click Web Settings, and then click the Database tab.
- Click the connection name in the list box, and then click the Verify button.
- Click the OK button.

To verify the database connection:

1. Click **Tools** on the menu bar, click **Web Settings**, and then click the **Database** tab. The Recipes database has a question mark in the Status column, indicating that the database connection has not been verified yet.

2. Click the **Recipes** connection, and then click the **Verify** button. The question mark in the Status column changes to a green check mark, indicating a valid connection. See Figure 8-8.

Figure 8-8   WEB SETTINGS DIALOG BOX

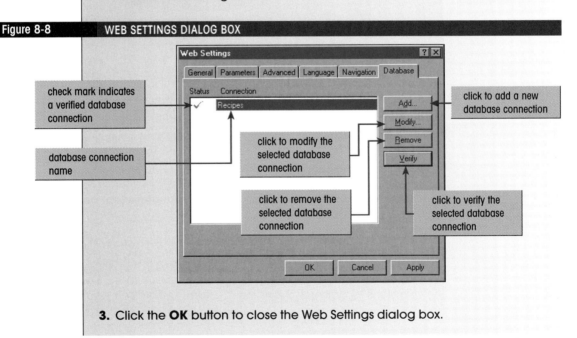

check mark indicates a verified database connection

database connection name

click to modify the selected database connection

click to remove the selected database connection

click to add a new database connection

click to verify the selected database connection

3. Click the **OK** button to close the Web Settings dialog box.

The Recipes database now exists on your computer's PWS as part of the recipes Web site, and it also exists as a separate file in the Tutorial.08 folder on your Data Disk. These two files have the same name, but they are not linked in any way. For example, if you open the Recipes database from the Tutorial.08 folder on your Data Disk and make changes to it, the Recipes database that is stored in your FrontPage Web will not reflect these changes. After you import a database into a FrontPage Web, it is important that you make changes only to the database that is stored in the fpdb folder in the Web site. To start Access and open the database stored in the Web site, just double-click the database filename in the fpdb folder.

Now that you have imported the Recipes database into your FrontPage Web and verified its connection, you can create a new Web page and use the Database Results Wizard to display the Customer Query from the database in the Web page.

Setting the Web Site to Run Scripts

Before you can insert a Database Results region in a Web page, you need to make sure that the Web site is enabled to use Active Server Pages (ASP). An **Active Server Page** is a Web page with an .asp filename extension that includes client-side and server-side scripts, which process the page. Because these scripts allow programs to run on the server, you must also configure your Web site's folder to run scripts. A folder on a Web server that permits the execution of scripts is called an **executable folder**.

You will change the Web site's settings before inserting the Database Results region. Normally, only the Web site's administrator can change a Web site's settings. If you are working on a server other than a Microsoft Personal Web Server, your instructor will provide you with alternate instructions.

To change the Web site's settings to run scripts:

1. Click **Tools** on the menu bar, and then click **Page Options**. The Page Options dialog box opens.

2. If necessary, click the **Compatibility** tab to display those settings.

3. If necessary, click any empty check boxes in the Technologies section to select them. Every check box should contain a check mark. Notice that the Browser versions list box now shows the "Custom" setting. See Figure 8-9.

Figure 8-9   **ENABLING SCRIPTS FOR THE RECIPES WEB SITE**

browser version is set to "Custom" when you enable ActiveX controls

enables the Web site to use FrontPage Server Extensions

select all options in this section

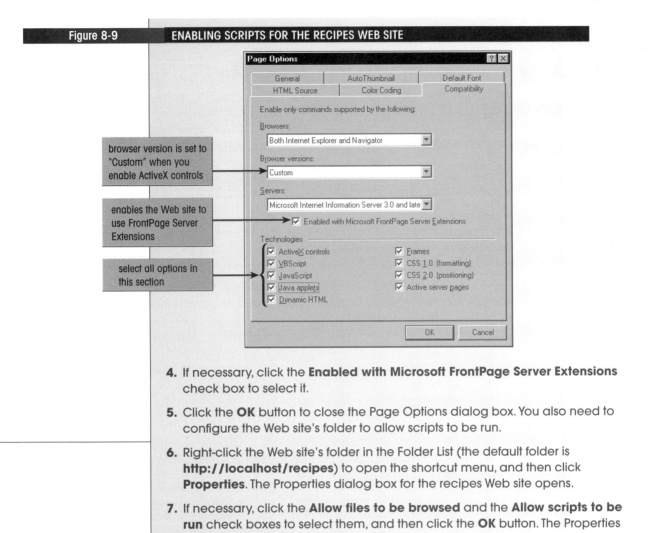

4. If necessary, click the **Enabled with Microsoft FrontPage Server Extensions** check box to select it.

5. Click the **OK** button to close the Page Options dialog box. You also need to configure the Web site's folder to allow scripts to be run.

6. Right-click the Web site's folder in the Folder List (the default folder is **http://localhost/recipes**) to open the shortcut menu, and then click **Properties**. The Properties dialog box for the recipes Web site opens.

7. If necessary, click the **Allow files to be browsed** and the **Allow scripts to be run** check boxes to select them, and then click the **OK** button. The Properties dialog box closes.

Now the Web site is configured to run scripts and Active Server Pages. Next you will insert the Database Results region in a new Web page.

Inserting a Database Results Region in a Web Page

David's planning analysis sheet shows that you will create a new Web page and insert a database into it. When you insert a database in a Web page, FrontPage calls it a Database Results region. A **Database Results region** is a component in a Web page that contains HTML code and client-side and server-side scripts that retrieve and display database data in the Web page. After inserting the Database Results region, the Database Results Wizard starts. The Database Results Wizard asks you a series of questions about the database, which database object to insert, and any special filters to apply to it. A **filter** is a set of restrictions that you place on the records in a table or query to display a subset of a table's records. For example, a filter might display records that contain the value TX in a State field to select records for people who live in Texas. A filter is different from a query in that a filter only *temporarily* displays a subset of data.

REFERENCE WINDOW   RW

Using the Database Results Wizard to Insert a Database Results Region in a Web Page

■ Open the existing page in which to insert the Database Results region in Page view.
  or
■ Create a new page in Page view.
■ Position the insertion point where you want to insert the Database Results region.
■ Click Insert on the menu bar, point to Database, and then click Results. The Database Results
  Wizard starts.
■ Click the Use an existing database connection option button, and then, if necessary, click the list
  arrow and select the database name. Click the Next button.
■ Click the Record source option button, click the list arrow and click the object in the database that
  contains the data you want to display, and then click the Next button.
■ If necessary, click the Edit List button to select and/or reorder the desired fields to display in the
  Web page, and then click the OK button. To apply a filter to the records, click the More Options
  button, use the More Options dialog box to create the filter, and then click the OK button. Click the
  Next button.
■ Select a formatting option for displaying the data, and then click the Next button.
■ Select an option for displaying returned records in the Web page, and then click the Finish button.

After inserting a Database Results region in a Web page, you can change its properties to customize its default appearance to meet your needs.

To insert a Database Results region in a new Web page:

1. Click the **Page** button on the Views bar to change to Page view. If necessary, click the **New Page** button on the Standard toolbar to display a new page. The new page uses the background picture from the Web site's theme and has the filename new_page_1.htm.

2. Click **Insert** on the menu bar, point to **Database**, and then click **Results**. The Database Results Wizard starts. By default, FrontPage assumes that you will be using the Recipes database for your Database Results region, because this database connection is the only one in the Web site. See Figure 8-10.

Figure 8-10   USING AN EXISTING DATABASE CONNECTION

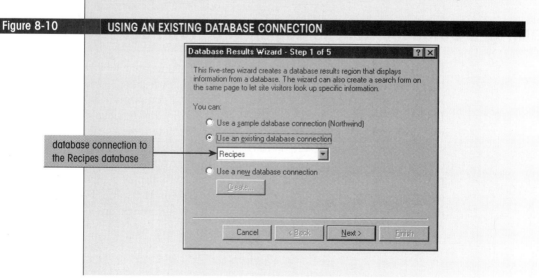

3. Click the **Next** button. The second dialog box lets you specify the database object that contains the data that you want to use in the Web page. The Recipes database contains four objects—the Customers, Subject, and Category tables, and the Customer Query. The Category table is selected in the Record source list box because it is first alphabetically in the list of objects. If you don't find a suitable object in the list, you can open the database from the fpdb folder of the Web site and then use Access to create the correct object. You will use the existing Customer Query object as the record source.

4. Click the **Record source** list arrow, and then click **Customer Query (VIEW)**. (The "VIEW" notation indicates that you will see the query datasheet in the Web page.) Click the **Next** button to continue. The third dialog box lets you specify the fields to include in the Web page, their order, and an optional filter. See Figure 8-11. David wants the person's phone number to be displayed as the third column in the Database Results region, so you need to change the field order.

Figure 8-11   **SELECTING AND ORDERING THE FIELDS TO USE IN THE DATABASE RESULTS REGION**

5. Click the **Edit List** button. The Displayed Fields dialog box opens. Notice that all of the fields from the Customer Query appear in the Displayed fields list box. See Figure 8-12.

Figure 8-12   **DISPLAYED FIELDS DIALOG BOX**

6. Click the **PhoneNum** field in the Displayed fields list box, and then click the **Move Up** button. Now the PhoneNum field appears third in the list.

7. Click the **OK** button to close the Displayed Fields dialog box. You will not create a filter for the database region, so click the **Next** button to go to the next dialog box. See Figure 8-13. In this dialog box, you select the formatting options to use in

the Web page. The default settings are to use one record from the table in each row, to format the table using a border and a header row with the field names, and to expand the table to the width of the page. You will accept these settings.

Figure 8-13	SELECTING THE FORMATTING OPTIONS FOR THE DATABASE RESULTS REGION

preview of the Database Results region using the current settings

8. Make sure that your default settings match those shown in Figure 8-13, and then click the **Next** button. The last dialog box lets you set the number of records to display in the Web page. A good rule of thumb is to split records into groups of five records each to make it easy for users to see each record without needing to scroll the Web page.

9. If necessary, click the **Split records into groups** option button to select it, click in the **Split records into groups** text box, and then type **5**.

10. Click the **Finish** button. The Web page now contains a Database Results region. See Figure 8-14.

Figure 8-14	DATABASE RESULTS REGION IN THE WEB PAGE

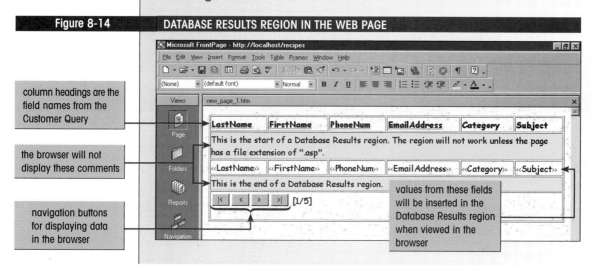

column headings are the field names from the Customer Query

the browser will not display these comments

navigation buttons for displaying data in the browser

values from these fields will be inserted in the Database Results region when viewed in the browser

Saving and Previewing the Database Results Region

FrontPage used the fonts and styles from the Web site's theme in the Database Results region. You can preview the page in the browser. First, however, you must save the page.

To save the Web page and preview it in the browser:

1. Click the **Save** button 🖫 on the Standard toolbar. The Save As dialog box opens.

2. Make sure that the recipes folder appears in the Save in list box, type **customer_query** in the File name text box, make sure that the Save as type list box displays the text "Active Server Pages," and then click the **Save** button. Notice that the Web page now has an .asp filename extension, indicating that it is an Active Server Page. The comment in the Database Results region reminds you that this page must have an .asp filename extension.

3. Click the **Preview in Browser** button 🔍 on the Standard toolbar to open the Customer Query page in the browser. See Figure 8-15.

Figure 8-15	CUSTOMER QUERY WEB PAGE IN THE BROWSER

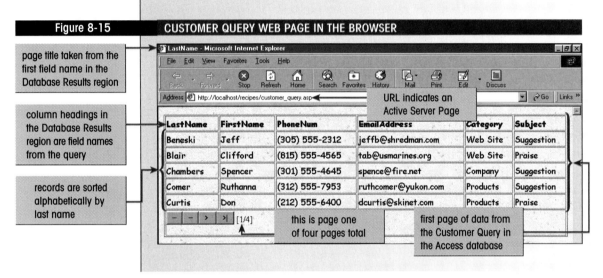

page title taken from the first field name in the Database Results region

column headings in the Database Results region are field names from the query

records are sorted alphabetically by last name

URL indicates an Active Server Page

LastName	FirstName	PhoneNum	EmailAddress	Category	Subject
Beneski	Jeff	(305) 555-2312	jeffb@shredman.com	Web Site	Suggestion
Blair	Clifford	(815) 555-4565	tab@usmarines.org	Web Site	Praise
Chambers	Spencer	(301) 555-4645	spence@fire.net	Company	Suggestion
Comer	Ruthanna	(312) 555-7953	ruthcomer@yukon.com	Products	Suggestion
Curtis	Don	(212) 555-6400	dcurtis@skinet.com	Products	Praise

this is page one of four pages total

first page of data from the Customer Query in the Access database

The Database Results region correctly grouped the records from the query and displayed the first five records in alphabetical order by last name. Notice that the PhoneNum column appears third, as you specified in the Wizard. Also notice the buttons that appear below the last record in the table. You can click these buttons to scroll through the table's records.

To scroll the table records:

1. Click the **Go to Next Page** button ▶ on the navigation bar. Internet Explorer displays the second page of the results. Notice that the navigation bar now displays the text "[2/4]" to indicate that you are viewing the records on page two of four pages total.

TROUBLE? If an Internet Explorer dialog box opens and asks if you want to send information to the local intranet, click the Yes button.

2. Click the **Go to Last Page** button ▶| on the navigation bar. Internet Explorer displays the fourth and final page of results.

3. Click the **Go to First Page** button |◀ s on the navigation bar. Internet Explorer returns to the first page.

Although the correct data is displayed, you notice several areas that you can improve. First, the page's title is "LastName," which is the first field name displayed in the Database Results region. You can change the Web page's title in Folders view to "Customer Query." Second, the column headings for the Database Results region are the field names from the Customer Query. You can change these column headings to use more meaningful names, and format them to use a style.

Changing the Page Title and Formatting the Database Results Region

David asks you to return to FrontPage to correct the problems that you identified.

To change the page title and format the Database Results region:

1. Click the **Microsoft FrontPage** program button on the taskbar to return to FrontPage.

2. Click the **Folders** button on the Views bar to change to Folders view.

3. Right-click **customer_query.asp** in the Contents pane to select the page and the filename and to open the shortcut menu, click **Rename**, and then press the **Tab** key to select the page's title and change to editing mode.

4. Type **Customer Query** and then press the **Enter** key.

5. Click the **Page** button on the Views bar to change to Page view. Notice that the LastName, FirstName, PhoneNum, and EmailAddress column headings have red wavy lines under them. These lines indicate that these words are not in the FrontPage dictionary. You can right-click a misspelled word to open a shortcut menu for the Spelling dialog box and then click the correct word. If the correct word is not in the list, you can edit the column headings just like any other text in the page.

6. Right-click the **LastName** column heading to open the shortcut menu, and then click **Last Name**. The column heading changes to "Last Name" and the red, wavy line disappears.

7. Right-click the **FirstName** column heading and click **First Name**, right-click the **EmailAddress** column heading and click **Email Address**, and then edit the PhoneNum field to change it to **Phone #**.

8. Select the first row in the Database Results region (the one that contains the column headings), click the **Style** list arrow on the Formatting toolbar, and then click **Heading 3**. The column headings change to the Heading 3 style.

9. With the column headings still selected, click the **Center** button on the Formatting toolbar to center the headings.

10. Click the **Save** button on the Standard toolbar to save the page, click the **Preview in Browser** button on the Standard toolbar to open the page in the browser, and then click the **Refresh** button on the Standard Buttons toolbar to refresh the page. See Figure 8-16. The page looks better with the new title and formatting.

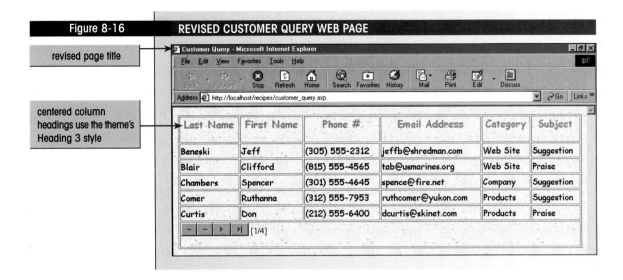

Figure 8-16	REVISED CUSTOMER QUERY WEB PAGE

revised page title

centered column
headings use the theme's
Heading 3 style

Customer Query - Microsoft Internet Explorer

Address http://localhost/recipes/customer_query.asp

Last Name	First Name	Phone #	Email Address	Category	Subject
Beneski	Jeff	(305) 555-2312	jeffb@shredman.com	Web Site	Suggestion
Blair	Clifford	(815) 555-4565	tab@usmarines.org	Web Site	Praise
Chambers	Spencer	(301) 555-4645	spence@fire.net	Company	Suggestion
Comer	Ruthanna	(312) 555-7953	ruthcomer@yukon.com	Products	Suggestion
Curtis	Don	(212) 555-6400	dcurtis@skinet.com	Products	Praise

[1/4]

Using a Web Page to Query a Database

In addition to displaying all of the records from a database object, such as a query, you might want to let users search for a specific set of records within an object. You can do this by creating a page that contains a Database Results region and a search form.

David wants you to create a second page that displays the query results from the Customer Query based on a category entered by the user. Instead of re-creating the Database Results region, you will copy the existing Customer Query Web page and then create a search form in the new page. Then you will rename the page's filename and title.

To create a copy of a Web page and change its filename and title:

1. Click the **Microsoft FrontPage** program button on the toolbar to return to FrontPage, and then click the **Close** button ⊠ on the Contents pane to close the Customer Query page.

2. Click the **Folders** button on the Views bar to change to Folders view.

3. Right-click **customer_query.asp** in the Contents pane to open its shortcut menu, and then click **Copy**.

4. Right-click any open area of the Contents pane to open the shortcut menu, and then click **Paste**. FrontPage creates a new Web page named customer_query_copy(1).asp and titled Customer Query. You will rename the page, and then open it in Page view.

5. Right-click **customer_query_copy(1).asp** in the Contents pane to select it and to open the shortcut menu, click **Rename** to change to editing mode, type **customer_query_search.asp**, press the **Tab** key to select the page title and change to editing mode, press the **End** key, press the **spacebar**, type **Search**, and then press the **Enter** key. The title changes to "Customer Query Search."

6. Double-click **customer_query_search.asp** to open the Customer Query Search page in Page view. This page contains a copy of the Database Results region that you created in the Customer Query page.

Now that you have copied and renamed the page, you can rerun the Database Results Wizard to create the search form.

Creating a Search Form to Query a Database

The search form that you will create to let users query the database is similar to the search form that you use to search a Web site for keywords. You must rerun the Database Results Wizard to create the search form. FrontPage will program the search form to query the database using the object from the database that you specify.

REFERENCE WINDOW   **RW**

Creating a Search Form in a Web Page That Queries a Database
- Open the existing page that contains a Database Results region.
- Right-click the Database Results region to open the shortcut menu, and then click Database Results Properties. The Database Results Wizard starts.
  or
- Create a new Web page, click Insert on the menu bar, point to Database, and then click Results. The Database Results Wizard starts.
- Confirm or set the options in the first two dialog boxes.
- In the third dialog box (Step 3 of 5), click the More Options button. The More Options dialog box opens.
- Click the Criteria button to open the Criteria dialog box.
- Click the Add button. The Add Criteria dialog box opens.
- Select the field name and comparison operator to use in the query.
- Click the Use this search form field check box to select it.
- Click the OK button. Click the Add button to specify additional criteria, or click the OK button to close the Criteria dialog box.
- Click the OK button to close the More Options dialog box.
- Confirm or set the options in the remaining dialog boxes, and then click the Finish button.

To create a search form in a page that queries a database:

1. Right-click the **Database Results region** to open the shortcut menu, and then click **Database Results Properties**. The Database Results Wizard starts.

   TROUBLE? If you do not see the Database Results Properties command on the shortcut menu, press the Esc key to close the menu, and then repeat Step 1, making sure to right-click the Database Results region and not a column heading.

2. Click the **Next** button twice to move to the dialog box that displays the text "Step 3 of 5" in the title bar.

3. Click the **More Options** button. The More Options dialog box opens.

4. Click the **Criteria** button. The Criteria dialog box opens.

5. Click the **Add** button. The Add Criteria dialog box opens. See Figure 8-17. You need to specify the Category field as the search field. In FrontPage language, you need to specify that *Category equals Category*, which means the category entered by the user in the search text box in the Web page must match a value in the Category field in the Customer Query to return a record.

Figure 8-17	CREATING A FILTER FOR A DATABASE RESULTS REGION

field to filter

comparison operator for the filter

6. Click the **Field Name** list arrow, and then click **Category**. The Comparison list box should display the operator "Equals" and the Value text box should display the field name "Category."

7. If necessary, click the **Use this search form field** check box to select it, and then click the **OK** button. The Add Criteria dialog box closes and the Criteria dialog box now displays the filter criteria. See Figure 8-18. You could specify additional criteria by clicking the Add button again. However, David only wants to use the Category field as a search field, so you can finish the Database Results Wizard.

Figure 8-18	CRITERIA DIALOG BOX

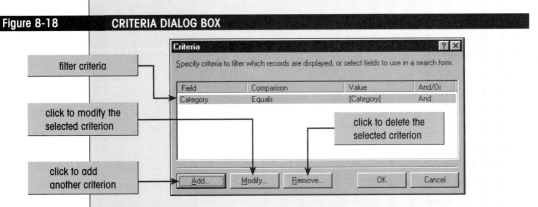

filter criteria

click to modify the selected criterion

click to delete the selected criterion

click to add another criterion

8. Click the **OK** button to close the Criteria dialog box, click the **OK** button to close the More Options dialog box, click the **Next** button two times, and then click the **Finish** button. The Database Results Wizard closes and the Customer Query Search page now displays the search form. See Figure 8-19.

Figure 8-19   **CUSTOMER QUERY SEARCH PAGE**

search form added by the Database Results Wizard

Submit and Reset buttons added by the Database Results Wizard

expression for selecting the Category field

Notice that the Database Results Wizard reset the column headings in the Database Results region to their field-name equivalents from the database. You will need to change the column headings to make them match the ones in the Customer Query Web page.

To change and format the column heading names:

1. Right-click the **LastName** column heading to open the shortcut menu and click **Last Name**, right-click the **FirstName** column heading and click **First Name**, right-click the **EmailAddress** column heading and click **Email Address**, and then edit the PhoneNum field to change it to **Phone #**.

2. Select the first row in the Database Results region (the one that contains the column headings), click the **Style** list arrow on the Formatting toolbar, and then click **Heading 3**. The column headings change to the Heading 3 style.

3. With the column headings still selected, click the **Center** button on the Formatting toolbar to center the headings.

You can test the search form by saving the page and opening it in the browser.

To test the database search form:

1. Click the **Save** button on the Standard toolbar to save the page.

2. Click the **Preview in Browser** button on the Standard toolbar to open the Customer Query Search page in the browser. See Figure 8-20.

Figure 8-20	CUSTOMER QUERY SEARCH PAGE IN THE BROWSER

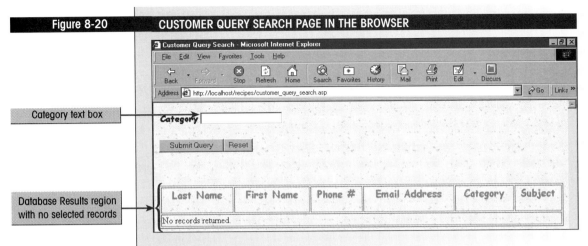

Category text box

Database Results region with no selected records

3. Click in the **Category** text box, and then type **Web Site**.

4. Click the **Submit Query** button. Internet Explorer displays the first of two pages that contain records matching your query request. Notice that all of the records contain the value "Web Site" in the Category column. See Figure 8-21.

Figure 8-21	QUERY RESULTS USING THE WEB SITE FILTER

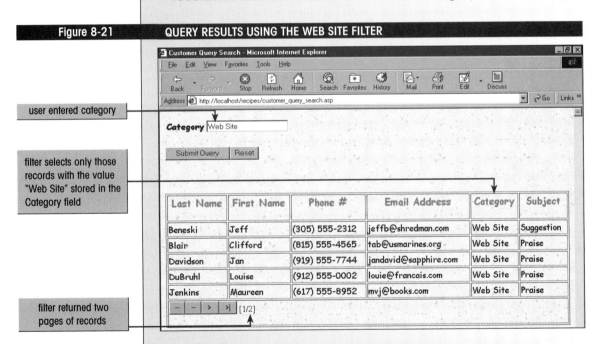

user entered category

filter selects only those records with the value "Web Site" stored in the Category field

filter returned two pages of records

TROUBLE? If an AutoComplete dialog box opens and asks if you would like to turn on this feature, click the No button.

TROUBLE? If you click the Submit Query button and the "No records returned." message appears in the table, instead of the records shown in Figure 8-21, make sure that you typed the category name ("Web Site") correctly in the Category text box. If you typed the category name correctly and you still do not see any records, ask your instructor or technical support person for help.

5. Select the text in the Category text box, type **Products**, and then click the **Submit Query** button. Internet Explorer selects the records that contain the value "Products" in the Category field.

The query works correctly, but you realize that you need to provide users with some instructions for using this page. Without any instructions, the user will not know what the Category values are. You can add instructions to the page in Page view, just like any other text.

To add text to the Customer Query Search page:

1. Click the **Microsoft FrontPage** program button on the taskbar to return to FrontPage.

2. Press **Ctrl + Home** to move the insertion point to the top of the page, and then press the **Enter** key to insert a new line. The insertion point is blinking on the new line.

3. Type the following text on the new line: **Type one of the following categories in the Category text box, and then click the Submit Query button: Web Site, Products, or Company.**

4. Click the **Save** button 🖫 on the Standard toolbar, click the **Preview in Browser** button 🔍 on the Standard toolbar, and then click the **Refresh** button 🖺 on the Standard Buttons toolbar. The revised Web page appears in the browser. See Figure 8-22. Now users of the page will know how to submit queries.

| Figure 8-22 | REVISED CUSTOMER QUERY SEARCH PAGE |

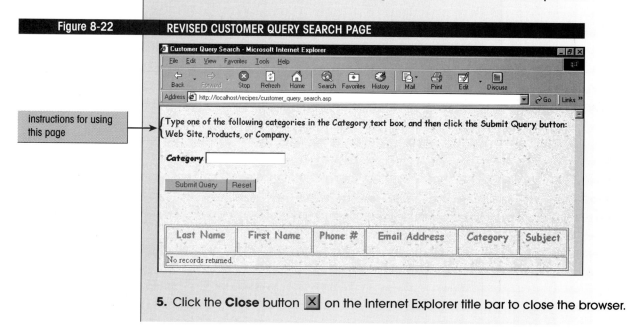

instructions for using this page

5. Click the **Close** button ⊠ on the Internet Explorer title bar to close the browser.

The real power and utility of the connection to a database is the ability to query the database after changes have been made to it. You will update the database and use the same Web page to view the changes next.

Updating a Database and Viewing the Changes in a Web Page

As more people visit the Sunny Web site, more names will be added to the Customers table in the Recipes database. David wants to make sure that the Customer Query and Customer Query Search Web pages always reflect the *current* data in the database, and not just the data that existed at the time that you created the database connection and its Web pages. As long as the changes are made in the database that is stored in the Web site, any Web page that uses that database connection will always reflect the current data. If you add, change, or delete records in the database, the Web pages that use that database connection will also reflect these changes.

To add a record to the Customers table:

1. If necessary, click the **Microsoft FrontPage** program button on the taskbar to return to FrontPage.

2. Click the **Folders** button 🖿 on the Views bar to change to Folders view, and then click the **fpdb** folder in the Folder List to open it.

3. Double-click **recipes.mdb** in the Contents pane. Microsoft Access starts and opens the Recipes database. You will open the Customers table and then add a new record to it.

4. If necessary, click the **Tables** object on the Objects bar, and then double-click **Customers** in the tables list to open the Customers table in Table Data-sheet view.

5. Click the **New Record** button 🔘 on the Table Datasheet toolbar. The current record indicator moves to row 21, the (AutoNumber) text in the CustomerID field is selected, and Access is ready to accept a new record.

6. Press the **Tab** key. The insertion point moves to the First Name column. Type **Betty**, press the **Tab** key to move to the Last Name column, type **Brask**, and then press the **Tab** key to move to the Email Address column.

7. Continue entering data and pressing the Tab key to enter the entire record using the following data: Email Address: **bettybrask@golden.net**; Phone #: **808-555-8751**; Category: **Web Site**; Subject: **Praise**. As you enter text in the Category and Subject fields, the Lookup Wizard will complete your entries.

8. Press the **Tab** key after entering the Subject field value to save the record in the table. The navigation bar at the bottom of the Table window now displays "Record 22 of 22" and (AutoNumber) is selected in the next row.

9. Click the **Close** button ⊠ on the Access program window title bar to close the table, the Recipes database, and Access.

10. If necessary, click the **Microsoft FrontPage** program button on the taskbar to return to FrontPage.

Now open the Customer Query Search page in Internet Explorer to make sure that the new record you added to the Customers table appears in the Web page.

To view the new database record in the Web page:

1. Click the Web site's folder in the Folder List (the default folder is **http://localhost/recipes**) to display all of its pages in the Contents pane, and then click **customer_query_search.asp** in the Contents pane to select it.

2. Click the **Preview in Browser** button 🔍 on the Standard toolbar to open the Customer Query Search page in the browser.

3. Click in the **Category** text box, type **Web Site**, and then click the **Submit Query** button. The new record for Betty Brask appears in the search results. See Figure 8-23.

Figure 8-23	NEW RECORD APPEARS IN THE CUSTOMER QUERY SEARCH PAGE

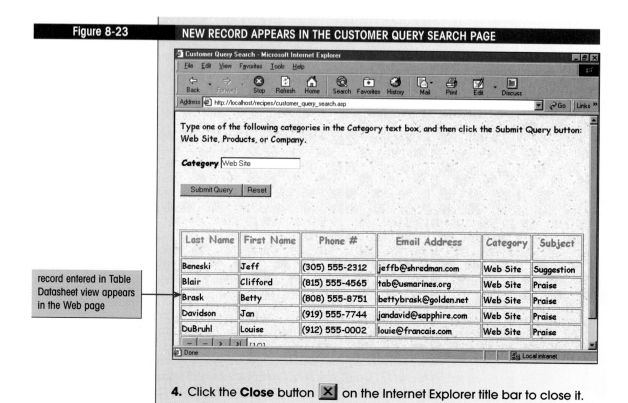

record entered in Table Datasheet view appears in the Web page

4. Click the **Close** button ⊠ on the Internet Explorer title bar to close it.

David wants you to examine the HTML code that created the search form and the Database Results region. To do this, you will view the HTML code for the Customer Query Search page.

Viewing **HTML Code for a Page with a Database Connection**

The Customer Query Search Web page contains complex HTML code that creates the querying capability for the Web page, the connection to the Access database, and the capability to display matching field values.

To view the HTML code:

1. If necessary, click the **Microsoft FrontPage** program button on the taskbar to return to FrontPage.

2. Double-click **customer_query_search.asp** in the Contents pane to open the Customer Query Search Web page in Page view, click the **HTML** tab to display the HTML code for the page, and then scroll down the page until the FORM tag is at the top of the Contents pane. See Figure 8-24.

Figure 8-24   HTML CODE FOR THE CUSTOMER QUERY SEARCH PAGE

creates the Category
text box

form fields in the page

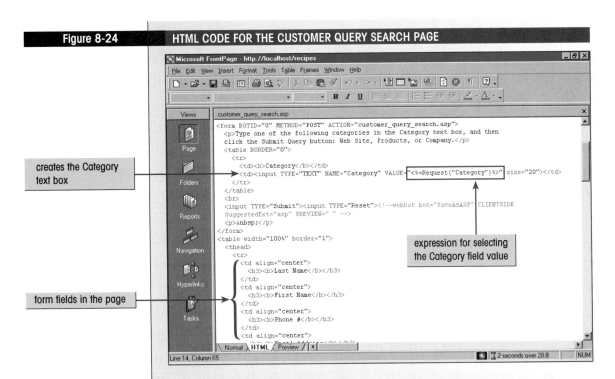

expression for selecting
the Category field value

3. Press the **Page Down** key to scroll the window down one page, and then scroll
the page so that the TBODY tag is at the top of the Contents pane. See Figure 8-25.

Figure 8-25   HTML CODE FOR THE CUSTOMER QUERY SEARCH PAGE, CONTINUED

Database Results region
code that selects records
and displays them in the
table

code to select records
from the Category value
supplied by the user

creates the message
that appears when no
records are selected

specifies the database
connection name

code that displays
returned records in a
table with five records
per page

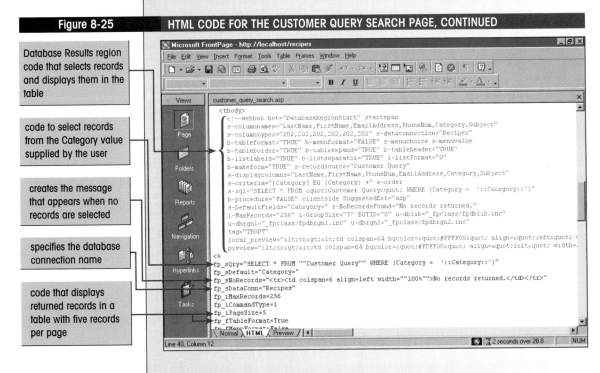

4. Continue pressing the **Page Down** key to scroll the window down one page at
a time. Notice all of the HTML code required to create the database connection and the Database Results region.

5. When you have examined the final page of HTML code, click the **Close** button
[X] on the FrontPage title bar to close FrontPage.

In the next session, you will create a form into which site visitors can enter information that is stored in the Recipes database. You will also create a data access page.

Session 8.1 QUICK CHECK

1. What is a database connection?

2. Describe how to import a database into a FrontPage Web.

3. What must you do prior to inserting a Database Results region in a Web page?

4. What is a Database Results region?

5. When you temporarily select a subset of records from a database table, you are using a(n) _____.

6. True or False: You cannot limit the number of records displayed in a Web page by a Database Results region.

7. True or False: You cannot change the properties of a Database Results region.

8. True or False: If you update a database that has a connection to a FrontPage Web and is stored in the Web site, any Web pages that use that database connection will display the revised data from the database.

SESSION 8.2

In this session, you will use a form in a Web page to send data to an Access database, and then you will view the changes in the Access database. You will also create a data access page to view, add, delete, browse, filter, and sort records from an Access table in the browser.

Creating a Form for Data Input

David wants you to create a form in the recipes Web site that will serve as an electronic guest book. The form will collect each visitor's first and last names, e-mail address, address, city, state, Zip code, and home telephone number. David also wants you to include a form field in the form that asks for permission to send promotional materials to the visitor's e-mail address.

The visitor will submit the form to the server, where it will be processed. The form results will be stored in an Access database. Storing the form results in an Access database will make the data accessible for many different needs. For example, the marketing department will use the mailing addresses to send printed promotional materials, it will use e-mail addresses to send electronic messages to promote new products at the Sunshine Country Store or new recipes in the Web site, and it will use the phone numbers to contact visitors for open-ended marketing research studies. By storing visitor data in an Access database, the marketing department gains the flexibility to produce reports about the data, to query the database for specific records, and to manage the data in many ways. These advantages are not readily available when you collect a form's results in an HTML or text file.

When creating a new database connection, you have the option of importing an existing database into the FrontPage Web, in which case FrontPage will create the database connection, or you can use the Database tab in the Web Settings dialog box to add a new database connection to a database that exists on the same file system or server as the Web site. For the guest book, you will import an existing database into the Web site. After importing the database, you will import into the recipes Web site a Web page David created that contains a form for collecting data.

Importing an Existing Database into a Web Site

David's existing database is stored in the Tutorial.08 folder on your Data Disk using the filename Guest. The database contains one table named Results, which has the structure shown in Figure 8-26. The database contains one query, named Results Query, which displays the LastName, FirstName, Address, City, State, Zip, Phone, EmailAddress, and Promotion fields from the Results table.

Figure 8-26	RESULTS TABLE DESIGN IN THE GUEST DATABASE		
FIELD NAME	**DATA TYPE**	**FIELD SIZE**	**DESCRIPTION**
ID	AutoNumber	Long Integer	An AutoNumber field that is created by Access adds the ID. IDs are assigned sequentially as new records are added to the table.
FirstName	Text	35	The customer's first name.
LastName	Text	35	The customer's last name.
Address	Text	70	The customer's street address.
City	Text	35	The customer's city.
State	Text	2	The customer's state.
Zip	Text	10	The customer's Zip code.
Phone	Text	15	The customer's phone number, area code first.
EmailAddress	Text	45	The customer's e-mail address.
Promotion	Text	3	A Yes or No response to indicate whether the customer has requested to receive promotional materials via e-mail.

To import the Guest database into the recipes Web site:

1. Click the **Start** button on the taskbar, point to **Programs**, and then click **Windows Explorer**.

2. Open the drive or folder that contains your Data Disk, and then open the **Tutorial.08** folder to display its contents.

3. Right-click the **Guest** file to open the shortcut menu, and then click **Copy**.

4. Click the **Close** button ⊠ on the Windows Explorer title bar to close it.

5. Start **FrontPage**, open the **recipes** Web site from your computer's PWS, and then, if necessary, change to Folders view. Because the fpdb folder already exists in the Web site, you can paste the file directly into that folder.

6. Click the **fpdb** folder in the Folder List to open it in the Contents pane, right-click any open area of the Contents pane to open the shortcut menu, and then click **Paste**. The Importing Files dialog box opens, and then the Add Database Connection dialog box opens on top of it. You will create a database connection named Guest.

TROUBLE? If you do not see the fpdb folder in the Folder List, turn on the display of hidden folders in the Web site.

7. Type **Guest** in the Name text box, and then click the **Yes** button. The Importing Files dialog box appears again and then it closes. The database is now stored in the fpdb folder of the recipes Web site. You can verify the database connection by using the Web Settings dialog box.

8. Click **Tools** on the menu bar, click **Web Settings**, and then click the **Database** tab. Click the **Guest** connection, and then click the **Verify** button. The question mark in the Status column changes to a green check mark, indicating a valid connection. The recipes Web site now has two valid database connections.

9. Click the **OK** button to close the Web Settings dialog box.

Now that the Guest database is stored in the Web site and its connection to the database has been verified, you can use the database connection to send data from a Web page to the database. David already created a Web page named GuestBk.asp that contains a form for collecting data, so you just need to import it into the Web site from the Tutorial.08 folder on your Data Disk. Then you will configure the form to send data to the Guest database.

To import the GuestBk Web page into the recipes Web site:

1. Click the Web site's root folder (the default is **http://localhost/recipes**) to select it, click **File** on the menu bar, and then click **Import**. The Import dialog box opens.

2. Click the **Add File** button. The Add File to Import List dialog box opens. You need to import the file from the Tutorial.08 folder on your Data Disk.

3. Click the **Look in** list arrow, change to the drive or folder that contains your Data Disk, double-click the **Tutorial.08** folder, and then double-click **GuestBk**. The Import dialog box appears again with the guestbk.asp page selected.

4. Click the **OK** button to import the Guest Book Web page into the Web site.

Now you can open the Guest Book Web page and make the necessary changes to it so that the server will send data collected from this Web page to the Guest database. You will need to add this new page to the Web site's navigation structure so that the page banner and navigation bar will be displayed correctly.

To open the Guest Book Web page and add it to the navigation structure:

1. Double-click **guestbk.asp** in the Contents pane to open the Guest Book Web page in Page view. The placeholders at the top of the page remind you to add the page to the Web site's navigation structure.

2. Click the **Navigation** button on the Views bar to change to Navigation view, and then drag the **guestbk.asp** page from the Folder List to the navigation structure, as shown in Figure 8-27.

Figure 8-27   ADDING THE GUEST BOOK PAGE TO THE NAVIGATION STRUCTURE

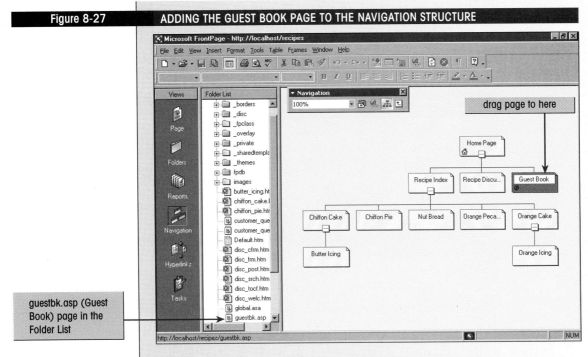

guestbk.asp (Guest Book) page in the Folder List

3. Double-click the **Guest Book** icon in the navigation structure to open it in Page view. Now the page banner and the navigation bar are displayed correctly. See Figure 8-28.

Figure 8-28   GUEST BOOK WEB PAGE IN PAGE VIEW

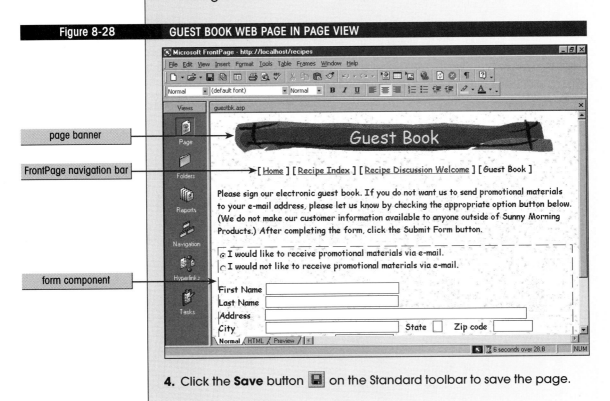

page banner

FrontPage navigation bar

form component

4. Click the **Save** button 🖫 on the Standard toolbar to save the page.

Configuring a Form to Send Results to a Database

Now you can configure the existing form to send its results to the Guest database in the Web site.

REFERENCE WINDOW   RW

Configuring a Form to Send Results to a Database
- Right-click the form component in the Web page to open the shortcut menu, and then click Form Properties.
- Click the Send to database option button, and then click the Options button.
- Click the Database Connection to Use list arrow, and then click the name of the database connection.
- Click the Saved Fields tab and then select the database field name that will store the data for each form field in the form component.
- Click the Additional Fields tab and select or remove any additional fields in which to store data.
- Click the OK button.

To configure the form to save results to the database:

1. Right-click the **form component** in the Web page to open the shortcut menu, and then click **Form Properties**. The Form Properties dialog box opens.

2. Click the **Send to database** option button to select this form handler, and then click the **Options** button. The Options for Saving Results to Database dialog box opens. FrontPage selected the first database connection—to the Recipes database—that appears on the Database tab of the Web Settings dialog box. You need to change the database connection to Guest.

3. Click the **Database Connection to Use** list arrow, and then click **Guest**. FrontPage connects to the Guest database and selects the Results table automatically. See Figure 8-29.

Figure 8-29   OPTIONS FOR SAVING RESULTS TO DATABASE DIALOG BOX

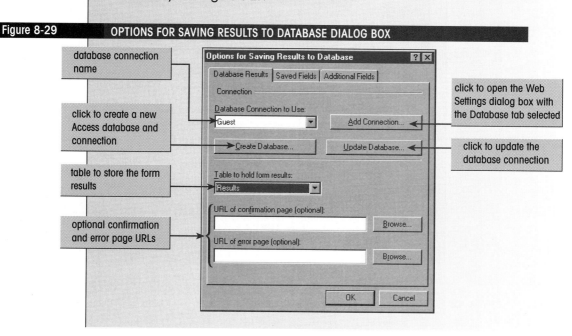

database connection name

click to create a new Access database and connection

table to store the form results

optional confirmation and error page URLs

click to open the Web Settings dialog box with the Database tab selected

click to update the database connection

4. Click the **Saved Fields** tab to display those settings. By default, FrontPage selected each field from the Results table in the Guest database; however, you need to tell FrontPage the name of the database field in which to store the values. See Figure 8-30. The values in the Form Field list are the form field names that David used when he created the form fields in the form. For example, the form field name of the one-line text box that is labeled "E-mail Address" is "EmailAddress."

Figure 8-30	SAVED FIELDS FOR THE RESULTS TABLE

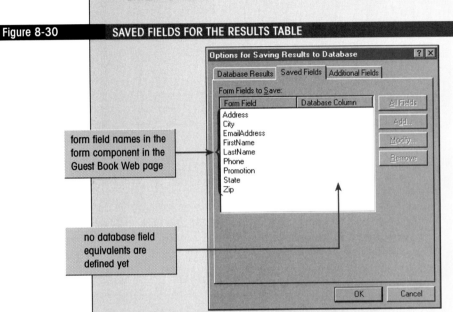

form field names in the form component in the Guest Book Web page

no database field equivalents are defined yet

5. Double-click **Address** in the Form Field list. FrontPage connects to the database, reviews the Results table structure, and then opens the Modify Field dialog box. FrontPage selected the Address field in the Results table as the one in which to store form results from the Address field. This selection is correct—the Address form field in the Web page will send data to the Address field in the Results table in the Guest database. If you need to change the field in which to save data, you could click the Save to database column list arrow and select a different field.

6. Make sure that Address is selected in the Save to database column list box, and then click the **OK** button to close the Modify Field dialog box. Notice that the Database Column value for the Address Form Field now displays the Address field. Because David's form fields and database columns have the same names, FrontPage should correctly select each database field in which to store the data. You can repeat Steps 5 and 6 for each form field to select the correct database field in which to store the results.

7. Repeat Steps 5 and 6 to supply the Database Column value for each field in the database.

8. Click the **Additional Fields** tab to display those settings. See Figure 8-31. David doesn't want to save information about the user's browser, user name, or time information, so you will remove these fields from the form results. If you select these options, the database connection will automatically add these fields to the table structure.

Figure 8-31 ADDITIONAL FIELDS TAB

optional fields to save information about the user's connection

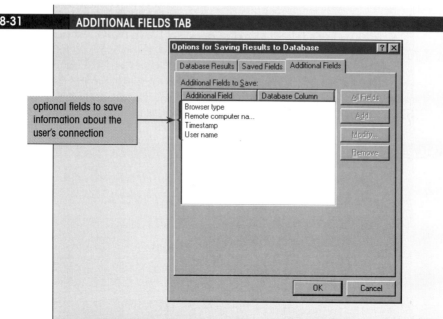

9. Click **Browser type** in the Additional Fields to Save list box, and then click the **Remove** button. The Browser type field is deleted and the Remote computer name field is selected. You can click the Remove button three more times to delete the rest of the fields.

10. Click the **Remove** button three times to remove all fields from the Additional Fields to Save list box, and then click the **OK** button to close the Options for Saving Results to Database dialog box.

11. Click the **OK** button in the Form Properties dialog box to close it.

12. Click the **Save** button 🖫 on the Standard toolbar to save the page.

Now you can open the Guest Book page in the browser and submit a form to the server. Then you will examine the Guest database to make sure that the server stored the form results as a record in the Results table.

To open the Web page in the browser and submit a form:

1. Click the **Preview in Browser** button 🔍 on the Standard toolbar. Internet Explorer starts and opens the Guest Book Web page.

2. Click the **I would not like to receive promotional materials via e-mail** option button to select it.

3. Click in the **First Name** text box, and then type **David**.

4. Press the **Tab** key to move to the Last Name text box, and then type **Harrah**.

5. Continue pressing the **Tab** key to enter the following data in the text boxes: Address: **8336 Seashore Drive**; City: **Los Angeles**; State: **CA**; Zip code: **90028**; Home Phone: **213-555-0725**; and E-mail Address: **dharrah@admin.sunnymorning.com**.

6. Click the **Submit Form** button. The default Form Confirmation page appears to confirm that your information was correctly submitted to the server.

7. Click the **Return to the form** hyperlink to return to the Guest Book page. The form fields are cleared, and the page is ready to accept another form submission.

8. Click the **Close** button ☒ on the Internet Explorer title bar to close it.

When you submitted the Guest Book page to the server, the server used the Guest database connection that you defined in the FrontPage Web to send the form results to the Guest database. You can open Access and the Guest database from FrontPage to make sure that the form results were correctly stored in the Results table.

To open the Access database and view the form results in a query:

1. If necessary, click the **Microsoft FrontPage** program button on the taskbar to return to FrontPage.

2. Click the **Folders** button ⬚ on the Views bar to change to Folders view.

3. Click the **fpdb** folder in the Folder List to display its contents in the Contents pane, click the **Refresh** button ⬚ on the Standard toolbar, and then double-click **guest.mdb** in the Contents pane. Access starts and opens the Guest database. David created a query in the database to display the data collected in the Results table, so you can just run the query to see if your form results were stored correctly.

4. If necessary, click the **Queries** object in the Objects bar, double-click **Results Query** in the queries list, and then click the **Maximize** button ⬚ on the Query window to maximize it. The Query window displays the record that you entered using the Guest Book Web page and that was stored in the Results table. See Figure 8-32.

Figure 8-32	RESULTS QUERY

record added to the table using the Guest Book Web page

TROUBLE? If your query does not display any records, close Access, and then return to the Guest Book Web page in Page view. Right-click the form component to open the shortcut menu, click Form Properties, and then click the Options button. Make sure that the settings on the three tabs in the Options for Saving Results to Database dialog box are set correctly using the information provided in the previous steps. If necessary, make any changes, save the page, and then preview the page in the browser again. Click the Refresh button ⬚ on the Standard Buttons toolbar, and then reenter the data into the form. Repeat Steps 1 through 4. If you still do not see any records in the query, ask your instructor or technical support person for help.

The form you used to store data in the database only accepts user input. If you want to use a Web page to display data from the table on which the form is based, you need to create a data access page.

Creating a Data Access Page

A **data access page** is a Web page that uses a form to display data from the Access table or query on which it is based. You use a data access page much as you would use a form in an Access database. The data access page has controls in it that let you add, delete, sort, filter, and change the records it displays. Only Internet Explorer 5.0 and higher can display data access pages. Normally, a data access page is available on an intranet, or it is hidden in a published Web site so that only authorized users can view its data. For example, in the recipes Web site, you won't want to allow users who are browsing the Web site to access the records stored in the Results table in the Guest database, so you will exclude this page when publishing the recipes Web site to make it unavailable to Internet users.

You must use Access to create a data access page. You will save the data access page in the recipes Web site.

REFERENCE WINDOW   **RW**

Creating a Data Access Page

- Double-click the database in the fpdb folder in the FrontPage Web to start Access and open the database.
- Click the Pages object in the Objects bar of the Database window.
- Double-click Create data access page by using wizard in the pages list.
- Select the table or query on which to base the data access page, select the fields to include in the data access page, and then click the Next button.
- Select an optional grouping level, and then click the Next button.
- Use the drop-down list(s) to select an optional sort order, and then click the Next button.
- Edit the suggested title or accept the default title, and then click the Finish button.
- Click the Save button on the Page Design toolbar, enter the page's filename and location in which to save it, and then click the Save button.

David wants you to create a data access page in Access that is based on the Results table. Then, instead of checking the records in the database by starting Access and opening the database and table, he can check the records using the data access page that is part of the FrontPage Web. Because the data access page will display customer information, you will set this page so it is not published with the rest of the site when the site is ultimately published on the server for Sunny Morning Products. The Guest database is already open in Access, so you are ready to create the data access page.

To create a data access page:

1. Click the **Close** button ⊠ for the Query window to close it. The Database window reappears.

2. Click the **Pages** object in the Objects bar of the Database window, and then double-click **Create data access page by using wizard** in the pages list. The Page Wizard starts and opens the first dialog box. See Figure 8-33. You use this dialog box to select the table or query in the current database that contains the fields you want to include in your data access page. The Results table is already selected; you will select all available fields.

Figure 8-33	USING THE PAGE WIZARD TO CREATE A DATA ACCESS PAGE

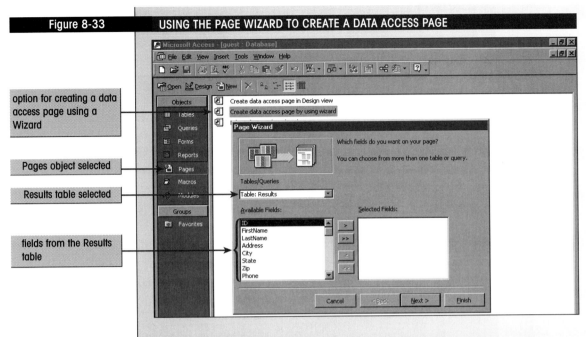

option for creating a data access page using a Wizard

Pages object selected

Results table selected

fields from the Results table

3. Click the [>>] button to select all available fields and to move them to the Selected Fields list box. Use the scroll box to make sure that the following fields appear in the Selected Fields list box: ID, FirstName, LastName, Address, City, State, Zip, Phone, EmailAddress, and Promotion.

   TROUBLE? If any other fields besides those listed in Step 3 appear in the Selected Fields list box, click the field to remove, and then click the [<] button to remove it. Repeat this process to remove all unwanted fields.

4. Click the **Next** button. The next dialog box asks you to specify any grouping levels for the data. You will not group the data, so you can click the Next button to continue.

5. Click the **Next** button. The next dialog box asks you to specify an optional sort order for the data. David wants to sort the records alphabetically by last name.

6. Click the **list arrow** for the first text box, and then click **LastName**. See Figure 8-34. An ascending sort order is already specified, so you can continue to the next dialog box.

Figure 8-34   **SPECIFYING A DEFAULT SORT ORDER FOR THE DATA ACCESS PAGE**

7. Click the **Next** button. The final dialog box asks you for a page title. You will accept the default title of "Results," so click the **Finish** button. After a few seconds, Access creates the data access page and opens it in Page Design view. If necessary, click the **Maximize** button ▫ on the Page Design window to maximize it. See Figure 8-35.

Figure 8-35   **DATA ACCESS PAGE IN PAGE DESIGN VIEW**

TROUBLE? If any other windows or toolbars are open in Page Design view, click the Close button ☒ on the title bar to close them.

8. Click the text at the top of the page (**Click here and type title text**), type **Guest Book Results Page**, and then click anywhere outside of the title to deselect it. You will not make any other design changes to the data access page, so you can save and close it.

Saving a Data Access Page

When you save a data access page, you can save it as an HTML file in any folder location on the computer's disk structure or in your Web site. You will save this page in the recipes Web site so that it will be accessible from the Web site. In order to do this, you will save it in the path c:\Inetpub\wwwroot\recipes, or the path to the recipes Web site on your server.

To save the data access page in the FrontPage Web site:

1. Click the **Save** button 🖫 on the Page Design toolbar to open the Save As Data Access Page dialog box.

2. Click the **Save in** list arrow and browse to the folder **c:\Inetpub\wwwroot** on your hard drive, and then double-click the **recipes** folder to open it.

TROUBLE? If you are storing published Web sites in another location, use the path to the recipes Web site on your server.

3. Click in the **File name** text box, type **ResultsDAP**, make sure that the Save as type list box displays the text "Microsoft Data Access Pages," and then click the **Save** button. Access saves the data access page as an HTML file in the recipes Web site.

4. Click the **Close** button ☒ on the Access program window title bar to close Access.

5. If necessary, click the **Microsoft FrontPage** program button on the taskbar to return to FrontPage.

Now the data access page is stored in the recipes Web site. You can open the data access page and use FrontPage to format it.

Modifying a Data Access Page in FrontPage

You stored the data access page in the recipes Web site. You will use FrontPage to open the page so you can edit it. David wants you to apply the Web site's theme to the data access page so it will match the appearance of other pages in the Web site. Then you will save the page and open it in the browser.

To open the data access page in Page view, apply the theme, and preview it in the browser:

1. Click the root folder of the recipes Web site (the default is **http://localhost/recipes**) in the Folder List to select it and to display its contents in the Contents pane.

2. Scroll down the list of files, and then double-click **ResultsDAP.htm** to open it in Page view. David wants you to apply the Web site's theme (Loose Gesture) to this new page.

TROUBLE? If you do not see the ResultsDAP.htm file in the Contents pane, click the Refresh button 🔁 on the Standard toolbar to refresh the file listing. If you still do not see it, then you may have saved it in the wrong folder of the Web site. Locate the file in one of the other folders of the recipes Web site, and then use drag and drop to move the file to the Web site's root folder (http://localhost/recipes). Repeat Step 2.

TROUBLE? If the data access page opens in Access, instead of in Page view, close Access, and then click the No button when asked to replace the file on the server. Right-click ResultsDAP.htm in the Contents pane to open the shortcut menu, and then click Open With. In the Open With Editor dialog box, click FrontPage (frontpg.exe), and then click the OK button. The Guest Book Results Page will open in Page view. Continue with Step 3.

3. Click **Format** on the menu bar, and then click **Theme**. The Themes dialog box opens.

4. Click the **Selected page(s)** option button to select it, and then scroll down the list of themes and click **Loose Gesture**.

   TROUBLE? If the Loose Gesture theme is not installed on your computer, select another theme.

5. If necessary, click the **Vivid colors**, **Active graphics**, and **Background picture** check boxes to select them, and then click the **OK** button. The page now uses elements from the Web site's theme.

6. Click the **Save** button 💾 on the Standard toolbar to save the page.

7. Click the **Preview in Browser** button 🔍 on the Standard toolbar to open the page in the browser. See Figure 8-36. The record that you entered into the Guest Book Web page appears in the Guest Book Results Page. As more records are added to the Results table, David will be able to use this data access page to view, delete, sort, and filter records as necessary.

   TROUBLE? If a Microsoft Data Access Components dialog box opens and asks if you want to allow data access to another domain, click the Yes button. If you click the Yes button and no records appear, then Internet Explorer is not configured to display records from an unknown Web site. Ask your instructor or technical support person for help.

   TROUBLE? If the Guest Book Results Page does not appear with the Loose Gesture theme (or the theme that you applied in Step 4), click the Refresh button 🔁 on the Standard Buttons toolbar.

Figure 8-36	DATA ACCESS PAGE IN THE BROWSER

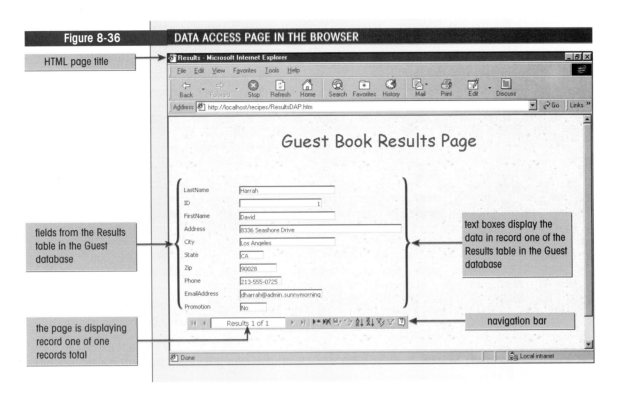

HTML page title

fields from the Results table in the Guest database

text boxes display the data in record one of the Results table in the Guest database

navigation bar

the page is displaying record one of one records total

The data access page contains the title that you created in Access Page Design view, the fields from the Results table in the Guest database, the values for the first record, and a navigation bar. Figure 8-37 describes the buttons that appear on the navigation bar.

Figure 8-37	DATA ACCESS PAGE NAVIGATION BAR BUTTONS AND THEIR DESCRIPTIONS

BUTTON	BUTTON NAME	DESCRIPTION
◄	First Record	Displays the first record in the table or query on which the data access page is based
◄	Previous Record	Displays the previous record in the table or query on which the data access page is based
►	Next Record	Displays the next record in the table or query on which the data access page is based
►◄	Last Record	Displays the last record in the table or query on which the data access page is based
►*	New Record	Clears the fields in the data access page so that a new record can be entered in the table or query on which the data access page is based
✗	Delete Record	Deletes the record that is displayed by the data access page from the table or query on which the data access page is based
🖫	Save Record	Saves the record in the table on which the data access page is based
✎	Undo Last Change	Reverses the previous action
A↓Z	Sort Ascending	Sorts the records in ascending order based on the current active field
Z↓A	Sort Descending	Sorts the records in descending order based on the current active field
⊽	Filter By Selection	Lets you set a filter to display a subset of the records in the table or query on which the data access page is based using the value in the current active field
⊽	Remove Filter	Removes the currently applied filter
?	Help	Opens the Microsoft Access Data Pages Help window

Adding a Record Using a Data Access Page

You can use the data access page to enter a new record, just as you would use the Guest Book page and its form component to add a new record. A customer won't use the data access page to enter a record, but David wants you to use the page to enter a new record so you can practice using the data access page.

REFERENCE WINDOW   **RW**

Adding a Record to a Database Table Using a Data Access Page

- Click the New Record button on the navigation bar in the Web page.
- Enter the data into the text boxes. Press the Tab key to move the insertion point to the next text box.
- Click the Save Record button on the navigation bar to save the record.

To add a record to a table using a data access page:

1. Click the **New Record** button 🔲 on the navigation bar in the Web page. Internet Explorer clears the fields. Notice that the insertion point is blinking in the LastName field.

2. Type **Bay** in the LastName text box, and then press the **Tab** key. The insertion point moves to the ID text box, but it is not blinking. Because this field has the AutoNumber data type, you cannot enter data into this field. Access will automatically enter a value in the ID field when you save the record.

3. Press the **Tab** key to move to the FirstName text box. The insertion point is blinking, which means that you can enter data into the text box.

4. Type **Amanda**, and then press the **Tab** key to move to the Address text box.

5. Press the Tab key as necessary to enter the following data into the remaining text boxes (do not press the Tab key after entering the data in the Promotion text box): Address: **5942 Los Verdes Drive**; City: **Los Angeles**; State: **CA**; Zip: **90026**; Phone: **213-555-0810**; Email Address: **abay@hotmail.com**; and Promotion: **Yes**.

6. After entering the data in the Promotion text box, click the **Save Record** button 🔲 on the navigation bar. Access saves the record in the Results table. The AutoNumber data type in the ID field added the value 2 to the ID text box. See Figure 8-38. Amanda's record is record 1 because the sort order that you specified—alphabetically by LastName—sorts the record with the LastName "Bay" before the record with the LastName "Harrah."

Figure 8-38   ADDING A NEW RECORD

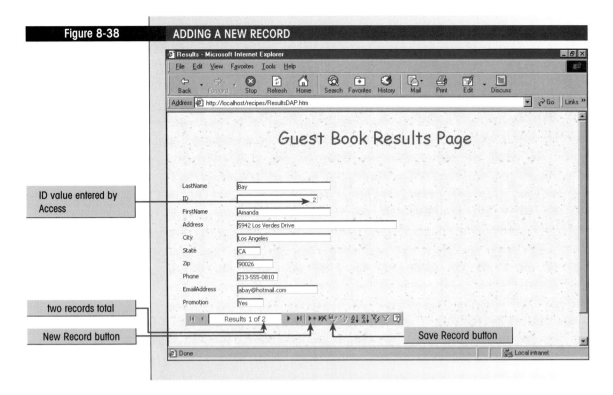

ID value entered by Access

two records total

New Record button

Save Record button

Viewing Records Using a Data Access Page

Now the Results table in the Guest database contains two records. The Results table will eventually contain hundreds of records. David wants you to use the buttons on the navigation bar to practice sorting and browsing records.

To view the records in the table using the data access page:

1. Click the **Last Record** button ▶| on the navigation bar. Internet Explorer displays the last record (for David Harrah), which has the ID 1.

2. Click the **Previous Record** button ◀ on the navigation bar. Internet Explorer displays the first record (for Amanda Bay), which has the ID 2.

3. Click in the **FirstName** text box, and then click the **Sort Descending** button ⇩ on the navigation bar. Internet Explorer sorts the records in descending order by the FirstName field, and then moves the insertion point to the LastName field. The record for David Harrah is displayed because the FirstName "David" comes first in descending alphabetical order. You can sort records based on any field by clicking the field prior to clicking a sort button.

4. Click in the **State** text box, and then click the **Filter By Selection** button ⍦ on the navigation bar. The filter will select only those records that contain the value "CA" in the State field. Two fields are selected, as indicated by the "Results 1 of 2" text in the navigation bar.

5. Click the **Remove Filter** button ⍦ on the navigation bar to remove the filter.

6. Click in the **Zip** text box, and then click ⍦. Only one record is selected because only one record in the Results table contains this Zip code.

7. Click ⍦ on the navigation bar to remove the filter.

8. Click the **Close** button ☒ on the Internet Explorer title bar to close Internet Explorer.

TROUBLE? If a Confirm Save dialog box opens and asks if you want to replace the fpdb/guest.mdb file, click the Yes button.

David wants you to view the HTML code for the Guest Book Results Page so you can see all of the HTML code required to create it.

Viewing **HTML Code for a Data Access Page**

When you created the Results data access page using Access and then saved it, Access created the HTML code for the page. The data access page includes code to define each field in the page, including its formatting properties and name, label, and position in the page.

To view the HTML code for the data access page:

1. If necessary, click the **Microsoft FrontPage** program button on the taskbar to return to FrontPage.

2. Click the **HTML** tab, press **Ctrl + Home** to scroll to the top of the page, and then scroll down the page so that the META tag for the theme appears at the top of the Contents pane. See Figure 8-39. Notice that each object in the data access page requires several lines of code to define its properties.

| Figure 8-39 | HTML CODE FOR THE DATA ACCESS PAGE |

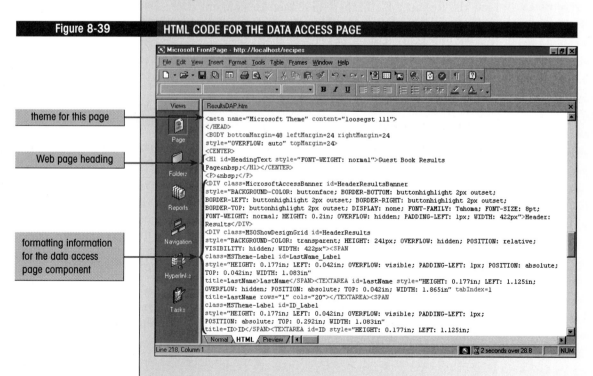

3. Press the **Page Down** key to see the HTML code for the rest of the objects in the data access page. Figure 8-40 shows the HTML code that creates the navigation buttons in the navigation bar.

Figure 8-40   HTML CODE FOR THE DATA ACCESS PAGE, CONTINUED

creates the navigation bar and its buttons and calls their functions (you might need to scroll the window to the right to see all of your code)

code that creates each button

4. Click the **Close** button ☒ on the FrontPage title bar to close the ResultsDAP.htm file, the recipes Web site, and FrontPage.

In the next tutorial, you will learn how to include Office components and a cascading style sheet in a Web page.

Session 8.2 QUICK CHECK

1. FrontPage saves database files used with database connections in the _____ folder of the Web site.
2. True or False: You use the Form Properties dialog box to configure the form fields to save in a database table using a database connection.
3. True or False: You can use a database connection to store information about the Web page user's browser type and computer name.
4. What is a data access page?
5. True or False: You can use FrontPage to create a data access page.
6. What settings are available when you use the Page Wizard to create a new data access page?
7. To add a new record to a table using a data access page, click the _____ button on the navigation bar.

REVIEW ASSIGNMENTS

The Web pages that you created in this tutorial have the functionality that David needs. However, the default pages created by the Wizards do not have the same appearance as other pages in the Web site. David asks you to format the Web pages and to finalize their appearance. In addition, you will also change the settings for pages that contain customer data so that they are not published when the Web site is ultimately moved to the Sunny Morning Products Web server.

If necessary, start FrontPage, insert your Data Disk in the appropriate disk drive, and then do the following:

1. Open the **recipes** Web site from your computer's PWS (http://localhost/recipes) in Folders view.

2. Open the Customer Query page (**customer_query.asp**) in Page view. Create a centered heading at the top of the page using the text "Customer List." (*Hint*: With the insertion point at the beginning of the first cell in the table, press the Enter key.) Apply the Heading 1 style to the heading.

Explore
3. Use the Database Results Wizard to change the message that appears when no records are returned in the query for the Customer Query page. (*Hint*: Click the More Options button in the Database Results Wizard – Step 3 of 5 dialog box.) The new message is "There are no records in the database that match your request." Go to the Database Results Wizard – Step 4 of 5 dialog box.

Explore
4. Change the formatting options for the Database Results region in the Customer Query page to display a list with one field per item. Add labels for all field values, place a horizontal separator between records, and use the Paragraphs list option. Click the Next button, accept the default settings in the last dialog box, and then click the Finish button.

5. Change the headings for each form field in the Customer Query page to Last Name, First Name, Phone Number, Email Address, Category, and Subject. (Keep the colon that follows each heading name.)

6. Add a normal, left-aligned paragraph under the heading that you added in Step 2 that says: "This customer list displays current data collected from the Feedback Web page in the Sunny Web site. Refresh the page to update the data. Records are sorted alphabetically by last name."

7. Save the page, and then preview it using the browser. (*Hint*: You might need to refresh the page to see the revised page.) Use the browser to print the first page of the Customer Query page, and then close Internet Explorer.

8. Change the settings for the Customer Query page to exclude it when publishing the Web site. (*Hint*: Click File on the menu bar, click Properties, click the Workgroup tab in the Page Properties dialog box, and then click the appropriate check box.) Save and close the page.

9. Open the Customer Query Search page (**customer_query_search.asp**) in Page view. Create a centered heading at the top of the page using the text "Customer List Search Page." (*Hint*: The heading will appear in the search form component in Page view, but it will appear as a heading when viewed using the browser.) Apply the Heading 1 style to the heading. Use the hint provided in Step 8 to exclude this page when publishing the Web site. Save and close the page.

Explore
10. In Folders view, change the page title of the data access page (**ResultsDAP.htm**) to "Guest Book Results Page." Then open the page in Page view. Change the labels that appear to the left of the LastName, FirstName, and EmailAddress text boxes to Last Name, First Name, and Email Address, respectively. (*Hint*: Click the label, click the insertion point in the label to position it, and then edit the label. You might not be able to see the insertion point.) Save the Guest Book Results Web page.

11. Use the browser to print the first page of data in the Guest Book Results Page, and then close the browser.

12. Close FrontPage.

CASE PROBLEMS

Case 1. Integrating a Database with the Web Site for Royal Hair Care Products As part of a new promotional campaign, Valerie Suarez wants to provide customers with a means of obtaining a product sample from a new product line of styling gels made from all-natural ingredients, including herbs and fruits. Royal Hair Care Products will use the styling gels to roll out a new product line next year that includes shampoos and conditioners. Valerie wants to include a new Web page in the Web site that collects interested visitors' first and last names, address, city, state, Zip code, and home telephone number.

Valerie asks you to create the following new pages: a "Request Product" page that includes a form that sends its results to an Access database named "Royal"; an Active Server Page named "Customer Information" that displays data in the Royal database; and a data access page named "Customer Data Access Page" that provides access to the table in the Royal database containing the data stored by the Request Product Web page.

If necessary, start FrontPage, insert your Data Disk in the appropriate disk drive, and then do the following:

1. Read all the questions for this case problem, and then prepare a planning analysis sheet for the enhancements to the royal Web site.

2. Open the **royal** Web site from your computer's PWS. The default location is http://localhost/royal.

3. Import the **Royal** database from the Tutorial.08 folder on your Data Disk into the royal Web site. Use the database connection name "Royal" and store all database files in the fpdb folder of the Web site.

4. Create a new page in Page view with the title "Request Product" and the filename **sendinfo.asp**. (*Hint*: Enter the page title before changing the Save as type option to "Active Server Pages.")

5. Add the Request Product page (**sendinfo.asp**) to the Web site's navigation structure as a child page of the Home Page. Position the Request Product page between the What's New and Feedback pages in the navigation structure.

Explore   6. Add a brief introductory paragraph under the navigation bar. Use the information in the Case Problem description to determine the appropriate content.

Explore   7. Insert a form component below the paragraph that you added in Step 6. The form component should contain the following one-line text box form fields: First Name, with the name FirstName and a width of 50 characters; Last Name, with the name LastName and a width of 50 characters; Address, with the same name and a width of 70 characters; City, with the same name and a width of 50 characters; State, with the same name and a width of 2 characters; Zip Code, with the name ZipCode and a width of 10 characters; and Phone, with the same name and a width of 15 characters. You choose the layout for the form fields in the form component.

Explore   8. Verify the Royal database connection, and then set the form to send its results to the Customer table in the Royal database stored in the fpdb folder of the royal Web site. Do not collect any additional fields.

9. Save the Request Product page, and then preview it in the browser. Complete the Request Product page using your own name and address information, print the page, and then submit the form to the server. Close Internet Explorer.

10. Open the **Royal** database from FrontPage, run the Customer Query, and then confirm that the form handler correctly stored your data. Close Access.

11. Close the Request Product page, and then create a new page in Page view with the title "Customer Information" and the filename **custinfo.asp**. Change the setting for the Customer Information page to exclude it when publishing the Web site. (*Hint*: Click

File on the menu bar, click Properties, click the Workgroup tab in the Page Properties dialog box, and then click the appropriate check box.) Then turn off the display of the top shared border for only this page. Save the page.

12. Add a centered heading with the Heading 1 style at the top of the page using the text "Customer Information." Then create a Database Results region that displays the records from the Customer Query in the Royal database. Include all fields from the query, accept the default formatting options, and display all records together. After the Database Results region is inserted in the Web page, change the column headings to more meaningful names, and then apply the Heading 4 style and center them. Save the page and preview it in the browser. Use the browser to print the page, and then close the browser.

13. Open the **Royal** database from FrontPage, and then click the Pages object in the Database window. Use a Wizard to create a data access page based on the Customer table. Include all fields in the page, do not use a grouping level, sort the records in alphabetical order by LastName, and change the default title to "Customer Data Access Page."

14. Enter the page title "Customer Data Access Page" at the top of the new data access page, and then save it as **custDAP** in the root folder of the royal Web site (c:\Inetput\wwwroot\royal). Close Access.

15. Open the Customer Data Access Page (**custDAP.htm**) in Page view, apply the Web site's theme to the page, and then exclude the page when publishing the Web site. (*Hint*: You might need to right-click the filename, and then click Open With and select the FrontPage option to open the page in Page view.) Save the page and then preview it in the browser. Use the data access page to add a new record to the table using real or fictitious data. Print the page using the browser, and then close the browser.

16. Close FrontPage.

Case 2. Integrating a Database with the Web Site for Buffalo Trading Post Donna Vargas, president of Buffalo Trading Post (BTP), knows that customer service is an important ingredient in the success of BTP. She realizes that many of her loyal customers might use a computer for business, but do not want to use their e-mail addresses for receiving personal correspondence. In response to customer requests, Donna wants to create a database of information that the promotion department can use to send advertisements about sales and promotions to customers. Donna wants you to create a Web page that will accept input from the user, a Web page that displays customer information, and a data access page that displays all records in the database and provides functionality to update them.

If necessary, start FrontPage, insert your Data Disk in the appropriate disk drive, and then do the following:

1. Read all the questions for this case problem, and then prepare a planning analysis sheet for the enhancements to the buffalo Web site.

2. Open the **buffalo** Web site from your computer's PWS. The default location is http://localhost/buffalo.

3. Import the **Buffalo** database from the Tutorial.08 folder on your Data Disk into the buffalo Web site. Use the database connection name "Buffalo" and store all database files in the fpdb folder of the Web site.

4. Create a new page in Page view with the title "Add to Mailing List" and the filename **mailinfo.asp**. (*Hint*: Enter the page title before changing the Save as type option to "Active Server Pages.")

5. Add the Add to Mailing List page (**mailinfo.asp**) to the Web site's navigation structure as a child page of the Home Page. Position the Add to Mailing List page to the left of the What page in the navigation structure.

Explore ▶ 6. Insert into the Add to Mailing List Web page a centered picture page banner and a centered FrontPage navigation bar with horizontal text hyperlinks to same-level pages and to the Home and parent pages. Then add a brief introductory paragraph under the navigation bar, but *not* in the bottom shared border of the Web page. Use the information in the Case Problem description to determine the appropriate content.

Explore

7. Insert a form component below the paragraph that you added in Step 6. The form component should contain the following one-line text box form fields: First Name, with the name FirstName and a width of 50 characters; Last Name, with the name LastName and a width of 50 characters; Address, with the same name and a width of 70 characters; City, with the same name and a width of 50 characters; State, with the same name and a width of 2 characters; Zip Code, with the name Zip and a width of 10 characters; Phone, with the same name and a width of 15 characters; and Email Address, with the name EmailAddress and a width of 50 characters. You choose the layout for the form fields in the form component.

Explore

8. Verify the Buffalo database connection, and then set the form to send its results to the MailingList table in the Buffalo database stored in the fpdb folder of the buffalo Web site. Do not collect any additional fields.

9. Save the Add to Mailing List page, and then preview it in the browser. Complete the Add to Mailing List page using your own name and address information, print the page, and then submit the form to the browser. Close Internet Explorer.

10. Open the **Buffalo** database from FrontPage, run the MailingList Query, and then confirm that the form handler correctly stored your data. Close Access.

11. Close the Add to Mailing List page, and then create a new page in Page view with the title "Mailing List Information" and the filename **maillist.asp**. Change the settings for the Mailing List Information page to exclude it when publishing the Web site. (*Hint*: Click File on the menu bar, click Properties, click the Workgroup tab in the Page Properties dialog box, and then click the appropriate check box.) Save the page.

12. Add a centered heading with the Heading 1 style at the top of the page using the text "Mailing List Information." Then create a Database Results region that displays the records from the MailingList Query in the Buffalo database. Include all fields from the query, accept the default formatting options, and display all records together. After the Database Results region is inserted in the Web page, change the column headings to more meaningful names, and then apply the Heading 3 style and center them. Select the database fields (the row between the start and end of the Database Results region), and then change the fields to 10-point text. Save the page and preview it in the browser. Use the browser to print the page, and then close the browser.

13. Open the **Buffalo** database from FrontPage, and then click the Pages object in the Database window. Use a Wizard to create a data access page based on the MailingList table. Include all fields in the page, do not use a grouping level, sort the records in ascending order by ID, and change the default title to "Mailing List Data Access Page."

14. Enter the page title "Mailing List Data Access Page" at the top of the new data access page, and then save it as **mailDAP** in the root folder of the buffalo Web site (c:\Inetput\wwwroot\buffalo). Close Access.

15. Open the Mailing List Data Access Page (**mailDAP.htm**) in Page view, apply the Web site's theme to the page, and then exclude the page when publishing the Web site. (*Hint*: You might need to right-click the filename, and then click Open With and select the FrontPage option to open the page in Page view.) Save the page, and then preview it in the browser. Use the data access page to add a new record to the table using real or fictitious data. Use the browser to print the record that you added, and then close the browser.

16. Close FrontPage.

Case 3. *Integrating a Database with the Web Site for Garden Grill* Nolan Simmons wants to include a new Web page in the Web site for Garden Grill that lets customers enter comments into a form whose results are stored in an Access database. Nolan hopes to use this information to gather information about regional trends, which might lead to new menu items. He wants the form to contain a scrolling text box that lets users enter information about whatever is on their minds—including the restaurant, service, menu, etc.

When the menu is updated, Nolan can use the information stored in the database to provide mailing lists to the marketing department so it can mail coupons and new menus to current and past customers.

If necessary, start FrontPage, insert your Data Disk in the appropriate disk drive, and then do the following:

1. Read all the questions for this case problem, and then prepare a planning analysis sheet for the enhancements to the garden Web site.

2. Open the **garden** Web site from your computer's PWS. The default location is http://localhost/garden.

3. Import the **Garden** database from the Tutorial.08 folder on your Data Disk into the garden Web site. Use the database connection name "Garden" and store all database files in the fpdb folder of the Web site.

4. Create a new page in Page view with the title "Customer Comments" and the filename **comments.asp**. (*Hint*: Enter the page title before changing the Save as type option to "Active Server Pages.")

5. Add the Customer Comments page (**comments.asp**) to the Web site's navigation structure as a child page of the Home Page. Position the Customer Comments page between the Career Opportunities and Feedback Web pages.

Explore　6. Add a brief introductory paragraph under the navigation bar in the Web page. Use the information in the Case Problem description to determine the appropriate content.

Explore　7. Insert a form component below the paragraph that you added in Step 6. The form component should contain the following one-line text box form fields: First Name, with the name First and a width of 50 characters; Last Name, with the name Last and a width of 50 characters; Address, with the same name and a width of 70 characters; City, with the same name and a width of 50 characters; State, with the same name and a width of 2 characters; Zip Code, with the name Zip and a width of 10 characters; Phone, with the same name and a width of 15 characters; and Email Address, with the name Email and a width of 50 characters. Also create a scrolling text box named Comments, with the same name, a height of five lines, and a width of 70 characters. You choose the layout for the form fields in the form component.

Explore　8. Verify the database connection, and then set the form to send its results to the Comments table in the Garden database stored in the fpdb folder of the garden Web site. Do not collect any additional fields.

9. Save the Customer Comments page, and then preview it in the browser. Complete the Customer Comments page using your own name and address information, print the page, and then submit the form to the browser. Close Internet Explorer.

10. Open the **Garden** database from FrontPage, run the Comments Query, and then confirm that the form handler correctly stored your data. Close Access.

11. Close the Customer Comments page, and then create a new page in Page view with the title "Comments from Customers" and the filename **custinfo.asp**. Change the settings for the Comments from Customers page to exclude it when publishing the Web site. (*Hint*: Click File on the menu bar, click Properties, click the Workgroup tab in the Page Properties dialog box, and then click the appropriate check box.) Turn off the top shared border for this page, and then save the page.

Explore　12. Add a centered heading that uses the Heading 2 style at the top of the page using the text "Comments from Customers." Then create a Database Results region that displays the records from the Comments Query in the Garden database. Include all fields from the query. Sort the records in ascending alphabetical order by the Last field. Accept the default formatting options and display all records together. After the Database Results region is inserted in the Web page, change the column headings to more meaningful names, and then apply the Heading 4 style and center them. Select the database fields (the row between the start and end of the Database Results region), and then change the fields to 10-point text. Save the page, and then preview it in the browser. Use the browser to print the page, and then close the browser.

Explore   13. Open the **Garden** database from FrontPage, and then click the Pages object in the Database window. Use a Wizard to create a data access page based on the Comments table. Include all fields in the page except for the ID field, group the records using the State field, and change the default title to "Customer Comments Data Access Page."

14. Enter the page title "Customer Comments Data Access Page" at the top of the new data access page, and then save it as **custDAP** in the root folder of the garden Web site (c:\Inetput\wwwroot\garden). Close Access.

Explore   15. Open the Customer Comments Data Access Page (**custDAP.htm**) in Page view, apply the Web site's theme to the page, and then exclude the page when publishing the Web site. (*Hint*: You might need to right-click the filename, and then click Open With and select the FrontPage option to open the page in Page view.) Save the page, and then preview it in the browser. How did the grouping option that you set using the Database Results Wizard change the way that data is displayed in the page? What happens when you click the ⊕ icon to the left of the GroupOfComments – State label? How can Garden Grill use the grouping levels to improve the menu?

16. Close FrontPage.

Case 4. Integrating a Database with the Web Site for Replay Music Factory Charlene Fields wants to let customers browse the inventory of Replay Music Factory (RMF) using a Web page. She wants customers to be able to select a category of music and then display the store's inventory. Alec Johnston will be in charge of entering the records for in-stock items into a database. While he is working on this extensive project, Charlene asks you to create the Web pages in the Web site that will let customers browse the site. Eventually, Charlene will add additional pages to the Web site that accept online orders.

If necessary, start FrontPage, insert your Data Disk in the appropriate disk drive, and then do the following:

1. Read all the questions for this case problem, and then prepare a planning analysis sheet for the enhancements to the replay Web site.

2. Open the **replay** Web site from your computer's PWS. The default location is http://localhost/replay.

3. Import the **Replay** database from the Tutorial.08 folder on your Data Disk into the replay Web site. Use the database connection name "Replay" and store all database files in the fpdb folder of the Web site.

4. Verify the database connection.

Explore   5. Open the **Replay** database from FrontPage, and then click the Pages object in the Database window. Use a Wizard to create a data access page based on the Inventory table. Include all fields in the page, do not specify a grouping level or a sort order, and change the default title to "Replay Music Inventory."

6. Enter the page title "Replay Music Inventory" at the top of the new data access page, and then save it as **invDAP** in the root folder of the replay Web site (c:\Inetput\wwwroot\replay). Close Access.

Explore   7. Open the Replay Music Inventory page (**invDAP.htm**) in Page view, and then apply the Web site's theme to the page. Change the AlbumTitle, StockID, and YearReleased labels to Album Title, Stock ID, and Year Released, respectively. Save the page, and then preview it in the browser. Use the data access page to enter one record for a real or fictitious album. Save the record. (*Hint*: The valid categories are Pop, Rock and Roll, Country & Western, Classical, Spanish, Children's, and Comedy. The valid ratings are Adult, General, Youth, and Not Rated. The ID field is an AutoNumber field. The StockID field can contain letters and digits to make a product code.) Use the browser to print the record that you added.

Explore   8. Use a button on the navigation bar to delete the record that you entered in Step 7.

Explore   9. Use a filter to sort the data access page to display records from the Classical category. How many records were selected?

Explore   10. Remove the filter that you applied in Step 9. Sort the records in ascending alphabetical order by album title. Which album is listed first?

Explore   11. Sort the records in descending order by artist name. Which album is listed first?

12. Close Internet Explorer and FrontPage.

QUICK | CHECK ANSWERS

Session 8.1

1. A database connection specifies the name, location, and type of database that you want to access from a FrontPage Web.

2. Copy the database file in Windows Explorer, open the Web site in FrontPage, right-click the Folder List, click Paste on the shortcut menu, enter the name of the database connection, and then click the Yes button. Click the Yes button again to store the database's files in the fpdb folder of the FrontPage Web.

3. You must enable the Web site to use Active Server Pages and to run scripts.

4. A component in a Web page that contains HTML code and client-side and server-side scripts that retrieve and display data from the database in the Web page.

5. filter

6. False

7. False

8. True

Session 8.2

1. fpdb

2. False

3. True

4. A Web page that uses a form to display data from the Access object on which it is based; the page has controls that let you add, delete, sort, filter, browse, and change the data displayed by the page.

5. False

6. The available settings are: select the table or query on which to base the data access page, select the fields to display in the data access page, select an optional grouping level, select optional sort orders, and enter a title.

7. New Record

LAB ASSIGNMENTS

Databases

These Lab Assignments are designed to accompany the interactive Course Lab called Databases. To start the Databases Lab, click the Start button on the Windows taskbar, point to Programs, point to Course Labs, point to New Perspectives Applications, and then click Databases. If you do not see Course Labs on your Programs menu, see your instructor or technical support person.

Databases   The Databases Lab demonstrates the essential concepts of file and database management systems. You will use the Lab to search, sort, and report the data contained in a file of classic books.

1. Click the Steps button to review basic database terminology and to learn how to manipulate the classic books database. As you proceed through the Steps, answer the Quick Check questions that appear. After you complete the Steps, you will see a Quick Check Summary Report. Follow the instructions on the screen to print this report.

2. Click the Explore button. Make sure you can apply basic database terminology to describe the classic books database by answering the following questions:
   a. How many records does the file contain?
   b. How many fields does each record contain?
   c. What are the contents of the Catalog # field for the book written by Margaret Mitchell?
   d. What are the contents of the Title field for the record with Thoreau in the Author field?
   e. Which field has been used to sort the records?

3. In Explore, manipulate the database as necessary to answer the following questions:
   a. When the books are sorted by title, what is the first record in the file?
   b. Use the Search button to search for all books in the West location. How many do you find?
   c. Use the Search button to search for all books in the Main location that are checked in. What do you find?

4. In Explore, use the Report button to print a report that groups the books by Status and sorts them by title. On your report, circle the four field names. Draw a box around the summary statistics showing which books are currently checked in and which books are currently checked out.

OBJECTIVES

In this tutorial you will:

- Insert a spreadsheet component in a Web page

- Insert a chart component in a Web page

- Resize Office components in a Web page

- Get Help for an Office component

- Understand how to use a PivotTable list component in a Web page

- Create user-defined styles for fonts, paragraphs, and hyperlinks

- Link a Web page to a cascading style sheet

- Create a new Web page and its content in HTML Page view

- Modify HTML tags and verify results using Reveal Tags

LABS

Spreadsheets

USING OFFICE COMPONENTS AND STYLES, AND WORKING WITH HTML CODE

Using Components and Styles in the Recipes Web Site

CASE

Sunny Morning Products

The recipes Web site will include hundreds of new pages within the next few months. David Harrah wants to make sure that the Web site development team has the resources it needs to make appropriate decisions on expanding and improving the site as it is introduced to customers. David is confident that the Web site will meet its original goals of featuring recipes for popular products and for collecting information about the site's visitors.

David wants you to include two new components in a Web page that he created so the Web site development team can easily determine which Web pages are the most popular. David wants to include a spreadsheet in a Web page that contains data about the number of times that each Web page in the Web site is opened. The spreadsheet will show the results by category. This information will help the team determine whether some recipes are more popular than others. David also wants this information to appear in a chart format to help illustrate Web site usage visually.

The team also expressed an interest in using a different format for new Web pages to distinguish them from existing pages. Currently, all Web pages use the same Web theme. The team feels that this approach makes it difficult when browsing the Web site to distinguish Web pages that promote special sales and events. David wants you to create a style sheet that authors can use to format new Web pages in a different way. For example, the style sheet will include different styles for headings, text, and hyperlinks to distinguish it from the ones used in the Web theme.

Finally, throughout this book you have examined the HTML code that FrontPage uses to create your Web pages. As your final assignment, David wants you to use HTML Page view to create a new Web page and add content to it. Then you will use Normal Page view to display some of the HTML tags used to create the page.

When you are finished with this tutorial, the Web site development team will be ready to create new pages using your style sheet and to use data collected by Sunny Morning Products to plan future enhancements to the Web site.

SESSION 9.1

In this session, you will insert a spreadsheet and chart component in a Web page. You will change the characteristics of these components by resizing them and using the commands in the Toolbox to change their properties. You will also learn how to get Help while using a component. Finally, you will learn how pivot tables are used to display data.

Using Pre-built Office Components in a Web Page

FrontPage includes many tools that let you view and display information in a Web page. The Office 2000 programs—Word, Excel, Access, and PowerPoint—all include commands that let you save their documents as Web pages so you can include these pages in a FrontPage Web. In many cases, you must have the original Office 2000 program installed on your computer to update the Web page that you created; you cannot use FrontPage to make the update. For example, if you use Excel to create a chart and then save the workbook that contains the chart as a Web page in a FrontPage Web, you must use Excel to make any changes to that chart.

You can use FrontPage to create a worksheet, chart, or pivot table in a Web page by inserting an Office component into the Web page. An **Office component** is a self-contained object in a Web page that includes the commands and tools required to use it—but it is important to note that an Office component is *not* an embedded object from another Office program. A **worksheet**, or **spreadsheet**, is a tool that lets you analyze and summarize data. A **chart** displays spreadsheet data as a picture, such as in a pie chart or a bar chart. A **PivotTable list** is an interactive spreadsheet that lets you quickly summarize, organize, and display large amounts of data.

When you insert an Office component in a Web page, FrontPage creates the object and the tools and commands necessary to manipulate it. For example, to create a Web page that contains spreadsheet data, you could create an Excel workbook and save it as a Web page. Another option would be to create a Web page in FrontPage, insert an Office spreadsheet component in it, and then enter the data directly into the component. An Office component does not include the same powerful functionality as an Excel workbook, but the component does contain tools to let you perform calculations and to format the data's appearance and change its characteristics.

You insert each object in a Web page by clicking the Insert Component button on the Standard toolbar and then clicking the component name. If you do not see the component that you want to insert in the list of choices, the Office components are not installed on your server or your FrontPage Web is not configured to support them.

David wants to include a spreadsheet and a chart in a Web page that display the Web site's activity by category. Figure 9-1 shows David's planning analysis sheet for the enhancements that you will make to the recipes Web site in this tutorial.

| Figure 9-1 | DAVID'S PLANNING ANALYSIS SHEET FOR ENHANCING THE RECIPES WEB SITE |

Planning Analysis Sheet

Objective

Enhance the recipes Web site by adding spreadsheet and chart components to the Activity Report Web page to show the Web site's activity by category and by creating a Web page that contains styles to use in the new recipe pages. Also, to practice entering and formatting Web page content and features using HTML Page view.

Requirements

Activity Report Web page

Excel workbook that contains the Web site's statistics by category

Results

A Web page that includes a spreadsheet and chart showing the Web site's statistics by category, and a style sheet that authors can use to create special styles in future Web pages for new recipes.

Inserting a Spreadsheet Component in a Web Page

When you need to display spreadsheet data in a Web page, you can select one of two methods to include the data. The first method is to create the workbook in Excel and then save it as a Web page by clicking File on the menu bar, clicking Save as Web Page, and then saving the file in the desired Web site as an HTML document. For this method, you must have Excel installed on your computer to create the spreadsheet.

When you don't have Excel on your computer, you can still insert spreadsheet data in a Web page by inserting an Office spreadsheet component. The **Office spreadsheet component** will provide the capability to enter, format, and update spreadsheet data using only FrontPage. When you insert a spreadsheet component, you are really inserting an object that includes spreadsheet commands and tools *similar* to those found in Excel. In fact, the object itself looks like a miniature Excel program window, and the commands and tools provided by the spreadsheet component are also similar to those found in Excel.

REFERENCE WINDOW　　　　　　　　　　　　　　　　　　　　**RW**

Inserting a Spreadsheet Component in a Web Page

- Create a new Web page to contain the spreadsheet component, or open an existing Web page and click the insertion point in the location in which to insert the component.
- Click the Insert Component button on the Standard toolbar, and then click Office Spreadsheet.
- Click in the Microsoft Office Spreadsheet window that opens, and then enter the data that you want to include in the Web page.
- Click the Property Toolbox button on the Microsoft Office Spreadsheet toolbar to open the Spreadsheet Property Toolbox. Use the commands and tools in the Toolbox to calculate and format the data.
- Click anywhere outside the Microsoft Office Spreadsheet window to deselect it.

David has been collecting information about the Web site's statistics in an Excel workbook that he saved in the Tutorial.09 folder on your Data Disk. He obtained this data from the network administrator at Sunny Morning Products. He wants to create a Web page in the recipes Web site that the Web site development team can use to determine which recipe categories are the most popular, as indicated by the number of times that users have opened pages from each category. After examining this data, the team can make decisions about future expansions to the site. For example, the team might find that recipes for cakes are opened frequently, but recipes for butters are not.

Because several members of the Web site development team do not have Excel installed on their computers, David wants you to insert a spreadsheet component in the Web page to display this information. He already created the Web page that will contain the spreadsheet component and the Excel workbook that contains the data. You will import both of these files into the Web site from your Data Disk. After inserting the spreadsheet component in the Web page, you will use the Spreadsheet Property Toolbox to import the data from David's Excel workbook into the spreadsheet component.

To import the Web page and data file, and then insert the spreadsheet component:

1. Start **FrontPage**, open the recipes Web site from your computer's Web server (**http://localhost/recipes**), and then, if necessary, change to Folders view.

2. Click **File** on the menu bar, click **Import**, and then click the **Add File** button. The Add File to Import List dialog box opens.

3. Click the **Look in** list arrow, change to the drive or folder that contains your Data Disk, and then double-click the **Tutorial.09** folder.

4. Click **Activity**, press the **Ctrl** key, click **Openings**, release the **Ctrl** key, and then click the **Open** button. Click the **OK** button to import the Activity and Openings files into the recipes Web site.

5. Double-click **activity.htm** in the Contents pane to open the Activity Report Web page in Page view. Notice that David created two placeholders in the page to indicate where to insert the spreadsheet and chart components.

6. Select the text **Insert spreadsheet component here**, click the **Insert Component** button 🖼 on the Standard toolbar, and then click **Office Spreadsheet**. A Microsoft Office Spreadsheet object is inserted in the Web page.

TROUBLE? If you do not see the Office Spreadsheet option on the Insert Component button list, press the Esc key to close the list. Click Tools on the menu bar, click Page Options, and then click the Compatibility tab. If necessary, click the ActiveX controls and the VBScript check boxes to select them, click the OK button, and then repeat Step 6. If you still do not see the Office Spreadsheet option, ask your instructor or technical support person for help.

7. Click the **Microsoft Office Spreadsheet** component to select it. Sizing handles appear around the component to indicate that it is selected. See Figure 9-2.

Figure 9-2   SPREADSHEET COMPONENT INSERTED IN THE WEB PAGE

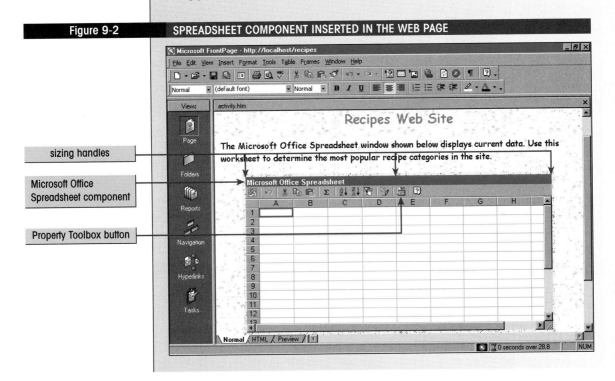

After inserting the spreadsheet component, you can either click in a cell and enter data just as you would in Excel, or use the Spreadsheet Property Toolbox to import data into the spreadsheet component. Because David already created the data that you need and you already imported his file into the Web site, you will use the Import Data command to enter his data into the spreadsheet component.

Importing Data into a Spreadsheet Component

You already imported the file that contains the data you will import into the spreadsheet component. After you insert a spreadsheet component in a Web page, you can use the commands on the Spreadsheet Property Toolbox to manipulate the data. The Toolbox contains commands similar to those found in Excel.

To open the Spreadsheet Property Toolbox and import the data:

1. Click the **Property Toolbox** button 🖻 on the Microsoft Office Spreadsheet toolbar to open the Spreadsheet Property Toolbox. See Figure 9-3. Depending on your installation of FrontPage, the Toolbox might appear in a different location

or the bars for one or more menus might be expanded to show commands. You can move the Toolbox anywhere on the screen by dragging its title bar. In addition, you can click the Close button ☒ on the Toolbox title bar to close it.

Figure 9-3	SPREADSHEET PROPERTY TOOLBOX

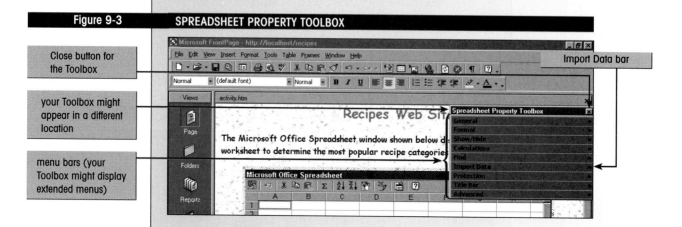

Close button for the Toolbox

your Toolbox might appear in a different location

menu bars (your Toolbox might display extended menus)

Import Data bar

You need to expand the Import Data bar to display the command to import the data.

2. Click the **Import Data** bar in the Toolbox. The Import Data commands are visible. See Figure 9-4. You will provide the URL to the openings.htm file in the Web site and then import the file into the spreadsheet component.

Figure 9-4	EXPANDED IMPORT DATA BAR

Spreadsheet Property Toolbox
General
Format
Show/Hide
Calculations
Find
Import Data
URL:
[   ]
Import Now
☐ Refresh from URL at run time
Protection
Title Bar
Advanced

3. Click in the **URL** text box, and then type
http://localhost/recipes/openings.htm

TROUBLE? If you are storing your Web site on a computer with a different name or on a different server, use the path for your server instead of the one provided in Step 3.

4. Click the **Import Now** button in the Toolbox. The data from the openings.htm file is entered into the spreadsheet component. Notice that the Refresh from URL at run time check box becomes active. See Figure 9-5. You can select this check box to ensure that the data in the spreadsheet component always displays current data from the data source (openings.htm) when the Web page is

opened or refreshed in the browser. However, the data source must be a file that exists in the Web site on the server. You cannot use this feature when you are importing data from an outside data source, or the browser will issue an error message. David doesn't want you to use this feature.

| Figure 9-5 | IMPORTING DATA INTO THE SPREADSHEET COMPONENT |

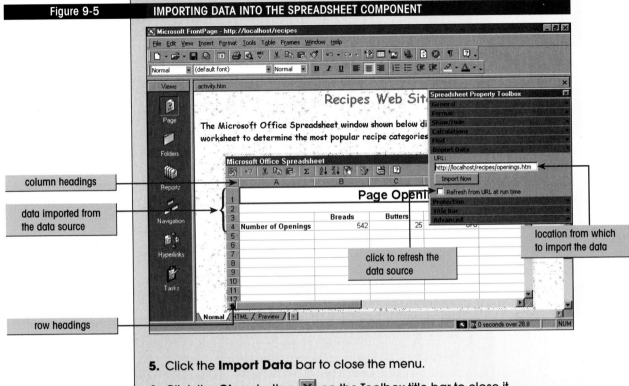

column headings

data imported from the data source

row headings

click to refresh the data source

location from which to import the data

5. Click the **Import Data** bar to close the menu.

6. Click the **Close** button ☒ on the Toolbox title bar to close it.

Resizing Worksheet Columns

Notice that the spreadsheet component has vertical and horizontal scroll bars. Users can click the scroll arrows on the scroll bars to scroll the worksheet. However, David doesn't want users to need to scroll the data in the spreadsheet component, so he asks you to resize the columns.

To resize the worksheet columns:

1. Point to the column heading labeled **A** in the worksheet so that the pointer changes to a ⊹ shape.

2. Click and hold down the mouse button, and then drag the pointer to the column heading labeled **G** to select columns A through G. When you move the pointer over the column heading labeled E, the window will scroll to the left so you can see the column heading labeled G. When you have selected the column headings A through G, release the mouse button. The columns are selected. See Figure 9-6.

Figure 9-6 **SELECTING COLUMNS IN A WORKSHEET**

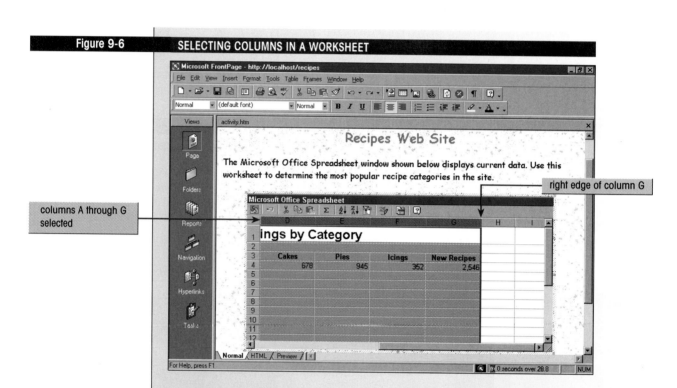

columns A through G selected

right edge of column G

3. Point to the right edge of the column heading labeled **G** so that the pointer changes to a ✛ shape, and then double-click the right edge. The columns are resized to their best fit, which means that each column is slightly wider than the data it contains.

4. Press **Ctrl + Home** to scroll to column A in the worksheet. See Figure 9-7. Now the data in the worksheet fits in the spreadsheet component better.

Figure 9-7 **RESIZED WORKSHEET COLUMNS**

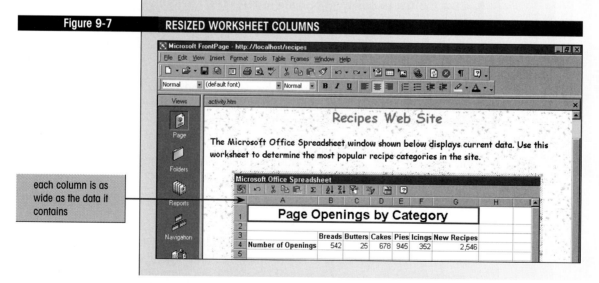

each column is as wide as the data it contains

Getting Help When Using the Spreadsheet Component

Regardless of your experience using Excel, you might need help using the commands in the Spreadsheet Property Toolbox. Fortunately, the spreadsheet component has its own Help system to help you use the commands in the Toolbox. The Help command is available on the General menu. David suggests that you use the Help window to learn about formatting data in a spreadsheet component.

To get Help while using the spreadsheet component:

1. Click the **Property Toolbox** button 🖼 on the Microsoft Office Spreadsheet toolbar to open the Toolbox.

2. Click the **General** bar to display those commands. See Figure 9-8.

Figure 9-8	GENERAL BAR SELECTED

3. Click the **Help** button 🔲 in the Toolbox. The Microsoft Spreadsheet Help window opens. If necessary, click the **Maximize** button 🔲 on the Microsoft Spreadsheet Help title bar to maximize the window. See Figure 9-9. Just like other Microsoft Help windows, the Microsoft Spreadsheet Help window has a Contents tab and a Search tab. You use the Contents tab to search for Help by category, and you use the Search tab to search for Help using a key term. You will use the Contents tab to search for Help on formatting data.

Figure 9-9	MICROSOFT SPREADSHEET HELP WINDOW

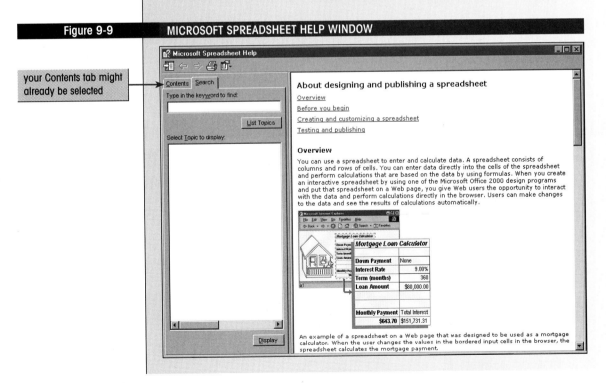

4. If necessary, click the **Contents** tab to select it, and then click ⊞ for the Formatting Spreadsheets and Data category.

5. Click **Change the appearance of data in a spreadsheet**. The Help window displays links to pages that describe how to change the format and alignment of data. Click some of the links and read the Help pages that open to learn about formatting and aligning spreadsheet data.

6. After reading the information about formatting and aligning data, click the **Close** button ☒ on the Microsoft Spreadsheet Help window to close it.

7. Click the **Close** button ☒ on the Toolbox title bar to close it.

When you need information about other formatting options, performing calculations, or other topics of interest, you can open the Help window to obtain information about your task.

Resizing a Spreadsheet Component in a Web Page

The spreadsheet component that you inserted in the Web page is an object, just like a picture or text. The spreadsheet component is selected when sizing handles appear around its outside border. You drag a sizing handle to resize the component.

David thinks that the spreadsheet component might look better if you resize it to fit the data in the worksheet, making it smaller.

To resize the spreadsheet component:

1. Make sure that the spreadsheet component is still selected. Sizing handles appear around the component.

2. Click the middle-right sizing handle, and then slowly drag it to the left so that the right edge of the component is slightly to the right of the column labeled **G** in the worksheet.

3. Click the middle-bottom sizing handle, and slowly drag it up so that the bottom edge of the component is slightly below row **4** in the worksheet. See Figure 9-10.

Figure 9-10	RESIZED SPREADSHEET COMPONENT

no empty cells appear in the component

> TROUBLE? If you cannot see all of the data in the worksheet, click and drag a sizing handle to make the spreadsheet component larger or smaller as necessary so that your component looks like the one shown in Figure 9-10.
>
> 4. Click the **Save** button 🖫 on the Standard toolbar to save the page.

Inserting a Chart Component in a Web Page

When you need to display data in a Web page graphically, you can insert an **Office chart component** to create many types of charts. Before inserting the chart component, you first must create a data source on which to base the chart. The most common data source for a chart is the data contained in a spreadsheet component. A **data source** is an ActiveX control that links the chart component to its data. When the Web page in which you are inserting a chart component contains a link to a valid data source, a Microsoft Office Chart Wizard starts and lets you select a chart type and subtype, the data source for the chart, and the data range to use to create the chart. After inserting the chart component, you can change its properties using the Chart Property Toolbox, which contains commands for working with charts.

The spreadsheet component that you added to the Activity Report Web page is a valid data source that you will use to create the chart. David wants to create a pie chart. A **pie chart** displays data as pieces of a pie to show the relationship of each piece to the whole. David feels that a pie chart will make it easy to determine which recipe category is the most popular.

REFERENCE WINDOW   **RW**

Inserting a Chart Component in a Web Page That Contains a Data Source

- Open the Web page that contains the data source in Page view, and then click the insertion point in the desired location for the chart.
- Click the Insert Component button on the Standard toolbar, and then click Office Chart. The Microsoft Office Chart Wizard starts.
- Select the desired chart type and subtype, and then click the Next button.
- If necessary, select the data source that contains the data you want to display in the chart, and then click the Next button.
- Click the Set this chart's data in one step button to open the Data Range dialog box. If necessary, enter the range reference that contains the data you want to chart in the Data range text box. Click the Rows or Columns option button to indicate where the data is stored.
- Click the OK button.
- Click the Finish button.

David wants you to create a pie chart using the data in the spreadsheet component. You will use the Microsoft Office Chart Wizard to create the pie chart.

To create the pie chart:

1. Scroll down the Web page as necessary so that you can see the "Insert chart component here" text. This is where you will create the chart.

2. Select the text **Insert chart component here**.

3. Click the **Insert Component** button 🖳 on the Standard toolbar, and then click **Office Chart**. FrontPage inserts a chart component in the Web page and starts the Microsoft Office Chart Wizard. See Figure 9-11.

| Figure 9-11 | INSERTING A CHART COMPONENT IN A WEB PAGE |

selected chart type

available subtypes for the selected chart type

description of the selected chart subtype

data source for the chart component

chart component inserted in the Web page

selected text in the Web page

4. Click **Pie** in the Chart type list box. Notice that the Chart sub-type area displays the three different types of pie charts from which you can select. The box at the bottom of the dialog box shows a description of the selected chart subtype. You will use the default pie chart subtype, which is the first one on the left.

5. Make sure that the Pie sub-type is selected, and then click the **Next** button. The second dialog box asks you to select a data source for your chart. Because the Web page contains only one valid data source, the data source is already selected for you. If the Web page contained multiple data sources, then you would need to select the one that contains the data you want to chart. See Figure 9-12.

| Figure 9-12 | SELECTING A DATA SOURCE FOR THE CHART COMPONENT |

spreadsheet component in the Activity Report Web page

default spreadsheet component name

6. Click the **Next** button. The final dialog box of the Microsoft Office Chart Wizard opens. FrontPage added the spreadsheet component's title (Page Openings by Category) to the Series list box. You need to identify the cells in the spreadsheet component that contain the chart's data.

7. Click the **Set this chart's data in one step** button [icon] in the dialog box. The Data Range dialog box opens. The range reference in the Data range text box identifies the data values to use to prepare the chart. For the spreadsheet component, the data is in the range =A3:G4, or cells A3 through G4. The Series in setting tells the chart component where your data is located—in rows or in columns. The data in the spreadsheet component is located in rows, so you will need to select the Rows option button.

8. Select the value in the Data range text box, type **=A3:G4**, and then click the **Rows** option button, even if it is already selected. See Figure 9-13. The chart in the Wizard changes to reflect the new settings.

TROUBLE? If you do not see the sample pie chart in the Microsoft Office Chart Wizard dialog box, click the Rows option button in the Data Range dialog box.

Figure 9-13   **SELECTING THE DATA RANGE TO CHART**

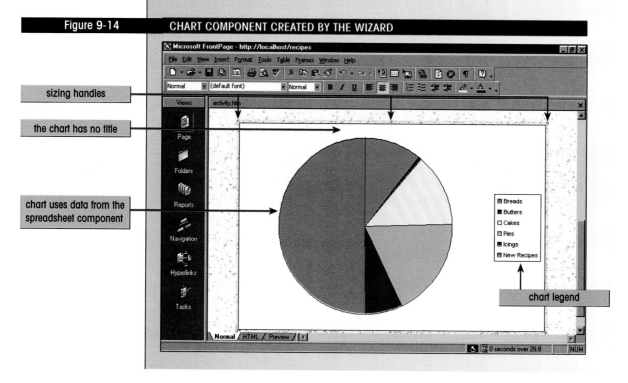

preview of the chart

chart legend

the data to chart
appears in rows

the data to chart is
in this range

9. Click the **OK** button to close the Data Range dialog box, and then click the **Finish** button to close the Wizard and create the chart. See Figure 9-14.

Figure 9-14   **CHART COMPONENT CREATED BY THE WIZARD**

sizing handles

the chart has no title

chart uses data from the
spreadsheet component

chart legend

Resizing a Chart Component in a Web Page

You can resize the chart component using the sizing handles, just as you resized the spreadsheet component. David thinks that the chart component is larger than it needs to be, so he asks you to resize it.

To resize the chart component:

1. Make sure that the chart component is still selected. Sizing handles will appear around the chart component's border.

2. Scroll up the Web page so that you can see some of the spreadsheet component and some of the chart component.

3. Click and drag the top-left sizing handle on the chart component down and towards the pie chart to resize the chart so that it is approximately the same width as the spreadsheet component. See Figure 9-15.

| Figure 9-15 | **RESIZED CHART COMPONENT** |

4. Click the **Save** button 🖫 on the Standard toolbar to save the page.

You can change the properties of the chart component by opening the Chart Property Toolbox. This Toolbox provides access to some of the same charting commands that you would find in Excel.

Changing the Properties of a Chart Component

The chart component does not include a toolbar. To open the Chart Property Toolbox, right-click the part of the chart that you want to format, and then click Property Toolbox on the shortcut menu. Different menu bars will be available in the Toolbox, depending on what you selected in the chart component when you opened it. David wants you to include the chart's title in the chart component.

To open the Chart Property Toolbox and add the chart's title to the chart component:

1. Click the **chart component** to select it, right-click the **chart component** (but not the chart itself) to open the shortcut menu, and then click **Property Toolbox**. The Chart Property Toolbox opens.

   TROUBLE? If you do not see the Property Toolbox command on the shortcut menu, the chart component was not selected when you right-clicked it. Press the Esc key to close the shortcut menu, and then repeat Step 1.

2. Click the **Chart** bar to show those commands.

   TROUBLE? If you do not see the Chart bar on the Toolbox, then you right-clicked the pie chart in Step 1. Click the Close button ⊠ on the Chart Property Toolbox to close it, and then repeat Steps 1 and 2.

3. Click the **Show title** check box to select it. The title "Number of Openings" appears in the chart component. This title was taken from the row heading in the spreadsheet component that contains the data. See Figure 9-16.

Figure 9-16	CHART PROPERTY TOOLBOX

chart title is the row heading for the row that contains the chart's data

expanded Chart bar

4. Click the **Chart** bar to close the Chart commands, and then click the **General** bar. Notice that the Chart Property Toolbox also contains a Help button. Clicking the Help button in this Toolbox opens the Microsoft Office Chart Help window, which provides Help for creating and formatting charts.

5. Click the **Help** button 🔲 in the Toolbox to open the Microsoft Office Chart Help window. Explore some of the topics in the window. When you are finished, click the **Close** button ⊠ on the Help window to close it.

6. Click the **Close** button ⊠ on the Chart Property Toolbox to close it.

7. Click the **Save** button 🖫 on the Standard toolbar to save the page.

Examining a Data Source Icon

When you created the chart component in the Web page, FrontPage inserted an ActiveX control icon in the page. Because you used a data source that exists in the same Web page, you don't need to configure an external data source. (Configuring an external data source is beyond the scope of this book.) However, you can examine the icon so you know what it is.

To examine an ActiveX control:

1. Press **Ctrl + Home** to scroll to the top of the Web page. The ActiveX control icon appears at the top of the page. This icon will not appear in the browser.

2. Double-click the **ActiveX control** icon. The ActiveX Control Properties dialog box opens. See Figure 9-17.

Figure 9-17	ActiveX CONTROL PROPERTIES DIALOG BOX

default object name for the ActiveX control

layout options for the ActiveX control

URL of the file on the network or server that contains the ActiveX control

a Web browser that does not display ActiveX controls will display the HTML name (when one is used) instead of the control

3. Click the **Close** button ⊠ on the ActiveX Control Properties dialog box to close it.

Now that you have finished creating the page, you can preview it using the browser. When you insert an Office component in a Web page, you provide the Web page's user with the capability to change the data in the spreadsheet component. Changing data in the spreadsheet component will also change the way that data is displayed in the chart component.

To preview a Web page that contains Office components and update data:

1. Click the **Preview in Browser** button 🔍 on the Standard toolbar. Internet Explorer opens and displays the Activity Report Web page. Notice that the ActiveX control icon does not appear at the top of the page.

   TROUBLE? If a dialog box opens and asks you to save your changes, click the Yes button.

2. If necessary, scroll down the Web page to see the chart component. The chart is displayed with a legend and title.

3. Double-click cell **C4** in the spreadsheet component, and then type **350**. Watch the chart as you press the **Enter** key. The pie slice that represents the Butters category increases in size to reflect the increased value in the spreadsheet component. See Figure 9-18.

Figure 9-18	CHANGING SPREADSHEET DATA USING THE WEB PAGE

new value

chart title

You changed the value for the Butters category in the Web page that is displayed in the browser. However, the spreadsheet component in the Web page in FrontPage still contains the original value. If you refresh the page, Internet Explorer will display the changed data in the spreadsheet component and in the pie chart, and not the original stored value. The value stored in the spreadsheet component in the Web page in FrontPage is still 25.

4. Click the **Refresh** button 🗘 on the Standard Buttons toolbar. The Butters value is still 350 in the spreadsheet component.

5. Click the **Close** button ⊠ on the Internet Explorer title bar to close it. If necessary, click the **Microsoft FrontPage** program button on the taskbar to return to FrontPage.

6. Click 🔍 on the Standard toolbar to open the Activity Report Web page in the browser. Notice that the value 25 still appears in cell C4.

7. Click ⊠ on the Internet Explorer title bar to close it, and then click ⊠ on the Microsoft FrontPage title bar to close FrontPage.

Inserting the spreadsheet and chart components provides you with worksheet capabilities in the Web page, without requiring you to use Excel.

Using a PivotTable List Component in a Web Page

The last type of Office component—the **PivotTable list component**—is an advanced tool that you can create using data from a spreadsheet, database, or other source. Before inserting a PivotTable list component in a Web page, you first must design a pivot table using a program that supports it. Access and Excel both include commands for creating pivot tables. In this section, you will not create a PivotTable list component in a Web page, but you will learn the general steps for creating one in a Web page.

Figure 9-19 shows how you might use a pivot table to display starting salary information for men and women working in four professions. The first figure shows the data on which the following four pivot tables are based. The data is stored in an Excel workbook. The first pivot table shows the minimum salary for each profession, arranged by gender. The second pivot table shows the maximum salary, and the third pivot table shows the average salary. The fourth pivot table shows the number of positions held in each profession by gender. To create each pivot table, the developer simply changed the formula that Excel uses in the computation by selecting MIN, MAX, AVG, or COUNT from a list. After the developer selected the function, Excel automatically changed the pivot table to display the requested data. As you can see, the pivot table did the work of organizing, formatting, and performing calculations on the original data.

Figure 9-19 — SAMPLE USES OF A PIVOT TABLE

Worksheet data on which the pivot table is based

PROFESSION	GENDER	SALARY	PROFESSION	GENDER	SALARY
Accountant	Male	$23,415	Journalist	Male	$32,546
Accountant	Female	$29,000	Journalist	Female	$21,543
Accountant	Female	$31,020	Journalist	Female	$24,556
Accountant	Female	$29,150	Journalist	Male	$36,487
Accountant	Male	$23,774	Journalist	Male	$35,000
Accountant	Male	$35,121	Registered Nurse	Female	$36,000
Computer Programmer	Female	$33,541	Registered Nurse	Female	$38,000
Computer Programmer	Male	$38,465	Registered Nurse	Male	$40,543
Computer Programmer	Female	$39,451	Registered Nurse	Male	$33,000
Computer Programmer	Female	$29,465	Registered Nurse	Female	$33,500
Computer Programmer	Male	$38,461	Registered Nurse	Female	$38,465
Computer Programmer	Male	$38,946	Registered Nurse	Female	$30,000
Journalist	Male	$20,167	Registered Nurse	Female	$31,573
Journalist	Male	$22,675`			

Pivot table showing the minimum
salary for each profession by gender

Min of Salary	Gender ▼		
Profession ▼	Female	Male	MIN
Accountant	$29,000.00	$23,415.00	$23,415.00
Computer Programmer	$29,465.00	$38,461.00	$29,465.00
Journalist	$21,543.00	$20,167.00	$20,167.00
Registered Nurse	$30,000.00	$33,000.00	$30,000.00
MIN	$21,543.00	$20,167.00	$20,167.00

Pivot table showing the maximum
salary for each profession by gender

Max of Salary	Gender ▼		
Profession ▼	Female	Male	MAX
Accountant	$31,020.00	$35,121.00	$ 35,121.00
Computer Programmer	$39,451.00	$38,946.00	$ 39,451.00
Journalist	$24,556.00	$36,487.00	$ 36,487.00
Registered Nurse	$38,465.00	$40,543.00	$ 40,543.00
MAX	$39,451.00	$40,543.00	$ 40,543.00

Pivot table showing the average
salary for each profession by gender

Average of Salary	Gender ▼		
Profession ▼	Female	Male	AVG
Accountant	$29,723.33	$27,436.67	$ 28,580.00
Computer Programmer	$34,152.33	$38,624.00	$ 36,388.17
Journalist	$23,049.50	$29,375.00	$ 27,567.71
Registered Nurse	$34,589.67	$36,771.50	$ 35,135.13
AVG	$31,804.57	$32,200.00	$ 31,994.96

Pivot table showing the number of positions
held in each profession by gender

Count of Salary	Gender ▼		
Profession ▼	Female	Male	COUNT
Accountant	3	3	6
Computer Programmer	3	3	6
Journalist	2	5	7
Registered Nurse	6	2	8
COUNT	14	13	27

In addition to recalculating the data, you can click the list arrow on the Profession or Gender button to exclude data from the pivot table. For example, clicking the Profession list arrow and then clicking Computer Programmer would cause Excel to exclude the Computer Programmer data from the pivot table and then redisplay it. You can use the list arrows to exclude or include information from the pivot table instantly.

After you complete the pivot table, you need to associate the data source for the pivot table with the pivot table itself. After you complete all of these steps, you can insert a PivotTable list component in the Web page using the Insert Component button. When users open the Web page that contains the PivotTable list component, they will be able to change its values to arrange the data in an acceptable manner, similar to how the data is displayed in Figure 9-19.

It is important to note that some browsers cannot display PivotTable list components in a Web page. You should plan your PivotTable lists carefully to ensure that all users of your Web site will be able to display and use them. For more information about creating and using pivot tables, consult the Help system for Access or Excel. After inserting a PivotTable list component in a Web page, click the Help button in the General bar of the PivotTable Property Toolbox for more information about using this component in a Web page.

In the next session, you will create a style sheet that formats text, paragraphs, and hyperlinks in Web pages.

Session 9.1   QUICK | CHECK

1. What are the three types of Office components that you can create in a Web page?

2. When should you use a spreadsheet component to display spreadsheet information in a Web page?

3. True or False: You can use the Help button in the Toolbox for an Office component to open a Help window that contains Help topics specific to the selected Office component.

4. True or False: You cannot resize an Office component after inserting it in a Web page.

5. In order for the Microsoft Office Chart Wizard to start, your Web page must contain a(n) _____.

6. What is the data range for a chart component?

7. True or False: To open the Chart Property Toolbox, click the Property Toolbox button on the chart component toolbar.

8. True or False: When you insert a spreadsheet component in a Web page, FrontPage inserts an ActiveX control icon in the Web page.

9. The two Office programs that you can use to create a pivot table are _____ and _____.

SESSION 9.2

In this session, you will create a cascading style sheet that contains user-defined styles for HTML tags. You will link the cascading style sheet to a new Web page and use it to format headings, text, and hyperlinks in the new Web page.

Using User-Defined Styles in a Web Page

Throughout this book, you have used the Style list box on the Formatting toolbar to apply different styles to text in a Web page. For example, when you select text in a Web page that does not use a theme and then apply the Heading 1 style to it, FrontPage applies the default font and paragraph settings for that specific style to the text that you selected. In this case, the default style for the Heading 1 style is 24-point, bold, Times New Roman, black, left-aligned text. When you apply a theme to the same Web page, the Heading 1 style changes to match the defined style of the theme for the Heading 1 style; for example, it might be 24-point, Comic Sans MS, purple, centered text. In other words, you might apply the Heading 1 style to selected text in several Web pages and the Heading 1 style might have different characteristics in each page.

In any single Web page, the defined style for an HTML element will be the same throughout the page. If your Heading 2 style is defined as 12-point, bold, Times New Roman text, then all text that uses the Heading 2 style in that Web page will be 12-point, bold, Times New Roman text.

Creating a Cascading Style Sheet

When you want to change the default style that is associated with an HTML element in a Web page, you can use the Style dialog box to apply new characteristics to a specific HTML tag. For example, if you want the Heading 2 style to use 12-point, Arial text, then you would select the H2 tag in the Style dialog box and change its font specifications to 12-point, Arial text. Then all text in the Web page—or throughout an entire Web site—that uses the Heading 2 style will change to 12-point, Arial text. After you modify an HTML tag in the Style dialog box, the tag that you modified becomes a **user-defined style**. You can list user-defined styles separately so you know which ones have been redefined from the default settings in the Web page.

Using styles is handy when you want headings and other elements that appear within a Web page to have the same appearance. You could format each heading separately using the Formatting toolbar, but creating a user-defined style is much easier and ensures that all similar elements in the Web page have the same appearance.

If you want to apply your user-defined styles to every page in a Web site, you can create those styles in an *empty* Web page and then save the Web page as a cascading style sheet (CSS). A **cascading style sheet** is a template that you use to link other Web pages to the user-defined styles you have created. For example, you might create a cascading style sheet that uses a specific background sound and applies user-defined styles to the Heading 1, Heading 2, and Heading 3 styles. When you create a new Web page in a Web site, you can link the cascading style sheet to the new page to make these styles available immediately. The only exception to this rule is when the Web page uses a theme. In this case, the theme provides the styles that define the different HTML elements in the Web page. To change the appearance of HTML elements in a Web page that uses a theme, click the Modify button in the Themes dialog box and then click the Color, Graphics, or Text button to change the style of different elements used in the theme. You can still use a cascading style sheet to make changes to a theme; however, it is better to use the Themes dialog box to make most changes, as the theme's settings will override most user-defined styles.

During your meeting with the Web site development team, one team member suggested creating a new page in the recipes Web site that will promote special sales and events at Sunny Morning Products. For example, during the first two weeks in November, customers who order online from the Sunny Morning Products Web site will receive a 10 percent discount on all sales as a bonus for ordering holiday gifts early. David wants these "specials" pages to have an appearance different from other pages in the Web site to distinguish them from the recipe and discussion group pages. He suggests that you create a cascading style sheet and define some of the styles that will be used in the specials pages.

REFERENCE   WINDOW   RW

Creating a Cascading Style Sheet

- Open a new Web page in Page view.
- Click Format on the menu bar, and then click Style.
- Click the HTML tag that you want to modify in the Styles list box to select it, and then click the Modify button.
- Click the Format button in the Modify Style dialog box, and then click the characteristic that you need to modify (Font, Paragraph, Border, Numbering, or Position).
- Make the desired changes in the dialog box that opens, and then click the OK button.
- Click the OK button three times to close the dialog boxes.

To create a cascading style sheet, you define the styles in a Web page and then save the Web page as a HyperText Style Sheet in the Web site. After saving the cascading style sheet, you can link it to other Web pages using the Style Sheet Links command on the Format menu. It is important to remember that the Web page that you save as a cascading style sheet must not contain any content—it must be empty, except for the defined styles.

David wants you to create a style sheet in which the Heading 1 style uses a centered, maroon, 24-point, Arial Rounded MT Bold font. The Heading 2 style should use left-aligned, maroon, 14-point, Arial Rounded MT Bold font. Regular text in the Web page should use 12-point, Arial Narrow font. Finally, hyperlinks should use 12-point, navy blue, underlined, bold Arial Narrow font. David feels that these different settings, in addition to not using the Web site's theme, will make these pages stand out effectively. You will create a new Web page that does not use the Web site's theme, and then you will open the Style dialog box.

To create a new Web page and open the Style dialog box:

1. Start **FrontPage**, open the recipes Web site (**http://localhost/recipes**) from your computer's PWS, and then, if necessary, change to Page view. If necessary, click the **New Page** button 🗋 on the Standard toolbar to create a new page. A new, blank page that uses the Web site's theme opens in Page view. You will change this page so that it will not use the theme.

2. Click **Format** on the menu bar, and then click **Theme**. The Themes dialog box opens.

3. Click the **Selected page(s)** option button to select it.

4. Click **(No Theme)** in the list box, and then click the **OK** button. The page background changes to white, indicating that the theme was removed from this page.

5. Click **Format** on the menu bar, and then click **Style**. The Style dialog box opens. See Figure 9-20.

Figure 9-20   **STYLE DIALOG BOX**

HTML tag names

all standard HTML tags are listed alphabetically

preview of the paragraph style for the selected HTML tag

preview of the character style for the selected HTML tag

Modifying an HTML Tag's Default Style

The Styles list box includes all HTML tags available for use in your document. You might recognize some of the tags immediately—for example, the BGSOUND tag is used to define a background sound in a Web page. Other tags, however, are not as easy to decipher. Unfortunately, FrontPage does not include a resource to help you interpret the HTML tags listed in the Styles list box. If you need help identifying the HTML tag to change in your Web pages, search the Internet for Web sites that describe HTML tags or consult an HTML reference book.

You will change the Heading 1 style first.

To modify the Heading 1 style:

1. Scroll down the **Styles** list, and then click **h1**. H1 is the HTML tag equivalent for the Heading 1 style.

2. Click the **Modify** button. The Modify Style dialog box opens. Notice that the HTML tag name appears in the Name (selector) text box.

3. Click the **Format** button. See Figure 9-21. You will change the font first.

Figure 9-21   MODIFY STYLE DIALOG BOX

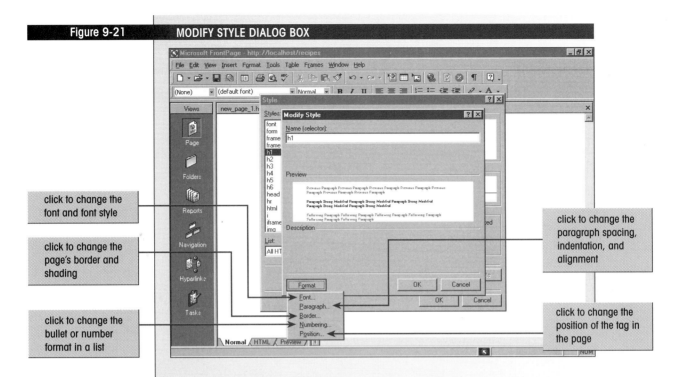

click to change the font and font style

click to change the page's border and shading

click to change the bullet or number format in a list

click to change the paragraph spacing, indentation, and alignment

click to change the position of the tag in the page

4. Click **Font** in the Format button list. The Font dialog box opens. You need to change the font to 24-point, maroon, and Arial Rounded MT Bold.

5. Click **Arial Rounded MT Bold** in the Font list box, scroll down the Size list box and click **24pt**, click the **Color** list arrow, click the **Maroon** color in the list, and then click the **OK** button. The Font dialog box closes, and the Modify Style dialog box now displays a preview and description of the new style. See Figure 9-22.

Figure 9-22   MODIFIED H1 TAG

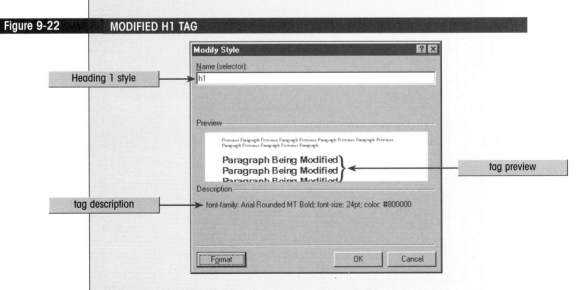

Heading 1 style

tag preview

tag description

font-family: Arial Rounded MT Bold; font-size: 24pt; color: #800000

You still need to change the paragraph alignment to centered, so you will not close the Modify Style dialog box yet.

6. Click the **Format** button, and then click **Paragraph**. The Paragraph dialog box opens.

7. Click the **Alignment** list arrow, and then click **Center**. See Figure 9-23.

Figure 9-23	PARAGRAPH DIALOG BOX

center alignment selected

8. Click the **OK** button to close the Paragraph dialog box, and then click the **OK** button in the Modify Style dialog box to close it. The Style dialog box is displayed again. The H1 style now appears in the Styles list box as a user-defined style. See Figure 9-24.

Figure 9-24	USER-DEFINED STYLES IN THE WEB PAGE

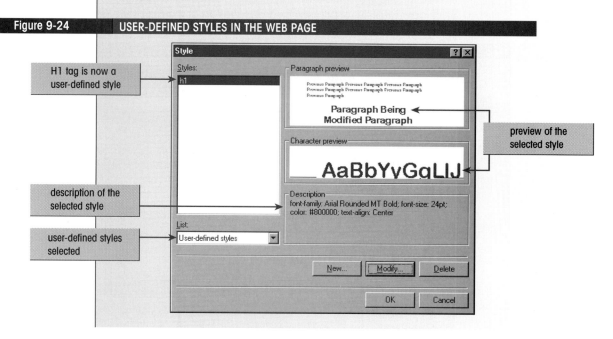

H1 tag is now a user-defined style

preview of the selected style

description of the selected style

user-defined styles selected

You can redefine other styles by changing the List list box to display all HTML tags again. Next you will redefine the Heading 2 style using David's specifications.

To redefine the Heading 2 style:

1. Click the **List** list arrow, and then click **All HTML tags**. The Styles list box now displays all HTML tags available for use in the document.

2. Click **h2** in the Styles list, and then click the **Modify** button. The Modify Style dialog box opens. You will change the font first.

3. Click the **Format** button, click **Font**, click **Arial Rounded MT Bold**, scroll down the Size list box and click **14pt**, click the **Color** list arrow, click the **Maroon** color, and then click the **OK** button. The Font dialog box closes and the Modify Style dialog box is displayed again. Next, change the alignment to left.

4. Click the **Format** button, click **Paragraph**, click the **Alignment** list arrow, click **Left**, and then click the **OK** button. The Paragraph dialog box closes. The Modify Style dialog box now displays the settings for the Heading 2 style. See Figure 9-25.

Figure 9-25	MODIFIED H2 TAG

Heading 2 tag name

tag preview

tag description

5. Click the **OK** button. The Style dialog box is displayed again and displays all HTML tags in the Styles list box.

   TROUBLE? If necessary, click the List list arrow, and then click All HTML tags to display that list.

Now you can redefine the style used for hyperlinks. By default, hyperlinks appear as blue, underlined text. You will change the hyperlinks to match David's specifications. The HTML equivalent for a hyperlink is the A tag.

To change the hyperlink style:

1. Scroll up the **Styles** list, click **a**, and then click the **Modify** button. To change the appearance of a hyperlink, you use the Font dialog box.

2. Click the **Format** button, and then click **Font**. The Font dialog box opens.

3. Click **Arial Narrow** in the Font list box, click **Bold** in the Font style list box, scroll down the Size list box and click **12pt**, click the **Color** list arrow, click the **Navy** color, click the **Underline** check box to select it, and then click the **OK** button. The Font dialog box closes and the Modify Style dialog box now displays the description for the A tag. See Figure 9-26.

Figure 9-26	MODIFIED A TAG

4. Click the **OK** button to close the Modify Style dialog box. The Style dialog box is displayed again and shows all HTML tags.

TROUBLE? If necessary, click the List list arrow, and then click All HTML tags to display that list.

David also wants to change the default font used with the Normal style to 12-point, Arial Narrow text. The HTML tag for normal text in a Web page is the BODY tag.

To change the Normal text style:

1. Click **body** in the Styles list box, and then click the **Modify** button. The Modify Style dialog box opens.

2. Click the **Format** button, and then click **Font**. The Font dialog box opens.

3. Click **Arial Narrow** in the Font list box, scroll down the Size list box and click **12pt**, and then click the **OK** button.

4. Click the **OK** button in the Modify Style dialog box to close it. You can view the styles that you modified by changing the Styles list box to display user-defined styles.

5. Click the **List** list arrow, and then click **User-defined styles**. The Styles list box now displays the H1, H2, A, and BODY tags.

6. Click the **OK** button to close the Style dialog box. The Web page in which you just created these styles does not contain any content in Page view. The only "content" contained in the unsaved Web page is the styles. You can view these styles in HTML Page view.

7. Click the **HTML** tab. The styles for the H1, H2, A, and BODY tags appear as gray text in the HTML document. See Figure 9-27.

Figure 9-27	HTML CODE FOR A CASCADING STYLE SHEET

STYLE tags enclose the user-defined styles that you created

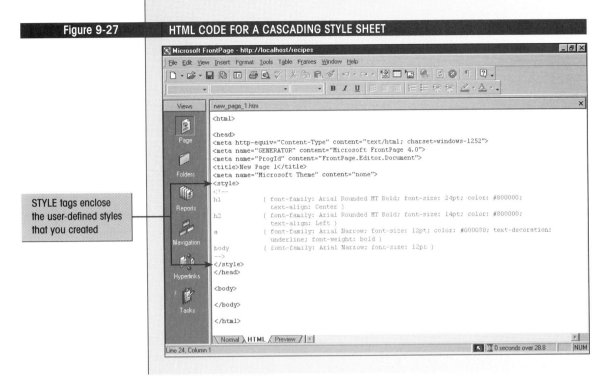

Saving a Web Page as a Cascading Style Sheet

The Web page doesn't contain any content—it contains only the styles you created. If you entered and formatted content in this Web page, you could apply the new styles to text that uses the Heading 1, Heading 2, Normal, and hyperlink styles. However, you will save this Web page as a cascading style sheet to make it available to use with other pages. If you don't save a Web page that contains user-defined styles as a cascading style sheet, then the user-defined styles are available *only* in the Web page that contains them.

To save the Web page as a cascading style sheet:

1. Click the **Save** button 🖫 on the Standard toolbar. The Save As dialog box opens.

2. Click the **Change** button to open the Set Page Title dialog box, type **Cascading Style Sheet** in the Page title text box, and then click the **OK** button.

3. Click the **Save as type** list arrow, and then click **HyperText Style Sheet**.

4. Select the text in the File name text box, and then type **Specials**.

5. Click the **Save** button. The title bar for the Contents pane displays the page's filename, Specials.css, indicating that this page is a cascading style sheet.

Creating a New Web Page and Linking It to a Cascading Style Sheet

Now the cascading style sheet is saved in the recipes Web site. You can use the styles in this page by linking it to a Web page. You will close the Specials.css style sheet, create a new Web page, remove the theme, and enter some sample text in the new page. Then you will link the cascading style sheet to the Web page. The new Web page will use the user-defined styles that you created in the Specials cascading style sheet.

To create a new Web page that uses the cascading style sheet:

1. Click the **Close** button ☒ on the Contents pane to close the Specials.css page.

2. Click the **New Page** button ☐ on the Standard toolbar to create a new Web page. The new Web page uses the Web site's theme. The theme's styles will override most user-defined styles, so you will turn off the theme for this page.

3. Click **Format** on the menu bar, click **Theme**, click the **Selected page(s)** option button to select it, click **(No Theme)** in the list box, and then click the **OK** button. The Themes dialog box closes and the new Web page displays a white background. You will enter some sample text in the new Web page before linking this Web page to the cascading style sheet.

4. Type **Heading 1**, press the **Enter** key, type **Heading 2**, press the **Enter** key, type **Normal**, press the **Enter** key, and then type **Hyperlink**.

5. Use the Style list box on the Formatting toolbar to format the Heading 1 text with the **Heading 1** style and the Heading 2 text with the **Heading 2** style. The Normal text that you typed already uses the Normal style, so you don't need to change it. You can create a hyperlink to test the hyperlink style.

6. Select the **Hyperlink** text, click the **Hyperlink** button 🖼 on the Standard toolbar, and then scroll down the list and double-click **Default.htm**. The Create Hyperlink dialog box closes and the Hyperlink text changes to underlined, indicating that it is now formatted as a hyperlink.

   Now you are ready to link the new Web page to the cascading style sheet.

7. Click **Format** on the menu bar, and then click **Style Sheet Links**. The Link Style Sheet dialog box opens. Notice that you can apply a cascading style sheet to all pages in the Web site or to only the selected page. You will apply the cascading style sheet named Specials.css to the selected page.

8. If necessary, click the **Selected page(s)** option button to select it, and then click the **Add** button. The Select Hyperlink dialog box opens.

9. Double-click **Specials.css** in the list box. The Select Hyperlink dialog box closes, and the Link Style Sheet dialog box now displays the Specials.css file in the URL list box. See Figure 9-28.

   TROUBLE? If necessary, navigate to the recipes folder to select the Specials.css file in the list box.

Figure 9-28   LINK STYLE SHEET DIALOG BOX

text in Web page uses the H1, H2, BODY, and A styles

link to the cascading style sheet

links the cascading style sheet to only the current Web page

click to add another cascading style sheet link

click to remove the selected cascading style sheet link

10. Click the **OK** button, and then click anywhere in the Web page to deselect any selected text. The text you entered and formatted in the Web page now uses the styles that you defined in the cascading style sheet. See Figure 9-29. Any time you use these styles in this Web page, they will be formatted using the specifications from the cascading style sheet.

Figure 9-29   WEB PAGE USES STYLES FROM THE CASCADING STYLE SHEET

H1 style

H2 style

BODY style

A style

When you don't need to use the cascading style sheet any longer, you can remove the link by clicking Format on the menu bar, clicking Style Sheet Links, selecting the cascading style sheet filename to remove in the URL list box, and then clicking the Remove button. When you remove the link to the style sheet, the styles in the Web page return to the default settings.

Viewing **the HTML Code for a Cascading Style Sheet**

David wants you to examine the HTML code that creates the styles in the cascading style sheet so you are familiar with this type of document. You will also view the HTML code for the new Web page that you created to see how it is linked to the cascading style sheet. You will close this Web page without saving it, and then view the HTML code for the Specials.css page.

To view the HTML code for a linked page and a cascading style sheet:

1. Click the **HTML** tab. The HTML code for the unsaved Web page appears in Page view. See Figure 9-30. The Web page contains a LINK tag to the Specials.css file. This link connects the Web page to the cascading style sheet so the page can use the defined styles. If you changed the defined styles in the Specials.css page, any pages that are linked to the cascading style sheet will be updated automatically.

| Figure 9-30 | HTML CODE FOR THE UNSAVED WEB PAGE |

link to the Specials cascading style sheet

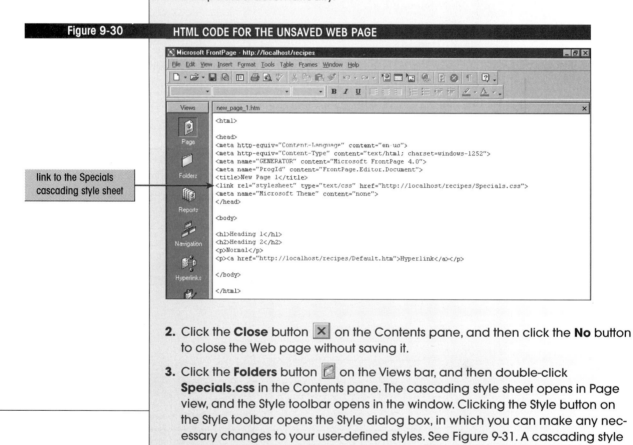

2. Click the **Close** button ⊠ on the Contents pane, and then click the **No** button to close the Web page without saving it.

3. Click the **Folders** button 📁 on the Views bar, and then double-click **Specials.css** in the Contents pane. The cascading style sheet opens in Page view, and the Style toolbar opens in the window. Clicking the Style button on the Style toolbar opens the Style dialog box, in which you can make any necessary changes to your user-defined styles. See Figure 9-31. A cascading style sheet only contains HTML code so it is only displayed in HTML Page view. The cascading style sheet includes a comment section that includes the names and definitions of the styles it contains. Otherwise, the page contains only the standard opening and closing HTML tags for a Web page.

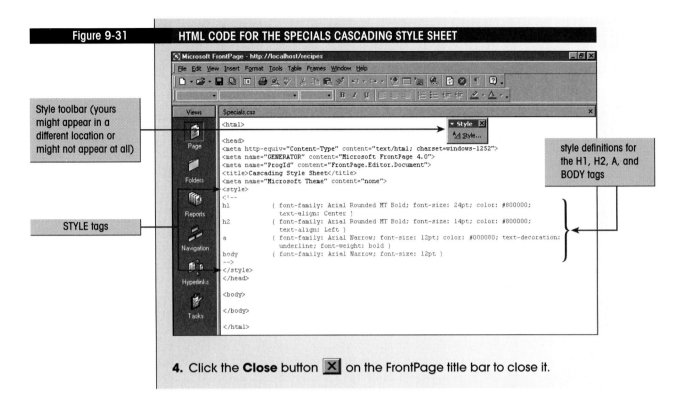

Figure 9-31   HTML CODE FOR THE SPECIALS CASCADING STYLE SHEET

Style toolbar (yours might appear in a different location or might not appear at all)

STYLE tags

style definitions for the H1, H2, A, and BODY tags

4. Click the **Close** button ☒ on the FrontPage title bar to close it.

In the next session, you will learn how to enter and view HTML code in Page view.

Session 9.2   QUICK CHECK

1. True or False: You can define more than one style for the same HTML tag in a single Web page.

2. True or False: A theme contains a set of styles that you might also find in a cascading style sheet.

3. When you save a Web page as a cascading style sheet, choose the _____ option in the Save as type list box.

4. True or False: You can modify any HTML tag to create a user-defined style.

5. You use the _____ dialog box to link a Web page to a cascading style sheet.

6. A Web page that was saved as a cascading style sheet has a filename extension of _____.

7. True or False: You can open a cascading style sheet in Normal Page view.

SESSION 9.3

In this session, you will create a new Web page in HTML Page view and enter HTML code into the page to create its content. You will also use the Reveal Tags command to display HTML code in Normal Page view.

Working Directly with HTML Code

As the last part of your Web site training, David wants you to learn how to use some important FrontPage features to manipulate HTML code. Throughout this book, you have viewed and examined the HTML code for different kinds of Web pages that include many features. You can use the menus and toolbars in FrontPage to make changes to the Web page, which also changes the Web page's HTML code, but it is still important to understand the code and how it works. Some Web page authors prefer to make changes directly in the HTML code because they feel that this approach gives them more control over page features. Sometimes you might need to do something in the Web page that you can't do using the menus and toolbars in FrontPage. In these cases, you will need to make your changes by entering code directly into the HTML document.

When you create a new Web page using the HTML tab in Page view, you have access to some of the menus and toolbars for Normal Page view. To implement features for disabled menu and toolbar commands, you can enter the HTML tag for the feature directly.

When you create a blank page, FrontPage will automatically create the HTML and BODY tags and the default META tags for the "empty" HTML document. If you display the HTML tab, you can add features to the Web page using most of the same menu commands and toolbar buttons that you use in Normal Page view. However, instead of seeing the element, you will see its HTML code.

Entering Text in HTML Page View

David wants you to practice using the HTML tab to enter text and other features in a Web page. The page that you will create is just a practice page. You won't create an actual page for the recipes Web site, although you will save the page in the site.

To create a new Web page and enter text in HTML Page view:

1. Start **FrontPage**, open the recipes Web site (**http://localhost/recipes**) from your computer's PWS, and then, if necessary, change to Page view. If necessary, click the **New Page** button ▢ on the Standard toolbar to create a new page. A new, blank page that uses the Web site's theme opens in Page view.

2. Click the **HTML** tab. FrontPage created the HTML, HEAD, TITLE, and BODY tags, along with META tags that identify the character set, the program used to create the page, and the Web site's theme name. The insertion point is blinking before the closing BODY tag. This location is where the insertion point would appear in Normal Page view. See Figure 9-32.

| Figure 9-32 | HTML CODE FOR A NEW WEB PAGE |

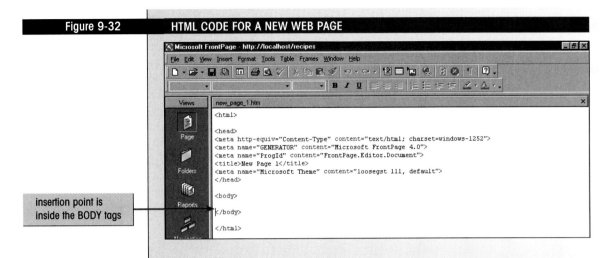

insertion point is
inside the BODY tags

3. Type **This is a Web Page Heading**, and then press the **Enter** key. Notice that as you type, the text changes color from blue to black. In HTML Page view, remember that HTML code appears as blue text and content entered by the user appears as black text. Now format the text that you entered with the Heading 1 style. The Heading 1 style uses the H1 tags.

4. Press the **up** arrow key ↑ to move to the beginning of the text that you typed in Step 3, and then type **<h1>**. FrontPage recognizes this text as an HTML tag and displays it as blue text. The H1 tag is a two-sided tag, so it also requires a closing tag.

5. Press the **End** key to move to the end of the line, and then type **</h1>**. FrontPage formats the closing tag as blue text. Now enter some text.

6. Press the **Enter** key, and then type **This is a normal paragraph.** FrontPage formats your content as black text. You can use the Formatting toolbar to change the style of your text to bold.

7. Select the text **This is a normal paragraph.** and then click the **Bold** button ⊞ on the Formatting toolbar. FrontPage adds the opening and closing tags for applying boldface to the selected text. See Figure 9-33.

| Figure 9-33 | INSERTING TEXT IN AN HTML DOCUMENT |

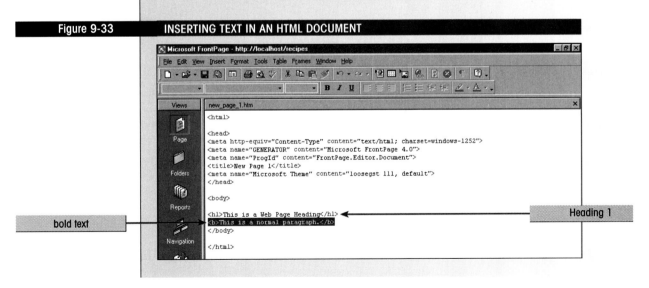

bold text

Heading 1

Changing Font Size in HTML Page View

Some menu and toolbar commands are dimmed in HTML Page view, but you can still apply these formats by entering the HTML code for them manually. You will change the "This is a normal paragraph." text to 14 points. When you work in HTML view, you must use the HTML equivalent of 14 points, which is a font size of 4. Other HTML equivalents for fonts are font size 1 (8 points), font size 2 (10 points), font size 3 (12 points), font size 5 (18 points), and font size 6 (24 points). The HTML tag that controls font size is FONT SIZE, and its value must include the equals sign and the font size value in quotation marks.

To change the font size of text in HTML Page view:

1. Select the text **This is a normal paragraph.** but do not select the opening and closing B tags.

2. Click **Format** on the menu bar. Notice that most of the commands on this menu are dimmed. In addition, the Font Size list arrow on the Formatting toolbar is also dimmed. You could change to Normal Page view, where these commands are active, to change the font size. However for now you will enter the HTML code directly into the HTML document.

3. Click between the <b> tag and the "T" in "This" to insert the insertion point there, and then type **<font size="4">**. See Figure 9-34. The FONT SIZE tag doesn't require a closing tag.

Figure 9-34	CHANGING THE FONT SIZE OF TEXT

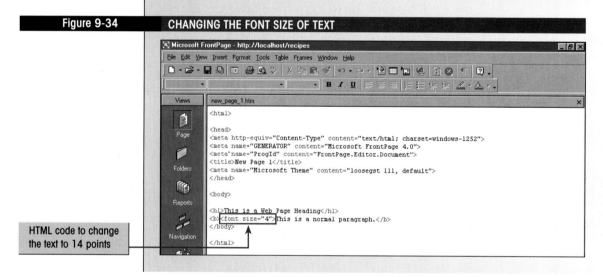

HTML code to change the text to 14 points

Inserting a FrontPage Component in HTML Page View

You can insert some FrontPage components into a Web page displayed in HTML Page view by using the toolbar buttons or the menu bar. You will insert a hit counter in the Web page.

To insert a hit counter in HTML Page view:

1. Press the **End** key to move the insertion point to the end of the line and to the right of the closing B tag, and then press the **Enter** key to create a new line.

2. Type **You are visitor number** and then press the **spacebar**.

3. Click the **Insert Component** button on the Standard toolbar, and then click **Hit Counter**. The Hit Counter Properties dialog box opens.

4. Click the **Reset counter to** check box to select it, press the **Tab** key, and then type **1000** so the counter will begin with the value 1000 instead of zero.

5. Click the **Fixed number of digits** check box to select it, press the **Tab** key, and then type **4**.

6. Click the **OK** button. The Hit Counter Properties dialog box closes, and FrontPage enters the HTML code to create the hit counter in the HTML document. Notice that the HTML comment tags surround the code that FrontPage created. A FrontPage Server Extension will create the actual hit counter in this page.

7. Press the **End** key to move the insertion point to the end of the selected text, press the **spacebar**, and then type **to our Web site.**

You have entered a heading, some formatted text, and a hit counter in the HTML document. Next you will preview your document using the Preview tab.

To preview the HTML document:

1. Click the **Preview** tab. All of your elements are displayed as expected. See Figure 9-35. (The browser would display the actual hit counter in the page.)

| Figure 9-35 | PREVIEW OF THE WEB PAGE |

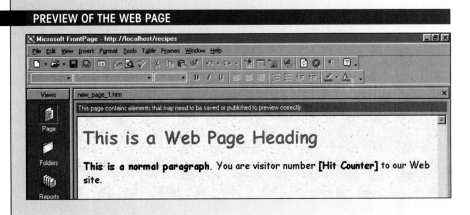

Displaying **HTML Tags in Normal Page View**

You can also work with HTML code in Normal Page view by turning on the Reveal Tags feature, which displays some HTML tags in Normal Page view. When you click an HTML tag, FrontPage selects the text that the tag affects. For example, if you click a B tag, FrontPage will select the text that the B tag applies bold formatting to.

To use the Reveal Tags command in Normal Page view:

1. Click the **Normal** tab. The Web page is displayed in Normal Page view.

2. Click **View** on the menu bar, and then click **Reveal Tags**. The HTML tags for HTML elements appear in the Web page. Notice that there are no HTML tags for the hit counter; the hit counter is really a comment that calls a FrontPage Server Extension to display it in the Web page. See Figure 9-36.

Figure 9-36   **REVEAL TAGS FOR THE WEB PAGE**

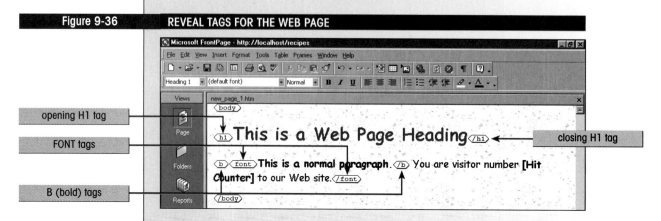

opening H1 tag

FONT tags

B (bold) tags

closing H1 tag

3. Point to the **h1** tag. A ScreenTip shows the HTML code for this tag.

4. Click the **h1** tag. FrontPage selects the text "This is a Web Page Heading;" the H1 tag affects this line of text.

5. Click the **body** tag. FrontPage selects the entire Web page; the BODY tag affects all of the text in the Web page.

6. Click anywhere in the Web page to deselect the BODY tag. You can create a new paragraph for the sentence that includes the hit counter and FrontPage will display the HTML tags for this action.

7. Click after the closing B tag, and then press the **Enter** key. FrontPage creates a new paragraph, moves the sentence that contains the hit counter to the next line, continues the FONT tags to the new line, and adds the P tags to indicate the beginning and end of the new paragraph. See Figure 9-37.

Figure 9-37   **CREATING A NEW PARAGRAPH**

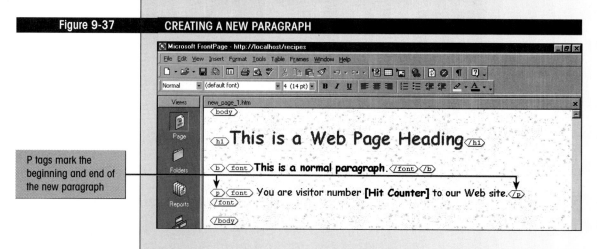

P tags mark the beginning and end of the new paragraph

You can preview your changes using the Preview tab.

8. Click the **Preview** tab. The Web page now displays three lines of text.

You can save the Web page in HTML Page view to see how FrontPage adds the Web page's title to the HTML document.

To save the Web page in HTML Page view:

1. Click the **HTML** tab and then click the **Save** button 🖫 on the Standard toolbar. The Save As dialog box opens.

2. Click the **Change** button to open the Set Page Title dialog box, type **Sample HTML Web Page** in the Page title text box, and then click the **OK** button.

3. Select the text in the File name text box, and then type **Sample**.

4. Click the **Save** button. FrontPage adds the TITLE tags to the Web page.

   TROUBLE? If the TITLE tags enclose the text "New Page 1," instead of "Sample HTML Web Page," click the Refresh button 🛃 on the Standard toolbar to refresh the page.

5. Click the **Close** button ☒ on the Contents pane to close the Web page.

The Reveal Tags command will stay on until you turn it off. Before turning it off, you can examine the HTML tags for another Web page to see how the Web page is created. You will examine the Recipe Index Web page, and then turn off the Reveal Tags command.

To open the Recipe Index Web page and then turn off Reveal Tags:

1. Click the **Folders** button 🗀 on the Views bar to change to Folders view, and then double-click **site_map.htm** in the Contents pane. The Recipe Index Web page opens in Normal Page view. See Figure 9-38.

| Figure 9-38 | REVEAL TAGS FOR THE RECIPE INDEX WEB PAGE |

2. Click some of the HTML tags in the Web page to see what text they affect.

3. Click **View** on the menu bar, and then click **Reveal Tags** to turn off this feature.

4. Click the **Close** button ☒ on the FrontPage title bar to close FrontPage.

Some Web page authors prefer to work with the tags displayed in Normal Page view because it lets them see the HTML code in the context of the Web page. When you have problems while working in a Web page, sometimes turning on the Reveal Tags feature lets you see something in the HTML code that you need to change to correct an error. You can change to HTML Page view to make the correction or try to correct the problem in Normal Page view.

Session 9.3 QUICK CHECK

1. True or False: A Web page that contains no content in Normal Page view does not contain any HTML code in HTML Page view.

2. In HTML Page view, content entered by the user is _____ in color.

3. In HTML Page view, HTML tag names are _____ in color.

4. The HTML tag that creates a new paragraph in a Web page is _____.

5. The HTML tag that creates bold text in a Web page is _____.

6. When you turn on the Reveal Tags feature, what happens?

REVIEW ASSIGNMENTS

David wants you to customize the default components that you created in the Activity Report Web page by formatting the title bar, changing the window name of the spreadsheet component, adding data labels, and formatting the title of the chart component. You will also create a custom theme for the Activity Report Web page and set the properties for this page and the data source for the spreadsheet component so they are not published with the Web site.

If necessary, start FrontPage, insert your Data Disk in the appropriate disk drive, and then do the following:

1. Open the **recipes** Web site from your computer's PWS (http://localhost/recipes) in Folders view, and then open the Activity Report Web page (**activity.htm**) in Page view.

Explore

2. Use the Themes dialog box to create a customized theme for this page only. Use the Colors button to change the Heading 2 style color to bright blue. (*Hint*: Click the Custom tab, and then select Heading 2 from the Item list.) Use the Graphics button to change the font used in the page banner to 24-point, regular, Impact font. (*Hint*: Click the Font tab, use the Item list arrow to select the page banner settings, and then select the Impact font and settings from the list.) Save the theme using the default name, and then close the Themes dialog box.

3. Add the **activity.htm** page to the Web site's navigation structure as a child page of the Home Page. (Add the **activity.htm** page to the right of the Guest Book page.) Then insert a centered picture page banner at the top of the Activity Report Web page. Save the page.

Explore   4. Click the spreadsheet component to select it, and then open the Spreadsheet Property Toolbox. Click cell A1 in the spreadsheet (this cell contains the title "Page Openings by Category"). Use the Format menu items in the Toolbox to change the heading to 20-point, bold, blue, Verdana font.

Explore   5. Use the Title Bar menu to change the background color of the title bar to blue. Change the title of the spreadsheet component to "Microsoft Office Spreadsheet - Openings.htm." Close the Toolbox and save the Web page.

Explore   6. Select the chart component in the Activity Report Web page, and then open the Toolbox. Open the General menu, click the list arrow, and then click Chart 1 Title. Use the Font menu to change the font of the title to 20-point, bold, blue, Verdana font.

Explore   7. Use the Microsoft Office Chart Help window to learn how to add data labels for the category names to each slice in the pie. After you add the data labels, change the font of the data labels to 12-point, bold, Verdana font. Close the Toolbox.

8. Change the value in cell C4 (the value for Butters) to 322. Save the Web page, and then preview it using the browser. Print the Web page using Internet Explorer, and then close the browser.

9. Change the properties of the **activity.htm** and **openings.htm** pages so they will not be published with the Web site.

10. Close FrontPage.

CASE PROBLEMS

Case 1. Determining Appropriate Marketing Channels for Royal Hair Care Products

Valerie Suarez is planning to expand the way that Royal Hair Care Products delivers its products to customers. In the next year, Valerie will change the Web site to accept online orders from customers and retailers. In the meantime, she wants to focus the Royal sales force on promoting its new styling gel products with an emphasis in the places where most customers purchase Royal products. To help determine the most appropriate channels, she wants you to create a Web page with spreadsheet data that displays the data in a stacked column chart. The data you will use is collected from a form field in the Feedback Web page that asks users to specify where they purchase the product most frequently.

If necessary, start FrontPage, insert your Data Disk in the appropriate disk drive, and then do the following:

1. Read all the questions for this case problem, and then prepare a planning analysis sheet for the enhancements to the royal Web site.

2. Open the **royal** Web site from your computer's PWS in Folders view. The default location is http://localhost/royal.

3. Create a new Web page in Page view, and then save it using the title and filename **Sales**. On the first line of the Web page, insert a centered spreadsheet component. Import the file named **RFBakDat.htm** from the Tutorial.09 folder on your Data Disk into the royal Web site, and then import its data into the spreadsheet component. Do not select the option to refresh the data at run time.

4. Select the columns in the spreadsheet component that contain data (columns A and B), and then size them to their best fit.

Explore   5. Add a new label in cell A8 with the value "Total." Change the label to 10-point, Arial, bold, blue font.

Explore   6. Create a formula in cell B8 that calculates a sum of the values in cells B2 through B7. (*Hint*: Click in cell B8, click the AutoSum button on the Microsoft Office Spreadsheet toolbar, make sure that the range B2:B7 is selected, and then press the Enter key.)

7. Insert a chart component below the spreadsheet component that you created in Step 3, with one blank line separating the components. Use the Column chart type and the Stacked Column subtype, the data range A1:B8, and the series in columns.

Explore   8. Change the value in cell A3 to "DiscStore," the value in cell A4 to "DeptStore," and the value in cell A6 to "Supermkt." What happens in the chart component?

Explore   9. Click the labels in the chart component (DrugStore, DiscStore, etc.) to select them, right-click the selected labels to open the shortcut menu, and then click Property Toolbox. Open the Ticks and Gridlines menu, and then turn on the major gridlines. Use the Font menu to change the text format of the labels to bold text. Then use the Axis menu to add the axis title "Location" to the chart. (*Hint*: Click the Show Axis Title button, click the Axis Title that appears in the chart component, open the Title menu in the Toolbox, and then change the caption.) Change the axis title to 14-point, bold, Arial font.

10. Turn off the shared borders for the Sales Web page, and then insert the text "Purchase Locations" at the top of the Web page. Change the text to use the Heading 1 style. Then insert a heading using the Heading 1 style on the blank line between the spreadsheet and chart components using the text "Purchase Locations Column Chart."

Explore   11. Change the theme for *only* the Sales Web page so that the Heading 1 style (h1) uses a centered alignment and purple, bold text. (*Hint*: Click the Modify button in the Themes dialog box, click the Text button, change the item to Heading 1, and then click More Text Styles. Use the Style dialog box that opens to make the changes to the Heading 1 tag. Save the theme using the default name.) Save the Web page, preview it using the browser, and then print the page. Close Internet Explorer.

12. Change the properties of the Sales Web page so it will not be published when the Web site is published to the Royal Hair Care Products Web server, and then save the page.

13. Close FrontPage.

Case 2. Creating a Sales Data Web Page for Buffalo Trading Post Donna Vargas wants to use the Web site for Buffalo Trading Post (BTP) to track sales in different retail categories. She wants to be able to use a Web page to compute the values given to her by her accountant, Cody Susen. Cody doesn't have this data in an electronic format, so Donna will need to input it manually into a spreadsheet. Instead of using an Excel workbook to create the data, Donna wants to be able to use a Web page. Donna wants you to create the Web page for her. Donna also wants to create a pie chart in the Web page to show the relative amounts for each category.

If necessary, start FrontPage, insert your Data Disk in the appropriate disk drive, and then do the following:

1. Read all the questions for this case problem, and then prepare a planning analysis sheet for the enhancements to the buffalo Web site.

2. Open the **buffalo** Web site from your computer's PWS in Folders view. The default location is http://localhost/buffalo.

3. Create a new Web page in Page view with the title "Sales Data" and the filename **SaleWkbk.htm**.

4. On the first line of the Web page (but not in the bottom shared border), create a heading using the Heading 1 style and the text "Sales Data by Category."

5. On the next line, insert a centered spreadsheet component. Enter the data shown in Figure 9-39 into the spreadsheet component. Format the column headings (cells B1 through D1) as 10-point, Arial, bold, centered text. Format the row headings (cells A2 through A7) as 10-point, bold, Arial text. Resize all columns to their best fit.

Figure 9-39

	Revenue ($)	Inventory Amount ($)	Sales Percentage
Women's	254,165	354,811	72%
Children's	25,644	84,511	30%
Accessories	10,264	11,265	91%
Men's	1,254	9,558	13%
Hats	157	865	18%
Shoes	2,955	6,988	42%

Explore   6. Insert a formula in cell B8 that computes the total of the values in cells B2 through B7, and then insert a formula in cell C8 that computes the total of the values in cells C2 through C7. In cell D8, enter a formula that computes the sales percentage, which is the revenue divided by inventory amount. Use the Toolbox to format the resulting value as a percentage. In cell A8, enter the label "Totals." Use the Toolbox to format the values in cells A8 through D8 as 10-point, Arial, bold, red text. (*Hint*: Use the Microsoft Spreadsheet Help window to get Help while completing Step 6.)

7. Resize the spreadsheet component to display only the data in the worksheet and no empty cells.

8. Change the title of the spreadsheet component to "Sales Data by Category" and the title bar background color to red.

Explore   9. Turn off the display of the vertical and horizontal scroll bars in the spreadsheet component. (*Hint*: Use the Advanced menu in the Toolbox.) If necessary, resize the spreadsheet component again so that it only displays the data.

10. Insert a chart component below the spreadsheet component that you created in Step 5, with one blank line separating the components. Use the Bar chart type and the 100% Stacked Bar subtype, the data range A1:C7, and the series in rows.

Explore   11. Use the Toolbox to add the minor gridlines to the chart. (*Hint*: Click the percentage labels in the chart component to select them, right-click the selected labels to open the shortcut menu, and then click Property Toolbox. Open the Ticks and Gridlines menu.) Close the Toolbox and then save the Sales Data Web page.

Explore   12. Change the Heading 1 style for all pages in the Web site to centered without changing the Web site's theme. (*Hint*: Create and save a cascading style sheet, and then link it to all pages in the Web site. Use the filename **styles.css** and the title "Style Sheet.")

13. Change the properties of the Sales Data Web page and the cascading style sheet so they are not published when the Web site is published to the BTP Web server.

14. Preview the Sales Data Web page in the browser, and then print it. Close Internet Explorer.

15. Use FrontPage to print the HTML code for the cascading style sheet that you created in Step 12.

16. Close FrontPage.

Case 3. Displaying Salary Data in a Web Page for Garden Grill Garden Grill has always attracted the most qualified applicants for management and staff positions in its restaurants. One of the reasons for its well-trained staff is that Garden Grill pays its employees higher salaries than other national restaurant chains. To keep employee morale high, management makes an effort to conduct salary research to show that Garden Grill employees are enjoying a higher reward for their work.

Nolan Simmons just finished a study of starting salaries for three other national restaurant chains. He wants to include a Web page in the Garden Grill Web site that shows his study's results in a spreadsheet and chart. This Web page will be available only on the company's intranet; it will not be published on the Internet Web site.

If necessary, start FrontPage, insert your Data Disk in the appropriate disk drive, and then do the following:

1. Read all the questions for this case problem, and then prepare a planning analysis sheet for the enhancements to the garden Web site.

2. Open the **garden** Web site from your computer's PWS in Folders view. The default location is http://localhost/garden.

3. Create a new Web page in HTML Page view with the title "Salary Data" and the filename **Salary.htm**. On the first line of the Web page, create a heading using the Heading 1 style and the text "Salary Data by Position." Return to Normal Page view, and confirm that you created the heading correctly.

4. On the next line, insert a centered spreadsheet component. Import the file **GData.htm** from the Tutorial.09 folder on your Data Disk into the Web site, and then import the data from this file into the spreadsheet component.

Explore ▶ 5. Insert a formula in cell B8 that computes the average of the values in cells B2 through B7. Then copy and paste the formula from cell B8 into cells C8, D8, and E8. Use the Toolbox to format the values in cells B2 though E8 as currency. In cell A8, enter the label "Average." Use the Toolbox to format the values in cells A8 through E8 as 10-point, Arial, bold, violet text. (*Hint*: Use the Microsoft Spreadsheet Help window to get Help while completing Step 5.)

6. Resize the spreadsheet component to display only the data in the worksheet and no empty cells.

7. Change the title of the spreadsheet component to "Starting Salary Data" and the title bar background color to violet.

Explore ▶ 8. Turn off the display of the vertical and horizontal scroll bars in the spreadsheet component. (*Hint*: Use the Advanced menu in the Toolbox.) Resize the component as necessary so that no empty cells are displayed.

9. Insert a chart component below the spreadsheet component that you created in Step 4, with one blank line separating the components. Use the Column chart type and the Clustered Column subtype. Chart the data in the rows in cells A1 through E8.

Explore 10. Use the Toolbox to change the background color of the chart to white. (*Hint*: Right-click the chart background to open the shortcut menu, click Property Toolbox, open the Format menu, and then change the interior color.) Close the Toolbox and then save the Salary Data Web page.

11. Turn off the display of shared borders in the Salary Data Web page, and then set the properties for this page and the **GData.htm** page so that they are not published with the Web site.

12. Save the Salary Data Web page, preview it in the browser, and then print it. Close Internet Explorer.

13. Close FrontPage.

Case 4. Customizing the Appearance of the Replay Music Factory Web Site Charlene Fields is pleased with the progress that you are making towards completing the Web site for Replay Music Factory. Charlene anticipates that the online ordering system will be ready to go in a few weeks. While the company's music inventory is being entered into an Access database, she asks you to customize the appearance of the Web site to ensure that all elements will look the same. She likes the Spiral Web theme that is currently applied to the Web site, but she feels that some of its elements could be redesigned to work better.

If necessary, start FrontPage, insert your Data Disk in the appropriate disk drive, and then do the following:

1. Read all the questions for this case problem, and then prepare a planning analysis sheet for the enhancements to the replay Web site.

2. Open the **replay** Web site from your computer's PWS in Folders view. The default location is http://localhost/replay.

3. Open the Themes dialog box. Make sure that the changes you will make will apply to all pages in the Web site.

Explore 4. Change the color for active and regular hyperlinks to navy and for followed hyperlinks to purple. (*Hint*: Modify the color options using the Custom tab.)

Explore 5. Change the body text to use the Garamond font. Then change the Heading 1, Heading 2, and Heading 3 styles to use MS Sans Serif font. (*Hint*: Modify the text options using the Text button.)

6. Save the theme using the name "Copy of Spiral," and apply it to the entire Web site.

Explore 7. For only the Home Page (**Default.htm**), change the theme so that the background picture is not displayed. Then change the background color to light yellow. (*Hint*: Modify the background color options using the Custom tab. Use the More Colors option to select a color that ensures readability of the text in the Web page.) Close the Themes dialog box, and save changes to the Copy of Spiral theme.

Explore 8. Change to HTML Page view for the Home Page, and then change the title of the Home Page to "Replay Music Factory Home Page." Then change the heading "Welcome to Replay Music Factory!" to use the Heading 1 style.

9. While still in HTML Page view, insert a hit counter on a new line between the last paragraph in the Web page and the footer. Use a style of your choice for the hit counter, a starting value of 1000, and four fixed digits. Insert appropriate text around the hit counter to describe its function, which is identifying the number of visitors to the Web site. Center the hit counter in the Web page.

10. While still in HTML view, insert a horizontal line below the hit counter. Use the default settings for the horizontal line.

11. Save your changes, and then preview the Replay Music Factory Home Page in the browser. Print the Web page, and then close Internet Explorer.

Explore   12. Return to FrontPage and then print the HTML code for the Replay Music Factory Home Page. On the printout, circle the HTML code that implements all of the changes that you made in this Web page.

13. Close FrontPage.

QUICK CHECK ANSWERS

Session 9.1

1. spreadsheet, chart, and PivotTable list
2. You should use a spreadsheet component in a Web page when you (or other Web site developers) do not have Excel installed on your computer or when you want to create a spreadsheet that is self-contained.
3. True
4. False
5. valid data source or a link to a valid data source
6. A cell or group of cells in a spreadsheet component that contain the data you want to chart.
7. False
8. False
9. Excel, Access

Session 9.2

1. False
2. True
3. HyperText Style Sheet
4. True
5. Link Style Sheet
6. css
7. False

Session 9.3

1. False
2. black
3. blue
4. P
5. B
6. In Normal Page view, the HTML tags for elements in the Web page appear as tags in the Web page. Clicking a tag selects the text or object that is affected by the tag.

Spreadsheets

LAB ASSIGNMENTS

These Lab Assignments are designed to accompany the interactive Course Lab called Spreadsheets. To start the Spreadsheets Lab, click the Start button on the Windows taskbar, point to Programs, point to Course Labs, point to New Perspectives Applications, and then click Spreadsheets. If you do not see Course Labs on your Programs menu, see your instructor or technical support person.

Spreadsheets Spreadsheet software is used extensively in business, education, science, and the humanities to simplify tasks that involve calculations. In this Lab you will learn how spreadsheet software works. You will use spreadsheet software to examine and modify worksheets and to create your own worksheets.

1. Click the **Steps** button to learn how spreadsheet software works. As you proceed through the Steps, answer all of the Quick Check questions that appear. After you complete the Steps, you will see a Quick Check Summary Report. Follow the instructions on the screen to print this report.

2. Click the **Explore** button to begin this assignment. Click the **OK** button to display a new worksheet. Click **File** on the menu bar, and then click **Open** to display the Open dialog box. Click the file **Income.xls**, and then press the **Enter** key to open the Income and Expense Summary worksheet. Notice that the worksheet contains labels and values for income from consulting and training. It also contains labels and values for expenses such as rent and salaries. The worksheet does not, however, contain formulas to calculate Total Income, Total Expenses, or Profit. Do the following:

   a. Calculate the Total Income by entering the formula =sum(C4:C5) in cell C6.
   b. Calculate the Total Expenses by entering the formula =sum(C9:C12) in C13.
   c. Calculate Profit by entering the formula =C6-C13 in cell C15.
   d. Manually check the results to make sure you entered the formulas correctly.
   e. Print your completed worksheet showing your results.

3. You can use a spreadsheet to keep track of your grade in a class. In Explore, click **File** on the menu bar, and then click **Open** to display the Open dialog box. Click the file **Grades.xls** to open the Grades worksheet. This worksheet contains all of the labels and formulas necessary to calculate your grade based on four test scores.

   Suppose you receive a score of 88 out of 100 on the first test. On the second test, you score 42 out of 48. On the third test, you score 92 out of 100. You have not taken the fourth test yet. Enter the appropriate data in the **Grades.xls** worksheet to determine your grade after taking three tests. Print your worksheet.

4. Worksheets are handy for answering "what if" questions. Suppose you decide to open a lemonade stand. You're interested in how much profit you can make each day. What if you sell 20 cups of lemonade? What if you sell 100? What if the cost of lemons increases?

   In Explore, open the file **Lemons.xls** and use the worksheet to answer questions a through d, and then print the worksheet for question e.

   a. What is your profit if you sell 20 cups a day?
   b. What is your profit if you sell 100 cups a day?
   c. What is your profit if the price of lemons increases to $.07 and you sell 100 cups?
   d. What is your profit if you raise the price of a cup of lemonade to $.30? (Lemons still cost $.07; assume you sell 100 cups.)

e. Suppose your competitor boasts that she sold 50 cups of lemonade in one day and made exactly $12.00. On your worksheet adjust the cost of cups, water, lemons, and sugar, and the price per cup to show a profit of exactly $12.00 for 50 cups sold. Print this worksheet.

5. It is important to make sure the formulas in your worksheet are accurate. An easy way to test this is to enter the value 1 for every value in your worksheet, and then check the calculations manually.

In Explore, open the worksheet **Receipt.xls**, which calculates sales receipts. Enter **1** as the value for Item 1, Item 2, Item 3, and Sales Tax %. Manually calculate what you would pay for three items that cost $1.00 each in a state where sales tax is one percent (.01). Do your manual calculations match those of the worksheet? If not, correct the formulas in the worksheet and print a formula report of your revised worksheet.

6. In Explore, create your own worksheet showing your household budget for one month. You can use real or fictitious data. Make sure that you put a title on the worksheet. Use formulas to calculate your total income and your total expenses for the month. Add another formula to calculate how much money you were able to save. Print a formula report of your worksheet. Then print your worksheet showing realistic values for one month.

OBJECTIVES

In this case you will:

- Create a new Web site and import pages into it

- Add and format shared borders in a Web site

- Add pictures to Web pages and change their properties

- Create a cascading style sheet and apply it to every page in a Web site

- Change cell properties in a table

- Add new pages to a Web site using Navigation view

- Apply a theme to a Web site

- Change the properties of a form component

- Add a discussion group to a Web site

- Import a database into a Web site

- Create Active Server Pages

CREATING A WEB SITE FOR SECURITY SHREDDING, INC.

CASE

Security Shredding, Inc.

When Mary Schmidt retired from her career as a systems analyst, she realized that she still wanted to work. Her husband, Bob, was also retiring from his career as a computer programmer. Together, along with the help of their two sons, Jeff and Brad, Mary started a business that shreds documents and other materials. She started Security Shredding, Inc. in 1990 as many state agencies and public companies were realizing the benefits of having their sensitive documents destroyed by independent specialists instead of using in-house resources. At first, Security Shredding primarily shredded documents, including personnel records, classified information, and financial information. The business quickly grew to include the destruction of non-salable materials such as unsold magazines and paperbacks, expired lottery scratch-off cards, and security tapes.

Security Shredding soon outgrew its small storage area and relocated to a warehouse that now houses several commercial shredders, paper bailers, and the company's offices. Security Shredding also leases several unmarked trucks that are used to pick up documents from its clients. Security Shredding's warehouse is also unmarked to guarantee the security and privacy of sensitive documents while they are being destroyed.

As business at Security Shredding continues to expand, Mary realizes that the creation and management of a Web site might increase the efficiency of the company's operations, in addition to marketing the company's services. Mary wants you to help her create a Web site with the following pages and features:

- A Home Page that describes the business and includes a picture and a hit counter
- An Experience page that describes the company's experience in shredding documents and lists its professional affiliations
- A 3 S's of Shredding page that answers the question, "What should be shredded?"
- A Pickup Request Form page that lets clients use a form to request document pickups
- A Pricing page that identifies the company's pricing policies
- A Size page that describes the company's equipment and location
- A Services page that describes the company's services, including pickup services, recycling efforts, and policies
- A Security page that describes the company's security measures and policies for ensuring the privacy and protection of materials it handles
- A Recycling Program page that includes information about how recycling efforts benefit the environment
- An E-Mail page that includes the e-mail addresses of the company's managers
- A protected discussion group of pages, which allows managers at Security Shredding to post information about the business or the industry in general to enhance interoffice communication

In addition to these Web pages, Mary wants to include pictures showing the company's operations. Mary wants the Web site to use a Web theme to ensure a consistent appearance among pages in the site. She also wants the company's logo, name, address, phone number, fax number, and e-mail address to appear at the top of each page.

If necessary, start FrontPage, insert your Data Disk in the appropriate disk drive, and then do the following:

1. Read all the questions for this case problem, and then prepare a planning analysis sheet for creating the Web site for Security Shredding.

2. Prepare a Web site plan that shows the desired Web pages and the expected hyperlinks from the Home Page.

3. Use the Import Web Wizard to import all of the files except for **Shred.mdb** that are saved in the AddCase1 folder on your Data Disk into a new Web site named **shred**. Save the Web site in the folder on your computer that stores server-based Webs (the default folder is http://localhost/shred).

4. Use drag and drop to move all picture files into the Web site's images folder.

5. Use Navigation view to create the Web site's navigation structure. All pages in the Web site are child pages of the Home Page. Change the title of the **Default.htm** page to "Home Page."

6. Open the Home Page in Page view. Add top and left shared borders to every page in the Web site. The left shared border should include navigation buttons. On the first line of the top shared border, insert the company's logo file (**logo.jpg**) from the Web site's images folder, resize it to approximately two inches high and wide, and then center it. Change the logo so its background is

transparent. One space to the right of the logo, enter the company's name (Security Shredding, Inc.), and then format it using the Heading 2 style. On the next line of the top shared border, insert the company's mailing address, phone number, fax number, and a mailto with the company's e-mail address using the following information: P.O. Box 20996, Austin, TX 78716-0996, Phone 512-555-1104, Fax 512-555-0922, mail@securityshreddinginc.com. Format the company's information as 10-point, centered text. Then insert a horizontal line under the address information.

7. Edit the left shared border so that all the pages in the Web site include vertical button links to child pages and to the parent page. The top shared border should contain only the items that you added in Step 6. Save your changes.

8. Create appropriate META descriptions and keywords for the Home Page, and then save the Home Page.

9. Insert the **paper.jpg** picture from the Web site's images folder between the first and second paragraphs of the Home Page. Center the picture, resize it to make it smaller, and bevel its edges. Add the alternative text "Paper Shredding" to the picture. Save the page.

10. Create a cascading style sheet using the filename and title **styles** that changes the Heading 1 style to use a centered alignment. Then apply the cascading style sheet to all pages in the Web site. Set the properties of the styles page so that it is not published with the Web site.

11. Open each Web page in the Web site and review its contents. For each page, format lists using bullets and headings using the Heading 1 style. Insert at least one picture from the Web site's images folder in three different Web pages. Make sure that the pictures are relevant to the content of the pages in which you insert them. Use alternative text to describe each picture, and resize the pictures as necessary to make them fit well in the pages. Save each page.

12. Open the 3 S's of Shredding Web page (**What.htm**) in Page view. Format the list in the second column of the table with bullets. The heading "The Three S's of Shredding" should use the Heading 1 style. The heading "Secure, Smart, Safe" should use the Heading 2 style. Then format the heading "What to Shred" in the first column of the table as bold, navy, 12-point Arial text.

13. Change the 3 S's of Shredding Web page so the right column in the table uses a customized, light yellow background color. Change the left column in the table to use a customized, light blue background color. Make sure you select colors that maintain the readability of the table's data.

14. Change the heading "Secure, Smart, Safe" in the 3 S's of Shredding Web page to use an animation of your choice that draws attention to these three words when the page is loaded. Save the page.

15. Open the E-Mail Web page (**Email.htm**) in Page view. Change the four names listed in the page to mailtos. The e-mail addresses are the person's name in all lowercase letters, with no spaces, followed by the domain securityshreddinginc.com.

16. If necessary, save any Web pages, and then preview the entire Web site using the browser to make sure that the pictures, links, and lists are working as expected. Return to FrontPage and make any necessary corrections.

17. Apply an appropriate theme to the entire Web site.

18. In Navigation view, add a new Web page to the shred Web site using the title and filename "Search." Then open the Search Web page and add a title and a

search component. Make sure that the new page uses the Web site's shared borders and the cascading style sheet. Add text to the Search Web page that describes how to use the search component, and then save the page.

19. Open the Pickup Request Web page (**Pickup.htm**) in Page view. Insert a form component in the page, and then cut and paste the information that is displayed below the first paragraph in the page into the form component. Use the existing labels in the page to create appropriate form fields to store the data the form will collect. Change the default form field settings to use appropriately sized form fields and meaningful names. Set validation criteria for form fields that require it. Save the form's results as comma-delimited text in a file named **Pickup.txt** in the _private folder of the Web site. Save the Pickup Request Web page, and then open the page in the browser and submit one form to the server.

20. Add a hit counter to the Home Page with your choice of specifications, location, and style.

21. Change the name of the Recycling Program Web page to **Recycle.htm**.

22. Use the Discussion Web Wizard to add a discussion group to the Web site. The discussion group should have the following features:

   a. Include all of the main features (Submission Form, Table of Contents, Search Form, Threaded Replies, and a Confirmation Page).

   b. The title of the discussion group is Security Shredding Discussion. The discussion folder name is _disc1.

   c. Choose the subject and comments input fields for the Submission Form.

   d. The discussion group is protected.

   e. Sort the messages in order from newest to oldest.

   f. Do not replace the existing Home Page in the shred Web site.

   g. The Search Form should report only the subject for matching documents.

   h. Use a dual interface frames page.

23. Add the Security Shredding Discussion Welcome page (**disc1_welc.htm**) to the navigation structure as a child page of the Home Page. Then change the title of this page to "Discussion."

24. Open the Discussion Web page in the browser, and then post a new article to the Web site and refresh the main page. All managers at Security Shredding will be authorized users, and they will use this discussion group for internal communications. (The Contents page will not display names because your discussion group does not have any registered users. Registered names are automatically added to the Contents page when registered users post messages.)

25. Mary wants to store information from the pickup form in an Access database, instead of storing it in a file on the server. Import the **Shred** database from the AddCase1 folder on your Data Disk into the shred Web site. Use the database connection name "Shred," and store all database files in the fpdb folder of the Web site. Change the Web site's settings to display hidden folders, and then verify the database connection.

26. Change the form component in the Pickup Web page (**Pickup.htm**) to send its results to the Shred database in the fpdb folder of the Web site. Set the form fields so that their data is stored in the correct field in the Results table of the Shred database. Do not save any additional fields.

27. Save the Pickup Request Web page, and then preview and refresh the page in the browser. Complete the Pickup Request Form using your own name and address information, and then submit the form to the server.

28. Open the **Shred** database from FrontPage, run the Results Query, and then confirm that the form handler correctly stored the record you added in Step 27. Close Access.

29. Create a new page in Page view with the title "Pickup Information" and the filename **pickinfo.asp**. Change the setting for the Pickup Information page to exclude it when publishing the Web site. Add a heading with the Heading 1 style at the top of the page using the text "Pickup Information." Link this page to the **styles** cascading style sheet, and make sure that the page uses the Web site's shared borders. Create a Database Results region that displays the records from the Results Query in the Shred database. Include all fields from the query, accept the default formatting options, and display all records together. After the Database Results region is inserted in the Web page, change the column headings to more meaningful names, and then apply the Heading 4 style to the headings and center them. Save the page and preview it in the browser.

30. Recalculate the hyperlinks in the Web site, verify all hyperlinks in the Web site, and then run a Site Summary report. Correct any errors that are listed in Reports view. (*Hint*: You can ignore any broken links to discussion group files.)

31. Use the browser to thoroughly test the Web site. Return to FrontPage as necessary to correct any errors that you discover.

32. Close Internet Explorer and FrontPage.

In this case you will:

- Create a new Web site, import pages into it, and change the Web folder's settings

- Create a Web site's navigation structure using Navigation view

- Add and format shared borders in a Web site

- Add pictures to Web pages and change their properties

- Apply a customized theme to a Web site

- Create a form component in a Web page that sends its results to a database

- Import a database into a Web site

- Create and format Active Server Pages in a Web site

- Create spreadsheet and chart components in a Web page

CREATING A NEW WEB SITE FOR PET ADOPTION SERVICES, INC.

CASE

Pet Adoption Services, Inc.

Pet Adoption Services, Inc. is a not-for-profit organization that cares for lost, abandoned, and neglected dogs and cats in its shelters located throughout the United States. Pet Adoption Services finds caring homes for all healthy and non-aggressive pets brought to its shelters. The organization provides affordable veterinary services through its shelters, and all adopted pets must be neutered before leaving the shelter. Pet Adoption Services relies on time donations from local veterinarians to make the clinics more affordable for the entire community.

Until recently, Pet Adoption Services has relied on radio advertising to communicate information about its pet adoption weekends across the country. Community reaction to these adoption events has been overwhelming. However, Madison Somero, president of Pet Adoption Services, has received feedback from the shelter directors across the country indicating a need for a Web site. The center directors want to include a Web page for each pet offered for adoption in the weekend events. Madison wants the Web site to have a Home Page, a Dogs page, and a Cats page. Child pages of the Dogs and Cats pages will include brief descriptions of each pet and the pet's photograph.

Because Pet Adoption Services is a not-for-profit organization, it relies heavily on the generosity of the community to ensure that each animal is cared for properly. Madison wants to include a Guest Book page in the Web site to collect information about potential donors of cash, food, and time. She hopes that the Web site will attract many donors, including veterinarians who can donate their services and provide inexpensive vaccines and medications. Because she hopes to collect a lot of information using the Guest Book page, Madison wants to use a form that sends its results to an Access database. She wants to view the data in the database using an Active Server Page and a data access page. She also wants to create a Web page that shows the dollar amounts for donations received over the past four years by donation category.

Finally, Madison wants the Web site to have a consistent, professional appearance. She asks you to use the pages that she created and stored in the AddCase2 folder on your Data Disk to begin work on the new Web site.

If necessary, start FrontPage, insert your Data Disk in the appropriate disk drive, and then do the following:

1. Read all the questions for this case problem, and then prepare a planning analysis sheet for the Pet Adoption Services Web site.

2. Prepare a Web site plan that shows the desired Web pages and the expected hyperlinks from the Home Page.

3. Use the Import Web Wizard to import all of the files except for **Pets.mdb** that are saved in the AddCase2 folder on your Data Disk into a new Web site named **pets**. Save the Web site in the folder on your computer that stores server-based Webs (the default folder is http://localhost/pets). Make sure that the Web site is enabled for Active Server Pages and ActiveX controls.

4. Use drag and drop to move all picture files into the Web site's images folder.

5. Use Navigation view to create the Web site's navigation structure. The **Dogs.htm, Cats.htm,** and **Guest.htm** pages are child pages of the Home Page. The following are child pages of the **Cats.htm** page: **Buster.htm, Phoebe.htm, Tex.htm, Thomasina.htm,** and **Zoe.htm.** The following are child pages of the **Dogs.htm** page: **Chance.htm, Maple.htm, Rocky.htm, Scout.htm,** and **Spike.htm.**

6. Add a top shared border to all pages in the Web site that includes a centered page banner, and add a left shared border to all pages in the Web site that includes a vertical navigation bar with buttons and links to child pages, the parent page, and the Home Page.

7. Insert the pet's picture in each page on a new centered line below the pet's description. The filename of the picture is the same as the Web page's filename, except that it begins with "P_". (All picture files are saved in the Web site's images folder.) For each picture, add alternative text using the pet's name, resize the picture to approximately four inches wide and three inches high, and apply a beveled edge. Overwrite the existing picture files when you save each page.

8. Create META descriptions and keywords, and include them on the Home Page.

9. Apply a customized version of the Clear Day theme to the entire Web site. The theme should use vivid colors, active graphics, and a background picture. (If you do not have the Clear Day theme, select another theme.) Before applying the theme, change the body font to Bookman Old Style and the page banner text and the text for the vertical navigation buttons to Arial Rounded MT Bold font. Save the new theme as Copy of Clear Day, and apply the theme to all pages in the Web site.

10. Open the **Guest.htm** page in Page view. Insert a form component in the page, and then cut and paste the existing form field labels from the page into the form component. Create appropriate form fields for each label, rename the form fields to have meaningful names, and set each form field to store a reasonable number of characters. Define any necessary validation criteria to ensure that data is correctly entered by the user. Change the Submit and Reset buttons

to have meaningful names and the labels "Submit Form" and "Clear Form," respectively. Save the Web page.

11. Import the **Pets** database from the AddCase2 folder on your Data Disk into the pets Web site. Use the database connection name "Pets," and store all database files in the fpdb folder of the Web site. Change the Web site's settings to display hidden folders, and then verify the database connection.

12. Change the form component in the Guest Book Web page (**Guest.htm**) to send its results to the Guest table in the Pets database that is stored in the fpdb folder of the Web site. Set the form fields so that their data is stored in the correct field in the Guest table. Do not save any additional fields.

13. In Navigation view, create a new child page of the Home Page using the title "Guest Book Info." Open the Guest Book Info page in Page view. Then change to Folders view and change the page's filename to **GuestInfo.asp**.

14. Enter the following description at the top of the Guest Book Info Web page: "This page displays data collected from the Guest Book Web page and stored in the Pets database." On the next line, insert a Database Results region that displays the records from the Guest Book Query in the Pets database. Change the Database Results region so that it displays fields from the Guest Book Query in the following order: LastName, FirstName, EmailAddress, Address, City, State, Zip, HomePhone, WorkPhone, Extension, CashDonor, FoodDonor, TimeDonor, and ContactMe. Sort the fields in ascending order using the LastName field. Change the message that is displayed when there are no returned records to "There are no records in the database that match your request." Use the default formatting options, and split records into groups of 10 records each.

15. Change the column headings in the Database Results region in the Web page to more meaningful names, and apply the Heading 5 style to the headings and center them. Change the headings for the LastName, FirstName, EmailAddress, HomePhone, WorkPhone, CashDonor, FoodDonor, TimeDonor, and ContactMe columns to be displayed on two lines, and then change the Extension column heading to "Ext." Select the database fields (the row between the start and end of the Database Results region), and then change them to use 10-point text. Set the Guest Book Info Web page so that it does not use the Web site's left shared border and will not be published with the Web site on the Pet Adoption Services Web server. Save the page.

16. Open the Guest Book Web page (**Guest.asp**) in the browser, and then complete the form using data that you make up and submit it to the server. Use the Home hyperlink in the Guest Book Web page to link to the Home Page, and then click the Guest Book Info link to open that page. Make sure that the record you entered into the database is displayed in the Guest Book Info Web page.

17. Open the Pets database from FrontPage, and then create a data access page based on the Guest table. Include all fields in the page, do not use a grouping level, sort the records in ascending order by LastName, and change the default title to "Guest Book Data Access Page."

18. Enter the page title "Guest Book Data Access Page" at the top of the new data access page, and then save it as **guestDAP** in the root folder of the pets Web site (c:\Inetput\wwwroot\pets). Close Access.

19. Open the Guest Book Data Access Page (**guestDAP.htm**) in Page view. Apply the Blends theme to this page only, and then exclude the page when publishing the Web site. Save the page, and then preview it in the browser. Use the data access page to add a new record to the database using real or fictitious data. (*Hint*: Enter the value "Yes" or "No" for the CashDonor, FoodDonor, TimeDonor, and ContactMe fields.)

20. Create a new Web page in Page view with the title "Donation Data" and the filename **Donation.htm**. Add the page to the Web site's navigation structure as a child page of the Home Page.

21. On the first line of the Web page, insert the following paragraph: "The following spreadsheet shows the monetary amounts of donations received by Pet Adoption Services, Inc. for food, cash, veterinary services, vaccinations, and medications. Veterinary services, vaccinations, and medications are valued at the market rate in the community in which they were donated."

22. On the next line, insert a centered spreadsheet component. Enter the data shown in Figure AC-1 into the spreadsheet component. Format the column headings (B1:F1) as centered, bold, 10-point Arial text. Format the row headings (A2:A7) as left-aligned, bold, 10-point Arial text. Format the data as currency. Change the color of the "Totals" and "Grand Totals" headings to red.

Figure AC-1

	1997	1998	1999	2000	Grand Totals
Food Donations	84,511	95,842	152,132	189,665	522,150
Cash Donations	102,465	118,549	187,456	254,139	662,609
Veterinary Services	167,995	145,884	159,643	162,513	636,035
Vaccinations	94,123	89,569	88,641	87,035	359,368
Medications	54,216	26,843	15,469	38,654	135,182
Totals	503,310	476,687	603,341	732,006	2,315,344

23. Resize the spreadsheet component to display the data in the worksheet and no blank cells.

24. Change the title of the spreadsheet component to "Donation Data by Category" and the title bar background color to red. Then turn off the display of the vertical and horizontal scroll bars in the spreadsheet component.

25. Insert a chart component below the spreadsheet component that you created in Step 22, with one blank line separating the components. Use the Column chart type and the Clustered Column subtype, the data range A1:E6, and the series in rows. Add the title "Donation Data" to the chart. Format the title as 24-point, bold, Arial text. Save the page.

26. Recalculate the hyperlinks in the Web site, verify all hyperlinks in the Web site, and then run a Site Summary report. Correct any errors that are listed in Reports view. (*Hint*: You can ignore any broken links to files with XML and CAB filename extensions.)

27. Save all pages in the Web site as necessary, and then use the browser to thoroughly test the Web site. Return to FrontPage as necessary to correct any errors that you discover.

28. Close Internet Explorer and FrontPage.

OBJECTIVES

In this case you will:

- Use the Import Web Wizard to create a new Web site

- Add a shared border to all pages in a Web site

- Create a new frames page in a Web site and set it to open existing pages

- Animate text in a Web page

- Create hyperlinks to new and existing pages

- Add pictures to Web pages using absolute positioning

- Create META tags for a Web page

- Apply a theme to a Web site

- Create hover buttons in a Web page

- Search for information using a browser

- Create a form component and set it to send results to a database

- Create an Active Server Page in a Web site

- Create a site map

- Check the spelling across an entire Web site

CREATING A NEW WEB SITE FOR MARTY SHARIK, REALTOR

CASE

Marty Sharik, Realtor

Marty Sharik has been an independent Realtor in West Lafayette, Indiana, for more than 25 years. In the past, he has relied on personal and professional referrals as his primary source of listings for residential properties. He has consistently been one of the top agents in West Lafayette.

Recently, Marty began worrying about competitors who were getting new listings from people who normally would work with him. He soon discovered that these new agents had Web sites that promoted listings in West Lafayette. The new agents would use the Web site to promote their services with people who are moving to West Lafayette and its surrounding areas. When a potential homebuyer indicated an interest in a certain type of neighborhood, the agent could respond immediately with information about listings, the community, and relocation assistance.

Marty decided to expand his business by creating a Web site that includes information about the community, his services, and his listings in West Lafayette. He wants to include a Web page for each property that he lists. Marty hopes that his new Web site will boost his listings, and that the service he provides will help him to establish new relationships with the new members of his hometown.

If necessary, start FrontPage, insert your Data Disk in the appropriate disk drive, and then do the following:

1. Read all the questions for this case problem, and then prepare a planning analysis sheet for Marty's Web site.

2. Prepare a Web site plan that shows the desired Web pages and the expected hyperlinks from the Home Page.

3. Use the Import Web Wizard to import all of the files that are saved in the AddCase3 folder on your Data Disk into a new Web site named **realtor**. Save the Web site in the folder on your computer that stores server-based Webs (the default folder is http://localhost/realtor). Make sure that the Web site is enabled for Active Server Pages and ActiveX controls.

4. Use drag and drop to move all picture files into the Web site's images folder.

5. Add a bottom shared border to all pages in the Web site. Replace the comment text with a left-aligned footer that consists of a copyright symbol and Marty's name on the first line. On the second line, add the text "Last updated" and a date field that indicates when the page was last edited. Format the date with the day of the week and the full date, with the month spelled out. Format the footer as 10-point, Arial, bold, italic text.

6. Create a new page in the Web site using the Contents frames page template. The frames page should open initially with the **Contents.htm** page in the contents frame and the **Marty.htm** page in the main frame. Save the frames page using the filename **Default.htm** and the title "Marty Sharik." Overwrite the existing file with the same name.

7. Create hyperlinks from the list in the Contents page to open the Marty Sharik page (**Marty.htm**), Listings page (**Listings.htm**), Relocation Services (**Relocation.htm**), About Marty Sharik (**About.htm**), and Information Request (**Info.htm**) pages in the main frame.

8. Turn off the display of the bottom shared border in the Contents page, and then save it.

9. Change the text "Over $100 million sold since 1974" in the Marty Sharik page (**Marty.htm**) to use an animation effect of your choice.

10. Open the Listings page in the frameset using the hyperlink that you created in Step 7. Change the listing number in each row in the table to a hyperlink that opens the Web page with the same title in the main frame. For example, create a hyperlink from the 51642 entry in the first row of the table to the **51642.htm** page in the Web site. Some listings do not have associated Web pages yet. In these cases, create a hyperlink from the listing number to a new Web page in the Web site that has the same name and title, and add the task of creating the Web page to the Web site's Tasks list.

11. Insert each picture file that is stored in the Web site's images folder in the Web page with the same filename. For example, insert the picture file **P_57495.jpg** in the **57495.htm** Web page. Insert each picture on the first line of the Web page, resize the picture to approximately three inches wide and high, and then use absolute positioning to position the picture to the right of the first five lines in the Web page. If no picture file is available for a Web page that contains a property description, use absolute positioning to position text where the photograph will appear. The text box should tell the Web page user that the photograph is not available at this time.

12. Create META descriptions and keywords and include them with the Marty Sharik page (**Marty.htm**). Save the page.

13. Apply a theme of your choice to the entire Web site. Make sure that the theme uses vivid colors, active graphics, and a background picture.

14. Open any Web page that includes a property description. Add a new, centered line below the property description. On the new line, create a hover button that includes the text "Request More Information" and contains a mailto to Marty's e-mail address (marty@martysharikinc.com). Use 18-point, bold, yellow, Arial font on the hover button and complementary colors and a mouse over effect of your choice. Save the page and then test the hover button in the browser to make sure that you are satisfied with its appearance and that the mailto works correctly.

15. Return to FrontPage, and then copy the hover button that you created in Step 14 and paste it in the same location in the other Web pages that contain property descriptions. Center each hover button in the page. Save each page.

16. Open the Relocation Services Web page (**Relocation.htm**) in Page view. Use your Web browser and your Internet connection to search for at least four Web sites that provide information about the community of West Lafayette, Indiana. When you locate an appropriate site, enter its URL in the Web page. Format the list of four hyperlinks as a bulleted list.

17. Open the Information Request Web page (**Info.htm**) in Page view. Insert a form component, and then cut and paste the existing form field labels into the form component. Insert the appropriate form fields for each label, change their properties, and create validation criteria as necessary. Save the Web page.

18. Set the form component that you created in Step 17 to store its results in a new Access database. In the Options for Saving Results to Database dialog box, click the Create Database button so FrontPage will create a database and a Results table for you. Do not include any additional fields. Follow the instructions to finish configuring the page, and then verify the database connection. Save the page.

19. Open the Information Request Web page in the browser, and then enter data for three different users.

20. Create a new Web page in Folders view using the filename **InfoReq.asp** and the title "Information Request Data." Open the Information Request Data Web page in Page view. Insert a Database Results region in the Web page using the database connection you created in Step 18. Remove the ID field and the additional fields from the Database Results region, and then sort the records in ascending order by last name. Create a search form in the Web page that lets Marty filter records using the "What can I help you with?" values. Use a formatting option of your choice and display all records together. After creating the Database Results region and the search form, add instructions above the search form to tell Marty how to use the page. (*Hint*: List the values that Marty can use to filter the Database Results region records.)

21. Assign the Web pages in the Web site that include property descriptions to appropriate categories that you create, and then create a new page in the Web site to serve as a site map. Save the site map Web page using the filename **site_map.htm** and the title "Site Map." Include descriptive text in the Web page to let Web site visitors know how to use the page. Give the page an appropriate title using the Heading 1 style. After you save the Site Map page, add it to the frames page to open in the main frame. (*Hint*: Create a link to the Site Map page in the Contents page.)

22. Create a Search Web page in the Web site using a template. After creating the page, delete the placeholder footer text at the bottom of the page. Save the page using the filename and title "Search."

23. Recalculate the hyperlinks in the Web site, verify all hyperlinks in the Web site, and then run a Site Summary report. Correct any errors that are listed in Reports view. (You can ignore broken hyperlinks to external URLs and to mailtos.)

24. Perform a spell check of all pages in the Web site and correct any errors that you discover. (*Hint*: Start the spell check from Folders view to check the entire Web site.)

25. Save all pages in the Web site as necessary, and then use the browser to thoroughly test the Web site. Return to FrontPage as necessary to correct any errors that you discover.

26. Close Internet Explorer and FrontPage.

TASK	PAGE #	RECOMMENDED METHOD
Access database, import into a FrontPage Web	FP 8.07	See Reference Window: Importing an Access Database into a FrontPage Web
Access query, open in Query Datasheet view	FP 8.06	Click the Queries object in the Database window, double-click the query name
Access table, open in Table Datasheet view	FP 8.05	Click the Tables object in the Database window, double-click the table name
Access, start and open an existing database	FP 8.04	See Reference Window: Starting Access and Opening an Existing Database
Action, undo previous in a data access page	FP 8.39	Click
Active Server Page, go to first page in the browser	FP 8.15	Click
Active Server Page, go to last page in the browser	FP 8.15	Click
Active Server Page, go to next page in the browser	FP 8.15	Click
Active Server Page, go to previous page in the browser	FP 8.15	Click
Active Server Page, save	FP 8.15	Click , type the filename in the File name text box, click the Save as type list arrow, click Active Server Pages, click Save
Alternative text, add to a picture	FP 2.33	See Reference Window: Adding Alternative Text to a Picture
Background color, change for a table	FP 4.26	See Reference Window: Changing a Table's Background Color
Background color, change for a Web page	FP 2.25	See Reference Window: Changing the Background Color of a Web Page
Background picture, insert in a Web page	FP 2.28	See Reference Window: Inserting a Background Picture in a Web Page
Background sound, add to a Web page	FP 2.36	See Reference Window: Adding a Background Sound to a Web Page
Background, specify common	FP 3.05	In Page view, click Format, Background, click the Get background information from another page check box, click the Browse button, select the filename of the page to use, click OK
Banner ad, create in a Web page	FP 6.50	See Reference Window: Creating a Banner Ad
Bookmark, create hyperlink to	FP 3.17	See Reference Window: Creating a Hyperlink to a Bookmark

TASK	PAGE #	RECOMMENDED METHOD
Bookmark, create nontext-based	FP 3.19	Click the location to create the bookmark, click Insert, Bookmark, enter the bookmark's name in the Bookmark name text box, click OK
Bookmark, create text-based	FP 3.14	See Reference Window: Creating a Text-Based Bookmark in a Web Page
Border color, change for a table	FP 4.27	See Reference Window: Changing a Table's Border Color
Broken link, update for a picture	FP 3.48	Right-click ⊠, click Picture Properties, click the Browse button, click 🔍, browse for the file, double-click the file, click OK
Browser version, enable a Web site for	FP 7.07	Click Tools, Page Options; click the Compatibility tab; set the browser name, browser version, and server version; select the Internet technologies; click OK
Caption, add to a table	FP 4.25	See Reference Window: Adding a Table Caption
Cascading style sheet, create	FP 9.23	See Reference Window: Creating a Cascading Style Sheet
Categories, create for a Web site	FP 7.09	See Reference Window: Creating Categories and Assigning Pages to Them
Categories report, create	FP 7.11	Click 📦, click the Report list arrow on the Reporting toolbar, click Categories
Cell, merge in a table	FP 4.16	See Reference Window: Merging Table Cells
Cell, split in a table	FP 4.15	See Reference Window: Splitting Table Cells
Chart component, create in a Web page	FP 9.11	See Reference Window: Inserting a Chart Component in a Web Page That Contains a Data Source
Chart Property Toolbox, open	FP 9.16	Select the chart component, right-click the object in the chart component that you want to modify, click Property Toolbox
Check box, add to a form	FP 6.25	Click the desired location, click Insert, Form, Check Box
Column, delete from a table	FP 4.14	See Reference Window: Selecting and Deleting Rows or Columns in a Table
Column, insert in a table in a Web page	FP 4.13	See Reference Window: Inserting Rows or Columns in a Table
Column, resize in a table	FP 4.18	See Reference Window: Resizing a Row or Column in a Table
Column, select in a table	FP 4.14	See Reference Window: Selecting and Deleting Rows or Columns in a Table
Columns, distribute selected evenly in a table	FP 4.19	Click 🔲
Columns, resize in a spreadsheet component	FP 9.07	Select the column(s), double-click ↔ on the right edge of a selected column
Data access page, create	FP 8.34	See Reference Window: Creating a Data Access Page
Data source icon, examine	FP 9.17	Double-click the ActiveX control icon in the Web page

TASK REFERENCE

TASK	PAGE #	RECOMMENDED METHOD
Data, import into a spreadsheet component	FP 9.05	Select the spreadsheet component, click ▣, click the Import Data bar, click in the URL text box, type the path to the data, click Import Now
Database connection, verify in a Web site	FP 8.09	See Reference Window: Verifying a Database Connection
Database Results region, insert in a Web page	FP 8.12	See Reference Window: Using the Database Results Wizard to Insert a Database Results Region in a Web Page
Discussion group, create	FP 7.24	See Reference Window: Using the Discussion Web Wizard to Create a Discussion Group
Drop-down menu, add to a form	FP 6.16	Click the desired location, click Insert, Form, Drop-Down Menu
Embedded file, save with a Web page	FP 2.29	See Reference Window: Saving a Web Page That Contains an Embedded File
File, insert in a Web page	FP 3.06	See Reference Window: Inserting a File in a Web Page
File, move in a Web site using drag and drop	FP 6.53	In Folders view, drag and drop the desired file in the Contents pane to the new folder in the Folder List
Filename, rename in Folders view for a disk-based Web	FP 5.21	See Reference Window: Renaming a Page's Filename and Title in Folders View
Filename, rename in Folders view for a server-based Web	FP 6.56	See Reference Window: Renaming a File in Folders View
Filter, remove in a data access page	FP 8.41	Click ▽
Folder List, show or hide	FP 1.29	Click ▦
Folders view, change to	FP 1.27	Click ▱
Form component, add to a Web page	FP 6.12	See Reference Window: Creating a Form Component and Adding Form Fields to It
Form component, send results to a database	FP 8.30	See Reference Window: Configuring a Form to Send Results to a Database
Form field properties, change	FP 6.15	Double-click the form field
Form field, validate	FP 6.24	Right-click the form field, click Form Field Validation
Form results file, examine contents of	FP 6.46	Open the server-based Web in FrontPage, double-click the _private folder, double-click the form results file
Form Web page, use	FP 1.21	See Reference Window: Using a Form Web Page

TASK REFERENCE

TASK	PAGE #	RECOMMENDED METHOD
Format Painter, use to copy and paste text formatting	FP 2.20	Click the text whose format you want to copy, click [icon], click the text to which to copy the format
Frame, add new to a frames page	FP 4.46	See Reference Window: Adding a New Frame to an Existing Frames Page
Frame, edit size of in a frames page	FP 4.39	Point to the frame's border, drag the border to the desired size, release the mouse button
Frames page, create	FP 4.33	See Reference Window: Creating a Frames Page
Frames page, print in Internet Explorer	FP 4.48	Click File, Print, click desired option in the Print frames section, click OK
FrontPage navigation bar, add to a Web page	FP 5.36	Click in the desired location, click Insert, Navigation Bar, select the navigation bar options, click OK
FrontPage navigation bar, revise	FP 5.32	Right-click the navigation bar component, click Navigation Bar Properties
FrontPage, start	FP 1.26	Click the Start button, point to Programs, click Microsoft FrontPage
Heading, create in a Web page	FP 2.15	See Reference Window: Creating a Heading in a Web Page
Help, get in FrontPage	FP 1.42	Click Help, Microsoft FrontPage Help
Help, get while using a data access page	FP 8.39	Click [icon]
Help, get while using an Office component	FP 9.08	Click [icon]
Hit counter, create in a Web page	FP 6.47	See Reference Window: Creating a Hit Counter in a Web Page
Horizontal line, add to a Web page	FP 2.34	See Reference Window: Inserting a Horizontal Line and Changing Its Properties
Hotspot, create in a picture	FP 3.32	See Reference Window: Creating a Picture Hotspot
Hotspot, highlight in a picture	FP 3.34	See Reference Window: Highlighting Hotspots on a Picture
Hover button, change characteristics of	FP 5.12	In Page view, right-click the hover button, click Hover Button Properties
Hover button, create	FP 5.09	See Reference Window: Creating a Hover Button in a Web Page
HTML code, view for a frames page in FrontPage	FP 4.36	In Page view, click the Frames Page HTML tab
HTML code, view for a No Frames page	FP 4.36	In Page view, click the No Frames tab
HTML code, view for a Web page using FrontPage	FP 1.41	In Page view, click the HTML tab

TASK	PAGE #	RECOMMENDED METHOD
HTML code, view for a Web page using Internet Explorer	FP 1.42	Click View, Source
HTML tag, modify style	FP 9.23	Click Format, Style, click the tag in the Styles list, click the Modify button, modify the desired characteristics, click OK
Hyperlink, create to another Web page	FP 3.22	See Reference Window: Creating a Hyperlink to Another Web Page
Hyperlink, create using drag and drop	FP 3.24	See Reference Window: Creating a Hyperlink Using Drag and Drop
Hyperlink, follow in Internet Explorer	FP 1.14	Click the hyperlink
Hyperlink, follow in Page view	FP 1.29	Press and hold down the Ctrl key, click the hyperlink
Hyperlinks view, change to	FP 1.34	Click 🔲
Hyperlinks view, print	FP 3.38	In Hyperlinks view, press the Print Screen key, start WordPad, press Ctrl + V, click 🖨
Hyperlinks, recalculate	FP 6.57	In Hyperlinks view, click Tools, Recalculate Hyperlinks, click the Yes button
Hyperlinks, show or hide to pictures	FP 3.38	In Hyperlinks view, right-click the Contents pane, click Hyperlinks to Pictures
Hyperlinks, verify	FP 6.58	In Reports view, click 🔲 on the Reporting toolbar, click the Start button
Initial page, set for a frame	FP 4.38	Click the Set Initial Page button, browse for and select the page to use
Internet Explorer, start	FP 1.08	Click 🔲 on the Quick Launch toolbar
List, create bulleted	FP 3.10	See Reference Window: Creating a Bulleted List
List, create definition	FP 3.08	See Reference Window: Creating a Definition List
List, create nested	FP 3.11	See Reference Window: Creating a Nested List
List, create numbered	FP 3.11	See Reference Window: Creating a Numbered List
Mailto, create	FP 3.26	See Reference Window: Creating a Mailto
Marquee, create in a Web page	FP 2.38	See Reference Window: Creating a Marquee in a Web Page
Message, post to a discussion group	FP 7.30	See Reference Window: Posting a Message to a Discussion Group
Message, reply to in a discussion group	FP 7.33	See Reference Window: Replying to a Message
Message, search for in a discussion group	FP 7.35	See Reference Window: Searching a Discussion Group
META tag, insert in a Web page	FP 2.41	See Reference Window: Inserting META Tags in a Web Page

TASK REFERENCE

TASK	PAGE #	RECOMMENDED METHOD
Music, stop playing in Internet Explorer	FP 1.13	Click ⊗
Navigation structure, create	FP 5.23	In Navigation view, drag and drop filenames from the Folder List into the Navigation pane
Navigation view, change to	FP 1.33	Click ▣
Nonprinting characters, show or hide in a Web page	FP 4.09	Click ¶
Office component, resize in Page view	FP 9.10	Select the component, drag a sizing handle to resize the component
One-line text box, add to a form	FP 6.18	Click the desired location, click Insert, Form, One-Line Text Box
Page banner, create	FP 5.37	See Reference Window: Creating a Page Banner
Page transition, create	FP 5.13	See Reference Window: Applying a Page Transition
Page view, change to	FP 1.28	Click ▤
Permissions, set for a Web site	FP 6.59	Click Tools, Security, Permissions
Picture, add to a Web page	FP 2.31	See Reference Window: Adding a Picture to a Web Page
Picture, animate in a Web page	FP 5.15	See Reference Window: Creating Animated Text or Pictures in a Web Page
Picture, change characteristics of	FP 5.05	See Reference Window: Changing Picture Characteristics
Picture, change color to transparent	FP 3.30	See Reference Window: Changing a Color in a Picture to Transparent
Picture, convert to another format	FP 3.29	See Reference Window: Converting a Picture to Another Format
Picture, position absolutely in a Web page	FP 7.18	See Reference Window: Inserting Text or a Picture in a Web Page Using Absolute Positioning
PivotTable list component, insert in a Web page		Click ▣, click Office PivotTable
Program window, maximize	FP 1.10	Click ▣ on the program's title bar
Program, close	FP 1.24	Click ✕ on the program's title bar
Push button, change properties of	FP 6.27	Double-click the push button, change properties, click OK
Radio button, add to a form	FP 6.14	Click the desired location, click Insert, Form, Radio Button

TASK	PAGE #	RECOMMENDED METHOD
Record, add to a database table	FP 8.23	Click the Tables object in the Database window, double-click the table name, click ▶✳, enter the new record
Record, add to a database using a Web page	FP 8.40	See Reference Window: Adding a Record to a Database Table Using a Data Access Page.
Record, delete from a table using a data access page	FP 8.39	Display the record, click ▶✕
Record, go to first in a data access page	FP 8.39	Click ⏮
Record, go to last in a data access page	FP 8.39	Click ⏭
Record, go to next in a data access page	FP 8.39	Click ▶
Record, go to previous in a data access page	FP 8.39	Click ◀
Record, save in a table using a data access page	FP 8.40	Click 💾
Records, filter by selection in a data access page	FP 8.41	Click in the field to filter, click 🖅
Records, sort in ascending order in a data access page	FP 8.39	Click in the field to sort, click ᴬ↓
Records, sort in descending order in a data access page	FP 8.39	Click in the field to sort, click ᶻ↓
Repeated hyperlinks, show or hide in Hyperlinks view	FP 1.36	Right-click the Contents pane, click Repeated Hyperlinks
Reports view, change to	FP 1.32	Click 🏢
Row, delete from a table	FP 4.14	See Reference Window: Selecting and Deleting Rows or Columns in a Table
Row, insert in a table in a Web page	FP 4.13	See Reference Window: Inserting Rows or Columns in a Table
Row, resize in a table	FP 4.18	See Reference Window: Resizing a Row or Column in a Table
Row, select in a table	FP 4.14	See Reference Window: Selecting and Deleting Rows or Columns in a Table
Rows, distribute selected evenly in a table	FP 4.20	Click ☰
Save Results component, configure	FP 6.28	Right-click in the form component, click Form Properties
Scrolling text box, add to a form	FP 6.20	Click the desired location, click Insert, Form, Scrolling Text Box

TASK	PAGE #	RECOMMENDED METHOD
Search component properties, change	FP 6.07	Right-click in the search component, click Search Form Properties
Search form, add to an Active Server Page	FP 8.18	See Reference Window: Creating a Search Form in a Web Page That Queries a Database
Search Web page, use	FP 1.19	See Reference Window: Using a Search Web Page
Shared border, edit	FP 5.29	In Page view, click the shared border to select it, make changes
Shared border, turn off for a Web page	FP 5.35	See Reference Window: Turning Off Shared Borders for a Single Web Page
Shared borders, create for a Web site	FP 5.25	See Reference Window: Turning on Shared Borders for a Web Site
Shared template, save in a Web site	FP 7.20	See Reference Window: Saving a Shared Template
Site map, create	FP 7.12	See Reference Window: Creating a Site Map
Source control, disable for a Web site	FP 7.16	Click Tools, Web Settings, click the General tab, click the Use document check-in and check-out check box to clear it, click OK, click Yes
Source control, enable for a Web site	FP 7.15	See Reference Window: Enabling Source Control for a Web Site
Special character, insert in a Web page	FP 2.18	Click the desired location, click Insert, click Symbol, select the desired character, click the Insert button, click the Close button
Spreadsheet component, insert in a Web page	FP 9.04	See Reference Window: Inserting a Spreadsheet Component in a Web Page
Spreadsheet Property Toolbox, open	FP 9.05	Click
Table, align in a Web page	FP 4.10	See Reference Window: Aligning a Table in a Web Page
Table, create in a Web page	FP 4.08	See Reference Window: Creating a Table in a Web Page
Table, create nested	FP 4.21	See Reference Window: Creating a Nested Table
Tags, reveal or hide in Page view	FP 9.37	Click View, Reveal Tags
Target frame, specify	FP 4.45	Click , click , select the target frame, click OK, click OK
Task history, show or hide	FP 3.49	Right-click in the Tasks pane, click Show Task History
Task, add in Tasks view	FP 3.43	See Reference Window: Adding a Task in Tasks View
Task, change in Tasks view	FP 3.45	Double-click the task to change, change the settings, click OK
Task, delete from the Tasks list	FP 3.49	See Reference Window: Deleting a Task from the Tasks List
Task, mark as completed	FP 3.48	See Reference Window: Marking a Task as Completed

TASK	PAGE #	RECOMMENDED METHOD
Tasks list, sort	FP 3.45	In Tasks view, click the column heading for the task by which to sort
Tasks view, change to	FP 1.37	Click 📋
Text, add over a picture	FP 5.06	See Reference Window: Adding Text Over a Picture
Text, align in a Web page	FP 2.16	See Reference Window: Aligning Text in a Web Page
Text, animate in a Web page	FP 5.15	See Reference Window: Creating Animated Text or Pictures in a Web Page
Text, change color of selected in a Web page	FP 2.19	Click the list arrow for **A**, click desired color
Text, change font of selected in a Web page	FP 2.17	Click the Font list arrow, click new font name
Text, change selected to bold	FP 2.19	Click **B**
Text, change selected to italic	FP 2.17	Click *I*
Text, change selected to underlined	FP 2.14	Click U̲
Text, change size of for selected in a Web page	FP 2.18	Click the Font Size list arrow, click the desired font size
Text, find and replace in a Web site	FP 6.54	Click Edit, Replace, specify the text to find in the Find what text box, specify the text to replace it with in the Replace with text box, click the Find In Web button
Text, find in Web site	FP 6.53	Click Edit, Find, specify the text in the Find what text box, click the Find Next button
Text, position absolutely in a Web page	FP 7.18	See Reference Window: Inserting Text or a Picture in a Web Page Using Absolute Positioning
Theme, add to a Web site	FP 5.39	See Reference Window: Applying a Theme to a Web Site
Theme, change attributes of	FP 5.42	Click Format, Theme, change attributes, click OK
Theme, customize	FP 5.43	Click Format, Theme, click the Modify button, change the desired settings, click OK, click OK
Thumbnail picture, create	FP 5.03	See Reference Window: Creating a Thumbnail Picture
Title, rename in Folders view	FP 5.21	See Reference Window: Renaming a Page's Filename and Title in Folders View
Title, rename in Navigation view	FP 5.25	See Reference Window: Renaming a Page's Title in Navigation View
Toolbar, show or hide	FP 1.32	Click View, Toolbars, click the name of toolbar to show or hide

TASK	PAGE #	RECOMMENDED METHOD
Views bar, show or hide	FP 1.29	Click View, Views Bar
Web page, add to navigation structure	FP 5.34	See Reference Window: Adding a New Page in Navigation View
Web page, check spelling in	FP 2.10	See Reference Window: Spell Checking a Web Page
Web page, check in	FP 7.14	Close the Web page in Page view, click [icon], right-click the Web page, click Check In
Web page, check out	FP 7.14	Double-click the page name in Folders view, click Yes
Web page, close in Page view	FP 2.12	Click [X] on the Contents pane
Web page, create new and add to the Tasks list	FP 3.41	See Reference Window: Creating a New Web Page and Adding It to the Tasks List
Web page, delete from navigation structure	FP 5.33	See Reference Window: Deleting a Page from the Navigation Structure
Web page, link to a cascading style sheet	FP 9.30	Click Format, Style Sheet Links, click the Selected page(s) option button, click the Add button, double-click the style sheet's filename, click OK
Web page, import into a Web site	FP 3.03	See Reference Window: Importing an Existing Web Page into a Web Site
Web page, preview in browser	FP 1.30	Click [icon]
Web page, preview using FrontPage	FP 1.29	In Page view, click the Preview tab
Web page, print using Internet Explorer	FP 1.24	Click [icon]
Web page, save as a cascading style sheet	FP 9.29	Click [icon], click the Change button, enter the page's title, click OK, click the Save as type list arrow, click HyperText Style Sheet, enter the page's filename in the File name text box, click Save
Web page, save from a World Wide Web site	FP 4.03	See Reference Window: Saving a Web Page from a World Wide Web Site
Web page, save in Page view	FP 2.12	See Reference Window: Saving a Web Page
Web page, scroll to bottom	FP 1.16	Press Ctrl + End
Web page, scroll to top	FP 2.17	Press Ctrl + Home
Web page, test	FP 2.22	See Reference Window: Testing a Web Page
Web page, print using FrontPage	FP 2.23	Click [icon]

TASK	PAGE #	RECOMMENDED METHOD
Web site, close in FrontPage	FP 1.37	Click File, Close Web
Web site, create new	FP 2.07	Click File, New, Web, enter the Web site's name in the Specify the location of the new web text box, double-click the template or Wizard to use to create the Web site
Web site, create new and import pages into	FP 5.19	See Reference Window: Using the Import Web Wizard to Create a New Web Site
Web site, display hidden folders	FP 7.35	See Reference Window: Displaying a Web Site's Hidden Folders
Web site, open existing from PWS	FP 7.25	Click the list arrow for 📂, click Open Web, click the Web Folders button, click the Web site folder, click Open
Web site, open using FrontPage	FP 1.25	See Reference Window: Opening a Web Site
Web site, open using Internet Explorer	FP 1.12	See Reference Window: Opening a Web Site in Internet Explorer
Web site, publish	FP 6.39	See Reference Window: Publishing a Web Site to Your Computer's Server
Web site, publish changed pages	FP 6.42	See Reference Window: Publishing Changes to a Server-Based Web Site
Web site, set to run scripts	FP 8.10	See Reference Window: Setting a Web Site to Run Scripts

Standardized Coding Number	Certification Skill Activity — Activity	Tutorial Number (page numbers)	End-of-Tutorial Practice — Exercise	Step Number
FP2000.1	**Create a new Web site**			
FP2000.1.1	Save a FrontPage Web	2 (2.06–2.09)	Case Problem 1 Case Problem 2 Case Problem 3 Case Problem 4	3 3 3 3
FP2000.1.2	Create a Web site using a Web wizard	5 (5.18–5.20)	\<none\>	
FP2000.1.3	Create a Web site using a Web template	2 (2.06–2.09)	Case Problem 1 Case Problem 2 Case Problem 3 Case Problem 4	3 3 3 3
FP2000.2	**Open and edit an existing FrontPage-based Web site**			
FP2000.2.1	Open an existing FrontPage Web	1 (1.25–1.27) 2 (2.15)	1: Review Assignment Case Problem 1 2: Review Assignment	1, 11 1, 13 1
FP2000.2.2	Modify and save changes to the Web site	2 (2.12)	Review Assignment Case Problem 1 Case Problem 2 Case Problem 3 Case Problem 4	2–4 4–14 4–14 4–14 4–14
FP2000.3	**Apply and edit a Theme across the entire Web site**			
FP2000.3.1	Apply a Theme to entire Web site	5 (5.38–5.42)	Case Problem 1 Case Problem 2	8 7
FP2000.3.2	Apply a custom Theme across entire Web site	5 (5.43–5.45)	Case Problem 2	7
FP2000.4	**Add a new Web page**			
FP2000.4.1	Create and Preview a new Web page using a FrontPage page template or wizard	4 (4.32–4.35) 6 (6.03–6.05, 6.08)	4: Case Problem 1 Case Problem 2 Case Problem 3 Case Problem 4 6: Case Problem 1 Case Problem 2 Case Problem 3 Case Problem 4	3 3 3 4 3, 6 8 3, 4, 7 3, 4, 7, 9, 10
FP2000.4.2	Create a new page within Page View	4 (4.32–4.35)	Review Assignment Case Problem 1 Case Problem 2 Case Problem 3 Case Problem 4	10 3, 4, 7, 9 3, 4, 7 3, 5, 7, 11 4, 6

Standardized Coding Number	Certification Skill Activity / Activity	Tutorial Number (page numbers)	End-of-Tutorial Practice	
			Exercise	Step Number
FP2000.5	**Open, view and rename Web page**			
FP2000.5.1	View a Web document in Normal, HTML and Preview view	1 (1.28–1.30,1.41) 2 (2.22, 2.43)	2: Review Assignment Case Problem 1 Case Problem 2 Case Problem 3 Case Problem 4	4 16 16 16 16
FP2000.5.2	Open an Office document in a FrontPage Web	6 (6.32–6.33)	\<none\>	
FP2000.5.3	Rename page title and change page URL	5 (5.21)	\<none\>	
FP2000.6	**Import text and images onto Web page**			
FP2000.6.1	Add or import images into a Web page (automatically converted to GIF/JPEG)	2 (2.31–2.32) 3 (3.28–3.30)	2: Case Problem 1 Case Problem 2 Case Problem 3 Case Problem 4 3: Review Assignment Case Problem 1 Case Problem 2 Case Problem 3 Case Problem 4	11 11 7, 10 11, 12 7, 11 4, 11, 16 4, 6, 13, 18 4, 13, 15 6, 7
FP2000.6.2	Add or import text to a Web page (automatically converted to HTML)	3 (3.06–3.07)	Case Problem 1 Case Problem 2 Case Problem 3	6 7 6
FP2000.6.3	Add or import elements from a Web site to a FrontPage Web	4 (4.02–4.05)	\<none\>	
FP2000.7	**Type and format text and paragraphs and create hyperlinks**			
FP2000.7.1	Type and format text/fonts on a Web page	2 (2.09, 2.14–2.21)	Case Problem 1 Case Problem 2 Case Problem 3 Case Problem 4	4, 6–8, 12 4, 6, 7, 9 4, 6, 8, 9, 12 4, 6–9
FP2000.7.2	Add multi-level bulleted or numbered lists to Web page	3 (3.11–3.12)	Case Problem 1 Case Problem 2 Case Problem 3 Case Problem 4	7 8 7–9 4
FP2000.7.3	Format bulleted or numbered lists	3 (3.09–3.12)	Case Problem 1 Case Problem 2 Case Problem 3 Case Problem 4	7 8 7–9 4

Standardized Coding Number	Certification Skill Activity		Tutorial Number (page numbers)	End-of-Tutorial Practice	
	Activity			Exercise	Step Number
FP2000.7.4	Add hyperlinks pointing to: an existing page in the current site, the WWW, or a brand new page		3 (3.21–3.25)	Review Assignment Case Problem 1 Case Problem 2 Case Problem 3 Case Problem 4	14 13, 14, 17 15, 19 14, 15 9, 10
FP2000.7.5	Use the Format Painter to apply formats		2 (2.20–2.21)	Case Problem 2	9
FP2000.7.6	Use the Clipboard		3 (3.38–3.39) 6 (6.07–6.08)	3: Review Assignment Case Problem 1 Case Problem 2 Case Problem 3 Case Problem 4 6: Review Assignment Case Problem 1 Case Problem 2 Case Problem 3	3, 12, 13 19 22 20 12 2 3 3 3
FP2000.8	**Edit images, apply image effects; create hotspots**				
FP2000.8.1	Rotate, flip, bevel, or resize images on a Web page		5 (5.05–5.06)	Review Assignment Case Problem 1 Case Problem 3	3 4 3
FP2000.8.2	Add text over image		2 (2.33–2.34) 5 (5.06)	2: Case Problem 1 5: Case Problem 1	11 4
FP2000.8.3	Create a hotspot (clickable imagemap)		3 (3.32–3.35)	Case Problem 2 Case Problem 3 Case Problem 4	16 14–16 10
FP2000.9	**Create and edit tables on a Web page**				
FP2000.9.1	Create tables on a Web page		4 (4.05–4.09)	Review Assignment Case Problem 1 Case Problem 2 Case Problem 3 Case Problem 4	4, 7, 8 4 4, 8 4, 5 3, 5, 6
FP2000.9.2	Erase or delete table rows or columns		4 (4.14–4.15)	Review Assignment Case Problem 1	2, 13 7
FP2000.9.3	Draw or add table rows or columns		4 (4.11–4.14)	Review Assignment	2, 13
FP2000.9.4	Resize tables and cells		4 (4.09, 4.18–4.20)	Review Assignment Case Problem 2	4 8
FP2000.9.5	Select and merge table cells		4 (4.14–4.18)	Review Assignment	2

Standardized Coding Number	Certification Skill Activity — Activity	Tutorial Number (page numbers)	End-of-Tutorial Practice — Exercise	Step Number
FP2000.10	**Insert dynamic, Active Elements and FrontPage components on a Web page**			
FP2000.10.1	Add a Hit Counter to Web page	6 (6.47–6.49)	Case Problem 1	9
FP2000.10.2	Format Page Transition for Web page	5 (5.13–5.14)	Review Assignment Case Problem 1 Case Problem 3	5 7 7
FP2000.10.3	Add or edit scrolling Marquee text on a Web page	2 (2.38–2.40)	Case Problem 1 Case Problem 2 Case Problem 3 Case Problem 4	12 12 12 9
FP2000.10.4	Add a Search Form to Web page	6 (6.03–6.08)	Case Problem 1 Case Problem 3 Case Problem 4	3 3 3
FP2000.11	**View and organize Web site documents**			
FP2000.11.1	View a Web site in Reports View, Hyperlinks View, or Folders View	1 (1.31–1.32, 1.33–1.36) 3 (3.35–3.39) 4	1: Review Assignment Case Problem 1 3: Review Assignment Case Problem 1 Case Problem 2 Case Problem 3 Case Problem 4 4: Case Problem 1 Case Problem 2 Case Problem 3 Case Problem 4	13, 14 13 13 19 21, 22 19, 20 12 13 12, 13 14, 15 12, 13
FP2000.11.2	View your Web site structure and print it from Navigation View	1 (1.32–1.33) 5 (5.23–5.25)	1: Review Assignment 5: Review Assignment Case Problem 2 Case Problem 4	11 11 3 5
FP2000.11.3	Move and organize files using drag and drop in Folders View and Navigation View	5 (5.23–5.25) 6 (6.52–6.53)	5: Review Assignment Case Problem 2 Case Problem 4	8 3 5
FP2000.12	**Manage a Web site (including all files, pages and hyperlinks) and automatically keep contents up-to-date**			
FP2000.12.1	Check spelling on a page or across a Web site	2 (2.09–2.10) 6	2: Case Problem 1 Case Problem 2 Case Problem 3 Case Problem 4 6: Case Problem 4	4 4 4 4 12

Standardized Coding Number	Certification Skill Activity		Tutorial Number (page numbers)	End-of-Tutorial Practice	
		Activity		Exercise	Step Number
FP2000.12.2		Change file name in Folders View and update its hyperlinks	5 (5.21) 6 (6.56–6.57)	5: Case Problem 3	4
FP2000.12.3		Verify hyperlinks	6 (6.57–6.59)	Review Assignment Case Problem 1 Case Problem 2 Case Problem 3 Case Problem 4	7 7 7 8 8
FP2000.12.4		Use Global Find and Replace across a Web site	6 (6.53–6.56)	Case Problem 1	10
FP2000.13		**Manage tasks**			
FP2000.13.1		View task history	3 (3.49)	<none>	
FP2000.13.2		View and sort tasks in Tasks View	3 (3.45–3.46) 4 (4.02) 6 (6.02)	3: Review Assignment Case Problem 1 Case Problem 2 Case Problem 3 Case Problem 4 4: Review Assignment 6: Case Problem 1	11 15, 18 20 18 11 14 8

Standardized Coding Number	Certification Skill Activity / Activity	Tutorial Number (page numbers)	End-of-Tutorial Practice Exercise	Step Number
FP2000E.1	**Create a FrontPage Web using existing resources**			
FP2000E.1.1	Use Import Wizard to import an existing Web site from a file into FrontPage	5 (5.18–5.20)	<none>	
FP2000E.1.2	Use Import Wizard to import an existing Web site from a URL into FrontPage	7 (7.04–7.05)	<none>	
FP2000E.1.3	Modify HTML tags and verify results using Reveal Tags	9 (9.37–9.40)	<none>	
FP2000E.1.4	Use buttons and drop–down menus to insert code directly in HTML View	9 (9.36–9.37)	Case Problem 4	8–10
FP2000E.2	**Apply and change Themes for an entire Web site and individual Web pages**			
FP2000E.2.1	Select a new Theme and apply to an individual Web page	5 (5.38–5.41)	Review Assignment	8
FP2000E.2.2	Change attributes (Vivid Colors, Active Graphics, Background Image) for a currently selected site-wide Theme	5 (5.42–5.43) 9	9: Case Problem 4	3–6
FP2000E.2.3	Create a custom Theme and apply it to an individual Web page	5 (5.43–5.45) 9	5: Case Problem 2 Case Problem 3 9: Review Assignment Case Problem 4	7 4 2 7
FP2000E.3	**Create and organize navigational structure for entire Web site**			
FP2000E.3.1	Rename new pages in Navigation View	5 (5.25)	Review Assignment	8
FP2000E.3.2	Add new pages to Navigation View	5 (5.33–5.35)	Review Assignment	8
FP2000E.3.3	Add existing pages to Navigation View	5 (5.23–5.24)	Case Problem 2 Case Problem 4	3 5
FP2000E.3.4	Use drag and drop to organize/re-structure pages in Navigation View	5 (5.23–5.24)	Review Assignment Case Problem 2 Case Problem 4	8 3 5
FP2000E.4	**Modify the Web page layout**			
FP2000E.4.1	Position graphics on a page	7 (7.18–7.20)	Review Assignment Case Problem 3	2, 4 7
FP2000E.4.2	Position text on a page	7 (7.18–7.20)	Review Assignment	4
FP2000E.5	**Add or edit Shared Borders across entire site and on individual Web pages**			
FP2000E.5.1	Turn off (deselect) site-wide Shared Borders for the current Web page	5 (5.35–5.36)	Review Assignment	10

Standardized Coding Number	Certification Skill Activity — Activity	Tutorial Number (page numbers)	End-of-Tutorial Practice — Exercise	Step Number
FP2000E.5.2	Edit content within Shared Borders for an entire Web site	5 (5.29–5.32)	Review Assignment Case Problem 2	9–10 4–5
FP2000E.5.3	Edit content within Shared Borders for current Web page	5 7 (7.39–7.40)	5: Review Assignment Case Problem 2 7: Case Problem 1	9–10 4 8
FP2000E.5.4	Turn on (set) alternate Shared Borders for the current Web page	5 (5.25–5.29)	Review Assignment Case Problem 2	10 4
FP2000E.6	**Automatically add navigation bars and page banners to Web pages**			
FP2000E.6.1	Add Navigation Bar to the top of a Web page	5 (5.36–5.37) 7 (7.18, 7.41)	5: Case Problem 4 7: Review Assignment Case Problem 2 Case Problem 4	7–8 12 6 5
FP2000E.6.2	Add Page Banner to the top of a Web page	5 (5.37–5.38) 7 (7.18, 7.41)	5: Case Problem 2 Case Problem 4 7: Case Problem 1 Case Problem 2	9 6 6 6
FP2000E.6.3	Select/change levels of navigational buttons to include in navigation bar on Web page	5 (5.30–5.32) 7 (7.18, 7.41)	5: Review Assignment Case Problem 4 7: Case Problem 1 Case Problem 2 Case Problem 4	9 7–8 6 6 5
FP2000E.7	**Add background elements to Web pages**			
FP2000E.7.1	Add a background image on a Web Page	2 (2.28–2.31)	Case Problem 3 Case Problem 4	10 11
FP2000E.8	**Manipulate table contents on a Web page**			
FP2000E.8.1	Center image or text within a table cell	4 (4.22–4.23)	Review Assignment Case Problem 1 Case Problem 2 Case Problem 3 Case Problem 4	3 4 8 4–5 5–6
FP2000E.8.2	Add a custom background color or image to an entire table and to individual table cells	4 (4.26–4.27)	Review Assignment Case Problem 1 Case Problem 3	5, 6, 8 5 9
FP2000E.8.3	Add a table within a table	4 (4.21–4.22)	Case Problem 4	3

Standardized Coding Number	Certification Skill Activity — Activity	Tutorial Number (page numbers)	End-of-Tutorial Practice — Exercise	Step Number
FP2000E.9	**Enhance or edit a Web page with custom text/hyperlink styles and formatting**			
FP2000E.9.1	View page Estimated Time to Download	2 (2.32)	<none>	
FP2000E.9.2	Resample/ Restore image on Web page	5 (5.05)	<none>	
FP2000E.9.3	Format special styles for fonts, paragraphs, and hyperlinks	9 (9.21–9.31)	Case Problem 1 Case Problem 2	10–11 12
FP2000E.10	Customize a Web page with dynamic, Active Elements and FrontPage components			
FP2000E.10.1	Add Hover Button to Web page	5 (5.08–5.12)	Review Assignment Case Problem 1 Case Problem 3 Case Problem 4	2, 4, 10 5 5–6 4
FP2000E.10.2	Edit Hover Button transitional effect	5 (5.12–5.13)	Review Assignment Case Problem 3 Case Problem 4	2, 4, 10 5–6 4
FP2000E.10.3	Change FrontPage component properties	5 (5.12–5.13) 6 (6.06–6.08)	6: Review Assignment Case Problem 1 Case Problem 2 Case Problem 3 Case Problem 4	5 3–4 3, 8 3, 4, 9 3, 4, 9, 11
FP2000E.10.4	Insert pre-built and Office Web components into a page	9 (9.02–9.21)	Review Assignment Case Problem 1 Case Problem 2 Case Problem 3	4–8 3–9 3–11 3–10
FP2000E11	**Build a Web site for user input**			
FP2000E.11.1	Add text boxes, check boxes, radio buttons, drop down pick lists, and push buttons	6 (6.13–6.21, 6.25–6.27)	Review Assignment Case Problem 1 Case Problem 2 Case Problem 3 Case Problem 4	3 4 3 4 4
FP2000E.11.2	Save form to file	6 (6.28–6.31)	Case Problem 1 Case Problem 2 Case Problem 3 Case Problem 4	4 3 4, 9 4
FP2000E.11.3	Add Search Form to a Web page	6 (6.03–6.08)	Case Problem 1 Case Problem 3 Case Problem 4	3 3 3

Standardized Coding Number	Certification Skill Activity Activity	Tutorial Number (page numbers)	End-of-Tutorial Practice	
			Exercise	Step Number
FP2000E.11.4	Save form to email	6 (6.29)	<none>	
FP2000E.11.5	Create a custom form on a Web page	6 (6.08–6.32)	Case Problem 1 Case Problem 2 Case Problem 3 Case Problem 4	4 3, 8 4 4, 9
FP2000E.12	**Integrate databases**			
FP2000E.12.1	Create a form that sends data to an Access database	8 (8.26–8.33)	Case Problem 1 Case Problem 2 Case Problem 3	4–10 4–10 4–10
FP2000E.12.2	Incorporate data access pages into a Web page	8 (8.34–8.42)	Case Problem 1 Case Problem 2 Case Problem 3 Case Problem 4	13–15 13–15 13–15 5–11
FP2000E.12.3	Incorporate database queries using the Database Results Wizard	8 (8.11–8.24)	Review Assignment Case Problem 1 Case Problem 2 Case Problem 3	3–4 11–12 11–12 11–12
FP2000E.13	**Use collaboration features**			
FP2000E.13.1	Check in and check out FrontPage files	7 (7.14–7.16, 7.38)	<none>	
FP2000E.13.2	Set rights to a FrontPage Web and sub-Webs	6 (6.59–6.60)	<none>	
FP2000E.14	**Create and edit a Frames Web page**			
FP2000E.14.1	Edit size of existing frames in Frames page using drag and drop of border lines	4 (4.39–4.40)	Case Problem 2	5
FP2000E.14.2	Edit actual content within a frame on the Frames page	4 (4.40)	Review Assignment Case Problem 1 Case Problem 2 Case Problem 3 Case Problem 4	11–13 7–10 4–8 7–11 6–9
FP2000E.14.3	Create a new Frames page from template or using Frames Wizard	4 (4.32–4.35)	Case Problem 1 Case Problem 2 Case Problem 3 Case Problem 4	3 3 3 4
FP2000E.14.4	Add target content within a frame	4 (4.37–4.40)	Case Problem 1 Case Problem 2 Case Problem 3 Case Problem 4	4, 6–7, 9–10 4, 7–8 7–8, 10–11 7–9

Standardized Coding Number	Certification Skill Activity	Tutorial Number (page numbers)	End-of-Tutorial Practice	
	Activity		Exercise	Step Number
FP2000E.15	**Publish a Web site**			
FP2000E.15.1	Publish a Web from one server to another	6 (6.60–6.61)	\<none\>	
FP2000E.15.2	Use FrontPage or Microsoft Personal Web Server as appropriate	6 (6.36–6.61) 7 8 9	6: Review Assignment Case Problem 1 Case Problem 2 Case Problem 3 Case Problem 4	1–7 6–10 6–9 7–11 7–12
FP2000E.15.3	Set FrontPage/server permissions as appropriate	6 (6.59–6.60)	\<none\>	

File Finder

Tutorial	Location in Tutorial	Name and Location of Data File or Web Site	Files or Web Sites the Student Creates from Scratch
Tutorial 1			
	Session 1.1	A:\Disk1\My Webs\SunnyMorningProducts	
	Session 1.2	A:\Disk1\My Webs\SunnyMorningProducts *(Continued from Session 1.1)*	
	Session 1.3	A:\Disk1\My Webs\SunnyMorningProducts *(Continued from Session 1.2)*	
	Review Assignments	A:\Disk1\My Webs\SunnyMorningProducts *(Continued from Session 1.3)*	
	Case Problem 1	A:\Disk1\My Webs\Carpenter	
	Case Problem 2	No Data Files are used in this Case Problem.	
Tutorial 2			
	Session 2.1		A:\Disk2\My Webs\Sunny
	Session 2.2	A:\Disk2\My Webs\Sunny *(Continued from Session 2.1)*	
	Session 2.3	A:\Disk2\My Webs\Sunny *(Continued from Session 2.2)* A:\Disk2\Tutorial.02\WB00791.gif A:\Disk2\Tutorial.02\smplogo.gif A:\Disk2\Tutorial.02\minuet.mid	
	Review Assignments	A:\Disk2\My Webs\Sunny *(Continued from Session 2.3)*	
	Case Problem 1	A:\Disk3\Tutorial.02\Royal01.gif A:\Disk3\Tutorial.02\Quantum.mid	A:\Disk3\My Webs\Royal
	Case Problem 2	A:\Disk4\Tutorial.02\Buffalo1.gif A:\Disk4\Tutorial.02\Cheers.mid	A:\Disk4\My Webs\Buffalo
	Case Problem 3	A:\Disk5\Tutorial.02\Garden01.gif A:\Disk5\Tutorial.02\WB02245.gif A:\Disk5\Tutorial.02\Casper.mid	A:\Disk5\My Webs\Garden
	Case Problem 4	A:\Disk6\Tutorial.02\WB00760.gif	A:\Disk6\My Webs\Replay
Tutorial 3			
	Session 3.1	A:\Disk2\My Webs\Sunny *(Continued from Tutorial 2 Review Assignments)* A:\Disk2\Tutorial.03\EmpPage.htm A:\Disk2\Tutorial.03\Customer.doc	
	Session 3.2	A:\Disk2\My Webs\Sunny *(Continued from Session 3.1)* A:\Disk2\Tutorial.03\Employ.jpg	
	Session 3.3	A:\Disk2\My Webs\Sunny *(Continued from Session 3.2)* A:\Disk2\Tutorial.03\Company.htm A:\Disk2\Tutorial.03\Profile.gif	Products.htm Company.htm Investor.htm
	Review Assignments	A:\Disk2\My Webs\Sunny *(Continued from Session 3.3)* A:\Disk2\Tutorial.03\whatsnew.htm A:\Disk2\Tutorial.03\WhatLogo.gif	
	Case Problem 1	A:\Disk3\My Webs\Royal *(Continued from Tutorial 2)* A:\Disk3\Tutorial.03\Rcompany.htm A:\Disk3\Tutorial.03\Royal02.gif A:\Disk3\Tutorial.03\Distrib.doc A:\Disk3\Tutorial.03\Up.gif A:\Disk3\Tutorial.03\RNews.htm A:\Disk3\Tutorial.03\RNewsLog.gif	RNews.htm RFeedbak.htm REmploy.htm

File Finder			
Tutorial	**Location in Tutorial**	**Name and Location of Data File or Web Site**	**Files or Web Sites the Student Creates from Scratch**
Tutorial 3 *(Continued)*			
	Case Problem 2	A:\Disk4\My Webs\Buffalo *(Continued from Tutorial 2)* A:\Disk4\Tutorial.03\Bhow.htm A:\Disk4\Tutorial.03\BHowLogo.jpg A:\Disk4\Tutorial.03\BWMark.gif A:\Disk4\Tutorial.03\HowWorks.doc A:\Disk4\Tutorial.03\BWho.htm A:\Disk4\Tutorial.03\BWhoLogo.gif	Up.gif BWhat.htm
	Case Problem 3	A:\Disk5\My Webs\Garden *(Continued from Tutorial 2)* A:\Disk5\Tutorial.03\GEmploy.htm A:\Disk5\Tutorial.03\GNavBar.gif A:\Disk5\Tutorial.03\Manager.doc A:\Disk5\Tutorial.03\Up.gif A:\Disk5\Tutorial.03\GAbout.htm	GAbout.htm GFeedbak.htm
	Case Problem 4	A:\Disk6\My Webs\Replay *(Continued from Tutorial 2)* A:\Disk6\Tutorial.03\Deal.gif	Students create a new Web page using a filename of their choice.
Tutorial 4			
	Session 4.1	A:\Disk2\My Webs\Sunny *(Continued from Tutorial 3 Review Assignments)* http://course.com/downloads/ newperspectives/fp2000/investor.htm A:\Disk2\Tutorial.04\Invest.gif A:\Disk2\Tutorial.04\Finperf.gif	
	Session 4.2	A:\Disk2\My Webs\Sunny *(Continued from Session 4.1)* A:\Disk2\Tutorial.04\Banner.htm A:\Disk2\Tutorial.04\Basket.htm A:\Disk2\Tutorial.04\Contents.htm A:\Disk2\Tutorial.04\Drink.htm A:\Disk2\Tutorial.04\Fruit.htm A:\Disk2\Tutorial.04\Ordrform.htm A:\Disk2\Tutorial.04\Ordrinfo.htm A:\Disk2\Tutorial.04\Catalog.gif A:\Disk2\Tutorial.04\Juice.gif	Products.htm
	Review Assignments	A:\Disk2\My Webs\Sunny *(Continued from Session 4.2)* A:\Disk2\Tutorial.04\Orngback.jpg	A:\Tutorial.04\Table Clothing.htm
	Case Problem 1	A:\Disk3\My Webs\Royal *(Continued from Tutorial 3)* A:\Disk3\Tutorial.04\RStock.htm	RInvest.htm RFinInfo.htm Banner.htm Contents.htm
	Case Problem 2	A:\Disk4\My Webs\Buffalo *(Continued from Tutorial 3)* A:\Disk4\Tutorial.04\BWhatLog.gif A:\Disk4\Tutorial.04\BNavHome.gif A:\Disk4\Tutorial.04\BNavWho.gif A:\Disk4\Tutorial.04\BNavHow.gif A:\Disk4\Tutorial.04\BNavWhre.gif A:\Disk4\Tutorial.04\BNavCtct.gif	BWhat.htm Banner.htm Contents.htm
	Case Problem 3	A:\Disk5\My Webs\Garden *(Continued from Tutorial 3)*	GMenu.htm Contents.htm Contact.htm
	Case Problem 4	A:\Disk6\My Webs\Replay *(Continued from Tutorial 3)*	MSpecial.htm Contents. htm Students will create three new Web pages using filenames of their choice.

File Finder

Tutorial	Location in Tutorial	Name and Location of Data File or Web Site	Files or Web Sites the Student Creates from Scratch
Tutorial 5			
	Session 5.1	A:\Disk2\My Webs\Sunny *(Continued from Tutorial 4 Review Assignments)* A:\Disk2\Tutorial.05\Map.gif A:\Disk2\Tutorial.05\MapPage.htm	
	Session 5.2	A:\Disk2\Tutorial.05\Bread.htm A:\Disk2\Tutorial.05\Cake.htm A:\Disk2\Tutorial.05\Icing.htm A:\Disk2\Tutorial.05\Pie.htm A:\Disk2\Tutorial.05\Recipes.htm	A:\Disk2\My Webs\Recipes cranberry_bread.htm
	Review Assignments	A:\Disk2\My Webs\Sunny *(Continued from Session 5.1)* A:\Disk2\Tutorial.05\Beach.gif A:\Disk2\My Webs\Recipes *(Continued from Session 5.2)*	
	Case Problem 1	A:\Disk3\My Webs\Royal *(Continued from Tutorial 4)*	
	Case Problem 2	A:\Disk4\My Webs\Buffalo *(Continued from Tutorial 4)* A:\Disk4\Tutorial.05\BD14530_.gif	
	Case Problem 3	A:\Disk5\My Webs\Garden *(Continued from Tutorial 4)*	GSpecial.htm
	Case Problem 4	A:\Disk6\My Webs\Replay *(Continued from Tutorial 4)*	
Tutorial 6			
	Session 6.1	A:\Disk2\My Webs\Sunny *(Continued from Tutorial 5 Review Assignments)* A:\Disk2\Tutorial.06\Search.gif A:\Disk2\Tutorial.06\Feedback.htm A:\Disk2\Tutorial.06\FormLogo.gif	Search.htm
	Session 6.2	A:\Disk2\My Webs\Sunny *(Continued from Session 6.1)* A:\Disk2\Tutorial.06\Form.doc	feedback.txt
	Session 6.3	A:\Disk2\My Webs\Sunny *(Continued from Session 6.2)* A:\Disk2\Tutorial.06\Banner1.gif A:\Disk2\Tutorial.06\Banner2.gif	C:\Inetpub\wwwroot\Sunny
	Review Assignments	C:\Inetpub\wwwroot\Sunny *(Continued from Session 6.3)* A:\Disk2\Tutorial.06\Banner3.gif	
	Case Problem 1	A:\Disk3\My Webs\Royal *(Continued from Tutorial 5)*	RSearch.htm RFeedbak.htm C:\Inetpub\wwwroot\Royal RFeedbak.txt
	Case Problem 2	A:\Disk4\My Webs\Buffalo *(Continued from Tutorial 5)* A:\Disk4\Tutorial.06\B_contac.gif A:\Disk4\Tutorial.06\B_where.gif	Contact.txt Contact.htm C:\Inetpub\wwwroot\Buffalo Confirm.htm
	Case Problem 3	A:\Disk5\My Webs\Garden *(Continued from Tutorial 5)*	Search.htm GFeedbak.htm Feedback.txt C:\Inetpub\wwwroot\Garden Feedback.htm FranInfo.htm

File Finder

Tutorial	Location in Tutorial	Name and Location of Data File or Web Site	Files or Web Sites the Student Creates from Scratch
Tutorial 6 *(Continued)*	Case Problem 4	A:\Disk6\My Webs\Replay *(Continued from Tutorial 5)*	Search.htm Feedback.txt Feedback.htm C:\Inetpub\wwwroot\Replay Confirm.htm FAQ.htm Students will create or import three image files into the Web site for use in a banner ad.
Tutorial 7	Session 7.1	Import the files butter_icing.htm, chiffon_cake.htm, chiffon_pie.htm, Default.htm, nut_bread.htm, and site_map.htm from the URL http://course.com/downloads/newperspectives/fp2000/recipes A:\Disk1\Tutorial.07\style.htm	http://localhost/recipes
	Session 7.2	http://localhost/recipes *(Continued from Session 7.1)*	disc_cfrm.htm disc_frm.htm disc_post.htm disc_srch.htm disc_tocf.htm disc_welc.htm _disc folder with the files 00000001.htm, 00000002.htm, and tocproto.htm _borders folder with the files disc_aftr.htm, disc_ahdr.htm, disc_foot.htm, and disc_head.htm
	Review Assignments	http://localhost/recipes *(Continued from Session 7.2)* A:\Disk1\Tutorial.07\CCake.gif A:\Disk1\Tutorial.07\orange_pecan_bread.htm A:\Disk1\Tutorial.07\orange_cake.htm A:\Disk1\Tutorial.07\orange_icing.htm A:\Disk1\Tutorial.07\orange_ck.jpg	
	Case Problem 1	http://localhost/royal	disc2_cfrm.htm disc2_frm.htm disc2_post.htm disc2_srch.htm disc2_tocf.htm disc2_welc.htm _disc2 folder with the files 00000001.htm, 00000002.htm, and tocproto.htm _borders folder with the files disc2_aftr.htm, disc2_ahdr.htm, disc2_foot.htm, disc2_head.htm, and top.htm

File Finder

Tutorial	Location in Tutorial	Name and Location of Data File or Web Site	Files or Web Sites the Student Creates from Scratch
Tutorial 7 *(Continued)*	Case Problem 2	http://localhost/buffalo	disc3_cfrm.htm disc3_frm.htm disc3_post.htm disc3_srch.htm disc3_tocf.htm disc3_welc.htm _disc3 folder with the files 00000001.htm, 00000002.htm, and tocproto.htm _borders folder with the files disc3_aftr.htm, disc3_ahdr.htm, disc3_foot.htm, disc3_head.htm, and bottom.htm
	Case Problem 3	A:\Disk1\Tutorial.07\GAngel.htm A:\Disk1\Tutorial.07\GPasta.htm A:\Disk1\Tutorial.07\GPecan.htm A:\Disk1\Tutorial.07\GPudding.htm A:\Disk1\Tutorial.07\GPiePic.jpg A:\Disk1\Tutorial.07\GAnglPic.jpg A:\Disk1\Tutorial.07\GPuddPic.jpg A:\Disk1\Tutorial.07\GPastPic.jpg	site_map.htm
	Case Problem 4	http://localhost/replay	disc4_cfrm.htm disc4_frm.htm disc4_post.htm disc4_srch.htm disc4_tocf.htm disc4_welc.htm _disc4 folder with the files 00000001.htm and tocproto.htm _borders folder with the files disc4_aftr.htm, disc4_ahdr.htm, disc4_foot.htm, disc4_head.htm, and top.htm
Tutorial 8	Session 8.1	A:\Tutorial.08\Recipes.mdb http://localhost/recipes *(Continued from Tutorial 7 Review Assignments)*	customer_query.asp customer_query_search.asp
	Session 8.2	A:\Disk1\Tutorial.08\Guest.mdb http://localhost/recipes *(Continued from Session 8.1)* A:\Disk1\Tutorial.08\GuestBk.asp	ResultsDAP.htm
	Review Assignments	http://localhost/recipes *(Continued from Session 8.2)*	
	Case Problem 1	http://localhost/royal *(Continued from Tutorial 7)* A:\Disk1\Tutorial.08\Royal.mdb	sendinfo.asp custinfo.asp custDAP.htm
	Case Problem 2	http://localhost/buffalo *(Continued from Tutorial 7)* A:\Disk1\Tutorial.08\Buffalo.mdb	mailinfo.asp maillist.asp mailDAP.htm

File Finder

Tutorial	Location in Tutorial	Name and Location of Data File or Web Site	Files or Web Sites the Student Creates from Scratch
Tutorial 8 *(Continued)*			
	Case Problem 3	http://localhost/garden *(Continued from Tutorial 7)* A:\Disk1\Tutorial.08\Garden.mdb	comments.asp custinfo.asp custDAP.htm
	Case Problem 4	http://localhost/replay *(Continued from Tutorial 7)* A:\Disk1\Tutorial.08\Replay.mdb	invDAP.htm
Tutorial 9			
	Session 9.1	http://localhost/recipes *(Continued from Tutorial 8 Review Assignments)* A:\Disk1\Tutorial.09\Activity.htm A:\Disk1\Tutorial.09\Openings.htm	
	Session 9.2	http://localhost/recipes *(Continued from Session 9.1)*	Specials.css
	Session 9.3	http://localhost/recipes *(Continued from Session 9.2)*	Sample.htm
	Review Assignments	http://localhost/recipes *(Continued from Session 9.3)*	
	Case Problem 1	http://localhost/royal *(Continued from Tutorial 8)* A:\Disk1\Tutorial.09\RFBakData.htm	Sales.htm
	Case Problem 2	http://localhost/buffalo *(Continued from Tutorial 8)*	SaleWkbk.htm styles.css
	Case Problem 3	http://localhost/garden *(Continued from Tutorial 8)* A:\Disk1\Tutorial.09\GData.htm	Salary.htm
	Case Problem 4	http://localhost/replay *(Continued from Tutorial 8)*	
Additional Case 1		A:\Disk2\AddCase1\bales1.jpg A:\Disk2\AddCase1\bales2.jpg A:\Disk2\AddCase1\cans.jpg A:\Disk2\AddCase1\Email.htm A:\Disk2\AddCase1\Experience.htm A:\Disk2\AddCase1\index.htm A:\Disk2\AddCase1\logo.jpg A:\Disk2\AddCase1\paper.jpg A:\Disk2\AddCase1\Pickup.htm A:\Disk2\AddCase1\Pricing.htm A:\Disk2\AddCase1\Secure.htm A:\Disk2\AddCase1\Security.htm A:\Disk2\AddCase1\Services.htm A:\Disk2\AddCase1\Shred.mdb A:\Disk2\AddCase1\Size.htm A:\Disk2\AddCase1\What.htm	http://localhost/shred styles.css disc1_cfrm.htm disc1_frm.htm disc1_post.htm disc1_srch.htm disc1_tocf.htm disc1_welc.htm _disc1 folder with the files 00000001.htm and tocproto.htm _borders folder with the files disc1_aftr.htm, disc1_ahdr.htm, disc1_foot.htm, disc1_head.htm, top.htm, and left.htm pickinfo.asp

File Finder

Tutorial	Location in Tutorial	Name and Location of Data File or Web Site	Files or Web Sites the Student Creates from Scratch
Additional Case 2		A:\Disk2\AddCase2\Buster.htm A:\Disk2\AddCase2\Cats.htm A:\Disk2\AddCase2\Chance.htm A:\Disk2\AddCase2\Default.htm A:\Disk2\AddCase2\Dogs.htm A:\Disk2\AddCase2\Guest.htm A:\Disk2\AddCase2\Maple.htm A:\Disk2\AddCase2\P_Buster.jpg A:\Disk2\AddCase2\P_Chance.jpg A:\Disk2\AddCase2\P_Maple.jpg A:\Disk2\AddCase2\P_Phoebe.jpg A:\Disk2\AddCase2\P_Rocky.jpg A:\Disk2\AddCase2\P_Scout.jpg A:\Disk2\AddCase2\P_Spike.jpg A:\Disk2\AddCase2\P_Tex.jpg A:\Disk2\AddCase2\P_Thomasina.jpg A:\Disk2\AddCase2\P_Zoe.jpg A:\Disk2\AddCase2\Pets.mdb A:\Disk2\AddCase2\Phoebe.htm A:\Disk2\AddCase2\Rocky.htm A:\Disk2\AddCase2\Scout.htm A:\Disk2\AddCase2\Spike.htm A:\Disk2\AddCase2\Tex.htm A:\Disk2\AddCase2\Thomasina.htm A:\Disk2\AddCase2\Zoe.htm	http://localhost/pets guestDAP.htm Donation.htm GuestInfo.asp
Additional Case 3		A:\Disk3\AddCase3\51642.htm A:\Disk3\AddCase3\57495.htm A:\Disk3\AddCase3\74862.htm A:\Disk3\AddCase3\75436.htm A:\Disk3\AddCase3\78456.htm A:\Disk3\AddCase3\87462.htm A:\Disk3\AddCase3\88462.htm A:\Disk3\AddCase3\About.htm A:\Disk3\AddCase3\Contents.htm A:\Disk3\AddCase3\Marty.htm A:\Disk3\AddCase3\Info.htm A:\Disk3\AddCase3\Listings.htm A:\Disk3\AddCase3\P_51642.jpg A:\Disk3\AddCase3\P_57495.jpg A:\Disk3\AddCase3\P_75436.jpg A:\Disk3\AddCase3\P_78456.jpg A:\Disk3\AddCase3\P_87462.jpg A:\Disk3\AddCase3\P_88462.jpg A:\Disk3\AddCase3\Relocation.htm	http://localhost/realtor Default.htm Info.mdb InfoReq.asp site_map.htm search.htm